The Teaching of Instrumental Music

Third Edition

RICHARD J. COLWELL

New England Conservatory, Boston

THOMAS W. GOOLSBY

University of Victoria, British Columbia

Prentice
Hall

Upper Saddle River, New Jersey 07458

Library of Congress Cataloging-in-Publication Data

COLWELL, RICHARD J.
   The teaching of Instrumental music / RICHARD J. COLWELL, THOMAS
GOOLSBY. — 3rd ed..
      p. cm.
   Includes bibliographical references and index.
   ISBN 0-13-020689-X
   1. Instrumental music—Instruction and study. I. Goolsby,
Thomas, [date]. II. Title
MT170.C64 2002
784'.07—dc21   2001056021

VP, Editorial Director: *Charlyce Jones Owen*
Acquisitions Editor: *Christopher Johnson*
Editorial Assistant: *Evette Dickerson*
Senior Managing Editor: *Jan Stephan*
Editorial/Production Supervision: *Joanne Riker*
Prepress and Manufacturing Buyer: *Benjamin D. Smith*
Director of Marketing: *Beth Gillett Mejia*
Marketing Manager: *Chris Ruel*
Cover Art Director: *Jayne Conte*
Cover Designer: *Bruce Kenselaar*

This book was set in 10/12 New Baskerville by East End Publishing Services, Inc.
and was printed and bound by Courier Companies, Inc. The cover was
printed by Phoenix Color Corp.

 © 2002, 1992, 1969 by Pearson Education, Inc.
Upper Saddle River, New Jersey 07458

Printed in the United States of America

10 9 8 7 6 5 4 3 2 1

ISBN 0-13-020689-X

Pearson Education LTD., *London*
Pearson Education Australia PTY, Limited, *Sydney*
Pearson Education Singapore, Pte. Ltd
Pearson Education North Asia Ltd, *Hong Kong*
Pearson Education Canada, Ltd., *Toronto*
Pearson Educación de Mexico, S.A. de C.V.
Pearson Education — Japan, *Tokyo*
Pearson Education Malaysia, Pte. Ltd
Pearson Education, *Upper Saddle River, New Jersey*

Brief Contents

Contents

Preface

We have been students of public and private school bands and orchestras for our entire professional careers, both of us having begun as teachers of these groups. We are impressed with the continual improvement of these ensembles, and the inspired teaching and commitment to music education that brought about the improvement. We hope that the first two editions of this text have contributed in a small way to the growth of instrumental music.

The basic thrust of the first edition has been retained in this expanded third edition. Good instrumental music teaching has not changed significantly, although today's teachers have more responsibilities. Teachers, whether in private or public schools, must inspire students, establish clear standards and insist that they be met, and most importantly provide students with accurate information that enables them to develop the musical skills, insights, understandings, and the sense of responsibility to themselves and others that make group performance both fun and satisfying.

Schools have changed considerably since the first edition of this book was published in 1969 with more required subjects, new ways of scheduling instruction, graduation standards, the availability of technology, and the unfortunate too-frequent need for teachers to secure the resources that enable today's musical outcomes. Colleges have modified teacher education to meet new teacher certification requirements, often resulting in less time for the pedagogy of instrumental music. Thus, books such as this one have become more valuable not only as a text but as a reference for teachers in the field. This third edition reflects these changes in expanded coverage of issues such as formulating objectives, evaluating, motivating, and recruiting students, as well as administering a program that depends upon its own unique philosophical justification. Secondary school ensembles no longer emulate college organizations; they have their own literature and rationales for existing.

We continue to emphasize a "centrist" approach to each of the instruments, we do not advocate a particular teaching approach by a master teacher. Students are individuals, each with strengths, weaknesses, and potential, requiring that the teacher approach each teaching venture with a flexibility that can best facilitate the student's musical growth. Thus, we have resisted providing examples of the teaching techniques of the master teachers of any instruments. The critics and reviewers of this edition have been public school teachers and excellent music educators at the college level. The credits for careful reviews from the first and second editions remain applicable; we are indebted to them. String pedagogues Bret Smith of the University of Maryland, Joanne Irwin of Oberlin College, Pat D'Ercole of the University of Wisconsin—Stevens Point, as well as brass expert Eric Ledebuhr provided us with important suggestions.

In an attempt to reduce the length of the Second Edition, we omitted the section on string instruments. This was clearly a mistake, as the continued growth of orchestras depends on the willingness of all instrumental teachers to provide both band and orchestra experience for their students. The many stunning all-city youth orchestras should inspire all students to have an orchestral experience. In this Third Edition, the addition of five string chapters plus an enlarged coverage of various additional responsibilities of the instrumental music teacher has resulted in a lengthy book which still cannot address all of today's educational issues that the instrumental teacher must confront and solve. Appropriate sections of the book have been successfully used as a text; other sections such as the trouble-shooting charts serve as a reference for the prospective teacher during his or her field experience; the book as a whole offers information that the authors hope will continue to be relevant to the instrumental teacher throughout his or her career.

We have attempted to improve the reference section by indicating which references are "out of print" at the time of publication of this book, but are texts that remain in circulation due to their availability in a large number of college and university libraries. Out-of-print books, no matter how excellent but not generally owned by these libraries, have been dropped. Most troublesome was providing accurate information about the important references still in print but not available from the original publisher. We believed it necessary to accurately identify our source and have done so, but many texts are now distributed by other publishers or music houses that purchased the remaining stock of the original publisher, or in some cases are reprinting the original text with a new copyright date.

Two individuals deserve special recognition. Joanne Riker of East End Publishing Services, Inc. designed the new format and supervised each step of the production process. Dr. Ruth Colwell, an impeccable editor who is fluent in many disciplines, music and English being two that were of inestimable value to us.

Richard J. Colwell
Thomas Goolsby

History of Instrumental Music

Knowledge of the history of instrumental music is not essential for success as a band or orchestra conductor. Still, it seems appropriate to begin a book on instruments and instrumental teaching with a brief historical survey. Besides the intrinsic interest which history holds for us, there is a practical value in the perspective gained from knowledge of history. One can become aware of trends; observe the ways in which things were done at previous times; make contact with objectives, procedures, and methods; and gain a greater understanding of the reasons behind present practices and present situations. One hopes that such knowledge will help the teacher plan upon sound bases, avoid mistakes of the past, and shape the future intelligently.

THE DEVELOPMENT OF THE ORCHESTRA

The earliest common use of instruments, recognizable ancestors of our modern woodwinds, strings, drums, and brasses, dates to several thousand years B.C.

Instrumental ensembles may be traced to groups of flutists and lyres used at the time of the Greek dramas of Aeschylus and Sophocles although Eastern music may have used grouped instruments at an even earlier date. Little development of group instrumental music occurred until the modern orchestra had its beginnings with the creation of opera at the close of the sixteenth century. It grew in size and importance as opera became more and more a public favorite. With one of the first operas, Monteverdi made an important contribution to the orchestra when he used instrumental tone color to portray mood and character, perhaps the first such use of instruments for their unique, individual qualities. Rudimentary in nature, the early orchestra used imperfect instruments and had no set instrumentation. For the public school teacher, the relevant history of bands and orchestras begins with the development and use of relatively modern instruments and instrumentation.

Because the violin is the heart of the orchestra, the modern orchestra was not possible until the seventeenth century, when the great Italian violin makers perfected their craft and created the master instruments. The first good orchestra is considered to be the "Twenty-Four Violins of the King," in the service of Louis XIII of France, which reached its peak of excellence some 40 years later under Lully, during the reign of Louis XIV. Lully was a great conductor who demanded perfection. He conducted with a cane to ensure rhythmic unity and created a balanced ensemble of violins, flutes, oboes, bassoons, and double basses. In France the orchestra was a vehicle for the private entertainment of the nobility; during the same period, however, the first recorded public concert by an orchestra took place in London, in 1673. By the time of Corelli, a generation later, the modern violin had taken precedence over its competitors as the heart of the orchestra; viola, vielles, and lutes were rarely used except as solo instruments or for special effects.

Corelli, a noted performer as well as composer, is often given credit for originating the practice of matched bowing for orchestra. Alessandro Scarlatti increased the importance of the operatic orchestra, often dividing the strings into four parts and balancing them with the winds. The brasswinds became a legitimate part of the orchestra about 1720. Thus, the French and the Italians had developed the orchestra into a well-established entity before the time of Bach. During the time of Bach they continued to increase its importance. It was therefore capable of a high level of technique and emotional expression before Germany became the primary musical center in Europe.

Bach himself was a master of orchestral writing. He contributed his unique voicing of the instruments in which each is treated as a solo instrument. Handel also, although perhaps to a lesser extent than Bach, used instruments for their individual timbre, obtaining novel effects. The cello became important as soloist and as orchestra member; the full range of the bassoon was exploited; kettledrums were used for a solo part in *Semele;* and the oboe was often featured for its hauntingly beautiful tone quality.

Any list of individuals important to the development of the orchestra must include Gluck. He not only made innovations in the use of instruments but also, more significantly, made radical changes in the type of music played by the orchestra. He introduced the use of the clarinet, omitted the harpsichord, and gave the orchestra music to play that was genuinely expressive and dramatic, mirroring the scenes and action of the opera. With Gluck the orchestra discarded its role as simple accompaniment and became an independent dramatic force.

The classical era of Haydn and Mozart created the balanced instrumentation and the musical forms that have for the past few hundred years made the symphony orchestra the chief of musical structures, first in popularity with the public and greatest in challenge to the composer. During the nineteenth century, the number of orchestras multiplied rapidly in Europe and were eventually established in America as well. The first symphony orchestra to be organized was the London Philharmonic in 1813. The New York Philharmonic, formed in 1842, has been in existence since that date. The Boston Symphony and the Chicago Symphony, founded in 1881 and 1891, respectively, have also survived to the present. Several events gave impetus to the orchestral movement. One of these was the visit of the Jullien orchestra to America in 1853–1854. Jullien was a spectacular showman whose antics not only fascinated the audience but also made a real and positive impact upon the American public.

> Jullien was always dressed in an extravagantly embroidered shirt front, glistening white waistcoat, with a great black mustache and lavishly bedecked in gold chains, rings and pendants. He stood on a crimson platform edged in gold, tapestried with crimson velvet. He had white kid gloves brought to him on a silver platter before conducting Beethoven. Before the Firemen's Quadrille commenced, the audience was warned that something unusual might happen. Jullien loved to spring a surprise but a lot of fainting women

might be too much of a good thing. Wiping his brow with his gorgeous silk handkerchief, he arose and faced his men. The piece started quietly like a nocturne or lullaby, a hush through the house made the suspense more thrilling. Then the music picked up a bit, the violins fluttered as they told of the awesome mystery of darkness. You could almost see ghosts. Suddenly the clang of fire-bells was heard outside. Flames burst from the ceiling. Three companies of firemen rushed in, dragging their hoses behind them. Real water poured from the nozzles, glass was broken. Some of the women fainted, and the ushers were rushing here and there yelling that it was all part of the show. And all the while the orchestra was playing at a tremendous fortissimo. When Jullien thought they had had enough, he signaled for the firemen to go, and in a glorious blare of triumph the orchestra burst into the Doxology. Those of the audience who were conscious joined in the singing.[1]

Of more lasting value and genuine artistic merit was the work of Theodore Thomas, who toured the country with his own orchestra in 1863. He served as inspiration for the founding of the Boston Symphony and himself founded the Chicago Symphony. His interest in education led him to start a school in Cincinnati for the training of professional musicians.

Two major events made a difference in professional orchestras during the past half century. The first was the Ford Foundation's midcentury allocation of some $80 million to stabilize the financial situation of major and regional symphony orchestras. This grant, carefully coordinated not to interfere with music programs being promoted by the cash-poor National Endowment of the Arts, provided such a psychological and financial boost that by the mid-1980s the question was whether all of the orchestras initiated by this money could continue to flourish. Most, with some effort, were able to find support to replace this one-time largesse of the Ford Foundation, thus enriching communities with professional and semi-professional orchestras and so widening the availability of orchestral music and exemplary soloists. The second event was the popularization of the symphony orchestra by the charismatic conductor Leonard Bernstein of the New York Philharmonic and the institution of concerts on public television.

Of note is the founding of "pops" orchestras, a movement that began in the mid-1920s with the formation by Arthur Fiedler of the Boston Symphony Orchestra of a small symphonette designed to play music more accessible to untrained audiences. The "pops" name was adopted to insure audiences that the music was listener-friendly; this style of orchestral programming was adopted by other symphony orchestras to attract larger audiences and to build a firmer financial support base for the orchestra's primary activities. The popularization of orchestral music expanded to include concerts for the community's school-age children supported by funds from the National Endowment of the Arts, integration funds, the symphony's own budget, and corporations that believed in this approach to education.

THE DEVELOPMENT OF THE BAND

The growth of the band movement is much less clearly defined. In the late sixteenth century, Venice was the center of a group of composers who wrote for brass ensembles, primarily trombones and cornetts. These ensembles performed prin-

[1] T. F. Normann (1931), quote from J. T. Howard, *Our American Music.* New York: Thomas Crowell, pp. 230-231; and in *Instrumental Music in the Public Schools* (1939), Byrn Mawr, PA: Oliver Ditson, p. 5.

cipally in the church. They were followed by other brass groups throughout Europe in the seventeenth and eighteenth centuries, usually civic or military bands. Their only similarity to present-day bands was in their use of wind rather than string instruments. The typical instrumentation was oboes, clarinets, horns, and bassoons. Considering the state of those instruments at the time, one would agree that their sound was primarily useful for battle commands rather than as musical entertainment. Bands as we know them today seem to have stemmed from the formation of the 45 piece band of the National Guard in Paris in 1789. Sarrette conducted this band for one year. In 1790 its number was increased to 70, and Francois Gossec became the conductor. Two years later the band was dissolved, but its members eventually became the nucleus of the French National Conservatory, founded in 1795.

America has been a leading country in the formation of bands, with groups that antedate the Paris Band of the National Guard by more than a decade. (For an excellent treatment of this subject, see Richard Franko Goldman [1974], *The Wind Band,* Westport, CT: Greenwood Press.) Josiah Flagg, often known as the first American bandsman, was active as early as the 1700s. The Massachusetts Band, formed in 1783, later became the Green Dragon Band, then the Boston Brigade Band. In 1859 the Boston Brigade Band acquired a 26-year-old conductor, Patrick Gilmore, who changed its name to Gilmore's Band, took it to war, and made it famous. The Allentown Civic Band, formed in 1828, still performs today. These and similar groups were presumably small, comparable to the U.S. Marine Band, founded in 1798, which at the turn of the century was composed of two oboes, two clarinets, two horns, a bassoon, and a drum. The usual size of the early American bands was between 8 and 15 players, with instrumentation similar to that of the U.S. Marine Band. Bands soon increased in size. Beethoven wrote his military march in D (1816) for a minimum of 32 players, an average group for the time. To honor the visit of the Russian Emperor Nicholas to Prussia in 1838, Wieprecht combined the bands of several regiments and conducted more than 1,000 winds plus 200 extra side drummers.[2]

Of major significance to the band movement was the invention of the valve for brass instruments by Blumel (c. 1813) and the subsequent improvement of the piston by J. P. Oates in 1851. These two events occurred during the rapid improvement of European bands in the first half of the nineteenth century that reached a peak with the international contest in the 1860s and 1870s. Perhaps the greatest band contest of all time was that held in Paris in 1867, with nine nations competing. According to Goldman[3], the numbers played included the "Finale" of the *Lorelei* by Mendelssohn, "Fantasy" on the *Prophet* by Meyerbeer, Rossini's *William Tell Overture,* the "Bridal Chorus" from *Lohengrin* by Wagner, plus a "Fantasy on the Carnival of Venice."

The cornet, vastly improved by the invention of the valve, assumed the same role in American bands that the violin held in the orchestra. Many of the conductors were virtuoso cornet soloists. In fact, the band in America was for the three decades prior to the Civil War primarily a brass band. This can be attributed at least in part to the influence of the Dodsworth Band, one of the first professional bands and perhaps the best band in New York City prior to Gilmore's heyday. In 1853, two New York bandmasters, Kroll and Reitsel, began to use woodwinds with the brasses, thereby greatly expanding the band's musical potential as well as its repertoire.

---

[2] R. Goldman, (1962), *The Wind Band: Its Literature and Technique;* reprint (1974), Westport, CT: Greenwood Press, p. 28.
[3] Ibid., pp. 29.

Bands increased in importance during the Civil War years, but although most of the members of the regimental bands enlisted together, they were mustered out in a year and the bands were dispersed. The real impetus to the band movement came from an event designed to celebrate the peace, stemming from the inventive genius of Gilmore. After his band was mustered out of the army, Gilmore had gone with General Banks into the South. An opportunity in 1864 to form a "grand national band" of 500 army bandsmen and a chorus of 5,000 schoolchildren whetted his appetite for massed festival performances. Accordingly in 1869 he organized the National Peace Jubilee at which a band of 1,000, an orchestra of 500, and a chorus of 10,000 were brought together. The event appealed to patriotism, to education, and to Gilmore's spirit of business enterprise. Its immense attraction may be gauged by the fact that members of Congress, the entire Cabinet, and President Grant himself attended. Three years later, a World Peace Jubilee was organized on an even grander scale. The performing groups were twice as large as those of the national event, and many of the finest musical organizations of Europe participated. Not only did these huge festivals attract the public and popularize better music, but they also served to raise American performance standards. The visiting European groups dazzled the audiences with their skill; it was obvious that American bands and orchestras were no match for them.

American professional bands improved rapidly after the Jubilees. Gilmore took over the leadership of the 22nd Regimental Band in 1873 and directed it until his death in 1892. He was succeeded by the unlikely personage of Victor Herbert, whose well-loved melodies seem to have been little influenced by the military march. From 1880 until 1892, John Philip Sousa conducted the Marine Band and gave it a national reputation. Sousa and Gilmore toured extensively, bringing fine performances of both great music and popular music to audiences who had little other opportunity to hear professional concerts. Many fine local bands sprang up whose repertoire's included transcriptions of orchestral favorites, music written especially for band, and virtuoso solos with band accompaniment. For millions, the local bands represented the only avenue to good music of any sort.

The size and scope of the band movement would not have been possible without the British band libraries. Published arrangements had become possible due to the standardized instrumentation encouraged by Kneller Hall, the Royal Military School of Music. British firms such as Boosey and Company were able to publish band arrangements of general high quality that stimulated and influenced the course of band music in both Great Britain and the United States.

Standardized instrumentation in the United States came about through the influence of leaders such as Herbert L. Clarke, Albert A. Harding, Frederick Stock, John Philip Sousa, E. F. Goldman, Taylor Branson, and C. M. Tremaine. When contests began in the mid-1920s, the Committee on Instrumental Affairs of the Music Supervisor's National Conference, which formulated the rules for band contests, instituted severe penalties for those organizations that did not have the recommended instrumentation, thus assuring standardization.

Although professional bands in America did not find fertile soil or financial support comparable to that of the symphony orchestras, the armed forces have supported a band program of excellence for more than half a century. World War II provided the service bands the opportunity to select excellent performers from the 16 million Americans serving in the Armed Forces during that period of time. The tradition of excellence continued after the war as the military musicians found that a career in band performance was both possible and rewarding, and the public had come to expect performance excellence from at least the four military ensembles based in the nation's capital. In the twenty-first century, the Washington,

DC. service bands and their supporting ensembles at military posts and bases provide the counterpart in the band field to the national and regional professional symphony orchestras.

THE GROWTH OF PUBLIC SCHOOL MUSIC

The year 1925 marks the end of the Sousa era and with it the abrupt decline of the professional band, although the Goldman Band and a few radio bands did maintain their popularity. Many factors contributed to the decline. The advent of the radio, the phonograph, the moving picture, even the popular-priced automobile diverted attention from the bands. Two musical trends may have contributed to the lessening of interest in professional bands. One was the rise of the symphony orchestra, perhaps itself brought about by the increased desire for good music that the band era had inspired. The greatest single figure of this development was Theodore Thomas. Between the years 1880 and 1933, nearly all of today's major symphonies were established. The band was unable to compete with the symphony in performances of the traditional classics because these, with few exceptions, suffered when transcribed for band.

The second trend was the increasing excellence and popularity of public school performing groups. School music seems to have been given impetus by the Peace Jubilees of Gilmore, and as public education broadened, so did the school music organizations. Freeport, Illinois, schools have had a continuous orchestra program since 1864, when an individual was hired specifically for this task.

> In 1864, Miss Francis Rosebraugh was called by the Freeport Board of Education from New York, where she had just completed two years of work in mathematics in a small up-state college. It was understood that in addition to her classes in mathematics she was to form an orchestra that would be the official group for plays, operettas, commencement exercises, etc. Our first orchestra consisted of two violins, one cornet, one clarinet, and a piano. The orchestra gradually grew in size and ability through the years until in 1913 some of the boys petitioned the principal to form a school band. This he granted on provision that the string players buy their own band music. From that year on our band has flourished along with our orchestra.[4]

An extracurricular student-run orchestra was formed in Aurora, Illinois, in 1878. Around the turn of the century the outstanding instrumental work of Jessie Clark in Wichita, Kansas (1890), and Will Earhart in Richmond, Indiana (1898), was evident. Despite the impact of the professional band movement in the last third of the nineteenth century, school bands were generally started after the orchestras. Freeport, Illinois, for example, had no band until several decades after the inception of the orchestra. By 1910 some 100 school orchestras existed. There are references to school bands at this time, but primary emphasis seems to have been on the civic boys' bands that flourished in nearly every town at the turn of the century. In the first 15 years of the twentieth century, several notable instances of real pioneering may be found. A few schools with vision and foresight were far ahead of the general public in adopting instrumental programs. In Los Angeles in 1904 grade school orchestras were formed to provide good players for the high school organi-

---

[4] Excerpts from a letter to the senior author written in 1967 by Mr. Ernie Seeman, director of Music Education, District 145, Freeport, IL.

zations. In 1905, A. A. Harding came to the University of Illinois and began the college band that set the standard for the next half century. A few years later, around 1912, A. R. McAllister instituted in Joliet, Illinois, a band program whose reputation for excellence continued for half a century. School boards as far apart as Oakland, California, and Rochester, New York, allotted $10,000 and $15,000, respectively, to purchase band and orchestra instruments for their school systems (this in the years 1913 and 1918 when that amount of money was a princely sum). Such instances were the exception, but they provided the leadership and inspiration for others.[5]

The great growth of public school bands after World War I has often been attributed to the war and the attraction of the military band during this period. It was believed that musicians who returned home after playing in military bands created an abundant supply of teachers for the schools. This is only partially true. School orchestras and bands abounded before the supposed influx of teachers. A survey of 375 schools in 1919 showed that three-fourths of them had orchestras and one-fourth had bands. Numerous other sociocultural factors contributed to the sudden growth that had begun prior to the postwar period.

The same cultural changes that affected the decline of the professional band contributed to the rise of the school band. The schools broadened their outlook to take in a number of activities not previously within their scope: vocational, athletic, artistic, and recreational. Music became important to competitive athletics, for public relations purposes, and for civic advertisement. Service clubs experienced a sudden growth, the National Band Association was formed, the Cardinal Principles of Secondary Education were proclaimed by the National Education Association, all of these directly and advantageously affecting the school band. Youth was changing; students were staying in school longer, and the band appealed to them with its color, group spirit, military apparel, and the chance for recognition.

Bands have always marched and they continue to do so. The primary purpose of the military band was to march into battle or to perform for those who were marching. The first college bands (shortly after the Civil War) were small military organizations supported by the military departments in the land grant institutions. When these bands became associated with Schools of Music, their size increased. With Albert Austin Harding's initiation of homecoming at the University of Illinois and the integration of a half-time show into this event, the growth of the marching band was assured. Music and showmanship combined to fill an important niche in American culture.

Although America still looked to Europe as its mentor in things musical and artistic, music in the schools cannot be said to be influenced directly by European practices. No such school instruction existed on the Continent; the skilled professional musicians of Europe either did not know how to teach groups of children or did not care to do so. One exception was the Maidstone movement in England, around 1908, which presented group instrumental instruction to children. This movement was studied by the supervisor of music in the Boston public schools, who introduced its principles and methods into the schools of that city around 1910.

With the introduction of music into the curriculum came the problem of credits. The members of the very early groups, from the Farm and Trade Band of Boston Harbor in 1858 to those existing at the end of the century, usually met after school hours and received no academic recognition or credit. As far as we know, the first instance of students receiving credit for school music was in Richmond, Indiana, in 1905, whereby students gained one-half credit for playing in the

---

[5] Edward Bailey Birge (1928), *History of Public School Music in the United States;* reprint (1966), Reston, VA: Music Educators National Conference, p. 192.

orchestra that met after school. The following year Osborne McConathy in Chelsea, Massachusetts, secured school credit for students who took music lessons after school from private teachers. In 1920 Charles McCray in Parsons, Kansas, gained both school time for the orchestra and credit for the students.

The next major innovation in school music occurred in 1923 when the instrument manufacturers sponsored a national band contest in Chicago as a promotional device. As with Gilmore's Jubilees, the commercial venture proved to be a powerful influence, and the success of the contest was unquestionable. The manufacturers wisely turned the management of future contests over to the school. State contests were held in Kansas in 1912 and by 1925 were coordinated by a Committee on Instrumental Affairs of the Music Supervisors National Conference. The first school-sponsored national contest was held in 1926 in Fostoria, Ohio. The competitive spirit of the American people insured the immediate success of the contests; as with athletic competition and debate tournaments, the American community had a chance to test its superiority against its neighbors in a music contest. The history of the contest became the history of the school band.

At almost the same time, school orchestras received impetus from a different source—the formation of a national high school orchestra. Joseph Maddy—who made an outstanding reputation as a high school orchestra conductor in Kansas, New York, Indiana, and Michigan, and who started orchestral tryouts and high school vocational music programs—took his orchestras to conventions where they could be heard. The response to the Parsons, Kansas, orchestra at the Music Supervisors National Conference in 1921 inspired him to form a National Conference Orchestra for Detroit in 1926. Accordingly, he advertised in music journals and from 400 applications selected 238 students for the orchestra.[6]

The music for the conference was of such quality that Maddy was invited to form a second national student orchestra to play for the 1927 Dallas meeting of the Department of Superintendence, the official national organization of school superintendents. The audience of school superintendents was highly impressed by the orchestra's performance and passed this resolution:

> We would record our full appreciation of the fine musical programs and art exhibits in connection with this convention. They are good evidence that we are rightly coming to regard music, art, and other similar subjects as fundamental in the education of American children. We recommend that everywhere they be given equal consideration and support with other basic subjects.[7]

The resolution resulted in the initiation of hundreds of instrumental programs in schools across the country. Music was the "new thing" established as a worthwhile area deserving both school time and credit. Maddy organized a third national orchestra for the 1928 Music Supervisors National Conference in Chicago. Administrators at these conventions were impressed by the healthy experiences of students working together; the excellent discipline (much of which Maddy had learned from T. P. Giddings); and those by-products of citizenship, health, and useful recreation that were considered so important at this time. Thus the success of Maddy's orchestra coincided with the requisite cultural and social conditions of the time to bring about music's firm establishment in the schools.

---

[6] Norma Browning (1963), *Joe Maddy of Interlochen*, Chicago: Henry Regnery, p. 178; reprint (1992), Chicago: Contemporary Books.

[7] W. F. Weber "Music and the Sacred Seven," as quoted in Gerald Prescott and Lawrence Chidester (1938). *Getting Results with School Bands.* New York: Carl Fischer; and Minneapolis: Paul A. Schmitt, p. 15.

Superintendents and music supervisors returned home from the conventions to find that administrative problems were involved in setting up instrumental programs. In the smaller schools there were too few students to support both a band and an orchestra; instructors who could teach both were scarce; financial support for two instrumental groups added a sizable amount to the budget. Because the same musical and extramusical values were claimed by both, the band took precedence over the orchestra partly because of its greater flexibility, greater usefulness to the community and to athletics, and its greater appeal to youth. Bands therefore became ascendant, and orchestras failed to get a major start.

The influence of the band instrument manufacturers and the uniform companies should not be overlooked nor discounted. When the town bands declined, they provided temporary funding for school band directors' salaries, and they offered attractive instrument rental and purchase programs. In addition, they actively supported contests, supplied financial aid to Joseph Maddy in the founding of the National Music Camp at Interlochen, Michigan, and later established yearly conventions that offered conductors new ideas and new materials to help build successful band programs.

The Midwestern Band and Orchestra Clinic held annually in Chicago, sponsored by industry, has been a major influence on public school ensembles, introducing new literature to teachers and providing a venue for school ensembles to perform before large numbers of music educators. Likewise, the monthly publication *The Instrumentalist* has provided the primary source of professional development for ensemble conductors, highlighting issues of concern to public school instrumental instructors. According to *The Instrumentalist*, public school bands have continued to grow in membership. Although they have remained unaffected by economic conditions (as was largely true during the Great Depression), these organizations presently raise their own funds for a large percentage of their operating budget, with some ensembles charging tuition for membership. However, ensembles that must seek total external funding are truly extracurricular. Travel to festivals, to holiday parades, even overseas, has become common for performing ensembles, dramatically escalating the operating expenses for such groups. Live American band music, whether at athletic events or concerts, is accessible to the majority of Americans, and they support the practice of having a school ensemble experience available to all interested students. There is scant evidence that educational factors such as the school reform movement or the Voluntary National Standards have affected instrumental music in any substantial way. Issues of school scheduling arising from reform movement suggestions appear to be the dominant factor of interest and importance to high school ensemble teachers.

The college band, along with the military ensembles, has provided the model and standard for the public schools, reaching its peak with Harry Begian and the University of Illinois bands in the 1980s.

With the formulation of the Eastman Wind Ensemble by Frederick Fennell in 1952 a new literature for school bands was promulgated. Ensembles playing original music written for winds sprang up at Eastman, the University of Illinois, and Northwestern University and were quickly emulated by colleges and large public schools. The idea of one-on-a-part wind instrument experiences enhanced the education arguments for school bands; extensive lists of excellent, usable literature were collected by David Whitwell and Robert Gray. The leading advocate for encouraging composers to write for the wind ensemble and to commission these compositions has been Frank Battisti, first with the Ithaca New York High School Band and for more than a quarter of a century with the New England Conservatory Wind Ensemble. The wind ensemble and, to a certain extent, renewed interest in the British brass band, balanced the influence of the concert band at the beginning of the twenty-first century.

Shinichi Suzuki was primarily responsible for demonstrating the viability of string instrument instruction at an early age and the advantages of continued participation. The "Suzuki movement" created and has sustained the present interest of American parents in string instruction for their children. Beginning about 1958, this movement grew steadily, influencing private string instruction more than any methodology being taught in the public schools and resulting in stunning youth orchestras (not associated with a single school system) in all parts of the country, a marked increase in string enrollment at the college level, and improved college orchestras. Interested parents request a Suzuki teacher, rather than a violin instructor, "Suzuki" becoming synonymous with string instruction. More recently the methodology has spread to other instruments, primarily piano and flute, but is best known for its major contribution to string education.

The small instrumental ensemble has existed throughout the history of instrumental music. Chamber music, however, can be traced primarily to the Renaissance period, although examples are to be found in the Middle Ages. Cultural changes, including public and university societies, aristocratic connoisseurs, and the improvement of instruments, provided a favorable climate for chamber music. All composers wrote for small ensembles, much of the music dependent upon the musicians and instruments available. Brass choirs (tower music) were important ensembles to the Gabrielis and others; string ensembles were popular in the more intimate palace settings. As with large ensembles, improvement of instruments affected the quality and quantity of small ensemble music to a greater extent than the influence of any composer or exemplary small ensemble. On occasion, a composer has been more daring in his or her music for the small ensemble, but for the most part, small ensemble literature parallels the literature of the large ensembles. (Vocal ensembles were likely an important influence on the acceptance and popularity of instrumental chamber music.)

The public school music program has long championed small ensembles as a means of continued music participation after graduation, as an instructional device, as a performance outlet, and as a source of motivation. The ensemble program has been, however, largely an after- or out-of-school experience, with students receiving no academic credit for participation. In the twentieth century, the most visible small ensemble has been the school stage band and later the jazz/rock band. The general policy for all ensembles has been for membership to be limited to students formally enrolled in a large ensemble, but the exceptions have been numerous. The public school music contests have consistently allowed private piano students to participate, thus increasing the futility of the struggle to limit access to a "select" experience to those students enrolled in school music courses. The music education profession itself holds diverse options here—jazz/rock bands have needed guitar and keyboard players, individuals who may not have had a second instrument that would enable membership in a concert band or orchestra.

Schools with eight or more periods in the school day may be able to schedule small ensembles (sometimes instructional time is available with block scheduling), but jazz/rock and stage bands are customarily after-school experiences. As public school music ensembles have always modeled themselves on those at the college level, the history of stage and jazz bands in the schools follows the history of college stage and jazz bands by a couple of decades. The colleges, of course, taking their cue from professional ensembles.

According to the *American Groves Dictionary*, jazz cannot be categorized as folk, popular, or art, as it shares commonalities with all three types of music. The cultural context, however, has been a major factor in the history of jazz in the public schools. The roots of jazz in the speakeasies of the Prohibition era made this music suspect and seem inappropriate in the public schools and on many college campuses. The college ensembles took the lead in introducing jazz to their students, lagging behind musical trends in the professional world by at least a decade. The Big Bands that flourished in the 1930s were not common on college campuses until the 1940s, nor numerous until after World War II. For the most part, the history of jazz is a history of individuals who introduced new rhythms, harmonies, and tone colors in their solos or ensembles, making any history a chronology of individuals. The respectability of jazz grew slowly in the 1920s and 1930s with the popularity of social dancing and the ready availability of sound recordings. American society was bent on seeking pleasure in life, and jazz was one of those pleasures. The Great Depression did reduce the accessibility of jazz, and only the better ensembles survived.

Present-day jazz represents a culmination of influences from the African and American cultures. The recreating and improvising of counterrhythms is an African contribution, whereas Paul Whiteman's contribution was to meld these creative improvisations with traditional music forms. The history of jazz is a continuing search for a balance between the influence of Western classical music and that of native African music, as the music of Whiteman and Jelly Roll Morton illustrate. The balancing act continued through Fletcher Henderson, Duke Ellington, Benny Goodman, Charlie Parker, Dizzy Gillespie, and on to Miles Davis. These individuals provided the intellectual and musical components that made it possible to have jazz criticism and for jazz to be accepted on college campuses. Jazz on college campuses and the Newport Jazz Festival both can be traced to the mid-1950s. The incorporation of rock into jazz in the 1960s provided it with new life, as did the interest of Gunther Schuller in his seminal publication and his effort to institutionalize "third stream" music. One can describe a jazz concert as a type of ritual with interaction occurring between players and the audience—an equal sharing among musicians based on a melody that can be shaped by the performers. Beyond that, the eclecticism present at the beginning of the twenty-first century makes any description of what constitutes jazz difficult.

At some time in the 1960s, jazz ensembles in the public schools began to be accepted, a decade after their acceptance on college campuses. Courses in jazz study became common at the collegiate level in the late 1970s. Whether the after-school small ensemble experience consisted of chamber music or jazz, the ensemble experience enriched and furthered the goals of school music programs. The objectives of musical independence, imagination, leadership, and performance excellence were more easily garnered in the small ensemble than in the increasingly large bands and orchestras. As official records are not maintained on voluntary, elective, or after-school groups, an accurate history of the growth of school small ensembles is difficult to develop. Further, many small ensembles are organized to exist for only a portion of the year, often prior to contests. The jazz band is an exception, having a full schedule of appearances and contests. It is not unusual for jazz groups to participate in a dozen or more festival/contests in a year, requiring school administrators to establish limits even on extra-curricular experiences. (There are considerable administrative issues with any ensemble that represents schools and uses school resources and facilities.) It is safe to assume that at the beginning of the twenty first century, most high schools (and a few middle schools) offer experience in jazz, with fewer schools offering experience in jazz choirs, woodwind quintets, and string quartets. Contests such as the annual, nationally publicized contest at Lincoln Center with Wynton Marsalis attract high school jazz bands of dazzling proficiency; such events contribute greatly to the viability of this genre of music.

BIBLIOGRAPHY

Indicates out of print in 2001.

*BAINBRIDGE, CYRIL (1980). *Brass Triumphant.* London: Muller.

*BERGER, KENNETH (1957). *The March King and His Band: The Story of John Philip Sousa.* New York: Exposition Press.

*BIERLEY, PAUL (1986). *John Philip Sousa, American Phenomenon,* rev. ed. New York: Integrity Press.

BIRGE, EDWARD BAILEY (1928) *History of Public School Music in the United States.* Boston: Oliver Ditson; reprint (1966) Reston, VA: Music Educators National Conference

*BRAND, VIOLET, and GEOFFREY BRAND (1979). *Brass Bands in the 20th Century.* Letchworth, England: Egon.

*———— (1986). *The World of Brass Bands.* Baldock, England: Egon.

*BROWNING, NORMA (1963). *Joe Maddy of Interlochen: Profile of a Legend.* Chicago: Henry Regnery Reprinted 1992 by Contemporary Books, Chicago.

*FENNELL, FREDERICK (1954). *Time and the Winds: A Short History of the Use of Wind Instruments in the Orchestra, Band, and the Wind Ensemble.* Kenosha, WI: G. Leblanc.

*FERGUSON, TOM, and SANDY FELDSTEIN (1976). *The Jazz Rock Ensemble: A Conductor's and Teacher's Guide.* Port Washington, NY: Alfred.

*GOLDMAN, RICHARD FRANKO (1938). *The Band's Music.* New York: Pitman Publishing.

*———— (1945). *The Concert Band.* New York: Rinehart and Co.

———— (1962). *The Wind Band: Its Literature and Technique.* Boston: Allyn and Bacon; reprint (1974) Westport, CT: Greenwood Press.

HITCHCOCK, WILEY H., and, STANLEY SADIE (1986). *The New Grove Dictionary of American Music,* Vol. II. New York: Grove's Dictionaries of Music.

*KEENE, JAMES A. (1982). *A History of Music Education in the United States.* Hanover, NH: University Press of New England.

MARK, MICHAEL L., and CHARLES GARY (1999). *A History of American Music Education,* 2nd ed. Reston, VA: National Association of Music Educators (MENC).

*NEWBOROUGH, GARY (1990). *Brass Bands in the 1990s.* Rochdale, England: British Federation of Brass Bands.

NORCROSS, BRIAN H. (1994). *One Band That Took a Chance: The Ithaca High School Band from 1955 to 1967 Directed by Frank Battisti.* Ft. Lauderdale, FL: Meredith Music.

*NORMANN, THEODORE (1939). *Instrumental Music in the Public Schools.* Bryn Mawr: Oliver Ditson.

*PRESCOTT, G. R., and L. W. CHIDESTER (1938). *Getting Results with School Bands.* New York: Carl Fischer, Minneapolis: Paul A. Schmitt.

WHITE, W. C. (1974). *A History of Military Music in America.* Westport, CT: Greenwood Press; reprint of (1944), New York: Exposition Press.

WHITWELL, DAVID (1984). *History and Literature of the Wind Band and Wind Ensemble.* Northridge, CA: Winds (Box 513, Northridge, CA, 91328, a multi-volume set).

*WRIGHT, A.G., and S. NEWCOMB (1970). *Bands of the World.* Evanston, IL: Instrumentalist.

2

Objectives

THE PURPOSE OF OBJECTIVES

Objectives are at the heart of teaching and every instrumental teacher has a pocketful. Writing objectives as part of lesson plans seems to be the essence of many teacher education programs. Every profession has at its heart objectives, goals, targets, quotas, or aims. Breaking a hundred, scoring (as in soccer), completing an assignment or the Boston Marathon, making a sales quota, quitting smoking, are only a few of the objectives that control our lives. Some are secret individual objectives (eating less fat) whereas others are group objectives and very visible (the band's extra morning rehearsals to compete in the state's marching band contest). Objectives can beget other objectives. An objective to win the New York Marathon requires training objectives, eating and drinking objectives, as well as altered relationships with job and family. One might have to learn to be comfortable driving a Porsche should that continue to be part of the New York prize. Not only *could* a book be written about objectives, but many already have. Although many universities are establishing a partnership with public schools, we advocate a partnership with the U.S. Marine Corps, whereby student teachers who fail to write adequate lesson plans with clearly stated well-thought-out objectives are sent to boot camp for the weekend.

To speak of objectives is fashionable but their importance extends beyond the latest Calvin Klein trend. They are the essential but most neglected step in teaching. Every experienced teacher knows objectives are indispensable to good teaching. Emphasis on goals, aims, and objectives often amounts to no more than lip service, too time-consuming and too complicated to be included in the practical business of organizing the materials of teaching. Theory and practice diverge considerably when one moves away from the printed page, the college course, or the professional symposium to the daily routine—teachers still teach as they *think* they were taught, not necessarily as they were taught to teach or actually experienced.

Objectives provide a structure for the music program. It is in terms of objectives that the teacher decides what shall be taught, when, and how. It is in terms of objectives that the teacher asks: "Is this worth knowing or doing? What difference will it make in the lives of the students? What difference will it make to them as adults?" The careful construction of objectives is the only way in which music instruction can become meaningful. Unless one clearly knows where he is going, he cannot know how far he has progressed toward his goal or whether he has reached it. These goals, however, must lie within the goals of the school, or music will be as extracurricular as the athletic program.

Experienced music ensemble directors often have trouble articulating their objectives. They can, however, tell you about their plans and these might be quite detailed. Successful conductors and teachers have plans for every rehearsal as well as a planned day, week, and semester. Planning is a critical survival technique. Adequate planning cannot only prevent failure but can result in success and even a happy teacher. Planning books are everywhere, designed for myriad purposes. Plans are related to New Year's resolutions; they indicate your best intentions. (Actually plans are also made to rob banks and accomplish other feats not intended for publication.) Plans seem to be semiprivate and individual, shared only when they require the cooperation of others to complete.

An objective differs from a plan in being more specific and focused but, most importantly, in requiring accurate assessment, most often immediate. When the military has an objective of crossing the line of departure at 0400 to capture a hill (a second objective), some leader evaluates the time of crossing the line, probably at 0401, and reports not only the time of the crossing but also whether the hill was captured and also the consequences, resources expended, and preparedness to accept another objective. You can imagine the many subobjectives, individual and group, public and private, in this situation. The group objective is obviously to plant the flag on top of the hill; an individual objective (shared by most fighting personnel) is to reach the top of the hill unharmed—hardly any individuals yearn to be Teddy Roosevelt–type heroes

This chapter has as its primary goal the extermination of vagueness and the promotion of clarity in the objectives for the instrumental music program. As the teaching of objectives requires that these objectives be assessed, the second goal is to stress the importance of immediate feedback to the student of his or her success or failure accompanied by recommendations that aid improvement. Determining priorities, articulating objectives, and accessing students' learning are the keys to successful teaching.

Long-term, intermediate, and short-term objective goals are part of every teacher's life and each has its own degree of importance. Learning to play the bassoon is no simple task; it is a *content,* not a *performance,* objective and is not accomplished in a single semester. The performance objective states how well the bassoon is to be played. Capable music teachers are able to articulate long-term goals for each student clearly, objectives that are realistic when considering the student's talent, interest, background, and competing interests. It is difficult for the student to have clear long-term goals—her worries are reasonably short term, maybe extending to lunch period—but most importantly she doesn't know what is required to become an accomplished bassoonist nor does she know what rewards she will receive from the accomplishment. Expert teachers understand long-term sequencing and instructional pacing.[1]

To teach as much good music in the time available is at best a hazy goal. If one is unable to visualize how this objective can be assessed and feedback provided to each individual, the objective should be rethought. Good objectives are articulated by the teacher and shared with the students so that they become public for everyone in the school and community to assess. These instructional objectives are

---

[1] A phase of professional development is for teachers to listen to the competence of students and ensembles in exemplary communities and revise upward their aural standards of what can be accomplished

termed *behavioral* objectives, as it is possible to observe a change in the learner's behavior. They can be either individual or group objectives. (Example: The student playing the right notes, the correct rhythm, and with tone satisfying to the instructor is an individual behavioral objective.)

Distinguishing between group and individual objectives is critical to the success of instrumental teachers. There must also be a priority assigned to these objectives. A rehearsal of the New York Philharmonic Orchestra or the Canadian Brass has as its primary purpose the attainment of group objectives. Each member of these two ensembles can already accurately and musically play his or her part. The focus is on group unity, interpretation, blend, balance, and more. The public school instrumental teacher may wish to imitate Kurt Masur but cannot, often having to spend considerable time on teaching students basic performing skills, knowledge of terminology, and details about the composition. A group objective may be expressed as follows: In performing the *Holst First Suite*, no individual clarinet player should be identifiable—the section should sound as if only one member were playing the part. The assessment measure is to listen to hear if any student's tone quality, intonation, or playing style "sticks out." With most school ensembles, instructional time is devoted to group objectives although the teacher may be keenly aware of individual progress—not an easy task with 100 students with unique competencies and needs. *The basic purpose of the school music program, however, is to teach musical independence.*

Teaching music is unique in the responsibility a teacher has for assisting others to accomplish the widest possible range of individual *and* group objectives. Music educators work on both simultaneously, which is challenging for anyone. No other school subject equals the complexity of objectives in the music program; individual students are uneven in individual skills and their personal objectives for each rehearsal differ. Theatre and dance have individual and group objectives but their individual objectives are broader than those in bands, orchestras, wind ensembles, and jazz groups. The genius in teaching is providing specific feedback to each individual student on his or her present performance competency and also aiding that individual to attain excellence on objectives important to the ensemble and/or society. Being helpful does not imply providing positive or negative comments; it implies providing fair and objective comments. The setting of individual objectives in music has been greatly aided by the existence of the Music Educators National Conference's (MENC) Voluntary National Standards, by more specific outcome content statements in state curriculum frameworks, by methods books, and by extensive professional development offered by school districts to aid teachers in assessing the progress of their students toward meeting challenging *performance* standards.

Music can be important in the lives of individuals only when individual, group, and program objectives that have real meaning are attained and at rather high levels. (Program objectives are not discussed in this chapter; such objectives assure the public that the school has a complete music program, well supported by those with authority over school matters.) It is not absolutely clear what the minimum skill level must be in the nation's schools in order to bring about a positive result; but, broadly put, each student must independently be able to perform one's part as soloist or in an ensemble, with appropriate music. Certainly, a semester's acquaintance with the violin in third grade won't satisfy an objective of "musical intelligence." John Kinyon suggests a typical performance standard: "when a concert is scheduled (at the end of one semester of instruction or later) students should be able to proficiently sight-read music of comparable difficulty." There are, of course, musical experiences other than performance; however, performance objectives remain the strongest and most memorable part of any music program.

It is probably impossible to teach music in the most efficient manner at all times, because emphasizing one type of objective will result in the temporary neglect or abandonment of other areas. The second orchestra and other technique classes need objectives as badly as the top organizations—perhaps more so—if they are to produce results and retain students' interest. Objectives unquestionably contribute to student achievement and satisfaction at every level, and the challenging objectives stretch the teacher's abilities as well as those of the students. The terms *lesser groups* and *remedial band* should not be used any more than labeling freshman English a "lesser" course than senior English, as the objectives are not less challenging.

The teacher must always be concerned with individual differences, because the progress of each individual within her groups will depend on the individual's background, aptitude, interest, private study, peer group, and home cooperation, perhaps more so for music than for any other course in which the student engages. In spite of the teacher's desire to retain students in her groups, the teacher must be honest in evaluating their progress and reporting it to them and their parents. The common practice of giving everyone As and Bs or bland, nonspecific comments will help to keep some students in performing groups, but if this practice is accompanied by low aims and low standards, it will quickly breed contempt.

OBJECTIVES FOR SPECIAL POPULATIONS

The instrumental program has long been successful in accommodating students with special needs. For those students who have individual educational programs (IEPs), it is important to discuss the music program with the student's counselor and with the parents to insure that appropriate objectives are included in the IEP along with pedagogically sound methods to accomplish them. Frequently the primary reasons for providing musical experiences for these students center on therapeutic rather than musical goals. Both can be accommodated with proper coordination and planning. The instrumental music program has included many different etiologies and different special-needs cases; a description of a few specifics may serve to illustrate the conduct of instrumental music education with this population.

The gifted are included in today's description of students with special needs, and students musically gifted should not be ignored. They need challenges and opportunities to develop their musical giftedness and meeting these needs is basic to the success of instrumental music in the public schools. As most music educators themselves were musically gifted, an understanding of this population usually presents no problem. The new understanding needed is how to provide for those students who are mentally, physically, behaviorally, socially, and emotionally different.

In the mid-1970s, Paul Rosene completed a doctoral dissertation that documented an instrumental music program in a public school for students with IQs ranging from around 50 to 80. He was able to attain the goals of the instrumental music program by conducting the instruction at a slower pace and providing additional individualized instruction. The accommodations that he made included more one-on-one instruction, the use of iconic notation, extensive rote learning, and direct instruction on several topics including care of instruments.[2]

Many of Rosene's students became sufficiently competent to qualify for membership in the school's regular instrumental program. Although mainstreaming of

---

[2] Paul Rosene, (1976), *A Field Study of Wind Instrument Training for Educable Mentally Handicapped Children*, unpublished doctoral dissertation, University of Illinois, Urbana-Champaign.

students is an important educational concept, tracking that provides the necessary basic skills in an accepting atmosphere remains the most viable solution to preparing students for any mainstreamed instrumental music experiences. Once these students have developed skills on their instrument and understand rehearsal routines, they can be mainstreamed without seriously impacting the group goals of the traditional program. Heterogeneity is basic to any instrumental group: It already includes students of as many as four age levels, students with different years of experience and background, including private lessons. Such a group provides a hospitable atmosphere for other students requiring individual objectives. Rosene's findings match the research in general music that indicates that students with mental handicaps should be compared on expectations with nonmentally handicapped students of comparable *mental*, not chronological, age. Special-needs students may present behavioral problems due to their shorter attention span or other variables in their backgrounds. Any classroom disruptions should be handled fairly and equitably. Young students often perform less well when learning music of slow tempos due to their mental age or even ADD. These students are more likely to have educational problems related to their musical memory than with basic musical perceptional tasks, although Ellis found that mentally handicapped students did as well on the *Music Achievement Tests* as did nonhandicapped students, except on pitch perception.[3]

Folklore has it that blind students have superior musical abilities; the truth is that their musical abilities are comparable to students who are not visually impaired. They may be more alert to aural stimuli and often have developed work habits that assist them in completing musical tasks. Braille music can be procured at no cost from the Library of Congress for these students, although time constraints may make this approach infeasible. The instructor may need to make an audio tape of the student's music that enables the student to do the practicing necessary to learn the music. Visually impaired students often have excellent attention spans due to the need to rely on their ears and their memories for large blocks of instruction in all subjects. If the student's aide does not attend rehearsals, the student's stand partner should relay nonverbal information such as cutoffs and the occasional frown by prearranged signals such as a touching of knees.

The director must, however, be continually mindful of the need to accommodate the presence of students with special needs. In the case of the visually impaired, he or she needs to provide additional verbal instructions to include "counting off" as preparation for the downbeat and allowing for the possible embarrassment of the student who may continue to play after the ensemble has been stopped. A full understanding of the possible and likely problems in accommodating students with special needs is justification for course work in teacher education and for attendance at workshops at which various strategies are suggested.

We know of a totally blind student who, through effort and perseverance, not only became solo clarinet in his high school band but also marched with the band. During his senior year in high school he served as the drum major! Present research data indicate that it may require the visually impaired student triple the practice time to accomplish the same objectives. Understanding those students with special needs must extend well beyond instructor knowledge, as the provisions for accommodation need to be part of the education of every student in the ensemble. When the peers are accepting and understanding of the extra accommodations that need to be made, parents and administration become equally supportive.

---

[3] Donald L. Ellis (1982), *Differences in Music Achievement Among Gifted and Talented, Average, and Educable Mentally Handicapped Fifth-and Sixth Grade Students*, unpublished doctoral dissertation, University of North Carolina, Greensboro.

A considerable body of literature exists on music for the deaf, although little research is pertinent to the schools. Students with partial deafness require special consideration due to their hearing aids and an inability to understand all of the instructions or cues from the teacher and other students. Evelyn Glennie has demonstrated that a deaf percussionist can rise to the top of the profession. She is, of course, an exceptional case but she demonstrates what is possible with appropriate accommodations. Although the deaf can lip-read and see the signals and gestures in the rehearsal, special assistance is necessary because of the difficulty in communicating instructions through modeling as well as verbal instruction. The inability to hear the humor in the director's voice can lead to misunderstandings.[4]

The physically handicapped are the easiest to accommodate if the school building and buses meet mandated standards. It has become commonplace to see in the televised holiday parades a student in a wheelchair in one of the participating bands being pushed by a friend. The public generally understands the needs of the physically handicapped and does not find a student and his wheelchair on stage for the spring concert particularly unusual. Greater understanding of the physically handicapped has been aided by the success and efforts of musicians such as Itzhak Perlman.

The teacher needs to reduce distracters, especially for the mentally handicapped student. The teacher also needs to ensure that all students in the ensemble or class understand the issues and why the pace of the rehearsal may have to be slow or the instructions exaggerated. The teacher should seek information about the particular handicapping etiologies of students in the ensemble. Students with Down syndrome are not, as often supposed, more musical than the average student but often are equally competent on rhythmic tasks.

Students with special needs may be discouraged from becoming involved in instrumental music by guidance counselors who believe that the emphasis should be on developing independent living skills or that the student needs additional time on the basic subjects. Instrumental music, however, can provide a needed balance to their general education. The field of special education is developing at a rapid pace, especially since the 1978 integration regulations. With special-needs students representing about 10 percent of the population, a wealth of potential talent is available, as are new understandings to the remaining 90 percent. Special-needs students may have multiple handicaps, which takes the issues discussed here to a different plane, requiring the assistance of the special education teacher, aides, and/or a level of special instruction and accommodation that may be beyond the resources available to the instrumental music department. In such cases, the school administration must be responsible.

ORGANIZING OBJECTIVES

The effective teacher needs to organize objective domains not only by individual and group objectives but also according to what he or she wants the student to know (*cognitive*), wants the students to be able to do (*psychomotor*), and wants the students to value (*affective*). A cognitive objective might require the student to trace the history of his or her instrument and know artists' names. A psychomotor objective would be to play a chromatic scale of two octaves ascending and descending at MM=120 quarter notes with no errors. An affective objective expressed in behavioral terms might be that the student earns money to purchase the complete recordings of Otto Klemperer. We have previously stressed the possibility for a

[4] Evelyn Glennie (1990), *Good Vibrations: My Autobiography,* London: Hutchinson.

fourth taxonomy of learning, that of *perception*. Although perception is often included as a cognitive activity, perception is not well served by Bloom's taxonomy. In organizing music instruction, it is helpful to distinguish between knowing and perceiving. Perceiving is the skill of hearing—hearing melodies, rhythms, harmonies, and timbres when performed and hearing them in one's head. The teacher's responsibility is to assist those students with talent and interest to attain standards in all domains—knowledge, perception, skill, and valuing. Mediocrity of achievement, usually resulting from low expectations, destroys interest, frustrates talent, and kills passion for the subject.

With the abundance of knowledge to be learned and skills to be attained in all types of music, only the trained teacher can chart each student's objectives toward musical excellence. An amateur would leave gaps in the learning sequence and thus misuse the appropriate time for learning. Educational theorists speak of organizing instruction according to a need to know (problem solving) or according to the great literature being studied, but unfortunately music doesn't work this way. One can't wait until a high C appears in the music to learn to play high C. There is no instant Stravinsky mix that takes only 20 minutes in the microwave when the need occurs. Knowing what Stravinsky often demands of his players, however, makes practicing exercises more meaningful. Instruction books and materials are important and plentiful—so plentiful that lucid objectives are needed to provide additional structure, to weight priorities, and to focus activities and experiences into meaningful learning.

The role of instructional objectives is not confined to a clear statement of *behavioral* objectives for individuals and groups. *Experiential* objectives, both focused and unfocused, are also a valuable part of musical goals. For example, a required experience might be to attend two live concerts each year, as attendance at concerts can result in considerable learning. Although the learning will differ among jazz concerts or between a wind ensemble and an orchestra concert, students who pay attention (*to something*) will learn something. Attending a concert is only one important experience; participating in a music contest and going to a record store to buy one's first CD are additional examples of important *experiences*. Experiences can also be focused toward specific ends, in which case the probability of learning is higher and more controlled. Selected students may be asked to speak before the school board about the importance of the music program in their lives (and all students could assist in assembling data and testimonials). Other focused experiential activities would include reflecting on their most *memorable* musical experiences, to think about the "Aha!" when a rehearsed piece of music first became meaningful and fun to play, or to report what they told their parents they were learning in orchestra. Focused response to experiences could compare and contrast the music heard, evaluate the performance, or describe the perceived receptivity of the audience. Incorporating experiential objectives into the sequence of instruction of objectives makes learning come alive.

Instrumental objectives include the encyclopedic number of nonmusical objectives that are important to the vitality of school music. Students learn to cooperate, to defer, to respect the situation, to take pride in their ensemble and themselves, to concentrate, and to be responsible; the list could go on to fill a small encyclopedia. A well-run, challenging music program has many nonmusical outcomes; students are less likely to drop out of school before graduating, and they learn the importance of community service (having to parade on every holiday). Their good musical work habits transfer to in- and out-of-school assignments. School attendance and punctuality frequently improve in members of well-run bands and orchestras. Good musicians take responsibility for their own health and conduct as well as responsibility for their instrument and music. These *instrumental* objectives are very visible—even the good physical condition of drum and bugle corps members is noticed by the community, and it is no surprise that instrumental objectives have received more press than the student's ability to manipulate her way through two modulations and three modes. The mindful teacher cannot ignore instrumental objectives. The first required general music instruction was justified on the basis of health and moral outcomes, and later (1850–1940) when delinquent children (boys mainly) were sent to state reformatories, participation in the reformatory band was considered one of the most important "reform" experiences.

The various objectives—cognitive, psychomotor, affective, perceptual, and experiential—must at times be considered by teachers as process or developmental objectives. In this event, their assessment will focus entirely on improvement; and the polished performance evaluation will be delayed.

Objectives should relate to standards and eventually, once the decision is made as to what all students should know and be able to do, to a coherent curriculum. The greater task is to establish priorities and communicate these to your students and other stakeholders. Students have so many opportunities in many fields that they continually establish priorities while accepting some by default. The sequence for connecting objectives to standards seems to be the following:

1. Identify the (long-term or short-term) objective so that its content standards and the performance standards are well defined and clear. Expectations must be reasonable. On a daily, weekly, or monthly basis, every student is informed as to what he or she is expected to hear, to know, to understand, to be able to perform—in what context and with what music.

2. Identify the evidence the student must provide to indicate that she has attained adequate, proficient, or advanced levels in knowing, understanding, hearing, and doing. Again, clarity is of utmost importance—on one hearing, at sight or rehearsed, oral, performed, or written. Trained music educators can, with some thought, describe the expected conditions but must provide a model of the level of skill expected before all students understand.

Identifying the enablers falls into place once the objectives are clear. Methods and techniques are determined by the objectives—selection of a band or orchestra method book is not the way to begin. To begin, make a list of the desired concepts, principles, facts, and experiences that are potential objectives, then consider the ways of assessing each. After this list is formulated, the objectives can be formulated and sequenced, and the instructional time and other required resources estimated. With the objectives of the instrumental program and the potential of each experience in mind, the teacher can formulate goals for the year. From the year's objectives, one can derive weekly, monthly, and sometimes daily goals. When written, these become a blueprint for teaching. When directors skip lesson plans, this omission usually indicates a focus on the performance of music rather than on music as a vehicle for learning. The music performed must be partially determined by objectives; not every class is based entirely on specified instructional objectives, but every successful class is based on a well-formulated plan. The intensity with which any particular composition is rehearsed will depend upon what it offers in terms of objectives; whether a festival is attended or ignored will depend upon how it fits into the objectives for the group. The amount of drill, section rehearsal, listening to records, and/or marching practice will also be determined by the objectives.

To formulate a set of objectives for the total program is a large task. But a careful formulation of objectives is the best starting point for productive teaching and frequent reference to the objectives is the best method for evaluating the quality of the teaching.

Music instruction, however, is often an exception to the teaching models in education because there is no "ideal time" at which the concert music is selected. Great music has seldom been written with student performers in mind and very little good music fits a neat pattern of sequenced instruction. This difference in instructional materials explains why difficult concert passages may have to be taught by rote or require intense, time-consuming drill. Although many teachers begin with the music as the teaching objective, a better approach is to select the music at the same time the instructional goals are identified. The music, however, remains more important than any *single* knowledge or skill, which explains the need for *occasional* rote drill.

THE RELATION OF STANDARDS TO OBJECTIVES AND ASSESSMENT

The Voluntary National Standards list nine content areas for music students, preschool through grade twelve. Although instrumental teachers will be most interested in the *performance* standards, the content standards are important. How well do we expect students to perform the content standards? The expectation of the national standard is that students will be required to select one of the four art forms (music, visual arts, theatre, dance) to study at the high school level and that states will use these standards as a reference to assess the teaching and learning. If the assessment is high stakes (the performance will determine whether the student can graduate from high school), careful selection of the objectives that conform to the content standards is necessary. These nine standards require considerable thought and discussion; their definitions follow in the order of their prominence in instrumental music education.

Content Standard 2 addresses performing on instruments, alone and with others; here a varied repertoire of quality music is obviously of importance. At the high school level, students should adequately perform music of difficulty level 4 on the six-point New York scale. Students at this age are expected to perform well alone and in small and large ensembles.

Content Standard 5, reading and notating music, is a corollary to being able to perform in instrumental music ensembles. Directors are expected to introduce students to more than the single line in their parts, perhaps requiring the reading (singing or playing) of four-part music to offer an idea of chords and harmony. The notating music objective is not accomplished if students cannot write out an improvisation or original composition, take dictation, or transpose their part. All percussionists are expected to be competent with mallet instruments that require music reading ability. Instrumental music students are expected to master *Content Standard 6*— listening to, analyzing, and describing music using their knowledge of the technical terms and the expressive devices in various genres. *Content Standard 7* is also a part of learning to play an instrument, as it requires that students should evaluate music and music performances. Students should be able to compare and contrast music identifying the important specifics and using the vocabulary that would be expected of a music critic. *Content Standard 3* asks that students improvise melodies, variations, and accompaniments. Too often students can neither harmonize nor add the bass part, both of which are reasonable expectations of high school students studying instrumental music. Students should also develop the ability to sing alone and with others a varied repertoire of music, *Content Standard 1*.

Whether students have time to learn to compose well or to relate music to the other arts and to disciplines outside the arts is difficult to conjecture, *Standards 4 and 8. Standard 9*, understanding music in relation to history and culture, is a more viable objective for the orchestra member than for the member of the wind ensemble, as a major part of the wind ensemble literature has been composed within the past few years and predominantly by American composers.

The National Standards are not objectives; an objective is more specific and will state clearly not only the content but also how well a student is to perform. Formulating objectives requires consideration of three standards—the content standard, the performance standard, and the opportunity-to-learn standard. The distinction is clearer if one thinks in terms of grades or contest ratings—what would you expect of an A student? a B student? a C student? Or, think in terms of a solo chair performer, an advanced performer, a good performer, a proficient performer, a performer at the basic level, and an unsatisfactory performer. The number of levels depends on the teacher's ability to distinguish among them. These descriptors could be part of a rubric, a statement that describes the degree of accuracy expected—no more than one sloppy attack, two wrong notes, or whatever for each standard. When language fails, the teacher should have a taped model of every level of performance, thus enabling the student to compare his or her own performance with that of the ensemble's standard of excellence.

The basic performance standard or assessment might be this: Two weeks prior to any public performance, without advance notice, each student will perform any of the music programmed with no more than two errors in pitch, one error in rhythm, and with tone quality, attacks, and releases acceptable to the instructor and matching the taped example.

Every facet of instruction must be supported by well-understood (printed) performance standards (and objectives) that every student must meet to remain in the ensemble, to participate in small ensembles, or whatever performance criteria are agreed upon between students, teachers, and administration. Standards and objectives must have consequences, good and bad. Teachers must convey the idea that some students will have to make a greater effort than others to meet the standards the group has agreed upon. Effort is part of ability and should be acknowledged. Instruments differ in their complexity as well as does the music. The required effort is not standardized in any ensemble.

Regardless of how specific the objectives are, they are only a list of good intentions. Any number of bad music programs possesses good objectives. Each objective must have a minimum standard representing a specific accomplishment toward which the pupils' energies and efforts are directed.

EXTRAMUSICAL VALUES

The school's broad objectives for the total life of the student—citizenship, literacy, moral responsibility, critical thinking, and skill in problem solving—often say very little about selecting appropriate objectives or meeting the standards of the music program. Nevertheless, the teacher must balance the music program's musical goals with the school's broad objectives, recognizing how effective musical participation can be in reaching valuable nonmusical goals for both the individual student and the school as a whole.

Two basic objectives seem prominent in today's schools. One is to fit the student into the complex twenty-first-century American definition of democracy and life as contributing citizen and productive individual. The other is to prepare the student for some form of endeavor after graduation, either further education or a vocation. The school has the continuing problem of balancing these two broad aims—personal development and mastery of subject matter. Each of these goals' appeal has fluctuated to reflect changing social demands since 1900. At present the pendulum has swung rather sharply in the direction of subject matter after an era in which personal development was emphasized. Music contributes to each in varying degrees, and what it cannot do it should not attempt. Music is well fitted for developing a number of nonmusical values promoted by the culture, as our discussion of instrumental objectives indicated. Because music integrates so well with a variety of other subjects and values, teachers have been known to lose sight of their own goals while pursuing secondary objectives. With today's emphasis on subject matter, however, music educators have the opportunity to speak up for the quality of their course content and that of the music studied and performed.

At the same time, the effectiveness of the extramusical values in program support must not be underestimated. Consider the history of instrumental music. Though the orchestra came into the public schools first, the marching band has been the vehicle through which the instrumental music program has flourished, obtaining equipment, literature, building space, professionally educated teachers, and public attention, in a manner that was impossible for the wind ensemble or the orchestra. Music found a fairly secure place, not because it caused a noticeable upgrading of musicianship in society or in the school, but because the marching band publicized the school, created excitement and spirit for competitive athletics, and made patriotic holidays more colorful. The music contest, with its often nonmusical but clearly defined goals, has also been one of the primary sources of support for the entire music program. The effective teacher utilizes the colorful, attention-getting facets of the music program, but keeps them in proper relationship to the actual teaching content of music. It is fortunate that some of these goals are compatible with musical goals; for example, discipline, cooperation, leadership, fellowship, and individual responsibility.

The Cardinal Principles of Secondary Education were formulated in 1918 by a commission of the National Education Association. They are outmoded in today's educational thought but are not quite out of style. Books and curriculum goals written in the past have offered as the *raison d'être* of school music as its ability to contribute to health, command of fundamental processes, vocation, responsible home membership, worthy use of leisure time, civic education, and ethical character. Many of these, including character education, are also twenty-first century objectives. Some of the attractions of school music are that it promotes informality, makes use of physically healthful activities, and involves interrelationships with the student's home life. Music can provide the benefits of teamwork, yet it has an advantage over competitive athletics in its utilization of larger numbers of students and wider ranges of student ability. Compared to the first 10 players in basketball, the "first-string" band contains a greater number of students, many of whom have not developed skills comparable to the first-string basketball team. Still, they derive the same feeling of accomplishment from concert and competition, even when sitting last chair. The fact that music can accommodate groups of widely varying size with a wide variety of ability and interest levels is strongly in its favor. In addition, one of the important benefits the successful player acquires is a self-imposed discipline in developing the competencies that allow music to be an emotional outlet and a means of self-expression.

In formulating objectives, some account should be taken of the goals of personal development and how these can be furthered within the music program. If the aims are more than musical, the student who is not particularly talented can be enrolled, knowing that she will have an opportunity to develop important competence through interaction with her peers even if she does not progress very far musically. A place will be found for her, though maybe not in the best performing group, so that she can have the experiences music offers that help her grow as an individual and a member of society.

The value of the marching band as a device for public relations and a source of enjoyment for students is a reality that the director cannot ignore, regardless of how much he prefers to conduct the symphonic band or the wind ensemble. The marching band must have objectives and the members must be skillful—both in marching and in playing. The director cannot afford to feel that the marching band is an inferior part of the year's activities, simply to be tolerated. The marching band is the student's first introduction to the year's activities. To wait for enthusiasm and interest to flourish with the first concert is hazardous—the group may by that time reflect carelessness and negativity produced by the chore of weekly football shows under an indifferent director. There are always opportunities to teach some music, technique, range, breathing, endurance, and even musical understanding. Good and bad arrangements can be compared, marches can be learned well enough to improve fingers and ears, and the quality of the music played in field shows can be discussed for comparison with other kinds of music.

THE PRIORITY OF OBJECTIVES

Music's firm position in the school curriculum may be due primarily to its power as an activity, but its basic essence is art. Public school music may seldom reach the level of art, yet it retains the drawing power of art—the ability to symbolize the feelings of humankind that cannot be put into conventional language. Like most adults, children are not aware of the symbolic quality of music but they react to it. Any teacher of the arts must be concerned primarily with guiding the student's growth in aesthetic sensitivity and understanding—in helping him learn the principles of that particular art, what the artist is trying to do, and how to find meaning in the great works of art.

Teaching for aesthetic growth is not simple. It is seldom accomplished by using vague terms (cool or awesome) to describe to the students the beauty of a work. It is accomplished by helping students recognize what they hear in a composition—balance, contrast, tension, relaxation, form, texture, color, mood—and how these are related. The teacher's purpose is to develop in the student the ability to hear music, understand its structure, and know whether the work he has heard is great music, good music, or trivial music, and why. Such teaching requires teachers who can really *hear* music and understand it well enough to explain and model it.

Aesthetic growth has as its objective music "appreciation" in the genuine sense—not appreciation as it denotes a course in which many compositions are heard, their composers discussed, and their dates pinpointed in a time continuum, but instead, denoting careful attention to a few compositions. Music being performed or studied should be examined to hear how it is put together, how melodies interact, how harmonies create tension and resolve, how instruments blend and stand out, how phrases return and lead to other phrases. Aesthetic growth means that the student should learn what makes the quality of Franz Schubert's music better than that of John Williams's— the student should hear for himself the difference, not simply be told of it—and should be at least respectful, if not loving, in the presence of Bach.

To teach music as an art is difficult because it requires skill and preparation on the part of the teacher. Directors of performing groups tend to slide over this objective, presuming that as students play more music and play it well they will acquire understanding and appreciation. This is simply not so. The third horn player, struggling with her part, does not pay much attention to the principal themes and perhaps not even to the harmonic structure of which she is a part. The oboe player knows melodies he himself plays and probably hears more than the third horn player, but hearing the melody is not tantamount to listening with understanding. Players should be aware of the harmonic structure of the music they play—where key changes occur, where unusual chords appear, and how unexpected harmonies heighten tension or create suspense in the music. Can students recognize the thematic material when it appears in an inner voice or in altered form? Do they understand how the composer uses motives and themes both to hold the work together and to give it contrast and variety? Because these things differ in every musical work, the teacher must talk about the music itself as well as about the fingering for fifth-line F♯.

At times students should listen rather than play. Listening to recorded versions of the music they are rehearsing or compositions with similar form or style can broaden understanding. But one does not become aware of all the things happening within a complex piece of music simply by sitting passively and listening—the process is active and takes expert guidance. Being proactive is the teacher's job, whether she is an instrumental director or a grade school music teacher.

Music understanding and satisfaction depend upon skill. Around the turn of the century, when choral music was required and was taught as an academic class, the skill of reading music was emphasized to the exclusion of other facets of the art. The movable *do* system, with its chromatics up and down, was drilled into every pupil. Some students learned to read music fairly well but often opened a songbook for the last time at the graduation exercises. Overemphasis on music-reading ability was replaced by "pleasure in music," "experiences with music," "discovering music," and "music for every child." To deride the philosophy of pleasurable experiences in music is easy, but this philosophy has much to recommend it. We would never return to the older drill method that recognized so little of the joyous, free response to music that is part of the child's nature, nor limit ourselves to the narrow use of materials and activities that the singing classes exemplified. The rich variety of approaches to music that the fivefold program and its successors brought into being is taken so much for granted that we fail to appreciate it. Singing, rhythmic, listening, instrumental, and creative activities all serve to keep children interested and actively engaged in music, preparing them for the band and orchestra programs and choral groups in the later public school years.

Musical activities should be varied because all children do not respond to the same musical stimuli. Diversity, however, is a mixed blessing. The activities themselves rather than the learning they embody tend to become the focus. Today rhythmic activities are conducted but students learn little about rhythm. Students sing but do not grow in reading skills nor in beauty of singing. Rhythm instruments are employed but students have little conception of the patterns created or the rhythm symbols that denote these patterns. Two- and three-part harmony is attempted with no knowledge of what a major chord or a tonal center is. Individuals listen to music as if it were the background score for an imaginary television drama instead of catching the return of themes and the building of climaxes. As students pass from elementary into secondary school, they are forced to become more specialized. Choosing between performing groups, music appreciation, and music theory is a matter of priorities. The performing groups expect skill, but in varying degrees. It is no secret that performing levels are uneven in bands and orchestras. The sad truth is that without thoughtful practices including sequenced objectives, children exposed to 10 to 12 years of music are badly lacking in tangible skills and musical understanding.

Valid music programs need objectives that focus on mental skills, aural skills, and physical dexterity on an instrument, along with musical understanding. Knowledge of key signatures, time signatures, clefs, and tempo indications is not enough. The player must also hear the notes as he sees them on the page; he must listen intelligently to hear and understand key centers and modulations, meter changes, return of previous thematic materials, and changes of mode and texture in the music. He must be able to look at his part in the score and play it musically, with thought for line and phrase. He must manage the technical requirements of his part—if not the first time through, then with a little practice. He should be able to concentrate sufficiently on a three-minute piece of music to keep his mind actively on it from beginning to end. He ought to have sufficient tonal memory to retain obvious themes after he has heard them a few times. The fact that music is for all does not invalidate the importance of learning musical skills in the public school. The student who wishes to play but not to develop any musical skills should be guided rather than accommodated. The purpose of the schools is to change the individual into something more than he is now.

The experience of skillfully performing a piece of music should not be underestimated. Skillful group performances are important both for the thrill they offer and for the high standard they set. Playing music badly is a waste of time. A polished performance of concert music encompasses a majority of the important goals of music: good tone, correct notes, technical skill, knowledge of musical symbols and terms, awareness of the style and form of the music, control of tone quality and intonation, and ability to follow the conductor. Each student must excel on his or her part, even though it may be simple; the necessity for excellence from everyone in the group is the primary reason why performance is of such value for learning.

No book can allocate the distribution of time for performance or for any other aspect of learning; the teacher herself will have to decide how much emphasis to place on developing skills, on the basic understanding of music, and how much of the year's music should be performed with the goal of perfection in mind. If flawless performance alone is the goal, students tend to become mechanical wonders who can play with precision but often without musical independence or understanding. On the other hand, the goal of excellent performance is both the inspiration and the chief learning vehicle of the music program. In formulating objectives, therefore, the music teacher must realistically consider all types of objectives as important, with individual outcomes the highest priority. Students try to make music an activity rather than a course. But—and the teacher must not overlook this—students like to learn, enjoy challenges, and like to progress in knowledge as well as skill; their pride in achievement is spontaneous and great.

Often the high school director does not consider her groups to be a continuation of the music program at the lower levels and she does not recognize the performing groups as a vehicle for progress built on previous attainment. When she thinks about the music program at the lower levels, she is inclined to complain about what her students failed to learn instead of taking responsibility for these objectives and making the process a continuous one. The high school band and orchestra share the same broad goals as the kindergarten and fourth-grade music classes and the high school appreciation class. Instrumental teachers might do well to visit grade school music classes occasionally, talk with elementary teachers and music supervisors, help with rhythmic activities or pre-instrumental instruments, and discuss common goals and how to reach them.

Finally, the director must be willing to work cooperatively with a number of individuals and community groups who want her services but who do not necessarily contribute to her objectives. To deal with administrators, athletic directors, and civic leaders who wish to have bands and orchestras perform for various school or community functions, the instrumental teacher has to sacrifice some orderly, logical scheduling of learning experiences despite the importance of a sequential curriculum based on the discipline of music. A sequential curriculum within high school bands and orchestras, with twelfth-grade students undergoing different experiences from ninth graders, makes little sense. The theory of asking each student to work to her fullest potential throughout high school, however, is sound, as is the concern for a rich, pedagogically based program designed to enhance musical understanding.

BIBLIOGRAPHY

Texts

* Indicates out of print in 2001.

ABELES, HAROLD, CHARLES HOFFER, and ROBERT KLOTMAN (1994). *Foundations of Music Education*, 2nd ed. New York: Schirmer Books.

AMERICAN SCHOOL BAND DIRECTORS ASSOCIATION (1997). *The New ASBDA Curriculum Guide.* Miami: Warner Brothers.

ANDERSON, LORIN, DAVID KRATHWOHL, and BENJAMIN BLOOM (2000). *A Taxonomy for Learning, Teaching, Assessing: A Revision of Bloom's Taxonomy of Educational Objectives.* New York Longman Publishing.

*BLOOM, BENJAMIN (1956), *Taxonomy of Educational Objectives: The Classification of Educational Goals.* New York: Longman.

COLWELL, RICHARD (1991). *Basic Concepts in Music Education*, II. Niwot, CO: University Press of Colorado.

*——— (1992). *Handbook of Research on Music Teaching and Learning.* New York: Schirmer Books.

CSIKSZENTMIHALYI, MIHALY (1993). *Flow: The Psychology of Optimal Experience.* New York: Harper & Row.

DARLING-HAMMOND, LINDA (1997). *The Right to Learn: A Blueprint for Creating Schools That Work.* San Francisco: Jossey-Bass.

ELLIOTT, DAVID J. (1995). *Music Matters: A New Philosophy of Music Education.* New York: Oxford University Press.

ELLIS, DONALD L. (1982). *Differences in Music Achievement Among Gifted and Talented, Average, and Educable Mentally Handicapped Fifth- and Sixth-Grade Students.* Unpublished doctoral dissertation, University of North Carolina, Greensboro.

*FLETCHER, PETER (1987). *Education and Music.* New York: Oxford University Press.

*GLENNIE, EVELYN (1990). *Good Vibrations: My Autobiography.* London: Hutchinson.

GRONLUND, NORMAN E. (2000). *How to Write and Use Instructional Objectives*, 6th ed. Upper Saddle River, NJ: Merrill.

HALL, LOUIS O. (ed.) (1997). *Strategies for Teaching: Guide for Music Methods Classes.* Reston, VA: Music Educators National Conference.

*HARROW, ANITA J. (1972). *A Taxonomy of the Psychomotor Domain: A Guide for Developing Behavioral Objectives.* New York: Longman.

HINCKLEY, JUNE (ed.) (1994). *Music at the Middle Level: Building Strong Programs.* Reston, VA: Music Educators National Conference.

HOFFER, CHARLES (1993). *Introduction to Music Education*, 2nd ed. Belmont, CA: Wadsworth.

——— (2001). *Teaching Music in the Secondary Schools*, 5th ed. Belmont, CA: Wadsworth.

*HOUSE, ROBERT (1958). "Curriculum Construction in Music Education," in *Basic Concepts in Music Education, 57th Yearbook of the National Society for the Study of Education, Part I,* Nelson Henry, ed. Chicago: University of Chicago Press.

JENNINGS, JOHN F. (1998). *Why National Standards and Tests? Politics and the Quest for Better Schools.* Thousand Oaks, CA : Sage.

KOHUT, DANIEL L. (1973). *Instrumental Music Pedagogy.* Upper Saddle River, NJ: Prentice Hall; reprint (1996) Champaign, IL: Stipes.

KRATHWOHL, DAVID, BENJAMIN BLOOM, and BERTRAM MASIA (1964). *Taxonomy of Educational Objectives: The Classification of Educational Goals. Handbook 2: Affective Domain.* New York: D. Longman; reprint (1999) New York: Longman Publishing.

*LEONHARD, CHARLES, and ROBERT W. HOUSE (1972). *Foundations and Principles of Music Education*, 2nd ed. New York: McGraw-Hill.

MAGER, ROBERT F. (1997). *Preparing Instructional Objectives*, 3rd ed., Vol. 2 of *The New Mager Six-Pack.* Atlanta: The Center for Effective Performance.

MARZANO, ROBERT (2001). *Designing a New Taxonomy of Educational Objectives.* Thousand Oaks, CA: Corwin.

MEIER, DEBORAH (1995). *The Power of Their Ideas: Lessons for America from a Small School in Harlem.* Boston: Beacon Press.

MUSIC EDUCATORS NATIONAL CONFERENCE (1996) *Performance Standards for Music: Strategies and Benchmarks for Assessing Progress Toward the*

National Standards, Grades K-12, Reston, VA. (Author)

———— (1996). *Aiming for Excellence: The Impact of the Standards Movement on Music Education.* Reston, VA: Music Educators National Conference.

———— (1994a). *Music for a Sound Education* (with videotape). Reston, VA: Music Educators National Conference.

———— (1994b). *National Standards for Arts Education: What Every Young American Should Know and Be Able to Do in the Arts.* Reston, VA: Music Educators National Conference.

NODDINGS, NEL (1998). *Philosophy of Education.* Boulder, CO: Westview Press.

*NORMANN, THEODORE (1939). *Instrumental Music in the Public Schools.* Byrn Mawr, PA: Oliver Ditson.

REIMER, BENNETT (1989). *A Philosophy of Music Education,* 2nd ed. Upper Saddle River, NJ: Prentice Hall.

ROSENE, PAUL (1976). *A Field Study of Wind Instrument Training for Educable Mentally Handicapped Children.* Unpublished doctoral dissertation, University of Illinois, Urbana-Champaign.

SCRUTON, ROGER (1999). *The Aesthetics of Music.* New York: Oxford University Press.

SINGLETON, IRA, and SIMON ANDERSON (1969). *Music in Secondary Schools,* 2nd ed. Boston: Allyn and Bacon.

SIZER, THEODORE R. (1996). *Horace's Hope: What Works for the American High School.* Boston: Houghton Mifflin.

———— (1999). *The Students Are Watching: Schools and the Moral Contract.* Boston: Beacon Press.

SMITH, RALPH A. (1994). *General Knowledge and Arts Education,* Urbana: University of Illinois.

SWANWICK, KEITH (1988). *Mind, Music, and Education.* London: Routledge.

———— (1999). *Teaching Music Musically.* London: Routledge.

*TAIT, MALCOLM, and PAUL HAACK (1984). *Principles and Processes of Music Education.* New York: Teachers College Press.

VAN BODEGRAVEN, PAUL (1966). "Music Education in Transition." In *Perspectives in Music Education, Source Book III,* ed. Bonnie C. Kowall. Washington, DC: Music Educators National Conference.

Instructional Videos

Conference for National Standards for American Education, 7 vols. (Olga Davis 1994). Oklahoma City: Oklahoma State Department of Education.

3

Evaluation

Evaluation is the keystone of the teaching process, yet it is an area largely neglected by the music teacher. Too often the teacher thinks of evaluation in terms of pupil selection, identifying those students best fitted for instrumental instruction or for membership in advanced groups or ensembles, as a means of motivating students by giving grades, or as an administrative necessity. Though important, these uses are minor when compared with the real purposes of evaluation.

DEFINING EVALUATION IN MUSIC

Good teaching that includes evaluation is illustrated by the private music lesson. This form of instruction has always been, and continues to be, the most effective vehicle for teaching music as an art and as a skill. The chief activity that distinguishes a private lesson from other music teaching is evaluation: The teacher continually evaluates the student's performance, making suggestions, changes, and assignments based on his appraisal of the student's progress. The objectives of the private lesson may seldom be stated or carefully thought out, but they are made clear to the student by the teacher's concern for specific strengths and weaknesses in the pupil's performance. At the end of each lesson and, indeed, within the lesson, teacher and student know what the student can do well and what needs attention. Evaluation is consistently made in terms of the music, the present or past assignment, and the student's ability. If classroom teachers, and we include ensemble conductors under this label, were to spend the same proportion of time on evaluation, they would soon make sound improvements in methods, materials, and approaches. However, the classroom teacher, busy keeping a roomful of pupils actively engaged in music making, tends to forget that activities can be meaningless without knowledge of intent and constant appraisal of results.

In the classroom, evaluation is facilitated by a precise definition of the objectives, stated in behavioral terms when possible. Good teaching can happen without stated objectives, but it is just that—a happening. These chance occurrences of exemplary teaching appear throughout the public school system, but are seldom permanent. Without objectives that can be verbalized, good music programs and good bands and orchestras come and go with the director. Music teachers give grades and counsel students without a consideration of their objectives, rendering their grading and counseling ineffective if not harmful. In music as in other areas, evaluation, recommendations, and advice should be as accurate as the science of music teaching allows. Evaluation can prescribe the objectives, but it should not. The teacher's philosophy and the school's philosophy dictate what is important in music and what should be taught.

Evaluation is often thought of only in terms of what the teacher does to the student—the kind of test created, the tryout or challenge system used or the point system enforced. However, one of the greatest benefits of evaluation is how it works *for* the student. Louis Thorpe states in the NSSE Yearbook, "Learning to play an instrument or to sing proceeds with greatest effectiveness when the individual periodically is provided with clear knowledge of progress made toward his goal."[1]

Any student can relate to the importance of evaluation. The first question by students in a new course is "How many tests and what kind?" Equal to her anxiety over a grade are (1) the student's pleasure in recognizing progress and (2) a need for structure in the learning process. The knowledgeable teacher uses this interest and concern to motivate learning. There is little doubt that most students work best under some pressure, so that those activities not evaluated tend to be neglected even if valued, under the demands of the educational process. Thus, evaluation when used for motivation is more than the mere giving of grades.

Measurement and evaluation are not synonymous. Measurement, the use of tests and scales that produce a specific grade, is a part of evaluation. Evaluation, however, encompasses a host of other factors and tools, including observation, interviews, checklists, and subjective appraisal. The giving of grades, so often considered the sum total of evaluation, frequently depends upon a single act of measurement, one test or one tryout. This not only is unfair to teacher and pupil but also is a complete misrepresentation of the role of evaluation.

Most important, to be effective evaluation must be systematic as well as comprehensive. Frequent, carefully planned steps will give the most accurate and complete appraisal of the teaching–learning situation. In music, with its many subjective judgments, the need for frequent, organized evaluative procedures is great.

PRINCIPLES FOR EVALUATION

In one sense, all teaching can be looked upon as an experiment, a continual process of improving learning through more effective materials and instruction. But simple trial and error is neither good teaching nor good experimentation. The knowledgeable teacher approaches instructional problems with some insight and can reject many approaches without trial in the classroom. Effective teaching, like effective experimentation, cannot take place without tools for determining the success of the endeavor. Once proven successful, methods and materials should be retained, but with the recognition that each combination of learning experience and student potential is new. The alert teacher must observe daily the results of the teaching situation.

Evaluation is dependent upon objectives, and, similarly, objectives cannot function without evaluation. The importance of this statement cannot be overstressed, but it has had little visible effect upon the teaching profession. Objectives are still often considered by themselves. Unfortunately, they serve little purpose when stated in such general terms that progress toward them cannot be evaluated. A common objective in music circles is "awareness", but it is like the pot at the end of the rainbow, vague

---

[1] Nelson Henry, ed. (1958). *Basic Concepts in Music Education*, in *The 57th Yearbook of the National Society for the Study of Education, Part I*, Chicago: University of Chicago Press, p. 192.

and unattainable. The objective "to improvise" is not much better as it also lacks specificity. Although broad program objectives cannot be systematically evaluated each day, some reasonable indication of their success or failure must be found.

Goals for the band or orchestra must primarily be those taught and reasonably attainable. One common set of objectives for all school situations is not feasible due to the students' differing backgrounds. Evaluation must be based upon a realistic appraisal of what is possible. The concept of a sequential curriculum in band and orchestra would be more difficult to implement than in any other subject. Not only are students different, but the demands of the parts in any piece of music differ in complexity and requisite skill. The most successful teacher considers the student and his instrument in formulating objectives and conducting systematic evaluation.

Evaluation cannot begin after the learning process has started. It must be part of the curriculum planning, taking place at every stage. In other disciplines, it is termed a *needs assessment.* Teachers tend to teach and emphasize favorite materials, ones they enjoy teaching, rather than basing content on an objective appraisal of student *needs.* Ensemble directors can often be typed by the kind of music performed and the manner of performance. With valid means of evaluation, these materials and methods can be appraised by experts, other faculty, and administrators, as well as by the teacher, to shape course content and keep it in line with student needs. Proper planning and frequent evaluation can minimize the need for radical revision later.

Evaluation in music must take into consideration the influence of noncurricular factors. Because music has entertainment and activity value, much learning takes place outside school. The effect of private music instruction, church or club music groups, performance in a combo or ensemble, and the exposure to music in the home environment must be accounted for before the school can take credit for student achievement. The factors that impact upon student outcomes also affect teacher evaluation plans.

It has become educationally fashionable to compare students, schools, teachers, buildings, states, and even nations with respect to school achievement, and it is incumbent upon all teachers to have data indicating that students are learning what they should know and be able to do. The public seems to accept football shows, exciting concerts, and contest wins as evidence of a solid music program. Most teachers and thoughtful school board members will require additional evidence if music teachers claim to be teaching musical understanding, appreciation, ability to read music, and knowledge about music, in addition to those skills needed for a successful performance. The best plan is to establish the objectives for the year cooperatively with students, administrators, and parents, and for the teacher to provide data at the end of the year that reflects the extent to which these goals have been met. One cannot expect that 100 percent of the students will meet the goals established for the ensemble or class; a reasonable expectation might be that 70 or 80 percent of the students will meet the standards established by group consensus.

Some schools have adopted a "gain score" or "value-added" approach to evaluation. The objective is to pre-evaluate all students and judge adequacy of the program on the year's gain. Although such a plan has obvious strengths and can be used to the teacher's advantage, sufficient weaknesses render it inappropriate as the sole evaluative criterion. Gain depends on one's initial ability and achievement level. Students could show marked gain and remain below acceptable standards, or show little gain and be among the nation's finest. And with high ability or achievement it is more difficult to demonstrate gain in raw scores or in percentages; the most advanced artist may spend months to improve the most subtle interpretations.

Much damage to music programs has come from those who insist that what they teach—the arts—cannot be evaluated. Such statements lack credibility. Any subject—and its subdomains of artistry, reflection, skill, and experience—that can be systematically taught can be systematically evaluated. "Experiences" as such, which are not objectives taught but are prepared for, are the one type of objective that is difficult to evaluate; yet even these can be tabulated and reported at the end of the year. We may not know what each student has learned from attending a concert of the New York Philharmonic, but we are still accountable in providing that experience for all students whose music education has been assigned to us. The emphasis in this chapter is on assessment measures that can be given to a group; ensemble directors always seem to be pressed for time.

EVALUATING MUSIC AS AN ART

To acquire an understanding of music as an art is far more difficult than to participate in music as an activity. Yet music is from first to last an art; activity and skill are only facets of learning this essential quality. As art eludes definition, it eludes evaluation. Most appropriate in instrumental music is to differentiate among the various kinds of learning that assist aesthetic development and to evaluate them. Such learning may also fit into the category of skills because certain skills are required in the aesthetic response. The learning related to understanding music as an art includes factual knowledge; discernment; understanding of style, orchestration, and structure; and perceptual listening skills. For the director who is teaching music through participation, it may be difficult to measure objectively the student's awareness of music as an art. However, evaluation devices can be used that are pertinent to the understanding of music from the listener's viewpoint.

Factual Knowledge

Measurement of factual knowledge is relatively easy. The problem is not testing for knowledge but preventing knowledge tests from becoming the only type of evaluation used. Too often a hastily constructed knowledge test is given in order to have a grade for semester reports, a practice that has little place in either good teaching or evaluation. Some factual knowledge is related directly to growth in musical skills—key and time signatures, pitch and rhythm symbols, tempo, and expression terms. These are found on the musical page and must be understood for skillful performance of the piece. They relate only indirectly to growth in musical understanding, however. The type of knowledge essential to musical understanding is that concerning the music itself, including its historical place and significance, form and structure, style, instrumentation, and social or extramusical connections. The more the student knows about the way music is put together, the people who put it together, the way "putting together" differs in various historical periods and countries, and the reasons for those differences, the greater will be his musical understanding.

The type of paper-and-pencil test with which to measure such knowledge is the teacher's option. Recognition tests (multiple choice), recall tests (short answer), essay tests, and occasionally a true–false test, can accurately measure factual knowledge. Of greater importance is measuring the student's ability to apply his knowledge when listening and performing. For listening, the test may consist of listening to a short composition one or more times and answering questions directly related to that piece of music. The piece may be familiar, perhaps one the group has been rehearsing, or it may be unfamiliar, depending upon the teacher's purpose. Questions asked may pertain to such items as form, style, possible historical period, possible composer, instruments used, tempos, dynamic levels, or texture. In performance, that performance should exude musical understanding.

Musical Discernment

Discernment is more than recognition of tunes or moods. It indicates the ability to follow the music as it unfolds, to distinguish great music from good music, to recognize the style of the composition, to understand the composer's message as reflected in the structure and style of the work, and to evaluate accurately the quality of the performance. Evaluation can take the form of the critical-incidence test, in which the student listens to music and answers questions about it. Or the student may be asked to listen to two or more compositions and, state which is the superior piece of music and why. In creating such tests, the teacher needs to be certain that she herself understands the music well and has formulated questions that truly reveal the acuity of the student's listening.

Recognition of Style and Structure

Recognition of style and structure is a part of both factual knowledge and discernment. It is mentioned separately because of its importance in understanding music as an art. One possible essence of an art object is its structure or form, and the style through which the form is displayed alters with each historical or cultural period. Therefore, the knowledgeable listener must know what to expect from a piece of music. He must not be bored or displeased when a classical symphony sounds different from late nineteenth-century, large-orchestra, "movie-mood" music. After he has become familiar with the baroque concerto style, the classical chamber music style, or a contemporary style, he is free to follow the form, to set up expectations as to what will happen in the music, and to take pleasure in how the composer fulfills or alters his expectations.

Tests in this area may take several forms. First, the simple objective test may be used, in which the student lists the characteristics of an art period, selects the correct answers from a given list, or answers true–false questions. The same can be used to test knowledge of form by asking the students to identify, label, or define certain musical forms such as rondo, sonata, or tone poem. These tests give no indication of her ability to apply the knowledge to her listening, however. A more revealing tool is the single-line score test. The student follows the score of the melody as she listens to a composition and indicates in the appropriate measures items that reveal style or form. She may be asked simply to check the measures in which important things happen in the music, or she may be asked to describe what is happening in certain important measures. A single-line score test can be as simple or as complicated as the situation requires; the teacher's responsibility lies in selecting a composition that can elicit good answers and in developing complete answers by which to evaluate the student's responses. A third type of test for this area is that described in the previous section, in which the student listens to a work and reflects and writes answers to specific questions about it, having no score to read from.

Auditory Skills

Because music is primarily a listener's art, listening skills are a necessary part of music participation. The relationship between seeing and hearing music is close; to mentally hear what is seen in the score and to visualize what is being heard are usually the marks of the skillful listener. However, some auditory skill can be developed without any accompanying visual skills: The student can learn to hear scales, key center and key changes, mode and mode change, meter, common chord progressions, dynamics, and tempo without being able to read music. Teachers can measure skill in these items the same way the items are taught, by playing examples and asking for identification. When the student is able to identify these elements, the hearer has made progress toward musical understanding.

Auditory–visual skills are commonly measured by tests requiring the student to follow short musical items (usually four or eight measures) in a score and to determine where the score differs from the musical items played. There are standardized tests of this type as well as of the type measuring only auditory skills.

EVALUATING MUSICAL SKILLS

In the majority of public schools, music was for many years thought of primarily as a skill and usually in the narrow sense of *performance* skill. This is natural, because music depends on performance; but other skills must also be developed if performance is to lead to a life-long interest in music. Chiefly, these other skills fall into two categories: *reading* skills and *auditory–visual* skills.

Performance Skills

Any number of vehicles exist for evaluating performance skill. The most familiar of these are private lessons, section rehearsals, daily rehearsals, tryouts or challenges, concerts, contests, and festivals—in short, any type of student performance. These vary in value because group situations of any type increase the difficulty of objective measurement of individual performance skill. In order to avoid a subjective judgment, the teacher should use a list of specific objectives. For example, objectives for performance include the following: production of a good tone throughout the pitch range and the dynamic range, the ability to change tone quality to suit the music, accurate intonation, a pitch range sufficiently wide for the level of music played, dynamic range from pianissimo to fortissimo, and accurate and rapid use of fingers. Each of these objectives could be measured on a point scale, ranging from 1 to 25 or more. When ratings are made using multiple anchor points (terms) such as *poor, good, excellent*, and *superior*, the student can more easily understand the expected standard.

Surprisingly, performance skill, which receives much teaching emphasis, has had little attention from test makers. Only one test is in print, *the Watkin–Farnum Performance Scale*, which is available for wind, string, and percussion instruments. In this test, 14 graded melodies of 16 bars each are given to the performer to play. These range from the easiest type to one of near-professional grade. The performer is graded on the number and type of errors she makes.

Reading Skills

Reading skills are the key to pleasure in musical participation. When the player can understand the musical page by himself without direction from the teacher, he can learn new music on his own, play in ensembles, enrich the family music circle, and in general enjoy musical freedom. Any good sight-reading test will follow somewhat similar lines of construction as the Watkins–Farnum test. In sight-reading, the student should see more than the notes. Evaluation should include awareness of the key signature, all accidentals, dynamic markings, accents, phrase and tonguing (bowing) markings, and recognition of the phrase so that proper articulation is observed. A teacher-constructed test can include a single piece of unfamiliar music or exercises of graded difficulty, as long as it contains sufficient variety of musical elements for the teacher to check each item to be evaluated.

Auditory–Visual Skills

The third area of skill is auditory–visual discrimination. Included are those skills that depend basically on the ear and its relationship to the eye: the ability to visualize what is being heard and to hear inwardly what is seen on the musical page. It differs from sight-reading in that an instrumentalist may successfully sight-read by allowing the notation to indicate what fingers to put down rather than hearing inwardly what she reads—she may have to play a melody before she knows how it sounds. Auditory–visual skill is what the sight singer uses, for he must hear the music inwardly before he can sing it accurately. Objectives for auditory–visual skill include ability to visualize simple melodies heard and, conversely, to inwardly hear simple melodies seen in the score. They also include the ability to recognize the tonal center and modulations, and commonly used chords and unexpected harmonies; the ability to remember melodies adequately for following simple formal structure; the ability to follow parts other than the principal melody; and the ability to recognize timbre and texture.

Music education has often divided its objectives by process or product. Process objectives are indicators that the student is learning how to learn rather than producing a product such as a musical performance. No one denies the importance of the process but it cannot substitute for outcomes. Understanding the compositional process is not the same as composing well. Students can meet a teacher's expectations in a music-focused process class without developing any valued musical competencies as is evident from a generation of graduates of general music classes. Evaluating process provides critical feedback on how to learn (learning can be effective or ineffective) and should not be ignored.

OBSERVATION

Teachers who don't observe miss a most valuable evaluation tool. In fact, the teacher who does not habitually and systematically observe his students as a group and individually is not nearly the teacher he could be. Aural and visual observation are critical with ensembles, in which each member's input affects the result. Most instructional objectives can best be assessed by listening and observing. With beginning students, visual observation is used to supplement ear assessments. (Visually noting incorrect fingering may be more obvious than listening for the nascent sound to emerge from the instrument.) As valuable as observation is, however, it is notoriously unreliable. In the midst of a class lesson or ensemble rehearsal, teachers observe selectively. Adults have learned to screen out much of what crosses the visual, aural, and olfactory senses to avoid information overload. Teachers learn to "eye" potential problem areas (the trombones?). Ensemble conductors attend to section leaders, those with solo parts, and in early rehearsals those who have yet to come in at the right time. The director who listens to his best player and to his own singing has an unearned opinion of his teaching.

A second and related concern with observation as an assessment tool is the lack of objectivity. Teachers are caring human beings and their judgments are affected by knowing their students. The talented lazy kid, the untalented but hardworking plugger, the special education student, the troubled student from a broken home, or the star athlete who is the first violist in the orchestra—each must be evaluated with care. Schools operate on instructional time whereas they should be structured on goal attainment. Individual differences are poorly accommodated by the clock, and when the bell rings some have succeeded while others are in various stages of disarray.

Important objectives that can be evaluated by observation are:

- Posture—from head to toe
- Bowings
- Finger position
- Embouchure
- Percussion playing position
- Rehearsal decorum and procedures
- Behavior
- Fingerings and slide positions
- Attitude
- Cooperation
- Responsibility
- Pencil availability
- Time on task
- Concentration (attentiveness)
- Care of instrument
- Uniform or concert attire
- Absence of instrument from school locker
- Breathing
- Punctuality
- Readiness

Evaluating students every day or periodically is not done easily. Teaching well is intense work. Students treasure fairness; the subjectivity of observation poses this criticism.

LISTENING

Related to observation is assessment through listening—undoubtedly the most important assessment tool for improving the quality of the ensemble and the learning of its members.

1. The most accurate listening assessment is when one student performs at a time. Assessment for blend, balance, matching pitch, maintaining one's own part, and so forth must be done in a group situation, but ideally it should take place in small groups.
2. It is difficult to make sensible judgments about beginners who have little embouchure control. Timbral differences are easily mistaken for pitch and intonation problems; ear training of musicians seldom extends to sounds of crows, donkeys, and beginning oboists.
3. Again, listen for specifics to improve listening reliability—listen for tone quality, attacks and releases, centered tones, clarity of production, as well as the correct notes and correct (approximate) rhythms.
4. Hearing incorrect notes, rhythms or even harmonics in a large ensemble of beginners is not easy and cannot be expected of most beginning teachers.

Sectional rehearsals provide the instructor with an opportunity to evaluate individual performers. In the full rehearsal, it is often difficult even for conductors of advanced groups to know who is participating wholeheartedly, playing accurately and musically, and paying attention. When sectionals are student led, the teacher has a better opportunity to observe and judge. Whenever ratings are made in sectional rehearsals, full rehearsal, private lesson, or other learning situations, they must be systematic, complete, and analytical. Superficial observations often lead to erroneous conclusions that hinder rather than aid the learning process.

Contemporary method books encourage assessment and include achievement charts that can be prominently posted. These method books emphasize skills on an instrument, requiring visual and aural observations as an assessment technique. The teacher must have aural models available, models representative of "superb," "wonderful," "magnificent," and "unsatisfactory" performances. These models should be familiar to the students so that they learn to listen critically with their judgments matching the teacher's. Evaluation is to a standard, not between students.

Students should improvise, understand more than the music performed, improve their musical memories, discover how music is put together, and discriminate among the good and less good in music and performance. Each student could and should be a *musical* leader as his assessment skills mature. In the educational reform movement, in which music is a core subject, it is possible that students who cannot demonstrate competency in required music will not graduate or they will receive a lesser diploma.

PORTFOLIOS

Much contemporary literature indicates that a portfolio is an assessment device. It is not. A portfolio is part of a student's locker, a place to store important and trivial items of interest and of value. It is a place of opportunity (or missed opportunity). Items in a portfolio still must be evaluated by one or more of the means suggested in this chapter. A disadvantage to the portfolio is that delayed feedback lacks the power and importance of immediate feedback. The portfolio may contain homework assignments and any extended research projects—although these still have to be graded. Students collect awards, trophies, newspaper articles, contest sheets, practice cards, letters of appreciation for community service, CDs, mementos of trips, athletic event souvenirs—almost anything that documents their participation and competence in music and music ensembles. A major advantage of the portfolio occurs when students *reflect* on the substance of their accomplishments.

Should students be interested in their improvement over time (we would hope that most would be), a tape of their solo and ensemble playing at two or more different time periods during the year can be included in the portfolio, though such recordings are probably more motivational than evaluative as they are indicators of improvement. Recordings in a portfolio can serve as baselines to refresh the director's memory, as well as the student's of how far he has come. Tapes are most impressive when the students were not initially proficient. Thus, tapes are valuable but the best assessment is "live" assessment.

Closely related to the portfolio is the student log. The log is a record maintained by the student of his musical experiences and his reactions to them. To be most helpful, the log should include both formal and informal encounters with music: concert attendance, recorded performances heard, musical participation in organized groups such as church or club ensembles and unorganized happenings such as campfire singing, combos, and family music making. Items in a portfolio or log are quantitative and qualitative keepsakes varying in assessment usefulness. Student comments on concerts and comments on their own performances are a measure of reflection. These comments provide a way of getting students to think about what they are doing. Our mental picture of the music room has a huge THINK poster attached to the wall in the most obvious location—thinking and reflecting are to be habitual and should not be identified solely as an evaluation device.

RUBRICS

A rubrics book for the ensemble should be considered, one that describes as clearly as language can portray the established local standards of excellent, proficient, basic, and unsatisfactory. (These rubrics, whether four, five, or six, should be established locally and their meaning made clear to the users.) Students should assist in building this book—using their own terms that are sufficiently explicit that agreement among the students is possible. Descriptors need to be formulated for levels of pitch and rhythmic accuracy, tone, aural perception, error identification, and even musical understanding. The rubrics book describes how accurate, how musical, how expressive, how rhythmic a performance need be to meet the performance standards that have been cooperatively established. A rubric accompanied by an aural recording that provides a clear example is optimum.

The use of standardized or formal tests is important even with ensemble teaching but other valid evaluative techniques must be used to ensure the improvement of learning and instruction.

1. Measures of musical aptitude have value. The effectiveness of teaching can best be measured in terms of a student's potential, although it is important that the students understand the importance of effort and that musical aptitude is not an absolute. The job of the teacher is to develop each student to her fullest potential, to cultivate the ability a student possesses for a subject. The teacher who helps the slow and average students to achieve deserves respect, but he does not fulfill his responsibilities unless he also provides the talented students with appropriate challenge and opportunity. The *Seashore Measures of Musical Talents* measured some skills expected of all good musicians but is generally unavailable today. Contemporary tests promoted by instrument manufactures are based on Seashore principles. The *Musical Aptitude Profile*, and its related aptitude tests, also provides an indication of a student's potential. In addition to published measures, the teacher can obtain indications of potential from private instructors, from the level of the student's performing ability, from the classroom teacher, and from the student's past achievement. All indications of talent should be noted.

2. Measures of music achievement, both standardized and teacher constructed, should be used. Achievement tests will reflect not only aptitude but also motivation, hard work, parental support, interest, good teaching, and a host of other known and unknown factors that contribute to success in instrumental music. Published measures of musical achievement are scarce but many states are initiating interesting measures. Tests based solely on Arts Propel are too narrow to provide a comprehensive measure of learning.[2] Teacher-construct-

---

[2] Lyle Davidson (1992), *Arts PROPEL, a Handbook for Music,* Harvard Project Zero: Educational Testing Service.

ed achievement tests are of value only when based on principles of good test construction and valid testing procedures are followed.

3. Audio and video taperecorders, including interactive video, are evaluative tools. Like the proverbial picture, recorded sound can be worth a thousand words. Used with rehearsals and classes as well as with concerts, recordings provide an opportunity for the teacher to examine at leisure the strengths and weaknesses of any performance. Often sections that sound good in rehearsal contain flaws when heard later, and those that were annoying in the stress of drilling are okay. The videotape recorder allows students and director to see as well as hear themselves and to adjust accordingly.

4. Students can judge themselves and judge each other. Making critical decisions about one's own performance or that of another provides a means for motivation, for developing values, and for increasing aural attention to the details of performance. Often, students set higher standards for themselves than those set by the instructor. The effectiveness of group opinion and peer standards is well known.

5. Computers can judge performances in pitch and rhythm to whatever degree of precision is desired. The computer is patient, and there is no opportunity for personal embarrassment when a machine judges and provides the feedback.

6. The music contest or festival can furnish an ideal evaluation situation. To do so, however, both teacher and pupil must view it as an opportunity to learn rather than as glorification of a cause. Adjudicators are always hurried and sometimes biased, but they usually offer some suggestions of value that either reinforce the viewpoint of the teacher or offer a new insight. In either case, the adjudication sheet or tape should be pondered carefully before it is posted with pride or destroyed in anger.

7. The private lesson, as previously discussed, is a fine vehicle for evaluation. When possible, the private teacher's opinion should be solicited and compared with other data on the student's progress. Whether information from private teachers is obtained by interview or written inquiry, a definite set of questions should be formulated in advance. General statements seldom offer enough details to be of value as an evaluative tool.

8. Interviews with students can reveal special strengths, interests, background, and environment, as well as prejudices, weaknesses, and dislikes. Although time may not be available to interview all students, an interview can be a valuable device for evaluating students who are not responding favorably to the present teaching process.

9. The critical-incidence test is a successful tool for measuring a student's perception in musical situations. The test consists of having the student describe the best and the worst moments of yesterday's concert or Friday's football show. The teacher should also take such a test; in so doing he must remain open-minded to students' reactions and to their various degrees of understanding.

10. Attitude scales are used in many areas of education to discover how students feel about something. The attitude scale is usually a list of statements, each reflecting a slightly different point of view, to which the individual responds with a "strongly agree," "agree," "no opinion," "disagree," "strongly disagree," or a similar set of choices. In the most carefully constructed attitude scale, each statement is given a numerical weight that indicates the negative or positive value of the attitude it reflects. Less objective scales reveal information by the type of answers given and the number and degree of negative and positive statements. These may take the form of open-ended statements to be com-

pleted by the student, matching of pictures to feelings, or essays for which the student answers a set of questions. A valid scale is one constructed so as to not reveal the attitude being sought, as students usually prefer to make the "right" response rather than the honest one. Statements must be of sufficient variety, contain different viewpoints, and offer an occasional "distracter" to conceal the purpose of the scale. Having the student complete the scale in homeroom or some other neutral situation helps elicit honest responses.

11. Preference scales are easier than attitude scales to construct and are of value but are seldom instructional and objective. In this scale the student ranks in order of preference such items as school classes, recreational activities, musical compositions, recording artists, tone quality, and others. As with attitude scales, in order to minimize attempts to give the "right" answer, preference scales should be completed in homeroom or other neutral situations with sufficient distracters to disguise the purpose of the scale.

12. Practice cards on which the student records the amount of daily practice on her instrument can be useful. They do not reveal the student's achievement, but when filled in honestly, they are an indication of interest and effort. In well-run ensembles, students are surprisingly honest.

13. Student demonstrations, whether spontaneous or planned, afford opportunities to evaluate skill and understanding. Spontaneous demonstrations occur when correct performance of some musical passage or pattern is requested of individuals or sections by the director or section leader. Planned demonstrations of technique, tone, or timbre, performed in public or rehearsal, are an effective device for motivation and learning. The teacher must observe these demonstrations carefully and record his reactions objectively.

14. Point systems are effective in motivation and evaluation. As an evaluative tool, the point system is most valid when it is broadly inclusive, covering as many aspects of student development as possible.

15. Checklists ensure greater objectivity and coverage of the factors of musical performance. Checklists are applicable to all forms of evaluation, including teacher self-evaluation. One common use of a checklist might be to rate the student's performance on a number of items such as tone, articulation, expression marks, phrasing, pitch accuracy, rhythm accuracy, rests, keys, breathing, practice routines, and style. Checklists are beguilingly simple. Like all evaluation devices, they can be misused. It is easier to violate the principles of good assessment with the checklist because of their simplicity and openness to bias and selectivity. Few teachers think about the checklists' validity and reliability. Checklists, however, capture musical competence in its most valid form. A student can be appraised on a ten-point checklist (ranging from awful to stellar), on ability to sing his part, perform on his instrument, warm-up intelligently, perform required skill exercises for endurance, range, bowing, tonguing, and fingering skills required of the instrumentalists to perform musically. (The importance of reliability is demonstrated by action of the New York School Music Educators Association, which requires training before one is allowed to assess solo and ensemble events.) The checklist is good for assessing abilities; it is not strong as a diagnostic instrument. Group objectives of balance, blend, common interpretation, diction, and "maintains own part" can also be partially assessed with a checklist. And the list goes on. Composing, improvising, knowing, using knowledge, using musical terminology, conducting, experiencing, as well as posture, attitude, effort, intonation, expressiveness, musicality, self-criticism, independence, helpfulness, going beyond, modeling for the group, audiates, values, attends

concerts, understands musical form, corrects immediately, writes excellent essays, is articulate, are a few of the competencies that ensemble directors teach and should assess.

16. Teacher-constructed tests are most successful when used to measure knowledge. Specific items that have been taught and emphasized in class or rehearsal are appropriate material for paper-and-pencil tests. Of course, many items are difficult to measure, but those that are measurable should be tested. A danger occurs when recall tests become speed tests; in other words, when there are more questions than the slowest student can do in the time available; the faster student can then score higher than the slower student who knows as much.

17. Collecting data on student achievement must always be made with reference to objectives. Frequently, tests or other evaluative tools are selected that do not reflect the actual objectives or content of the music class. The result is that the test shapes the content of the course. To be genuinely appropriate for a music program, a test must enhance progress toward the accomplishment of objectives already determined. The purpose of instruction is not to provide material for testing; rather, the purpose of testing is to provide information for the improvement of instruction.

In closing this section, it must be emphasized that evaluation requires a careful, systematic approach. Inspection of only the final test scores will seldom improve the teaching–learning process. Use of any one or all of the suggested tools will not in itself ensure good evaluation. It must be carefully planned, frequent, varied, and objective. Spurious judgments harm both the student and the program. With so many options, what does one use for awarding a grade? Evaluation in music has primarily been to improve instruction not to judge, thus grading has frequently emphasized responsibility. Grades should reflect the priority placed on the many objectives, priorities that are cooperatively established and are subject to change.

EVALUATION OF INSTRUMENTAL OBJECTIVES

Music involves participation and participation fosters attitudes and habits. The effectiveness of music participation to nurture instrumental objectives is at present the focus of much research, discussion, and publicity, but this aspect of musical participation is not new. Good habits, attitudes, and values have always resulted from engaging in music, and these have their appropriate place in assessment. The complexity of checklists can be understood by a discussion of these objectives that do not relate to music as an *art* and so are of lesser importance in any program.

Participation

1. Is the student dependable and punctual? Full participation in a musical group requires regular attendance. Is she responsible for her share of any activity? Does she take initiative appropriately?

2. Does the student participate wholeheartedly in rehearsal activities? Reading books, doing assignments, and gossiping during rehearsal are negative indicators of participation. Evaluation may indicate whether the fault lies with the students or with a rehearsal that lacks challenge, interest, or musical satisfaction.

3. Does the student use her music skills in leisure activities?

4. Does she participate in civic and/or church music organizations?

5. Does she take full advantage of school music offerings?

6. Does she attend concerts?

7. Do the good habits of group participation carry over into her everyday life?

8. Participation can be evaluated by student logs, checklists, interviews, critical-incidence measures, practice cards, and point systems. The method of evaluation depends only on the imagination and desires of the instructor.

Attitude

1. Does the student participate fully and willingly? Does he act in a democratic and cooperative spirit?

2. Where does music rank in the student's preference for school subjects? In his preference for recreational activities?

3. What selections and kinds of music does the student prefer?

4. Attitude can be appraised using the questions under participation and by sophisticated attitude scales. Degrees of agreement with statements or preference can be obtained. Students can be asked to caption pictures, to supply nonexistent subjects for described situations. Attitudes can be changed by effective lecturing, reading, relating of interesting facts, and similar endeavors, however, change is most effective when the student, through participation, discovers for himself how satisfying experiences with good music can be. The major task of the instructor is to provide skills and knowledge, including reading, ear training, and performance skills, and to provide musical experiences in large and small ensembles where attitude formation and change can be expected to occur.

Habits

1. Does the student have a regular daily practice routine?

2. Does she consistently warm up or warm down properly?

3. Does she routinely take care of her instrument?

4. Is concert attendance and record buying habitual within her means?

5. Good habits do not spring automatically from a good music program. Like transfer of training, habits must be specifically taught by insistence on schedule and routine. In habit formation, regularity is more desirable than spontaneity. In the same way that habits are hard to break, some are hard to form. They are generally reached gradually through the careful attention and dogmatic insistence of the instructor rather than through inspired teaching.

This chapter should not end on objectives of a lesser kind. Teaching requires making choices, establishing priorities. Musical *understanding* is a high priority for objectives and for assessment. High-level skills and copious knowledge do not guarantee understanding although they are important components. Those who understand can apply and use their skills and knowledge in unfamiliar musical terrain—because understanding transfers.

BIBLIOGRAPHY

Texts

*Indicates out of print in 2001.

AIRASIAN, PETER W. (2001). *Classroom Assessment: Concepts and Applications.* Dubuque, IA: McGraw-Hill.

ANASTASI, ANNE (1988). *Psychological Testing,* 6th ed. New York: Macmillan.

ARMSTRONG, CARMEN (1994). *Designing Assessment in Art.* Reston, VA: National Art Education Association.

AYRES, LINDA R. (1994). *Becoming Reflective Students and Teachers: With Portfolios and Authentic Assessment.* Washington, DC: American Psychological Association.

BLACK, PAUL J. (1998). *Testing, Friend or Foe?: Theory and Practice of Assessment and Testing.* London: Falmer Press.

BLACKING, JOHN (1995). *How Musical Is Man?* Seattle: University of Washington Press (reprint of 1973 ed.).

BLOOM, BENJAMIN S. (1956). *Taxonomy of Educational Objectives; Book 1, Cognitive Domain.* New York: Longman Publishing.

BOUGHTON, DOUGLAS GORDON. (1994). *Evaluation and Assessment in Visual Arts Education.* Geelong, Victoria: Deakin University Press.

BOWMAN, WAYNE (1998). *Philosophical Perspectives on Music.* New York: Oxford University Press.

*BOYLE, J. DAVID, and RUDY RADOCY (1987). *Measurement and Evaluation of Musical Experiences.* New York: Schirmer Books.

BOYLE, WILLIAM F., and TOM CHRISTIE (1996). *Issues in Setting Standards: Establishing Comparabilities.* London; Falmer Press.

BRUNER, JEROME S. (1994). *Acts of Meaning.* Cambridge, MA: Harvard University Press.

CENTER FOR PERFORMANCE ASSESSMENT (1998). *Making Standards Work,* 2nd ed. Denver: Center for Performance Assessment.

CHELIMSKY, ELEANOR, and W. R. SHADISH (1997). *Evaluation for the 21st Century: A Handbook.* Thousand Oaks, CA: Sage.

COLWELL, RICHARD (1968–1970). *Music Achievement Tests.* Author: 34 Cleveland Hill Road, Brookline, NH 03033.

*——— (1970). *The Evaluation of Music Teaching and Learning.* Upper Saddle River, NJ: Prentice Hall.

CONSORTIUM OF NATIONAL ARTS EDUCATION ASSOCIATIONS (1995). *Opportunity-to-Learn Standards for Arts Education.* Reston, VA: The Consortium.

CRONBACH, LEE (1990). *Essentials of Psychological Testing,* 5th ed. New York: HarperCollins.

DARLING-HAMMOND, LINDA (1998). *Teaching for High Standards: What Policymakers Need to Know and Be Able to Do.* New York: National Commission on Teaching and America's Future.

*DAVIDSON, LYLE (1992). *Arts PROPEL, Handbook for Music.* Harvard Project Zero: Educational Testing Service.

*FARNUM, STEPHEN E. (1953). *Farnum Music Notation Test.* New York: Psychological Corp.

*HENRY, NELSON, ed. (1958). *Basic Concepts in Music Education,* Part I. The 57th Yearbook of the National Society for the Study of Education. Chicago: University of Chicago Press.

*LEHMAN, PAUL (1968). *Tests and Measurements in Music.* Upper Saddle River, NJ: Prentice Hall.

LINN, R. L., NORMAN GRONLUND, and K. M. DAVIS (1999). *Measurement and Evaluation in Teaching,* 8th ed. New York: Macmillan.

MARZANO, ROBERT (2001). *Designing a New Taxonomy of Educational Objectives.* Thousand Oaks, CA: Corwin Press.

MENC (1996). *Performance Standards for Music: Strategies and Benchmarks for Assessing Progress Toward the National Standards, Grades K–12.* Reston, VA: Author

*NATIONAL INTERSCHOLASTIC MUSIC ACTIVITIES COMMISSION OF THE MUSIC EDUCATORS NATIONAL CONFERENCE (1963). *NIMAC Manual: The Organization and Management of Interscholastic Music Activities.* Washington, D.C.: Music Educators National Conference.

NITKO, ANTHONY J. (2001). *Educational Assessment of Students.,* 3rd ed. Upper Saddle River, NJ: Merrill.

PAGE, NICK (1995). *Music as a Way of Knowing.* Los Angeles: Galef Institute.

PARIS, SCOTT, and LINDA AYRES (1994). *Becoming Reflective Students and Teachers: With Portfolios and Authentic Assessment.* Washington, DC: American Psychological Association.

PHYE, GARY D. (1997). *Handbook of Classroom Assessment: Learning, Adjustment, and Achievement,.* San Diego: Academic Press.

*PIZER, RUSSELL (1987). *Instrumental Music Evaluation Kit: Forms and Procedures for Assessing Student Performance.* West Nyack, NY: Parker Publishing, Co.

*——— (1990). *Evaluation Programs for School Bands and Orchestras.* West Nyack, NY: Parker Publishing, Co.

REEVES, DOUGLAS (1998). *Making Standards Work: How to Implement Standards-Based Assessments in the Classroom, School, and District* 2nd ed. Denver, CO: Center for Performance Assessment.

ROSSI, PETER H. (1999). *Evaluation: A Systematic Approach.* Thousand Oaks, CA: Sage Publications.

SEIDEL, KENT (2000). *Assessing Student Learning: A Practical Guide* (CD-ROM). Reston, VA: The Alliance for Curriculum Reform (distributed by MENC).

WEISS, CAROL H. (1998). *Evaluation: Methods for Studying Programs and Policies* 2nd ed. Upper Saddle River, NJ: Prentice Hall.

WIGGINS, GRANT P. (1998). *Educative Assessment: Designing Assessments to Inform and Improve Student Performance.* San Francisco: Jossey-Bass.

WILSON, BRENT (1997). *The Quiet Evolution: Changing the Face of Arts Education.* Los Angeles: Getty Education Institute for the Arts.

Instructional Video

Assessing the Whole Child. (Jay Comras, and Michael K. Hibbard, 1995) Livingston, NJ: Instructivision, Inc.

4

Motivation

A successful music program is one in which participation results in musical learnings. A good teacher is one whose basic musicianship and knowledge enable her to produce good performances of good music, and whose grasp of pupil psychology helps her produce enthusiastic participation leading to greater skill and positive attitudes toward music. These qualities are essential for good teaching. Without musicianship and technical knowledge the teacher may produce participation but little student achievement; without an understanding of her pupils, the teacher may develop a program that involves only the highly motivated few, depriving many others of the enjoyment of participating in music as adults.

It is simply not true that good music in itself furnishes sufficient motivation for public school pupils. For the more advanced pupils, good music can and should be the strong central attraction. For the beginner or the pupil of limited ability, however, other factors influence his participation and affect his learning. Even for the advanced pupil, teacher personality, classroom atmosphere and organization, as well as teaching and learning procedures are of crucial importance.

American industry places a high priority on motivation of the workforce, often failing to understand why workers give priority to TV, sports, and their home over their job and job advancement. The factors that shape our priorities are many, but center on personal incentives. Some individuals who are initially motivated by money find that money itself loses its ability to satisfy. Others seek power or recognition. Still others are competitive and strive for excellence. Most individuals have a need to be with others and to be accepted. Groups promote social concerns, a desire to help others. And we all want to be competent, to have self-esteem, and to feel that others have confidence in us throughout a range of interpersonal relationships. The psychologist Csikszentmihalyi suggests that tasks themselves can be motivating; we can become so interested in pursuing a goal that we lose all track of time and if interrupted can't wait to return to the task. Teachers make a continuing study of motivation as students differ from each other as well as responding differently in specific social or economic situations.

The importance of motivation to learning is well established. Any teaching, whether of an individual or a group, has as its aim the development of musical knowledge, good practice habits, technical proficiency, and musical understandings; therefore, the suggestions for motivation given here can be applied to either individual or group situations, although some will, of course, be more appropriate for one than for the other. The ideas presented in the next few pages fall into two categories: first, those pertaining to long-range planning, representing intrinsic values; and second, those relating to day-by-day, immediate goals, representing extrinsic motivation. When used together, these two kinds of motivation can do much to promote interest and stimulate better performance and better learning.

Although motivation in school is directly related to the student's *goals*, both short term and long term, the teacher should remember that motivation is also based upon the student's *preferences, feelings*, and *values*. [1]

Carol Dweck has suggested that a student's concept of ability, whether fixed or developmental, is a critical factor in motivation. For her, individuals who believe they "can do" love learning, seek challenges, value effort, and persist in task accomplishments. These human characteristics determine the extent of the student's personal investment in any subject or experience. Instrumental music is almost always an elective experience, and students give up many other alternatives to participate in it. Success in instrumental music may sometimes represent the attainment of a dream; when this is the case, other motivational factors such as pride in the group effort become much less important.

Whether the characteristic of fun is intrinsic or extrinsic, the study of music must be fun. The fun of being in band or orchestra may be the student's goal—and the student determines whether the fun and enjoyment of performance justifies the extensive study and practice. The list of motivational factors presented in the following pages should help ensure that enjoyable experience.

INTRINSIC MOTIVATION

1. Use good music. The music itself should be the central motivating force for any musical learning, though it is rarely the only factor. To furnish genuine motivation, music must be of high quality, for poor music soon becomes tiresome and boring. Also, poor music is so easily available to the student on tape or television that she does not need to participate in school music groups in order to find it. Teachers are tempted to make one of two mistakes regarding the quality of the music to be used. The first is that of using popular commercial music on the ground that it will interest the student. The fallacy in this approach is that the basic goal—that of developing a discriminating love of good music—can never be reached, even though the student may acquire considerable performing skill. The second mistake is to set unrealistically high standards for the music used. To use good music does not necessarily mean to use only great music. The skillful teacher begins where the student is—selecting music that will appeal to her at her present level of understanding—and gradually introduces her to better music as she becomes ready for it. A variety of types of music is more satisfying than a steady diet of one kind, and its use can teach the student to judge between varying qualities. As long as the music is well written, challenges the student with something new, has genuine musical worth, and is not trite or shallow—in short, as long as it broadens the student's appreciation—it is good music and should be used.

2. Use wide musical repertoire. New music is the most obvious way to maintain interest. Even if the individual or the group is not able to perform old music perfectly, there comes a time when a change is necessary. Nothing brings on boredom faster than working continually on the same few pieces or trudging wearily over the

---

[1] Carol Dweck (1999). *Self-Theories: Their Role in Motivation, Personality, and Development,* Philadelphia: Psychology Press.

same exercises until all is perfected. If a long period of time is needed to learn a piece well, the selection is probably too difficult. The use of much music of varied levels not only helps maintain interest but also contributes to the sightreading skill of the learners. This principle holds for both individual and group instruction. Many music teachers seem to feel that only one instruction book or one solo should be used at a time. Limiting a student's musical experiences in this way contributes to a loss of interest.

3. Have a goal. Each student should know why he is practicing and what his objective is. Similarly, the teacher should make clear in rehearsals where she is leading the group. Like the proverbial carrot in front of the donkey, the goal should be visible. Unlike the carrot, it should be attainable. The teacher must have long-range goals that shape her planning and programming, but short-range goals are also necessary.

For the greatest effectiveness, a goal must be fairly specific. If the group is working toward a concert performance, members will put forth more effort if the date has been set and the numbers selected. When time is given to drill, to sightreading, to listening, or to factual or technical learning, the students will respond more readily if they know what the purpose of the activity is.

4. Relate technical drill to real music. Scales, studies, and exercise material should be used in anticipation of the difficult spots in music being learned. Until the student encounters a particular technical problem in a piece of music, she will see little reason for practicing exercises designed to give her that facility. Treat technical studies like vitamins: they are to be taken as needed, but never as the main ingredient of the diet. As with all rules, the exceptions are many—for example, producing long tones and extending one's range are daily habits.

This is not to suggest that technical studies be omitted—far from it. Because technical drill focuses on particular kinds of learning, it can help the student to become technically proficient much more rapidly than if only musical pieces are practiced. Drill needs to be meaningful and relevant, but if omitted altogether, the individual and the group will suffer.

5. Develop musicianship skills and factual knowledge. Factual knowledge about music and the ability to perform some of the musicianship skills, such as transposing, reading several clefs, and improvising, are both goals of the music program and real motivators. Like good music, skill and knowledge are of intrinsic value and furnish valid ends of motivation. Students like to know, for instance, the problems that double-reed players have with reeds—how difficult they are to make, how scarce good cane is, and how much adjusting is necessary. They can be interested and inspired by details about composers and about music itself—how a fugue is put together, the background for a Wagner composition, or the type of social system in which Haydn lived and worked. The more the student knows and the more she can do in any area, the more she is likely to retain a lively, active interest in it.

6. Develop a tradition of excellence. Music programs with a reputation for quality provide a momentum that motivates students to practice and minimizes discipline problems. When there is an established standard to measure up to, students usually accept the challenge. High school students are idealistic, and they take pride in doing things well, even though they often talk to the contrary. They can derive satisfaction from meeting high standards whether in personal or group achievement; they develop loyalties toward organizations and individuals that expect much from them, and enjoy living up to those expectations.

A tradition of excellence is not established overnight. If a teacher moves into a school without such a tradition, she must build it by starting with the younger students. Older players unaccustomed to high standards will resist drastic reforms and may retain their habits of sloppy practice or halfhearted participation. Sometimes such students respond to the challenge from younger players who begin to surpass them and occupy first-desk positions. Sometimes the best way of dealing with these students is to be patient and let them graduate.

7. Help the student to arrange enjoyable, independent musical activities other than the private lesson and the large group rehearsal. Try to arrange schedules and assignments to make it possible for students to work together toward a common goal. Practicing alone can be boring and take considerable inner discipline, whereas working on parts with other students is much more enjoyable. This is especially true for students who play such nonmelody instruments as tubas and horns. Two or three students practicing together, all on the same part or each on a different part, can increase the pleasure of each participant and also help to develop musicianship.

Supply duets, trios, and other kinds of ensemble music to interested students. Whether the group remains together for a long period or simply reads through the music a few times, such activity should be encouraged. A good library of ensemble music representing a variety of instrumental combinations and levels of difficulty is a must in a good instrumental program.

8. Encourage the establishment of small ensembles. The small chamber group presents the greatest musical challenge, the best training, the heaviest individual responsibility, and the highest musical pleasure of any activity. Some special problems are involved in establishing small ensembles; these include scheduling, grouping students of similar levels of ability, and helping the groups become independent of teacher supervision. To create an ensemble of students whose levels of ability are comparable is perhaps possible only in a large school. In smaller schools the group will usually be uneven, and the more capable students will have to wait for those less capable or even help them with their parts. This in itself can have learning advantages if it is properly handled to avoid resentments or antagonisms. The learning derived from small ensemble work is likely to be more valuable if the teacher does not have to supervise the small ensemble rehearsal regularly, and the saving of time to the teacher will be great. It is important to promote an atmosphere in which independent rehearsal is desirable and expected. Whether small ensembles perform in public, go to festivals and contests, or play only for their own pleasure is the decision of the individual teacher. Performances for appropriate community groups, however, bring added motivation and also strengthen public relations.

9. Select music in which supporting players can star. The second-desk viola player and the third snare drum are likely to lead humdrum existences musically. When it is possible to do so, the teacher should use music that gives solo passages to the little-heard supporting players. Such music may be short on artistic value but it is long on psychological value. Even a short solo passage may offer incentive for additional practice, and the chance to be heard is something every player deserves.

10. Hear good performances. Players should not play all of the time. They should occasionally listen. Listening should include both live and recorded performances, amateur as well as professional. Older, advanced players may perform or demonstrate for younger players. Pupils are always interested in performances by groups at their own age level, whether these are semiprofessional or simply outstanding public school organizations. Some students will be more encouraged by virtuoso displays and master performances. An occasional poor performance on record or tape may serve as an opportunity for intelligent criticism. Opportunities to hear an occasional professional concert, informal presentations by adult members of the community whose skill would be an inspiration, and exchange concerts with other schools—these live performances can supplement the recorded ones.

11. Obtain good equipment and facilities. Much has already been said on this point. Good tools help to produce good results. Poor instruments affect both the group and the individual; an inferior instrument handicaps the student and may embarrass her as well. The teacher should see that both school-owned and student-owned instruments are of the best quality the financial situation will permit. Lack of practice areas or a good rehearsal room can also be a handicap. The players of large instruments such as the tuba, string bass, or drums especially need an in-school practice room, and these rooms may be a great convenience to other students whose schedules would permit practice time within the school day.

Regardless of the physical facilities in which teacher and students work and learn, a room that is efficiently arranged, neat and ready for work, provides a certain motivation. A room in disarray sends a message of laxness and lack of concern. If a room presents the impression that efficiency and industry are the rule, the likelihood of this being true is enhanced.

12. Develop favorable attitudes. Students will accomplish little without the proper attitude. Attitudes are contagious—especially among teen-agers—and so the attitude of a few may set the pattern for the group. The teacher needs to communicate to the students a sense of responsibility for their own individual parts in the organization, together with a pride in the organization and a desire to work for it. The student needs to feel that his practicing is important, not only for his own improvement but for the improvement of the group as a whole. The teacher can instill a sense of responsibility by taking notice of those students who are responsible, commending sections that have improved, pointing out areas that are weak, and helping students who need extra practice find the time and place to do so. Pride in the organization can be encouraged by stressing honestly the achievements of the group, by planning attractive activities, and by reporting to the group any commendations that come from the community, the student body, or school officials.

13. Build esprit de corps. Pride and responsibility are least successful when they spring solely from teacher inspiration, though in the beginning it may be necessary for the teacher to be the main source of inspiration. A group spirit of unity is the best source for control; the desire to belong and be accepted will lead a student to adopt the ideals of the group. If the group is included in appropriate decision making, a spirit will be fostered that will spread to new members coming into the group. Because high school students are not yet mature adults, group spirit can be strongly influenced by such extrinsic values as uniforms, contests, social affairs, and good publicity, as well as by successful performances.

14. Use student leaders. Esprit de corps can be enhanced through the selection of the right student leaders. In addition, some of the less talented students can find recognition and satisfaction in performing organizational tasks or becoming student officers. Student government not only aids in developing morale but also in lessening the load for the director and providing a chain of command through which the teacher may channel authority and needed regulations. Some positions are best filled by popular election whereas others should be appointed by the director.

15. *Treat all students and student ideas with respect.* Students need to feel that their ideas contribute to the selection of music, procedures, organizational rules, and even the amount of practice expected of every member.

It must be clear that the director makes the final decision in all matters but that she is also a good listener. If the atmosphere is such that all students believe they and the group can improve, the students will establish higher standards and expectations for themselves, often exceeding even those of the director.

16. *Plan a sensible schedule.* The schedule should make it possible for students to practice and to attend all extra rehearsals. Performance goals should be reasonable so that the students are not discouraged. If too many events are scheduled there may be continual frantic efforts to prepare for the next performance or activity, and students may be deprived of participation in other worthwhile activities. Always present is the danger of exploiting the talented student. Often she is capable in many areas, and many teachers wish her to participate in their particular fields. Because of this, such a student can become accustomed to doing rapid, superficial work and forget the importance of sustained effort. The teacher must be willing to think of the student's welfare first, to help her acknowledge her limits and budget her time wisely.

17. *Take into consideration the motivational force of the teacher.* The teacher is the decisive element in providing inspiration, motivation, and learning. Much has been said about what the teacher does; of more basic importance is who the teacher is. Her level of musicianship, technical facility as a performer, command of musical knowledge, leadership, and depth and breadth as a human being can inspire students to imitation and emulation. The necessity to be both musician and teacher has already been discussed; the inspiration that comes from a fine musician and a fine teacher is the point here.

In addition to being timely, motivational goals and activities must not be too specific. Teachers should apply the Goldilocks principle and pursue programs that are "just right." Students do not study instrumental music because it is a medium for the creation and expression of beauty or because they sense their aesthetic needs are unfulfilled. Neither do they enroll in instrumental music to learn more about the music of Francis McBeth or Gustav Holst or to learn the relationship of key signatures to the circle of fifths. "Just right" programs and goals are understandable, meaningful, and attainable.

The foregoing suggestions are of a long-range type; they are based primarily on a belief in the motivating force of good music and in the importance of psychology in working with students. These suggestions should be the basis of the teacher's planning and decision making. A second group of suggestions related to motivation is most pertinent to temporary or short-term goals. These suggestions alone would never be adequate to provide a healthy atmosphere or a firm basis for musical learning, but they can serve to create temporary inspiration and day-to-day interest. The suggestions that do not relate directly to music provide extrinsic rather than intrinsic motivation.

EXTRINSIC MOTIVATION

1. *Praise is effective when properly used.* Most students will respond to a deserved compliment from a teacher whom they respect, and they will work to earn one. Praise can be directed at the entire group or focused on one section or one individual. The praise must be honest and must not be so frequent as to become meaningless. Students should not be led to think their work is better than it is, but improvement and effort as well as good performance can call forth praise. The teacher should be careful that her praise does not always fall on the same heads, but that the little-noticed plodders are also given credit.

Praise and approval can come from other sources than the teacher. The commendation of the administration and the student body are important in forming a group's opinion of itself, and such commendation is a legitimate goal for which to work. One excellent way in which to see that a music group receives deserved recognition is to publicize its activities. Newspaper, television, and radio publicity concerning group activities foster both school and public awareness, and encourage the student to take pride in her organization.

2. Criticism and disapproval also have a place in motivation. Being inspirational should not imply that the teacher is the Good Humor Man. She should use praise liberally when it is merited but be firm when the situation demands it. Because psychologists have spent years sending animals through mazes and giving them electric shock treatments, it is fairly well established that punishment as well as reward is effective in learning. Many successful teachers create a lasting enthusiasm for music while at the same time arousing a certain amount of apprehension at the weekly lesson or the daily rehearsal. When the student can relax without fear of criticism regardless of what she does, the atmosphere no longer contains that creative tension in which learning takes place. However, as a general rule, sarcasm, ridicule, and other unfair practices have no place in good teaching, and criticism and disapproval do not have to be couched in these terms. Students respect firmness and want to be challenged to meet high standards. Respect for the teacher may often be based on the number of mistakes she identifies and the helpfulness of the suggested corrections. And it may be that at the immature level, mild fear is the strongest motivator.

When offering criticism, teachers need to know whether performance failure is due to lack of ability or lack of effort. Mild punishment works wonders when the problem is a lack of effort; however, when the untalented student is doing everything she can, criticism and punishment lead to discouragement.

3. Keep parents informed regarding practice requirements and objectives. Enlist parents' support but never allow home practice to be used as a form of punishment for any students. Many directors send a periodic progress report to the parents in order to maintain a close relationship between the music program and the home. Emphasis on a regular time for practice may help serve as a kind of motivator for the student. If he feels that practice is important enough to be done at a particular time each day, with this time to be sacrificed only under exceptional circumstances, an aura of significance develops around the practice hour. Because consistent practice is of great intrinsic value, the teacher need not hesitate to enhance it any way she can.

4. Grades are as valid in music as in other areas. Although some teachers recommend grading as a disciplinary measure—that is, the student who manages to avoid breaking the rules receives a high grade—it seems more psychologically sound to accept the traditional view of grading as a reward for good work. Many systems of grading are used in music programs, including the following:

    a. Practice charts. Students are required to practice a specified amount each day. Those who exceed the minimum get higher grades. The drawback to this approach is that it rewards effort rather than results. Also, it is difficult to be certain that practice reports are accurate.

   b. Progress charts. Students are graded for completing specified objectives. Such a chart has the advantage of establishing definite goals and of rewarding actual attainment rather than putting in time. It gives the teacher an impartial and objective vehicle by which to determine grades and places music on the same plane with the more academic subjects, in which grades are determined objectively on the basis of work accomplished.

   c. Point system. Like progress charts, the point system rewards achievement and in addition may cover a wide range of other accomplishments. Point systems may also be useful to determine annual awards to members of the organization. Some teachers object to the clerical effort involved in keeping an accurate record of earned points for each student, but student help can be successfully used in keeping records.

One of the important values of a systematic grading procedure is that the student can examine his progress and see his results. He can see a graphic illustration of progress for the year, the relationship between work and achievement, and he can make a personal evaluation of this progress.

5. Competitive seating plans are an excellent stimulus. When there is a competitive seating plan, the better players are encouraged to work for the honor of retaining their positions as first-desk players, while those beneath them strive to catch up. For this plan to be effective the teacher needs to schedule tryouts at fairly regular intervals. The importance of the first-chair position for every part should be stressed (e.g., first chair, third clarinet), not simply the solo chairs. Whether tryout times are announced ahead of time or scheduled without notice is the teacher's decision. Each has advantages. Some teachers feel that announced tryouts stimulate more energetic practicing, wheareas others have discovered that their students practice more consistently when they have to be ready for unannounced tryouts.

6. Challenge systems are a corollary of the competitive seating plan. Students in the lower ranks may aspire to the higher chairs through testing the occupant in a fair match. The director should make the challenge system as democratic and fair as possible, probably by including students on the judging committee and by having a clear challenge procedure that will also serve to produce added practice. In order not to spend too much class time on challenging, it is better to have a set time or schedule in which challenges may take place.

7. Tryouts for chair positions or ensemble membership are important. As in other subjects, the music teacher should make specific assignments and then test all students on the preparation of the assignments. Such testing may take place at rehearsals, sectional practices, or at lessons, but regardless of the method students should be expected to do the work assigned and to be graded accordingly. Whether such tryouts affect seating is up to the teacher.

Some teachers succeed in holding tryouts during regular rehearsals, calling on individuals to play the assignments in front of the group. The director should use discretion and not force unwilling students to submit to such a practice if it seems too harsh. Once the routine is established, however, it may encourage students to be well prepared in order to avoid making a poor showing before their peers.

8. Competition on technical proficiency has a place. Students can derive a great deal of fun and inspiration from an occasional contest for sheer technical proficiency—players compete to see who can play the greatest number of scales correctly, play the fastest, hold notes the longest, and so forth. Such contests would not be considered a serious part of any evaluation but should be used simply to stimulate interest and challenge students to greater technical mastery.

9. An occasional written test may be of value. Tests of musical learning, used infrequently, may result in extra effort from students. Such examinations may test knowledge of music fundamentals: terms, keys, scales, and tuning. Although these tests give no indication of the student's playing ability, they help to emphasize the importance of basic musical knowledge. Written tests take up valuable time, but even in performing groups an occasional written test can provide motivation for learning and give the teacher some valuable insights.

10. Various methods of evaluation may add to the perceived importance of the group and its goals. Public performance evaluation, properly handled, can contribute both to the level of motivation and to musical understanding. For example, an outside critic may be employed during the regular rehearsal period to listen to individuals and sections, to comment to the group on its performance, and to offer suggestions for improvement. Or students may perform their parts for the entire ensemble, analyze their own weaknesses, and suggest how they will improve their parts by tomorrow or by next week. Such an activity can be great fun, constitute public testimony of intent, and act intrinsically and extrinsically as a motivator for musical excellence. In addition, members may comment on their section's progress toward the overall goal and what they need to do to improve. The more specific the suggestions, the more helpful this activity will be. Comments like "take your parts home and practice" may be on target but lack sufficient specificity to ensure meaningful improvement. Comments about how better or more intelligent use of warm-ups and home drill and practice can improve the intonation, balance, or musical line of the performance can be especially worthy.

11. Membership standards for all groups, beginning through advanced, are desirable. Although there must be some flexibility in selecting members for each group, students should have a fairly accurate idea of what must be accomplished in order to gain membership in the group. A clear set of standards is one way to encourage practice and achievement. In addition, standards can help dispel any feeling that the teacher is partial or unfair. Published rules must be followed; the fewer exceptions made, the more important these rules will become in the eyes of all members. Moreover, there is a natural desire to be a member of those groups having an aspect of selectivity. The Marine Corps, Phi Beta Kappa, and Who's Who would lose their appeal if open to all comers. Musical organizations should not be exclusive, cliquish bodies, but membership in them should imply that certain standards have been met and that each member is characterized by a certain level of achievement.

12. Awards provide another stimulus to effort. They may take the form of letters, medals, sweaters, service stripes, or certificates. An award has no intrinsic value of its own and is important only as a means to promoting greater musical growth. Even so, students often prize an award highly, taking pride in earning it and pleasure in others' recognition of it. As with membership standards, a definite system for giving awards should be established that the group knows and understands. If the point system or competitive chairs are an accepted practice, the awards system should be related to these and to other administrative practices. To be most effective, awards should be presented in public, with at least a modicum of ceremony.

13. Scholarships are an even more effective incentive to achievement. The scholarship should relate to the music program—for instance, a scholarship to an outstanding summer music camp. This kind of award may be used to sustain the interest of the best students in the organization. Funds for scholarships may be secured through money-raising projects by the group itself or by the parents' group; or they may come from one or more civic groups or from private individuals. To be most effective, the scholarship should be publicized throughout the year and should be awarded at the close of the year.

14. Section rehearsals are a necessity for all good bands and orchestras. They have been discussed at some length already. Sectional rehearsals not only help the student with specific difficulties but also provide some additional incentive for outside practice. When the whole group always rehearses together, the student may not hear his mistakes or realize how important it is that he perform his part correctly. If scheduling makes extra section rehearsals impractical, the director should consider using some of the regularly scheduled large-group rehearsal time for concentrated work with various sections. Where feasible, several sections might be scheduled at the same time with responsible students in charge.

15. Summer music camps offer students a chance to improve their musical skills in new and stimulating surroundings. The inspiration of a music camp comes from excellent teachers, the outstanding ability of other students, and a high level of performance. The director should encourage any student who can attend summer camps to do so. A local summer camp can often be organized with successful results. The staff may consist of college music students, teachers with free time, or guest conductors from college campuses or other school systems. If an actual campsite is available the experience is enhanced, but even without an outdoor atmosphere the local music camp can be worthwhile.

16. New instruments provide a reward for work well done. The teacher should encourage her students to own the best instruments they can afford. When a new instrument is obtained, the teacher should make the acquisition known to the group and help the student attract attention to his new possession.

17. Tape recordings and videotapes allow students to hear and see their efforts and point up shortcomings as well as achievements. Problems of intonation, wrong notes, and poor attacks and releases often show up more vividly on tape than in actual rehearsal. An impending recording session furnishes another incentive for additional work and is in this sense a close kin to the live performance.

18. Social activities can be a way to develop greater interest. Special dances, banquets, and trips foster a spirit of unity and help maintain interest. These events also provide a welcome change from the routine of daily rehearsals, concerts, and sports events. In addition, they help the director become acquainted with her students on a different basis.

OTHER POSSIBILITIES

High schools should consider commissioning works and inviting the composer to attend and conduct the premier performance of the work. Frank Battisti initiated this idea more that 40 years ago with the Ithaca New York High School Band, an idea that has been adopted by many fine ensembles. The thrill of playing a number at its first public performance with the composer in attendance is a special, memorable event.

State and local arts councils will support an artist-in-residence program in your school. Select the instrument you wish to promote, write a proposal, and submit it to the arts council. There are many superb performers graduating in applied music from American universities who will willingly teach and perform in all of the district's schools. They are inspirational for both strong and weak performers.

Form a jazz band, a brass band, a drum and bugle corps, or other attractive ensemble. Enlist students who play in garage bands on piano, guitar, and other instruments. Encourage them to find their place in the orchestra or wind ensemble as well. These students are enthusiastic, often have special musical skills, and can motivate other students.

Scheduled Saturday morning sessions at which older students can assist younger students and the entire music faculty is in attendance have advantages far beyond the extra rehearsal. Older students gain a feeling of accomplishment; younger students are inspired by the performing abilities of the high school students. All participants gain an appreciation for the size and diversity of the school system's instrumental music program. When the high school ensembles perform for the grade and middle schools, the recognition that then occurs will inspire other students to begin instrumental music study.

Make a CD, have your organization perform on TV, furnish pictures and stories to the yearbook and school newspaper—all public recognition in which students can take pride.

The opportunity to use interesting computer programs continues to be a motivational tool. Take the opportunity to incorporate music theory and music history into your programs. Computer programs also can judge pitch and rhythm accuracy should your teaching space allow for this configuration.

PERFORMANCE

Theoretically, the music program does not exist for the sake of performance. In practice, however, most of the efforts of both teachers and students focus on performance as the conscious or unconscious goal; the opportunity to perform represents the greatest single motivating factor. This is natural; music is a listening art and the greatest satisfactions come when performers feel their music has reached a listening ear. Therefore, the instrumental music teacher finds occasions for a variety of kinds of performances, knowing that the opportunity to perform will stimulate more conscientious and concentrated practice, prompt interest in concomitant musical learning, provide an outlet and a reward for students, and serve as a demonstration of the accomplishments of the music program. The danger is that this last consideration will take on undue importance and that performance will become the goal of the program rather than a vehicle for greater learning. In considering performance and motivation, one should remember that performance is encouraged primarily because of its motivation power, not the reverse. On the other hand, the group that does not perform at least once a semester will almost always be a dying organization. Students need to be challenged to do their best and to attain what is possible; with most music groups that means a reasonably active performing schedule.

Performance can take several forms. Contests and festivals are a common and valuable form of public performance. In some instances, these occasions are the only times groups play good music. The challenge to compete successfully is strong, so that the music for contests and festivals is learned more thoroughly and played more adequately than that for any other occasion. If the pressure to succeed in the competition is too great, however, the psychological negatives can outweigh the pluses. It is the teacher's responsibility to see that the efforts of the group are focused on excellence for the sake of excellence and for the sake of the music, not for the sake of winning the highest rating.

Concerts hold a place of equal importance and nearly equal intensity to contests and festivals. Here again, the music should be carefully chosen for its value and played as well as possible, so long as rehearsals do not become drudgery for the sake of unattainable perfection. The music chosen should be well within the ability of the group, so that a satisfactory performance does not demand an unreasonable amount of preparation.

Exchange concerts have all the advantages of regular concerts, with addition of the value of competition—the student's desire to excel in comparison with another group, school, or town. The teacher should not make a competition a major consideration and should be careful to emphasize good and bad features of both groups so that the students profit both from their own playing and from listening to the exchange group.

Special performing events are another form of motivation. Bringing in a guest conductor or guest artist to work with the group, hearing an artist perform, attending a clinic, or playing in select groups such as all-state or all-city organizations can result in great inspiration for a young player. Membership in all-state ensembles or the biannual National Youth Orchestra is a major accomplishment and should be publicized. Such opportunities are probably greater now than ever before.

Tours, though often viewed with dismay by teacher and administrator alike, have high appeal for students. Performing tours are probably never worth the agony involved, but great value is to be gained from them even if not equal to the effort expended. The kind of "professionalism" gained from performing well day after day is a fine experience for the student. However, the teacher must decide whether she can justify the expenditure of time and effort for value received.

Solo, small-group, and large-group performance before civic organizations has been emphasized. The more students who can participate in such programs, the more value for the students and the more interest promoted in the entire music program. When one or two highly touted groups are sent out exclusively, these tend to become exploited, the learning values diminish for them, and other deserving students are barred from the opportunity to perform.

This chapter has put forth sound educational principles translated into terms and situations applicable to the instrumental music program. The casual reader may feel that these principles are things she can take or leave, utilize or ignore. Sound motivation, however, is not simply something with which the music program is better, but which it cannot do without. Motivation is the *sine qua non* for learning, musical or any other kind. The teacher cannot take or leave it as she desires, for if there is no motivation there will be no learning, and where there is thoughtless or misguided motivation there may be negative learning. Motivation comes from within, but the teacher can provide day-to-day situations that are as desirable as possible so that the student's interest grows and he becomes motivated to develop in those areas that are the teacher's goals. Basically, every individual is motivated by his own needs. The psychological and physical conditions that hold promise of answering these needs can stimulate him to respond.

Motivation, however sound, is not in itself educational. Even the best motivation does not necessarily lead to learning. In music, we often forget that not all experience is educative, just as not all experience is motivating. To be educative, experience must be purposeful. Psychological studies have indicated that people attending lectures or reading material gain widely differing information from what they read or hear, depending on what they expect to gain. Sometimes their impressions vary so greatly that one person's bear no resemblance to another's. When purposes differ, the resulting learning also differs. To apply this to music is not difficult; merely practicing or reading through music or drilling perfunctorily on exercises is not educative. A purpose must be present, the student's purpose as well as the teacher's. Instrumental teachers continue to teach primarily in the "drill" fashion; the paucity of results attests to the failure of this method. Kurt Lewin said, "It seems easier for society to change education than for education to change society."

BIBLIOGRAPHY

Texts

* Indicates out of print in 2001.

CHEARY, JOHN M., and JACQUELINE J. CHEARY (1987). *The Band Awards System.* Oskaloosa, IA: C. L. Barnhouse.

CSIKSZENTMIHALYI, MIHALY (1991). *Flow: The Psychology of Optimal Performance.* New York: HarperPerennial.

———, KEVIN RATHUNDE, and SAMUEL WHALEN (1993). *Talented Teenagers: The Roots of Success and Failure.* New York: Cambridge University Press.

DECKERS, LAMBERT (2001). *Motivation: Biological, Psychological, and Environmental.* Boston; Allyn and Bacon.

DWECK, CAROL (1999). *Self-Theories: Their Role in Motivation, Personality, and Development.* Philadelphia: Psychology Press.

GREEN, BARRY, and TIMOTHY W. GALLWEY (1986). *The Inner Game of Music.* Garden City, NY: Anchor Press/Doubleday.

KEMP, ANTHONY (1996). *The Musical Temperament: Psychology and Personality of Musicians.* New York: Oxford University Press.

*MAEHR, MARTIN, and LARRY BRASKAMP (1986). *The Motivation Factor: A Theory of Personnel Investment.* Lexington, MA: Lexington Books.

RADOCY, RUDOLF E., and DAVID J. BOYLE (1997). *Psychological Foundations of Musical Behavior,* 3rd ed. Springfield, IL: Charles C. Thomas.

SARASON, SEYMOUR B. (1999). *Teaching as a Performing Art.* New York: Teachers College Press.

Instructional Videos

Increasing Student Effort: The Role of Attribution Theory (Marijana Weiner, James Popham, Sarah Stanley, 1991). Los Angeles, CA: IOX Associates.

Using Nine Powerful Motivators in the Classroom (Master Teacher Video Series, 1991). Manhattan, KS: Master Teacher.

5

Administration

ORGANIZATION

The orchestra director couldn't find his baton—again. His small (but appreciative) orchestra waited patiently for him to locate the missing baton. He was an excellent musician. He just couldn't get organized.

Across the hall in the band room the director stepped up on the podium and his band snapped to attention with military precision. Today they were going to play the latest band overture.

And so it goes. We might imagine a musical seesaw with the perfect musician on one end and the perfect administrator on the other. To stay on an even keel a balance must be struck between music and administration. At times one is clearly more administrator than musician, and fortunately there are many other times when one can be foremost a musician—the resulting combination equals a "music teacher." One director thinks of administration as forms, record keeping, inventories, and bids; another thinks that objectives, evaluation, and curriculum development are the essence of administration. Neither aspect should be neglected.

Though it is often said that good musicians are poor administrators, this is not so. Music educators have spent many years developing high-level skills in making music, but attention to administrative tasks is often learned on the job. The teacher who understands how to run his program with the maximum of smoothness and the minimum of fuss has more time for making music, selecting and learning scores, and organizing his teaching. Record keeping does not have to be a full-time job. A stockpile of good ideas has accumulated over the years based on the successful routines used by good teachers. A director should know the tricks of administration and select from them. Nevertheless, he does not need to use all of them to keep his musical house in order. The prospective music teacher should begin to collect his own private store of good administrative techniques: sample seating plans, records, forms, and the like. Numerous computer programs are available to help keep records and do other tasks such as organizing the music library, the instrument inventory, and uniform inventory/assignments. Such programs save both time and space and need to be included in the budget.

The first item required for organization is a calendar. It is useful for the director to carry a pocket calendar or to have a "pocket PC," have a "master calendar" on his desk, and post a large wall calendar in the rehearsal room. One of the first tasks for new directors is to contact the state music educators association or district band or orchestra division president to join the organization and receive a calendar of the year's events. (Addresses and contacts are available through MENC's Web site.) These events should be placed on the calendars of the instrumental teachers at all levels.

From this schedule, the instrumental music teacher can plan his concerts, band camps, recruiting activities, and any other events (such as trips) that vary from year to year. Each of these dates should be cleared with each school's principal and coordinated with other music teachers. All possible performance dates should be mailed to students' parents in the summer with an update of the handbook plus a note to contact the director immediately if these dates conflict with previously scheduled family activities. Early notification can help prevent many scheduling conflicts.

Coordination between music teachers is important. In school systems that have a music supervisor, coordination presents fewer problems. When a school system has no designated "chair" of the music program, the high school band or orchestra director should simply assume the role of coordinator by asking the other music teachers for their schedule of activities. If other teachers have not planned ahead, the director can simply provide them with a list of his dates (i.e., whoever is most organized gets to be the chair). The high school orchestra and band directors should also work with the middle school and elementary teacher(s), because these individuals can make or break the secondary music program.

It is virtually impossible for an instrumental music teacher to accomplish by herself all the administrative chores needed for a band or orchestra to function smoothly (unless the program is small or not very active). Students, parents, and even local service clubs can handle many responsibilities. Students may be elected to positions of president, secretary (to check roll), quartermaster (to oversee the uniform distribution, collection, and storage), property manager (to keep track of and maintain all equipment, stereo system, video cameras, etc.), and treasurer; students may be *appointed* by the director to the positions of student conductor, librarian, publicity chairman, section leader, and drum major.

Parents' organizations can handle a variety of tasks such as helping with concerts, trips, fund-raising when necessary, and chaperoning.

All of the effort put into administration will be enhanced by the practice of consistently keeping the principal informed.

BUDGETING AND PROPERTY

Budgets are provided to the instrumental music program on a yearly basis. If additional funds are not requested, additional funds will not be appropriated; if parents are willing to make up the difference between the required funding and that allocated by the principal or board of education, then the administration will be less inclined to provide additional funding. If the band and orchestra have a good history of retaining their membership, and if the ensembles and individuals perform as frequently as possible for as many people as possible, then the community and school administrators will feel they are getting their money's worth.

Ideally, every dime used for the instrumental music program should come from the board of education. In the 1980s and 1990s, as taxes became a major political issue, taxes were not raised even though the cost of education continued to rise; in some areas of the country they were actually lowered. Yet bands and orchestras continued to do what they were doing—playing concerts, participating in contests, and traveling.

This dilemma has been resolved in various ways by instrumental music teachers. Some have gone into fund-raising and tour management as a second profession; those who in the mid-1970s foresaw the growing needs of marching band programs have been financially successful. Some teachers have thrown up their hands in despair, met their classes, and let the chips fall where they may, leaving everyone the poorer. And some—perhaps most—have simply taught music well, supplementing the resources they had with required fund-raising.

When budgets are inadequate, it is very easy to exploit parents' organizations, or assess the students, constantly to raise funds. The better approach is to continue to seek funds from the principal, letting the parents raise money only for those items the director *knows* the school cannot afford. Although students should be entitled to a free public education, most instrumental programs are not cost free.

Budgets are usually presented to the principal each spring for the following school year and take effect on the first of July. New teachers should ask to see the budgets for at least the three previous years to determine any growth or reduction and to know on what items the funds were spent. Most school systems use a numbered code to denote what the funds were used for (equipment will have a number, instrumental music supplies a number, office supplies a number, additional staff or assistants a number, etc.). The beginning teacher should learn this code in order to present his budget in as orderly and accurate a fashion as possible. All teachers must discover the process by which money is spent, that is, to whom they submit their requests for purchases. And most importantly, teachers must determine to whom the funds are allocated. Site-based budgeting has changed the rules of the game. In some systems the upper administration will directly provide the instrumental music program with a budget; in others, the principal is provided with a budget and she allocates it based on individual school priorities.

The budget request should be as exact as possible, using round figures only on items that are impossible to determine precisely (such as instrument maintenance or telephone calls). A short explanation justifying each request can help facilitate a principal's decision, and attached bids indicating that the director has done his homework also help. For example, in the budget request under the line item *educational equipment*, the figure may represent the total sum for a cello, an oboe, a euphonium, and two marching mellophones (plus shipping). Attached to the budget request should be a paragraph listing how that sum breaks down and a sentence or two about why each instrument is needed, including how long the instrument will last. A long-range purchase program helps the school board determine the reasonableness of the music department's requests.

Instrumental budgets are usually divided into supplies (expendable items that normally do not last more than a year or so), equipment ("permanent supplies"), music (which may fall into either of the previous two categories), instructional staff (clinicians, honoraria, color guard instructors, arrangers, or director's pay for summer band camp—although putting the instrumental music instructor on an eleven- or twelve-month contract seems to be an increasingly common practice), and instrument maintenance (for yearly overhauls of selected school-owned instruments and minor repairs for numerous other school-owned instruments).

The director must attempt to prevent items such as file cabinets, stereo and recording equipment, and office furniture from being part of the yearly budget. These items should be from funds other than program funds. It is better for the director to bring a kitchen chair from home than to sacrifice a needed instrument.

Early on, all new teachers need to create a wish list, numbering each item in order of priority. This list should be submitted annually and updated as items are acquired and new needs identified. Such a list is helpful in long-term planning, and every teacher must approach his job as a long term career.

The new teacher should check last year's inventory and immediately delete missing items, such as school-owned instruments that are not worth repairing, and request restitution.

A time-consuming task for the instrumental teacher is to list the missing scores and parts. The first year's appropriation for music may be spent on missing first violin parts and needed flute music, resulting in no new music being purchased.

PURCHASING

Valve oil, cork grease, violin strings, reeds, tape for repairing music and scores, "pop" tunes, and a host of other supplies that the school does not stock and that need to be on hand should be purchased as soon as the new fiscal year begins. Otherwise, the director will have a quadruplicate form to fill out the day of a performance or each time he wants a roll of adhesive tape.

The most economical method for school instrument purchase is to advertise for bids. The disadvantage of doing this is that it may not be possible to obtain the exact instrument desired unless the bid is drawn up to indicate that only one specific brand and model will meet the requirements. A bid should specify make, model, key, finish, special features, accessories, case, acceptable standards (provision for rejection of shipment), acceptable alternates, desired method of shipment (if important), latest date for delivery, and possible trade-ins. The teacher who does not draw up the bid carefully and neglects to obtain several bids harms the program. Occasionally, a company may try to substitute a less expensive item for the one specified, omitting certain features or making what it considers to be relatively unimportant changes in the specifications. Usually, however, instrument companies are eager to have their best instruments in the schools and cooperate in providing competitive prices. If a trade-in is involved, it is even more important to see that multiple bids are obtained, because trade-ins are more valuable to some firms than others.

The greatest disadvantage in bidding for instrumental purchases is that tax dollars may not flow to the local merchants. These businessmen feel, with some justice, that they support the schools and that the schools should in turn support them. The director may thus be forced to choose between saving money and gaining goodwill, and is hard pressed to know which is more precious. A major advantage of dealing with local businesses is that they can rescue one in an emergency. For example, if the school gives a local dealer its business, then the director is much more likely to be able to "borrow" a drumhead to replace the one broken hours before Friday evening's performance.

A major purchase from year to year is music. Band directors must be careful to purchase a balance of marching band music, light works, and serious works for concert band (knowing that arrangements of popular music become quickly dated). Orchestra directors must purchase a balance of arrangements and compositions for string and full orchestra, both light and serious works. Undoubtedly the most neglected music is that for solos and small ensembles. Although this music is fairly inexpensive and absolutely essential to the program, band and orchestra directors are usually more familiar with many good large-ensemble works, as they hear new ones at conventions, on demo CDs distributed by publishers, and at other band and orchestra concerts. Selecting brass quintet, string trio, and woodwind quintet music at appropriate levels for different students will require additional learning on the part of most instrumental music teachers. Music for pep and jazz bands as well as rental charges for music for the annual musical cannot be overlooked.

Accountability

Once acquired, an inventory of equipment must be maintained. As with all public property, the teacher is responsible for the equipment in his area, so he must always know who has what. He should be able to account for stands, normal classroom furniture, instruments, uniforms, music, computers, and stereo and recording equipment—those items that are part of his standard paraphernalia and are movable.

School-Owned Instruments

Keeping records on instruments can become very extensive, but making duplicate copies is not difficult, especially with computers and the availability of paper that does not require carbons for producing multiple copies. Thus, the teacher can have sign-out cards for all equipment filed alphabetically by student, maintain a file by instrument indicating those checked out and those still available, give a copy to the student so that the student knows what she is responsible for, and have a copy available for the business office, principal, or other interested parties. The same applies to a bond, which in elementary and junior high schools is more common than a sign-out card because the parents are usually the responsible parties.

Some practical suggestions pertaining to record keeping follow:

1. The record should have the student's name, address, phone number, and ID number (in computerized schools). A complete description of the instrument, including all of its parts and its replacement value, is a *must*. A statement that sets the limits of responsibility and the uses prescribed for the instrument is also desirable.

2. It is a good legal precaution as well as good psychology to have both the parent and the student sign for the instrument. Both will then feel responsible for its care.

3. The form should tell whether the school or the user is obligated to pay for normal repairs during the year, and it should give a monetary limit.

4. The same form may be used to record the repair work done on the instrument: the date, cost, type of repair, and a yearly depreciation record showing percentage of depreciation each year and the present value of the instrument. If it seems more desirable to use separate forms for signing out the instrument and for recording its year-to-year history, a note on the sign-out form stating the present value of the instrument is important.

5. If rental fees are charged, the form should include a statement of the fee and should show payments. Rental of instruments is not always the best idea, however. To most people, rent of any kind, whether house, lawn mower, or musical instrument, implies that the owner assumes the cost of all repairs. This often entails having to render judgment throughout the year such as: Did that pad fall out as the result of use over the years or through the fault of the present user? A rent-free system, one making the user responsible for repairs during the time he has the instrument and obliging him to return the instrument at the end of the period in as good condition as when he received it, entails fewer problems for the director and may be just as feasible economically.

6. If rental fees are charged, the director can save himself many problems by having them paid directly to the business office, even if they go into a general fund rather than into the music fund. If the business office assumes responsibility for collecting fees and issuing the necessary bills, hours of teacher

time will be saved. It is possible in most situations to have the rental funds deposited into a specific account for yearly repairs.

7. A good suggestion often made but worth repeating is that the signing out of all school property, including that of the music department, should be handled by the school office. When this route is taken, the instrumental teacher's sole responsibility is to fill out an authorization slip indicating who is to have which instrument. The school office may then decide upon the necessary forms or bonds and make decisions about rentals, deposits, and repairs for damages as well as rules for use of the instrument.

Other records on instruments may include any of the following:

1. A record of repairs for each instrument allows a systematic approach to overhauls and helps avoid serious last-minute repairs. To wait until the instrument breaks down completely is no wiser than to ignore preventative maintenance on a car. Keeping track of what has been done helps the director decide what should be done to maintain the instrument in good working order. A long-range schedule can be based on a revolving system in which two or three instruments receive an extensive overhaul every several years.

2. A repair list on each instrument furnishes valuable information about which brands and models have given the best service. In addition, it may be used as a guide for the purchase of new instruments, because it can show at what date it would have been cheaper to invest in a new instrument rather than to repair the old one.

3. A checklist for student maintenance of the instrument is helpful. Some directors set aside a class period twice a year in which the energy of all students is devoted to a thorough cleaning job on every instrument—whether it needs cleaning or not.

4. A standard method should be followed for getting school instruments to the repair shop and for picking them up when repairs are completed. The director should see to it that he does not have to do this himself: The duty can be delegated to some responsible student or to someone in the school administration.

5. Instruments and cases should be marked. The manufacturer's serial number is the best and easiest way to keep track of the equipment; it is already on the instrument, it is not easily removed, and it will probably not duplicate any other number. A school number can be put on the case, neatly and in small-size numbers, by use of a stencil and an aerosol paint can.

School-Owned Uniforms

Uniforms are probably the most difficult item for the director to handle efficiently. Each separate part of the uniform should be numbered for record keeping. A set of records by number should be maintained so that if a shortage is discovered (e.g., belt 45 is missing) a check can easily be made. However, it is just as necessary to have a record of every part of the uniform each student is using—Freddie Jones has coat number 32, trousers 39, plume 67, and so on. The director also likes to know what sizes he has available, so a master sheet should be posted stating the size and number of every item. Size designations are not too reliable, however, as most students have alterations made initially and again as they change shape in the course of their school years.

A tailor is more practiced in judging which basic sizes can be successfully altered to fit any particular individual. It is important to get the largest possible number of students fitted well; so, having a tailor do the fitting and the major alterations will be a wise expenditure of time and money. A tailor shop will often issue uniforms for a school in return for the alteration and cleaning business.

Having the student maintain his own uniform is often unsatisfactory. Some parents are more frugal than others, so that whereas one mother carefully "spots" the uniform and presses it, another sends it to the cleaners before every appearance. At the end of the year one uniform is darker from having dirt pressed into it, and the other is lighter from excessive cleaning. For this reason, many schools keep the uniforms at the school; students change immediately before and after the performance and never take the uniforms home. Cleaning is paid for by the school or by charging the students.

When uniforms are left at school rather than kept at home, two other problems are avoided, the first being that after a concert or a sports event students often begin to shed their uniforms bit by bit, thus creating a sloppy impression of the band. The second is the problem of students arriving with part of the uniform missing—"I thought you said no belts tonight!" Keeping the uniforms at school may also help minimize the game of trading for a better fit, which wreaks havoc with the most careful record keeping.

In some school situations parents sign bonds for the uniform just as for the instrument, and often, damage deposits are charged. There are situations in which use of the uniform is entirely free; in some places the student is required to purchase the uniform for the period of time he is in band—from one to four years—and sell it back to the school at the end of that time at its depreciated value. In four years' time a new uniform depreciates perhaps 40 percent; the student absorbs this loss.

MUSIC LIBRARY

As any professional librarian can tell you, there is practically no limit to what can be done in the library routine. Besides listing the music by composer, a cross-filing system by titles is useful, and this can be expanded to cross-filing by the filing numbers, type of composition, required instrumentation, date of publication, date of last performance, and on and on. Library work is one area in which the job expands to fill the time available.

In organizing the instrumental music library, two areas must be considered: music in the library and music in the hands of students.

Music in the Library

In the library, it is absolutely necessary to have a system that allows the teacher or ensemble librarian to go to the files, find the desired composition quickly, and know that all parts are there. The teacher may not always know just what composition he wants but may have only a set of stipulations in his mind (especially when pulling a selection for sight-reading). Therefore, two things are essential: (1) a means for storing music so that browsing is facilitated and (2) a listing of the holdings by composer.

Nothing has yet replaced a heavy manila folder and a regular filing cabinet for storing music—the music is placed in the folder on which is printed the title, composer, and file number, and the folder is put in its numerical place in the filing cabinet. The filing drawer can be filled as tightly or as loosely as one desires, but it must support the music upright in a way that its name is easily seen. Music is often stored in paper envelopes, but this has disadvantages: it is less accessible for browsing; the top corners of the music get ragged, bent, and illegible; the temptation is always present to try to squeeze in that last single piece of music without taking the envelope out of the file, and they promote paper cuts. With the use of folders, instrumentation can be printed on the folder or on a separate sheet inserted in it or stapled to it.

Narrow shelves are also often used for storing music, but they waste space. The shelves are either too narrow to accommodate the thick symphonic parts of larger works or are too wide to be well utilized for the thinner numbers.

Filing cabinets built for march-size and for octavo-size music can also be obtained. Music should be filed by number as it is acquired rather than alphabetically. The latter is too time consuming, because it means rearranging almost every drawer and changing the labels on the outside of the drawers when a quantity of new music is purchased. New music can be given the next higher number above the last acquisition and placed behind it in the newest file. The card file can easily tell where the composition is to be found, simply by its number, for example "4–A–12" means cabinet 4, drawer A, folder 12.

A separate filing system should probably be set up for chamber music, jazz-band music, and small ensemble music. These should be cross-indexed according to ensemble type: woodwind quintet, string trio, string quartet, brass sextet, stage band, and so on. Percussion ensembles are best filed by the number of players required, for example, trios or quartets.

Every piece of music must be stamped with the name of the school to establish ownership. Stamping should be done in an obvious spot and should be neat—straight with the page and not smeared.

A library should be equipped to mend, file, and distribute music. A paper cutter, a large-carriage typewriter, tables, and sorting racks are minimal. The distribution of music should be done from a movable folder cabinet that can be placed inside or outside the rehearsal room.

The computer is useful for any number of administrative tasks. Pygraphics publishes *Pyware The Music Administrator* as well as *Pyware Charting Aid for Marching Band* (Pygraphics, P.O. Box 399, Argyle, Texas). Computer assisted instruction is a rapidly changing field; many excellent programs are being written by individuals, marketed from their basements, and eventually incorporated into the catalogs of major distributors. We recommend that teachers obtain the annual directory of the Association for Technology in Music Instruction (Barbara Murphy, Department of Music, University of Tennessee, Knoxville).

Music in the Hands of Students

It is easier to identify folders and to pass out music when the small shelves on the folder cabinet are labeled with an individual's name, part assignment, and a number (shelves should be arranged in score order). Folders (supplied as advertisement by music dealers) protect the music and are useful any time music must be taken outside the classroom. Many directors forbid students to take single pieces of music from the folder, stipulating that the entire folder must be taken by the student who wants to practice at home. The object of this rule is to prevent lost and mutilated parts of music.

Less important, but contributing to efficiency, are these practices:

1. Keeping music in a certain order in the folder, separated as to size and arranged perhaps numerically, will save rehearsal time when the folder contains a number of selections.

2. In putting music in the folders, the librarian should leave a note in the folder when a part is missing so that the player does not hunt and hunt—or ask for it, taking rehearsal time to settle his problem.

3. If the performing group has an instrumentation requiring extra parts beyond the publisher's normal set, give the local music dealer a list of these additions. She can see that these parts are included in the order, saving time that would be wasted by treating each order as a unique request. Every music educator should have the integrity to follow copyright laws.

FACILITIES

Most of the time a director doesn't choose the physical characteristics of his rooms—he inherits them, to suffer with or enjoy. Knowledge of the ideal specifications for rehearsal and practice rooms is important, if only to determine how far from the ideal one's own conditions are. The MENC has published an excellent pamphlet on the subject, covering the number of cubic feet per person, types of acoustical treatment, the height of ceilings, and the use of windows.[1]

When a new rehearsal room is being built or an old one remodeled, the director can get the most accurate information about acoustical materials and their sound-absorbing qualities from a basic acoustics book. Architects are not always well informed on the subject of acoustics, so the director should know what he wants by doing some research himself.

If the rehearsal room is not carpeted, it may be possible to solicit used carpet from someone in the band parents' organization. A carpeted floor or wall deadeners are among the most essential acoustical treatments of a rehearsal room. Air conditioning is also frequently a necessity so that doors and windows can be kept shut to prevent rehearsals from disrupting other class, and make summer programs feasible.

Permanent risers have both advantages and disadvantages. The disadvantages are chiefly that they severely limit flexibility of seating, and they make coping with changes in the size of a section difficult. They also discourage experimentation with seating effects. In addition, they make small ensemble arrangement troublesome because they are usually not wide enough to permit the V-or U-shaped seating of quartets and sextets. In rooms without satisfactory ventilation, players on the top risers may be playing in a tropical climate, adding to intonation problems and encouraging sleepiness. On the other hand, permanent risers are an asset for two reasons. First, they make it possible for both students and the director to see and be heard. If risers are used in concert, it makes good sense to use them in rehearsal. Second, they discourage use of the room for meetings and academic classes scheduled during the room's free hours. Because such meetings can leave the room in a state of chaos, this advantage should be given serious consideration. Risers should have an approximate six inch increment and be deep enough to accommodate all the necessary equipment and players, allowing for breathing space.

Instrumental practice rooms are costly to build and must be used if the expense is to be justified. Not many students find it possible to practice during the day, and when the practice rooms are not used they become storage places and eyesores. Administrators should be aware before having practice rooms built that they will be used largely before and after school rather than during the school day. The advent of computer-assisted instruction and programmed learning such as the

[1] Harold Geerdes (1987). *Music Facilities: Building, Equipping, and Renovating,* Reston, VA: Music Educators National Conference.

Temporal Acuity Products rhythm and pitch machines may increase the opportunity for individual study and the use of practice rooms during the school day.

Other rooms included in the ideal situation are a director's office with a soundproof glass wall into the rehearsal room; a library with sorting racks, worktables, and files; a small repair shop; and a uniform storage room. Others could be added, but these offer the most in efficiency and usefulness.

Equipment for the rehearsal room can be extensive and expensive. It can also be excessive if not properly used. Among the articles that have been useful to most instrumental groups are the following:

1. Numbered chairs with a straight back and with metal or rubber tips on the legs
2. A sufficient number of music stands of the pneumatic type
3. An electronic tuner
4. A quality digital tape recorder with high-grade microphone
5. A high-fidelity stereo system that allows for burning CDs
6. Music cabinets, storage, reed supplies, basic repair items, and other daily needs such as valve oil, pencil sharpeners, and metronome
7. A movable chalkboard or dryboard and a bulletin board
8. Stands for large instruments such as sousaphones and baritone saxophones; lockers or cabinets for all instruments, including percussion
9. A piano
10. Indirect lighting or lighting from the rear
11. A sound system including microphones, mixing board, and speakers for the jazz groups

PUBLIC RELATIONS

Publicity through newspapers, radio, and television is an important way of strengthening community relations. Any band or orchestra activity is of potential interest if the announcement is attractively written and accompanied by well-chosen pictures; for example, activities of parents' groups, trips, fund or membership drives, work with other departments such as drama or athletics, twirlers, and new instruments or new uniforms. Work by students, parents and service clubs should be recognized at programs and in public service announcements. Unique features of the group may furnish material for a story: Examples might be rare instruments, an unusual library collection, a musical family with members in the band or orchestra. The director should take the time to submit a short press release on individual band or orchestra students' accomplishments even if these achievements are not related to the music program. Headlines such as "High School Band Member Is National Merit Scholar" can do wonders for public relations. Publications designed to help the director with publicity are available.[2]

Press releases should be fairly short and to the point. (Most newspapers like to create their own "catchy" headlines.) Several short paragraphs indicating who, what, when, where, how, and why are all that is needed. Students' names and grade levels should be included.

---

[2] For example, Kenneth L. Neidig (1973), *Music Director's Complete Handbook of Forms*. West Nyack, NY: Parker Publishing; Guy S. Kinney (1987), *High School Music Teacher's Handbook: A Complete Guide to Managing and Teaching the Total Music Program*, West Nyack, NY: Parker Publishing.

Some directors shy away from writing press releases because of the time involved and because the director may feel that he does not write well. This task, however, cannot be ignored. Publicity is required to make the community aware of these activities, especially those citizens who do not have students in school.[3]

One of the most important benefits of good public relations is to prevent administrators or boards of education from neglecting or overlooking the instrumental music program in their attempts to conduct the school's business. If the public is unaware of the numerous and varied activities of the instrumental music program, boards of education are more likely to take funds from this "expensive" activity to fund other areas.

When photographs are scheduled, everything should be ready when the photographer arrives—including the human elements. This is especially important for large groups. Many a photographer has wasted her time and lost her temper waiting for the orchestra or band to collect itself. It is better to spend group time beforehand than to waste a paid professional's time. The position of every chair on the stage should be marked in advance, and the players in their positions. The seating arrangement should enable every player to be seen. Chairs should be placed so that proud parents can spot their child playing third sax or fourth horn.

Optional Activities

The teacher should consider the values of a scrapbook. If well kept, scrapbooks give pleasure to alumni, present players, and interested townspeople as well as material for publicity.

An up-to-date list of the alumni of the organization can be useful. To have alumni appear at concerts and rehearsals sparks interest, provides for publicity, and heightens the prestige of the organization.

Displays in store windows, for concerts and for recruitment, arouse interest. The displays—usually posters, but even a mannequin dressed in a high school band uniform—must look good. When the director has attractive posters announcing concerts, he should assign responsible students to ask permission of merchants to place them in their windows. Of equal importance is poster pickup after the event.

RELATIONSHIP WITH PARENTS

The relationship with parents can be the difference between a smooth or a thorny path for any teacher. A director cannot handle all of the details of trips and performances; he needs either a parents' organization or the cooperation of individual parents. Contests, trips, housing, food, festivals, games, fund-raisers, the problems of uniforms, instruments, stands, and music, to say nothing of props for half-time shows, are part of a director's everyday work. The best ways to gain parental cooperation are (1) to earn the admiration of the students and (2) to keep parents well informed.

Policies and procedures governing uniforms, practice, attendance, regulations on instruments, grades, point systems, merits and demerits, and rental fees, as well as a brief statement of objectives, will be welcomed by parents. For each performance, the parents should be informed what time the student is to arrive and at what place, what uniform is required, how long the performance will last, and whether the public is welcome. Parents should not simply be invited to attend a

[3] Kinney, *Ibid.,* p. 71.

rehearsal—they should be requested to come. Their attendance is an opportunity for them to see what the director does in a class period.

Music parents' clubs are not essential; they can be helpful except for an occasional one that definitely belongs in the "how-to-waste-time" category. The parents' organizations must always have a project. Parents' clubs can be actively involved in recruiting, in organizing trips, and in publicity and money raising, but they *should not* expect to have a part in formulating objectives or running the program.

Though there are obviously views to the contrary, money raising and fee collecting for special events should not be necessary. Students should not be expected to pay extra fees for contests or for all-state festivals of any sort. If these events are educational experiences, the school should be willing to underwrite them; if they are less educational than staying in school, then students should not be allowed to go.

In the real world of the twenty-first century, fund-raising has become the norm, especially for bands. A balance between educational priorities and the local political climate is necessary in establishing procedures for the use of nonappropriated funds. The primary issue of balance before embarking on any fund-raising is one of determining the educational needs of the students and the responsibility of the school board and administration to provide for program costs. Once there are multiple sources of support that result from fund raising, there is the issue of ownership and use. In theory, all equipment should appear on the school inventory, but the local culture may dictate more imaginative arrangements. An external organization that has purchased major equipment or even a vehicle may need to retain ownership and establish a long-term lease arrangement with the school system. The educational and legal issues that can arise when multiple funding sources are required to support a musical program of excellence would entail a lengthy treatise. For example, parent clubs often raise funds to pay for auxiliary instruction—drum line expertise, supervisors of flags or majorettes, or even clinicians and sectional help. When these individuals are not employees of the school district, interesting legal issues of responsibility and accountability can arise as laws differ by state and there are often different legal interpretations of the same law. We recommend that all possible legal situations be submitted to the school administrator with a request for a ruling from the school attorney. All travel, including that by commercial companies, the role and responsibilities of parents and chaperones, performances in public and private buildings, use of school instruments when students receive remuneration, acceptance of prize money, concert receipts, and surplus and deficit fund-raisers are a few of the "legal" situations. Teachers should not exaggerate the possible negative consequences of an active program but they must act to keep the best interest of the students and the program in the forefront of all decisions. Only important administrative issues and responsibilities should be published in the instrumental music department handbook; once published, the handbook should be widely distributed. Even the word responsible must be carefully considered and selectively used. For example, holding parents and students responsible for damage to school owned equipment is a tricky matter in a court of law—it is best to convey the impression of responsibility and omit explanation of any exception.

RELATIONSHIP WITH STUDENTS

First and last, the success of the director's program depends on student response. Although his ability as musician and teacher is decisive for the achievement of his objectives, he must be able to enlist students and keep them interested before he can teach these objectives. One of the most important considerations is realizing that the band or orchestra is not the most important thing in his students' lives—though it may be in his life.

The basic relationship between the director and the band or orchestra should be the typical student–teacher relationship. Because the high school band or orchestra director has the same students for four years (and possibly in the elementary or middle school before that) and extra time is often spent in working/rehearsing, most directors develop special relationships with students. This relationship must be all business whenever the director is on the podium but can be more relaxed when off. Directors should take an interest in students' activities outside of band or orchestra, but listening to students talk negatively about other teachers or other students is never appropriate. The director should *never* speak negatively about other students, parents, administrators, or other music programs. He should be careful to say only those things that he does not mind having spread throughout the entire community. Every director must strive to give the same attention to every student, even to those with little promise—acceptance is important to adolescents and lack of acceptance is the most common and serious threat to a student's self-esteem.

And remember, respect is a bit like smiling: When one gives a little, the recipient reciprocates.

Student Responsibility

One cautionary note: When student responsibility and efficiency are emphasized, a complex military structure can evolve, with superior and subordinates, fines and prizes, demerits and awards, and rules and regulations for everything. Students are extremists about most things and if sold on an idea they will carry it as far as the director allows. He must know, then, just what kind of atmosphere he wants and patiently but firmly work for the appropriate balance of control and relaxation.

The delineation of the authority of the officers is another important area that should be clearly spelled out so that they and the rest of the students know the limits of their authority. Doing so saves many complaints such as "John fined me fifty cents last night for doing ... and I was really, only ... just like you told us to!" If the delineation of authority is not clear, the director becomes a full-time adjudicator rather than one preparing for adjudication.

If there seem to be only a few rules that the teacher wants enforced, a single page containing instructions may be sufficient. These instructions should be given to every student so that no pleas of ignorance are possible. Most instrumental teachers will find, however, that much more than a single page is necessary, in which case a band or orchestra booklet is warranted.

Rather than a list of rules, the booklet should contain procedures. For example, behavior at a football game should be a procedure ("this is what we do") rather than a list of "don'ts." Behavior at games is a good illustration of what can be included. What are the procedures for getting up to buy food and soft drinks? Students do not always appear to be in their right minds at athletic events; the quiet, hardworking oboe player in the concert band goes wild with her cymbals at a basketball game. Some written procedures may help to curb her enthusiasm and outline what behavior is expected.

Travel

Travel is the student's great delight and the bane of the teacher's existence. Even for a short trip to a neighboring town for a game, there are so many things to load and unload that a check sheet of some sort is standard equipment. For a long trip there are additional considerations, such as meals, lodging, chaperones, loading crews, and schedules, to mention a few.

Lost among the many details may be the need to attend to adequate insurance coverage in case of accident, plus the need to have full administrative approval of every detail so that the teacher himself will not be liable. If a student rides across town with the teacher to pick up an instrument from a repair shop, the director and the school are assuming responsibility. All types of releases have been required of parents by school districts in the case of travel; however, no release will stand up if some negligence can be proved. Recent court decisions have found schools liable to the extent that the legislators in many states are passing laws to cap the amount of liability. The teacher cannot be too careful nor overinform the administration.

Students should never be allowed to come to an event by school transportation and return home by other means. The only exceptions to this should be if they are going home with parents, and this only when the proper release has been executed before the trip begins. Even if the student's parents have given him permission to ride home with someone else, he should not be allowed to do so. The best policy is to allow no exceptions to the rule, even to parents. Always use a school bus (even if it may be only partially filled) or commercial transportation, so that all students come and go by the same means.

RELATIONSHIP WITH ADMINISTRATORS AND COLLEAGUES

One element in developing and maintaining a good relationship with the school principal is that every act discussed in the preceding sections should be cleared through the principal's office. In matters of curriculum, discipline, budget, scheduling, and giving permission, most authority for the important decisions lies with the principal. Simply stated, it is virtually impossible for the instrumental music teacher to provide too much information to the principal. The principal should be kept well informed of every aspect of the total program.

The first point to clarify with administrators is the amount of school time allowed for extra appearances such as pep rallies, team send-offs, and similar spontaneous outbursts of goodwill toward defenders of the school's honor. Administrators must be informed that when a pep rally is scheduled for the last 15 minutes of the school day, the band must be called out 15 or 20 minutes earlier so that equipment can be readied and some coordination with the cheerleaders can take place. In addition, the band and orchestra director should send memoranda to other teachers giving as much advance notice as possible of any activity for which students must miss class, and reminders should be sent out closer to the event.

BIBLIOGRAPHY

TEXTS

Indicates out of print in 2001.

BROWN, FRANK. (1979). *A Band Director's Handbook of Problems and Solutions in Teaching Instrumental Music.* Lebanon, IN: Studio P/R.

*BUTTS, CARROL M. (1981). *Troubleshooting the High School Band: How to Detect and Correct Common and Uncommon Performance Problems.* West Nyack, NY: Parker Publishing.

COWDEN, ROBERT L. (1991). *Administration and Supervision of Music.* New York: Schirmer Books.

FLEMING, DOUGLAS S. (1997). *How to Manage Instruction in the Block.* Upper Saddle River, NJ: CPDR.

GAROFALO, ROBERT (1983). *Blueprint for Band,* rev.

ed. Ft. Lauderdale, FL: Meredith Music.

GEERDES, HAROLD (1987). *Music Facilities: Building, Equipping, and Renovating.* Reston, VA: Music Educators National Conference.

HAZARD, WILLIAM R. (1979). *Tort Liability and the Music Educator.* Reston, VA: Music Educators National Conference.

HOFFER, CHARLES R. (2001). *Teaching Music in the Secondary Schools,* 5th ed. Belmont, CA: Wadsworth.

HOFSTETTER, FRED T. (1988). *Computer Literacy for Musicians,* Upper Saddle River, NJ: Prentice Hall.

*INTRAVAIA, LAWRENCE J. (1972). *Building a Superior School Band Library.* West Nyack, NY: Parker Publishing.

*KINNEY, GUY S. (1987). *High School Music Teacher's Handbook: A Complete Guide to Managing and Teaching the Total Music Program.* West Nyack, NY: Parker Publishing.

KINYON, JOHN (1982). *The Instrumental Music Director's Source Book.* Sherman Oaks, CA: Alfred.

*KUHN, WOLFGANG E. (1970). *Instrumental Music, Principles and Methods of Instruction,* 2nd ed. Boston: Allyn and Bacon.

LABUTA, JOSEPH A. (1997). *Teaching Musicianship in the High School Band,* rev. ed. Ft. Lauderdale, FL: Meredith Music.

MUSIC EDUCATORS NATIONAL CONFERENCE (1994). *Opportunity-to-Learn Standards for Music Instruction: Grades PreK–12.* Reston, VA: Author.

NEIDIG, KENNETH L. (1973). *Music Director's Complete Handbook of Forms.* Reprinted 1997, Ft. Lauderdale, FL: Meredith Music.

OTTO, RICHARD A. (1997). *Effective Methods of Building the High School Band.* Ft. Lauderdale, FL: Meredith Music.

Instructional Videos

Educational Use of Copyrighted Material (John McCaa, et al., 1993). Reston, VA: Music Educators National Conference.

6

Recruiting and Scheduling

Recruiting students for the instrumental program is the responsibility of all music instructors, not a task solely for the classroom teacher. To attract new members, the instrumental staff should cooperate to (1) demonstrate a successful quality program; (2) develop positive relations with other teachers, administrators, the community, and parents of present students, (3) meet the needs of the local community; (4) demonstrate attainment of the objectives of band or orchestra, and; (5) work as consistently as possible in a planned recruiting program.

Successful recruiting varies with the personality and preferences of the teacher as well as with community tradition. Visiting grade school classes or appearing at grade school assemblies to talk about the music program or having a school ensemble perform for the youngsters may be effective for one teacher, whereas another has more success when high school students talk, perform, and demonstrate. Elementary school students should attend concerts by their own high school orchestras and bands before being bused to the local symphony orchestra youth concerts. The opportunities for education and for recruiting within school district performances are great. A third scenario might find last year's beginners involved in the recruiting demonstrations. In programs limited to starting beginners in middle school, these activities would occur during the spring prior to the elementary students' entering middle school.

Letters to parents explaining the program, summer music programs, instrument displays in elementary school buildings; encouraging local music stores to advertise; capitalizing on visiting bands or orchestras; disseminating news of high school group activities, (e.g, tours, honors, and awards); working with arts advocacy groups publicizing individual and group achievements—all are legitimate ways of capturing interest.

Making the instrumental program visible is important. Many activities compete for students' time including sports, the mall, MTV, church and clubs, required and elective school subjects, goofing off, computer surfing, and video games. Marketing is a part of even the youngest students' lives, and they expect to be given choices and to be persuaded. The instrumental teacher has available to her a rich array of resources provided by music advocacy organizations and community partners interested in furthering the arts.

Among all of the possibilities there are national, regional, and local resources. On the national scene, VH1's efforts to provide instruments to school systems have become well known and now the accompanying instructional materials are available at no charge to applicant schools. The National Association of Music Manufacturers (NAMM) is a continuing source of support, including recruiting strategies (see chapter bibliography for address). In one recruiting pamphlet, the national band instrument manufacturers state that many talented students do not know they have talent and must therefore be evaluated and interviewed. If a student with low initial interest and high talent is recruited, he is likely to remain in the program throughout school; success is a marvelous thing. If recruiting is successful and there is a high demand for membership in the performing ensembles, instrumental music will have administrative and community support and not be affected by the vagaries of financial and curricular support.

PRELIMINARIES FOR SUCCESSFUL RECRUITING

First, recruiting is not just a one-shot (one week or one month) event that takes place in kindergarten (Suzuki) or third or fourth grade. Recruiting is a yearlong endeavor and can be effective with students at any age. Students change rapidly— their interests, their abilities, and sometimes their potential. Consequently, flexibility in beginning instrumental programs should be maintained and instruction offered when the student is interested. Second, recruiting requires energy and an enthusiastic approach to music education. Enthusiasm is contagious; excitement about what is being accomplished in the instrumental music class influences students' attitudes and provides intrinsic motivation. Third, the maxim "Nothing succeeds like success" is certainly true in instrumental music. Peer acceptance of the program is important; having a large number of students participate encourages other students to enroll. When one has recruited half the students in a classroom, the interest of others is almost automatic. The recruiting plan should promise something for everyone. It must be attractive to boys and girls, rich and poor, extroverts and introverts, and all races—it is diversity in action.

When to Begin

Instrumental music should begin in the elementary school. When instruction cannot be scheduled until middle school, having instruction five days per week is a possible benefit, but clearly the students are delayed a year or two and some students will miss the opportunity to particpate. In those middle schools where the sixth graders are normally limited to the number of terms they can take an exploratory course, one must work closely with the administration to devise a schedule in which instrumental music is an exception and may be repeated each term.

Instrumental music instruction should be available in the elementary schools and students should be allowed to begin at any time during the school year. Most successful elementary music programs employ a "pullout" arrangement whereby students leave their regular class to participate in organized instrumental music instruction, organized by competence, instrument, or instrument family. Organization by classroom does not make educational sense. Being excused from class has no negative impact upon the instrumental student's academic course work, as the research of Ed Kvet, James Littlefield, Michael Wallick, and David Holmes has found.[1]

[1] Ed Kvet, (1982), *Excusing Elementary Students from Regular Classroom Activities for the Study of Instrumental Music: The Effect on 6th Grade Reading, Language, and Math Achievement,* unpublished doctoral dissertation, Cincinnati: University of Cincinnati; James Littlefield, (1986) *An Analysis of the Relationship between Academic Achievement and the Practice of Excusing Elementary Students from Class for the Study of Instrumental Music,* unpublished thesis for the Specialist in Music Education degree;

Even reading class need not be sacred; reading is taught in small groups and thus may be one of the classes in which being absent for 20 to 30 minutes has the least impact. An established beginning time facilitates one type of organization and group psychology is effective with youngsters—learn an instrument with your friends. Instrumental rental programs and computation of teacher loads make it advantageous to have multiple starting dates for instruction.

There is no best time of the year to begin instrumental music instruction. State aid may be available to pay for the teacher's summer salary, and though family vacations will interrupt instruction, summer offers time for both practice and lessons. Fall is also a good time to begin class or individual instruction, as the instrument rental period ends about Christmas, an appropriate time for a first public "concert" and for the purchase of the rental instrument as a cherished Christmas present.

Recruiting intensifies as students enter third grade. Students can successfully begin instruction on strings at age five and most other instruments when eight or nine years of age; most are ready by fourth grade, while a few may not catch the fever or be sufficiently mature until fifth grade. The American Music Conference data indicate that 79 percent of Americans began their study of instrumental music when they were between the ages of six and eleven. Recent research results indicate that involvement with music at the earliest ages is especially beneficial. With proper parental support it is almost never too early to begin the study of music. Piano teachers and Suzuki specialists have demonstrated that preschoolers can successfully participate in beginning instrumental music classes. When the physiological and psychological attributes of a child indicate readiness, let instruction begin.

It is essential that the director have access to students, support of their classroom teachers, and some knowledge of their academic achievement and their work habits to see tasks through to completion *prior* to the demonstration with parents. Instrumental teachers must provide guidance in the selection of the instrument to ensure the best "balanced" ensemble is recruited each year to avoid having twice as many high school saxophones as clarinets. Persuasion can be done in any number of ways, such as pep talks, modeling, stressing the importance of low brass, violas, and cellos, or others.

How to Begin the Demonstration

The instruments available for starting wind and string players should be brought to an evening meeting to which parents and students are invited. This event should be preceded by hype and classroom discussions. Retail music dealers will usually lend instruments or set up their own instrument displays. Students from the high school band and orchestra should be at the meeting, dressed in their concert attire, and prepared to demonstrate the instruments and help with details such as sterilizing the mouthpieces between each student's attempt at producing a sound. Recruiting is a serious "petting zoo." Parents of students from the high school ensemble should be solicited for assistance: setting up chairs for the audience, displaying the various instruments, making coffee—but most importantly, answering questions based on their experience of having a child in band or orchestra.

Atlanta: Georgia State University; David Holmes (1997), *An Examination of Fifth Grade Instrumental Music Programs and Their Relationship with Music and Academic Achievement.* unpublished doctoral dissertation, Seattle: University of Washington; Michael Wallick, (1998) "A Comparison Study of the Ohio Proficiency Test Results Between Fourth-Grade String Pull-Out Students and Those of Matched Ability," *Journal of Research in Music Education,* 46 (2).

Time should be allocated for students and/or parents to ask questions of both the director and the high school students. If a supportive administrator will attend, a spot on the program should be arranged. Parents are influenced by observing their child's excitement and enthusiasm about the instruments and the instrumental music program. Parents are part of the decision-making process and parent and child join the program together. Suzuki's ideas do work.

Useful information to distribute to the parents should include a list of acceptable or preferred brands for each instrument. This information prevents parents from purchasing an off brand instrument through the local discount store. Limiting the list to only one brand, however, puts unnecessary restraints on parents and is likely unethical.

Registration forms that parents may take home, complete, and return within the next week should be provided at the meeting. These registration forms should be accompanied by complete information about the instrumental program, costs, obligation, grading practices, and rules, regulations, and expectations.

The most burdensome decision concerning recruiting meetings for parents is whether to ask retail music instrument companies to send representatives or to have the music teacher provide all the information concerning instruments. Companies often have superb sales personnel—but they can be too high pressure. All interested companies should be invited. Being sued along with your principal and/or superintendent for omitting a company can ruin a perfectly good day.

Testing

Testing a student for his or her musical aptitude is an important part of recruiting even if you accept all applicants. If the student and the parents are given evidence that the student has sufficient musical aptitude to make the investment and effort worthwhile, most students will enroll. If the parents believe the student has exceptional music talent, almost no price is too great to pay to provide the child an opportunity for instruction. The instrument manufacturers learned the importance of aptitude testing some 50 years ago, and most of the manufacturers publish their own talent test. All of these tests are limited in their ability to determine musical aptitude, but most are based on good common sense and are certainly preferable to no test at all. The no-testing approach is a no-recruiting approach.

The Froseth recruiting pamphlet published by the National Band Instrument Manufacturer Association in 1972 recommends a specific aptitude test, probably because the association funded the longitudinal research that helped to establish the test's validity. That test, the *Musical Aptitude Profile* (authored by Edwin Gordon), although dependable, requires a testing time of three 50-minute periods, too much for most teachers. The advantage is that the test will identify a small percent of the student body with talent who would not normally try out for instrumental music. If the instrumental teacher uses an aptitude or an achievement test plus information from teachers and parents about student interests, along with a sound recruiting program, most students with the potential for musical success will be identified.

INSTRUCTION

In many schools, the instrumental music teacher instructs the general music class on song flutes or recorders for a month or six weeks; the results of this instruction and the teacher's impressions are helpful in recruiting.

Song flutes, penny whistles, and recorders teach basic music reading skills, develop finger dexterity and coordination, and generate interest. A final recorder concert may be part of the demonstration night for parents or may be used as a separate recruiting event. In recorder/song flute classes, the teacher can discover individual traits such as eye–hand coordination or aural acuity as well as any physical attributes that may hinder or help a student's progress in learning an instrument.

The disadvantages to teaching the six-week recorder program are the time involved and the fact that the instrument blows so easily that students get in the habit of overblowing. Unless carefully controlled, early recorder instruction can result in students' insensitivity to pitch and tone quality.

A truthful, honest recruiting program is the only way to longterm success. Any misconception of instrumental music as all fun, trips, uniforms, concerts, and immediate success will bring negative reactions as soon as the child is into the program. The recruiting program is directly affected by how well the teacher does the following:

- Deals with the parents of students
- Relates to the members of the band or orchestra
- Deals with the administrators at the various levels of the school hierarchy
- Instills in students, parents, and administrators a feeling of pride, accomplishment, and value in the instrumental program
- Articulates the objectives and benefits of the program

RETENTION

Retention is, of course, even more important than recruiting. A high attrition rate reflects negatively on the instrumental music program, but some should be expected and may be good for the program. Although students should be provided every opportunity to join the program, it is important that students and their parents understand that instrumental music is a long-term commitment. Music classes can and should be fun, but instrumental music should not be treated as a home video game to be shelved as soon as the student becomes the least bit bored. In every music program there are times when at least some of the students will be bored or too busy to practice, and virtually every student will at one time or another encounter frustration. Parents and students must keep in mind that frustration is part of life, and the instrumental music program can help students in an "extra-musical" way, teaching them to deal with the less glamorous as well as the glamorous periods of any experience. Long lists of reasons for dropouts have been prepared by industry and researchers, and each begins with "loss of interest" as the primary reason for a student's dropping out. Use of the ideas in other chapters of this book, and a personal concern for every student are the most effective methods for retaining students in the program.

One of the most important tasks facing the instrumental music teacher is scheduling. The task is difficult due to the limitations imposed by available facilities, the size of the instrumental staff, and demands on student and faculty time. Instructional time has been a major concern in virtually every school since the mid-1980s when a strong emphasis on basic education began to be felt in all fifty states. This emphasis and a lengthening list of core subjects has limited students' electives and oriented parents to greater concern for academics (a positive development and one that should enhance instrumental music rather than threaten it), but in many instances this emphasis has also brought about after-school scheduling for school music.

The schedule can make the difference between a successful and an unsuccessful program. The director should distribute an approved schedule to parents during the recruiting meeting—a schedule that shows how their children can complete a "college prep" diploma and yet take instrumental music through middle and high school. The music teacher must therefore be able to hold her own in discussions about the desired "approved" schedule with school staff including guidance counselors and principals. Access to students is critical. The general rule is that to make instrumental music available to all students, students must be scheduled by the administration into these courses first. There are multiple sections of other courses and more scheduling flexibility even with single section courses. Parents, teachers, administrators, and students must know that participation in instrumental music does not place the student at risk in any school subject or experience. Instrumental teachers often have limited flexibility in their own schedule (due to commitments in more than one building, travel time, and extra rehearsals), so that a careful consideration of the possibilities to adjust schedules of other courses is important.

Scheduling problems are not new but they have become more acute due to changes in the organization of the schools and increased graduation requirements. The problems and suggestions presented in this chapter are organized by elementary, middle, and high school.

ELEMENTARY SCHOOL

Initiating instrumental music in third or fourth grade is appropriate because it allows more years for learning and for finding the student's real interest, it allows for a more flexible pace, and it establishes instrumental music more firmly in the elementary school curriculum. If instrumental music is delayed until fifth grade, there will be a move to remove it completely from the elementary school by suggesting one year is too short and it belongs in the middle school curriculum. There will be arguments that mature students progress faster; this is true, but the advantage is always with the earlier start. Tiger Woods was hitting a golf ball at the age of two.

The pullout program, often on a rotating schedule, offers the most viable scheduling solution in the elementary school. The instrumental teacher, however, needs to be sensitive to the classroom teacher's problems—one of which is that she has had to expand her teaching to accommodate a world with rapidly expanding knowledge. A pullout schedule by specific instrument affects the fewest students in a class at any one time but means more interruptions.

Instrumental music teachers must learn as much as possible about the priorities and philosophy in each elementary school and work to obtain teacher support for the music schedule. Scheduling is truly a case in which the rich get richer—the better your program and the more students involved, the more easily administrators find ways to overcome obstacles and work for the continued success of the instrumental music program. The largest middle school in the country (over 3,000 students) recently discussed the subject of organizing schools within schools, and what advantages and disadvantages this offered. In the discussion, the principal made it clear that scheduling instrumental music came first, as more than 600 students in her school participated. She knew these students were getting something special in their education, something not provided in the rest of the school day. Parents also need to be informed about scheduling, because a supportive group of music parents is of value at any level of instruction.

MIDDLE SCHOOL

According to the Carnegie report *Turning Points*, emphasis at this level should be on self-esteem, on inculcating the belief in each individual that he or she can succeed, and that each person, different as each may be, is OK. Middle school becomes a time to *explore* not only ideas of self but also academic subjects and a world of experiences. Academic course content, although important, is often not considered as important as learning how to learn and deciding on long-term goals. Formative instruction takes place at the middle school level; it is the age when attitudes are established including attitudes toward band and orchestra. To accomplish the Carnegie Foundation's *Turning Points* objectives, students are to be members of small groups that are supervised by the same teacher for all of middle school.[2] Instruction is to be coordinated by team leaders who supervise the teachers of the core subjects for a pod of 100 students or so. The teams are assigned a large block of time to be divided as the team sees fit. These teams plan their days and weeks and are understandably possessive of their time. The team does not object if its pod of 100 students is scheduled into electives or exploratories at the same time, because this frees them of teaching duties and facilitates cooperative planning. This schedule, however, means that a pod of students must fit their electives into a period or two, bringing about competition among the teachers of electives. Students might be forced to choose between orchestra, chess club, or Tai Kwon Do. If a student took orchestra as an elective every quarter with such a schedule, he could miss out on interesting exploratories. In some schools competition has been lessened, but instrumental music instruction destroyed, by shortening the exploratory to six weeks, with the student abandoning strings after six weeks to take keyboarding, visual arts, physical education, or something else.

The centrality of teams often has meant that the orchestra and band were not scheduled so all members could attend at one time. In another scheduling variation, the ensembles are scheduled by grade level—bringing together one-third or fewer of the members of the band or orchestra with no concern for ability or instrumentation.

The third situation is a middle school in name that operates as a junior high school with subjects offered at prespecified times. Scheduling is similar to the scheduling in high school.

Our suggestion for the instrumental teacher parallels that of the elementary school—learn as much as possible about middle schools and the philosophy that presently dictates scheduling. Middle school philosophy can be quite opposed to instrumental music per se, as shown by the following statement from Paul George and William Alexander's *The Exemplary Middle School:* "Further, others argue that the traditional approach to instrumental music in the middle grades (an intensive focus on the few and the talented) when judged by the criterion of continued participation in high school, college, and adult bands is a staggering failure."[3]

One final alternative is to convince the administration of the need for a daily activity period scheduled at the same time throughout the school, or the lunch hour scheduled in such a way that instrumental students eat together, leaving at least 45 minutes for rehearsal.

HIGH SCHOOL

Curriculum reform in the secondary schools has had an impact on instrumental music programs. The "back-to-basics" and "arts are basic" movements often lump all the fine arts together, making little distinction among them. Additional

---

[2] *Carnegie Foundation Turning Points: Preparing American Youth for the 21st Century* (1989), New York: Carnegie Council on Adolescent Development; *Great Transitions: Preparing Adolescents for a New Century,* (1995) New York: Carnegie Corp.

[3] Paul George and William Alexander, (1993), *The Exemplary Middle School,* 2nd ed., Ft. Worth: Harcourt, Brace, Jovanovich, p. 75.

required courses leave little room for students to participate in band or orchestra every semester.

The highest dropout rate in band and orchestra occurs when students transfer schools or transition from middle to high school. There is a natural concern for the unknown: Will the next grade or school be more difficult? Will I still have time to practice? High school graduation requirements affect college choices. Pressure on teachers to improve learning has resulted in more homework and higher course demands. Again, it is an advantage for the high school directors to distribute schedules to parents that indicate how their children can complete the high school requirements and remain in the instrumental program all four years.

The optimum secondary school scheduling for instrumental music is to schedule it first period in the day (accommodating all students in grades 9 to 12 or 10 to 12) and to schedule concurrently only those courses with multiple sections. With the increasing importance of advanced placement (AP) subjects (some 33 are presently available), students should not have to choose between an AP core subject and instrumental music because instrumental music students are also likely to be AP students.

High schools are increasingly adopting some form of block scheduling. The *Instrumentalist* magazine indicates that its readership is concerned about the negative effects of block scheduling on high school bands and orchestras, with some states affected more than others. There is no one block schedule but dozens of variations.

Block scheduling is not always bad; some variations are advantageous to instrumental music. For example 90-minute blocks can be broken into full ensemble rehearsal, then sectionals with specific goals set for each section, then the full ensemble. Another advantage is that the longer period allows for listening activities so essential to learning. It is essential, however, that students are motivated to practice when they rehearse only every other day. Precious rehearsal time cannot be used for practicing the music.

Students can take more subjects—eight each year—with 4x4 block scheduling (see Figure 6–1). The illustrated version has students finishing a year's course work in one semester by meeting daily in double periods. A double period schedule means that students have only four subjects a day, thus reducing time devoted to passing and to class start-up and winddown compared to that needed with six or more subjects. The disadvantage is that this schedule cannot accommodate year-long subjects such as foreign language or music. A philosophical issue arises when students elect to take instrumental music all eight semesters in high school, as this would result in 25 percent of their high school education consisting of ensembles. At issue also is whether ensemble grades should be included in computing a student's high school grade average, whether colleges should consider these grades in admission decisions, and whether there is grade inflation in music courses.

4 x 4 Block Schedule	First Semester	Second Semester
90-Minute blocks	Course 1	Course 5
	Course 2	Course 6
	Course 3	Course 7
	Course 4	Course 8

Figure 6–1 4 x 4 Block Schedule, the "Purist" Form of Block Schedules. *Source:* T. N. Conners (1997). *A Survey of Block Scheduling Implementation in the Florida Public Secondary Schools and Its Effect on Band Programs,* unpublished doctoral dissertation, Florida State University, Tallahassee; R. L. Canady and M. D. Rettig (1995), *Block Scheduling: A Catalyst for Change in High Schools,* Princeton, NJ: *Eye on Education,* p. 69; J. Carroll (1987), "The Copernican Plan: A Concept Paper for Restructuring High Schools," *American Association of School Administrators Report,* EA019, 373.

AB Rotating Block Schedule Alternating Daily	A Day	B Day
Full School Year Schedule **90-Minute Blocks**	Course 1	Course 5
	Course 2	Course 6
	Course 3	Course 7
	Course 4	Course 8

Figure 6–2   AB Rotating Block Schedule, the Second Most Popular Type of Block Schedules. A compromise designed to facilitate courses that may be sacrificed under the 4 x 4 schedule—those courses that benefit from meeting throughout the year. It does defeat the purpose, however, of limiting students to only four courses each semester.

Visual arts teachers are often satisfied with longer periods in a single semester experience (as are theater and dance—advantages outweigh disadvantages) whereas music teachers expect and need the same students in the large ensembles for all six or eight semesters of high school. The formation of small schools of no more than 400 students within the larger school (schools within schools) heightens the scheduling problem, as each school is independent. Athletics, which is always after school, can assemble all the soccer players from the schools within schools to form a winning team, whereas band and orchestra are expected to meet during the school day and offer *academic* credit. Double periods in block scheduling are optimum for doing experiments in science and cleaning up afterward; double periods also allow students to do their homework in school with a teacher, a library, and a computer nearby as important resources.

A second iteration is to have classes meet every other day (four periods per day) for an entire year. Under this "AB Rotating Block," two days one week, three the next, music can be scheduled along with other core courses (Figure 6–2).

Still another variation is to employ a modified block schedule for core courses and regular scheduling for two or more "singleton" courses that meet for the entire year (Figure 6–3). This form of block scheduling is the most flexible.

Additional block schedules extend the school day for students but not for teachers, or have semesters of 75 days of core subjects and a 15-day term for makeup work and enrichment activities.

Modified Block Schedule	
First Semester	*Second Semester*
Block 1 (90 minute block)	Block 5 (90 Minute block)
Split Block 2A (40–45 minutes) for entire school year	
Split Block 2B (40–45 minutes) for entire school year	
Split Block 3A (40–45 minutes) for entire school year	
Split Block 3B (40–45 minutes) for entire school year	
Block 4 (90 Minute block)	Block 6 (90 Minute block)

Figure 6–3   Modified Block Schedule. The most flexible, allowing for 45-minute periods throughout the school year (eight periods) or collapsing split blocks into 90-minute blocks (also resulting in eight periods).

Block scheduling must account for not only the needs of instrumental ensembles but also the need for two or three lunch periods to accommodate students attending large middle and high schools. Block scheduling is complex and worthy of study by all music educators. The block schedule in which a year's course is completed in one semester has significant consequences for a student who fails—not only is it a "big" failure (two semesters of traditional work) but the student may need to wait until the next year to retake the course. The student who falls behind academically may not be able to schedule music, or music may conflict with an AP or other desired course, requiring that the student drop out of music for a year. Although most scheduling plans make it difficult for a student to participate in more than one music organization, the right block scheduling (more periods—eight rather than six or seven; as in Figures 6–1 and 6–2) allows for this richer high school music experience.

A block schedule with only one singleton to accommodate yearlong courses is not recommended. AP courses require the yearlong experience (the tests are always given in the spring), foreign language becomes a competitor, and with only one singleton a choice has to be made whether the band, orchestra, or chorus is scheduled for that singleton slot, requiring the other ensembles to meet for a double period for only one semester. Physical facilities in most high schools would seldom allow three or more music organizations to be scheduled at the same time.

In the worst-case scenario, as the course requirements for high school graduation become more stringent and student schedules more difficult to manage, periods are added to the school day. The extra period may be a "zero period," beginning an hour or so before school "technically" begins, or an additional period after school. In other schools an extra period may be created by lengthening the school day by thirty minutes with five minutes borrowed from each of the regular periods.

A high school instrumental teacher needs the strategic foresight of a Napoleon, aligning herself with powerful allies and equipping herself with knowledge of the strengths and weaknesses of block schedules and the arguments for and against the many variations. Advocates of block scheduling cite that presently the typical high school is organized with a six-period day and that only about 41 percent of the instructional time is devoted to core subjects. Such data have prompted school supporters to accept these scheduling changes! The longer time blocks allow students time to think, to research, and to solve problems, thereby achieving greater understanding and mastery in block-schedule subjects.

Today's challenge is to secure a schedule for those teachers who wish to *build* strong instrumental programs in schools with no tradition of excellence in ensembles or in schools whose administrators are unfamiliar with the educational benefits of excellent bands and orchestras. That challenge can be met only if the instrumental teacher possesses knowledge of the total educational program scheduling, plus a bit of charisma and considerable leadership skills.

SUMMER PROGRAMS

In addition to summer high school marching camps, many school systems schedule six-week summer programs for beginning and advanced students, grouping them by ability level and/or by instrument. The one- or two-week summer music camps that are available on many college campuses provide wonderful experiences for high school and middle school players. These programs provide many students with their initial introduction to music theory and history, an opportunity to interact with other motivated and gifted players, and a unique performing experience unobtainable in the regular school program.

PRIVATE LESSONS

Elementary and middle school students as well as high school students can benefit from year round or summer private lessons. Because parents of students still struggling to play "The Old Gray Goose" may be reluctant to spend dearly on private lessons, advanced high school or college players provide a pool of teacher/coaches at reasonable fees. These lessons motivate both the teacher and learner to greater achievement, as teaching is among the best ways to learn to perform. Middle school string, wind, and percussion players teaching elementary students is a win–win situation in which a nominal fee is charged, but the real prize is that both levels gain in performance skills. Allowing high school students to teach middle school students for slightly higher fees has the same effect on performance—students who teach begin to give much more thought to the performance process and greater credence to what their teachers have told them.

HONORS COURSES

One trend emanating from the educational reforms that began in the 1980s has been honors or advanced placement courses. These courses often receive more units of credit than other courses. In school systems that use some form of course weighting, the ambitious and bright students may believe they have no choice but to drop out of music and take honors courses in order to attain the highest possible GPA. and to be admitted to the best colleges. Fortunately the best colleges value ensemble participation. Countering negative feelings from other teachers, administrators, and critics toward schedules and grading practices requires both initiative and patience. Each school system appears to be unique in its priorities and traditions but solutions can usually be found.

SCHEDULING ELECTIVE COURSES

Each scheduling option depends on a number of factors. Where the instrumental program is fairly small, all players should be scheduled into a single performing ensemble with separate technique classes for beginning strings, winds, and percussion, if this is feasible. Where a program has a strong performing tradition, the quickest way to improve the top-performing ensemble is to start a second one. The improvement results not only from grouping the more proficient players together but also from a sense of pride, esprit de corps, and a general positive attitude. Again, to group by ability is possible only if music is scheduled before all other courses.

The purpose of a second group is also to prevent the weaker players from becoming buried in the second violin section or relegated to a four-year tenure on third trumpet. In the second ensemble, less advanced musicians play first parts and establish a second leadership corps. The second group is expected to play with the same tone quality, intonation, and as cleanly; though some allowance may need to be allowed for late starters.

One final point about scheduling a first and second ensemble: Students, parents, and administrators should be informed whether students will be selected according to an audition process in which students who score below a set standard will be assigned to the second group, or if standards will vary according to instrumentation. Selection for two different orchestras or bands may be influenced by the concert literature and thus display a double standard; that is, a weaker student may qualify if he plays bassoon but not if he plays violin. In such a case, directors must avoid placing unreasonable demands on weaker players simply because the instrument is needed in the top ensemble. Private lessons can assist the weaker player to "catch up" with the other members of the top group—plus obviously allow them to contribute more to the ensemble.

SMALL ENSEMBLES

Another effective way to improve the high school instrumental music program is to require membership in small ensembles that rehearse on a regular basis before or after school. If bus travel is a concern, discussion with administrators and/or parents may result in a solution. Another option is to have students meet in chamber groups at a centrally located home after school to which the parents car pool or perhaps some students walk. If such an arrangement is established, the teacher needs to hear the group on a regular basis and provide guidance for what the students are accomplishing on their own.

Small ensembles place unique technical and musical demands on individual students who generally rise to these new demands. In a small ensemble, performance errors and intonation problems are immediately apparent, and aural skills are developed more quickly. It is easier for students to perceive and comprehend style when four to eight players are trying to achieve a uniform style; players can quickly become sensitive to the necessity for a uniform interpretation (e.g., articulation, nuances, and tempo). Students should not be allowed to form their own in-school ensembles as they may become cliquish and not be organized educationally. The instrumental music teacher should assign each student to at least one ensemble and carefully avoid assigning the best players to more than two. Students should be grouped according to interest and ability levels. Players of average ability and those sitting toward the bottom of sections can benefit greatly from small ensembles in which each player is responsible for a part and cannot depend on other players.

Mixed-instrument small ensembles have a distinct advantage over ensembles of like instruments because through them players can learn more about balance and blend. There are, of course, benefits from participating in ensembles comprised of like instruments. Regular meetings and rehearsals of a clarinet choir, flute choir, cello choir, or percussion ensemble can be held in lieu of rehearsal time for sectionals. In those homogeneous groupings, clearer instruction in tone production, embouchure, technique, bowing, intonation, and articulation can be provided.

SCHEDULING HONOR/COMMUNITY ENSEMBLES

Honor groups provide additional motivation and musical challenges. The best examples are the stunning youth symphonies in many cities. An all-county or all-city band/orchestra comprised of the better players from each of several groups in a geographic area, which rehearses once a week on a regular basis throughout the school year, provides additional learning opportunities. Such all-city groups can perform more challenging music than any one school can attempt, as well as constituting an additional source of visibility for instrumental music. The high school and/or middle school conductors who provide students for the group could take turns conducting or a college or professional conductor be employed. This ensemble can offer inspiration to teachers as well as students. Any rivalries among directors and/or students should be set aside and not allowed to enter into decisions regarding the honor group (e.g., chair placement, soloists, literature, and more).

BIBLIOGRAPHY

Texts

* Indicates out of print in 2001.

*BOYER, ERNEST L. (1983). *High School: A Report on Secondary Education in America.* New York: Harper & Row.

*CONNERS, T. N. (1997). *A Survey of Block Scheduling Implementation in the Florida Public Secondary Schools and Its Effect on Band Programs.* Unpublished doctoral dissertation, Florida State University, Tallahassee.

DILLON-KRASS, JACQUELINE, and DOROTHY A. STRAUB (1991). *TIPS: Establishing a String and Orchestra Program.* Reston, VA: Music Educators National Conference.

FLEMING, LISSA A. (1994). *Getting Started with Jazz Band.* Reston, VA: Music Educators National Conference.

*FROSETH, JAMES (1974). *NABIM Recruiting Manual.* Chicago: GIA Publications.

GAROFALO, ROBERT (1976). *Blueprint for Band.* Portland, ME: J. Weston Welch.

GEERDES, HAROLD P. (1987). *Music Facilities: Building Equipping, and Renovating.* Reston, VA: Music Educators National Conference (reprint of 1987 ed.).

GORDON, EDWIN (1995). *The Musical Aptitude Profile,* rev. ed. Chicago: GIA Publications.

Great Transitions: Preparing Adolescents for a New Century (1995). New York: Carnegie Corp.

A Guide to Successful Recruiting. (n.d.) Durham, NC: Pearson Music Company.

*HOLMES, DAVID (1997). *An Examination of Fifth Grade Instrumental Music Programs and Their Relationship with Music and Academic Achievement.* Unpublished doctoral dissertation, University of Washington, Seattle.

*KINNEY, GUY S. (1980). *Complete Guide to Teaching Small Instrumental Groups in the High School.* West Nyack, NY: Parker Publishing.

*——— (1987). *High School Music Teacher's Handbook: A Complete Guide to Managing and Teaching the Total Music Program.* West Nyack, NY: Parker Publishing.

*KLOTMAN, ROBERT (1968). *Scheduling Music Classes.* Reston, VA: Music Educators National Conference.

*KVET, ED (1982). *Excusing Elementary Students from Regular Classroom Activities for the Study of Instrumental Music: The Effect on 6th Grade Reading, Language, and Math Achievement.* Unpublished doctoral dissertation, University of Cincinnati, Cincinnati, OH.

LEHR, MAJORIE R. (1998). *Getting Started with Elementary Level Band.* Reston, VA: Music Educators National Conference.

*LITTLEFIELD, JAMES (1986). *An Analysis of the Relationship between Academic Achievement and the Practice of Excusing Elementary Students from Class for the Study of Instrumental Music.* Unpublished thesis for the Specialist in Music Education degree, Georgia State University, Atlanta.

MILES, RICHARD B. (1996). *Block Scheduling: Implications for Music Education.* Springfield: Focus on Excellence.

*MUSIC ACHIEVEMENT COUNCIL (1986). *A Recruiting Guide for Band and Orchestra Directors.* Carlsbad, CA: Author.

MUSIC EDUCATORS NATIONAL CONFERENCE (1995). *Scheduling Time for Music.* Reston, VA: Author.

NAMM. *Dropouts: Reasons, Preventives, and Cures.* Carlsbad, CA: The Music Achievement Council, (1998). (Available from NAMM Web site.) www.namm.com

Turning Points: Preparing American Youth for the 21st Century (1989). New York: Carnegie Council on Adolescent Development.

WALLICK, MICHAEL (1998). "A Comparison Study of the Ohio Proficiency Test Results Between Fourth-Grade String Pull-Out Students and Those of Matched Ability," *Journal of Research in Music Education, 46* (2).

Instructional Videos

The ABC's of Block Scheduling. (Ben Swecker, 1996). Sheffield, MA: Educational Reform Group.

Alternative Scheduling (Elliot Merrenbloom and Robert Canady, 1999). Alexandria, VA: Association for Supervision and Curriculum Development.

Alternative Scheduling (John Health, John Checkley and Jim Oppenheimer, 1996). Three volumes; Alexandria, VA: Association for Supervision and Curriculum Development.

Band Scheduling: A Crisis is at Hand. (Bands of America, 1997). Palatine, LI: Sharper Video.

Block Scheduling and the Music Program. (Gerald Kember, 1995). Madison, WI: WMEA.

Block Scheduling: Time to Learn. (1997). Palatine, IL: IRI/Skylight Training and Publishing.

Elementary Parallel Block Scheduling for Enhanced Teaching and Learning. (Robert Canady, 1994) Salt Lake City, UT: Video Journal of Education.

High School Alternative Scheduling to Enhance Teaching and Learning. (Robert Canady, 1994). Salt Lake City, UT: Video Journal of Education.

Making the Transition from the Traditional Seven-period Day to Block Scheduling. (Mary A. Haley and Deborah Reed, 1998).

ASCD. Middle School Block Scheduling (2 vols.) (Michael Rettig, 1996). Salt Lake City, UT: Linton Professional Development Corp.

The New American High School. (Paul George, 1998). Gainesville, FL: Teacher Education Resources.

Planning and Implementing Instruction in the Block Schedule. (David H. Colley, 1998). Association for Supervision and Curriculum Development.

7

Principles of Winds
and Acoustics of Strings

Each wind instrument has its unique characteristics including: fingerings, inherent intonation problems, and timbre. The wind instruments also have common characteristics. Each instrument's "tone generator" is dependent on air, affecting tone quality and intonation.

This chapter is devoted to common characteristics of wind instruments, primarily addressing similar and dissimilar factors of the woodwind family and, to a lesser extent, similar factors of the brass family—these are covered more thoroughly in Chapter 13.

First and foremost, the brass or woodwind player must have a good sound. No matter how well developed her other musical skills are, if the student plays with a bad tone all else is of little concern. Tone quality is determined by a number of factors: equipment, embouchure, and breathing. The first two are covered in the chapters for individual instruments and each instrument's different requirements.

Each instrument produces a unique timbre, determined by the overtones present, their strength, and the degree to which they are audible. The harmonic overtone tone that predominates helps create the unique timbre. Whenever a particular musical pitch is produced by a wind instrument, one or more overtones of that pitch also sound. With modern technology these overtones can be measured, as well as the degree to which they are audible. This technology has enabled electronic synthesizers to duplicate the sound of the various wind, string, or percussion instruments. The details of sound production and perception make up the discipline of acoustics.

BREATHING

Proper breathing is that which maximizes the amount of air drawn into the lungs to support the tone plus the process of exhaling that supports the tone.

Posture. Establishing good breathing habits is possible only when the performer establishes and maintains good posture. Though the position for playing a wind instrument may appear unnatural, the proper position need not and should not strain any part of the body. The neck, throat, shoulders, chest, and arms must be free of tension; the upper part of the body rests naturally on the lower part, and the

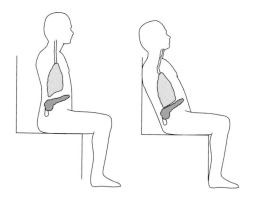

Figure 7–1 Proper and Improper Posture: The Affect on Breathing

player is alert but relaxed. Good performance posture is difficult to attain if the student has used the wrong muscles for years and incorrect posture has become habitual. Figure 7–1 illustrates the difference between proper and improper posture and the effect of the breathing system. Figure 7–2 illustrates proper posture for playing a wind instrument.

Note that the player pictured appears to be relaxed and comfortably seated. His arms are free, extended from the body. Elbows are comfortably away from the rib cage, feet are flat on the floor, balancing any weight. The instrument is held with the hands and neck strap, not propped on a leg or chair. His body is erect, eyes straight ahead, no neck tension is apparent.

The "rag doll" approach is frequently used to eliminate tension throughout the body so that the right muscles for playing can take over. To be a rag doll, flop over from the hips, let the top of the body fall in a limp, rag doll fashion, and rotate the head in a large arc. In rehearsal this exercise can be used as part of the warmup before students take their seats. Exercises to loosen facial muscles, such as dropping the jaw and taking deep relaxed breaths through a "throat as open as a tunnel," yawning, and extending a pencil straight out of the middle of the lips for 30 seconds, then yawning more, will further aid relaxation. Encouraging relaxation techniques as the first item of business in rehearsals and lessons can establish good habits. Relaxation exercises are limited only by the teacher's imagination.

For all winds, the correct playing position is based on moving the *instrument to the player,* the mouthpiece or reed to the embouchure. In no case, not even the sousaphone, tuba, or baritone saxophone, is it desirable to bring the player to the instrument or to adjust the head and shoulders to the position of the mouthpiece. On the larger instruments, any supporting stand should be adjusted, extra shanks used, or even a towel folded to the correct width for (baritone) to bring the mouthpiece to the player. The player should sit or stand tall (sitting away from the back of the chair), the spine straight to prevent bending the trachea. The notion of a string attached to the top of the head will help create a posture in which the air column is not constrained at the throat or by the rib cage.

**Figure 7–2
Proper Posture While Playing**

A relaxed but erect posture is also necessary in marching band. Players must remain erect ("stand tall") without tension and allow the breathing apparatus to remain relaxed in order to maximize the airstream necessary to adequately project the sound. A beginning band or orchestra director may observe the importance of posture by watching top-quality drum and bugle corps rehearsals.

Diaphragm. Proper breathing involves the diaphragm as well as the lungs. With hands on the waist just below the rib cage, thumbs in front and fingers in back, one can feel movement in the lower torso when breathing properly. If the diaphragm draws the maximum amount of air into the lungs, the lower torso will expand in the back as well as the front. It is impossible to expand the back of the abdominal cavity without expanding the front, but it is possible for the front to expand without the back expanding.

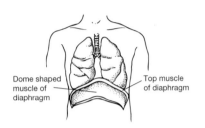

Dome shaped muscle of diaphragm

Top muscle of diaphragm

Figure 7–3 Drawing of Upper Torso Showing Location of Diaphragm

The diaphragm is a rather large, flat muscle located in a plane parallel with the floor (Figure 7–3) that separates the upper body from the lower. When the diaphragm is relaxed, it has the shape of a dome lying over the abdomen. When this muscle contracts, it flattens to create a vacuum, drawing air into the lungs and displacing the organs in the abdomen, resulting in a slight projection of the abdominal wall. Due to the fixed nature of the abdominal viscera, there is a limit to how far this projection can extend; consequently, full and deep breaths result in the rib cage expanding.

Proper breathing does *not* raise the shoulders. One inhales *downward*, drawing air toward the waist, a practice that eliminates raising the shoulders and helps ensure the proper use of the diaphragm. The feeling for a deep breath can be developed by taking a sudden inward gasp, with the fingers positioned to feel the expansion of the lower back and stomach, then shouting "hey" in a deep voice and feeling what happens to the muscles. Practicing Santa Claus belly laughs or panting like a tired puppy on a hot day can reinforce these sensations. The following devices are helpful for teaching the student to inhale correctly.

1. Imagine stepping into a cold shower on a hot day. The result is a sudden gasp as the air rushes deep inside, seemingly to the stomach.

2. Imagine taking an unmannerly "slurp" of soup. Actually make the sound, *then* duplicate the sound silently.

3. Sit in a chair and lean forward with the chest touching or almost touching the knees and the arms extending beside the legs to the floor. Breathe as deeply as possible. In this position it is difficult to inhale incorrectly.

4. Inhale several short breaths in sequence. For instance, before playing a whole note, inhale on the four preceding counts.

5. Stand with the heels and shoulder blades touching the wall. Inhale without moving the shoulders or chest.

6. Lying on a rug on the floor, inhale slowly, the small of the back touching the floor.

Whereas these exercises communicate the feel of proper breathing, in actual performance the majority of breaths are taken very quickly. Therefore, breathing exercises should also be practiced rapidly.

Controlled proper breathing means inhaling sufficient air and then exhaling it under pressure. Many players run out of air because they force it out too fast, an almost universal problem with beginning flute players. The player who can sustain a long phrase is one who has (1) a good embouchure that enables an economical use of air and (2) good control over the muscles used for exhaling. Although most students can learn to inhale properly, the process of exhaling correctly has the most direct effect on tone quality, pitch and intonation, and range. To exhale properly, the following exercises are helpful:

1. Hiss in imitation of a teakettle (being careful to make sure that the sound is produced by air rushing by the tongue and not produced by a tense, tight throat).

2. Blow up a balloon.

3. Whistle a note in a comfortable register and sustain it as long as possible without diminuendo.

4. Blow a stream of air against the hand, holding the hand a few inches in front of the lips (ask students to exhale air as hot as possible, then exhale air as cold as possible—the process used for blowing cold air is that required for playing a wind instrument).

Exhaling is often neglected or taught in such a manner as to increase tension or pressure in the body. The first exhale following a slow inhale should be like a sigh. The inhale should be silent as any noise indicates tension in the throat or mouth, and the sigh should expel all the air in a second or less. Exercises to assist in controlling the exhale might include a slow, four-count, relaxed inhale followed by blowing out 16 separate candles ("hooing") and observing the belly bouncing. Initially, some students will have difficulty hooing 16 times; others may cheat, holding back the air to have enough air remaining in the lungs at the end of the count. One give-away of an incorrect exhale is that the belly is not bouncing. Another exhalation exercise is have the students hold a sheet of music in the middle and at the top about 6" in front of their face. Then they should take a slow full, relaxed breath and exhale toward the paper attempting to blow it straight away from the face. Any exercise that attempts to blow the paper straight out also reduces unnecessary pressure from the muscles surrounding the lungs. Students who hear the term *push* often try to do strange things with the airstream. Better are terms such as *support, fast, cold, warm*; these may achieve the desired results quicker and without tension.

Here are additional inhaling and exhaling exercises that may speed the development of proper breathing habits.

1. Inhale as though yawning and exhale by sighing to promote relaxation through both the inhale and the exhale.

2. Inhale as in a relaxed gasp.

3. Inhale rapidly.

4. Pretend to blow out the candles on the birthday cake at your one-hundredth birthday.

5. Inhale while the teacher counts aloud to four, then exhale hot air in four counts at the same tempo.

6. Inhale while the teacher counts aloud to four, then exhale cold air in eight counts.

7. Inhale while the teacher counts aloud to four, then exhale while hissing for twelve counts.

A helpful concept is to think of blowing the air *through* the horn, *through* the stand, and *through* the wall. The idea of projecting air through the instrument rather than just into the mouthpiece helps both inhaling and exhaling and creates a more centered tone.

Tense throat muscles that constrict the throat and affect the free passage of air are a common breathing problem. Symptoms of a closed throat include raised shoulders, tense neck muscles, slightly protruding tendons and blood vessels in the neck, a pinched sound in the upper register, a weak lower register, and the inability to tongue rapidly. A closed throat may result from attempting to play in the upper register before the muscles are developed (usually to satisfy the demands of the performing situation, as in jazz and marching band). For players with a closed throat, the remedy lies in pretending to yawn, relaxed gasping, and fogging a mirror while saying "ah" (i.e., slower inhalation and exhaling a warm airstream). When practicing to correct a closed throat, the student should avoid playing in the upper register of his instrument, concentrating on the registers in which playing is comfortable, relaxed, *and* in which he produces a good sound. *Tension must be avoided in all parts of the body for good wind (and string) playing.*

Playing with the teeth together (a problem with young brass players), blocking the air passage with the tongue, or failing to exhale completely can restrict breathing.

The quantity of air required for good tone quality varies with the different instruments. Among woodwind instruments, the oboist requires the least amount of air, the bassoonist and clarinetist the most. With the brasses, the air required is proportionate to the overall length and diameter of the various instruments: The tuba requires the most, the trombone more than the trumpet, and the horn the least. Young players often confuse the *quantity of air* with the *speed of the airstream. The quantity of air determines the volume level, and the speed of the air determines the pitch of the note.* Students frequently exhale too much air when they should be blowing the same amount of air faster. The steadiness of the speed of the airstream is crucial both to good tone quality and to good intonation.

Learning the benefits of breathing exercises and proper breath support takes time—months and years—not a few focused rehearsals. Band rehearsals should frequently start with breathing exercises. Breathing exercises in the midst of a rehearsal are also a valuable way to refocus a group after a break or intensive rehearsing.

Full ensemble practice on breathing exercises should include the percussionists as proper breathing improves virtually every aspect of band performance (e.g., entrances) and emphasizes the importance of proper breathing in daily life. The exercises should start with a relaxed, slow inhale that fills the lungs at the bottom, then the middle, then the upper part without raising the shoulders. Having students extend both hands/arms above their head and inhale a large amount of air demonstrates filling the bottom part of the lungs. A student may attempt to please the teacher by pushing the stomach out—muscles that obviously are not related to the breathing apparatus. Teachers must emphasize relaxation during inhaling to allow the appropriate parts of the body to expand. As the daily breathing exercises progress, the inhaling should become more rapid, with continual emphasis on a relaxed, erect body.

ACOUSTICAL PRINCIPLES FOR WINDS

Although more detailed and technical explanations are available, some knowledge of the acoustics of woodwind and brass instruments is useful for clarifying any misconceptions from "common wisdom."

Two important terms for *all* musical instruments are resonance and damping. Everything that can vibrate has a resonant frequency, the "pitch" at which it will vibrate most freely when set in motion. Some objects have more than one resonant frequency. Multiple resonant frequencies are related mathematically, as one frequency is twice as fast as its fundamental, or three times as fast, and so on. The resonant frequency is the frequency with the greatest amplitude (loudness), or the longest sound. Tuning forks are labeled with their resonant frequencies, and it is this frequency's pitch that is heard when a tuning fork is made to vibrate.[1]

---

[1] Arthur H. Benade, (1992), *Horns, Strings, and Harmony*, New York: Dover Publications, pp. 29–31.

Damping. All sounds have a measurable decay. A pen striking the desk is dampened very quickly—in a matter of a few milliseconds. The water glass has a longer damping time and the tuning fork still longer. Factors such as friction, mass, and shape affect the damping time. Mass and shape along with the damping time affect resonance.[2]

Frequency of a pitch is the number of wavelengths per second (e.g., A=440). The sound perceived is comprised of the pitch's fundamental frequency plus pitches derived from its multiples or overtones. "Pure" sounds that are generated electronically have only one frequency.

Upper harmonics, overtones, or partials are present in the tone produced by all musical instruments; their amplitudes vary with the instrument. A glockenspiel sounds brighter than a marimba due to the upper partial being much stronger (greater in amplitude). The presence of specific partials (multiples) when a fundamental pitch is sounded, as well as the partials' individual amplitudes, gives each musical instrument its own timbre.

A musical instrument achieves its maximum amplitude (loudness) at its resonant frequency. The resonant frequency is also the least damped frequency. When a trumpet player attempts to make a piano string sound by playing a specific note, he will obtain soft and quickly decaying sounds from the piano string if he is slightly out of tune. When he is sounding exactly the same pitch, the piano string will vibrate.

Air contained in bottles, jugs, pipes, and other solid containers will all vibrate at their resonant frequencies if some type of *tone generator* (vibrating reed, plucked string, buzzing lips) sets the air molecules in motion at the appropriate speed. Wind instruments are lengths of plastic, wood, or metal tubing in which the air column inside the tube is set into motion at a resonant frequency; string instruments are a somewhat oddly shaped box that encloses the air, providing a multitude of resonant frequencies due to its shape. For winds, the vibrating air column is called a *standing wave*, as it primarily remains in the tubing with very little air escaping due to the difference in air pressure on the "bell end" (or open tone holes) and the tone generator on the other end. The cymbals and timpani are particularly useful for coloring effects due to their relatively long damping time.

The bursts of air from brass instruments pass through the mouthpiece and create a pressure wave inside the brass tubing where air molecules push against each other traveling longitudinally through the horn (as opposed to transverse motion when a violin string is plucked). The longitudinal pressure wave is kept in motion by a stream of tiny bursts of air at an appropriate frequency or speed. These standing waves are stationary between points called nodes— points where the longitudinal motion is reversed—for brasses the vibrating air column in the tubing is reversed at the bell and at the mouthpiece where the air column is reenergized (see Figure 7–4); for woodwinds it is at the bell or last open hole reversed to the point where the reed reenergizes the air column.[3]

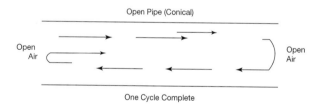

Figure 7–4   Illustration of the Standing Wave of Most Wind Instruments

Brass

A *standing wave* in a brass instrument is created by exciting the enclosed air column with a steady stream of tiny bursts of air. These tiny bursts of air are created by the performer opening and closing his lips very, very rapidly (appearing to buzz the

[2]Ibid., pp. 145–147.
[3]A. H. Benade, (1990), *Fundamentals of Musical Acoustics,* New York: Dover Publications, p. 406.

Partial

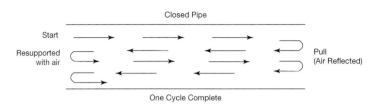

Figure 7–5
Change of Pressure at Bell

Figure 7–6
Illustration of the Standing Wave of a Clarinet

lips) and are controlled (i.e., contained, directed, and even altered) by the shape and size of the mouthpiece. This air passing through the lips is needed to resupply the vibrating air inside the instrument as there is a large amount of friction and a mass of air escaping from the bell—both producing a damping effect.

The change of air pressure at the bell of a brass instrument is enough to reflect the pressure wave back toward the mouthpiece (Figure 7–5). Only a slight amount of air escapes the bell of a brass instrument; this phenomenon can be observed by placing the hand over the bell of an instrument being played at a high pitch and at a very loud dynamic level. Pressure waves that start at the player's lips and travel through the tubing are reflected at the bell (by the change in air pressure), and travel back to the player's lips where they are resupplied with air (energy) (Figure 7–6). This type of vibration air column is defined as a "standing wave."

Because the lips are more pliable than the reeds used by woodwind players, brass players have more control over the frequency of the pitch. When the brass player creates greater tension in his lips in order to produce a stream of airbursts at twice the speed, a new resonant frequency is heard. This frequency, twice that of the fundamental, becomes the new primary pitch. The process of mathematically increasing the speed of the "tiny burst of air" (or what we view as buzzing lips) can be repeated in order to continue raising the fundamental pitch through the overtone series.

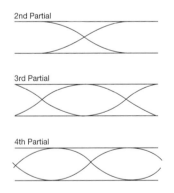

Figure 7–7
Illustration of the Standing Wave of a Brass Instrument with a Node Halving the Standing Wave that Increases Frequency

The instant the initial vibration is doubled, a node appears approximately half the length of the tube (slightly toward the mouthpiece or the energy source) of the brass instrument. A node is a spot inside the tube that remains stationary when the speed of the vibrating standing wave changes, dividing the standing wave into two equal waves that are half its length. The node cuts the standing wave by half and the frequency is doubled. The doubling of the air column is achieved by the player's lips buzzing twice as fast as he projects tiny bursts of air at a sufficient speed to sustain the faster vibration of the air column. This new pitch enhances the higher partials (overtones) that give brass instruments their unique timbre (Figure 7–7).[4]

Brass players are prone to miss the initial pitch as the first tiny bursts of air sent through the instrument must wait for the wave to be reflected at the bell before the pressure wave and lips work together to "lock" onto the desired pitch; during that brief instant, one occasionally hears brass players "crack" pitches.

This "coordination" between air, lips, and brass instrument becomes a performance problem when a musical passage requires frequent and rapid changes between partials. Experience and practice develop the kinesthetic skill required to create the necessary firmness in the embouchure to obtain the desired pitch.

[4]Ibid., p. 412.

The simplest illustration of the overtone series is the valveless bugle. The bugler is capable of producing at least the second to eighth partials in the overtone series shown in Figure 7-8. The fundamental is B♭ (extremely difficult to play due to the small diameter of the tubing in proportion to the length). Each pitch has its resonance frequency and each pitch also contains the higher overtones, although some are barely audible. These overtones can be heard by playing a pitch into a piano soundboard with the damper pedal depressed and listening to hear the resonate frequency dominate and the upper partials ring.

Figure 7-8   The Overtone Series for a B♭ Brass Instrument

Each pitch in the overtone series can be lowered to pitches of the chromatic scale by adding the appropriate length to the bugle's tubing (this is how the trombone operates). For trumpet, cornet, baritone, euphonium, trombone, and tuba, the largest interval among the "usable" notes in the overtone series is that which occurs between the second and third partials (the interval of a perfect fifth). There are six pitches missing between these two notes. Consequently the trombone is designed with six slide positions beyond the first position. Each slide position on the trombone progressively lowers the pitch one half step, enabling the trombone to bridge the gap between the second and third partials.

The valve brasses produce each of the six missing pitches between the second and third partials (the perfect fifth). The middle valve adds tubing to the extent that the partial is lowered one half step, the first valve lowers the partial by two half steps, and the third valve lowers the partial by three half steps (as do the first and second valves in combination). Different combinations of these valves are used to lower the third partial four, five, and six half steps in order to play chromatically to the second partial. Today, many of the brass instruments have devices to enhance the lower register to reach the first partial: F and G attachments on trombones, a fourth valve on baritones and euphoniums, and four or five valves on the tuba.

A musical instrument achieves its maximum amplitude (loudness) at its resonant frequency. The resonant frequency is also the least damped frequency. If one blows into an empty soft drink bottle at just the right angle, the air inside the bottle will respond at its resonant frequency. Altering the angle and/or the speed of the air inside the bottle will set the "trapped" air in motion at a faster or slower frequency, but only the resonant frequency will respond at maximum amplitude. This resonant frequency can be altered by changing the shape and size of the trapped air by partially filling the bottle with water.

Woodwinds

With the woodwinds, there are exceptions to virtually every common denominator. For example, all woodwinds are (or were) made of wood—except the saxophone; all use a wooden reed as a tone generator—except the flute; all have undergone extensive improvements to the key mechanisms during the last century—except the bassoon; all overblow the octave for their second register—except the clarinet; all of the upper woodwinds have one register key—except the oboe; all are based on the acoustics of a pipe closed at one end—except the flute; all have been manufactured with open tone holes that are covered with the fingers—except the saxophone; all behave acoustically as a conical bore instrument—except the clarinet; all are suitable for beginners—except the bassoon; all have bells—except the flute … and so on.

Woodwind instruments, like the brasses, produce sound from the longitudinally vibrating air column contained inside the instrument. Air enters a woodwind instrument through the mouthpiece, vibrating the reed that acts as the tone generator to force the air column inside the instrument to vibrate. The air molecules move longitudinally back and forth between nodes at a frequency equal to the pitch being played. As with the brasses, the basic node is at the bell of the instrument where the air column is reversed; unlike the brass, the last open key can also be a node that shortens the fundamental and reflects the air column in the opposite direction.[5]

The length of the air column is determined by the length of the instrument (which is shortened or lengthened by the tone holes). There is always at least one node present when the low register is played on any woodwind; this node forms near the bell (or the first opened tone hole) where the change in air pressure is sufficient for the air column to be reflected. As tone holes are uncovered, the node moves up the instrument to the highest open hole; consequently, the air column is shortened and the pitch is raised proportionately. The sound is projected through the first open tone hole where the air column is reversed, and the air surrounding the instrument is set into motion, carrying the sound to the listener (the same as the node at the end of a brass bell and the f-holes in a string instrument. The air remains in the instrument, but the air directly at the node radiates in all directions).

One important feature that makes woodwinds different from the brass is that each makes extensive use of its fundamental pitch and uses its second partial for the middle registers (except the clarinet). The woodwinds have six tone holes that are uncovered one at a time to produce a seven-note scale. The upper tonic of the scale is played by again covering all of the tone holes and overblowing the fundamental frequency to sound the second partial—this point between the first and second registers is called "the break." Additional tone holes and keys are added to extend the range downward and to play the chromatic scale. For all of the woodwinds, keys extend the range and create chromatic pitches.

The exception to the above is the clarinet, the only truly cylindrical instrument in the woodwind family, which overblows a twelfth skipping the even numbered partials. If one depresses all the keys, the lowest note is a written E. Overblowing to the next partial sounds a B (an octave and a fifth). The notes in the gap between that upper fifth (B) and the missing octave (E) are achieved by "throat tone" keys located near the middle of the instrument where a node is needed to divide the vibrating air column to half its length.

On all woodwinds, the second register is made accessible by use of an octave or register key that opens a vent hole closer to the mouthpiece than to the open end. (On the clarinet this is not an octave but a twelfth.) The octave or register key makes the lower register (fundamental pitches) impossible to sound due to an opened vent hole that changes the instrument's resonant frequency. In short, the octave key does not facilitate the second register, it simply makes the lower register difficult to play. The left thumb operates the register or octave key.

Woodwind players often have difficulty developing a good tone quality, due to the woodwind players' dependence upon the reed and the instruments' unforgiv-

---

[5]For a more detailed explanation, see John Backus (1969), *The Acoustical Foundations of Music*, New York: W. W. Norton; Benade, *Horns, Strings, and Harmony*; or Everett Timm (1971), *The Woodwinds: Performance and Instructional Techniques*, 2nd ed. Boston: Allyn and Bacon.

ing reliance on a proper embouchure. Woodwind beginners should be instructed in homogeneous classes to avoid the mistake of matching the brass players, with resulting poor tone quality. Homogeneous ensembles such as woodwind choirs, clarinet or flute choirs, and saxophone quartets also promote better intonation, balance, blend, and tone quality.

Woodwind performers are expected to be able to play lush, lyrical, or fast and technically demanding passages equally well, and with proper style and precision. For example, the clarinet and trumpet are both pitched in B♭, but due to the clarinet's ability to play lower and higher than the trumpet, as well as its ability to play larger intervals with ease, the music considered idiomatic for each is quite different. Fast passages are found more frequently in woodwind than in brass music. And while double- and triple-tonguing are becoming more commonplace among reed players, they must first learn to single-tongue at rapid tempos. Consequently, technique is an element of woodwind performance that is constantly practiced and improved. Because technique is a psychomotor skill not unlike a sport, woodwind players must continually work to retain the skills they have, plus work toward faster fingers and a faster tongue, all with control and precision.

Technique is the synchronization of the embouchure, the fingers, and the tongue with the brain. The way the instrument is held is essential to finger dexterity. Almost all beginners initially find the woodwind holding position awkward. Scales and arpeggios are the basis of at least 75 percent of all finger technique required of school bands and orchestras, and form the foundation of exercises designed to improve finger dexterity. Scales should be practiced systematically in all major and minor keys (plus chromatic); the maximum tempo should be established at which the student can play evenly and accurately with good tone quality and intonation. Scales are best practiced beginning on the tonic, playing up to the highest note learned (or possible) in that key, then down to the lowest note learned (or possible) in that key, and back up to the tonic.

Due to the fact that woodwinds raise their pitch by uncovering tone holes, adjacent notes are often different in tone color. This is especially apparent when the break (or octave) is crossed. Practice on scales while listening and thinking about tone color helps the student maintain good tone quality throughout the range of the instrument. Arpeggios are excellent means for practicing raising and lowering more than one finger at a time and for raising and lowering fingers simultaneously. Arpeggios also help develop the embouchure, secure good tone quality across registers, and train the ear.

Flute

The sharp outer edge of the embouchure hole splits the airstream. This split airstream is a simple division, some of the air going into the flute and the rest blown across the top of the embouchure hole. Almost all of the airstream is directed into the head joint (which fills with air in milliseconds); the airstream is deflected out of the embouchure hole and "across the room" until the air pressure in the head joint is lowered again and the airstream is again pulled into the head joint (again, taking only milliseconds). This "up-and-down" motion across the sharp edge of the embouchure hole creates turbulence that triggers one of the flute's resonant frequencies (depending on how many tone holes are covered and the speed of the air); a fundamental pitch should sound.

Increasing the speed of the airstream will cause a slight rise in pitch (but only within the confines of the length of the flute's bore). A greater increase in the air speed with a slight change of direction of the airstream will cause the vibrating air column to double in frequency and the second partial will sound (the second octave).

This principle of a sharp edge splitting the airstream to produce a sound is also how a recorder works—the performer blows through a rectangular chamber which controls the direction of the airstream and the amount of air that is allowed to reach the sharp edge (consequently determining the tone quality, the volume level, and to an extent the pitch). The flute embouchure serves the same function but the flutist has greater freedom to alter the tone quality, volume, and pitch.

Reeds

The other woodwinds use a reed as the primary tone generator. The fundamental and second partial produce the first and second registers (except on the clarinet, previously discussed) and six tone holes are used to relocate the "last" node.

The reeds are flexible slivers of wood carefully carved to vibrate at the appropriate resonant frequencies. Because reeds are considerably less flexible than brass players' lips, woodwind players cannot manipulate pitch as easily. Whereas a brass player can play seven to ten pitches without changing the valves/slide combination, the woodwind player can play only one pitch (sometimes two and rarely three) using the same fingering.

Reed players learn to care for the reed early in their instruction (another advantage to homogeneous classes). Single-reed players do not make their own reeds; double-reed players, however, benefit from learning how to finish and make reeds.

Many single reeds are playable straight from the box, but most can be improved and adjusted to respond better. Basic care and adjustment of the reed includes sanding the back of the reed to make and keep it flat, lightly sanding or rubbing the beveled portion of the reed to close the pores, and clipping the tip if necessary. Unfortunately, accurate reed adjustments take a great deal of experience, and students will produce more poor than good reeds in the process of learning this skill. The ability to produce a good sound on a good reed is obviously a prerequisite to being able to evaluate and adjust a reed.

Single Reeds

When the air is expelled into the instrument, the resonant frequency determined by the fingering is set in motion and the instrument responds. Because the reed itself has a resonant frequency, care must be taken not to allow it to sound (this happens when the player bites); nor should it be allowed to squeak (as happens with incorrect embouchures).

As the air pressure inside the single-reed mouthpiece builds, it forces the flexible reed to bend open allowing more air to enter the mouthpiece but only if the air pressure in the performer's mouth is greater than that inside the instrument. This puff of air forces the "high-pressure area" inside the mouthpiece and down through the instrument that in turn creates lower pressure in the mouthpiece. The low pressure acts as a vacuum to pull the reed toward the mouthpiece, sealing off the player's airstream. This oscillation of the reed is very fast; it is considerably faster than the frequency of the pitch being sounded by the instrument.

Two factors make it difficult to play softly on a reed instrument. First, the frequency of the reed must be faster than that of the instrument's air column (which requires a fast airstream). And second, any slight drop of the performer's air pressure will force air into the mouth rather than into the instrument. Both factors require the player to blow a steady, supported, fast airstream into the mouthpiece. (It is often difficult for students to realize the difference between velocity of the airstream and the volume of the air blown.)

Clarinet. One limitation: A cylindrical pipe closed at one end produces only the odd-numbered partials of the overtone series. If a trumpet were genuinely cylindrical throughout its length, it would require several additional valves to "close the gap" between notes of the overtone series. Instead of missing a maximum of 6 half steps between playable notes of the overtone series, the trumpet would have 18 half steps missing between the first and third partials.

Missing 18 half steps is precisely how a clarinet works. The basic six-tone-hole scale produced is a G scale; tone holes and keys are added to extend the range down to an E and up to the G, G♯, A, and A♯ above the seventh. To play the next B, all of the tone holes are covered (as if fingering the low E), and the fundamental is overblown to the third partial (the interval of a twelfth). The second partial, or octave, will not sound; rather, the clarinet jumps to the third partial.

The second register is assisted by pressing the register key that opens an additional vent hole near the mouthpiece and destroys the resonant frequencies for all of the fundamental pitches. For some of the higher notes in the second register and for notes in the third register, additional tone holes covered by the first few fingers are opened to serve as additional vent holes.

The distinctive timbre of the clarinet is due to the odd-numbered partials sounding. When a low F concert is played the octave partial is not present. However, the third partial, C, is sounded and becomes the dominant pitch when the register key is pressed. The fifth, seventh, and ninth (A, E♭, and G) are also present.

Saxophone. The saxophone uses a single reed like a clarinet but is the most obviously conical instrument in the woodwind family. Because it is conical it overblows the octave with the help of an octave key that opens a vent hole on the neck. Its basic six-tone-hole scale is D, like the flute, but it has additional tone holes and keys to extend the range down to B♭ and to provide the chromatic scale.

Double Reeds

The tone generator for double reeds is also the reed—but in this case two reeds sounding simultaneously. Whereas the area inside a single-reed mouthpiece acts as a vibrating chamber, the double reed's vibrating chamber is the area between the two curved reed blade, and is much smaller in size. This vibrating chamber does, however, allow the performer to have more control over pitch, volume level, and tone color. The two flexible reeds vibrate toward each other and then away from each other to create the same effect as a single reed vibrating.

Oboe. The oboe is a conical-shaped instrument that overblows the octave. The basic six-tone-hole scale is D to C with keys to extend the range down to B♭. The octave key destroys the resonant frequencies of the lower octave. Some notes in the second octave and the third octave require additional octave keys. To compensate, the oboe is provided with several vent holes, and also uses a half-hole technique to provide a small vent for obtaining some pitches. Other pitches are played with upper tone holes opened while lower tone holes are covered to provide yet a third type of vent hole (called "forked fingerings"), and this technique is also used to improve intonation in the lower octave.

The oboe has virtually the same fundamental pitches as the flute. Though the oboe and clarinet are similar in size and shape, the pitch difference occurs because the clarinet is cylindrical and the oboe is conical.

Bassoon. The bassoon is also a conical-shaped double-reed instrument. Its total length is about 100 inches (over 8 feet), doubled up to position the six primary tone holes and keys within reach of an average-size adult hand. Even in this position the fingers must stretch for certain keys.

The double reed attaches to the bocal that is inserted into the wing joint. The wing joint derives its name from the shape of wood of this section of the instrument. If the first three tone holes were positioned properly in the bore of the bassoon, they would be too far apart for the fingers of one hand to cover all three. Wood has been added to this joint to make the wood thicker, allowing for the tone holes to be cut at an angle such that the first three fingers of the left hand can cover them and still open into the bore of the instrument with the correct distance between them.

The basic six-tone-hole scale is G to F. The range is extended down to a low B♭ with the addition of keys and tone holes. Because the tube is so long, there is no way for one vent hole to serve as an octave key for all pitches. As the notes ascend upward, additional octave keys are provided that open vent holes farther up the instrument.

ACOUSTICAL PRINCIPLES FOR STRINGS

Consider a string of fixed length that one cannot adjust, like piano (we know the piano is really a percussion instrument, but consider it a string). Each string is set vibrating by a sudden action or disturbance, and rings freely until the energy is completely spent and the string comes to a stop. Plucking and striking a string produce the same effect.

Glancing inside the piano, one notices that the lengths of strings vary from fairly short at the treble end to much longer at the bass end. Further, the strings on the bass side are wrapped with a metallic wire (usually copper). Consider these rules:

1. A longer string vibrates at a lower pitch than a shorter string (when tension is equal on both), so that the longer string must be twice the length of the shorter string to play an octave lower (Strings use the same harmonic series as brasses.)

2. The frequency of string sizes is proportionate with an increase in tension, so quadrupling the tension on a string will raise it an octave. Increase the tension on a string 16-fold and it will rise two octaves.

3. For fixed string tension and length, the frequency is determined by the diameter of the string and its mass.

If the piano string tension and diameter were held constant, the highest C is 2 inches long, the next C is 4 inches long, and so forth; the lowest C on an 88 key piano would have to be 21 feet long. The tone would be thin and "bright." Another approach is to make most of the strings three or four different lengths and adjust the pitch by altering the tension. This, however, has a detrimental effect on the tone quality because each "set" sounds different.

The third option is to increase the diameter of the string for the lower pitches to reduce the length. The same tension on all the piano strings would require the diameter of the lowest notes to be pencil size with the tone adversely affected.

The solution has been that from the highest C on the piano to the C an octave below middle C, the strings are lengthened by 1.94 rather than doubled while their diameters are increased by 9.3 percent (per octave). The notes are then tuned correctly by adjusting the tension.[6]

---

[6]Benade, *Horns, Strings, and Harmony*, p. 113.

Below this C, the strings are lengthened relatively little, and the pitch is lowered by increasing the mass by wrapping different diameters of copper wiring around the primary string so that the string itself doesn't have to be as stiff (as a steel bar). The diameter (and stiffness) of the last unwound C string is selected to match the next lowest C (which is wrapped in copper wire) to produce a perfect octave with similar tone quality. Most pianos produce an acceptable sound around middle C, but there is a difference in tone quality between upright and concert grand pianos in the lower register. One trivial point is that on the concert grand, the tension is over 400 feet per pound on some strings with the total "pull" on the frame being almost 20,000 feet per pound of torque.

In the string family, the best example of this compromise between tension, the string's mass, and length is the string bass. The resulting tension is so great that regular pegs cannot hold string bass strings in place. Rather a mechanical device is used to secure the string's tension and allow tuning, as illustrated in Figure 7–9.

**Figure 7–9
Mechanical Tuners
Required for String
Bass Strings**

The Bowed String Family

The violin, viola, cello, and bass incorporate the same acoustical principles as the piano. Instead of a flat soundboard, they have a characteristically shaped "box" with four strings stretched over it. The box has a bridge that elevates the strings and serves as a conduit to the box or body and the air that fills the body. The sound is produced by rubbing the hair on a stick across the strings and using the fingers of the other hand to shorten or lengthen the vibrating strings with the box acting as the resonating chamber.

The rosin rubbed on bow hair creates a vibrating motion when the bow is drawn across the string. A string player can choose where on the string to bow and how much bow hair (friction) to use. This action is like the pianist choosing a hammer (piano key) to strike a string.

The bow affects tone quality, as the friction created by the bow damps the strings (violin more than viola more than cello more than bass—which can be observed at the release of a fermata in a string orchestra: The basses are the last voice to decay). A pitch produced by a plucked violin string dies away faster than the same note played on a piano.

These and other factors determine why a string instrument produces a broad variety of sounds (both good and bad) with various uses of the bow.

Effect of the Instrument's Body

The purpose of the shaped body of a string instrument is to insure that the air inside has a large number of resonant frequencies (about 5,000 on a violin). When the box itself is set in motion via the bridge, the air oscillates violently and radiates from the f-holes.

The skilled violin makers of the past discovered through trial and error that positioning the bridge with its shaped feet resting over the bass bar on one side and near the sound post on the other side produced the best sound. Bowing a string causes a side-to-side rocking of the bridge about the sound post so that the bass bar sets the entire top of the instrument vibrating, spreading to the rest of the body and finally to the enclosed air inside.

Like the brass and wind acoustical principles, the string instruments make use of the harmonic series. Stopping a string at its midpoint produces an octave; one-half that length produces a twelfth and so forth.

BIBLIOGRAPHY

Texts

* Indicates out of print in 2001.

Woodwind and Brass Instruments

BLACKWOOD, ALAN (1987). *Musical Instruments.* New York: Bookwright Press.

*DONINGTON, ROBERT (1982). *Music and Its Instruments.* New York: Mehuen.

*ENGEL, CARL (1977). *Musical Instruments.* Wolfeboro, NH: Longwood Publishing.

*FENNELL, FREDERICK (1954). *Time and the Winds.* Kenosha, WI: G. Leblanc.

*HOLZ, EMIL A. (1966). *Teaching Band Instruments to Beginners.* Upper Saddle River, NJ: Prentice Hall.

*PORTER, MAURICE (1970). *The Embouchure* , rev. ed. London: Boosey & Hawkes.

REMNANT, MARY (1978). *Musical Instruments of the West.* New York: St. Martin's.

*THOMPSON, KEVIN (1985). *Wind Bands and Brass Bands in School and Music Centres.* San Antonio, TX: Southern Music.

*WINTERNITZ, EMANUEL (1979). *Musical Instruments and Their Symbolism in Western Art.* New Haven, CT: Yale University Press.

General Instrumental Music

*GALLO, STANISLAO (1935). *The Modern Band: A Treatise on Wind Instruments, Symphony Band, and Military Band.* Boston: C. C. Birchard.

*GOLDMAN, EDWIN (1934). *Band Betterment, Suggestions and Advice to Bands, Bandmasters, and Band Players.* New York: Carl Fischer.

*GOODMAN, A. HAROLD (1982). *Music Education: Perspectives and Perceptions.* Dubuque, IA: Kendall/Hunt.

KOHUT, DANIEL (1973). *Instrumental Music Pedagogy,* Upper Saddle River, NJ: Prentice Hall; reprint (1996) Champaign, IL: Stipes.

KUPPUSWAMY, GOWRI and M. HARIHARAN (1980). *Teaching of Music* , 2nd ed. New Delhi: Sterling.

*MOORE, E. C. (1963). *The Band Book,* rev. ed. Kenosha, WI: G. Leblanc.

Music Teacher Education: Partnership and Process, the Task Force on Music Teacher Education for the Nineties (1987). Reston, VA: Music Educators National Conference.

*NEIDIG, KENNETH (1964). *The Band Director's Guide.* Upper Saddle River, NJ: Prentice Hall.

*PRESCOTT, G. R., and W. L. CHIDESTER (1938). *Getting Results with School Bands.* New York: Carl Fischer; Minneapolis: Paul A. Schmitt.

READ, GARDNER (1976). *Contemporary Instrumental Techniques.* New York: Schirmer Books.

WALKER, ROBERT (1984). *Music Education: Tradition and Innovation.* Springfield, IL: Charles C. Thomas.

*WEERTS, RICHARD (1966). *Handbook for Woodwinds.* Kirkville, MO: Simpson Printing and Publishing.

Elementary Instrumental Music

*HOLZ, EMIL, and ROGER JACOBI (1966). *Teaching Band Instruments to Beginners.* Upper Saddle River, NJ: Prentice Hall.

KONOWITZ, BERT (1973). *Music Improvisation as a Classroom Method.* New York: Alfred.

KVET, EDWARD (1996). *Teaching Beginning and Intermediate Band.* Reston, VA: Music Educators National Conference.

LEHR, MARJORIE R. (1998). *Getting Started with Elementary-Level Band.* Reston, VA: Music Educators National Conference.

LOMBARD, PHILIP C. (1994). *Fingering Practice for Beginning Bands.* Portland, ME: J. Weston Walch.

Secondary Instrumental Music

GAROFALO, ROBERT (1995). *Instructional Designs for Middle–Junior High School Band Teacher's.* Ft. Lauderdale: Meredith Music.

HOFFER, CHARLES (2000). *Teaching Music in the Secondary Schools,* 5th ed. Belmont, CA: Wadsworth.

KOHUT, DANIEL (1985). *Musical Performance: Learning Theory and Pedagogy,* Upper Saddle River, NJ: Prentice Hall; reprint (1992) Champaign, IL: Stipes.

KVET, EDWARD, and JANET TWEED (1998). *Strategies for Teaching High School Band.* Reston, VA: Music Educators National Conference.

*LABUTA, JOSEPH (1972). *Teaching Musicianship in the High School Band.* West Nyack, NY: Parker Publishing Company.

*MERCER, JACK (1970). *The Band Director's Brain Book.* Evanston, IL: Instrumental Publishing Company.

STRAUB, DOROTHY A., LUIS BERGONZI, and ANNE C. WITTE (1996). *Strategies for Teaching Strings and Orchestra.* Reston, VA: Music Educators National Conference.

History of Instruments

BAINES, ANTHONY (1975). *Musical Instruments Through the Ages.* New York: Walker.

CARSE, ADAM (1965). *Musical Wind Instruments: A History of the Wind Instruments Used in European Orchestras and Wind Band, from the Later Middle Ages up to the Present Time,* 2nd ed. New York: Da Capo Press.

*GEIRINGER, K. (1978). *Musical Instruments: Their History in Western Culture,* 3rd ed. New York: Oxford University Press.

*SACHS, CURT (1940). *The History of Musical Instruments.* New York: W. W. Norton.

Tuning and Acoustics

BACKUS, JOHN (1977). *The Acoustical Foundations of Music.* New York: W. W. Norton.

BENADE, ARTHUR H. (1990). *Horns, Strings, and Harmony.* New York: Dover Publications.

_____.(1992). *Fundamentals of Musical Acoustics.* New York: Dover Publications.

BROADHOUSE, JOHN (1990). *Musical Acoustics: Or the Phenomena of Sound as Connected With Music,* 4th ed. Temecula, CA: Reprint Service Corporation.

*CAMPBELL, D. W., and CLIVE GREATED (1987). *Musician's Guide to Acoustics.* New York: Schirmer Books.

FLETCHER, NEVILLE and THOMAS ROSSING (1998). *The Physics of Musical Instruments,* 2nd ed. New York: Springer-Verlag, Inc.

HALL, D. E. (1980). *Musical Acoustics: An Introduction.* Belmont, CA: Wadsworth Publishing.

HIRSCHBERG, A. J. KERGOMAND. and G. WEINREICH (1996). *Mechanics of Music Instruments.* New York: Springer-Verlag.

HOWARD, DAVID M., and JAMES AGNUS (1996). *Acoustics and Psychoacoustics.* Boston: Focal Press.

HUTCHINS, CARLEEN (1976). *Musical Acoustics: Violin Family Functions,* 2 Parts. New York: Academic Press.

*KENT, EARLE (ed.) (1977). *Musical Acoustics: Piano and Wind Instruments.* Stroudsberg, PA: Dowden, Hutchinson and Ross.

NEDERVEEN, CORNELIUS (1998). *Acoustical Aspects of Woodwind Instruments,* rev. ed.. DeKalb, IL: Northern Illinois University Press.

RIGDEN, JOHN S. (1985). *Physics and the Sound of Music,* 2nd ed. New York: John Wiley.

Repairing Instruments

BURTON, STANLEY (1978). *Instrument Repair for the Music Teacher.* Van Nuys, CA: Alfred.

HINKLE, RUSSEL, WILLIAM WOODWARD, and JAMES R. McKAY (2001). *The Bassoon Reed Manual: Lou Skinner's Techniques.* Bloomington, IN: Indiana University Press.

*NILLES, RAYMOND (1959). *Basic Repair Handbook for Musical Instruments.* Fullerton, CA: F. E. Olds.

SASKA, RONALD (1987). *Guide to Repairing Woodwinds.* Mount Laurel, NJ: Roncorp Publications.

TIEDE, CLAYTON (1976). *The Practical Band Instrument Repair Manual,* 3rd ed. Dubuque, IA: W. C. Brown.

*WEISSHAAR, OTTO H. (1966). *Preventive Maintenance of Musical Instruments.* Rockville Center, NY: Belwin-Mills. The text is also available in separate publications for flute and piccolo, oboe and English horn, clarinet, saxophone, bassoon, piston valve instruments, rotary valve instruments, and percussion instruments.

Woodwinds

BAINES, ANTHONY (1963). *Woodwind Instruments and Their History*, rev. ed. New York: Dover Publications.

BARTOLOZZI, BRUNO (1982). *New Sounds for Woodwinds*, 2nd ed. New York: Oxford University Press.

HOVEY, N. (1978). *What to Look for When You Choose Your New Woodwind Mouthpiece.* Elkhart, IN: Selmer.

THE INSTRUMENTALIST CO. (1992) *Woodwind Anthology: A Compendium of Woodwind Articles from the Instrumentalist.* Northfield, IL: Author.

*KIRK, G. T. (1983). *The Reed Guide: A Handbook for Modern Reed Working for all Single Reed Woodwind Instruments.* Decatur, IL: Reed-Mate.

MERRIMAN, LYLE (1978). *Woodwind Research Guide.* Evanston, IL: Instrumentalist.

*OPPERMAN, KALMEN (1956). *Handbook for Making and Adjusting Single Reeds.* New York: Chappell and Company.

SAUCIER, G. A. (1981). *Woodwinds: Fundamental Performance Techniques.* New York: Schirmer Books.

*TIMM, EVERETT (1971). *The Woodwinds: Performance and Instructional Techniques,* 2nd ed. Allyn and Bacon.

*WEERTS, R. (1972). *How to Develop and Maintain a Successful Woodwind Section.* West Nyack, NY: Parker Publishing.

WESTPHAL, FREDERICK (1990). *Guide to Teaching Woodwinds*, 5th ed. Dubuque, IA: W. C. Brown.

Journals

The Instrumentalist. Monthly from Instrumentalist Company, 200 Northfield Road, Northfield, IL 60093.

Woodwind, Brass and Percussion. Eight issues/year from Evans Publications; 138 Front Street, Deposit, NY 13754.

8

The Flute

The flute is the soprano instrument of the wind family, together with the C piccolo, which uses the same fingerings as the flute and sounds one octave higher. Pitched in C, the flute is nontransposing. Other flutes include the E$^\flat$ flute, which is pitched between the regular C flute and the piccolo, the alto flute pitched in G and which is becoming more popular in jazz, and the bass flute in C pitched one octave below the regular C flute.

HISTORY

The flute has the longest history of any of the wind instruments. There are in existence today two flutes taken from Egyptian tombs, believed by scholars to date from about 2200 B.C.E. Amazingly, both are in playing condition. Wall drawings and paintings from this period show flute players at various court and religious functions. Around 1300 B.C.E., a double-pipe instrument related to the flute existed, each pipe with three finger holes. By C.E. 79 the art of music had advanced to the extent that a fifteen-hole instrument existed that was fitted with silver bands that slid or twisted to cover the holes not being played. Most of the ancient flutes were not transverse but held vertically, and the vertical flute, in its familiar form the recorder, was popular through Bach's time. Transverse flutes also existed in ancient times. Pictures of transverse flutes are found on Japanese monuments dating from about 50 B.C.E.

During the 1600s the flute began to take on its modern aspects. The first key, the D♯ (E$^\flat$) key, was added about 1600; the bore was changed from cylindrical to conical in 1680; the round embouchure hole was replaced by an oval hole in 1724. By the mid-eighteenth century, the flute was among the most popular wind instruments. Alterations continued for the next century, with the most significant by Boehm, who made the flute very similar to what it is today. In 1832 Boehm invented a ring-key flute; in 1847 he changed the conical bore back to cylindrical; and in 1851 he added covered, open-standing keys.

SELECTING THE INSTRUMENT

Most student-line flutes manufactured by reputable companies are fine for beginners. The majority of these flutes have a head joint bore that starts at 17 millimeters at the cork end and is graduated to 19 millimeters where it joins the main body. The remaining length of the flute is cylindrical, through the body and foot joint.

Various aspects of new flutes can provide evidence of the quality of craftsmanship. Those aspects include the keys, tone holes, post mounting, and optional keys. A good student-line instrument has forged keys as opposed to cast ones, "pulled" tone holes as opposed to soldered ones, and posts mounted on ribbing rather than directly on the body of the flute.

Optional keys may be added to the flute to mitigate technical difficulties such as an awkward fingering or trill. Perhaps the easiest to justify is the low B key, which primarily adds resonance and enhanced tone quality to the lower register. Other keys such as the split E key (to make the high E easier to play) and the C♯ trill key are recommended, as are the rollers on C♯ and D♯ to facilitate fingering. Other optional keys should be avoided except by the most advanced players. Adding keys complicates mechanical adjustment problems.

The closed-hole plateau instrument is easier to master in the early stages than an open-hole French flute. It is also less expensive. The primary advantages of the open-hole flutes are that (1) the player can control the intonation more exactly by partially covering the holes with his fingers (some avant-garde music requires pitches played by partially covered holes), and (2) the open hole promotes proper hand position. In fact, it cannot be played successfully *without* good hand position.

Used flutes should be inspected for common signs of use such as worn pads and for indications of abuse such as damaged keys and rods, and dents or scratches. These may indicate more serious neglect or excessive wear. Furthermore, the prospective buyer should make sure that the outer edge of the embouchure hole is still sharp to the touch, that the keys are in alignment and the pads seat properly, that the cork in the head joint is tight (if the crown can be turned easily with the fingers, the cork may be too loose), and most importantly, that the instrument fits together easily but not too easily. Although minor repairs may be inexpensive, too many repairs may warrant buying a new instrument.

A possible option for the young flutist is the curved head joint available from several manufacturers as shown in Figure 8–1. This option makes good hand position easier while enabling a satisfactory tone. As the student grows physically, this head joint should be replaced with a standard one.

Figure 8–1 Flute with Curved Head Joint

Piccolo

The piccolo is similar to the flute, and all accomplished flutists should also be able to play the piccolo. It has the following distinguishing characteristics:

1. Low D is the lowest note because the piccolo has no foot joint; otherwise, the piccolo plays the same range and notes as the flute but sounding an octave higher. The piccolo cannot go beyond a written C.
2. Although the C piccolo is almost universal today, the D♭ piccolo is scored in older march music and transcriptions. The ability to transpose is useful.
3. The piccolo lacks the pitch flexibility of the flute.

4. The wooden piccolo, more sonorous than the metal, is more desirable for orchestral playing. The metal piccolo is easier to blow and more brilliant in quality.

5. The piccolo requires firmer lips and more pressure on the extreme high notes to overcome the instrument's tendency to sound flat in this register; hence, it is more tiring to play than the flute.

6. Because there is greater resistance, a smaller quantity of air is required, but the airstream must move more rapidly.

7. Piccolos are made with either a cylindrical or a conical bore. Most flute teachers recommend the cylindrical-bore instrument for marching band and the conical-bore instrument for professional and orchestral players.

An advanced flutist with good intonation is the best candidate for playing the piccolo. Students with small, dexterous fingers and thin lips are usually the most successful.

ASSEMBLING THE FLUTE

Although assembling the flute is a simple matter, a few precautions may help establish good habits that contribute to playing technique and to keeping the instrument in good repair.

The flute consists of three pieces: the head joint, which includes the embouchure hole, the embouchure plate, and the cork; the body of the instrument; and the foot joint that contains three tone holes. Correct alignment of the three pieces is important. To align, the head joint should be grasped between the embouchure plate and open end with the left hand (where the label or manufacturer's name is engraved). The right hand gently picks up the body of the flute without grabbing the key mechanism any more than is necessary. The two pieces are twisted together, not pushed or wiggled. The center of the embouchure hole in the head joint should align with the center of the line of keys. The foot joint is grasped in such a way that the keys will not be damaged, then gently twisted onto the body of the flute. The rod on the foot joint should bisect the D key on the body of the flute. In correct position, with the fingers of the right hand on the keys, the little finger of the right hand can drop to the low C key without the right wrist having to move. If the foot joint is turned in too far, the little finger will hang over; if out too far, the little finger must poke at the key rather than depress it.

Student-line flutes are often made with an engraved mark on the head joint and a matching mark on the body. If the embouchure hole is turned in, a slightly covered sound and flat pitch result. If the hole is turned out, higher pitch and better projection are obtained. The correct alignment allows complete finger freedom, proper balance, and an embouchure hole parallel with the lips.

The beginning student must adjust his embouchure to the correct alignment, not the alignment to his embouchure. After a player has acquired considerable skill, he may turn the head joint slightly one way or the other, but experimenting should be postponed until the student has had considerable experience playing with the conventional alignment.

The head joint is not pushed all the way in, but is pulled from one-eighth to one-quarter of an inch, to allow for tuning with other instruments. The tenons, the ends of the joints where two pieces fit together, are somewhat delicate and can bend easily if assembled carelessly. The flute should be assembled with a smooth, circular movement, pushing and turning the parts together. If the flute is difficult to assemble, clean *only* the tenons with a mild silver polish. Using a lubricant causes the tenons to attract dirt and grime.

HOLDING THE FLUTE

Most students are uncomfortable when first attempting to hold the flute. Their fear of dropping the instrument often results in improper habits, and beginners must be monitored carefully. The size of the hand determines the hand position that will allow the fingers to rest properly on the keys. The flute is supported primarily by the base of the left forefinger and the thumb of the right hand, with the right little finger adding balance. The lips also serve to balance the instrument.

The right thumb supports the flute from below and should be placed *approximately* underneath the F key, or between the right index finger and middle finger (Figure 8–2). The thumb does not extend under and past the flute; it should be bent so the side of the thumbnail supports the instrument. The right wrist should not bend; it should be held straight with the fingers slightly curved, the hands forming a C, or as if holding a cup of water. When the water is poured out by turning the hand 90 degrees, the correct hand position is obtained.

Figure 8–2 Hand Position for the Flute

The pads of the four fingers should rest on their proper keys (rechecking the alignment of the foot joint is advised). The instructor must watch that the fingers do not overlap the keys, a practice that reduces finger dexterity and in extreme cases can cause uneven wear of the keypads.

In general, the left wrist must be curved, so that the base of the left forefinger touches the instrument for support but the left thumb is free to manipulate the B and B♭ keys. The fingers of the left hand, especially the forefinger and less so for each successive finger, are curved more than those of the right hand to allow easy manipulation of the proper keys. The left hand has a tendency to rotate to the left, forcing the fourth finger to stretch for the G♯ key, thus hindering technique. The fingers must be kept *very close* to the keys. The left thumb is placed on the B key at a slight tilt so that the edge of the thumb presses the key. Beginners often have a tendency to slide their thumb too far under the instrument to help hold it. The left thumb should not be used primarily to support the instrument; it must be able to move freely to manipulate the B♭ key. Initially, this position may feel somewhat artificial and unnatural to beginners. The teacher should check frequently to see that the player has not relaxed into habits that feel more natural but will eventually affect technique.

The position for playing the flute is shown in Figure 8–3. The flute is held approximately parallel to the line formed by the lips; that is, the embouchure hole should be parallel with the lips both horizontally and vertically. Proper position keeps the flute almost parallel to the floor—with the end joint a little lower than the rest of the flute (no more than a 20 degree tilt for the instrument). A slight tilt to the head is appropriate as long as it is not due to poor posture and does not restrict the airstream.

Figure 8–3 Holding Position for Flute

The right elbow is raised until the muscle in the upper part of arm begins to pull. The correct position is when the elbow is dropped to a point where pulling ceases. Beginning students often drop the right arm to a more comfortable position, but this cramps the hands, flattens the fingers, and hampers technique.

In playing while seated, the feet are flat on the floor with one foot slightly in front of the other; the body is erect and the back is away from the chair. Knees, chest, and head face the same direction, which may require pointing the corner of the chair at the conductor. The arms must be free of the body, not draped over the chair. The student should stand part of the time during lessons and during practice. Proper upper body position does not change when standing. For beginners, maintaining correct playing position may cause some fatigue; therefore, the beginning flutist should practice frequently for short periods of time.

Good flute playing depends upon good flute position. In slow passages students tend to raise their fingers far above the keys. Young players also learn incorrect fingerings. An example of the latter is the D♯ (E♭) key. This key should be used for most of the notes played on the flute. As the little finger is usually the weakest finger, many youngsters soon discover that the D♯ (E♭) key can be avoided completely and play these notes "close enough" to pitch that many teachers do not catch the error.

EMBOUCHURE AND REGISTER

The flute is not played like a pop bottle. This approach, taught all too often, results in a hollow sound. The air is directed primarily *across* the embouchure hole, although somewhat downward for the low register, slightly upward for the upper register, and more directly into the embouchure hole for louder volume.

The beginner should start on the head joint alone so that he can concentrate solely on the proper embouchure to produce an adequate tone and not get dizzy. He should be asked to relax his lips as if vocalizing "em" (this keeps the teeth apart and the lips together). The head joint is tilted upward ever so slightly. The bottom lip is spread gently across the embouchure plate and turned out as if slightly pouting (some of the pink should be visible). The lower lip covers approximately one-quarter of the embouchure hole. The corners of the lips are then tucked slightly to anchor the embouchure. See Figure 8–4a.

With the head joint closed by the palm of the right hand (see Figure 8-4b), the student should be asked to blow air as if vocalizing "pee" (syllables such as "poo" cause the embouchure to pucker too much and should be avoided). This

Figure 8–4a
Student Playing Head Joint—Open

Figure 8–4b
Student Playing Head Joint—Closed

small puff of air should produce second-space A; when the hand opens the head joint, an octave higher is sounded. Beginning students often use more air than is required and become dizzy when playing their first tones. Students should be encouraged to focus the airstream, keeping the aperture of the embouchure a small oval. The width of the embouchure opening should not exceed the width of the flute's embouchure hole.

The head joint should align on two planes—parallel to the lips and the embouchure hole centered *on* the chin. With this position the airstream (fast and focused) has the best chance to be directed to the edge of the embouchure hole where the airstream is split evenly without wasted air. The instrument should not be angled too far backward or forward. The head joint should not be rolled in too far, as this results in a muffled nasal sound; nor rolled too far out where the sound is thin and unfocused. A telltale sign of where the airstream is crossing the plate is the trail of condensation formed by the breath. The trail should look like a small triangle with the base at the far edge of the embouchure hole.

The "pee"-type articulation is recommended to help the student produce the beginning sounds, but its use should not become automatic because the syllable "pee" uses a burst of air to open the lips, whereas the player should form the embouchure opening prior to blowing the air. The Suzuki flute teacher Takahashi advocates that students "spit out one grain of rice at a time" to establish the embouchure. This task keeps the aperture in the embouchure small and the corners firm (but not too firm), and a burst of air pressure is required to send the rice flying.

When the student can sustain the two As on the head joint for three or four seconds without fainting, he should be guided to focus the airstream by making the aperture in the embouchure slightly smaller and blowing the air more toward the outer edge of the embouchure hole. He can accomplish this by moving his jaw forward slightly while maintaining the "spitting rice" embouchure. This change should produce the third harmonic, high E, when played on the closed head joint. In his first attempts, the student may blow *more* air rather than a *faster* airstream. Usually blowing "more air" results in blowing the aperture in the embouchure open, which in turn loses focus of the air and actually allows the air to slow down, defeating the intention. Encouraging students to maintain the size of the aperture and blow the wind faster helps students comprehend the difference between "amount" of air and air "velocity." The player should try to produce the upper harmonic by blowing *less* air faster. Beginners generally have a problem in focusing the airstream. It is common for these beginners to use excessive wind, most of it wasted, and find themselves short of air, dizzy, unable to complete a note or phrase, and completely frustrated.

Basically, the flutist's embouchure has these characteristics: (1) The corners of the mouth are stretched back, but not too firm or pinched or clamped; (2) the corners of the mouth are straight or even turned or tucked down rather than in a smiling position; (3) the lower lip is drawn back just enough to allow the upper lip to protrude over it slightly. If the lower lip is too far back, the air column is directed straight down; if it is even with the upper lip, the air column will go straight out as when blowing out a candle.

The correct embouchure is illustrated in Figure 8–5. The player may need to move the head joint up and down, raising and lowering the flute on his lip to find the best spot. Experimenting with very slight movements is necessary. The player may want to try two versions of correct embouchure to see which seems best.

Figure 8–5
Flute Embouchure

1. The upper lip is relaxed while the lips are held in an even position. Only enough pressure from the corners of the lips to smooth out the wrinkles in the lower lip is used. The lower lip will cover approximately one-fourth to one-third of the embouchure hole, and the column of air will be blown just inside the outer edge of the embouchure hole.

2. The upper lip is stretched tight against the teeth. This embouchure can be thought of as being long, straight, and thin, rather than round and open. Blow over the moist inner surface of the lower lip such as vocalizing "pee" with the corners of the mouth held firmly. While playing in the upper register, the student relaxes his lip and covers more of the hole.

With either approach, the lower register will require less of the embouchure hole covered and more of the air directed into the flute. The upper register requires the flutist to direct the air toward the outer edge of the embouchure hole and cover more of the embouchure hole with the lower lip.

For the low register, the mouth should be open about the width of the embouchure hole; narrower and more oval shape for the middle register; and a yet smaller oval for the upper register. The mouth aperture should not be round. Intonation should improve with these embouchure changes.

An embouchure opening that is too wide for any register produces a coarse, breathy, and inflexible tone. If the opening is too small, which seldom happens, the tone will be small and thin. Initially, the smaller the lip opening the better. It makes for more resistance to the airstream, enables production of a better tone, and helps avoid dizziness.

Correcting the Embouchure

If too little of the embouchure hole is covered, the tone will be breathy and require more air. If the lips are too tight and too far away from the hole, the air striking the sides of the aperture will cause extraneous vibration in the upper lip. The air column may not be focused, resulting in a thin tone with poor intonation. To improve focus, the student should cover more of the embouchure hole with his lip and attempt to direct more air into the flute while not changing his hand position.

If too much of the embouchure hole is covered, the tone will be small and thin, there will be a limited response, legato playing will be more difficult, dynamic range will be limited, and flexibility impaired. To correct this, the student should direct the airstream out across the hole (which may require pushing the jaw forward).

Variations in facial structure that affect the embouchure follow:

1. A relaxed or receding jaw results in a spread, unfocused tone. To correct, the student should bring the lower lip out or turn up the corners of his mouth.

2. A protruding jaw may produce a breathy tone or no tone at all. To correct, roll the head joint in more.

3. An overhanging upper lip may cause the mouth opening to be too wide and the lower lip to cover too much of the hole, letting air strike the sides of the embouchure. Use the same solution as for a receding jaw.

4. Thick lips will need to be compensated for by placing the flute higher onto the pink portion of the lower lip.

5. A slight dip in the center of the upper lip can be accommodated by keeping it raised and supported by the upper teeth. The student with a very pronounced dip may meet with some success by playing off center; the aperture

of the embouchure, however, should be centered on the embouchure hole. Students with the infamous "cupid's bow," however, will more likely be successful on another instrument.

Figure 8–6 illustrates the "split" vapor trail that is common to beginners with a "cupid's bow." This close-up shows a player who can be assisted by altering her upper lip and learning to play by directing as much air into the flute (rather than across it) as possible while achieving the correct pitch. Many such students can work toward adjusting their embouchure, but with a large bow most students should be directed to another instrument.

Figure 8–6
Split Vapor Trail Due To Cupid's Bow

INTONATION

Flute players are notorious for their intonation problems. Because the instrument's range is in the upper register of the grand staff (see Figure 8–7), the wavelengths are shorter, and pitch variations among players cause interference between the close sound waves. The points of interference occur two, three, or four times per second faster than for other instruments and are more easily heard. The result is considerably more annoying than when four tuba players play slightly out of tune.

Generally, the flute has these intonation problems: the low register is flat, the middle register is in tune, and the upper register is sharp. Both middle and upper registers, however, change with the volume—flatter when soft and sharper when loud. The flute player deals with pitch by applying two principle rules: (1) covering the embouchure hole or directing more of the air *into* the instrument, which lowers the pitch; and (2) uncovering the embouchure hole or blowing more air *across* the instrument, which raises the pitch. These two procedures are explained to students in a variety of ways, including "raising or lowering the head" (which can affect the airstream), directing the air "at the wall or at the floor" (keeping the head erect), and the most common, "rolling the flute in and out" (which usually results in poor hand position and should be avoided). The best is to encourage students to "direct the air to the floor or wall."

The flute tends to play flat in cold temperatures. The instrument should be thoroughly warmed before tuning by gently blowing air into the instrument with all keys closed. The flute can cool down so quickly that flutists need to warm it by blowing warm air into it prior to making an entrance after long rests.

The A or F without vibrato are good tuning notes, but one well-tuned pitch does not ensure correct intonation on all notes. Particular tones on the flute have their own intonation problems, as shown in Figure 8–8. The biggest offender is the C♯ in the staff and, to a slightly lesser extent, the C♯ above the staff. To correct sharpness, the player must lower the jaw very slightly to direct the air more into the

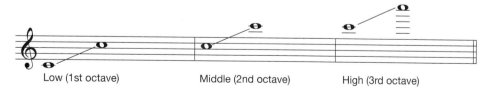

Low (1st octave)   Middle (2nd octave)   High (3rd octave)

Figure 8–7   The Three Registers (or Octaves) of the Flute

Figure 8–8 Intonation Characteristics of the Flute—Arrows Indicate Pitch Tendencies (hash marks indicate degree of tendency)

embouchure hole. The F is usually tested after tuning, as it is often flat. If higher notes sound flat in relation to lower notes, the cork (the stopper at the end of the head joint) is too far from the embouchure hole and needs adjusting.

Flute players have a tendency to go flat at the ends of phrases and sustained notes because the breath support diminishes. To counteract the sagging pitch on diminuendos, the player can direct the airstream up and protrude his jaw at the end of a note.

The greatest flutists disagree about whether the flute goes sharp or flat as the volume increases. When other factors are held constant, an increase in volume raises the pitch, but seldom are all other factors held constant. The player usually tightens his embouchure when he increases the volume to prevent the flute from skipping to the next octave higher, focusing the airstream more directly into the flute and lowering his head to compensate for the increased volume. As the air pressure builds, the pitch rises, and the player must blow more directly into the tone hole to compensate for the higher pitch. Some flutists drop the lower jaw rather than lowering the head. To keep forte playing from being sharp, the player needs to open or relax the throat, lips, or jaw. Blowing the air in an arc that follows the contour of the mouth and is aimed at the outer edge of the embouchure hole will help maintain an open throat and mouth. In soft playing, the lips must be stretched to raise the pitch.

The cork, at the end of the head joint, determines the intonation within the flute itself. Most of today's student-line instruments have replaced the cork with a synthetic material. The cork should not be tampered with once it is set, as moving it makes the pitch at both extremes harder to control. Adjustments are made only when necessary and then by a repairperson who unscrews the crown cap and moves the cork to the proper position. The possibility of adjustment is best kept a closely guarded secret from beginners and their parents.

In summary, to *lower* pitch on the flute:

1. Direct the airstream more into the flute.
2. Cover more of the embouchure hole with the lower lip.
3. Drop the lower jaw or lower the head.
4. Pull the corners of the mouth back and down slightly.
5. Roll the flute inward.

To *raise* pitch on the flute, do the opposite.

TONE QUALITY

A good sound should always be the primary consideration of any performing musician—especially flute players, who play in the upper registers of bands and orchestras and are easily heard. Good tone is dependent on (1) proper breathing, (2) good posture, and (3) embouchure formation (as well as good equipment). It also requires a solid mental concept of the sound desired, especially important for upper woodwind players as they are in larger sections and have difficulty hearing themselves in full ensemble rehearsals. Private teachers, recordings, concerts, master classes, and especially small chamber ensembles where the student can hear himself and focus on tone, intonation, and balance all help to develop a good tone.

A good flute tone is round and full-bodied, not thin, shrill, or breathy. As for all instruments, the tone should be well centered and focused, not spread. A "sweet" tone is not necessarily a good tone. It may be the result of covering too much of the embouchure hole with the lip or turning the flute in too far. Either of these habits limits the player's development, for both make lip slurs difficult and produce a delay in attacks. The embouchure plays an important role in flute tone. It controls the size of the airstream—as small and focused as possible but more open in the lower register.

One of the best ways to improve tone quality on all wind instruments is to practice long notes. Long tones are especially difficult for beginning flutists. The player's ability to create his own resistance in order to use the air efficiently is a skill learned over a period of time. B above the staff is one of the best notes for developing embouchure, and practicing long notes in the key of G centering on B is helpful. To develop richness and focus, the student should strive to project the tone. One good exercise is to take a deep breath, using diaphragm support, and then exhale all of the air in eight beats. When working for projection of the tone, the player must avoid the windy-sounding tone that comes from relaxing the cheeks and the corners of the mouth. The same embouchure and support are used for loud, driving tones as for softer tones.

The greatest difference in tone quality between adjacent pitches on the flute is found between fourth-space E and fourth-line D. E is a dark tone, D is bright. For a legato passage in which these notes occur in succession, the player must adjust his embouchure so the tones match.

Vibrato

Vibrato is essential to musical playing on the flute but it should not be used all the time. The flute sound is easily turned into a saccharine, overly sentimental one if vibrato is overdone. The flute can also have a pure, classical, crystal clear sound. The student should understand these opposites, learn how to produce both, and use each with discrimination. The great flute performer/pedagogue Marcel Moyse was one of many who compared flute vibrato to vocal vibrato—both in the production of vibrato and in its use. Vibrato is used to enhance the tone and provide expression and melodic direction, *not* to mask intonation or poor tone quality.

Diaphragm vibrato is preferred by most flutists. The teacher introducing vibrato to his student for the first time will probably have the best results when the student practices a slow alternation of loud and soft. Diaphragm vibrato is developed by having the student vocalize "ha—ha—ha—ha," gradually turning it into "a—a—a—a—a." The speed of the alternations should be increased until an even and real vibrato results. The slow vibrato should be practiced with a definite difference between the loud and soft, then as the speed increases the vibrato should become narrower until the flutist is able to produce fast and slow vibratos, wide or narrow. The normal vibrato is about seven pulsations per second.

Finally, the student should increase the pulsations in a way that follows the musical line—that is, not mechanical but changing speed with the phrasing. This stage is monitored to ensure that the vibrato is not (1) too fast when it should be slow or even stopped, (2) too slow and wide, or (3) moved too far up into the throat. In expressive performance the flute player, like the vocalist and violinist, uses a variety of speeds and pitch fluctuation as dictated by the music. Vibrato is mastered when the student uses it expressively with discretion.

TECHNIQUE: ARTICULATIONS AND FINGERINGS

Articulation for the flute player is similar to the tonguing technique used by brass players. The section on articulation in Chapter 13, "Principles for Brass," should be consulted, with "tee" substituted for "duh" or "doo." The flute player has available a great variety of articulations including double-, triple-, and flutter-tonguing.

Tonguing is best taught by having the student "hoo" the first few exercises; that is, use no tongue while playing the exercises ("hoot" can lead to the habit of stopping the note with the tongue). As the embouchure and playing position become more natural, tonguing is introduced by having the student vocalize "tee" while playing. The student should sustain a tone, holding a pitch steady for as long as possible, then repeat the tone while disrupting the steady airstream at a slow, regular pace. This is done by the tongue touching the spot on the roof of the mouth as for the syllable "tuh." "Tee," "kee," "lee," and "gee" are useful syllables to demonstrate various degrees of legato tonguing; the syllables "doo" or "loo" should be avoided because they adversely affect the student's embouchure.

The flute is the only woodwind on which it is easy to double- and triple-tongue without faking. For multiple tonguing, special attention is given to the "second" and "third" syllables, practicing them individually as if single-tonguing. The flute player double-tongues by rocking the tongue inside his mouth, alternating tongue placement for each note between the syllables "tee—kee—tee—kee" for a distinct definition to each note or a more legato double-tongue using the syllables "dee—gee—dee—gee." Triple-tonguing is achieved by rocking the tongue back across the roof of the mouth as though vocalizing: "tee—dee—kee, tee—dee—kee." Flutists are also called upon to flutter-tongue on occasion: rolling the tip of the tongue on the roof of the mouth as a child may do when pretending to be a motorboat.

Single- and multiple-tonguing should be practiced slowly and gradually increased in speed. Practices to be avoided are tonguing between the teeth and not retracting the tongue quickly enough. In learning staccato, players should not stop the note with the tongue; this creates a pitch change, leads to breathing problems, and makes it more difficult to control the next attack.

WHAT TO PRACTICE

Tone quality is the most important aspect of performance, and intonation and tone quality go hand in hand. Long tones should be omitted from the flute players daily practice until the economical use of the air supply is learned; control of the air supply is facilitated by playing simple melodies. When long tones are first introduced, they should be played in the middle register and gradually extended toward the upper and lower registers while a steady, clear uniform sound is attempted in all three registers. Long tones played while crescendoing and decrescendoing follow as the player begins to develop control.

Scales including the chromatic scale should be part of the daily routine, as should tonguing exercises at various tempos and in various styles. The different flute registers have different tonal characteristics, and even within one register the notes at the extreme ends have different timbres. Students should play a scale with the objective of not letting the "audience" know where the change in timbre takes place. Such a task is more difficult when playing arpeggios. Eventually larger and larger intervals are to be practiced.

Flexibility studies should be included in every flute student's daily routine. The control of airspeed and embouchure will promote flexibility. Unlike brass players, the flutist intent on improving flexibility is *also* confronted with the task of changing the direction of the airstream *and* using the jaw to cover and uncover the embouchure hole.

Harmonics can be sounded on a flute by fingering the fundamental and overblowing in a particular manner, namely, reducing the size of the oval-shaped aperture, increasing the air speed, and directing the airstream upward. Practicing harmonics is an excellent way for students to develop their embouchures so that they can change registers and play large intervals. It also helps in the high register and in teaching the player control of the decrescendo. Harmonics on the flute follow the pattern shown in Figure 8–9.

fundamental

Figure 8–9 Flute Harmonics Based on Low C

If the player has difficulty obtaining harmonics, it is usually due to lips that are too stiff. Harmonics are usually flat when played without adjusting the embouchure, so the player must direct the air more across the embouchure hole as he ascends, as well as tightening his embouchure. Harmonics can also be produced on the head joint alone—E above the staff and A above that. Harmonics are notated in contemporary music with a small circle above the note. The first four overtones above the fundamental are the most common flute harmonics.

CARE AND MAINTENANCE OF THE FLUTE

The bore of the flute should be swabbed and dried frequently during and after each playing, primarily so that dust does not accumulate in the damp interior. Some type of soft absorbent cloth is fine for a swab cloth. Most flute cases are equipped with a cleaning stick that also serves as a tuning rod. The swab should be inserted through the eye of the cleaning rod and then wrapped around the rod to prevent metal from touching metal and to avoid scratching the inside of the flute. The foot joint should be swabbed first as it collects the least moisture; then the body; then the head joint. When swabbing the head joint, care must also be taken to avoid poking the metal covering of the cork located inside.

The exterior of the flute does not need elaborate care. In fact, silver polish on a metal flute may damage it; all the finish needs is to be wiped off after each playing. Care should be exercised in wiping the head joint because excessive rubbing may dull the outer edge of the embouchure hole. The head joint should be cleaned two or three times a year with hot, soapy water, followed by thorough rinsing and drying. The body and foot joint should not be washed.

Sticky pads cause a delayed response when a finger is lifted from a key. To clean, the pad should be closed lightly over a clean coffee filter, which is then withdrawn with the pad closed. A simple item of preventive maintenance to teach flute players from their first day is to hold the instrument with the pads up when not playing, thus preventing moisture from collecting in the tone holes and being absorbed by the pads.

The pivot screws should be oiled at least once every four months to ensure that they work properly. Occasionally these screws must be loosened using a jeweler's screwdriver, oiled, then retightened.

If the tenons become dirty and sticky, they can be cleaned with denatured alcohol or with silver polish (the latter will remove a very slight layer of the finish as well as the grime). Protector rings for the end joints are frowned on for two reasons: They make it more difficult to keep the ends clean, and they add wear with the frequent removing and replacing. This wear can result in distortion of the dimension and parabolic construction of the head joint. In the days of wooden instruments and poorly constructed cases, protector rings were necessary for the preservation of the cork on the ends, but today there is no longer a reason for them, and most companies no longer make them.

TROUBLESHOOTING

Equipment

Sticky pads

1. Moisture absorbed by pads. (If pad is not damaged place lens paper between pad and tone hole, press key, and gently pull paper out; repeat several times pulling the paper out in different directions. As a last resort: Apply a *slight* amount of talcum powder to absorb the moisture, being careful to keep it off the mechanism.)
2. Bent rods. (Have repaired by competent repairperson.)
3. Worn springs. (Have repaired by competent repairperson.)
4. Pivot screw at end of rod through post may need oiling (one drop). Occasionally it may need to be loosened and partially removed, oiled, then retightened.

Pads not seating correctly

1. Leaking pads—usually discovered when lower register does not respond easily. (If pads are in good shape, readjustment of the adjusting screws may be necessary. Insertion of thin paper "washers" behind pad can be made by repairperson. Possibly bent rods to be repaired.)
2. Brittle or hardened pads. (Have replaced by competent repairperson.)
3. Torn pads. (Have replaced by competent repairperson.)
4. Loose pads. (Reheat the glue; seal the pad with gentle pressure.)

Tone

Breathy

1. Too much embouchure hole covered. (Move flute up or down to cover one-fourth to one-third of the embouchure hole.)

2. Airstream not centered with embouchure hole. (Practice in front of mirror to keep embouchure centered. In rehearsal, roll flute up to lips before attacks and entrances to make sure embouchure hole is centered. If due to physical shape of lip—such as a tear-drop-shaped upper lip—some have success playing off center, many switch to another instrument.)
3. Aperture in embouchure is too large or too round. (In upper register keep aperture small; in low registers keep embouchure flatter and slightly wider.)
4. Not enough air support. (Breathe correctly and let air flow, keeping constant pressure behind the airstream. Be careful not to overblow, however; keep airstream focused.)
5. In upper register, too much of a smile embouchure. (Make more rounded.)

Fuzzy, hollow

1. Not enough embouchure hole covered. (Move head joint up to cover one-fourth to one-third of the embouchure hole. Roll flute inward.)
2. Flute turned out too far. (Correct alignment of head joint or holding/hand position.)
3. Misdirected airstream. (Blow air slightly more into flute.)
4. Airstream not focused or incorrect shape of aperture in embouchure. (Aperture should be relatively flat and wide for lower notes and small and round for upper pitches. Physical shape of lip can prohibit focused airstream—attempt to pull upper lip more tightly against teeth.)
5. Aperture in embouchure too loose. (Focus airstream. Firm up corners of mouth slightly.)
6. If in low register, commonly due to too small an aperture. (Relax corners of mouth. Pull back and down on corners and attempt to raise center of upper lip.)
7. Leaky pads. (Have replaced.)

Thin, strident shrill

1. Too much tension in lip around embouchure hole. (Try to relax center of upper lip. Focus airstream. Form flatter, wider aperture for lower register, rounder for upper register.)
2. Playing on outer surface of lip. (Roll lips out to play more on the moist inner surfaces.)
3. Blowing too hard. (Blow easier yet maintain air pressure. Focus air more.)
4. Airstream not centered. (Roll flute up and down to center embouchure hole with embouchure. Hold flute so that embouchure hole is parallel with lips. Cover more embouchure hole, pull corners back and down more, roll flute in slightly—or a combination of these.)
5. In upper register—corners of lips too tense (i.e., too much of a smile embouchure). (Relax corners. Practice flutter-tongue.)
6. Too much air blowing over and out of flute. (Blow more air into instrument.)
7. If in lower register, aperture too small. (Attempt a wider, flatter embouchure.)
8. With poor flexibility—not enough embouchure hole covered. (Move head joint down, cover at least one-fourth of embouchure hole, but not more than one-third.)

Stuffy

1. Flute rolled in too far. (Roll out. Correct alignment of head joint.)
2. Too much embouchure hole covered. (Move head joint up to cover at least one-fourth of the embouchure hole. Roll flute out.)

Weak

1. Not enough air support. (Breathe correctly.)
2. Leaky pads.
3. Too much embouchure hole covered. (Move head joint up.)

Difficulty with the higher register

1. Bring jaw forward and cover more of the embouchure hole with the lower lip in upper register.

2. Use faster, more focused airstream.
3. On sharp notes such as C♯ direct air slightly more downward into embouchure hole or try arching tongue more toward roof of mouth.
4. Focus and direct air more toward outer edge of embouchure hole with more rounded embouchure aperture.

Difficulty with the lower register

1. Lips too open. (Direct airstream more downward.)
2. Lips too tense. (Practice softly, relaxed on lowest pitches. Blow more air being careful not to overblow.)

Flexibility problems

1. Too much embouchure hole covered. (Move head joint up or roll flute out.)
2. Aperture of embouchure too large. (Common problem when playing in low register—keep aperture only as wide and large as necessary.)

Pitch

Flat

1. Airstream is directed too much into the flute. (Raise head or lower jaw slightly, blow more toward outer edge of embouchure hole.)
2. Too much of the embouchure hole is covered. (Raise head joint, roll flute out.)
3. To avoid going flat when descending into the first octave, uncover embouchure hole while directing more air into the embouchure hole.

Sharp

1. Airstream is directed too much toward the outer edge of the embouchure hole. (Lower head or jaw slightly, blow more into the embouchure hole.)
2. Not enough of the embouchure hole is covered. (Lower head joint, roll flute in.)
3. In lower register—pull the corners of the mouth back and down slightly.
4. A C♯ is being played. (Lip down, fake it, or cough at the appropriate moment.)

BIBLIOGRAPHY

Texts

* Indicates out of print in 2001.

BATES, PHILIP (1979). *The Flute: A Study of Its History, Development and Construction*, (2nd ed. New York: W. W. Norton.

BOEHM, THEOBALD (1899); MILLER, DAYTON (1931 English Translation). *The Flute and Flute Playing in Acoustical, Technical, and Artistic Aspects*, 2nd English ed. by Dayton Miller, New York: Peter Smith.

CHAPMAN, F. B. (1973). *Flute Technique*, 4th ed. New York: Oxford University Press.

*COOPER, ALBERT (1980). *The Flute*, 2nd enlarged ed. London: Author.

DE LORENZO, LEONARDO (1992). *My Complete Story of the Flute: The Instrument, the Performer, the Music*, rev. and expanded ed. Lubbock TX: Texas Tech University Press.

DICK, ROBERT (1975). *The Other Flute: A Performance Manual of Contemporary Techniques*. London: Oxford University Press.

*FAIRLEY, ANDREW (1982). *Flutes, Flautists, and Makers (Active or Born Before 1900).* London: Pan Educational Music.

GALWAY, JAMES. (1982). *Flute.* New York: Schirmer Books.

HOWELL, THOMAS (1974). *The Avant-Garde Flute: A Handbook for Composers and Flutists.* Berkeley, CA: University of California Press.

MORRIS, GARRETH (1991). *Flute Technique.* New York: Oxford University Press.

*MOYSE, MARCEL (1974). *How I Stayed in Shape (Coment jai pu maintenir ma forme).* Trans. P. M. Douglas. West Brattleboro, VT: Author.

PHELAN, JAMES, and MITCHELL D. BRODY (1980). *The Complete Guide to the Flute from Acoustics and Construction to Repair and Maintenance.* Boston: Conservatory Publications.

PUTNIK, EDWIN (1970). *The Art of Flute Playing.* Evanston, IL: Summy-Birchard.

RAINEY, THOMAS E. (1985). *The Flute Manual: A Comprehensive Text and Resource Book for Both the Teacher and the Student.* Lanham, MD: University Press of America.

SHEPARD, MARK (1999). *How to Love Your Flute: A Guide to Flutes and Flute Playing.* Los Angeles: Shepard Publications; reprint of (1980) Portland, OR: Panjandrum Books.

SOLUM, JOHN (1992). *The Early Flute.* New York: Oxford University Press.

*STEVENS, ROGER S. (1967). *Artistic Flute; Technique and Study,* ed. Ruth N. Zwissler. Hollywood, CA: Highland Music.

TOFF, NANCY (1996). *The Flute Book: A Complete Guide for Students and Performers,* 2nd ed. New York: Oxford University Press.

Journals

The American Piper. The Official Publication of the Flute Club of America, P.O. Box 1021, Royal Oak, MI 48068.

Flute Talk. Ten per year from The Instrumentalist Publishing Co. 200 Northfield Road, Northfield, IL 60903.

Flute World. URL: http://www.fluteworld.com.

The Flutist. Out of print, published 1920–1929, Ashville, NC.

The Flutists Quarterly. Quarterly from: National Flute Association; URL: http://www.nfaonline.org/NFA.

The Woodwind Quarterly. URL: www.musictrader.com/wwqindex.html.

Flute Studies

Easy—Beginning (elementary or middle school)

Arnold. *Introduction to the Flute* (C. Hansen).
Buchtel. *Elementary Method for Flute* (Kjos).
Cavally. *Original Melodious and Progressive Studies* (Southern Music).
Eck. *Tone Development for Flute* (Belwin-Mills).

Gariboldi. *30 Easy and Progressive Studies* (Books I and II) (Edwin F. Kalmus).
Hart. *Introduction to the Flute* (Oxford University Press).
Kincaid. *The Art and Practice of Modern Flute Technique* (Vol. 1) (MCA Music).
LeJeune. *A Flutist's Manual* (Summy-Birchard).
———. *Pitch and Sound Search Studies for Flute* (Broude).
Moyse. *Beginner Flutist (Le De'butant Flutiste)* (Al. Leduc).
Pares. *Daily Exercises and Scales* (Carl Fischer).
———. *Pares Scale Studies* (Belwin-Mills).
Platanov. *School of Flute Playing* (Leeds).
Takahashi. *Takahashi Flute School* (Suzuki Method, Vols. 1–2) (Summy-Birchard).
Wye, Trevor. *Beginning Books for the Flute* (Vols I and II) (Novello).

Medium (middle school or high school)

Adler. *Harobed—7 Studies* (Southern Music).
Andersen. *18 Studies for Flute 41.* (International). Op.
Bona. *Rhythmical Articulation* (G. Schirmer).
Cavally. *Melodious and Progressive Studies* (Books 2 and 3) (Southern Music).
Gatti. *15 Studi Moderni* (Edizioni Berben).
Kincaid. *The Art and Practice of Modern Flute Technique* (Vol. 2) (MCA Music).
Koehler. *Romantic Etudes* (Southern Music).
———. *20 Easy Melodic Progressive Exercises* (Vols. 1 and 2) (Belwin-Mills).
Moyse. *Exercices Journaliers* (Al. Leduc).
———. *24 Etudes Petites Melodious* (Al. Leduc).
Pares. *Daily Exercises and Scales* (Carl Fischer).
Porcelijn. *Communication for Easy Flute and Modern Flute* (Vol. I) (Zalo Publications).
Steensland (ed. Ployhar). *Studies and Melodious Etudes for Flute* (Levels 2–3) (Belwin-Mills).
Taffanel (ed. Gaubert). *Complete Method for Flute* (especially "17 Daily") (Leduc).
Takahashi. *Takahashi Flute School* (Suzuki Method, Vols. 3–5) (Summy-Birchard).
Wye. *Practice Book for the Flute* (Vols. 1–4) (Novello).

Advanced (high school or college)

Andersen. *24 Exercises* (Southern Music).
———. *24 Studies* (Southern Music).
———. *24 Technical Studies* (Southern Music).
Barrere. *The Flutists' Formulae* (G. Schirmer).
Camus. *12 Etudes* (Al. Leduc).
Donjon. *The Modern Flutist* (includes Karg-Elert below) (Southern Music).
Drouet. *25 Etudes for Flute* (Al. Leduc).
Galli. *30 Exercises* (G. Ricordi).
Gates. *Odd Meter Etudes* (Fox Publishing).
Jean-Jean. *16 Modern Studies* (Al. Leduc).
Karg-Elert. *30 Caprices* (Southern Music).
Kincaid. *The Art and Practice of Modern Flute Technique* (Vol. 3) (MCA Music).
Moyse. *De La Sonorite* (Al. Leduc).

——. *Exercices Journaliers* (Al. Leduc).
——. *Scales and Arpeggios* (Al. Leduc).
Platanov. *30 Studies for Flute* (International).
Schade. *24 Caprices* (Southern Music).
Wye. *Practice Book for the Flute* (Vols. 5–6) (Novello).

Instructional Videos

Beginning Flute (1989). Atlantic City, NJ: Music Education Video.

Belwin 21st Century Band Method: Level I (Jack Bullock, 1996). Miami: Warner Brothers Music Publishing.

The Flute. (Rebecca Magg, 1998) Canoga Park, CA: Backstage Pass Instructional Videos.

Flute for Beginners (Rebecca Magg, 1995). Chatsworth, CA: Maestro Instructional Video Series.

Flute Seminars (Marcel Moyse, 1989). Eight videocassettes by six flutists including Marcel Moyse. W. Brattleboro, VT: Moyse Enterprises.

How to Play the Flute in the Traditional Irish Style (Mickie Zekley, 1986). Mendocino, CA: Lark in the Morning.

Play the Flute: A Beginner's Guide (Trevor Wye, 1988). Sevenoaks, Kent: Novello.

Steps to Excellence: a Flute Clinic (James Walker, 1985). Grand Rapids, MI: Yamaha Music Corporation.

Steps to Excellence: a Video Clinic, Vol. 1 (James Walker, 1984). Grand Rapids, MN: Yamaha Music Products.

Ultimate Beginner Series–Flute, Vols. 1 and 2 (Elizabeth Rowe, 1998) Miami: Warner Brothers Music Publishers.

Recommended Classical Flute Artists

James Galway playing Bach and Debussy
Jean-Pierre Rampal playing Haydn
Julius Baker playing Mozart, Vivaldi, and Telemann
Peter Graf playing Poulenc and Boccherini
Fenwick Smith playing Koechin, Rorem, and Pinkham

Recommended Jazz Flute Artists

Cool: Bud Shank
Post-Bop, New Age, World Music: Yusaf Lateef
Avant-Garde, Free Jazz: Eric Dolphy
Crossover, Afro-Cuban, Pop/jazz: Herbie Mann
Crossover, Classical, Hard Bop: Hubert Laws
Post-Bop, Avant-Garde, Contemporary: Robert Dick

FLUTE
Fingering Chart

9

The Oboe

The oboe has the most limited compass of any woodwind instrument and seems to resist any effort to achieve a good tone. However, when mastered its unique timbre and its expressive possibilities are ample reward to the player. When played correctly, it can express humor, satire, calm, mystery, and despair, among many others. Unfortunately, when played badly it can be downright unpleasant.

For years there has been a controversy over whether beginners should start on oboe or play a year or two on another instrument before switching to oboe. A fourth grader is fully capable of beginning on the oboe if the music teacher is able to devote a bit of extra attention to her; if not, there are advantages to starting on another woodwind instrument such as the clarinet.

One reason beginning oboists have problems is that most class method books start on concert F, a note that promises immediate success on trumpet, low brass, clarinet, and saxophone but for the oboist is one of the most awkward fingerings used, a forked F. These method books generally progress through E♭, D, and C, all of which are difficult notes for the young oboe player.

HISTORY

The double-reed instruments are nearly as old as the flute. Their record of use and popularity is perhaps greater because their fuller tone gave them a wide adaptability. Instruments with a double-reed mouthpiece of cane date from 3700 B.C.E.; an oboe is mentioned as early as 2000 B.C.E. in the literature of Mesopotamia. The instrument, appearing in many shapes and forms, dominated the music of the ancient world for centuries. It had only three or four finger holes up to about 400 B.C.E. Collars and half stops were added until the player had to operate as many as fifteen holes. Various forms of oboes are to be found in all parts of the East. They were used by shepherds and by fakir snake charmers in the old Turkish Empire, in the harems of Baghdad, and in the temples of Cairo. Egyptian oboe players who had the unique practice of breathing through the nose while they played, which enabled them to sustain a tone continuously.

The oboe belonged to the Asian world until Europe began to be aware of Near Eastern civilization in the late Middle Ages. About the thirteenth century the shawm, derived from the Arabian double-reed instruments called the "zamr," was introduced to Europe by returning Crusaders. This instrument was called the "bombarde" by the French, "pommer" by Germans. Its cousin was the "krummhorn," on which the reed was encased and could not be placed in the mouth, but was set in motion by blowing into an opening in a way similar to the manner organ pipes are sounded. With the exception of the krummhorn, these early instruments were played by taking the entire reed into the mouth, the lips resting against a metal disc.

From the high Renaissance through the Baroque period, the oboe was increasingly important. It was a popular member of Elizabethan bands. By the middle of the seventeenth century, the descant shawm had assumed the form of the oboe. It was introduced into the orchestra by Lully, and was a favorite instrument of Handel, whose orchestra contained 26 oboes, 46 first violins, and 47 second violins. Bach used the oboe d'amour for sprightly and plaintive effects; he was particularly fond of it in combination with the solo voice. By the time of Haydn, Mozart, and Beethoven, the oboe had become a standard part of the orchestra.

SELECTING AN INSTRUMENT

Let the buyer beware. The prospective automobile owner always kicks the tires and slams the doors in an involuntary admission that she doesn't know how to judge the quality of the engine. An oboe is an expensive purchase that one hopes to keep for many years. Knowing what to look for is vital, because good oboes are not mass-produced and one cannot always trust name brands.

As with any other musical instrument, the overall sound is the primary guide for selecting an oboe, whether new or used. Oboes differ in tone quality, even those made by the best manufacturers. Unless the instrumental music teacher is herself an accomplished oboe player, she may be unable to evaluate the potential of an instrument. A skilled oboe player should therefore be found to assist in selecting an oboe whether the buyer is the parents or the school.

The conservatory system, based upon the innovations and improvements of Boehm, is almost universal, but many different models exist within it. The plateau system has covered tone holes (vented plates with pads). This system was initiated about 1906 by F. Lorée, one of the most famous makers of oboes. The plateau oboe is preferred by the majority of professionals because it produces a rather dark sound.

Because there is such a great variance in oboes, a stable reed should be used when checking the overall pitch of the instrument, and each note should be checked with an electronic tuner. All notes throughout the registers of the instrument should respond freely, with a good tone quality and a full, resonating sound.

Oboes come with either a semiautomatic key or a fully automatic octave key. With a semiautomatic key, the player must add the side octave key to all high notes beginning with A above the staff. With a fully automatic key, one presses only the octave key on the back of the instrument to obtain the upper octave of any pitch. The semiautomatic system is best for beginning students. The fully automatic octave key is not recommended for two reasons: First, it has a temperamental mechanism that is usually in need of an adjustment; and second, it makes the harmonics from G♯ through C and some alternate fingerings impossible.

Both the oboe and the bassoon profit from the addition of extra keys. Of major importance for the oboe is the low B♭ key. An oboe without this key is not a good purchase. Though school-grade music seldom requires the low B♭, it must be available when it does appear, and it improves the resonance of low B and C.

The left F resonance key, once considered optional, is a feature common on most beginner-to professional-level oboes. It opens automatically when the forked fingering for F is used, eliminating the need for the E♭ key to be pressed with the right little finger. The standard order of importance for remaining optional keys might be the following: the B–C trill key, the left-hand A♭–B♭ trill, the C–D trill, the left little finger F key, and the B♭–B trill key.

Because a musical instrument is expensive to manufacture, ways are continually sought to lower the cost. One of these ways is to substitute plastic for wood. Experiments with plastic oboes have met with varying success, mostly unsuccessful—the basic element of tone quality is lacking. The traditional oboe is made of grenadilla wood, and the quality of the wood is crucial to the quality of the instrument. The instrument should be made of wood with the straightest grain possible. Secondhand instruments should be checked for cracks and for scoring inside the bore.

The reed is almost as important as the instrument and is a favorite topic of conversation among teachers and players. Reeds appropriate for beginners are essential for initial success. They may be purchased from a music retailer, but few of these are considered good reeds by the professional oboist. A better source for reeds is the professional who makes and sells them; these custom-made reeds are usually of good quality and the professional can make them for various levels of embouchure development. Reeds appropriate for beginners should have a relatively small opening and blow easily without changing pitch at different dynamic levels. More advanced students should learn to make their own reeds; this skill should be considered an essential element of any oboe player's instruction and development.

ASSEMBLING THE OBOE

The key mechanism of the oboe can be damaged when putting the instrument together or taking it apart, so care is encouraged. The oboe has four parts: the reed, the upper joint, the lower joint, and the bell. The beginner should learn to assemble it with careful movements, not by wiggling or forcing, because (1) the tenons are thin and easily broken, (2) the cork can be compressed or loosened, (3) the ends of the tenons can become rounded from wear, and (4) the keys can be easily bent. These four factors affect the snug fit necessary to prevent leakage of air around the joints and pads.

The upper and lower joints are assembled by placing the left hand at the top of the upper joint and the right hand over the rings or pads between the lower joint and the bell section. The keys on the lower joint and bell sections are not depressed when assembling because touching the F♯ tone hole or C–D trill key raises the bridge key. The two joints are pushed together with a gentle turning motion aligning the bridge keys. The corks at the ends of the joints (the tenons) may be greased slightly to make assembly easier.

The reed is grasped at the *cork* by the thumb and first finger and inserted in the upper joint by a slight downward push. If the reed is not pushed in all the way, an air pocket is created that affects intonation and tone. Grabbing the cane of the reed while inserting it will damage one or both blades or destroy the fit, causing air leaks. After the reed has been inserted, it can be easily turned so that the blades line up with the rest of the instrument. One of the two blades will always be stronger than the other; as the player gains experience she will notice that the instrument plays better when one particular side of a reed is up. To identify that side each time, she can place an ink mark on the cork.

HOLDING THE OBOE

The oboe is held with the left hand on the upper joint and the right hand on the lower joint, as shown in Figure 9–1. The fingers are slanted slightly downward

Figure 9–1
Hand Position for the Oboe

toward the bell to facilitate the use of the C and C♯ keys by the right little finger and enabling the left little finger to play the G♯, B, and B♭ keys more easily. The right thumb points slightly upward. The fingers should be slightly arched, with the fleshy pad of each finger centered on the tone hole. The little finger of the right hand rests lightly on the D♯ key and the little finger of the left hand on the B key. The inside edge of the right thumbnail is on the thumb rest. If the thumb is placed too far under the oboe, the right fingers will be cramped and unable to move rapidly. Hand position will vary somewhat according to the size of the hand, however. Freedom of finger movement and avoiding tension are the important considerations in thumb placement.

The left thumb rests against the instrument at an angle of approximately 60 degrees (approaching 90 degrees for students with small hands) just below the octave key so that it can activate the octave key by a rolling motion (i.e., not by lifting it and placing it on the key). The index finger of the left hand should be on the first tone hole; the first joint of that finger rests lightly on or over the second octave key. This position enables the index finger to do two things: (1) roll back and forth to half hole and (2) depress the second octave key with the first joint of the finger while keeping the other fingers of the left hand in place.

The oboe should be brought to the erect head, not the head to the oboe. The instrument should be centered on the embouchure. Movements of the head, body, and instrument are not necessary when playing the instrument and can in fact detract from the playing. When the head is moved, the embouchure is changed and the position of lips on the reed is altered, so control is lost, tone quality is distorted, and pitch and response are jeopardized.

The Angle of the Instrument

Figure 9–2
Sitting Position for Playing the Oboe

Correct position for playing the oboe is illustrated in Figure 9–2. The oboe is positioned directly in front of the player whether she is standing or sitting. Her head is kept erect. The oboe is held between 30 and 45 degrees from the body, supported primarily by the right thumb and steadied by the embouchure. Beginning students may try to copy clarinet positions, especially if the new oboists are former clarinetists, in which case the instrument will be held too low. Others may get into the habit of holding their head down, which is the same as holding the instrument too high.

As a general rule, the lower the instrument is held, the darker the tone; as the angle increases, the tone becomes brighter. The present trend is toward a brighter oboe sound. If the head is held erect and the student sits or stands tall, the angle of approximately 30 to 45 degrees will produce a bright tone and allow for a fast, light tonguing action. When the oboe is lifted too high, the reed is pulled away from the lower lip cushion and the upper lip presses too tightly on the reed. The result is a drop in pitch, particularly in the upper register, and a bright, harsh tone. Holding the oboe down to produce a dark tone with a mysterious, haunting quality must not be carried to the extreme. When the oboe is nearly parallel to the body, the upper lip is prevented from serving its normal function, the sound becomes not only dark but also hard, and the tone has a tendency to be sharp in all registers.

EMBOUCHURE

Embouchure formation is easier to explain than to do, and much easier to do than to maintain. The focus should be on the relationship of the embouchure and the reed.

1. The player drops her jaw about a half inch and relaxes her lips.
2. With the mouth slightly open, the reed is placed on the tongue, which can then guide the reed to the center of the lower lip. The top of the reed should be about halfway over the lip.
3. Roll the lower lip in while allowing the reed to follow the rolling motion into the oral cavity—students must experiment to determine exactly how much reed to be rolled in.
4. With the reed resting on the lower lip that serves as a cushion, form the vowel "ooo" while keeping the lower lip and reed in place.
5. Seal the lips around the reed with equal pressure from all directions.
6. The player should *feel* that he is holding the reed in place with the sealed lips and not from pressure through "biting."
7. At this point, with the reed sealed by the lips and pressure exerted from all directions, the student should attempt to lower the jaw as if to vocalize "ah."
8. In this position, the oral cavity is fully open, the teeth are apart, and the only pressure on the reed is from the lips.

If there is no response, gently press the reed blades together with the thumb and forefinger to change the size of the opening, or possibly soak the reed a bit longer. Frequently the new reed is too stiff; beginners may try a softer reed in order to obtain an immediate response, but tone quality and intonation will suffer. As the embouchure becomes stronger and more developed, the student should switch to stronger reeds.

The correct oboe embouchure is formed by rolling both lips in slightly over the teeth to form a cushion above and below the reed. Extreme overbite or underbite can prevent the player from applying equal pressure to both blades of the reed. Lips should be in a vertical line, usually with more of the pink of the lower lip rolled in. The edge of the lower lip (where the pink meets the flesh) should be directly over the teeth. A thick lower lip appears to be an advantage, as it forms the cushion necessary to avoid nasal quality. Figure 9–3 illustrates the lips rolled in and the alignment of the teeth.

The facial muscles form a gentle pucker that exerts pressure on the reed from all sides. The corners of the mouth are pushed in toward the reed. A "smile" pucker or "crocodile face" should be avoided. A flat chin, although not as important as for the clarinet, usually accompanies an embouchure that surrounds the reed with even pressure. If the corners of the mouth are held firmly and forward *toward* the reed, the chin will remain flat. Air bulges may appear in the cheeks, caused by lack of muscular control: unequal tension between the muscles pulling to a pucker and those pulling to a smile. A fleshy upper lip may only give the appearance of an air pocket; if probing with the index finger disturbs the embouchure, there is, in fact, an air pocket. The correct oboe embouchure is shown in Figures 9–4 and 9–5.

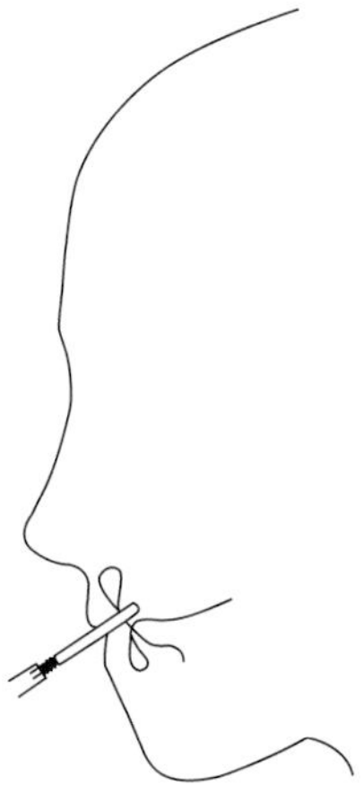

Figure 9–3
Oboe Embouchure: Teeth and Lips

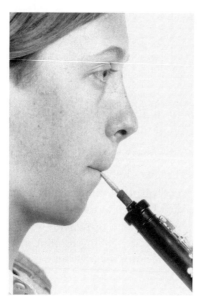

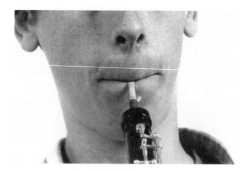

Figure 9–5
Oboe Embouchure

Figure 9–4
Oboe Embouchure (side view)

With the beginning student, one of these problems usually occurs: (1) Too much of the lip is turned in. Only enough lip needs to be rolled in to control the reed. (2) With a clarinet-type embouchure, too little lip is turned in. (3) When the upper lip is short and less flexible, it is often placed too far on the reed. The young oboist learns that the amount of reed inserted into the mouth depends on the tessitura of the music. A different lip cushion is required for each octave. The reed is placed farther in the mouth for the upper register and is moved out slightly for lower tones. A second factor is the type of tone desired. A third is the lip and jaw formation. A fourth factor is the reed itself.

Oboists must deal with a different kind of endurance challenge than do brass players. The oboist's endurance problems result from the amount of air pressure in the mouth as so little air goes into the instrument. Thus the oboe player must gain a great deal of strength in the embouchure muscles before she can play complete phrases or for long periods of time.

The framework of the embouchure is formed by the teeth. The teeth determine the size and shape of the embouchure and must be kept open so that the other elements of the embouchure function properly. There is no upward bite in the normal embouchure. The lower teeth and jaw drop away from the reed. Control is derived entirely from the lips.

Reed Placement

Usually the reed is positioned in the mouth with about one-third to one-half of the cane covered by the lips. To check placement, the student should play second-space A and slur down one step to G. If she has too much of the reed in her mouth, the A will sound wild and quite sharp in relation to the G. She should then experiment with less of the reed in her mouth until she can play the two-note slur with good intonation and consistent tone quality. If she has too little of the reed in her mouth, which rarely occurs, the G will be flat.

When a bright, hard tone is desired, more reed is put in the mouth, with adjustments to keep the intonation correct. If the player puts too little reed in her mouth, the tone may be fuzzy and weak as well as flat. As the beginner's control grows, the amount of reed placed into the mouth should change.

The Grip

There is no biting in a good oboe embouchure, but the lips must be firm enough to control the reed. The grip of the lips depends on the amount of reed in the mouth as well as the tessitura of the music. The firmness for the higher registers should not cause the throat to tighten. The student should start with a rather relaxed embouchure; it will soon tighten of its own accord. Regardless of the advancement of the player, too tight a grip on the reed will choke off the tone, cut off most of the lower overtones, or make the primary pitch sharp. The player should always be able to feel the reed vibrating, even when playing in the upper range of the instrument where the greatest firmness is required. Conversely, if the player relaxes the lips too much on the low tones, the reed vibrates excessively and some of the overtones become stronger than the fundamental.

The oboe requires different embouchures in different registers and for crescendos and decrescendos; these are opposite to those used by clarinet players. In playing crescendo passages many oboists allow their lips to roll out slightly, covering the teeth with somewhat less lip while relaxing the embouchure. This action counteracts the sharpness accompanying an increase in volume.

The Jaw

For most players, leaving the jaw alone is best. The lower jaw is normally pulled down and slightly back so the lower teeth drop away from the reed, thus forming the smile pucker. Probably the most common fault of the young oboe player is that she juts out the lower jaw, perhaps to create some feeling of needed support from the lower lip. A player with a receding lower jaw should hold the oboe at less than a 30-degree angle rather than push the jaw forward in an unnatural position.

INTONATION

Although professional orchestras tune to the principal oboist, the young oboist cannot be so confident of her pitch. She should use an electronic tuner to check individual pitches and adjust her overall tuning. If she finds herself adjusting each and every pitch, it is time to get a better instrument, learn to make reeds, or switch to percussion.

Intonation on the oboe is related to embouchure as well as to the position of the reed in the mouth. Specifically, sharp intonation is caused by

1. An embouchure that is too tight
2. Too much reed in the mouth (especially for the second octave)
3. Too stiff a reed
4. Holding the oboe at an angle of less than 30 degrees from the body
5. Too much of either lip turned under

The tone will be flat when the reverse errors occur. When a combination of faults occurs, intonation problems will be difficult to correct as there are so many variables to test. The ear is the key; students must learn to listen carefully and evaluate their pitch in relation to that of other players.

All intonation problems do not lie with the player. The instrument itself, no matter how fine, is never perfectly in tune. Usually, the ring keys played with the right hand and the low D♯, C, C♯, B, and B♭ keys of either hand should be tried to see if they improve intonation or enhance the resonance. Defects in the dimensions of the bore may make the low tones unstable. The very high pitches are often sharp and the low register flat with notes interspersed in the upper register that also tend to be flat.

As a new oboe is broken in, some of the keys will need adjusting to stabilize or correct pitch and enhance finger dexterity. Most oboes, including student-line instruments, have at least a dozen small set screws for regulating key height and the evenness of the mechanism. Because height and evenness of the keys affect intonation, pads must be adjusted. Until students learn to make these adjustments, the music teacher or a competent repairperson should do it. Although the oboe is tremendously difficult to play in tune if it is out of adjustment, having it in adjustment does not guarantee that it will play in tune.

However, the oboe is by no means the most difficult instrument to play in tune, being considerably easier to control than, for example, the clarinet or flute. Pitch can be altered by the reed itself and by the player's approach to the reed. A higher arch to the tongue raises the pitch and a lower arch lowers it. The arch changes as one goes from a high to a low register—moving from a position for vocalizing "ee" to one for vocalizing "ah." The temperature of the instrument and the amount it is pulled at the joints also affect pitch. Figure 9–6 illustrates notes that generally tend to be out of tune on the oboe.

Figure 9–6 Intonation Problems of Selected Pitches on the Oboe

If the pitch is unstable (some notes going sharp and others going flat within the same register), the player may not be blowing directly into the reed. To obtain consistent pitch both blades of the reed must vibrate equally. The player should try tipping her head up and down or slightly altering the angle at which the oboe is held while listening to the result. When experimenting, the player must play and listen throughout the entire range.

A problem known as "flat staccato" is not really related to intonation but to timbre that makes the pitch sound flat. Flat staccato is caused by having too much reed in the mouth, which forces the tongue to curl into an incorrect position in order to reach the tip of the reed for tonguing. The same term is sometimes applied to the poor tone quality that results when the angle of the reed is too great and there is too little bottom lip on the reed. This situation also impairs the accuracy of the attack and the speed with which the player can tongue.

In attempting to flatten the pitch, the oboist should not pull the reed from the upper joint. If the reed is pulled out more than just the slightest amount, an air pocket will form, causing the instrument to lose response. A general unevenness of sound will result: Low notes will tend to become wild and some tones will be difficult to attack clearly and will be fuzzy in quality.

TONE QUALITY

All performers should strive for beauty of tone, the oboe player among them. A good oboe tone depends upon four things: (1) the player's concept of tone, (2) breath control, (3) embouchure, and (4) a good reed. A beginner's tone that is usually coarse and uncontrolled is due to too much air going through the reed. If the tone is dead and unresonant, there is insufficient pressure. The abdominal muscles must pressurize the air, and the embouchure must be firm enough to control this pressure; a balance of these forces creates an appealing tone.

A small tone even when pleasant is limited in dynamic variety and carrying power. The reasons for a small tone are biting the reed, too little reed in the mouth, not enough lip over the teeth, and holding the instrument too close to the body. A squawky tone results from the opposite set of factors.

Sometimes a player becomes accustomed to a nasal tone and even strives to maintain it. The player must listen to her own playing and compare her tone with the sounds she would like to imitate.

Harmonics are useful. The oboe harmonic is the second overtone, an octave and a fifth (a twelfth) above the fundamental; for example, if the player fingers low B♭, top-line F will sound. Harmonics are produced by overblowing—tightening the lips more and using more pressure than necessary for the fundamental tone. Using the low C key with these harmonics will help keep them in tune; harmonics are usually flat. There are two uses for harmonics, the more common being tone color, the other, their use in quiet orchestral passages and for pianissimo notes.

Oboe players almost always double on the English horn, and this doubling can interfere with their oboe tone. Too much concentrated practice on the English horn can make the oboe tone hard and less controlled because of the difference in the reeds of the two instruments. The playing of the two instruments is nearly identical.

Vibrato

Oboe players in some countries disapprove of vibrato. They believe it destroys the characteristic oboe sound and prevents the instrument from blending well. Most players, however, feel that vibrato enhances the sound by adding warmth and expressiveness to the tone. Diaphragm vibrato seems to be preferred. Throat and jaw vibrato tend to constrict and tighten muscles, producing a disappointing, artificial sound. Vibrato on oboe is probably not for beginners.

REEDS

The world's greatest oboist would sound like a child on a kazoo without a good reed. The quest for good reeds has forced oboists to make their own; learning to play the instrument includes learning to make a satisfactory reed. The teacher must make the reeds or purchase them for the beginning player. Purchasing reeds does save time, but all reeds need adjustment, even those guaranteed to play. Purchased oboe reeds are usually too stiff for normal playing; minor adjustments are necessary.

The ideal reed is one that responds to louds and softs, highs and lows, and staccatos and legatos with little effort. On it the player can control pitch, tone quality, and dynamic changes with a minimum of embouchure manipulation. "The reed should sound good with no help, so that when there is help, it sounds great."[1]

Every player should have more than one reed ready to play. Clarinet and saxophone players rotate reeds, but this is not necessary for the oboist. It is, however, necessary to have another reed ready and broken in. One should not play on a reed

[1]Jay Light (1983), *The Oboe Reed Book: A Straight-Talking Guide to Making and Understanding Oboe Reeds*, Des Moines, IA: Drake University, p. 7.

until it is worn out, since the embouchure will compensate as the reed is wearing out. Players should switch to a new reed as soon as signs of the reed's final days are apparent—usually a lack of response or when the reed becomes difficult to control.

Selection of Cane

If students desire to make their own reeds, the cane can be purchased by the pound in tubes bundled together, but starting with uncut cane requires more tools than with precut cane. Most student oboists should purchase cane that has already been split, gouged, and shaped.

When purchasing either cane or ready-made reeds, the appearance of the cane and its pliability are guides to its selection. A shiny golden color to a brownish color with spots indicates sufficient ripeness and curing. Cane need not be spotted—this is not always an accurate indication of ripeness—but if too green it will not make a satisfactory reed.

Pliability and porousness are also considerations. On a ready-made reed, pliability can be checked with the thumbnail; if the nail makes too deep a mark, the cane is probably too soft. Cane that is hard to cut was harvested too late and is not pliable; cane that is too soft flakes off while being gouged and scraped. The porousness of the cane can be tested by wetting the butt end. If it darkens to an orange arc, it is properly aged. If bubbles appear when one blows on the butt end, the reed is too porous.

Selection of a Reed

Because the oboist is not likely to be able to play a commercial reed before purchasing it, the following points may serve her well:

1. The cane should match the staple so that the oval sides of the reed are flush with it and without cracks on the sides.
2. Slivers of cane appearing at the sides of the reed may not be serious unless their removal will leave a crack.
3. Reeds that have a feathered tip usually have faulty workmanship. The craftsman has feathered out a faulty stroke by scraping and sanding to make it appear acceptable. Reeds made with decisive, sure strokes are almost universally superior to those made by short, choppy strokes.
4. Thin reeds make good tone production easier.
5. The cane should fit snugly together past the staple and somewhat above the fishskin. The fishskin is immediately above the string wrapping and aids in preventing air leaks. The sides of the reed do not meet evenly at the tip, but should be slightly offset when the reed is dry; soaking will counteract the shape.
6. If the tips are flat and parallel rather than oval shaped when dry, too much offset will occur when the reed is soaked.
7. The reed should be held to the light to determine that the two sides of each blade are scraped symmetrically and the two blades are symmetrical with each other. (See Figure 9.7)

The general craftsmanship of the reed is important. These things indicate a good piece of work: Is the string even? Has it been waxed? Is there a good invisible knot? Is the fishskin on at the correct spot and evenly applied? So many items can

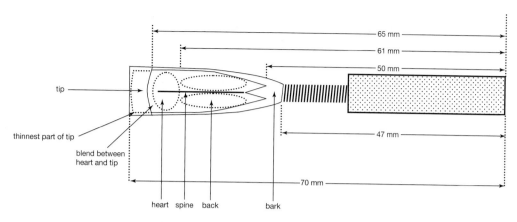

tip

thinnest part of tip

blend between
heart and tip

65 mm

61 mm

50 mm

47 mm

70 mm

heart   spine   back   bark

Figure 9–7   Illustration of Oboe Reed

be so skillfully hidden that making one's own reeds seems the only certain way to get a good product. On a commercial reed one cannot see how far onto the staple the cane was placed or whether the winding extends too far beyond the end of the staple. The winding should end exactly with the end of the staple or at most one thread beyond it. (But beauty is only skin deep; the best-looking reed may not play).

David Weber and Ferald Capps in *The Reed Maker's Manual* write, "deciphering the sound [of the crow] is all that is needed to determine where and how to scrape the reed."[2] Thus, learning about the crow is important. To produce a crow, one inserts the moist reed well into the mouth, closes the lips up to the string, and blows a stream of air through it. The crow should respond immediately and sound a C (or close) in at least two octaves. All new students must experiment with the help of their teacher as to how much reed is inserted in the mouth for the best, clearest, and fullest crow.

Figure 9–8 illustrates several cuts used by oboists. The more advanced player may be able to judge the type of cut that she prefers, whether V-shaped, U-shaped, W-shaped, and so forth; these can easily be identified by the eye.

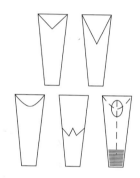

**Figure 9–8
Cuts of Oboe Reeds**

Care of Reeds

Store reeds in a reed case for protection and to insure proper drying. Plastic cases make it hard to return the reed to the case without damaging the tip; furthermore, they do not allow the reed to dry and may cause it to become moldy unless small holes are punched through the plastic. Reeds become dirty during playing and then tend to play flat. Lipstick clogs the pores, dust and lint cling to the moist reed, small food particles from the mouth become lodged in the reed—all unnecessary damage to the reed. To remove these particles, a small piece of paper is placed between the blades from the top and gently pulled back and forth a couple of times, with care taken to avoid breaking the delicate tip of the reed. Rinsing one's mouth at the water fountain before playing and avoiding lipstick and cookies during oboe practice and rehearsal are recommended.

---

[2]D. Weber and F. Capps (1990), *The Reed Maker's Manual: Step by Step Instructions for Making Oboe and English Horn Reed*, Phoenix, AZ: Authors, p. 70.

Adjustments While Playing

Before starting to play a passage one must check the reed opening and adjust it if needed. The player can pinch the reed to obtain the best opening for playing, but a clumsy squeeze, with too much pressure or in the wrong place, may split the blades down the middle. If the reed is too stiff or is not responding, the player may pinch the two pieces of cane together, pinching close to the wrapping on the flat of the blade. This adjustment may raise the pitch slightly. If the reed is soft and closing up, press at the sides, where the two pieces join. This is usually only a quick fix, but soaking it longer may also help. Besides pinching, another way of getting the reed to open up is to put more reed into the mouth, down past the beginning of the winding, and alternate between sucking and blowing air through the reed. The fishskin can be tightened to better support the blades if the tip is still too closed.

Use of the Knife in Reed Adjustments

Professional oboists appear to be as opinionated and exacting with regard to the knife they use (type, size, shape of blade, handle, weight, material, and so on) as what to do with the knife. They do agree that the knife should be very sharp. Only a few of the most common adjustments are given here. Each oboist, upon reaching the stage of adjusting her own reed, should possess three tools: a knife, a mandrel, and a plaque. The scraping of the reed is done in three sections: the tip, the grattage, and the back. (See Figure 9–7.)

Common adjustments for intonation include these: If low C and D are out of tune, open the reed by tightening the fishskin. This will involve inserting the plaque between the blades and scraping the tip of the reed to offset the stiffness coming from a tighter wrapping. If the general pitch is too flat, cut off some of the tip of the reed or trim it slightly on the sides to make it a bit narrower. If the reed is then too stiff, too sharp, or too dull in sound, scrape the tip. If some pitches are sharp, the scraped area should be lengthened or thinned at the lay; sometimes cutting the tiniest bit from the corners helps flatten the pitch. If the player cannot "crow" a C, then the reed is unequally scraped or too thin or too thick in the areas listed previously.

Comparing the pitch of second-line G with the one an octave higher is often used to test the intonation of a reed. The general rule for altering the reed to adjust intonation is this: If the top note is sharp, more of the reed should be scraped; if the top note is flat, the tip of the reed should be cut off or the sides of the reed narrowed. A reed that plays sharp can be scraped more, or the grattage or cut of the reed can be changed from a V-shape to a U-shape. For a reed that plays flat, filing the staple, not the tip, is preferable, but filing the staple should be a last resort. Sometimes "slipping" the reed, that is, moving the blades so that they do not coincide and are slightly offset, will help raise the pitch.

Tone quality, response, and intonation are affected by the various cuts of the reed. If the tone is shrill, bright, and brassy, lengthen the heart by scraping at the bottom, accentuating a U-form over a V-form, and diminishing the width of the sides toward the opening. Shrillness may also be caused by the winding being too far up the reed. If the top tones are dull and thick, scrape the tip slightly, or sometimes only the very end of the tip. Narrowing the sides of the reed will also brighten and harden the sound. If the low notes are difficult to play and are stuffy in sound, thin the bottom of the scrape, particularly at the sides, or else thin both sides of the scrape just below the tip of the reed. Poor response on low notes comes from too short a lay or unevenness in the thickness of the blades.

If the reed blows hard in the upper register, scrape more off the tip. If it blows hard in the lower register, scrape a little at the base near the bark. Whistling may result from unevenness in the thickness of the blades, too short a grattage, or a reed tip that is too thin or is too long for balance. When the reed seems to be causing uncertainty in attacks yet the cane itself is good, there are probably bumps or unevenness in the scrape.

If a new reed seems hard to play, delay making adjustments until the reed is sufficiently broken in and its opening has assumed its regular shape. New reeds and those not recently used will have wide openings that may narrow with playing. If the opening remains too wide, go lightly over the spine of the scrape, and lengthen or thin the V at the bottom of the scrape. If the opening is too small, the reed is probably excessively thin or soft and will produce a loose, edgy, thin tone or else a bright, wild sound. The reed can be improved by scraping the sides, with most of the scraping at the bottom of the scrape. In restoring the original length of the lay after trimming the tip, be careful not to make the lay too long, because then the high notes will not respond. There is an optimum ratio for each reed; when correcting one fault, don't create a worse one.

TECHNIQUE: ARTICULATIONS AND FINGERINGS

Good tonguing is inseparable from artistic playing. For the oboe, while the tone is being produced, the tip of the tongue touches the lower lip or rests on it slightly. To stop the tone, the tongue may stop both blades by touching the tip of the reed with the upper, flat part of the tongue, or stop the lower blade just under the tip of the reed with the very tip of the tongue. Both techniques are used by experts, but students find the second method easier. The oboist has less success with "doo" tonguing than does the clarinetist. A "t" motion gives a sharper, cleaner attack.

Double-tonguing on the oboe is seldom used. The "k" sound required in double-tonguing is not successful because it tends to produce a flat tone and a fuzzy, muddy attack. The oboe player should achieve a facile single-tongue and depend on it for fast passages.

The reed or the instrument itself can be twisted slightly to the left, making it possible to tongue on the corner of the reed. This achieves a rapid, clean tonguing action. The horizontal approach should be mastered first.

Finger dexterity is developed by practicing slowly then speeding up. Coordinating tonguing with fingering is absolutely essential. The young player should begin tonguing on a five-note-scale passage, concentrating on synchronization of fingers and tongue. Slow practice will allow time to listen and think about what is happening. Evelyn Rothwell explains the importance of conscientious practice of technique and the music beyond technique:

> When you play ... you may sacrifice—consciously or unconsciously—certain details for the effect of the whole. For instance, if you are in an orchestra, other instruments are playing at the same time as yourself and may cover up the imperfections in your own technique of which you may not be aware. You may, even when playing quite by yourself, be too carried away by the musical pleasures of what you are doing to listen critically enough to small technical faults, particularly to careless intonation. The purpose of real practice is to acquire complete coordination and control of the muscles you need, by conscious and concentrated mental discipline. No slip or fault, however slight, must be allowed to pass. Train your ears to observe imperfections, and use your brain to put them right.[3]

[3]Evelyn Rothwell (1982), *Oboe Technique*, 3rd ed., London: Oxford University Press, p. 61.

CARE AND MAINTENANCE OF THE OBOE

A well-fitting case is important. It protects the keys of the instrument against damage and it helps prevent extremes of heat and cold from damaging the wood. An outer vinyl or fleece-lined nylon case cover further protects against damage and sudden temperature changes. Always allow the outside of the wooden oboe to warm up before blowing through the instrument.

Dirt is more harmful to an oboe than to other instruments because the small tone holes are easily clogged. It should be swabbed after each playing. A swab of soft cloth is satisfactory for the bell and lower joint; for the upper joint a soft pheasant or turkey feather should be used. The feather sometimes may dry out tone holes or vents but will at least spread the moisture about to prevent a buildup. The feather should first be washed with soap to get rid of natural oils.

Many oboe players oil the bore to guard against splitting wood. However, most reputable manufacturers now guarantee their instruments against cracking, and preparation of the wood in the factory includes soaking it in oil. If oiling the instrument seems desirable, a small amount of bore oil should suffice. Too much oil remaining in the bore adds to the accumulation of dirt. The springs of the oboe should be oiled perhaps once a year and very lightly with key oil, which is available with a needle applicator.

Moisture that collects in the smaller tone holes and the octave keys can be blown out as a temporary solution, and a piece of coffee filter placed between the tone hole and the key, pressed gently, will absorb any remaining moisture. The tone holes should be cleaned regularly with a pin or with the quill of the feather.

The pads and keys of the instrument should be checked frequently because pads leak and keys are easily bent. The keys should be wiped occasionally with a soft cloth. They should not be polished with silver cleaners because this may clog the mechanism and destroy the silver plating.

TROUBLESHOOTING

Equipment

Difficulty in assembling

1. Grease corks on joints, including reed if necessary.

Sticky pads

1. Moisture in tone hole(s) or absorbed by pads. (If pad is not damaged, place tissue paper between key and tone hole and cover/hold gently for paper to absorb moisture; do not use talcum powder.)
2. Bent rods—probably the bridge keys. (Have repaired by competent repairperson.)
3. Worn springs. (Have repaired.)
4. Pivot screws at end of rods need oiling (one drop); occasionally screws may need to be loosened, oiled, then retightened.

Pads not seating correctly

1. Leaking pads—usually discovered when the lower register does not respond easily. (If pads are in good condition, adjusting of the screws may be required; possibly bent rods to be repaired by competent individual.)
2. Pads are damaged. (Replace or have replaced.)

Gurgling sound

1. Water collected in tone hole(s) under pads that usually remain closed. (Open appropriate key, blow water out of hole and into the bore—(blowing must be sudden and forceful). Clean with a feather; bore may need oiling.)
2. On low notes—often a tight throat—first overtone trying to sound. (Relax throat, drop jaw, blow steady air without forcing.)
3. Too much reed in mouth.

Tone

Reedy, nasal, harsh, rough

1. Head down or oboe held too high. (With head erect hold oboe at 30 to 45 degree angle.)
2. Biting on reed. (Drop jaw; lip down and blow faster air to compensate; use firmer lips/embouchure to control reed.)

3. Jaw protruding. (Correct embouchure including jaw.)

4. Reed too hard. (Try softer reed or scrape reed.)

Pinched, small

1. Oboe held too close to body. (With head erect hold oboe 30 to 45 degrees away from torso.)

2. Opening in reed too small—overall contour or sides too weak. (Trim end 1 millimeter at a time and scrape reed when necessary to reform the tip; keep lip pressure on sides of reed.)

3. Biting the reed. (Drop jaw; use more lip to control reed and use slightly faster air to compensate for pitch.)

4. Not enough reed in mouth. (Place more reed in mouth.)

5. Not enough lip over teeth for reed. (Check reed; use more lip over teeth—less red of lip showing.)

6. Not enough breath support.

7. First-space F♯ is weak or breathy. (Play F♯ with G♯ key down. If G♯ key does not close, replace the G♯ cork.)

Unresponding, cold

1. Reed too hard. (Adjust for free blowing or wrong cut—scrape.)

2. Inappropriate reed cut. (Try different brand of reed.)

3. Not enough air. (Blow more air after taking proper breath; use proper embouchure to hold the increased pressure.)

Squawky

1. Reed too stiff. (Player attempting to overblow; adjust reed or replace it with a softer one. Try playing softly or starting *mf* with decrescendos.)

2. Too much reed in mouth.

3. Too much lip over teeth.

4. Reed too open. (Carefully close reed between thumb and first finger to reduce stiffness.)

5. Embouchure too loose.

Trouble with control

1. Oboe too high or too low. (With head erect, hold oboe between 30 to 45 degree angle from body.)

2. At *pp* volume levels—reed too stiff; biting reed; lips in wrong place for reed.

3. Jaw protruding.

4. Reed too soft. (Try harder reed or trim tip.)

5. Cheeks puffing. (Firm corners to keep chin and cheeks flat.)

6. Embouchure too loose.

Trouble with flexibility

1. Too much lip rolled over teeth. (Let some red show.)

2. Too much reed in mouth.

3. Practice overblowing to obtain harmonics; practice slowly moving from note to note in middle of staff in which few fingers are used, gradually adding fingers as range increases.

4. Embouchure too loose.

Squeaks

1. Too much reed in mouth.

2. Bent bridge key to bell, pads not seating.

3. Biting reed with lower jaw. (Try dropping jaw as if lipping the note flat—increase airstream and firm up embouchure/lips.)

4. Oboe held too low. (With head erect, oboe should be 30 to 45 degrees from body; experiment for appropriate position.)

Pitch

Sharp

1. Embouchure too tight. (Use less lip over teeth; loosen embouchure; and/or drop jaw by trying to blow a pitch flat.)

2. Especially in second octave, too much reed in mouth. (Pull reed out.)

3. Reed too stiff. (Scrape reed or try a softer replacement.)

4. Holding oboe at less than 30 degrees from body.

5. Too much bottom and/or top lip turned in.

6. A combination of items 1–5.

7. On individual notes—keys/pads may be rising too far. (Adjust adjusting screws to open keys properly.)

8. Scrape both sides of reed.

9. Pull reed out of mouth.

Flat

1. Embouchure too loose. (Firm up lips especially corners; try more lip over teeth, that is, less red showing; blow faster airstream.)

2. Not enough reed in mouth.

3. Reed too soft. (Cut tip 1 millimeter at a time; scrape when necessary to reform tip to strengthen reed.)

4. Head down or holding oboe too high.

5. Too much red showing on bottom and/or top lip. (Correct embouchure)

6. Combination of items 1–5.

7. On individual notes—keys/pads not opening enough. (Adjustments to screws to allow for proper opening of pads.)

8. Tone holes or vent holes dirty. (Clean with feather or needle.)

9. Overall with reed inserted all the way. (Cut 1 millimeter at a time from reed, scrape when necessary to reform tip—repeat as needed; reed opening too large—press together with fingers to slightly weaken the reed—soak longer—scrape shoulder of reed; file staple to shorten.)

BIBLIOGRAPHY

Texts

* Indicates out of print in 2001.

BATE, PHILIP (1975). *The Oboe: An Outline of Its History, Development and Construction,* 3rd ed. New York: W. W. Norton.

FITCH, WILLIAM D. (1984). *The Study of the Oboe: A Method for the Beginner with Previous Beginner Music Experience,* 4th ed. Ann Arbor, MI: George Wahr.

GOOSSENS, LEON, and EDWIN ROXBURGH (1993). *Oboe.* Miami: Music Sales Corporation; reprint of (1980) London: Kahn and Averill.

HAYNES, BRUCE (2001). *The Eloquent Oboe: A History of the Hautboy from 1640 to 1760.* New York: Oxford University Press.

JOPPIG, GUNTHER (1988). *The Oboe and the Bassoon.* Portland, OR: Amadeus Press.

LEDET, DAVID (2000). *Oboe Reed Style—Theory and Practice.* Bloomington, IN: Indiana University Press; reprint of (1981).

*LIGHT, JAY (1983). *The Oboe Reed Book: A Straight-Talking Guide to Making and Understanding Oboe Reeds.* Des Moines, IA: Drake University.

*McFARLAND, PATRICK (1981). *The Oboist Adjustment Guide.* Atlanta: McFarland Oboe Shop.

OH, HAL (1998). "Oboe," in *Teaching Woodwinds* (Dietz, ed.). New York: Schirmer Books.

*PRODAN, JAMES (1983). *The Third Octave: A Study of the Oboe Altissimo Register.* Greensboro, NC: Spectrum Music.

*———, and PAUL B. REGISTER (1997). *Oboe Performance Practices and Teaching in the United States.* New Bethlehem, PA: Institute for Woodwind Research.

ROTHWELL, EVELYN (1982). *Oboe Technique,* 3rd ed. London: Oxford University Press.

*——— (1974). *The Oboist's Companion,* 3 vols. London: Oxford University Press.

*SPRENKLE, ROBERT, and DAVID LEDET (1961). *The Art of Oboe Playing.* Evanston, IL: Summy-Birchard.

WEBER, DAVID B. AND FERALD B. CAPPS VENDLA AND PAUL CRUTCHFIELD (1990). *The Reed Maker's Manual: Step-by-Step Instructions for Making Oboe and English Horn Reeds.* Phoenix, AZ: Authors.

Journals

The Double Reed (three per year) and *The Journal of the Double Reed Society* (one special issue). From The International Double Reed Society, Norma Hooks, Exec. Sec., 2423 Lawndale Road, Fredricksburg, MD 21048.

Oboe Studies

Easy–Beginning (elementary or middle school)

Andraud. *First Book of Studies for Oboe* (A. Leduc).

———. *Practical and Progressive Oboe Method* (Southern).

Edlefson/Weber. *Student Instrumental Courses: Oboe Student* (3 vols.) (Belwin-Mills).

———. *Tunes for Oboe Technique* (3 vols.) (Belwin-Mills).

Fitch. *Elementary School* (C. F. Peters)

Hinke. *Elementary School* (C. F. Peters).

Hovey. *Elementary Method for Oboe* (Rubank).

Langey-Fischer. *Tutor for Oboe* (C. Fischer).

Macbeth. *Learn to Play Oboe* (2 vols.) (Alfred).

Mayer. *Essentials of Oboe Playing* (Karnes Music)

Snavely. *Basic Technique for Oboe* (Kendor).

Medium (middle school or high school)

Andraud. *Practical and Progressive Oboe Method* (Southern).

Barret. (ed. Barre). *Complete Method for Oboe* (also available in parts) (Boosey & Hawkes).

Bozza. *18 Etudes* (A. Leduc).

Brod. *20 Etudes* (A. Leduc).

Dufresne and Voisin. *Developing Sight Reading* (Colins).

Ferling. *48 Famous Studies* (Southern Music).

Giampiori. *16 Daily Studies* (Ricordi).

Luft. *24 Studies for Oboe* (Billaudot).

Pares. *Daily Technical Exercise for the Oboe* (C. Fischer).

Prestini. *Collection of Studies for Oboe* (Ricordi).

Rothwell. *The Oboist's Companion* (2 vols.) (Oxford).

Teal. *Studies in Time Division* (Fox).

Tustin. *Daily Scales* (Southern).

Advanced (high school or college)

Bach/Rothwell. *Difficult Passages* (Boosey & Hawkes).

Barret. (ed. Barre). *Complete Method for Oboe* (Boosey & Hawkes).

Bassi. *27 Virtuoso Studies* (C. Fischer).

Bozza. *Graphismes* (A. Leduc).

Brown. *370 Exercises for the Oboe* (A. Leduc).

Debondue. *100 Exercises* (A. Leduc).

———. *32 Etudes* (A. Leduc).

Ferling. *48 Etudes,* Op. 31 (Costallat).

Flemming. *60 Progressive Studies* (3 vols.) (C. F. Peters).

Gillet. *Studies for the Advanced Teaching of the Oboe* (A. Leduc).

Karg-Elert. *Etuden-Schule* (Broude)
Loyon. *32 Etudes* (Billaudot).
Prestini. *12 Studies on Chromatic Harmonies* (Belwin-Mills).
Rothwell. *Difficult Passages for Oboe and English Horn* (Boosey & Hawkes).
Tomasi. *3 Concert Etudes* (Eschig).

Instructional Videos

Beginning Oboe (1993). Bowling Green, KY: Music Education Video.
Belwin 21st Century Band Method. Oboe, Level 1 (Holly White, 1996). Miami, FL: Warner Brothers Publications.
Oboe and Bassoon (Allen Signs, 1987). Bellingham, WA: Band Instrument Repair Video Company.
The Oboe Starting Right (Marc Fink, 1993). Madison, WI: University of Wisconsin, Madison.
The Reed Maker's Video: A Supplement to The Reed Maker's Manual (David Weber and Ferald Capps, 1990).
Understanding the Oboe (Kerry Wilinghem and Kurt Hider, 1997). Ft. Mead, Md: U.S. Army Field Band.

Recommended Classical Oboe Artists

Robin Canter playing Mozart and Vaughan Williams
Heinz Holiger playing Milhaud, Mozart and Handel
Joseph Robinson playing Rochberg and Barber
Kurt Meier playing Bach, Holzbauer and Ravel

Recommended Jazz Oboe Artists

Swing: Mitch Miller
Cool: Bob Cooper
Hard Bop, Post-Bop, World Music, New Age: Yusef Lateef
Avant-Garde: Ken McIntyre
Contemporary, Crossover, Bop, New Age: Paul McCandless (and with group Oregon)

OBOE
Fingering Chart

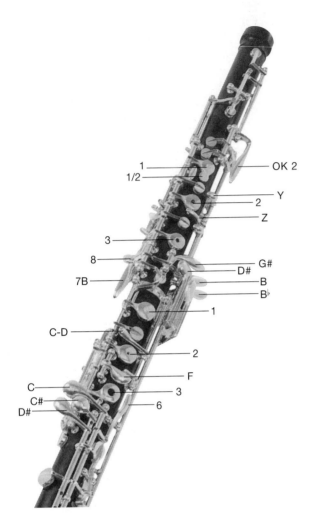

1
1/2
2 — Y
Z
3
8
7B
C-D
C
C#
D#

OK 2
G#
D#
B
B♭
1
2
F
3
6

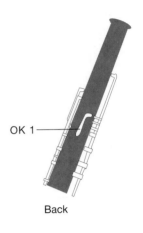

OK 1

Back

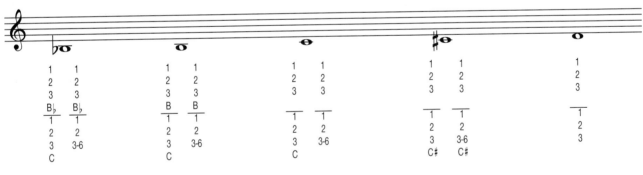

OBOE
Fingering Chart, *Continued*

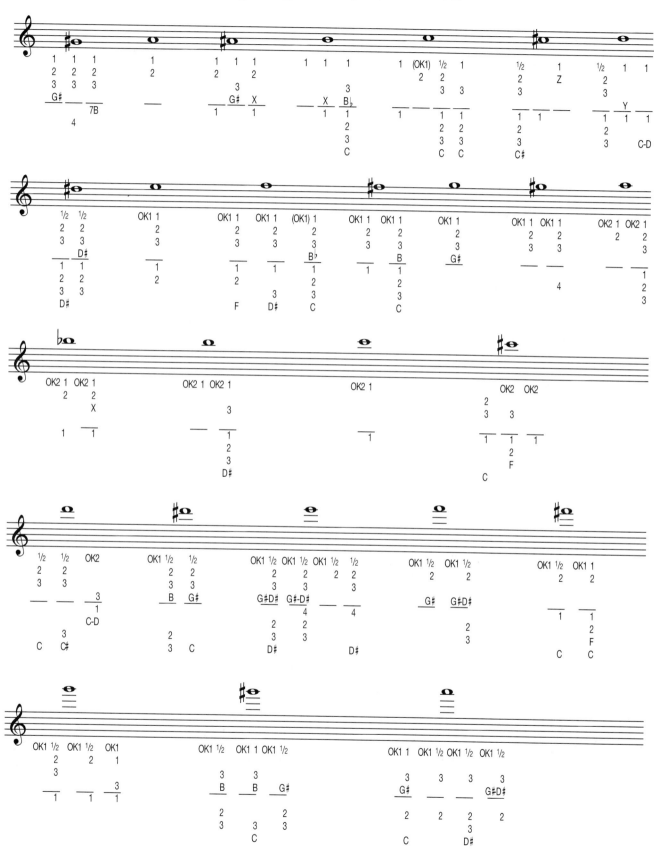

10

The Clarinet

HISTORY

The forerunners of the clarinet, the single-reed instruments, date back to 2700 B.C.E. when the double clarinet was used in Egypt. A triple instrument dating from this period, the launedda, is used in Sardinia to the present day. A clarinet-like instrument called the jaleika was found in Russia; it also dates from the pre-Christian era. The true forerunner of the present-day clarinet is a Greek single tube instrument called the chalumeau. This instrument was never as popular as the double reed shawm due to problems of mouthpiece construction and a short, incomplete scale that was hard to overblow. The chalumeau increased in popularity during the sixteenth century but was still not favored by the more important composers. Its first real use occurred in two obscure operas written in 1710: Keiser's *Croesus* and Bononcini's *Turno Aricino*. By this time, the chalumeau was already a thing of the past, for in 1690 Johann Christoff Denner had added two keys to create an instrument with a range of two octaves. By 1720, finger keys and the speaker key had been added. This clarinet, using a small reed, sounded a bit like an oboe. The clarinet remained a minor instrument and did not appear in scores until four concertos in 1747, followed by works of Arrein in 1762, Stamitz in 1765, and the Concerto for Clarinet in A by Mozart in 1791. Muller added a key system in 1810. The clarinet did not become a modern instrument until Klose added the Boehm system in 1843 making it possible to play in all keys. Numerous forms of the clarinet appeared in the nineteenth century with clarinets pitched in C and D, bass clarinets, the bathyphone (in E), and the basset horn—an alto clarinet pitched in F with a narrow bore and thin wall.

Today the clarinet has four chief registers: the low chalumeau register, the middle or throat-tone register, the upper register called the clarion or alt because it is loud and brilliant, and the high register (See Figure 10–1). Presently made in five or six different keys, ranging from the small sopranino to the contrabass, the clarinet is one of the most useful instruments. Since the time of Mozart, composers have given the instrument a superior repertoire.

The clarinet is the backbone of symphonic and concert bands. Ideally, the symphonic band has more B♭ soprano clarinets than any other single instrument.

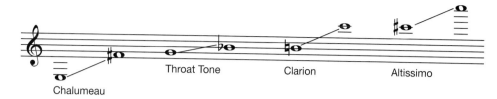

Chalumeau · Throat Tone · Clarion · Altissimo

Figure 10–1 The Four Registers of the B♭ Clarinet (written pitches)

The clarinet is popular as a jazz instrument, as a classically oriented solo instrument, and as an essential element in the orchestra. Its range extends almost an octave higher *and* lower than that of an oboe, giving it one of the widest ranges of all the wind instruments.

SELECTING THE INSTRUMENT

Knowledge of the troublesome idiosyncrasies of an instrument is important to teach or play it well. Clarinets are made of various materials, natural and synthetic; of these, grenadilla wood is the favorite. Several factors enter into the superiority of grenadilla wood: It is easy to work with; it is dense, which minimizes moisture absorption; and it is available in large enough quantities to keep it from being prohibitively expensive. The clarinet has been the most successful plastic instrument because the quantities sold have justified the research required to produce an adequate product. Plastic clarinets, especially the alto and bass, are now made that approach the evenness of scale, the intonation, and the tone quality of the wooden instrument.

Straight-grained wood is always desirable. On older instruments it is important to check whether the wood has dried out excessively or the posts have become loose. Small cracks are not serious if they have been repaired expertly; they can be pinned or banded so that intonation and response are not affected. The appearance of more than one crack may indicate that the wood was not originally aged and seasoned properly. The most important part of a clarinet to check is the joints; any chip in the joints will prevent a perfect seal, allowing air to leak and affecting the intonation. Some professional models (such as the Selmer Paris) have metal caps to reinforce tenon joints. Checking the interior of the barrel is essential because scratches and scorings affect intonation and tone.

One should always play an instrument before making a decision about its adequacy—there is no other way to estimate intonation and tone quality. Every clarinet will respond somewhat differently. Pitch should be checked by playing and listening. The performer testing the instrument should play octaves to determine intonation (with an electronic tuner) and then scales to determine that the intervals are in tune at various dynamic levels. The merits of a new or used clarinet are judged on its tone quality, intonation, and response.

At a pitch of A=440 the barrel should be pulled about one-sixteenth of an inch at 68 to 72 degrees Fahrenheit. This fraction of an inch gives the player freedom to push the barrel in when room temperatures and air density make a sharper pitch desirable. Because warmer rooms raise pitch at different rates for different instruments, the clarinetist needs to be able to match this sharpness when necessary. Sometimes clarinets cannot be adjusted to match the ensemble's pitch. If a particular clarinet plays under the pitch A=440 with the barrel pulled one-sixteenth inch, a shorter barrel will be necessary.

The quality of the keys should be considered. Keys should be made from good, forged nickel silver so they are not easily bent or broken. Bent keys are important on any woodwind, because a bent key may not open the proper distance, creating intonation problems. Bending the key back into place does not remedy the initial damage (or the intonation problem); it simply makes location of the problem more difficult.

The clarinet is far from a perfect instrument, and many compromises have been necessary in its manufacture. The register key (not an octave key) and the speaker key (for third-line B♭) are the same. To correct the problems caused by this doubling up, it would be necessary to place the speaker key higher on the clarinet and reduce it in size (its present placement results in clarinets having a flat fourth-line D and fourth-space E). Alto, bass, and contrabass clarinets often have both keys, one the B♭ and one the register key.

A single middle joint would allow a better C♯ and G♯ because that tone hole could be placed lower, but the loss of the option of pulling at this joint for intonation purposes has prevented this design from being adopted on better soprano instruments.

ASSEMBLING THE CLARINET

The various instruments of the clarinet family, ranging from the E♭ soprano to the contrabass, are constructed with similar parts. Precautions that apply to the assembling of one apply to all.

The B♭ soprano clarinet has five parts: the mouthpiece (which holds the reed by means of a ligature), the barrel, the upper joint, the lower joint, and the bell. The parts fit together tightly—the tenons, covered with cork, ensure a close fit. The pieces do not slide together easily but must be coaxed. The corks should be greased prior to attempting the first assembly and should remain greased. They should never be assembled by wiggling.

The left hand firmly holds the upper joint with the fingers depressing the three rings over the tone holes to raise the bridge key. The right hand holds the lower joint with the thumb just below the thumb rest and the fingers grasping the joint *without* depressing any key rings. The joints are coupled together using a slight twisting motion taking care not to bend the bridge key. A bent bridge key may prevent certain keys from closing, making some notes hard to play.

Next, holding the two joints in the right hand with the right thumb against the thumb rest, the bell is twisted on the bottom joint with the left hand. Then the barrel is twisted on the top joint—the wider end of the barrel is connected to the upper joint. The manufacture's labels on the barrel, the upper joint, and the bell should be aligned.

Finally, with the instrument still held carefully in the left hand, the mouthpiece is assembled so that the flat side, or table, is in line with the thumb rest and register key and the ligature is placed over the mouthpiece.

The reed is slipped under the ligature rather than the ligature placed over the reed and mouthpiece. For beginners the ligature screws usually go on the same side of the mouthpiece as the reed (although Bonade and similar ligatures are reversed). The bottom screw should be tightened just enough to hold the reed firmly in place. The upper screw should be tightened only enough to prevent it from vibrating and causing an unpleasant buzzing sound. Stein advocates tightening the top screw and leaving the bottom one loose, for greater elasticity throughout the entire reed.[1] Caution: If the ligature is screwed too tightly for too long or

[1]Keith Stein (1958), *The Art of Clarinet Playing*, Evanston, IL: Summy-Birchard, p. 6.

not loosened after playing, it may cause the mouthpiece to warp when the reed becomes soaked and expands. The type of ligature is important, as the object is to provide maximum vibration of the reed and avoid a choked or buzzing tone quality. The use of Velcro or string wound around the mouthpiece to hold the reed in place allows the reed great freedom to vibrate. For years David Pino has used a flat, cloth shoestring as a ligature.[2] There are many satisfactory ligatures.

A ligature placed too high on the mouthpiece hinders reed vibration, encourages squeaks, and results in a stuffy tone. When the ligature is positioned too low, the reed has too much freedom to vibrate and the tone becomes harsh; placing the ligature slightly below the lines marked on the mouthpiece is a valid recommendation.

The reed is placed so that it is centered on the mouthpiece and only a very slight "rim" of mouthpiece is visible when the tip of the reed is gently depressed. The mouthpiece cap should be a frequently used item.

HOLDING THE CLARINET

Two guidelines that are important in establishing a good position for holding the clarinet are (1) the angle at which the instrument is held and (2) the flexibility of the fingers and the hand position.

The angle at which the clarinet is held should be established first because correct embouchure depends in part on it. The player's posture should be erect whether sitting or standing (see Figure 10–2 for the correct posture when seated). Stiffness should be avoided. Neck, shoulders, and arms must stay relaxed with the head erect. Arms held too far out from the body can create tension in the neck and may cause tenseness in the fingers. One of the first impulses of the beginner is to lower the head to meet the mouthpiece. He should bring the instrument to his mouth, not his mouth to the instrument. Depending upon his embouchure formation, he should hold the clarinet directly in front of the body at an angle of about 30 degrees from the body. Each student has different posture habits, different teeth formation and lip structure, and the sensible teacher considers these in determining the angle that fosters the best embouchure.

Figure 10–2
Sitting Position for Playing the Clarinet

The student who rests the clarinet on one knee shifts the clarinet to one side and develops an improper embouchure and a rough tone. Some authorities feel that there is little harm in letting a beginner rest the bell on his knee if he is tall enough. These clarinet teachers advocate this practice with the belief that this will keep the hands and fingers relaxed and prevent their being used to support the instrument. Resting the instrument on the knee, however, can indeed lead to a misaligned embouchure, the development of the wrong facial muscles, poor breathing habits, and restricted finger dexterity. If the student finds the clarinet too heavy to hold without resting it on his knee, he should practice for shorter lengths of time. Proper position may not initially feel comfortable or natural, but if his embouchure seems correct and he is able to produce what promises to be a good tone, the student should be encouraged to adjust to the position. *Head up, horn down.*

If the student's head is lowered, or the instrument held too far out from the body, the lower jaw is positioned directly beneath the upper jaw when it should be

[2]David Pino (1980), *The Clarinet and Clarinet Playing*, New York: Scribner's, pp. 21–22.

farther down on the mouthpiece. When the lips are equidistant from the mouthpiece tip, the tone is less flexible and more uneven between registers, and the lower lip loses sensitivity. It is better to keep the lower lip about three-quarter inch from the tip of the reed and the upper lip about half inch from the tip. This is facilitated by holding the instrument at the appropriate angle. This quarter inch difference contributes to better tone, more flexibility, more consistency throughout the entire range of the clarinet, and a more focused tone. One common rule is that the lower lip should be placed as far down as possible without squeaking.

If the player has thin lips, he should decrease the angle of the clarinet; if he has thick or full lips, holding the instrument out more than 30 degrees may improve his embouchure and tone quality, the position depending upon the jaw. A player with a protruding jaw must hold the instrument at a greater angle from the body to compensate for increased pressure from the lower jaw. Generally, the smaller the angle at which the clarinet is held, the more shrill the tone. The tone mellows as the angle is increased. A completely dull sound is obtained, however, if the clarinet reaches a 90 degree angle, excluding the rare exceptions such as Benny Goodman and Buddy DeFranco, whose sounds in this position can hardly be described as dull, but such a position is inappropriate for most players when playing music of a classical nature.

Correct hand position is shown in Figure 10–3. The thumb rest should lie between the nail and the first end joint of the right thumb. The right thumb is responsible for supporting the clarinet, with the left thumb and embouchure only

Figure 10–3
Hand Position for the Clarinet

helping to balance or steady it—the right-hand and left-hand fingers cover the holes without gripping the instrument. If the player allows the thumb rest to slip farther back on the thumb, the right fingers curve excessively to fit over the keys, which produces a tense wrist. The right thumb must be firm but should not push the clarinet into the mouth. Deep teeth marks in the mouthpiece indicate excessive right thumb pressure.

The right hand should slant so the side keys are easily accessible to the middle of the index finger as the fingertip rests over the fourth tone hole. The left thumb rests over the register key at a 45 degree angle without touching it, and the fingers of the left hand lie almost at right angles with the clarinet. The left index finger is positioned over the G♯ and A keys. The slant necessary for the fingers to reach the auxiliary keys depends on the size and shape of the hands and the length of the fingers. The tips of the little fingers on both hands should rest on the tips of the F keys.

For dexterity and coverage, the pads of the fingers, not the flat or tips of them, are used to cover the tone holes. The fingers should be slightly curved in a natural, relaxed position so that the fleshy tip fits comfortably over the tone hole. Small air leaks caused by insufficient covering of the tone holes can cause large changes in intonation and tone.

Students should be encouraged to keep their fingers close to the keys and tone holes, especially the little fingers. The novice is apt to exaggerate each fingering motion and thereby slow his technique. Some teachers suggest raising the fingers high in order to ensure synchronization of the fingers, but this usually causes bad habits. From the beginning, students should use as little finger movement as necessary. The problem of synchronizing fingers is more a matter of paying close attention to the finger action than of exaggerating it.

Jazz clarinetists use alternate fingerings to alter pitches and shade the tone holes slightly to play micropitches, flat/sharp notes, but *all* clarinetists emphasize that one must learn to play correctly before experimenting with such special effects.

EMBOUCHURE

Clarinet embouchures vary a great deal: Some teachers prefer more bottom lip over the teeth; others prefer the corners of the mouth pulled downward, or outward, or inward or simply tightened. The upper teeth should not bite into the mouthpiece or push down on it; the mouth should simply be closed and the teeth vertically aligned. Blowing a fine stream of air or inhaling through the lips as if pulling through a soda straw is a good way to describe the action. Many players use a small piece of very thin vinyl glued to the top of the mouthpiece to prevent damage to the mouthpiece and to limit the vibrations felt by the teeth (known technically as the "heebie-jeebies"). Figure 10-4 illustrates the lips and teeth.

The corners of the lips are held together so that there is a firm grip all around the mouthpiece. The student should not think of forming a huge smile. The chin and jaw should be kept as still as possible, because any movement of the jaw tends to raise or lower the pitch. The final embouchure adjustment is based on tone quality; the mouthpiece may be pulled or pushed into the mouth while experimenting with more or less lip over the bottom teeth.

The pressure on the reed comes principally from the lips and corners of the mouth (Figure 10–5 and 10–6). In addition, the need for keeping the chin down has to be stressed often with the beginner, because the sensation is not natural. Practicing with a mirror or with a parent watching can help to keep the chin pointed. Positioning the chin in the proper position is relatively easy, but it tends to return to its natural position as soon as air pressure builds up. Unless the chin is held down and flat, intonation in the high register becomes difficult, the lower register loses some of its carrying quality, and the cheeks tend to puff out, especially in the lower register. Advanced players need not be so concerned about the pointed chin. With a well-developed embouchure the clarinet can be held down more with most of the support on the lower lip, the upper lip encasing the mouthpiece to prevent air leakage and produce the desired tone.

When the player has developed a good embouchure, he should initially take his breath slowly and avoid any disturbance of the embouchure. As he begins to

Figure 10–4
Clarinet: Lips and Teeth

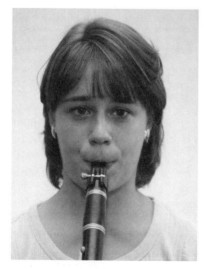

Figure 10–5
Clarinet Embouchure

Figure 10–6
Clarinet Embouchure (side view)

understand the "hows" and "whys" of a proper embouchure, he should be encouraged to breathe through the corners of his mouth, keeping the center of his lips on the mouthpiece. When the air is blown into just the mouthpiece, a tone approximating a high C or D will sound. Practicing on just the mouthpiece to obtain these pitches is fine although a room full of students eagerly practicing does contribute to noise pollution.

There should be minimal change of embouchure for different registers and for wide skips. A good exercise is to practice harmonics. If the player finds high E, F, and G difficult to produce, he may not have his lower lip low enough on the reed and should experiment with more of the mouthpiece in his mouth. He may have to stretch the corners of his mouth as the high register is reached, perhaps from about G above the staff. This stretch helps eliminate the "crying" effect so often heard in the high registers. Another recommendation is that the chin be pulled down farther than normal for the upper register without disturbing the basic embouchure. Experimenting is necessary. As the embouchure tires during a rehearsal or concert, more pressure will be needed to play the upper notes. Proper embouchure formation will prevent damage to the muscles.

The use of the lips helps determine quality and volume of clarinet tone, and the pressure of the lips alters according to the volume desired. For fortissimo playing, the pressure is shifted lower on the reed, farther from the tip; for pianissimo playing, closer to the tip. The embouchure does not change—the lip pressure is exerted in different areas for different dynamic levels. Adjusting lip pressure affects tone; a relaxed lip results in a bigger, unfocused, mellower sound, whereas more pressure against the reed by the lip provides increased intensity of tone.

Squeaks, one of the continual plagues of the beginning clarinet player, are usually due to (1) having too much of the mouthpiece in the mouth or (2) using an embouchure that is too tight, biting too much, or exerting too much jaw pressure. Squeaks may often be eliminated by a gentler attack on the mouthpiece. Squeaks are also caused by broken reeds, the fingers not covering the holes completely, a leaking instrument, or occasionally an inferior mouthpiece.

The members of the clarinet family are very similar and most playing techniques apply to the entire family. However, there are some important differences. In playing the E♭ and the B♭ soprano clarinets, the best embouchure is one in which equal pressure is exerted on the mouthpiece from above and below. The higher of these, the E♭ instrument, will be most easily controlled when less mouthpiece is placed in the mouth than that used for the other clarinets, along with a firmer embouchure and more breath support.

BASS CLARINET

When the bass clarinet squeaks in the high register, there is usually too much pressure being exerted from below by the lower lip and jaw, not enough pressure from the upper teeth, or an insufficient amount of the mouthpiece in the mouth. The general rule is that as one goes higher the pressure from the lower lip and jaw is shifted to the top and sides. The upper teeth continue to apply the same or slightly more pressure. Thus the player must take more of the mouthpiece into the mouth, relax the lower lip, drop the jaw, and at the same time slightly increase the pressure on the top and sides, pushing the instrument forward so a little more of the upper side of the mouthpiece enters the mouth. This procedure will help remove tension from the lower lip and eliminate much of the problem of high-register squeaking.

Figure 10–7
Bass Clarinet: Embouchure

A good bass clarinet embouchure (Figure 10–7) requires more mouthpiece in the mouth and less pressure. A slightly softer reed should be used than for the B♭ soprano because of the more relaxed embouchure. Tenor saxophone reeds are sometimes chosen for the bass clarinet, but this is not a good idea; reeds for the tenor saxophone are slightly longer and narrower than those for bass clarinet and will be unwieldy when used on the clarinet mouthpiece.

INTONATION

Some of the major problems of intonation arising within the band and orchestra stem from the built-in characteristics of even the best instruments. The solution is to teach the students to listen and adjust.

The clarinet is designed to overblow at the interval of a twelfth when the register key is depressed. In other words, the fingering that produces B♭ in the low register produces the F an octave and a fifth above when the register key is depressed. Unfortunately, these twelfths are not in tune with themselves.

The clarinet is built to play slightly sharp. As the clarinet is somewhat inflexible in pitch, tuning to it is not out of order. (The oboe, the traditional tuning instrument, is more flexible.)

Probably the best tuning notes on the clarinet once a student has a good embouchure are thumb F and open G, but for best results several notes in different ranges should be used. Changes in temperature and in the density of air affect the pitch; cold and heat, dryness and humidity alter the pitch just as change of volume does. In cold temperatures the pitch will drop; in warm temperatures it will rise. Thin, dry air gives a faster sound wave and a higher pitch, whereas moist air causes slower waves and a lower pitch. Changes of volume also have an effect: Pianissimo playing without adjustment will be sharp and forte playing flat (the opposite of the flute).

The clarinet tends to go sharp in the lower register and throat tones, and flat in the upper register, also opposite to the tendencies of the flute. To play in tune, soft tones should be produced by controlling the airstream with the large breathing muscles, but some players pinch off the air with their lips, thus tightening the embouchure and producing a sharper pitch. The fact that the tighter lips make a better tone quality in soft playing complicates the problem.

Figure 10–8 Pitch Tendencies of Certain Notes on the Clarinet

Sharp Tones

Pitches that are particularly sharp when played softly are shown in Figure 10–8. First-line E♭ may also be sharp when soft. To correct, open the throat more and use more breath support. Only as a last resort should one use less pressure from the lower lip.

Flat Tones

Low E and F may be flat in forte playing, even though generally sharp in normal and soft playing. The beginning player should constantly be reminded of intonation problems so that his ear becomes sensitive to small discrepancies.

Adjustments and Corrections

Tightening the lips will raise the pitch slightly. Adequate breath support will keep the pitch from sagging. When the throat is relaxed, the pitch will be steady as well as of better quality; tension in the throat will raise the pitch and adversely affect tone quality. Any jaw movement will alter the intonation, as will changing the angle at which the clarinet is held. None of these changes make large differences in the pitch; for larger differences, the player relies on alternate fingerings.

Physical Alterations

If the clarinet is consistently sharp, the player should pull slightly at the joints, the barrel, the middle joint, and the bell, although the lower joints have less effect. If the throat tones are in tune and the middle register sharp, he might pull the middle joint to improve the intonation of the middle register. However, pulling too much can add to intonation problems rather than eliminate them; for example, middle-line B♭ uses only one-fourth of the clarinet tube as its vibrating chamber, so pulling affects this four times as much as it affects the B natural one-half step above, which uses all the tube for its vibrating chamber.

Adding tuning discs to correct sharpness lengthens the clarinet without forming air pockets. A shorter barrel primarily raises the throat tones and the left-hand notes. A barrel that is too short produces the same general problems as if the player had failed to pull the barrel sufficiently: Throat tones or the entire register will be faulty and excessively sharp. Conversely, pulling the barrel too much will flatten the throat tones.

Other Factors

Other factors that may affect pitch relate to reeds, position of instrument, and use of the jaw. The most common are these:

1. A cheap mouthpiece may play extremely sharp. If the throat tones, G, G♯, and A, are out of tune, the fault may be with the mouthpiece rather than with the instrument. The tone chamber—that part of the mouthpiece that is immediately below the air entrance—is not proportioned correctly for the clarinet.

2. A mouthpiece with a bore slightly smaller than that of the instrument will raise the pitch of notes in the lower register. A mouthpiece bore slightly larger than that of the instrument will lower the pitch of the low notes.

3. The diameter of the barrel also makes a discernible difference in intonation as well as in tone quality.

TONE QUALITY

In the spectrum of instrumental sound, the clarinet's unique contribution is a quality that has both an edge and a large, full sound. Those who want to make the clarinet always sound mellow or who want a personal, romantic sound from the instrument fail to understand and appreciate the tonal possibilities of the clarinet.

The clarinet sounds like a clarinet due to the odd-numbered partials sounding. When a low F concert is played (see Figure 10–9) the second partial, the octave, is not present. The third partial, C concert, is sounded and becomes the predominate pitch when the register key is depressed, as well as the fifth, seventh, and ninth (A, E♭, and G). This effect is due to the clarinet's being a cylindrical pipe, closed at one end. Other wind instruments are either conical having the same acoustical properties as open pipes—that is, sounding all partials—or a combination of conical and cylindrical that results in a combination of odd-and even-numbered partials sounding.

Figure 10–9
B♭ Clarinet: The Odd-numbered Partials when a Low F Concert is Played

Hearing good clarinet tone is desirable but apparently not essential in concept formation as students have been known to overcome the models heard on MTV. D, E, and F at the top of the staff are considered model tones for tone production. Good tone is accomplished by practicing sustained tones, first within a narrow range then gradually enlarging the range as skill increases. An occasional good tone does not constitute good playing; tone quality must be attractive at all times and in all registers. It is easier for teachers to focus their attention on the more objective elements of performance, such as technique and dynamics, than to encourage good tone.

Variables in good tone production are the instrument and reed, the mouthpiece, the player's lip and facial structure, the embouchure, breath support, the amount of mouthpiece in the mouth, and the angle at which the clarinet is held.

The speed of the air determines the intensity of the tone, and good tone demands intensity. A small, flaccid tone is a result of playing with little air support. The beginner should play with as much air, or as big a sound, as he possibly can. He should learn to control the tone gradually, to focus it, and to reduce the volume while still keeping the intensity in the tone. Overblowing causes harsh sounds and incorrect intonation, especially in the high register. If the embouchure is correctly formed, the air support/pressure should be as great as the muscles of his lips and jaw will allow.

An open throat aids in the production of good tone. This is often taught with the help of vowels, an "ah" for the lower pitches and progressing toward "ee" as the pitch rises. The vowel "ee" helps to lift the tongue and compress the space through which the air must travel, thus helping to achieve the rapid air necessary for the high register tones. This vowel change, with its corresponding change of tongue position, can be acquired by practicing slurs of a tenth or a twelfth.

A good clarinet sound is generally described as being somewhere on a continuum between "dark" and "brilliant"— tone on the brilliant side is that most preferred. Others claim that the best clarinet tone is somewhat on "top of the pitch"—that is, approaching being sharp. Therefore, the player should play on top of the tone at all times. The only way to make the pitch any sharper at that degree of intensity would be to tighten the lip, producing a pinched sound and sacrificing tone quality.

Few approve of vibrato on clarinet. There are times, however, when it is appropriate. Traditionally the diaphragm vibrato has been preferred; however, most jazz clarinetists use jaw vibrato.

The Clarinet Mouthpiece

Double-reed players blame all faults on their reeds, clarinet players on their mouthpieces. The average player is advised to buy a good standard mouthpiece and adjust to it. The teacher should know what to look for in a good mouthpiece and what possible troubles may arise from poor or inadequate equipment. Many instrumental teachers request that the local music retailers supply a specific model mouthpiece with all clarinets sold or rented to their students. The slight difference in cost is built into the contract.

A clarinet mouthpiece is illustrated in Figures 10–10 and 10–11. Mouthpieces are made from a variety of materials: plastics of several kinds and rubber. Crystal mouthpieces come and go in popularity. Currently they are extremely popular among jazz clarinet players in Europe. An open crystal mouthpiece with a medium-hard reed is used to get a breathy tone quality.

Probably the best mouthpiece for the average student is made of hard rod rubber. It retains its shape, plays easily, and has the strongest fundamentals and more overtones than mouthpieces made from other materials.

Mouthpieces with shiny inside surfaces are usually molded rubber or plastic, and to date have not been successful because they warp easily. Warping, on better mouthpieces, is caused by temperature changes and by the ligature being consistently put on too tightly. Some temperature changes cannot be avoided, but one can avoid washing the mouthpiece in hot water.

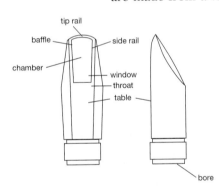

Figure 10–10
Clarinet Mouthpiece Viewed from the Top and Side

Although an average mouthpiece the width of the window is 11.5 millimeters and that of the tip 11 millimeters, there is no foolproof formula. The mouthpiece tip opening varies from 0.9 to 1.5 millimeters; knowledge, experience, instinct, and trial and error are required.

If the side rails of the mouthpiece are not identical, the clarinet will squeak. Where a set of feelers (used in checking pad closings) is available, the mouthpiece is placed on a piece of glass and the feelers pulled through to determine whether there is an equal amount of resistance. Another way of checking the rails and facing is to blow on a piece of glass or mirror so that it clouds over, then place the mouthpiece face down and roll toward the tip. When the mouthpiece is carefully removed from the glass, the points of contact can be checked by the impression left on the glass. The tip rail at the very end of the mouthpiece should be about 1/32 inch thick; excessive squeaking may be due to the fact that the tip rail is too thin. On the other hand, if the tip rail is too thick, there will be too much resistance. The

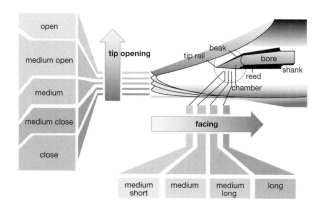

Figure 10-11
Clarinet Mouthpiece Viewed from the Side
Showing Tip Openings Between Reed and Tip
Rail and Length of Side Rails or Facing
Used by permission of Vandoren Paris ©2000 from
http://www.vandoren.com/Products/products.htm

tone produced will be a soft, clear tone, attractive to the beginning player, but not a characteristic clarinet tone.

The lay of the mouthpiece determines the amount of opening between the reed and the tip of the mouthpiece; it makes a large difference in the kind of sound produced. A wide variety of lays, or facings, is available because different people prefer different clarinet sounds. Some recommend the close, short French lay; "short" because the tip of the mouthpiece curves away from the reed a short distance; "close" because the opening that results at the very end of the mouthpiece is narrow. This lay is preferred because it is easier to control and does not require as much pressure.

Such a detailed discussion of the lay may seem unnecessary, but it is important because in a mouthpiece the lay itself and its relationship to the bore are the most important factors in sound production. For example, the quicker the mouthpiece curves away from the reed (which usually makes it more open), the harder the reed needed, and consequently, the more difficulty in controlling the tone.

The average mouthpiece is the medium French, with a lay of about 18 millimeters long. With a longer lay, the tip should be closer so that a long facing is not combined with too open a tip. A long, open lay would require such a soft reed that good control of the tone would be almost impossible; the sound would be easier to produce but the tone would have less body. A short, closed lay generally produces a harsh tone quality.

The tone chamber at the bottom of the curve of the mouthpiece influences the quality of the tone. A tone chamber with a small bore will tend to have a brilliant tone with an edge, and a pitch that is somewhat sharp. A tone chamber with a large bore produces a still more brilliant tone, but the quality is broader, with less edge. This latter sound is better for band work because it blends well with other instrumental timbres. The typical intonation produced by a large tone chamber is a flat chalumeau and clarion register, and a slightly sharp high register. The small tone chamber, conversely, produces opposite intonation effects, a flat high register and somewhat sharp low and middle registers.

The following list of mouthpiece faults is a guide in locating possible sources of common playing difficulties.[3]

Excessive Squeaks May Be Due To

A vent that is too straight
A thin tip rail
A facing that is too short
A convex baffle near tip rail
An uneven facing

[3]Ralph Ritchie (1961, Nov.), "The Clarinet Mouthpiece," *Instrumentalist,* p. 66.

An irregular tip rail
A facing that is too open

Hard Blowing May Be Due To

A wide tip rail
An excessively curved vent
A baffle that is too concave
A baffle that is convex
The pivot in the facing is too close to the tip

A rough Tone May Be Due To

An unduly flat facing
A facing that is too open
A facing that is too long
A facing that is both too open and too long
An extremely concave curve in the baffle

The taper of the barrel may be at fault if the problem is thin tone quality in the upper register or extremely coarse tone in the lower register. Intonation problems most characteristic of barrel trouble are these: If the clarinet appears to be a good instrument except for a tendency to sharpness in the upper register, there is a good chance that the bore of the barrel is too large at the mouthpiece end for the instrument. If throat tones have a tendency to sharpness in an otherwise satisfactory instrument, the barrel is probably too small at the end that joins the clarinet body.

Jazz musicians agree that the advertised "jazz mouthpieces" are "snake oil." Most play the same mouthpiece for jazz and classical playing. "Jazz sound" on the clarinet is merely alterations in articulations, rhythm, and drive. The difference in classical playing is in balance and blend—fitting into the band and orchestra.

TECHNIQUE: ARTICULATIONS AND FINGERINGS

Few successful musicians rate technique as more important to performance than good tone quality and expressive playing. Technique, however, is the control with which the performer manages the mechanized piece of expensive wood that comprises the clarinet. Technique can be fast and flashy, and many young clarinetists are impressed by such playing and focus their energy on developing it. Rapid practice merely enables the student to perform his bad habits more rapidly.

The most popular method of tonguing is to touch the reed with the tip of the tongue about one-eighth inch down from the tip of the reed. Beginners should be encouraged to touch the reed gently, just enough to stop the vibration.

When tonguing is introduced, the instructor explains that the tongue is like a switch that merely touches the reed to stop the vibration and then allows it to vibrate. The tongue moves to the bottom of the mouth to let the reed vibrate and returns to touch the reed to stop the vibration. Encourage students to play quarter notes while blowing air through the clarinet as if playing whole notes, while the tongue touches the reed gently on each beat (quarter notes).

This approach, legato tonguing, prevents the bad habit of starting and stopping the note with the tongue. It is particularly important for the player to think pitches as he tongues. Because playing is like singing, he invariably thinks a syllable, and the syllable he forms will influence the type of tone produced.

The type of articulation, legato to marcato, depends on how the tongue touches the reed; the amount of air determines the dynamic level as well as the style of articulation. Only the forward part of the tongue need move; excessive movement from the tongue or the jaw will reduce tonguing speed and control and can result in a tight throat, further affecting both tonguing and tone quality. The tongue should remain relaxed and resting at the bottom of the mouth as much of the time as possible.

As the player progresses, he will not try to form "t" with each stroke but will relax the tip of the tongue over the tip of the mouthpiece and let the movement itself become more flexible, omitting the hard, time-consuming "t" sound before the vowel.

Heavy, harsh tonguing is a major problem for many players. Directors may inherit these players and need suggestions for curing their faults. The use of legato studies and legato tonguing is one possibility. Another is to instruct students to coordinate their breathing with the tongue touching the reed. If air pressure is built up before the tongue "opens" the reed, an explosive articulation occurs.

FINGERINGS

Technique involves the development of correct, appropriate tonguings and the development of accurate fingerings. Simple scalewise and arpeggiated exercises for finger dexterity can be created by the teacher. Repeating a scalewise pattern over and over (up or down) and starting on different notes of the scale provide practice on lifting one finger at a time and then closing several together (or in descending, vice versa).

Occasionally, however, there is no alternative to the fingers sliding from one key to another. If a finger is raised and then presses another key, a "grace note" will usually sound or tempo/articulations will be impaired. The most common problem of this sort is playing an F♯ to an A in the throat register without sounding a G between the two.

The "diabolus in musica" (the tritone) was the most dreaded element in music in the Middle Ages; today, it can be helpful in teaching beginning clarinetists to cross "the break," that is, playing from the B♭ in the staff to the vast realm of the unknown notes above. Though students are anxious about crossing the break, it is a learned fear. If students are playing confidently in the chalumeau and throat registers, it is merely a matter of pressing the register key with the side of the thumb to play notes above the break. Having students play in the low register (low F to C) and then activate the register key is a much easier way to cross the break than to approach it scalewise; playing from second-space A to the third-line B requires changing from one key pressed with the left index finger to nine holes/keys pressed with eight fingers and a thumb. The right hand can continue to cover the tone holes/keys while playing the throat tones to reduce finger movement.

Many alternate fingerings are possible on clarinet. The instrumental music teacher should recommend alternatives when the need arises (e.g., to make rapid passages and trills easier and cleaner). The most common alternate fingerings are contained in the fingering chart at the end of this chapter.

REEDS

Clarinet players often become as fussy about selection and care of reeds as Stradivarius was about the varnish on his violin. Much of the concern over the right reed is unnecessary; the average student should select a brand and a strength that works well for him and stick with it. Contrary to common wisdom, even jazz clarinetists use medium-strength reeds.

It is nearly impossible to tell by looking at a reed whether it has the desired qualities. Green cane will absorb water readily and give a fuzzy tone, yet some artists like cane with a slightly green tint because it offers more resistance. The cane needs to be sufficiently dry, and spotted cane is often selected as indicating dryness. Coarse-grained cane, however, which is golden and spotted, soaks water readily and gives a harsh tone and is therefore no more desirable than green cane. The generally accepted characteristics that mark a good piece of reed cane are (1) straight grain, (2) heavy fibers evenly spaced, and (3) gold or darker color. Mottled or streaked cane is not necessarily bad when these spots are on the bark. Holding prospective reeds to the light to find those that have a well-balanced fiber structure is a good practice, but it is virtually impossible to obtain a reed that will be perfect without some additional work. One can wet reeds and expose them to sunlight for additional curing.

After well-aged golden cane with straight, even grain has been selected, the next problem is to obtain the proper degree of stiffness. The lay of the mouthpiece influences the appropriate playing stiffness of the reed; and each reed, being slightly different, will have to be placed slightly differently on the mouthpiece. General guidelines can nevertheless be established. Teachers who do not play the clarinet often recommend softer reeds, probably from lack of personal experience, but a stiffer reed (2-1/2 or 3) will produce a better embouchure if used from the beginning. Further, cane can be scraped or shaved from a reed, but cannot be added. The strength numbers cannot be taken as absolute; strengths vary.

After selecting his reed, the player should be able to make minor adjustments on it. To add life and resistance, a new reed should be well soaked with saliva and immediately massaged by the finger for about 30 seconds, or pressed hard on a piece of glass and rubbed vigorously up and down with the forefinger. The massaging closes the pores and prevents the reed from becoming soaked too quickly.

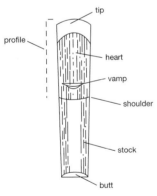

**Figure 10-12
Different Parts and Areas
of the Clarinet Reed
(same as saxophone)**

The stock of the reed is about 3 inches long. The tip of the reed is about one-eighth inch long and should not contain any fiber that runs the length of the reed. If the fibers or grains come closer to the end than one-eighth inch, the reed will tend to have a coarse sound; if they do not extend this close to the end, but stop farther down on the reed making the tip more than one-eighth inch deep, the reed will not have enough resiliency. The heart extends to within one-quarter inch from the end of the reed (Figure 10–12).

A good reed clipper, one that has the same cut as the mouthpiece, is necessary for successful work on reeds. The two cutting surfaces of the clipper should come exactly together—the cutting blade should not pass under the cutting edge but should strike it evenly so that clean cuts occur. Fine sandpaper or garnet paper can be used for sanding dry reeds; Dutch rush is used when the reed is wet. The end of the rush is used to remove specific spots, or it can be used lengthwise for broader areas.

Before working on the reed to correct apparent faults, it should be moved around on the mouthpiece and played in each position. For example, if the lower notes are heavy sounding, the reed may be moved lower on the mouthpiece, decreasing resistance. If this does not help, it may be moved slightly to one side of the lay. An extremely slight movement is all that is necessary. Shifting the center even minutely changes all of the dimensions of the reed. If moving it does not produce satisfactory results, then one can chop and scrape.

The two principal approaches to modifying a reed are sanding thick spots to a uniform thickness and clipping to alter the tip. To determine whether the reed is even or whether it has thick, heavy spots that need to be sanded, the reed may be flexed on the thumbnail. The following checklist includes reed problems that can be minimized or corrected by scraping.

1. If the sides of the reed are uneven, the player will blow harder because of the stiffer side, making the weaker side vibrate too fast and causing the reed to feel soft. Sand the stiffer side so that it matches the weaker side.

2. Low register: If the reed responds well except in the low register, remove some cane at the beginning of the cut. If the low notes are harsh with proper response, shave the entire reed.

3. High register: If high notes respond but are sluggish, thin the tip of the reed; If high notes fail to respond, work just below the point of resistance.

4. Staccato: If the staccato is poor, the reed is too heavy and should be sanded; if staccato is sluggish, there is a hard spot in the tip.

5. If the reed has a good forte but sounds tubby or otherwise poor when played *piano*, the tip or the left side is probably too thick.

6. If the reed blows hard, go over the entire reed; if it has a good sound but is a little too heavy, work on the lower edge, right side, to thin it down. If the reed gives a poor response, shift it slightly first to one side then the other to see if any improvement occurs; one side being stronger than the other may cause the poor response.

7. If the reed squeaks, one side is too resistant in the heart. Because this reed will have to be discarded if sanding cannot improve it, the player can feel free to work on the heart area to see if he can get rid of the squeak with some judicious sanding. Ordinarily the heart of the reed should be left alone, as faulty intonation will result if too much wood is taken off this area. If a reed causes faulty intonation, the heart is generally the cause and almost nothing can be done except to discard the reed. If the intonation fault is very minor, lightening the side of the reed may correct it.

8. If the reed is too stiff, sand on the sides near the tip. The tip plus the heart governs staccato, freedom, pitch, and squeaking.

The following defects can be improved or eliminated by clipping the tip of the reed, although clipping can add problems by changing the reed's proportions. In using the clipper, the reed should be damp and drawn down from the blade of the clipper. After clipping, the tip is often somewhat rough, but this can be smoothed down with garnet paper (Number 8–9) when the reed is dry.

1. The tone is thin and nasal.

2. The reed closes up on high notes, response is stuffy, or generally makes playing the high notes difficult.

3. High notes are flat. Clip the reed about .1 millimeter at a time, and scrape when it becomes necessary.

4. The reed plays too freely. Trim it down and then work it over with Dutch rush.

5. The reed is soft when playing forte passages, and too heavy or strong for pianissimo passages. Trim the tip or take some off at the lower left side.

6. The tone is buzzy. Trim the tip at each side slightly. However, buzzing usually indicates that the reed is very old or else split—throw it away.

Rotate reeds daily, keeping from four to six good reeds on hand and using a different one each day. Not only does this prolong the life of the reed but also it keeps the player's embouchure in better shape. When the same reed is used continually, the player tends to adjust his embouchure to it as it gradually alters, so that by the time he is forced to discard the reed his embouchure may be distinctly different than when the reed was new.

A few things can be done to rejuvenate an old reed. It can (1) be cleaned, (2) have a groove put in its back under the ligature screws and the ligature tightened somewhat more than normal, and (3) be placed in a hydrogen peroxide solution until the solution stops bubbling, then rinsed in cold water.

Emergencies

If the reed is squeaking during a concert, blowing some saliva into the mouthpiece between the rails and the reed and sucking it out just before the clarinet's entrance in the music will usually eliminate the danger of squeaks.

A partial solution to a soft reed is to keep the head up and the clarinet down—allowing more reed in the mouth and placing the lower jaw farther down on the mouthpiece than the upper teeth. With this change of embouchure, one can apply more pressure without closing the reed, as the lower jaw is positioned nearer the heart of the reed thus allowing the softer reed greater vibrancy and liveliness of sound.

The placement of the ligature can influence the stiffness of a reed; try raising the ligature if the reed is too stiff and lowering it if the reed is too soft.

WHAT TO PRACTICE

Practicing is the same for jazz or classical performers. If tonguing is practiced, it should be based on the concept that the tongue is used to stop the vibrations of the reed, the tongue "releasing" the reed to allow the air to vibrate it. One approach to fast, even tonguing is to tongue on the first beat of each 4/4 measure and to rest the tongue on the three succeeding beats without lessening the breath support. The player gradually tongues closer together—on every other beat, then every beat, and so on—as the tongue muscles develop. Any attempt to tongue short notes by using a "hard" tongue creates tension and reduces control. The tongue does not close off the reed during staccato tonguing; the airstream continues through the mouthpiece. The tongue's movement away from the reed produces the desired effect, not the tongue touching the reed.

A warm-up routine is valuable to get the air moving and the reed responsive. Long tones are essential for development of tone quality at various dynamic levels and in different registers. Students should start a note (alternating registers) as softly as possible, crescendo a specific number of beats and decrescendo an *equal* number of beats, and fade to air.

As new literature makes more demands on clarinet articulations (speed), most clarinetists must learn to double tongue. It is similar to the procedures described in "Principles for Brass" (Chapter 13), but on the clarinet, because the tongue works as a valve, the "tah" syllable is used as a valve on the reed, and the "kah" is used as a valve on the throat (or back of the mouth).

Students should start by repeating "tah–kah" over and over while riding the bus, watching television, and so on, then apply the tongue to the mouthpiece and barrel striving for evenness— starting slowly and gradually increasing tempo. Finally, add the instrument and play trumpet double—tongue exercises.

Slow octave slurs are useful as they develop endurance, greater air intake (striving to lengthen the notes over time), control of intonation, control of the extremes of dynamics, and improved tone quality. Warm-ups are not limited to long tones; arpeggios, technique exercises, rhythm patterns, and awkward fingering passages are all part of a systematic warm-up.

CARE AND MAINTENANCE OF THE CLARINET

All clarinets should be swabbed with a weighted cotton or linen swab after each use. Residual moisture will combine with dust and lint particles in the air to form a layer of sediment that gradually builds up in the bore, mouthpiece, and tone holes. This layer of dirt and sediment will make noticeable differences in the intonation of the affected notes and also a noticeable difference in the odor of the clarinet.

Swabbing should not be overdone—too much will wear down the bore of wooden instruments and round the edge of the tenons where the swab enters the instrument. A few times through with the swab is sufficient. Damage can also occur from dropping the metal weight of the swab into the clarinet, which after a while may chip the walls of the bore. Even tiny differences in the bore affect the instrument's response; chips in the mouthpiece are even more serious.

The mouthpiece, the most crucial part of the clarinet, should be treated with special care. The cotton or linen swab should be twisted and drawn through the mouthpiece (no weight). A chamois or the string on the swab should never be used to swab the mouthpiece, as the sharp edges will wear away with the continual application of the heavy material. Mouthpieces can be cleaned satisfactorily by running lukewarm water through them or by swabbing with a soft linen handkerchief. The mouthpiece will warp if left lying in the sun or close to a radiator. The reed should never be allowed to dry on the mouthpiece; it should be stored in a commercial holder that allows it to dry properly.

Because swabbing does not rid the tone hole of accumulated moisture, a piece of coffee filter can be kept in the case to blot the water from under the pads. The paper can also be used to clean pads by closing the pad gently on the paper and holding it for a few seconds.

Tone holes should be cleaned every month or so, using cotton ear swabs or a satisfactory substitute. Abrasive materials enlarge the tone hole, causing the pitch to rise.

The advisability of oiling the clarinet is debatable. A well-aged instrument adequately cured during the manufacturing process may never crack from lack of swabbing after use, but there are other reasons why the instrument should be oiled. Moisture from the player's breath penetrates the wood and will in time affect the resonating quality of the wood. Instruments dry out in heated homes during the winter. A clarinet should be oiled more often when new—perhaps as often as every two months, with a minute amount of olive oil or a commercial bore oil. Oiling is accomplished by placing a few drops of oil on the swab and running it through the barrel and through the upper and lower joints and bell. Gradually the oiling can be eliminated; twice a year is probably enough for a clarinet that has had good treatment. The chief disadvantage of oiling too often is that oil may get on pads and rot or harden them; oil may also add to the accumulation of dirt and lint on the key mechanism.

Some shrinkage can be expected to take place that may loosen posts and the rings on the ends of the joints. When the tenon rings become loose they should be tightened by inserting a small ring of cloth or paper under the ring to prevent the instrument from expanding and cracking. One should not be fooled if the bell or other ring has been crimped on and cannot be rotated—this offers no protection if it can be determined that it no longer fits.

Moving parts of the keys should be oiled very lightly every three to six months, depending on the use the instrument gets. If the climate is humid, a small amount of oil should occasionally be applied to the steel springs to prevent rusting. Springs become worn with time. They can be temporarily rejuvenated by carefully bending them. The cork tenons should be sparingly greased.

Post screws should be loosened and retightened once a year to prevent jamming, so when a pad needs to be replaced, the screw can be unscrewed instead of drilled out.

Equipment in the clarinet case should include (1) a camphor stick to help control humidity and prevent tarnishing of the keys, (2) cork grease, (3) a small screwdriver, (4) extra reeds, (5) a swab, (6) a pencil, and (7) possibly a lyre. In addition, a handkerchief in the case, spread over the clarinet, will protect the case lining from discoloration due to tarnishing keys and add a layer of insulation for the instrument. An outside covering for the case of any wooden instrument helps preserve the expensive case and offers protection against the effects of extreme temperature changes. When clarinets are brought in out of the cold they should be allowed to warm in the case before they come into contact with the even warmer human breath. A good rule would be never to take a quality wooden instrument outside unless it is in a case.

A check on the condition of the clarinet is to play the chromatic scale through the entire range of the instrument, listening carefully for fuzzy notes caused by swollen pads or keys that have become bent and are opening too far or not far enough. A light or a feeler should be used on each key. An important caveat for clarinetists is that not everyone should feel compelled to be an instrument repairperson.

TROUBLESHOOTING

Equipment

Sticky pads

1. Moisture absorbed by pads. (If pad is not damaged place thin paper between pad and tone hole, press key and gently pull paper out; repeat several times pulling paper out in different directions. Last resort—apply a slight amount of talcum powder to absorb the moisture being careful to keep it off mechanism.
2. Bent rods. (Have repaired by competent repairperson.)
3. Worn springs. (Have replaced by competent repairperson.)
4. Pivot screws at end of rods may need oiling (one drop); occasionally they must be loosened and oiled, then retightened.

Pads not seating

1. Leaking pads. (If pads are in good shape, heat back of key with match to melt "glue" and hold pad down firmly to correctly reseat—use soft rag over hot key; readjustment of the mechanism may be necessary to align keys; bent rods to be repaired by competent repairperson.)
2. Worn springs. (Have repaired by repairperson.)
3. Brittle, hardened or torn pads. (Have replaced.)

Gurgling sound

1. Water collected in tone hole(s) under pads that normally remain closed. (Open appropriate pad, blow water into bore; clean with a pipe cleaner.) This can usually be avoided by frequent, preventive swabbing.
2. Consistent water in one tone hole may indicate a path to that key; careful oiling or thorough swabbing may change the path.

Tone

Squeaks

1. Reed crooked on mouthpiece. (Realign reed.)
2. Too much mouthpiece in mouth. (Correct embouchure.)
3. Tone holes not covered. (Correct finger positions.)
4. Bent bridge key preventing pads on lower joint from closing. (Have repaired by competent repairperson.)
5. Leaky pads. (Replace or have replaced.)
6. Bad reed. (Try another reed.)
7. Inadvertently pressing side key with hand. (Correct holding position.)
8. Mouthpiece problems:
   a. A facing (or lay) which is too short
   b. An uneven facing
   c. A facing which is too open
   d. An irregular, thin tip rail

Small, pinched sound

1. Biting on reed. (Firm lips around mouthpiece while trying to drop jaw as if playing flat.)

2. Not enough reed in mouth. (Experiment to find the best and most appropriate sound.)

3. Throat/oral cavity too tight. (Hold shoulders down; keep tongue down inside mouth)

4. Reed too soft.(Try a harder reed, or clip tip of reed.)

Squawky, loud sound

1. Not enough lower lip over teeth. (Correct embouchure.)

2. Lips around mouthpiece not firm enough, especially corners. (Correct embouchure.)

3. Bad reed. (Usually too soft, or poorly made.)

4. Mouthpiece is too open at tip. (Try a different mouthpiece.)

5. Too much breath—overblowing. (Correct breathing.)

Hard, strident sound

1. Reed too hard. (Try softer reed or scrape reed.)

2. Lay is too open and/or too long on mouthpiece. (Try another mouthpiece.)

Control

Of soft

1. Not projecting a smooth, steady airstream into the instrument. (Check and correct breathing.)

2. Reed too soft. (Try harder reed or clip reed.)

3. Mouthpiece too open at tip. (Try different mouthpiece.)

4. Poorly shaped or too tight embouchure. (Work on all aspects of the embouchure.)

5. Cheeks puffing. (Firm up corners of mouth to flatten chin and keep cheeks flat.)

6. Upper teeth not on mouthpiece. (Correct embouchure.)

7. On "throat tones." (Try adding right hand keys to notes.)

Of loud

1. Underdeveloped embouchure—usually too loose or flabby. (Do not demand too much too soon; allow development; encourage and provide material for embouchure development.)

2. Overblowing. (Do not try to force too much air into instrument.)

3. Angle of mouthpiece too high or head too low. (Hold head erect; keep instrument no more than 45 degrees from body.)

4. Too much mouthpiece in mouth. (Correct embouchure.)

Pitch

Sharp

1. Embouchure too tight or biting on reed. (Correct embouchure.)

2. Reed too hard. (Try softer reed or scrape reed.)

3. Barrel too short. (Try longer barrel.)

4. Embouchure not relaxed enough for softer passages.

5. Clarinet held too low. (Correct holding position.)

6. Individual notes:

   a. Keys too open. (Have instrument readjusted.)

   b. Dirty tone holes. (Clean with pipe cleaner or needle.)

   c. Worn corks that determine the opening of keys. (Replace or have replaced.)

Flat

1. Reed too soft. (Try harder reed.)

2. Clarinet too high or head down. (With head held erect, clarinet should be about 30 degrees from body.)

3. Not enough mouthpiece in mouth. (Correct embouchure.)

4. Not enough air. (Correct breathing—both inhaling and exhaling.)

5. Embouchure not tightening for loud sections. (Correct embouchure—lips, especially corners, firm up for loud.)

6. Barrel too long. (Try shorter barrel.)

7. Individual notes.

   a. Keys not opening enough. (Have clarinet adjusted.)

   b. Barrel pulled out too far. (Push in barrel, pull at middle and bell.)

   c. Dirty tone holes. (Clean with pipe cleaner.)

8. Insufficient practice.

BIBLIOGRAPHY

Texts

* Indicates out of print in 2001.

ANDERSON, J. E. (1996). *Concepts for the Clarinet Teacher: The Study of the Clarinet as a Secondary Instrument for College Music Education Students,* 3rd ed. Minneapolis, MN: Jeanné.

GOLD, CECIL V. (1997). *Clarinet Performing Practices and Teaching in the United States and Canada* rev. ed. Akron, OH: University of Akron Press.

HEIM, N. D. (1993). *Ornamentation for the Clarinetist.* Hyattsville, MD: Norcat Music Press.

*KROLL, OSKAR (1968). *The Clarinet* Trans. by A. BAINES. New York: Taplinger.

LAWSON, COLIN (ed.) (1996). *The Cambridge Companion to the Clarinet.* London: Cambridge University Press.

PINO, DAVID (1998). *The Clarinet and Clarinet Playing.* New York: Dover Publications; reprint of (1980) New York: Scribner's.

PLATAMONE, VITO (1998). *Clarinet and Saxophone Reed Adjustments,* 2nd ed. Prescott, AZ: Author.

REHFELDT, PHILLIP (1990). *Study Materials for Clarinet,* 3rd ed. Mentone, CA: Mill Creek Music Publications (P.O. Box 556, Mentone, CA 92359).

———— (1977). *New Directions for Clarinet,* rev. ed. Berkeley, CA: University of California Press.

*RENDALL, F. GEOFFREY (1954). *The Clarinet: Some Notes Upon Its History and Construction,* 2nd rev. ed. New York: Philosophical Library.

RICHMOND, STANLEY (1972). *Clarinet and Saxophone Experience.* New York: St. Martin's.

SMITH, BILL (1993). *The Jazz Clarinet.* Seattle, WA: Parkside Publications.

SPRATT, JACK (1981). *How to Make Your Own Clarinet Reeds,* 2nd ed. Old Greenwich, CT: Jack Spratt Woodwind Shop.

STEIN, KEITH (1958). *The Art of Clarinet Playing.* Evanston, IL: Summy-Birchard.

*STIER, C. (1991). *Clarinet Reeds: Definitive Instruction in an Elusive Art.* Olney MD: Halcyon Productions.

*STUBBINS, WILLIAM. H. (1974). *The Art of Clarinetistry: The Acoustical Mechanics of the Clarinet as a Basis for the Art of Music Performance,* 3rd ed. Ann Arbor, MI: Guillaume Press.

*———— (1976). *The Study of the Clarinet: For Soprano, Alto or Bass Clarinet,* 5th ed. Ann Arbor, MI: George Wahr.

*———— (1991). *The Study of the Clarinet: An Introduction to the Problems of Clarinet Playing.* Troy, MI: Piansano Press.

THURSTON, FREDERICK (1985). *Clarinet Technique,* 4th ed. New York: Oxford University Press.

*TOSE, GABRIEL (1962). *Artistic Clarinet: Technique and Study.* Hollywood, CA: Highland Music Company.

*VAGNER, ROBERT (1966). *Single Reed Guide for the Clarinet and Saxophone Player.* Corvallis, OR: Oregon State University Book Stores.

*WESTON, PAMELA (1976). *The Clarinet Teacher's Companion.* London: Robert Hale.

Journals/Associations

The Clarinet. Quarterly from the International Clarinet Association. P.O. Box 7683, Shawnee Mission, KS 66207-0683.

Clarinet and Saxophone Association of Great Britain. 167 Ellerton Road, Surbiton; Surrey KT6 7UB England.

Clarinet Studies

Easy—Beginning (elementary or middle school)

Albert/Pares/Hovey. *Daily Exercises for Clarinet* (Belwin-Mills).

Buck. *Elementary Method for Clarinet* (Kjos).

Cailliet. *Elementary Clarinet Method* (Leblanc).

Hovey. *Elementary Method for Clarinet* (2 vol.) (Rubank).

———— *First Book of Practical Studies* (Belwin-Mills).

Klose. *Celebrated Method for Clarinet* (Book I) (C. Fischer)

Lester. *The Developing Clarinetist* (Belwin-Mills).

————. *Melodious Studies for Clarinet* (Henri Elkan).

Liegel. *Basic Method for Clarinet* (C. Fischer).

Opperman. *Clarinet* Vol. I (Pro-Art Music).

Perier. *La Debutante Clarinetistte* (A. Leduc).

Stubbins. *The Study of the Clarinet* (George Waln).

Waln. *Waln Elementary Clarinet Method* (Belwin-Mills).

Medium (middle school or high school)

Albert. *24 Varied Scales and Exercises* (C. Fischer).

Baermann. (ed. Langenus). *Complete Method for Clarinet* (2 vols.) (C. Fischer).

————. *Daily Studies* (Boosey & Hawkes).

Delecluse. *12 Easy Etudes* (A. Leduc).

Gambaro. *21 Caprices* (Billaudot).

Gee. *Style Etudes and Technical Exercises* (Southern Music).

Hite. *Melodious and Progressive Studies* (2 vols.) (Southern Music).

Hovey. *Second Book of Practical Studies* (Belwin-Mills).

Jean-Jean. *Etudes Progressive and Melodiques* (A. Leduc).

————. *16 Modern Etudes* (A. Leduc).

————. *25 Etudes Technique and Melodiques* (A. Leduc).

Klose. *Klose Method for Clarinet* (complete or in 2 parts) (C. Fischer).

Lester. *The Progressing Clarinetist* (C. Fischer).

Opperman. *Modern Daily Studies* (M. Baron).

Perron. *Daily Exercises* (Billaudot).

Stark. (ed. Barbarino). *24 Studies in All Tonalities* (Cundy-Bettoney).

Stubbins. *22 Etudes for Clarinet* (George Waln).

Advanced (high school or college)

Baermann-Langenus. *Complete Method for Clarinet* (3 vols.) (C. Fischer).

Bitsch. *Douze Etudes de Rhythm* (A. Leduc).

Bozza. *14 Etudes* (A. Leduc).

Cavallini. *30 Caprices* (A. Leduc).

Delecluse. *14 Grand Etudes* (A. Leduc).

Faulx. *20 Virtuoso Studies After Bach* (Henri Elkan).

Gabucci. *Dix Etudes Modernes* (A. Leduc).

————. *26 Cadences en Forme de Prelude* (A. Leduc).

Kroepsch. (ed. Bellison). *Progressive Daily Studies (Books III–IV)* (C. Fischer).

Langenus. *Complete Method for the Boehm Clarinet* (3 vols.) (C. Fischer).

Lazarus. *Method for Clarinet* (3 vols.) (C. Fischer).

Rose. *40 Studies for Clarinet* (Books I and II) (C. Fischer).

————. *32 Studies for Clarinet* (C. Fischer).

Perier. *20 Etudes de Virtuosite* (A. Leduc).

———. *21 Etudes Modernes* (A. Leduc).

———. *24 Grand Virtuoso Studies* (Cundy-Bettoney).

———. *331 Exercises Journaliers de Mecanisme* (A. Leduc).

Polatschek. *Advanced Studies* (G. Schirmer).

Instructional Videos

Belwin 21st Century Band Method. Clarinet, Level 1 (Jack Bullock & Anthony Maiello, 1996), Miami: Warner Brothers Music Publishers.

Clarinet in a Masterclass (David Shifrin, 1987). Clarksville, TN: Austin Peay State University.

Clarinet with Ron Reynolds for Beginners (Ron Reynolds, 1995), Van Nuys, CA: Backstage Pass Productions.

Getting Started with the Clarinet (James Schoepflin, 1996), Spokane, WA: Getting Started Productions.

Improving Your Clarinet Section Through the Use of Clarinet Quartets (Dennis Strawley, David Jones, Jim Hefferman: B♭ soprano; Jean Gould: B♭ bass, 1997), Ft. Mead, MD: U.S. Army Field Band.

The Master Speaks: Clarinet and Saxophone Principles Techniques That Work (Joe Allard. 1987), Seattle, WA: American Motion Pictures.

Ultimate Beginner Series—Clarinet, Vol. 1 & 2 (Malena Calle, 1998), Miami: Warner Brothers Music Publishers.

Recommended Classical Clarinet Artists

Jack Brymer playing Mozart and Weber
Richard Stolzman playing Fischer and Poulenc
Naomi Drucker playing Babbitt and Kuferman
Eduard Brunner playing Copland and Milhaud

Recommended Jazz Clarinet Artists

New Orleans Dixieland: Sidney Bechet and Johnny Dodds
Chicago Dixieland: Frankie Teschemacher
Swing: Benny Goodman, Woody Herman and Artie Shaw
New Orleans Revival: Pete Fountain
Bop, Cool: Tony Scott
Jazz Virtuoso Innovators: Buddy DeFranco and Eddie Daniels
Avant-Garde: Anthony Braxton and Don Byron

CLARINET
Fingering Chart

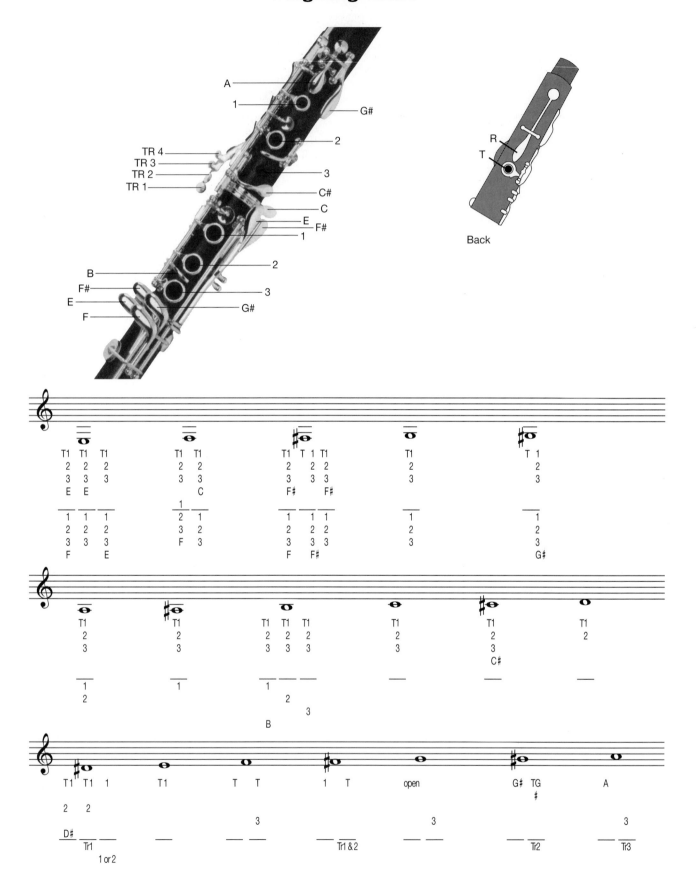

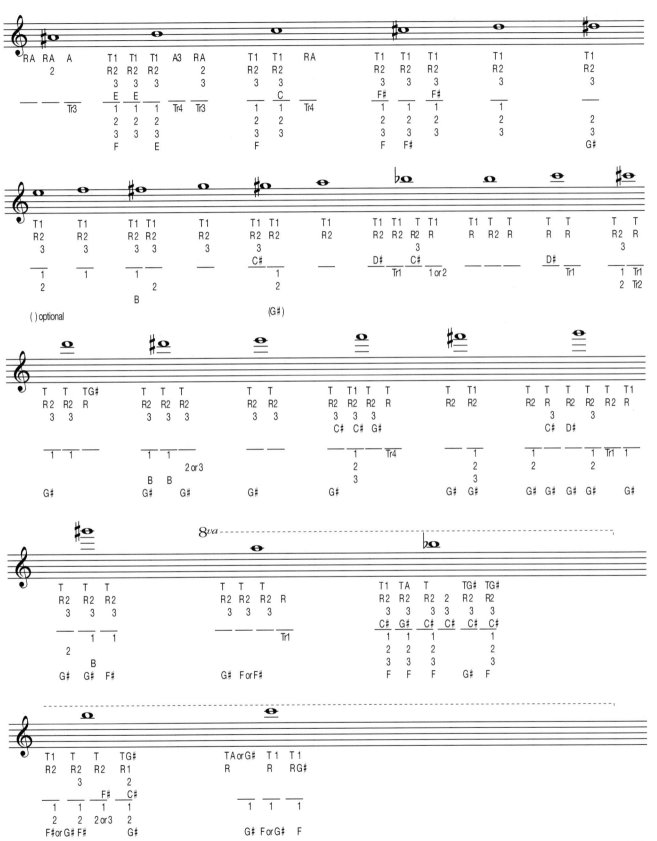

11

BASSOON

HISTORY

The origin of this strange and wonderful instrument is unknown, but it can be traced back to the "phagotus" which Afranio of Ferrara built in the early sixteenth century. Its name is derived from its resemblance to a bundle of sticks. Another early form of the bassoon was the "curtal," or short wood, which was about 40 inches long. The curtal, also dating from the sixteenth century, had a reed similar to that used today; its primary function was as an accompanying instrument, used in the church as the bass with cornetts and trombones. The French bassoon with its characteristic mellow sound grew out of this instrument sometime after 1675. Also appearing in the sixteenth century was a "dolcian," made from a single block of wood.

The bassoon was a favorite of the composers of the late baroque and the classical eras; Bach, Handel, Haydn, and Mozart all used its wide musical resources to good effect. However, the bassoon had gross instability of pitch and could be played in tune only by the most skillful players; it did not become widely used until after 1825 when Carl Almenrader made improvements on it. His innovations improved the pitch but in the process destroyed the bassoon's characteristic tone quality. J. A. Heckel in turn improved the bore of the Almenrader instrument until its tone quality was acceptable. The Heckel bassoons appeared in the early part of the nineteenth century. They became common after 1879. The Heckel family still makes bassoons that are considered the finest available. The Heckel system, also called the German system, has become widespread. French system bassoons are easily distinguished from the German type as they have fewer keys, especially on the boot joint; they are seldom found in the United States.

Many attempts have been made to refine the bassoon further, but all have resulted in a destruction of the tone quality, so musicians are forced to adapt themselves to its frailties. With all of its failings, the bassoon is one of the most delightful and beloved instruments, capable of every response from broad farce to genuine pathos.

SELECTING A BASSOON

Because the bassoon is handmade, there will be only general consistency between instruments of the same company, and each bassoon should be checked by both the eye and the ear. A list of things to look for helps in making a wise selection. Good bassoons are usually made of hard maple. A quality instrument is indicated by straight-grained wood, carefully made tone hole edges, and tenons that fit snugly. With a secondhand instrument, the wood should be checked for dryness; the clues to watch for are joints that no longer fit, loose keys and key posts, and cracks. A crack may not be important at the time the instrument is purchased, but it invariably gets bigger. Some cracks are easily repaired on the bassoon, others difficult or impossible. If an instrument with a crack seems acceptable in other respects, a competent repairperson should be consulted before the instrument is purchased. The lacquer and the stain on the wood are matters of personal taste and of minimum importance. Above all, the instrument must be played for tone quality, clarity, and intonation. If the intonation is poor, beware.

The purchaser has some option as to the number of keys on the instrument. The full Heckel system is usually considered to be 22 keys plus the F♯ trill key on the wing joint. The addition of one more key, the high D octave key, is very desirable, for without it several upper pitches are more difficult. A lock is advisable between the long and the wing joint to insure a minimum of damage in assembly. Post locks are standard on most instruments. To prevent clothing catching on the B♭ and F♯ keys, bassoons should have a protective plate covering these keys.

As with all good instruments, the bassoon should offer some resistance to the player, though not to the point where it becomes stuffy.

ASSEMBLY OF THE BASSOON

Proper assembling is one of the principal aspects of caring for the bassoon. Because the instrument is at the same time big and fragile, its assembly is both awkward and delicate. If the instrument survives the eager student's initial experiments, the teacher must make sure that correct assembly is one of the first things he learns.

If the bassoon has a locking mechanism between the long and wing joints, these two sections should be assembled first, locked and fitted into the boot joint. Inserting the long and wing joints into the boot, at the same time helps insure that they are not at an angle, which could damage the tenons. The two joints assembled together are heavy, and the disadvantage is that they may be dropped. If the instrument is not equipped with a lock, one should not try to put the two sections into the boot joint together. There are too many delicate keys and fittings that can be injured if either part slips from place. The bell is placed on the top of the long joint before it is inserted. Either the wing or long joint may be placed into the boot first and the other fitted carefully next to it with a pushing motion and a slight turning without wiggling. A small amount of cork grease on the tenons is recommended for corked tenons, vaseline for wrapped string. The joints fit tightly and are rarely pulled for tuning purposes. The last part of the instrument to be put into place is a fragile metal tube, or the bocal, often called the mouthpipe or crook, which is inserted into the upper end of the wing. The bocal should not be grasped on the curve or on the reed end, but coaxed into place gently by grasping the cork end. If forced, the metal may split. Although this can be repaired, tone is adversely affected. The bocal is usually not pulled for tuning. The tiny hole which the whisper key covers is on the bocal, and must fit under the key which extends up from the wing joint. Correct playing posture is made even more important by the whisper key. The player must sit so that he plays comfortably without moving the bocal to either side. Moving it will result in improper closing of the whisper key.

The bassoon may be held in two different ways.

1. The most widely used among student bassoonists is to hold it by the neck strap which hooks onto the instrument and can be adjusted for comfort. Often used with the neck strap is a crutch or widget which screws into the instrument near the top of the boot joint. This is a wing-shaped piece of wood which rests in the crotch of the thumb and forefinger of the right hand. It impairs right-hand flexibility somewhat and is not practical for bassoonists with short fingers. Without it, however, the instrument becomes less steady on the open or near-open tones when few fingers are down to help support it.

2. The seat strap is used by most professionals. It eliminates the need for the widget, offers maximum flexibility, and holds the bassoon firmly. The seat strap either hooks on to the end of the boot joint or is made in the form of a cup in which the bassoon sits. The other end of the strap is held securely at the right length by sitting on it, bringing the lower end of the instrument close to the body. The seat strap has the advantages of taking all the weight off the neck and freeing the right hand from supporting the instrument so that more rapid right-hand technique is possible.

POSITION FOR HOLDING

The bassoon is held in front of the player at an angle that allows the instrument to bisect the body of the player from lower right to upper left (see Figure 11–1). It will nearly rest on the right thigh and pass directly in front of the player's face, with the left-hand position almost directly in front of the player. One of the most common mistakes is to lean the bassoon out too far, forcing the wrists—the right wrist in particular—into an unnatural position.

The bassoon player seems irresistibly drawn to tip the bassoon down to where the bell touches the top of the music stand, to cross his left leg over his right knee,

and to hunch over his instrument. The player should sit on the edge of his chair with both feet on the floor. His posture should be erect and his head only slightly tilted to the left, if at all. His arms should not touch his body. His upper torso should be pulled up out of his hips so that his chest is lifted naturally and there is no cramping of the diaphragm. The bassoon should be brought to the player, not the player to the bassoon. Correct playing posture is essential to manipulating the whisper key. The player must sit so that he plays comfortably without moving the bocal to either side. Moving it will result in improper closing of the whisper key.

Figure 11–1
Bassoon: Position for Playing

Figure 11–2
Right-Hand

Figure 11–3
Left-Hand

Figure 11–4
Right Thumb

Figure 11–5
Left Thumb

Hand Positions for the Bassoon

As with all of the instruments, the fingers should be slightly curved with the balls of the fingers covering the keys and holes (Figures 11–2 and 11–3). With either neck or seat strap support, much of the balance of the bassoon is necessarily borne by the left hand. The weight then falls on the base of the fingers rather than on the fingertips. The right thumb rests over the pancake key, the right little finger over the low F key (Figure 11–4). The left thumb rests lightly on the whisper or adjacent key and the left little finger over the low C♯/D keys. The fingers remain over the holes at all times.

The bassoon should always be played sitting down. Standing only complicates embouchure problems and usually puts an unnecessary strain on the bocal as well as on the player. It is inconceivable that this instrument would be needed for marching (which only ruins player, reed, and instrument). It is done, however, and not infrequently. If the bassoonist wants to march, let him play the triangle.

EMBOUCHURE

In forming the bassoon embouchure, the player draws his lips over both his upper and lower teeth to form an ample cushion for the reed. The more lip cushion he provides, the more easily he can achieve a full, dark sound. His teeth are apart to avoid biting. His lips support the reed. Only rarely would a student have such long teeth as to affect the embouchure. A small school of bassoon players believes there is no need for the player's lips to be drawn over his teeth. These players develop their lip muscles to such an extent that their lips support the reed without assistance from an understructure of teeth. They are able to demonstrate this successfully. However, this embouchure is difficult to achieve and tires more rapidly. Figure 11–6 illustrates the teeth and lips from the first and more common school of thought.

The player should exert all the pressure toward the center of his lips (see Figure 11–7 on page 166). Playing is controlled where the lips touch the reed. The lips are primarily in front of the teeth, rolling over them only enough to gain support. Because the pressure is directed to the center of the lips, maximum pressure is against the edges rather than the flat sides of the reed, thus preventing the reed from closing. The jaw muscles should be relaxed. The use of the jaw in bassoon playing constricts the throat and causes

Figure 11–6
Bassoon Embouchure:
Teeth and Lips

Figure 11–7
Bassoon Embouchure

biting or pinching. The lower jaw should recede slightly behind the upper, with the reed anchored against the lower lip. The lower lip should be firm and straight with the reed centered on it. About one-quarter inch of the lower side of the reed goes into the mouth. The student should experiment with the exact placement of the reed, in and out, and with the relative positions of the upper and lower lip. A slight change can make a big improvement. This experimentation should continue for at least the first six months of playing. There is a danger that the student will produce an acceptable tone and be satisfied with it when with more searching he could find an embouchure that would give him a really fine tone.

With the player's lower jaw behind the upper, his top lip is set on the reed almost to the wire so that much more of the upper lip covers the reed than the lower. A very common embouchure fault with bassoon players is not putting sufficient reed into the mouth and not placing enough of the upper lip on the reed. The characteristic bassoon tone is due to the fact that the top half of the reed vibrates more than the lower. The embouchure must be formed so that this happens. Too little lip on the reed, almost invariably meaning too little upper lip, results in a nasal sound; too much lip, usually too much lower lip, produces a pinched, dark sound.

The teacher will rarely be confronted with a student who is unable to make a sound unless he is trying too hard, biting on the reed, and keeping it from vibrating. The problem is rather getting the right sound. Although whistling produces a pucker, it is not a good illustration of bassoon embouchure; the lips protrude too much and do not have the support of the teeth. Pronouncing the word "oh" is sometimes used, but this pulls the lips from the teeth. Some fine texts recommend finding the buzz point of the reed and straddling this for the correct embouchure. This can be successful with the teacher who is himself a performing bassoonist but has some hazards for others: (1) Poor reeds do not buzz or crow; (2) students who do not know what a buzz or crow sound is may get their reeds too far into the mouth, produce a weird sound, and declare that the reed has crowed; (3) the beginning student whose embouchure is undeveloped is inclined to pinch the reed and may have difficulty making the reed crow.

A player transferring to the bassoon from the flute or saxophone has fewer challenges to overcome than one who transfers from the clarinet. The clarinetist has learned to pull his chin tightly and produce too much of a smiling embouchure. A smile will make the bassoon tone windy, hard, and nasal because there is not enough cushion and not enough control in the lips. The chin has to be sufficiently relaxed to assure full support from the diaphragm. However, the idea of a relaxed embouchure can lead to the opposite fault, a loose chin that allows small pockets of air. With the bassoon, the lower lip is the anchoring point for the reed and the only place where a constant embouchure is maintained. Thus the chin has to be relaxed enough to let the sound come from the diaphragm but firm enough so that the chin muscles do not move during tonguing, breathing, or rapid leaps in pitch. If the chin moves, the lip is apt to be forced off its lower teeth support. The player needs to discover the combination of muscles that will give him a firm chin but not a stiff one, and ample support for the reed without biting or tensing the throat muscles.

The bassoon embouchure resembles the oboe embouchure in that it changes with the various registers. In the low register less lip is required. As the pitches ascend the lip must roll more, taking the reed with it. A similar requirement exists for dynamics: for extremely soft playing there may be less lip and less reed in the mouth; increasing volume demands that more lip be rolled in. The embouchure is not so relaxed and uncontrolled that it cannot move in and out continually. The movements should be very slight and are accomplished by applying a little more or a little less pressure. The player develops lip flexibility for adjusting quickly to large skips or sudden dynamic changes. Flexibility and control are synonymous in this respect, because without the first the second is impossible.

The bocal must have a slight downward slant if the reed is to enter the mouth correctly. Players who tilt the instrument forward are forced to lean over it in order to get any semblance of good embouchure, thus cramping the breathing apparatus and hindering good tone.

Although nothing helps develop an embouchure like playing and practicing, the bassoonist may not be aware when he is overworking his lips and may continue to play by expending a great deal of effort and using his lips in ways which destroy rather than build a good embouchure.

INTONATION

The bassoon is a very imperfect instrument with many intonation problems. It has 23 keys plus 5 holes that must be placed on a bore 8 feet in length. It is made from material that changes with the climate. The doubling back of the bore, the slanting holes, and the rods which run completely through the instrument all require an exactness of construction difficult to achieve. Tuning may be improved by moving the bocal in or out, but it can be moved only a very short distance without upsetting the relationship of the whisper key to its hole on the bocal. The whisper key is very important to the bassoonist's intonation for most pitches within the staff and for the clarity, response, and resonance of other notes.

Bocals affect the sound and feel of the bassoon. Five bocals of different sizes are manufactured to help the bassoonist adjust to ensemble pitch. They are numbered according to size: the Number 0 is for pitches higher than A=440, the number 1 is for standard pitch; 2, 3, and 4 are for flatter pitches. School instruments often have only one bocal, depending upon which of the two originally with the instrument has become broken or lost.

The bassoon is the least mechanically flexible of the orchestra or band instruments to tune. In theory, the band or orchestra should tune to the bassoon. The bassoon has flexibility in lipping, but it is not wise to use this method when mechanical means are available on other instruments.

It may be argued that the reed itself makes so much difference in the intonation that any quibble about the bocal becomes unnecessary. The reed is a large factor in bassoon pitch, but each factor must be recognized, and all utilized to make intonation as good as possible—the instrument, the bocal, the reed, and the player. Improving any one of these will improve pitch but will not make up for deficiencies in the others. The section on reeds offers some details, but the general rules are these: A stiff reed raises the pitch; a soft reed flattens it. Reeds that are old and water soaked are flat. The reed problem is compounded because the fit of the reed on the bocal is rather inexact. Bassoon reeds are not made on a staple like the oboe reed, but depend on the skill of the reed maker. There are variations in the size of the butt opening, which naturally affect the pitch.

Each bassoon has its own intonation problems and these display less uniformity than those of other instruments. More of the out-of-tune pitches tend to be sharp rather than flat (see Figure 11–8 on page 168).

very sharp   sharp   most are sharp   flat   sharp

Figure 11–8   Bassoon Intonation Tendencies

The teacher may suggest the student lower his pitch by

1. Adding a tuning ring
2. Half holing
3. Changing lip and breath pressure
4. Adjusting the bocal
5. Adding the right little finger
6. Adding the left-hand C♯ key
7. Adding the E♭ key
8. Opening the reed

The player should try these and others to determine which is most effective for his instrument.

Most texts refer to "lipping" a note in tune. Lipping means doing one of several things: receding the lower jaw, lessening the tension in the center of the lips, changing the direction of the air, loosening the firmness of the embouchure, reducing the speed of the air and the amount of breath support, and putting more reed into the mouth. All make the tone flatter. The opposite action will "lip up" the pitch. A tight throat and a pinched or bunched-up chin make the pitch sharper; to lower the pitch the player should maintain his breath support, drop his lower jaw, and play with an open, relaxed throat. A reed that is too soft or a key too closed tends to flatten. On the bassoon, alternate fingerings and trick fingerings are usually more successful than lipping the pitch in tune because changing the embouchure or airstream can affect the tone quality as much as, or more than it can change the pitch. For example, a low C♯ is usually played much better in tune with the low D key added by the left thumb, the third-space E is improved with the low C key in the right hand, and the written E♭ (half step down) is helped by pressing the low C♯ key and using the left little finger on low D. In addition, a different fingering may improve not only intonation but also tone quality.

Bassoons are so individual in character that each one could have its own fingering chart, worked out by a player who explored to see which fingerings are best for every note. Accomplished performers usually develop a set of fingerings for slow passages to produce the best pitch, quality, response, and resonance, then use the more standard fingerings for fast passages in which agility is decisive.

TONE AND EFFECTS

The bassoon has an established musical place today despite the same mechanical defects that have long since relegated the ophicleide, saxhorn, and serpent to the museum. Its popularity is due to its unique color possibilities. In the hands of an expert the bassoon can sound as mellow as a cello or as piercing as a trumpet. It can imitate with amazing fidelity the tone of a clarinet, baritone, or horn. It can be shrill, grotesque, pompous, and comical—in short, the clown of the orchestra—but it can be rich and powerful as well.

Good tone is not difficult to teach but it is difficult to talk about or explain in a text. This is truer with the bassoon than with the trumpet or flute whose good tone quality is commonly heard and can be easily imagined.

Good tone depends upon correct training and proper habits. Breath support and embouchure coupled with the reed and the instrument make the sound. If the reed and/or the instrument is average, good use of breath support and embouchure can produce a bassoon tone that is above average, even exceptional. Good exercises to strengthen embouchure and encourage breath control are sustained tones, slurs in one register, slurs across registers, slow scales that extend over more than one register, and intervals. The player should attempt to match each tone with the preceding one. He must remember, however, that the bassoon has three distinctly different registers. From low B♭ to second-space C is the bottom register, the next octave is the middle register, and the high register is the remainder of the range. Each register in the bassoon range has its own characteristic sound; if it does not, incorrect breathing is probable—tone is being controlled by the chest or throat and not by the diaphragm.

Not putting enough reed into the mouth, especially not covering the top of the reed with the upper lip, is usually the cause of an unpleasant or buzzing quality. If the lip position seems to be correct but the buzzing quality persists, the reed may be too soft at the tip or the player's lips may be too relaxed. To improve the reed, a very small amount of the tip may be cut off with a sharp knife or razor blade. If the tone quality is not improved, the student might pucker his lips around the reed more firmly, bringing more of the lower lip into contact with the reed. He should not cover more of the reed with his lower lip, but make his lower lip firmer.

Poor response and poor quality on the low notes may be due to a reed that has closed. It is easily opened by pressing in gently on the sides, or edges of the reed, though this is usually only a temporary remedy. If the reed is not closed, it may be dried out. It should be moistened well and frequently. If this does not help, the player may be pinching the reed. He should relax his embouchure, particularly his upper lip.

If the player produces a poor tone coupled with irregular response in the higher register, the problem may be with fingerings. He should check alternate fingerings and do some experimenting. His lower lip may be too relaxed, or the reed may be too soft. If only the tip is at fault, and the rest of the reed is not overly soft, cutting a bit off the tip can improve the reed and the player's tone quality.

Unsteady pitch on the middle E and F—usually flatness with accompanying bad tone quality—usually indicates that the reed is too soft. The tip may be cut off, one of the temporary cures tried, or the reed replaced.

Another common problem is a tone that cracks on the attack and often in the middle register. Cracking may indicate a faulty embouchure, too much pressure from the top and bottom, not enough from the sides. Students who transfer from other instruments in which the pressure is placed more up and down than into the center seem to have difficulty applying pressure to the sides of the reed. Cracking is also caused by a plugged hole under the whisper key. Finally, cracking may be due to a flaw in the instrument, and if so the instrument must be humored into a different response. Flicking one of several keys just as the note is attacked often mitigates cracking; it may help to flick the first hole of the left hand to allow a small amount of air in, flick the whisper key, or the D or A key just as the note is attacked. This requires some concentration until the player gets used to flicking one finger as he puts down other fingers for the desired pitch.

When the middle F♯ and G respond with poor tone quality or when they crack on the attack, other gradations of the half hole should be tried. The bassoon is temperamental and unpredictable; half holing with various fine shadings is one of the best ways to conquer the instrument's foibles.

The tones in the low register can be produced best by dropping the lower jaw and applying more pressure to the sides of the reed. The embouchure is not relaxed; the reed is given more freedom to vibrate. If the embouchure is relaxed, the pitch drops. For the upper register the embouchure is altered in the opposite direction: More pressure is applied from the top and the bottom, the lower lip and jaw are somewhat more firm, and the corners of the mouth exert less pressure.

As with other instruments, a change in the dynamic level must be accompanied by appropriate changes in the embouchure. Forte playing demands a relaxation of the embouchure so that the reed is more free to vibrate; pianissimo playing needs a more careful, restricted, cushioned embouchure. Soft playing should not be done by closing the throat; it is the embouchure that is more restricted and the throat remains open to support the tone.

Two important areas of learning are required of the bassoonist. First, he should begin reading the tenor clef as soon as possible. Adjusting to a second or third clef is not difficult even for a young pupil—young pianists learn to read two clefs simultaneously and think nothing of it. Second, he must have or develop a flexible thumb. The bassoonist needs to play eight or more keys with the left thumb, so he must adjust to this strange situation.

Finally, the instrument must be in good repair, and the bocal should not leak; the reed should be suited to the embouchure and in good condition. The student should check his posture and breath support, continually work for a better embouchure, and listen, listen, listen.

Vibrato

There are purists who insist that a really beautiful tone does not need vibrato to enhance its beauty and that vibrato is used only when it fits a style of music. However, most musicians seem to agree that no matter how fine a tone quality one produces, a good vibrato adds warmth and humanity. Because the human voice is the most expressive and personal of all musical instruments, other instruments imitate its qualities if not its timbre. Of the different ways to produce vibrato, both diaphragm and lip vibrato are acceptable on the bassoon. See the section on vibrato in Chapter 7.

TONGUING

Tonguing on the bassoon is somewhat different from the other reed instruments because the reed lies farther in the mouth, making it more difficult to tongue at the very tip of the reed. If the player uses the tip of his tongue on the tip of the reed, he will have to place his tongue high in the mouth for contact. This tends to tighten the throat and cut down on the resonance. Only the bottom half of the reed needs to be stopped in order to achieve a clean articulation. The tongue should touch the underside of the reed about one-quarter to one-eighth inch from the tip. When this is done naturally, the part of the tongue that touches the reed is not the tip but an area about a half inch from the tip on the top side of the tongue. The action of the tongue is more nearly up and down than forward and back. The player should find the easiest and most natural place for tongue and reed to come together. If his tongue is short, using the very tip of the tongue may facilitate articulation; if his tongue is long or thick, touching the reed at a spot farther back on the tongue may work more efficiently.

Double-tonguing is looked upon with skepticism by many reed players. However, William Spencer mentions a type of double-tonguing different from that ordinarily used. The technique consists of flipping the tongue rapidly up and down across the reed, producing one sound on the way up and another on the way down. This would be hard on both tongue and reed but could achieve great rapidity. There will be few passages, however, that the bassoonist cannot handle with well-developed single-tonguing.[1]

FINGERING

Many notes require awkward fingerings on the bassoon. Bassoonists and music educators joke about the dilemma encountered by the left thumb, which activates nine keys, sometimes as many as four at once (See Figure 11–9). Besides learning the basic fingering for each note, the young bassoonist must also learn how to move from one note to another smoothly and without tension, sliding the left thumb instead of letting it jump about. The position for holding the bassoon described earlier is essential to keep the hands relaxed. If the left wrist, for example, is forced into a tense, angled position, thumb dexterity is hampered.

**Figure 11–9
Left Thumb on Whisper Key
(flicker keys are top two
above the thumb)**

As with the flute, numerous notes can be played on the bassoon without pressing or lifting all of the keys. On the flute these fingerings affect pitch; on the bassoon these alternate fingerings affect not only pitch but also tone quality and control. For example, many notes that should be played with the whisper key pressed will sound without it, but lack control.

Unlike the oboe, intonation and tone quality can be greatly affected on the bassoon by half holing. The bassoon player needs to half hole certain notes, such as fourth line/space F♯, G, and G♯, which should be played with a half hole by the left first finger. These notes can be played with that finger completely lifted, but with poor intonation and a harsher tone quality. Players must learn to listen carefully and make adjustments with the embouchure, alternate fingers/keys, and the extent to which the first tone hole is opened.

While the bassoonist's thumb is extremely busy, the little fingers have fewer keys to operate than on the clarinet or oboe. The keys manipulated by the little fingers are used more in alternate fingerings. As the complexity of the music increases, the alternate fingerings should be taught and practiced. Teachers should always select the best fingerings for the young player until the student matures to the point where he can make those determinations himself. The fingering chart at the conclusion of this chapter indicates many bassoon fingerings: the first one for each note is the basic fingering, the rest are listed in approximate order of their use. Coordination of tongue and fingers is of great importance in good bassoon technique as with all the other winds. The bassoon reed takes slightly longer to begin to vibrate than do the other reeds. Although this delay is perhaps only 200 milliseconds, the delay is an aspect of technique with which the player must deal. A steady airstream with adequate breath support is essential.

[1]William Spencer (1958), *The Art of Bassoon Playing,* Evanston, IL: Summy-Birchard, p. 55.

REEDS

The first weeks of teaching the bassoon to a beginner are often the most pleasant, because he has not yet learned how much trouble the reed can be nor how it can enhance his prestige to be able to complain to the trombone player about his reed problems. The first sounds come easily from the bassoon, and the player is so busy holding the instrument and finding the right places for his fingers that he is bliss-fully unaware of the difficulties he will encounter. The wise teacher will not be too hasty in giving the beginner more awareness of reed problems than can be handled with understanding. The bassoon player who is given too much information about the reed too soon will spend all his time making and fixing reeds instead of prac-ticing. The student will never play better than his practicing has prepared him for, even though he has a reed worthy of a professional.

No reed lasts forever. When a player has a good reed, he must begin immedi-ately to work on or search for another. Like a good meal, a good reed gives tremen-dous satisfaction for a while, but will be consumed in time and need to be replaced. Public school students tend to believe a good reed is imperishable. As a reed is used it deteriorates, and the embouchure with it as the student tries to compensate for changes in the reed. Soon he has neither reed, embouchure, nor a concept of tone quality.

Although reeds are usually purchased, the student should learn to make them if only to learn to adjust them. Reeds should not be discarded, because they have a use: Students can learn from working on them, taking them apart and inspecting previous workmanship. The double reed is actually two reeds, held together with three pieces of wire and some string. To be satisfactory the cane will be golden in color rather than green, neither too soft nor too hard, and the fibers will run the full length of the reed. Cane which is only slightly green may improve if allowed to cure in the open air. Though most players look for a gold-en shade, various shades of yellow may be satisfactory, and so may be mottled, spotted cane. Coarse-grained cane does not produce satisfactory tone quality for most players, but it responds easily. Because of their easy response students often feel that these are the better reeds, but one with a harder response will produce a better tone. Because no sealing agent is used, the edges must fit all the way to the tip, and the tip opening should be oval or elliptical. The tone quality and response of the reed will be determined by the quality of the cane, the workman-ship and evenness of the reed, the shape of the tip opening, and the condition of the edges.

In selecting commercial reeds, several criteria besides the quality of the cane may be considered. Drawing the fingernail over the reed can show how hard the reed is. It should have a springy quality. If it is too hard, the fingernail will leave no mark; if it is too soft, the fingernail will leave an indentation. It is better to buy a reed that is too stiff than to buy one too soft, as the stiff reed can be altered with-out destroying its resistance. The sides should be of equal thickness for balance and taper without either thick or thin spots. The tips should be even. The corners should have even shading. One can insert a plaque into the reed to check this thickness and also to check the curve of the blades. Cracks and splits should be avoided, especially deep scoring marks on the butt, because they can extend onto the blade with the slightest pressure. If the throat of the reed is not completely formed, the reed will be unsatisfactory. Reeds that are alike in color, shape, thick-ness, and cut will not necessarily play alike. The workmanship varies and the cane even more so; reeds that look good and that have been selected with care may still prove to be unsatisfactory or beyond fixing. The experienced player becomes accustomed to this.

It is always difficult to criticize something that apparently works. The plastic reed works but is not recommended by professionals. It is, however, amazingly durable and difficult to crack, it can be worked and shaved like a cane reed, it is always ready to play without soaking, it has a consistent response regardless of the register, and it costs about twice as much as a regular reed while outliving a dozen. Transfers from clarinet like it because they can master it much more easily than a regular reed that demands a better bassoon embouchure. The plastic reed has serious drawbacks. The wide difference of tone colors possible in the various registers cannot be achieved with the plastic reed; in eliminating the undesirable variables the desirable ones have also been lost. Because the bassoon's great appeal lies in its tonal possibilities, the plastic reed detracts from rather than enhances the value of the instrument.

Bassoon reeds vary in size and shape to such an extent that it is often surprising to the novice that all can play in tune. There are two specific styles, the French and the German, and two general sizes, long and short. The French reed has less heart than the German reed. The French reed tip is about the same thickness at the edges as at the center, whereas the German is tapered from the center of the tip to the edges and comes to a point at each side where the two blades meet. This makes the French reed a thicker, heavier reed. Such characteristics make major differences in the tone quality. The French quality is lighter and more reedy, even nasal, whereas the German quality is darker and more mellow.

Spencer has an interesting picture showing the relative size and shape of 10 different bassoon reeds. They vary more than one-quarter inch in length and show different widths and bindings.[2]

They can all play in tune because they are cut with a lay that is in proportion to their length, a fact more essential to the pitch than the actual length of the reed. Tone quality differs more than pitch in different reeds. Beginners and even some advanced players will prefer the wide, thinner reed because it gives a rich, full sound, is easy to control, and is especially compatible to players who have transferred from the clarinet. A narrow, more resistant reed may be chosen by the professional or near-professional whose embouchure is highly developed and who wants to be able to control the upper register, the part of the range little used in school music but prevalent in symphonic literature. Longer reeds are usually preferred over the shorter ones.

Figure 11–10 designates the various parts of the reed. The lay is that part of the reed above the wire, thicker in the center, or heart, and tapering out to the edges and the tip. The shoulder is the small ridge where the lay ends and the tube begins. Three wires hold the two sides of the reed together. The throat is that part of the tube lying between the second wire and the shoulder.

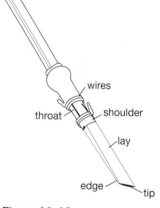

Figure 11–10
Bassoon Reed

Problems of Response

If the upper register is unresponsive, the reed may be either too stiff or too soft. For a low register which speaks slowly, the bottom third of the reed or the tip is too stiff and should be scraped.

If the tip is very thin, the reed may not respond readily in any part of the range; more should be taken off the edges, and the tip scraped. If the tip and edges are thin enough, cane in the area of the sides and around the heart should be removed. If cane has been removed at the sides of the reed and the response is still sluggish, one can take a little from the heart, but this must be done delicately and carefully as this area is best not tampered with. If too much is removed from the

[2]Ibid., p. 26.

heart, the reed will be thin and buzzy and impossible to improve. *The smallest change may be sufficient to improve or ruin the reed.*

Additional guidelines for adjusting reeds:

1. Reeds become stronger during the breaking-in period. Play only a few minutes a day for the first week or 10 days.
2. Make small adjustments and then try the reed; minute differences in scraping, sanding, and clipping can result in the change desired.
3. Do not scrape the reed until it has been well soaked.
4. Wires must always be tight. Tightening the wire takes care and practice; the wire is very fine and a single twist can break it. Wires that are too tight will choke the reed and prevent proper vibrating.
5. To improve quality, scrape below the tip.
6. To increase resistance, scrape the sides of the reed.
7. When scraping one blade of the reed, always support the other blade.
8. Sand only a dry reed; scrape a wet reed.
9. A reed with thin spots cannot be repaired.
10. A reed warped at the tip may right itself when soaked, but a wavy tip may indicate the tip has been scraped too thin.
11. If a reed produces a dull tone, thin the tip.

Pitch Problems

For general low pitch, the tip of the reed should be trimmed. For general sharp pitch, the lay or work on the bottom of the reed at the sides should be lengthened. Lengthening the lay will sometimes mean simply scraping the shoulder back a little, or it may be necessary to rework the entire reed. In selecting reeds or fixing them, C, D, E, and F in the staff are key notes for intonation. Flatness here indicates the reed is too soft, sharpness indicates too stiff.

Specific intonation problems include the following:

1. For sharp low notes, the back and sides of the reed are too heavy.
2. For sharp high notes, the reed is probably too closed and the top wire should be tightened.
3. For flat high notes, the reed is too open. Gentle pressure with the pliers on the first wire area of the butt can close the reed somewhat, but the reed must be well soaked and the pliers used carefully or the reed will be ruined. The reed should be squeezed on the flat sides; squeezing on the edges will serve to open it more.
4. For flat E and F in the staff, the tip of the reed is too long, the heart is too thin or the reed is old and soggy.
5. When fourth-space G and forked E♭ are very sharp, the reed is too heavy and needs general scraping. These notes are good notes on which to check intonation.

Wire adjustments control the size of the opening and change the quality of the tone. When the second wire is squeezed from the sides, a lighter sound results; tonguing will be easier but there will be less resistance and the reed will tend to close up on forte passages in the low register. If the second wire is squeezed on the top and bottom, the tone is somewhat heavier and the low register easier to obtain.

Squeezing the first wire produces the opposite effects. Squeezing the first wire on the top and bottom closes the reed, thins the tone, decreases the resistance, and improves the upper register. Because squeezing the wire usually loosens it, tightening the second wire before adjusting the first wire is recommended in order to keep from loosening the reed and destroying the fit at the edges. A test for proper adjustment of the opening is to tongue low F rapidly—the opening is not too small if low F is in tune and responds normally; play high F (F above middle C)—if this note is in tune and responds normally, the opening is not too large.

Tests for a good reed include the following

1. Put the reed well into the mouth and blow; the reed should crow. If the crow is too high and tight, the lay is too short, too thick, or both, and more scraping is necessary; if the crow is too deep the reed is too thin and the lay too long, the tip should be cut off and the reed reworked. If a reed does not crow, it may be leaking or the tip may be too far apart. Try tightening the wires and soaking.
2. Suck briefly on the reed, take it out of the mouth, put a finger over the butt opening, and wait a few moments. There should be a "pop" as it dries and the air pressure becomes equal. The reed that does not stay closed is too stiff or too open and needs more work; if the reed stays closed a long time, it indicates softness. The remedy is to cut off the tip and rework the reed.

Care of the Reed

Reeds should not be kept in the clear plastic containers. They are fairly airtight and do not allow a wet reed to dry as it should after each use. A Sucrets or Altoids box can be used for reed holders. The reed is cleaned with a small feather or even a pipe cleaner gently pushed through from the butt end of the reed. A completely clean reed does not play as well as one which has accumulated a little bit of scum inside, perhaps two or three days' worth. This saliva sediment acts as a cushion against excessive vibrating and helps produce a darker, clearer tone.

CARE AND MAINTENANCE OF THE BASSOON

Bassoons do not work well with bent or dirty bocals, loose reed wires, or accumulation of dust under the keys.

The bocal, small in diameter and fairly fragile, needs to be cleaned frequently and carefully. It should be carefully blown out after each playing and warm soapy water run through it occasionally, followed by thorough rinsing and swabbing.

The holes that are covered by the fingers accumulate grease and dirt from the hands and, because of the holding position of the bassoon, are susceptible to moisture from the inside of the instrument. This results in tiny layers of sediment around the edges of the holes that decrease the size of the hole and make the pitch sharper. They should be cleaned with a pipe cleaner, cotton swab, toothpick, or some similar tool. Wiping the wooden surface and the keys is a good idea, as it keeps the exterior clean and the finish intact.

Swabbing the entire bassoon is not a necessity, neither is oiling the bore. Most bassoons are made with partial rubber linings or specially treated interiors to protect the pertinent areas from moisture. Oil causes these materials to deteriorate. The nonlined portions—usually the larger part of the butt joint, the tenor, and the bell joints—may need an occasional slight oiling, but even a little too much oil aids in collecting dust and dirt. It is better not to oil at all than to use too much. Swabbing discourages the unpleasant smell that unswabbed horns inevitably acquire. The wing joint and the boot should be swabbed with a linen hand towel rather than a brush swab, as the latter leaves lint in the instrument. Springs and bearings, joints, posts, and rods need minute applications of oil about twice a year. Use a pin or an instrument screwdriver to apply the oil.

The bottom cap and tube of the boot joint should be cleaned occasionally with soap and water. The cap and the tube should be removed from the joint, then washed, rinsed, and dried before replacing. The gasket should not leak when reassembled, as a leak may affect tone quality and intonation of several pitches.

General care includes keeping the instrument away from excessive heat, and avoiding sudden extremes of temperature. When the instrument is cold, allow it to warm to room temperature before blowing through it. Check the spot where the bocal fits into the wing joint, as this occasionally leaks air.

TROUBLESHOOTING

Equipment

Difficulty in assembling joints

1. Grease corks on joints, petroleum jelly on threaded.

Sticky pads

1. Moisture in tone hole(s) or absorbed into pads. (If pad is not damaged, place piece of a coffee filter between the key and tone hole and cover gently for paper to absorb moisture.)
2. Bent rods or keys. (Have repaired by competent repairperson.)
3. Worn springs. (Have repaired.)
4. Pivot screws require oiling (one drop.)

Pads not seating correctly

1. Leaking pads. (Readjustment of mechanism may be required if some keys are remaining open.)
2. Pads damaged or hard and brittle. (Have replaced.)
3. Some pads that are worn but not damaged can be reseated by carefully heating the back of the key and pressing the key over the tone hole (being careful to cover the hot key with a soft cloth and realizing that the key may cause other leaks due to its new position).

Gurgling sound

1. Water in tone holes. (Blow water into bore; clean with feather or pipe cleaner; maintain instrument well—dry out after playing if possible.)

Tone

Raucous, loud sound

1. Too much reed in the mouth. (Try just a small amount of reed and gradually insert more until the desired sound is produced.)

2. Reed too hard. (Try softer reed or scrape and trim as needed.)
3. Cheeks puffing. (Firm up corners to flatten chin and cheeks.)
4. Embouchure too loose. (Correct embouchure.)
5. Reed too open. (Carefully close soaked reed between thumb and index finger to reduce stiffness.)

Pinched, small sound

1. Not enough reed in mouth. (Place more so that upper lip is at least one-quarter inch from first wire.)
2. Chin bunched. (Tighten corners of mouth or direct the corners more toward the reed.)
3. Not enough air. (Correct breathing, careful not to overblow.)
4. Throat or oral cavity too tight. (Try dropping lower jaw; use less jaw, more lower lip pressure.)
5. Biting on reed. (Drop jaw leaving lip pressure around contour of reed.)
6. Bad reed, poorly made. (Try new reed, perhaps a different cut.)
7. Bassoon held with boot too far back—bad angle for reed. (Boot should be by thigh, head erect.)
8. Reed not open enough. (Trim end of reed a very small amount at a time until the opening produces desired sound.)

Hard, strident, sound

1. Reed too hard or inappropriate cut for embouchure. (Try a softer or different cut reed.)
2. Biting on reed. (Drop jaw, more lip pressure under reed.)
3. Not enough breath support. (Correct breathing.)

Trouble with control

1. Not maintaining a smooth airstream. (Correct breathing.)

2. Biting on reed or poor embouchure. (Correct embouchure.)
3. Angle of reed entering mouth is too high or too low. (Correct holding position.)
4. Jaw not dropped or pulled back. (Correct embouchure.)
5. Reed too soft or too hard. (Adjust reed as above and in Chapter 9, "The Oboe.")
6. Embouchure too loose. (Keep firm embouchure around reed.)

Pitch

Flat

1. Bocal too long. (Try different bocal.)
2. Embouchure too relaxed. (Correct embouchure with pressure directed toward reed from all sides.)
3. Reed too long. (Shorten, trim and scrape.)
4. Individual notes—keys may not be opening enough. Have adjusted by competent bassoon

repairperson.) Or dirty tone holes. (Clean with a pipe cleaner or feather.)

Sharp

1. Problems with bocal. (Pull out bocal or try longer bocal.)
2. Embouchure too tight. (Occurs with a great deal of back pressure; student may be blowing too hard. Relax airstream—"let it flow"—and relax embouchure slightly.)
3. Reed too short. (Try new, longer reed.)
4. Biting on reed. (Drop jaw, more lip pressure under reed.)
5. Reed too hard. (Try softer reed or scrape or trim as needed.)
6. Not enough reed in mouth. (Place more reed in mouth.)
7. Individual notes—keys may be opening too far. (Have adjustments made by competent bassoon repairperson.) Or adjust embouchure. (Lipping up or down.)

BIBLIOGRAPHY

Texts

* Indicates out of print in 2001.

*ARTLEY, JOE (1968). *How to Make Double-Reeds for Oboe, English horn and Bassoon,* 4th ed. Old Greenwich, CT: Jack Spratt Woodwind Shop.

*BEST, A. S. (1959). *The Bassoon.* Elkhart, IN: Conn Corp.

*BRYANT, LETITIA (1987). *Bassoonist: Make Great Bassoon Reeds.* Tucson, AZ: Author.

*COOPER, LEWIS H., and HOWARD TOPLANSKY (1976). *Essentials of Bassoon Technique (German Technique).* Union, NJ: Howard Toplansky; reprint of (1968) ed.

FLETCHER, KRISTINE K. (1988). *The Conservatoire and the Contest Solos for Bassoon.* Bloomington, IN: Indiana University Press.

HECKEL, W. H. (1950) (translated by Langwill and Waples). *The Bassoon.* Old Greenwich, CT: Jack Spratt Woowind Shop.

*JANSEN, WILL. (1978). *Bassoon: Its History, Construction, Makers, Players, and Music, (5 vols.)* Buren, The Netherlands: Uitgeverij F. Knuf.

JOPPIG, GUNTHER (1988). *The Oboe and the Bassoon.* Portland, OR: Amadeus Press.

*KLIMKO, RONALD (1974). *Bassoon Performance Practices and Teaching in the United States and Canada.* Moscow, ID: University of Idaho, School of Music.

LANGWILL, LYNDESAY GRAHAM (1975). *The Bassoon and Contrabassoon.* New York: W. W. Norton.

MCKAY, JAMES, RUSSELL HINKLE, and WILLIAM WOODWARD (1999). *The Bassoon Reed Manual: Lou Skinner's Technique.* Bloomington, IN: Indiana University Press.

*PENCE, HOMER (1963). *Teacher's Guide to the Bassoon.* Elkhart, IN: Selmer.

*PESAVENTO, ANN (1972). *Design and Adjustment Principles of the Bassoon Reed: A Manual for the Intermediate Player.* Indianapolis, IN: Lang Music.

*SCHLEIFFER, J. ERIC (1974). *The Art of Bassoon Reed Making.* Oneonta, NY: Swith-Dorr.

SPENCER, WILLIAM (1958). COPYRIGHT RENEWED 1986 *The Art of Bassoon Playing,* Evanston, IL: Summy-Birchard.

VIGDER, SCOTT (1994). *The No-Nonsense Guide to Bassoon Reeds.* Los Angeles: author.

WEAIT, CHRISTOPHER (2000). *Bassoon Reed-Making: A Basic Technique,* 4th ed. New York: McGinnis and Marx Music.

Journals

The Double Reed (three per year) and *The Journal of the Double Reed Society* (one per year). From The International Double Reed Society, Norma Hooks, Exec. Sec., 2423 Lawndale Road, Finksburg, MD 21048

Bassoon Studies

Easy—Beginning (elementary or middle school)

Buck. *Elementary Method for Bassoon* (Kjos).

Gekeler–Hovey. *Belwin Bassoon Method Book One* (Belwin).

Hawkins. *Melodious and Progressive Studies for the Bassoon* (Southern Music).

Herfurth. *A Tune a Day for Bassoon* (Boston Music).

Jancourt. *26 Melodic Studies,* Op. 15 (Costellat).

Lentz. *Lentz Method for Bassoon* (vols. 1–2) (Belwin-Mills).

McDowell. *Practical Studies for Bassoon* (vols. 1–2) (Belwin-Mills).

McDowell–Hovey. *Daily Exercises for Bassoon* (Belwin-Mills)

Pares. *Scales and Daily Exercises for Bassoon* (C. Fischer).

Skornicka. *Elementary Method for Bassoon* (Rubank).

Weissenborn. *Bassoon Studies for Beginners* (Book I) (C. Fischer).

———. *Practical Method for Bassoon* (C. Fischer)

Medium (middle school or high school)

Fink. *Introducing the Tenor Clef for Trombone* (Bassoon) (Accura).

Gambaro. *18 Etudes* (International).

Giampieri. *16 Daily Studies* (G. Ricordi).

Jacobi. *6 Caprices* (International).

Jancourt. *26 Melodic Studies Op. 15.* (Costellat).

Kopprasch. *60 Studies for Bassoon* (vols. 1–2) (International).

Milde. *Concert Studies* (vol. 1) (International).

———. *25 Studies in Scales and Chords Op. 24.* (International).

Oubradous. *Gammes et Exercices Journaliers* (vols. 1–2) (A. Leduc).

Satzenhofer. *24 Studies for Bassoon* (International).

Weissenborn. *Practical Method for the Bassoon* (C. Fischer).

Advanced (high school or college)

Bitsch. *20 Studies for Bassoon* (A. Leduc).

Bozza. *12 Caprices* (A. Leduc). Op. 64

Giampieri. *16 Daily Studies for Perfection* (G. Ricordi).

Klengel. *Daily Exercises for Cello* (Breitkopf).

Milde. *Concert Studies for Bassoon* (vol. 2) (International).

———. *50 Concert Studies Op. 26* (Kalmus).

Oubradous. *Gammes et Exercices Journaliers* (vols. 2–3) (A. Leduc).

Piard. *90 Etudes* (vols. 1–2) (Theodore Presser).

Satzenhofer. *24 Studies for Bassoon* (International).

Schoenbach. *20th Century Orchestral Studies for Bassoon* (G. Schirmer).

Weissenborn. *50 Advanced Studies* (Books I–II) (C. Fischer).

Instructional Videos

Basics of Bassoon. (Richard Lottridge, 1993). Madison, WI: Univeristy of Wisconsin-Madison.

Bassoon (1976). Seattle, WA: University of Washington.

Bassoon Basics. (Richard Spittal, Lynn Peck, and Roy Carson, 1997). Ft. Meade, MD: U. S. Army Field Band.

Belwin 21st Century Band Method. Bassoon, Level 1. (Janet Polk, 1996). Miami: Warner Brothers Publications.

Oboe and Bassoon. (Allen Signs, 1987). Bellingham, WA Band Instrument Repair Video Company.

Techniques of Teaching Bassoon (Kenneth Evans, 1978). Greeley, CO: MusEdCo.

Recommended Classical Bassoon Artists

Stefano Conuti playing Rossini and Mendelssohn
Daniel Smith playing Bach and Vivaldi
Mauro Monguzzi playing Hindemith and Tansman
Christian Davidson playing Hummel and Schnitke

Recommended Jazz Bassoon Artists

Classic Jazz, Dixieland: Frankie Trumbauer
Swing, Bop, Hard Bop: Frank Tiberi
Hard Bop, Post-Bop: Michael Rabinowitz
Free Jazz, Avant-Garde: Karen Boca
Crossover: Janet Grice

BASSOON
Fingering Chart

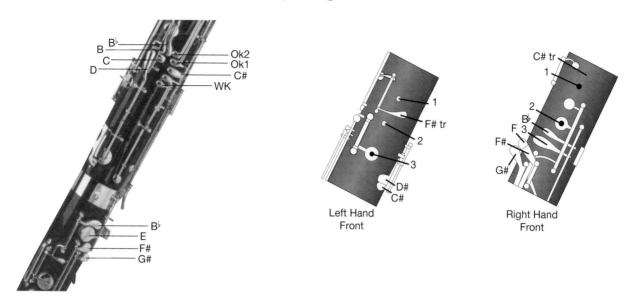

Left Hand
Front

Right Hand
Front

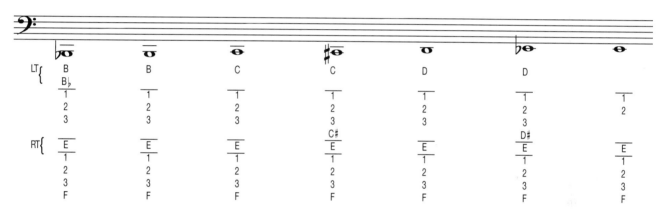

LT { B	B	C	C	D	D	
B♭						
1	1	1	1	1	1	1
2	2	2	2	2	2	2
3	3	3	3	3	3	
			C#		D#	
RT { E	E	E	E	E	E	E
1	1	1	1	1	1	1
2	2	2	2	2	2	2
3	3	3	3	3	3	3
F	F	F	F	F	F	F

WK	WK WK	WK	WK WK	WK
1	1 1	1	1 1	1
2	2 2	2	2 2	2
3	3 3	3	3 3	3
	F#		G#	
1	1 1	1	1 1	1
2	2 2	2	2 2	2
3	3 3	3	3 3	
F	F#		G#	

WK WK	WK	WK	WK WK	WK	WK WK WK	WK WK	WK
			DC# C#		C#		
1 1	1	1	1 1	1	1 1 1	1 1	
2 2	2	2	2 2	2	1 2		
3 3	3	3	3 3		3 3 3		
					D#		
B♭			(E)		B♭ B♭	E	
1 1	1				1 1		
2 2					2		
B♭			(F)				

179

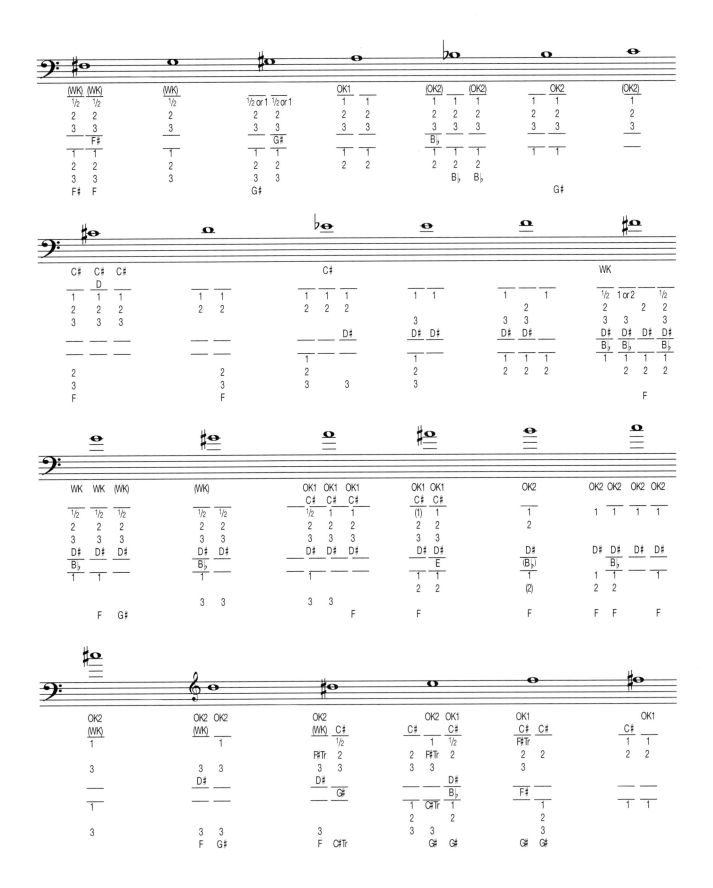

12

The Saxophone

HISTORY

The saxophone differs from the other instruments in that it did not gradually evolve, but was deliberately invented. When Deshontenelles produced a clarinet with a bent mouthpiece in 1807, and Lazarus a tenoroon in 1820, they created the closest predecessors to the saxophone. It is far younger than the other instruments, being little more than 150 years old, compared to the 4000-year evolution of the flute and 3000-year history of the trumpet. In 1840, Adolph Sax, an instrument craftsman of Brussels, set out to combine a woodwind mouthpiece with a brass body that would have woodwind fingering. The saxophone, an instrument similar to one created by Miekle some 20 years earlier, was the result, and except for a few minor changes remains today as Sax invented it. Its original popularity has not faded, due to its extreme dynamic range and the possibility for producing a very personal, intimate, and sentimental tone quality well suited to many kinds of music.

The instrument stands in a class by itself, being neither brass nor woodwind, having a clarinet mouthpiece, oboe fingering, and a brass body.

In America, the saxophone was once associated with only jazz and popular music. It is now accepted as a solo instrument of classical music and written for by contemporary orchestral composers.

SELECTING THE INSTRUMENT

The entire family of saxophones includes nine instruments ($E^\flat$, C, and $B^\flat$ sopranos; $E^\flat$ alto, C melody; $B^\flat$ tenor; $E^\flat$ baritone; and the $B^\flat$ bass and $E^\flat$ contrabass), each differing from the others in range, tone, appearance, and playing problems. The most commonly used saxophones include the $B^\flat$ soprano, made in curved and straight versions, sounds one step lower than the written notes; the $E^\flat$ alto, the most popular and useful of the family, which sounds a major sixth lower; the $B^\flat$ tenor, which sounds a ninth lower; and the $E^\flat$ baritone which sounds an octave and a sixth (a thirteenth) lower than the written notation.

The principal item to look for in purchasing a saxophone is workmanship. The horn should be well machined and of reasonably good-quality metal. The pads should be put on well and should close without leaks. The resonators on the pads should be carefully attached and centered, there should be no noisy keys, and the tone holes should open evenly. Playing the instrument will show the purchaser the quality of the response and the intonation. New instruments sometimes respond a little stiffly because the springs loosen with use.

Neither a new or a used saxophone should leak air around or under the pads. The key action should be even for all keys, with no "bounce" from the keys when they are released. Replaced springs must be regulated with the others to maintain even action. Bending springs often weakens them. Any drag in the keys is an indication of bent rods or posts that can be costly to repair.

Most pads on saxophones are leather and will show signs of wear with use. Torn or scuffed pads should be replaced by a competent repairperson.

When purchasing any used wind instrument, the prime considerations are tone quality, intonation (with itself), and response. The guidance of an expert is desirable, preferably a saxophone player well grounded in classical playing. This advice is especially important due to the relative high cost of upper-line used saxophones.

Special keys such as the low A for the baritone saxophone can be obtained on some saxophones. The standard model baritone saxophone is recommended for school use, although more and more pieces requiring the low A are finding their way into the high school repertoire.

ASSEMBLING THE SAXOPHONE

The saxophone is not as sturdy an instrument as it looks. The three sections—the mouthpiece, the neckpiece, and the body of the instrument—are simple to assemble and care for. Assembling the saxophone involves putting the neckpiece onto the body of the instrument. Like the flute, there is no cork on the joint where the two pieces fit together, so forcing or wiggling can damage the metal and alter the fit. The parts fit easily if placed together with a slight turning motion, but the clamp screw must be loosened. All too soon adolescent players learn that with a little force the saxophone can be assembled and the neckpiece moved without loosening the screw.

Some saxophones have an octave key lever that must go inside the octave key ring on the neck; this ring should not have to be bent because it is adjusted before the instrument leaves the factory, but if it does, it should be taken to a competent repairperson. Often a damaged ring is the result of good intentions backed up by the mistaken belief that the key ring should be round. In careful assembling, the octave key is *not* depressed, the neckpiece should be put on at approximately the proper angle because turning the neckpiece too much after it is on the instrument can cause damage.

The cork on the neckpiece should be greased to ensure proper fit. The mouthpiece, without the reed or ligature, is put on straight so that the player's head need not be cocked to either side when playing. The mouthpiece has no regular stopping place on the neckpiece such as a rim or edge beyond which it will not go, so it can be put on a small distance or pushed down nearly to the octave key depending upon the strength and determination of the student and the thickness of the cork. Intonation is directly affected by the distance the mouthpiece goes on the neck and disproportionately affects left hand placement, so careful listening and tuning are recommended. An ink mark should be placed on the cork as a starting position for good intonation, but small adjustments will have to be made to accommodate temperature and humidity and to adjust to the pitch of other instruments. Students generally fail to put the mouthpiece on far enough; the cork on a new instrument is initially a little too large, to allow for wear and shrinkage. Thus, it is understandable that students may play on instruments that are slightly flat and form bad habits.

The ligature is the metal band that holds the reed in its place on the mouthpiece. The ligature screws should be turned only enough to hold the reed centered on the mouthpiece without slipping. Players often turn the screws as far as they will go, which cuts into the reed and limits the vibration, making any musical tone quality impossible. The tip of the reed should be "about" even with the tip of the mouthpiece.

The neck strap is among the most neglected yet essential parts of the saxophone. The alto saxophone is larger and heavier than the flute, trumpet, clarinet, and other beginning instruments. The neck strap should be of sufficient quality and designed to disperse the weight across as much of the neck as possible; an inadequate strap or its lack of adjustment is the cause of many performance problems.

HOLDING THE SAXOPHONE

Contrary to widespread opinion, the angle of the alto saxophone is correct (whether the player is standing or sitting) when the instrument is held in front of the body and the player's head is in a normal upright position and his neck relaxed (this position is imperative when standing). When the saxophone is held at the side and the bottom crook of the instrument pulled too far back, there is tension in the right arm and fingers, and likely a bad embouchure as well. Alto saxophones should be held in front unless the performer's trunk is so short that the right wrist would be in a cramped position. Holding the instrument directly in front of the player results in fewer errors of posture and position. Positions for holding the saxophone are shown in Figures 12–1 and 12–2. It is not incorrect to play the alto saxophone to the side when seated, although the angle must be less than that of a

Figure 12–1
Sitting Position for Playing the Saxophone (saxophone held in front)

Figure 12–2
Sitting Position for Playing the Saxophone (saxophone held to the side)

tenor saxophone. Whether sitting or standing, the mouthpiece must be adjusted so that the head and neck remain in a straightforward, relaxed position. The practice of holding the instrument to the right side is so prevalent among younger students, that most manufacturers of student-line instruments have redesigned them so that the keys are on the right of the bell. The right arm is positioned slightly back to keep the right hand and wrist relaxed. When the saxophone is held to the side, the player's chair should be rotated approximately 30 degrees counterclockwise. This chair placement allows rotation of the player's trunk to the right, more closely approximating the front-held position.

The placement of the music stand deserves mention. Both beginning flute and saxophone players can develop bad habits because of crowded seating conditions. When players share a music stand, the result can be poor posture and playing position.

The tenor and baritone saxophones are usually held to the side along the leg, but not pulled all the way back to the hip unless the student is very small. These students must adjust their holding position as they grow physically. When the instrument is held too far back, the right arm is put in an awkward position, creating tension and forcing the head to be buried, which, in turn, restricts the airstream and makes the mouthpiece and reed enter the mouth at an inappropriate angle. For these larger instruments, the head remains in a normal, relaxed position with the mouthpiece straight with the player's mouth, not straight with the instrument. The tenor and baritone instruments can be held to the side because the neck of the instrument is a different shape and the mouthpiece will enter the mouth at the proper angle. With the largest instrument, the baritone saxophone, most players will rest the instrument on a stand.

The neck strap should be placed so that it is "correctly adjusted" when the student is playing in the correct posture and holding position—the purpose of the neck strap is to support the instrument while playing, not while counting rests. Neck strap adjustment is critical as a neck strap that is too short can make the head tilt down; one too long provides little support. No alteration of embouchure or hand position should be needed because of the strap.

Support comes from two areas: from the right thumb positioned on the thumb rest on the back of the instrument similar to the clarinet and from the neck strap attached to a ring midway on the back of the horn. The left hand merely serves to steady the saxophone. The right thumb, resting under the thumb rest, acts as a pivot point minimizing tension and allowing for right hand flexibility. The thumb, properly placed, is able to steady the saxophone at the place where it contributes most to comfort, good embouchure, and good tone quality.

The instrument is held with the left hand above, right hand below, and fingers placed similar to their position on the oboe, except that the pads of the fingers lie on pearl buttons positioned on the keys rather than on open tone holes. Left-hand fingers lie on the second, fourth, and fifth buttons with the little finger on the G♯ key (Figure 12–3). The left thumb rests below the octave key on a thumb rest at a 30- to 45-degree angle depending on student size, always touching the octave key. The right-hand fingers rest on the lower buttons with the little finger near the E♭/C keys and the thumb under the thumb rest. The fingers should not be flat and hang over the far side of the keys; neither should the hands be drawn away from the instrument so the fingers barely touch the keys. A relaxed arch to the fingers, with the pads of the fingers resting on the keys, will allow the most flexibility and synchronization of movement (Figure 12–4).

If the instrument is held too far from the body, not enough of the mouthpiece is in the mouth; if it is held too close to the body, the arms become cramped and tense. Some saxophone teachers advocate an instrument position that allows

Figure 12–3
Left-Hand Position for Playing the Saxophone

Figure 12–4
Right-Hand Position for Playing the Saxophone

the tip of the mouthpiece to point upward, resulting in more facile tonguing than when the mouthpiece is more horizontal. To point the tip of the mouthpiece upward, the player holds the instrument closer to his body. Experimenting is necessary to find the angle that produces the best sound with each individual's embouchure formation.

The player should sit or stand comfortably erect, allowing for full chest expansion—shoulders back but relaxed, and breath support from the depth of the abdomen. Saxophonists often lean forward in a tense position with the left shoulder high, right elbow back, head twisted with the entire upper torso showing obvious strain. The secret with saxophone, as with all instruments, is to avoid any position that causes tension.

EMBOUCHURE

The saxophone is among the easiest instruments on which to produce a sound but among the most difficult to master. The student should initially begin to play with only the mouthpiece so that the embouchure is the sole area of concentration. It is important to explain to aspiring saxophone beginners that their initial sounds may be less than desirable, but at the same time a good teacher provides models (i.e., demonstrations by high school players, recordings, or such) to reveal to the beginners "where they should be headed."

Beginners should use a reed that is a bit on the soft side, but no softer than a 2 lest improper habits be encouraged. To establish the proper feeling for the embouchure:

1. The student should vocalize "oou," then retain this general position while opening the mouth a little wider and pointing the chin.
2. The mouthpiece is then inserted rolling the lower lip over the teeth. An attempt should be made to align the edge of the lip that separates the red of

the lip from the flesh-colored part of the chin to a position directly above the teeth.

3. The lips and corners of the mouth close toward the mouthpiece from all directions and the teeth rest on top of the mouthpiece about a half inch from the tip (nylon or rubber pads are useful).

4. The upper lip should close around the mouthpiece and should be held firmly against the eyeteeth. Because most children have an overbite to varying degrees, slightly more of the lip is on the top than on the bottom.

The point where the mouthpiece begins to curve away from the reed is placed directly above the lower teeth. This detail will require experimentation by teacher and student to find the best position for the best sound—a difficult task with beginners. As with the clarinet embouchure, the lower lip should be held firmly against the lower teeth, with a feeling of tautness or "pointing" in the chin. It is important not to jut the lower jaw while trying to point the chin. The sound will be thin and nasal if there is not enough mouthpiece in the mouth, and wild and loud if there is too much. Approximately one-half to three-quarters inch of the mouthpiece should be inserted into the mouth, leaving the reed free to vibrate inside the mouth (see Figure 12–5).

Every note requires some minimum jaw support. The secret is to determine the minimum amount of lower jaw necessary. Biting always should be avoided. The student must not rest the saxophone on the lower lip or, worse, the lower teeth; the teacher should be sure that the student is using his hands (the right thumb) to push the instrument up and out, *anchoring it on the upper teeth.* The lower lip and corners push toward the mouthpiece. Donald Sinta recommends cutting a one-quarter to one-half inch plastic or rubber hose into sections for each beginner to hold in his mouth and squeeze to help develop embouchure muscles.

Figure 12-5
Saxophone Embouchure

One of the best ways to check a student's embouchure is by his pitch. When the alto saxophone mouthpiece is played alone, the pitch produced with a correct embouchure and mouthpiece placement approximates A-440. If the pitch is too high, the player probably has too tight a grip on the mouthpiece, usually by the lower teeth. If the pitch is too low, the embouchure is not sufficiently developed; the player has to learn to play with a tighter grip formed all around the mouthpiece.

As students progress they should be encouraged to alter the A played on the mouthpiece alone to a pitch almost a perfect fourth below. Students should be encouraged to play short melodies on their mouthpieces without an extreme or apparent change in the embouchure. Teaching the student to make changes inside the mouth and throat is much like singing. A bad saxophone tone is often caused by a clarinet embouchure; loosening the tension of the lips and checking for a horizontal pull at the corners of the mouth can help improve the quality. The embouchure for the higher, smaller saxophones is firmer than that for the larger ones, but still not as firm as for the clarinet.

The tongue is also in a sense part of the embouchure. It should be relaxed, but forward, and flat. The tongue does not strike the reed to begin a tone, but acts as a valve and pulls away and lets the reed vibrate. The tongue maintains contact with the reed prior to the attack. Although some air will build up behind the tongue, too much air pressure will produce a harsh attack. One of Sinta's suggestions to determine where the tongue touches the reed is to mark the reed with a "marker" and have the student tongue a few notes. Most beginners will show dots on the tongue in various places; expert saxophonists will have a single dot about a half inch from the tip of the tongue.

The middle of the upper lip stays on the mouthpiece at all times, except when breathing. The lower lip may be thought of as resting against the reed. The pressure is upward where the mouthpiece pushes against the upper teeth, and not downward where the reed meets the lower lip. The mouthpiece remains stationary for the entire saxophone range; it is not moved in and out to achieve the extreme ranges. The player breathes through the corners of his mouth without removing his upper teeth or lower lip from the mouthpiece. Dropping the jaw often causes the player to lose his embouchure and tends to move the mouthpiece in and out. Many jazz players change their embouchures in an attempt to get a bright or dark tone (e.g., Duncan Martin), but these are combo players and not section players who are expected to fit into a balanced, blended section.

With the correct embouchure, the corners of the mouth push toward the mouthpiece, a balance between the muscles pulling out to a smile and those pulling into a pucker—somewhat analogous to a rubber band around the mouthpiece. All pressure must be toward the mouthpiece, because horizontal pull at the corners of the mouth gives a squeezed, tight sound. If the embouchure has a tendency to stretch as well as push toward the mouthpiece, dimples will be apparent in the cheeks.

From the teacher's view, the mouthpiece should appear to be placed about 1 inch in the mouth. From the player's standpoint, the teeth are placed about a half of an inch on the mouthpiece for the alto saxophone, perhaps five-eighths of an inch for tenor saxophone, and slightly more for baritone saxophone (see Figure 12-6). The amount of mouthpiece in the mouth has a definite effect on the tone. The sound will be too thin if there is too little mouthpiece in the mouth and noticeably spread and uncontrolled if too much of the mouthpiece is taken in or if the chin is not down.

A good check for proper mouthpiece placement and lip tension is for the student to play octaves on the instrument. If both octaves respond with only the octave key manipulated, then the embouchure is close to being correct. If only the upper octave speaks, then the embouchure is too tight or there is not enough mouthpiece in the mouth; if only the lower octave speaks, then the embouchure is probably too loose or there is too much mouthpiece in the mouth.

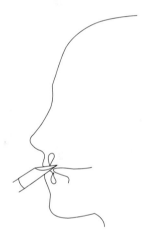

12-6
Saxophone Embouchure Showing Teeth and Lips

The following symptoms are clues to the types of problems that the student may be developing:

1. A quiver in the tone usually means that the throat muscles are too tight and breath support inadequate. To get the right feeling in the throat for an open, unobstructed flow of air, use the syllable "hoo." Using "hoo" must be understood as pertaining to throat relaxation and not to the syllable formed in the mouth. "Hoo" may be used for any instrument when the player needs a word to help her understand the feeling for throat relaxation.

2. A harsh tone and a low register in which the tones are difficult to produce may mean that the embouchure is too firm or the reed too stiff; working over the reed or changing to one of less resistance may help.

3. If the sound is deficient in resonance, the problem is usually that the mouthpiece tip is too closed. The lack of resonance may also be due to the player's embouchure: too much lower lip over the teeth.

4. A weak, breathy tone may be characteristic of the beginner who lacks sufficient wind to fill the mouthpiece. She can be helped to develop more air pressure and breath support, but her tone quality can be improved by changing to a more closed mouthpiece. The Meyer 5 with a medium chamber or the Selmer C* is of this type and is fine for beginners who have not developed enough air support to cope with a more open mouthpiece.

RANGE

No discussion of the saxophone would be complete without reference to the octave above top-line F. Today all fine saxophone players include these notes in their playing range, and music utilizing them is common. These pitches are harmonics and achieved by a firm embouchure and intense breath support. An advanced player does not necessarily find harmonics easier to play; she learns how by specific practice and such practice can be started as soon as the player has established a reasonably good embouchure. Harmonics require experimentation with air pressure, breath support, tongue, lip and teeth pressure, and so on, in addition to much work. The notes are there, and the ambitious student should learn to play them if she wants to consider herself competent. Good pitches to start on are the harmonic fingerings for high E and F. Another good exercise is to produce harmonics from the fundamental pitches of low B♭ to first-space F.

INTONATION

In listening to school saxophonists, one is often hard pressed to decide which is the more objectionable, the intonation or the tone quality. The sad part about this is that the poor sound is unnecessary; there is absolutely no reason for a beginning saxophonist (and his family and teacher) to suffer from bad intonation or lousy tone quality. The saxophone is one of the most perfect instruments and thus easier to play in tune than other instruments. It may be that the instrument is so easy to play initially that the instrumental teacher neglects the saxophonists. Poor band scoring also contributes to the problem; performance in saxophone ensembles and jazz groups helps.

Pitch problems depend partially on the instrument itself: how well it is cared for. For example, if the keys open too wide, the pitch will be sharp. Although the most perfectly in tune of all woodwinds, the saxophone still has built-in intonation flaws, as illustrated in Figure 12–7. The soprano saxophone has intonation problems similar to those of the E♭ clarinet; it is a smaller instrument that, even when of good quality, requires careful listening. The more common alto, tenor, and baritone saxophones are generally well made by leading manufacturers, and such instruments can be played well when their pitch characteristics are understood.

Basic tuning is accomplished by adjusting the mouthpiece on the neckpiece to lengthen or shorten the instrument. When vibrato is used, the instrument is frequently tuned slightly sharp. This practice is often overused, but it keeps the tone from dropping below pitch on the low side of the vibrato. Intonation is controlled

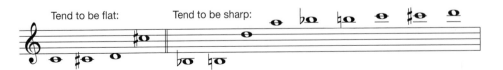

Figure 12-7 Intonation Problems on the Saxophone

by tightening and loosening a properly formed embouchure during performance. Without proper listening and control, most saxophonists will tend to blow flat on loud passages and sharp on soft passages. Jazz musicians make use of this technique constantly … but on purpose.

The double octave key mechanism makes intonation a series of compromises. The lower octave of the alto saxophone is usually sharp, the upper octave generally flat. The upper octave is especially flat when players have inadequately developed embouchures. For other flat notes, low C♯, low E♭, chromatic F♯, G♯, the S1, and the S2 keys may be added. Additional fingering changes that may improve intonation are as follows:

1. Third-space C♯ is always out of tune with the fingering ordinarily suggested for it; use of the low C♯ fingering makes the pitch quite sharp, and the right-hand keys can be added to lower the pitch.
2. The first-leger-line A♯ is out of tune and can be improved by the addition of the F♯ key, third finger, right hand.
3. The following chromatic fingerings are usually fingered for technical ease and not for intonation: (a) F♯, use forked F♯ key; (b), B♭, use the side key; (c) C, use the B key and the second trill key.
4. Third-space open C♯, which is almost always flat, may be corrected in one of two ways: open plus the side C key, or 3 left hand plus the octave key.
5. Right hand 1, 2, and 3 may be added for high notes as required above second-leger-line C♯.

In general, closing additional tone holes other than those required to produce a particular note will lower a pitch. At least one tone hole below the lowest one used for the actual fingering must obviously remain open, and the closer the open or closed tone hole is to those used for the actual fingering, the greater its effect on the intonation.[1]

The saxophone embouchure does not have as much lip flexibility as do other woodwind instruments. Advanced players learn to vocalize every note, placing every note as in singing. The player who tightens the throat slightly to make a minute adjustment in the pitch usually forms bad habits, constricts his throat muscles, and produces an inadequate tone. Some players find helpful a mouthpiece with a comparatively open tip because it allows use of a softer reed and a gain in pitch flexibility. Pitch problems can sometimes be corrected by changing the angle of the mouthpiece in the mouth, or varying the amount of bottom lip over the teeth. These adjustments should be used as a last resort. The same admonition applies to lipping up the pitch—changing it by raising the jaw to tighten the embouchure.

If the player's embouchure seems correct and still one or more individual notes are out of tune, the teacher should consider the excellent pitch alteration chart in the *Art of Saxophone Playing.* [2]

TONE QUALITY

True saxophone tone, with its own characteristic and beautiful sound, is not commonly heard by young instrumentalists. In the midtwentieth century, the *Saxophones of Paris* was one of the few recordings useful as a guide to good saxophone sound. Within 20 years, however, many recording artists, both jazz and classical,

---

[1]Frederick W. Westphal (1990), *Guide to Teaching Woodwinds*, 5th ed. Dubuque, IA: W. C. Brown.

[2]Larry Teal (1976), *The Art of Saxophone Playing*, rev. ed. Secaucus, NJ: Summy-Birchard.

contributed greatly to a growing discography of the saxophone. Listening still has to be selective, because the commercial music on radio and television, as well as many recordings, portrays the instrument with an unpleasant, blatant sound. For every instance in which the true sound of the instrument is heard, there are a hundred instances of bad sound.

Practicing on the mouthpiece and neckpiece can improve tone quality as this portion of the instrument responds quickly to embouchure changes and breath support. Later, remind the student to blow through the saxophone rather than into the mouthpiece. Practicing on the mouthpiece and neckpiece also allows students to get closer to a mirror and observe if the throat is moving while tonguing (it should remain still), and to ensure the embouchure remains still while playing long tones with crescendos and decrescendos and while tonguing on every beat.

The sound of E, F, and G at the top of the staff is most characteristic of the instrument's tone quality and an acceptable tone should be easiest in this range. The factors in bad tone quality are poor breath support and poor embouchure. The player should develop the muscles of the mouth and cheek to withstand additional air pressure so that a more intense column of air can be sent through the mouthpiece. The player should have the breath support and air pressure used by the trumpet player for his high notes; with these she will be well on her way to a disciplined tone.

The study of harmonics should begin early as an aid to good tone and successful altissimo performance. Harmonics help to develop breath control and support, a firmer embouchure, and a consciousness of pitch. In addition, harmonics themselves are useful, for they can literally add octaves to the top range of the saxophone.

Poor tone quality results when beginners are told to play softly. The student tightens his throat, ignores proper breathing, and finds no reason to work on a firmer embouchure because there seems to be no need for control. These habits stay with her when playing at other dynamic levels.

Vowel formation in the mouth will help produce the type of tone color desired. The more open vowels should be used in the middle and low registers, and the more closed vowels in the upper. An "oh" or "ooou" is often suggested to produce the fuller, rounder sound desirable for Romantic music, with "ay" or "ee" for classical repertoire, because it produces a brighter, less personal sound. For the upper register the "ee" or "i" sound will result in a brilliant yet free tone quality. Frequently the saxophone sound is spread, lacking brilliancy and beauty, with no center or focus to the tone. To obtain an edge or focus to the tone is not easy. The player must have the following:

1. A concept of the sound she wants
2. An unobstructed throat
3. A vowel formation in the mouth
4. Air pressure to support the tone
5. A well-controlled embouchure
6. Sufficient intensity of air pressure

When these six are present, the tone takes on a focus and edge that makes it beautiful and interesting.

Vibrato

A good vibrato enhances a beautiful tone, but an inappropriate vibrato can make the saxophone tone glaring and vulgar. Vibrato adds warmth when needed but is best used judiciously. The straight tone tends to sound somewhat manufactured except in the hands of a real artist, it is useful in rapid passages. In ensemble playing, vibrato must be judiciously used or avoided completely, because vibrato seldom blends with other instruments. Blend is particularly important for saxophones and horns (midrange instruments), whose range is such that unisons are frequent and especially obvious. One of the primary differences between classical and jazz saxophone playing is vibrato. In classical playing it is usually fast and very narrow; jazz musicians tend to play with a broader vibrato and adjust the speed to match the phrasing.

Unlike other instruments, the saxophone is not at its best with diaphragm vibrato and does make successful use of the jaw vibrato because it can be accurately controlled. Because the lower lip is only providing a cushion for the reed rather than support for the embouchure, jaw vibrato can be used without distorting the embouchure, provided the player has both correct embouchure and the correct approach to vibrato. The lower jaw may be moved with discretion to assist proper intonation. The jaw vibrato is an alteration of high and low pitch rather than of fluctuating intensity and must be handled with care. A definite change of vibrato speed is required for the high, low, and middle registers: Unless the music dictates otherwise, a slow and spare vibrato is used for the low register, faster and narrower for the high register, and medium pace and width for the middle register. In passages that require intensity for a specific musical effect, a fast, narrow vibrato will be required regardless of register. Because jaw vibrato does alter the pitch, one can readily see why the saxophone is usually tuned sharp enough for the bottom of the vibrato to be on pitch.

When should the student begin learning vibrato? Because control is not possible without training, many saxophonists advocate beginning vibrato study by the second or third week, with a few minutes' practice a day devoted to vibrato, striving for evenness. Other practicing to develop a solid embouchure, good breathing habits, and a pleasant and correct tone is done without vibrato. For some saxophonists, one to three years of playing without vibrato is not uncommon.

THE MOUTHPIECE

The saxophone mouthpiece, like the clarinet mouthpiece, is an important factor in the tone quality of the instrument (see Figure 12-8 on page 192). The size and shape of the tone chamber, the proportion of the facing, the type of baffle, and the material of the mouthpiece each influences the tone quality in specific ways. Unfortunately, mouthpiece selection is not simply a matter of determining what type of sound one wants and picking the appropriate mouthpiece to produce that sound. The student's facial characteristics, lip size, shape of teeth, and structure of the jaw must be considered. A major objective in selecting a mouthpiece is to neutralize those facial characteristics that could hinder the development of tone quality and enhance those characteristics that help in production of good tone.

One style of mouthpiece has a large, round tone chamber allowing a resonant, refined sound. Another type of mouthpiece with a smaller bore and elongated for volume produces a more piercing tone. A chamber with straight walls produces a slightly more brilliant sound.

The baffle, the part of the mouthpiece that lies immediately opposite the opening, influences the volume of the tone and the amount of air needed to produce it. A concave baffle gives a softer sound and requires more air for the tone. The convex baffle gives a louder sound and requires less air. (An extended or elongated baffle produces a very loud, harsh sound and will rarely be desirable.) One mouthpiece makes a good tone more difficult to produce and the other makes it more difficult to control.

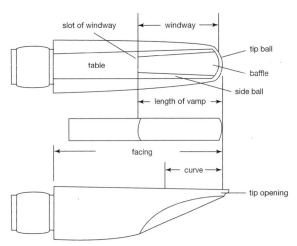

**Figure 12–8
Saxophone Mouthpiece**

The side rails on which the reed rests may also be found in a variety of shapes. For dance band work the usual requirement is straight, flat side rails similar to those of the clarinet. The side rails that best combine with a large tone chamber will be slightly convex to complement the shape of the chamber.

The facing is the curve on which the tip end of the reed rests; the curve and length of the curved rails of the facing determine the size of the tip opening. A short facing produces a smaller tip opening, and a long facing produces a larger one. The longer facing requires a firmer embouchure and a softer reed, which consequently reduces loud dynamic levels and makes the high register more difficult because more pressure is necessary to close the larger tip opening. With a well-developed embouchure, however, the longer facing provides additional pitch flexibility. At the other extreme, a shorter facing requires less embouchure pressure and a stiffer reed that results in greater control on the part of the player. The medium facing is the most useful unless the player is advanced enough to know his preferences and how to handle a differently proportioned mouthpiece facing.

Mouthpieces come in a variety of materials. Glass mouthpieces exist but are extremely rare. Plastic mouthpieces, formerly avoided because of their tendency to become brittle and crack, have improved greatly and may now be purchased with confidence. They are durable as well as inexpensive. Hard rod rubber, or ebonite, is the standard mouthpiece material because it combines high durability with a good tone quality. Metal mouthpieces are also acceptable for the saxophone. Their advantage is that they will never warp under misuse as will plastic and ebonite. Also, they can be made with slightly smaller exterior proportions because of metal's greater strength, which is a true advantage to smaller tenor and baritone saxophone players who often feel that they are playing with a baseball bat in their mouth. Both metal and ebonite can be retooled and refaced easily. At one point metal mouthpieces were the choice of jazz saxophonists, but in a survey of 38 jazz saxophone players only one presently plays a metal mouthpiece.

REEDS

Saxophone reeds are adjusted on the same basis as clarinet reeds (see Chapter 10). Beginners should replace the reed every four to six weeks. New reeds can be broken in as the old ones are wearing out. The resistance of the reed is the single most important factor. Saxophonists usually play with a number 2 or 3 reed. The player, the facing of the mouthpiece, and the reed itself vary, so any reed may be too soft or too stiff. If the tone becomes open, flat in pitch, and cuts out completely in the upper register, the reed is too soft. Other signs of an overly soft reed are these: The lower harmonic is heard when upper register notes are played, biting harder does not produce more edge to the tone, dynamic changes are difficult to produce, attacks tend to scoop, and releases drop in pitch.

For a guide to reed adjustment that presents excellent information in neat, accessible form, specifically for the saxophone, but also applicable to the clarinet, the reader may wish to look at the chart in *The Art of Saxophone Playing* .[3]

TECHNIQUE: ARTICULATIONS AND FINGERINGS

The placing of the mouthpiece in the mouth can help or hinder correct tonguing. If the mouthpiece is too horizontal, the action of the tongue will be impeded; if the tip of the mouthpiece points slightly upward, tonguing will be more easily mastered.

There are at least two correct ways to tongue; the one to use depends on the individual. The traditional method is to use the tip of the tongue to stop the reed, placing it lightly on the reed either at the tip or a little farther down. Rascher, for one, believed in touching the reed a short distance from the tip because it keeps the reed from closing up on the mouthpiece—the vibration of the reed is stopped for an instant but the air going through the mouthpiece is not halted. The tongue action must be as rapid and as slight as possible so that it does not interfere with the smoothness of the tone. Using the tip of the tongue can cause a small movement of the jaw, thus tightening the jaw and altering the embouchure.

The second type of tonguing is to rest the tip of the tongue at the base of the teeth, at the gum line, and to use the middle of the tongue to touch the reed. For many students this seems the natural way to tongue. The curved midtongue makes a small movement forward to contact the tip of the reed. Those players who can use this method find it to be as fast and as well controlled as the tip of the tongue, with the added advantage that there is no danger of moving the jaw. With either method, the tone is articulated by touching the reed with the tongue.

Moving the jaw results in flattened pitches on each tongued note and too much mouthpiece in the mouth. The problem can be helped by having the student tongue the same pitch repeatedly, gradually increasing the speed, while watching the embouchure in a mirror. As soon as the jaw starts to move, the student should reduce the speed in order to "lock in" the proper feel and coordinate the proper tonguing.

Two types of incorrect tonguing can be detected by the sounds that accompany them. A small "thud" with each tonguing action indicates that the player is placing too much of the tongue on the reed, often called a "slap tongue." Besides the unpleasant sound, this kind of tonguing can never be done with much speed or delicacy. The tip of the tongue should be touching only the tip of the reed. The second sound is a small "oink," present when the student is tonguing with the throat. Here, movement in the throat is visible with each tonguing. A player can become so skillful at throat articulation that it is both rapid and quiet. But even so, it is far from desirable because the throat action tightens the muscles and restricts the openness needed for tonal resonance. Tightening the throat is one of the most difficult habits to break.

Multiple tonguing can be done on single-reed instruments. The ability to single-tongue very fast and with control, however, is more important.

Hand position is critical for developing good technique. Young saxophonists often acquire bad habits since they do not have to cover tone holes directly with

[3]Ibid., p. 29.

their fingers. Supplementary exercises should be provided to young students to help develop finger coordination. Fingers must be lifted together, lowered together, and raised and lowered simultaneously. Slurs between certain notes, such as a D♯ to a G♯, help develop the coordination required for complex finger patterns.

The saxophonist can leave right-hand fingers down during certain passages, even though the normal fingering does not require them.

The fingering chart at the end of the chapter gives, under each note, the normal fingering that is usually taught to beginners. The fingerings that follow are given in the order that they least affect intonation. Beginners should learn one fingering for each new note. Alternate fingerings such as the B♭, the side key C, and the forked F♯ should be integrated into the regular fingering patterns. Other alternates can be introduced after the normal fingering is learned.

WHAT TO PRACTICE

Good tone quality, that most essential element in music whether classical or jazz, is best developed through the practice of long tones. Early development of good tone can be achieved through practice of simple melodies, because the embouchure, if properly established, does not change for register, dynamic level, articulation, or pitch. Beginners should form the correct embouchure, breathe carefully, and play these melodies while maintaining the correct embouchure and a steady airstream, with only the fingers moving.

Scales are excellent for practicing tone and intonation as well as finger dexterity. Scales demand use of different finger combinations and patterns beyond those required in the beginning method books, which are usually limited to the keys of G, C, and D for alto saxophone. Scales can also help develop good intonation.

CARE AND MAINTENANCE OF THE SAXOPHONE

Daily care of the saxophone involves the following: (1) tipping it upside down to drain the excess moisture; (2) swabbing it with a soft, lint-free cloth for sanitation and to extend the life of the pads; and (3) wiping and drying the mouthpiece. Every week the mouthpiece should be cleaned by running lukewarm water through it (hot water may warp it). Not advised is the use of a swab stick or a rough-surfaced object to pull the cloth through the mouthpiece because scratches or nicks on the interior of the mouthpiece can alter tone quality. A simple cloth such as the swab used by most clarinetists is fine. Dropping the mouthpiece can chip the facing. After each playing, the reed should be wiped off and put in a safe place to dry. To be avoided are the cardboard containers in which some reeds are purchased. Metal or plastic reed holders are better but can damage the heart of the reed if handled carelessly.

The neckpiece tends to collect dirt faster than the lower part of the instrument. The exterior of the end that fits into the body should be kept clean by wiping with a moist cloth. This makes a good fit easier. Two or three times a year the posts and pivots should be oiled, first loosening the rods to ensure a more even distribution of the oil. Pads should be checked periodically for air leakage by pulling a piece of sturdy thin paper gently through each closed key (if resistance is offered by the closed key it shuts sufficiently to form a seal), or shining a light in the instrument and examining for cracks of light from the closed key.

Bumper corks adjust the height of the key opening. Two important ones that tend to wear out are the tone hole above the first finger of the right hand for articulated G♯ and the forked B♭ fingering. The exterior of the instrument requires no particular care, although players who like a shiny surface will polish it with a soft cloth. Wiping off fingerprints is sufficient. To prevent damage to the instrument, one should replace the instrument plug when returning the saxophone to the case.

TROUBLESHOOTING

Equipment

Sticky pads

1. Moisture absorbed by pads. (If pad is undamaged, dry by placing tissue paper or small piece of coffee filter between pad and tone hole and closing gently.) (As a last resort: Apply a slight amount of talcum powder to pad, being careful not to get it on the mechanism.)
2. Bent rods. (Have repaired by a competent repairperson.)
3. Worn springs. (Have replaced by a competent repairperson.)
4. Pivot screws at end of rods may need oiling. (Usually these must be loosened to oil—oil sparingly, then retighten.)

Pads not seating

1. Leaking pads. (Even if pads are in good shape, they usually cannot be heated and reset like clarinet pads; they must be replaced.)
2. Bent keys or rods. (Have repaired by competent repairperson.)
3. Brittle or "scuffed" pads. (Have replaced.)

Gurgling sound

1. Water has collected at the bottom crook of the instrument or in a tone hole. (Dry with a swab.)
2. Water in mouthpiece or neckpiece. (Swab neckpiece; remove ligature and reed to dry mouthpiece.)

Tone

Squeaks

1. Worn pads or pads not seating correctly. (Have pads replaced by competent repairperson.)
2. Too much mouthpiece in mouth. (Use less mouthpiece, practice playing soft attacks and playing decrescendos.)
3. Unequal pressure on sides of reed. (Can especially occur when beginners hold instrument by their sides without adjusting neckpiece and/or mouthpiece, correct holding position; if due to leaking pads see above.)
4. Trying to articulate by biting and releasing reed with mouth. (Correct articulation.)
5. Inadvertently pressing side key(s). (Correct holding position)

Thin, pinched

1. Biting on mouthpiece. (Drop lower jaw—push mouthpiece toward upper teeth.)
2. Corners of mouth not pushing toward mouthpiece. (Correct embouchure.)
3. Not enough lower lip for cushion. (Either not enough lower lip over teeth or lower lip is stretched too thin and needs to be "bunched up" more ... or both.)
4. Mouthpiece entering mouth at too much of an angle. (Hold bottom of saxophone farther away from body or tilt head downward slightly.)
5. Not enough mouthpiece in mouth. (Insert more mouthpiece, being careful not to put too much inside the mouth.)
6. Throat too tight or oral cavity too tight. (Drop shoulders; practice "bending" or "lipping" notes as flat as possible—at least a full step—to open airstream; keep tongue down except when needed to articulate.)
7. Reed too soft. (Try stronger reed or clip reed and scrape as necessary.)

Loud, wild, harsh

1. Too much mouthpiece in mouth—makes it easier to play loudly. (Use less mouthpiece—may require loosening or tightening the embouchure—practice very soft attacks and decrescendos on long tones to reinforce softer tone.)
2. Too much lip over lower teeth. (Pull lip out—try to align the point where the red of the lip is directly over the lower teeth.)
3. Not enough pressure on reed from lower lip. (Careful not to encourage pressure from the jaw or teeth, ask student to tighten and direct muscular force toward reed.)
4. Corners and/or upper lip too loose. (Tighten corners and ask student to clamp together; upper lip should be firm and press against eye-teeth.)
5. Mouthpiece too open. (Try another, more appropriate mouthpiece.)
6. Reed too hard. (Scrape the reed or try a softer reed.)

Uncontrolled

1. Cheeks puffing. (Keep corners of mouth firm.)
2. Upper teeth not on reed (Correct embouchure.)
3. Embouchure too loose. (Direct all muscular pressure from lips and surrounding muscles toward mouthpiece.)
4. Corners of mouth not firm or smiling (Keep corners firm and direct toward mouthpiece.)

5. Throat too tight or oral cavity too small. (Keep tongue down except when needed to articulate; shoulders down; practice bending notes down a full step then back to pitch.)

6. Too much mouthpiece in mouth. (Correct position; try to align the point where the mouthpiece begins to curve away from the reed directly above the teeth.)

7. Reed too hard. (Try softer reed or scrape reed.)

Pitch

Sharp

1. Biting on mouthpiece. (Drop lower jaw and compensate by using more lower lip pressure against reed; practice bending notes flat; push or direct corners of mouth toward mouthpiece; push mouthpiece up, toward reed; or a combination of these.)

2. Reed too hard (Try softer reed or scrape reed.)

3. Mouthpiece at too much of an angle with embouchure (Hold bottom of saxophone away from body more and/or tilt head slightly downward.)

4. On individual notes: pads over tone holes too open (Have competent repairperson readjust.)

Flat

1. Reed too soft. (Try harder reed or clip reed.)

2. Embouchure too loose. (Direct all muscular pressure from lips and surrounding muscles toward mouthpiece.)

3. Saxophone held too far out so that mouthpiece enters mouth almost directly instead of at an angle. (Hold head up and/or pull bottom of instrument toward body.)

4. On individual notes: pads over tone holes too closed. (Have adjusted by competent repairperson.)

BIBLIOGRAPHY

Texts

* Indicates out of print in 2001.

*BAKER, DAVID (1978). *Charlie Parker, Alto Saxophone.* New York: Shattinger International Music.

*BENGER, RICHARD (1995). *Studies in Style: Classical, Traditional, Rock and Pop for Saxophone.* Monmouth: Spartan Press.

BROWN, JOHN R. (1993). *How to Play the Saxophone,* U.S. ed. New York: St. Martin's.

*FURSTNER, MICHAEL (1986). *Overtone Practice on the Saxophone: The Sure Method to Good Tone.*, St. Austine, FL: M. Furstner.

HARVEY, PAUL (1995). *Saxophone.* London: Kahn & Averill.

*HEMKE, FRED (1977). *Teacher's Guide to the Saxophone.* Elkhart, IN: Selmer.

INGHAM, RICHARD (1988). *The Cambridge Companion to the Saxophone.* New York: Cambridge University Press.

*LIEBMAN, DAVID (1994). *Developing a Personal Saxophone Sound,* 2nd ed. Medfield, MA: Dorn.

*LUCKEY, ROBERT A. (1992). *Saxophone Altissimo: High Note Development for the Contemporary Player.* Lafayette, LA: Olympia Music.

MCLAUGHLIN, PATRICK A. (1992). *Practical Owners Guide to the Saxophone.* Eustis, FL: Instrumental Press.

PARKER, CHAN (1999). *My Life in E-flat.* Columbia, SC: University of South Carolina Press.

PLATAMONE, VITO (1998). *Clarinet and Saxophone Reed Adjustments,* 2nd ed. Prescott, AZ: Author.

*RAE, JAMES (1993). *Introducing the Saxophone.* London: Universal.

REED, RAYMOND (1995). *The Saxophone Reed: The Advanced Art of Adjusting Single Reeds,* Encino, CA: Author (17608 Martha St., Encino, CA 91316).

RICHMOND, STANLEY (1972). *Clarinet and Saxophone Experience.* New York: St. Martin's.

RUSSELL, ROSS (1996). *Bird Lives!: The High Life and Hard Times of Charlie (Yardbird) Parker.* New York: Da Capo Press.

STEPHAN, KAREN (1995). *The Complete Guide to Saxophone Playing: For Classical and Jazz Musicians (w/ CD).* Jenison, MI: Stephan Publications.

TEAL, LARRY (1976). *The Art of Saxophone Playing,* rev ed. Secaucus, NJ: Summy-Birchard; reprint (2001) Miami, FL: Warner Brothers.

THOMAS, J. C. (1988). *Chasin' the Trane: The Music and Mystique of John Coltrane.* New York: Da Capo Press.

*TODENHOFT, NORMAN (1965). *The Proper Selection of Clarinet and Saxophone Mouthpieces.* Elkhart, IN: Conn Corp.

*VAGNER, ROBERT (1966). *Single Reed Guide for the Clarinet and Saxophone Player.* Corvalis, OR: Oregon State University.

*WEINSTEIN, IRA JAY (1988). *The Master Speaks: Joe Allard's Saxophone and Clarinet Principles,* 2nd ed. Seattle, WA: RIA Business Concepts.

*WEISSHAAR, OTTO H. (1966). *Preventive Maintenance of Saxophones.* Rockville Center, NY: Belwin-Mills.

Journals

Saxophone Journal and *Jazz Player* (for saxophone). Quarterly from Saxophone Journal, Inc. P.O. Box 206, Medfield, Mass. 02052. URL: http://www.dornpub.com

Clarinet and Saxophone Association of Great Britain. 167 Ellerton Road, Surbiton; Surrey KT6 7UB England. URL: http:// www.cassgb.co.uk.

Saxophone Studies

Easy—Beginning (elementary or middle school)

Cailliet. *Method for Saxophone* (Book I) (Belwin-Mills).
Cough. *Let's Play Saxophone* (Chapel Music).
Eisenhauer. *Elementary Supplement Studies for Saxophone* (Alfred).
Hegvik. *Modern Course for the Saxophone* (2 vols.) (Elkan-Vogel).
Hetzel. *Hetzel's Visual Method for the Saxophone* (Ditson).
Hovey. *Daily Exercises for the Saxophone* (Belwin).
———. *Elementary Method for Saxophone* (Rubank).
———. *Practical Studies for Saxophone* (2 vols.) (Belwin).
Lindeman. *Saxophone Made Easy* (2 vols.) (Colin).
Rossari-Iasilli. *53 Etudes* (2 vols.) (Southern).
Rousseau. *Eugene Rosseau Saxophone Method* (2 vols.) (Kjos).
Skornicka. *Intermediate Method for Saxophone* (Rubank).

Medium (middle school or high school)

DeVille. *Universal Method for the Saxophone* (Fischer).
Ferling. *48 Studies* (Southern).
Hegvik. *Modern Course for the Saxophone* (Vols. 3–4) (Rubank).
Iasilli. *33 Concert Etudes* (Fischer).
Klose. *25 Daily Exercises for the Saxophone* (C. Fischer).
Londeix. *Les Gammes Conjointes et en Intervalles* (Lemoines).
Loyon. *32 Etudes for Oboe and Saxophone* (Billaudot).
Pares. *Scales and Daily Exercises for Saxophone* (C. Fischer).
Rascher. *Top-Tones for Saxophone* (C. Fischer).
Sellner. *Etudes* (Vol. I, Elementary) (Robert Martin).
Small. *27 Melodious and Rhythmical Studies* (C. Fischer).
Teal. *The Saxophonist's Workbook* (University Music).
Vereecken. *Foundation to Saxophone Playing* (C. Fischer).
Voxman. *Advanced Method for Saxophone* (2 vols.) (Rubank).

Advanced (high school or college)

Bozza. *Twelve Etudes-Caprices* (A. Leduc).
Capelle. *20 Grandes Etudes* (A. Leduc).
Corroyez. *22 Pieces of J.S. Bach* (Billaudott).
DeVille. *Universal Method for the Saxophone* (C. Fischer).
Ferling. *48 Studies* (Southern).
Gates. *Odd Metered Duets* (Gornston).
Karg-Elert. *25 Caprices* (Zimmerman).
Labanchi (ed. Iasilli). *33 Concert Etudes* (C. Fischer).
Massis. *Capriccio-Studies* (A. Leduc).
Mule. *18 Etudes After Berbiguier* (A. Leduc).
———. *Enseignement for Saxophones* (A. Leduc).
Rascher. *24 Intermezzi* (Bourne).
Voxman. *Selected Studies for Saxophone* (Rubank).

Jazz Materials (high school and beyond)

Aebersold. *A New Approach to Jazz Improvisation* (nearly 80 vols. by 2000) (Aebersold Music).
Arnold. *Jazz Styles for Saxophones* (Music Scales).
Baker. *Techniques of Improvisation* (Studio P/R).
Berle. *Complete Handbook for Jazz Improvisation* (Music Scales).
Coker. *A Complete Method for Jazz Improvisation* (Studio P/R).
———. *Patterns for Jazz* (Studio P/R).
DiBlassio, D. *DiBlassio's Box Shop: Getting Started in Improvisation* (Kendor).
———. *DiBlassio's Box Shop: The Sequel* (Kendor).
Gerard, Charley. *Improvising Jazz Saxophone* (Colin).
Giuffre, H. *Jazz Phrasing and Interpretation* (Associated Music).
Hejda. *Selected Studies and Jazz Compositions* (Polskie Wydawnictwo).
McGhee. *Improvisation for Saxophone* (Colin).
Niehaus. *Basic* (and *Intermediate* and *Advanced*) *Jazz Conceptions* (Colin).
———. *Jazz Improvisation for Saxophone* (Colin).
Parker. *Charlie Parker Omnibook.* (Atlantic Music).
Viola. *The Technique of the Saxophone* (3 vols.) (Berklee Press).

Instructional Videos

The Art of the Saxophone (Steve Wilkerson, Llew Matthews, John Leitham, and Gregg Field, 1993), Timonium, MD: Reyner Products.
Basic Jazz Improvisation for Saxophone (Lynda Reid, 1988) Levelland, TX: Texas Music and Video.
Basic Jazz Saxophone Techniques (Lynda Reid, 1992). Levelland, TX, Texas Music and Video.
Belwin 21st Century Band Method. Alto Saxophone, Level 1 & 2 (James Houlik, 1996). Miami: Warner Brothers Music Publishers.
Belwin 21st Century Band Method. Tenor Saxophone, Level 1 & 2 (James Houlik, 1996). Miami: Warner Brothers Music Publishers.
The Complete Guide to Saxophone Sound Production (Dave Liebman and Gene Perla, 1989). Stroudsburg, PA: Caris Music Services.
Getting Started with the Saxophone (Robert Spittal, 1996). Spokane WA: Getting Started Productions.
The Master Speaks: Clarinet and Saxophone Principles Techniques That Work (Joe Allard, 1987). Seattle, WA: American Motion Pictures.
Rock and Roll Saxophone with Steve Douglas (Steve Douglas, 1998). Pound Ridge, N.Y.: Hot Licks Productions.
Saxophone (Ron Reynolds, 1994), Chatsworth, CA: Music Video Productions.

Saxophone Repair. (Allen Signs, 1987), Bellingham, WA: Band Instrument Repair Video Co.

Sinta on Sax (Donald Sinta, n.d.). Madison WI: University of Wisconsin Videotapes.

Steps to Excellence, A Video Clinic—Alto Saxophone Vol. 3. (Eugene Rousseau, 1984). Grand Rapids, MN: Yamaha Mucic Products.

Ultimate Beginner Series—Saxophone, Vol. 1 & 2 (Ed Calle, 1998). Miami: Warner Brothers Music Publications.

Recommended Classical Alto Saxophone Artists

Sophie Cherrier playing Berio, Takemitsu, and Boulez

Claude Delangle playing Stockhousen, Raskatov

Sohre Rahbari playing Debussy, Faure, and Milhaud

Timothy McAllister playing Mead and Carter

Recommended Jazz Saxophone Artists

Chicago Dixieland: Jimmy Dorsey, alto

Swing: Johnny Hodges, alto; Ben Webster and Coleman Hawkins, tenor

Early R&B: Louis Jordon, alto; Illinois Jacquet, tenor; Paul Williams, baritone

Bop: Charlie Parker, alto; Dexter Gordon, tenor; Serge Chaloff, baritone

Cool: Paul Desmond, alto; Stan Getz and Lester Young, tenor; Gerry Mulligan, baritone

Hard Bop, Post-Bop: Jackie McLean, alto; Sonny Rollins, tenor; Pepper Adams, baritone

Fusion: David Sanborn, alto; Michael Brecker and Grover Washington, Jr., tenor

Avant-Garde, Free Jazz: Ornette Coleman, alto; Roland Kirk and John Coltrane, tenor; Pat Patrick, baritone

Free Funk: Steve Coleman, alto; Eddie Harris, tenor

Most influential 1980–2000: Bobby Watson, alto; Wayne Shorter, tenor; Sahib Shihab, baritone

SAXOPHONE
Fingering Chart

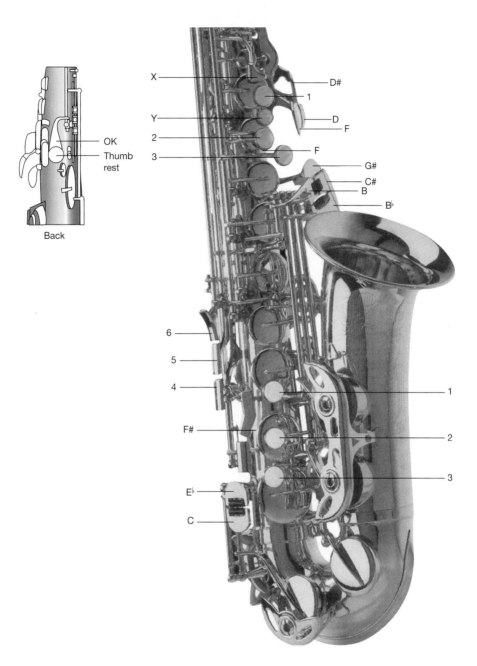

Back

OK
Thumb rest

X
Y

D#
1
D
F
F
G#
C#
B
B♭

6
5
4
F#
E♭
C

1
2
3

1
2
3

1	1	1	1	1	1
2	2	2	2	2	2
3	3	3	3	3	3
B♭	B		C#		
1	1	1	1	1	1
2	2	2	2	2	2
3	3	3	3	3	3
C	C	C	C		E♭

SAXOPHONE
Fingering Chart, *Continued*

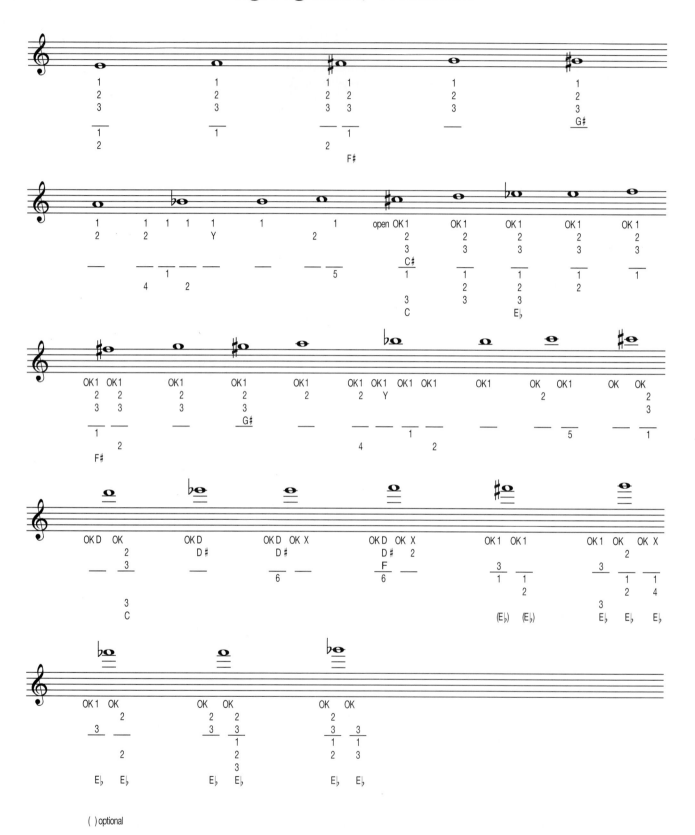

13

Principles for Brass

Brass instruments produce a sound from a vibrating column of air inside the tubing set in motion by the lips. All brasses play pitches based on the overtone series and are fitted with valves to play a complete chromatic scale. With the exception of fiberglass used for some sousaphones, all brass instruments are constructed of a brass alloy.

CONICAL AND CYLINDRICAL INSTRUMENTS

Brass instruments can be divided into two classes: those constructed of tubing that is primarily cylindrical throughout the bore and those that are completely conical. The cylindrical instruments have a slightly conical-shaped leadpipe (the first section of tubing—before the main tuning slide—in which the mouthpiece is inserted) and an exaggerated conical shape forming the bell. Roughly two-thirds of the total length, however, is cylindrical. Conical-shaped brass instruments are tapered almost completely from mouthpiece to bell. About one-third of the total tubing is cylindrical, consisting primarily of the section comprised of tuning and valve slides. The greatest difference occurs in the taper of the leadpipes.

  The acoustical difference is that a conical-shaped standing wave eliminates several of the upper partials from each pitch resulting in a less "brilliant" sound than that produced by cylindrical brass instruments. A more rapidly flaring leadpipe enables a brass player to change the speed of the air more easily, enhancing flexibility. A cylindrical leadpipe is less forgiving, reducing flexibility and affecting control on lip slurs. Thus, initial success is easier on the conical cornet than the cylindrical trumpet.

  Both classes of brass instruments are available in soprano, alto, tenor, and bass voicings in the brass section (see Figure 13–1 on page 202). Bands use both conical and cylindrical instruments within the same voice range (for example, the frequent use of both cornets and trumpets as well as euphoniums and trombones), as composers make use of the differing timbres.

Register	Cylindrical	Conical
soprano	trumpet*	cornet
alto	alto horn, mellophone	horn*
tenor	trombone*	euphonium
bass	sousaphone	tuba*

Figure 13–1 Brass: The Two Classes of Brass with those Most Commonly Used in the Orchestra Indicated by an Asterisk

SELECTING THE INSTRUMENT

Many manufacturers of brass instruments produce good-quality instruments. Used brass instruments are generally fine. One important consideration with all brass instruments is bore size. A medium- or medium-large-bore instrument is the most popular and generally offers the most immediate success. The common recommendation that beginners should select small-bore instruments is erroneous. Small-bore trumpets/cornets and trombones may enable the student to produce an initial sound with less effort, but only because the student does not have to breathe properly in order to produce the tone. Small-bore instruments are easily overblown, and good tone is fleeting. The distorted sound becomes hard to correct.

At the advanced and/or professional levels, the size and material of the bell becomes a matter of concern. The standing wave that produces the quality of tone in a brass instrument is established by the reflection of the pressure wave originating at the embouchure and is reflected by the change of air pressure at the bell. The greater flare has the effect of damping the upper partials, thus creating a "darker" tone quality. Less flare, or a slower flare, projects the upper overtones heard by the audience. Consequently, the darkest tone is produced by an instrument that has a small bore but a large bell, a horn producing the darker sound

Bells are made of various materials; most are of the same brass alloy as the rest of the instrument, but some professional-line manufacturers offer the player a choice of alloys for the bell. Opinions differ as to the value of these various brass alloys; many find no difference whatsoever between them. The effect, if any, seems to be in the degree of brilliance. To further complicate matters for the student, but to facilitate the tastes of the professionals, many brass manufacturers make instruments with detachable bells. Schilke invented the first to serve as a tuning device to avoid interruption of the main tuning slide.

The metal of the brass instruments is important for tone quality and most companies presently use a satisfactory grade. A yellow brass lacquer finish is the most common although silver plating is preferred by most professionals. Silver plating becomes a part of the instrument itself instead of an "overcoat" of lacquer; silver is thinner than lacquer and results in a darker tone quality.

Student-line instruments often are manufactured with nickel plate. These wear better and normally produce a slightly more brilliant sound. Most repair shops, however, do not have the facilities to replate nickel.

A number of professionals prefer a "raw brass" finish (or lack thereof) which produces the darkest or "purest" tone quality. Different alloys have been used for bells on trombones and trumpets such as red brass that has the most copper and results in the darkest tone quality, followed by gold brass that has less copper. Both of these are "stuffy" in soft passages but provide a rich, full sound at fuller dynamic levels. Yellow brass is the default of most brass instruments and has even less copper.

STARTING THE BEGINNER

Many brass methods, teachers, players, and texts list physical aspects necessary to learn a brass instrument. Some of these authorities recommend that the teacher inspect a child's teeth, lips, fingers, jaw, arms, hooves, and the like before allowing him to start a brass instrument. In reality, interest in the instrument is the primary predictor of success. The only characteristic of the child that the teacher can truly rely on is that the student will change. If Louis Armstrong had been assessed under these rules, he would have played bass drum.

Although some famous trumpet players have suggested that all they do is screw up their lips and blow, there are guidelines to initial production of tone. The following are helpful suggestions.

1. Wet the lips, then with the lips alone (and keeping the teeth apart), produce a puttering sound like a child imitating a motorboat. Increase the "speed of the motor" by tightening the corners of the mouth, to produce a buzz. Watch for excessive puckering. If buzzing is difficult and the tendency is to "flop" the lips "like a horse," curl the lips under more (so that less pink of the lip is showing) and place them closer together. Practice the buzzing until it comes naturally, feels easy, and can be sustained for several counts. At this point, place the mouthpiece lightly to the lips, avoiding any pressure other than the minimum amount necessary to seal off escaping air.

   Some teachers advocate first buzzing with the lips then with the mouthpiece for a week or two before buzzing on the horn. This routine requires unusual patience on the part of the student. Continuing to buzz with and without the mouthpiece enhances brass playing.

2. Place the lips together as if saying "em" (this keeps the teeth apart), firm the corners, add the mouthpiece and blow until a sound is produced. The student should be cautioned not to pull the mouthpiece back into the lips, but to let the airstream make the sound. Excessive pressure against the lips prevents the lips from flexing to change pitches. Excessive pressure is a natural tendency for the beginner, as he is using facial muscles in a different manner than he has before. Unfortunately, excessive pressure is among the more common bad habits for brass players and is the primary reason for poor upper register playing. Excessive pressure is usually a symptom of an under-developed embouchure or lack of wind.

3. Have the student gently blow into the instrument without firming the lips—as if "sighing" into the brass instrument; then very gradually bring the lips closer together; firming the corners until a pitch responds.

4. Place the mouthpiece against the lips and release a burst of air into the mouthpiece while simultaneously making a "toe" or "tah" syllable (depending upon the instrument) with the tongue touching the roof of the mouth near the teeth. Try the same procedure with the mouthpiece inserted into the instrument.

5. If none of the above helps produce a sound on the mouthpiece, the teacher has two alternatives: (a) try a brass instrument with a larger mouthpiece (if the student isn't already playing a tuba), or (b) let the student try blasting to produce the initial sounds. Brass playing is a vigorous physical activity; in some cases what feels like blasting is exactly what may be required. Blasting is never advocated, but it may be worth trying when all other means fail, especially if the term *blasting* conveys the concept of blowing a fast airstream.

When the student can consistently produce a tone with each attempt, he is ready to experiment with raising and lowering pitches by tightening and loosening the corners of the mouth. Playing short melodies with just the mouthpiece is valuable embouchure training; it is also fun, and it helps the all-important development of the ear.

EMBOUCHURE

The correct brass embouchure consists of a lip position that uses a balance of smiling and puckering muscles. Because individuals differ in facial structure, the safest way to help a student develop a correct embouchure is to have him close his mouth with the lips touching (but the teeth remaining slightly apart, as if saying "em"). The corners of the lips are held firm (which results in a flat chin) and the center of the lips will be loose enough to vibrate with the outgoing stream of air. Lip tension is adjusted by slightly tightening or loosening the strongest muscles in the face, those at the corners of the mouth (the corners of the mouth do not clamp on anything but themselves). The process works somewhat like a "zip-lock bag" in that the aperture at the center of the embouchure is closed by tension moving from the outside of the lips toward the inside. The chin is kept flat. This position makes it virtually impossible to puff out the cheeks.

When the airstream is increased in velocity to play pitches higher in the overtone series, the corners of the lips must become firmer to prevent the increased air pressure from blowing the lips open. The lips vibrate more rapidly when the airstream is moving more rapidly. Tension at the corners of the mouth makes the aperture smaller while retaining a similar shape. Initially, students should be encouraged to produce a higher pitch by simply tightening the corners of the mouth or lips. By "thinking" higher and lower pitches, the player can increase and decrease the speed in much the same way a singer produces higher and lower pitches.

The smile embouchure tends to produce lips that are stretched to produce higher pitches but results in a thin sound. The pucker-type embouchure creates tension in the center of the lip, a lip that needs to be free to vibrate. The pucker-type embouchure also makes it difficult for the chin to remain flat. The type of embouchure affects tone quality between registers.

Every effort should be made to center the mouthpiece on the lips horizontally and vertically. Though there are many shades of opinion regarding the vertical placement of the mouthpiece, most teachers prefer to have equal amounts of each lip vibrating for cornet, trumpet, and tuba, and more of the upper lip on the mouthpiece for horn and trombone. A mouthpiece rim or embouchure visualizer is helpful in checking the mouthpiece placement.[1] When one-third of the upper lip and two-thirds of the lower lip show from the outside, the placement is closer to half-and-half on the inside of the cup. The lip and jaw structure affect the placement. If the upper lip is fuller, the mouthpiece may be positioned slightly higher on the lip; if the lower jaw recedes, the mouthpiece will be positioned a bit farther down. The lower jaw should be exactly beneath the upper jaw, with the incisors aligned, making the lower jaw jut out in such a position that it sends the column of air almost directly into the mouthpiece, neither excessively upward nor downward. Most students need to be encouraged to move their lower jaw forward to align the teeth and lips.

[1]A device that consists of a rim (without the cup or shank) attached to a steel rod/handle. This visualizer can be "played" like a brass mouthpiece and allows the teacher to visualize what is normally hidden inside the cup

Although beginning players are encouraged to center the mouthpiece both vertically and horizontally, a slight drift to one side or the other may occur with students who have uneven teeth; this drift should be no cause for alarm. The teacher must maintain a careful watch, however, to make sure the drift does not extend to the point where the mouthpiece placement becomes detrimental to the player.

The direction of the air changes in different registers (more so with larger mouthpieces)—generally, the higher the register the more the air is directed downward, or toward the edge of the cup Figure 13–2. The embouchure remains basically the same, but there is a slight shifting of pressure from one lip to the other depending upon the register. Upper and lower lips and teeth may not remain perfectly vertically aligned, as the lips move into these slightly different positions. (The head or the instrument may be pivoted just enough to transfer pressure from one lip to another). According to the brass pedagogue Donald Reinhardt, the direction of the airstream in conjunction with the degree of lip tension and air speed determines the pitch. In addition, the tongue directs and governs the size of the airstream through the embouchure (generally, articulations such as "doe" are used in the lower registers and articulations such as "dee" are used in the upper registers; these two vowel sounds require a differ-

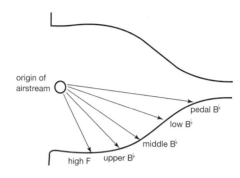

Figure 13–2
Direction of Airstream inside Mouthpiece

ent placement of the back of the tongue but use the same consonant for the beginning of the note). Articulations such as "toe" and "tee" are slightly more defined and are used for marcato or accented passages.

Both range and dynamics affect the size of the embouchure opening, the embouchure becoming smaller for higher notes and softer tones. Players who resort to a pucker for the lower register and a smile for the higher notes usually experience tension and fatigue. A more satisfactory solution seems to lie in pivoting—that is, in changing the position of the lower lip because it is not as crucial in producing the "buzz." Pivoting can also be accomplished by raising or lowering the lower lip by rolling it in and out or, in extreme cases, by slightly lowering the jaw.

If the teeth are sufficiently far apart it will be easier to get the right feeling in the lips. Some trumpet pedagogues say that the lips should form a small oval resembling the opening of an oboe reed. Beginning players may misinterpret this and open the lips too much, but the visual imagery of the opening of an oboe reed can help students in properly forming their lips. In higher brass, the opening is so small that it can hardly be felt by the player, but can be seen with a mouthpiece visualizer. An embouchure that is too open allows the air to "spread" and the sound loses focus. The tone produced by a too open embouchure will be soft and hollow with no center or resonance; the resulting tone is often airy or "fuzzy" sounding and pitch will sag. When the embouchure is too closed, articulations will usually be very explosive and the tones choked and pitch will rise.

Practicing in front of a mirror is an excellent way for the student to check his embouchure, mouthpiece placement, instrument position, and general posture.

Embouchure Faults

Too much mouthpiece pressure is the most common and the most destructive fault. Pressure affects the quality of tone, flexibility, endurance, and range. When the left hand pushes the mouthpiece into the lips, the sound will be thin and hard with little breath support, or the player overcompensates and the sound is harsh. Pressure should be only enough to create a seal between the instrument and the lips. An illustration in *The Art of French Horn Playing*[2] shows the author playing the horn resting on the mantelpiece; his only point of contact with the instrument is his lips on the mouthpiece. Herbert L. Clarke was famous for his apocryphal stunt of hitting high C with the horn suspended from the ceiling by a string. Both examples serve as superb illustrations that little mouthpiece pressure is necessary.

Pressure restricts the flow of blood to the lips causing them to tire quickly. The cure is to use less pressure, to remove the mouthpiece from the lips at every opportunity, and to increase air support. Insufficient air or an underdeveloped embouchure is a cause of excessive mouthpiece pressure as the player makes his lips vibrate by pulling the mouthpiece back into the lips rather than by relying on an adequate flow of air or firm corners of the mouth to create the lip vibration. Brass students should always be encouraged to rely on more air instead of a changed embouchure.

The player should feel as though the air is pushing the mouthpiece away from his lips rather than pushing his lips into the mouthpiece. When the lips are pushed into the mouthpiece (pucker), notes are scooped upward toward the center of the pitch. Also the tone will be stuffy and dull.

The lower brasses allow the player to assume a more relaxed embouchure that may give the feeling of more puckering, although tuba players must maintain firm corners and prevent the embouchure from "caving in."

Beginners often produce a strange, pinched sound for which the cause is not readily apparent. This sound may result from keeping the jaws too closed or bringing the teeth too close together. It may be caused by a lack of breath support, the player squeezing his throat to increase air velocity, or clamping his jaws together to keep the pitch up. To get the jaws separated properly, hold a long tone while slowly raising and lowering the lower jaw while carefully listening to identify the position where the best sound is obtained. The distance between the jaws differs for the trumpet and the tuba player.

Air in the cheeks causes the lips to stretch at the center, destroying the pucker and preventing the muscles at the corners of the mouth from working properly. The smiling embouchure has the same result as air in the cheeks, stretching the center of the embouchure and preventing a good tone.

To be sure the mouthpiece is centered during lengthy practice sessions, the player should take the horn away from his lips at every opportunity and reposition it correctly. As portions of the lips begin to tire or become irritated from constant contact with the mouthpiece, the mouthpiece will "slip" to a new position. As the embouchure develops, the mouthpiece will always fit into the same "grooves" nicely and comfortably. One of Louis Armstrong's unique traits as a trumpet player was his ability to play for hours seemingly without embouchure fatigue. Scholars have observed that this phenomenon was due to his having developed several embouchures. When he felt fatigue setting in, he moved the mouthpiece to a different spot.

ENDURANCE

Herbert L. Clarke said, "Endurance is 90 percent of cornet playing." On any brass instrument, endurance is the prize for practicing regularly and correctly. Some performers have unbelievable staying power as a result of hard work and their natural gifts. Many more are barely warmed up before they are all through for the day. A

---

[2]Philip Farkas (1956). *The Art of French Horn Playing.* Chicago, Clayton F. Summy, p. 66

majority of the brass players believe that endurance and range are the two most difficult aspects of performance. Both require physical and mental skills that are developed over relatively long periods of time.

Excessive mouthpiece pressure is also the primary enemy of endurance. A student who uses heavy pressure should endeavor to break the habit by relearning the fundamentals of tone production and proper breathing and temporarily limiting his playing range. Practice with only the mouthpiece helps as too much pressure prevents one from attaining a full, "loud" buzz. Another exercise is to support the instrument by balancing it on the thumbs instead of grasping it.

Careful practice is practice alternated with rest. The worst scenarios are those in which students do not practice all week and make up for it by practicing four or five hours Sunday afternoon. Those five hours equal thirty minutes of focused practice plus more than four hours of frustration and bad habits. During any practice, the brass player should remove the mouthpiece from his lips and rest a few seconds whenever he feels more than a slight strain. Most published exercises do not warn the player to rest after a few lines, with the result that the students often force themselves to play an entire exercise regardless of how fatigued their lip and embouchure.

As a student's embouchure becomes more stable, the muscles at the corners of the mouth become stronger. The result is greater staying power, increased range, greater flexibility, and more control at various dynamic levels.

Performance anxiety is also a common cause of poor endurance. And because a brass mouthpiece rests against the performer's mouth, it can shake and quiver. The student, unable to control those quivers, suffers from increased performance anxiety. A lack of confidence results in loss of mental control over the physical responses to the performance stimuli: physical tension, shortness of breath, and improper use of the embouchure. Teachers should concern themselves with development of the mental, as well as physical, attributes that enhance endurance.

Increased endurance and the development of a correct embouchure depend upon intelligent and conscientious practice. Control and flexibility, so necessary to the brass player, are gained by careful practice.

All brass players must also concern themselves with tension throughout the body, not just the embouchure. A sample of common tension points is illustrated in Figure 13–3. Tension in these areas of the body will cause fatigue that affects all aspects of performance. Because brass playing is such a physical endeavor, relaxation and flexibility of body parts is essential for accurate playing for any extended period of time and for good playing for *any* length of time.

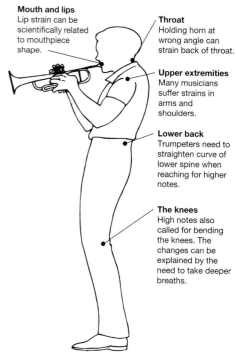

Mouth and lips
Lip strain can be scientifically related to mouthpiece shape.

Throat
Holding horn at wrong angle can strain back of throat.

Upper extremities
Many musicians suffer strains in arms and shoulders.

Lower back
Trumpeters need to straighten curve of lower spine when reaching for higher notes.

The knees
High notes also called for bending the knees. The changes can be explained by the need to take deeper breaths.

Figure 13–3
Common Areas Susceptible to Tension in Brass Playing © 1989 by The New York Times Company. Reprinted with permission.

WARM-UPS AND WARM-DOWNS

The daily warm-up is one of the most important activities of a practice routine. Although the warm-up affects the instrument itself (pitch), its essential purpose is to condition the player in much the same way the athlete's "daily dozen" keeps him in condition—the warm-up increases blood circulation throughout the body and especially the embouchure. For beginning brass players the warm-up is an "embouchure-training" exercise. The muscles used in brass playing must be loosened every day before placing the strain of actual performance on them, gently awakening the lips rather than announcing an abrupt reveille. The warm-up not only conditions the muscles for playing but also helps the player coordinate other physical processes before he starts to practice.

An athlete's calisthenics help him loosen up before a game and build stronger muscles for future endeavors. Similarly, a brass player's warm-up routine is also a muscle-building session that will result in good tone, breath support, tonguing, endurance, flexibility, control, good intonation, and range—in short, almost all the desirable elements of beautiful playing. The word routine is important here, because the warm-up is a daily process, not a spasmodic occurrence. Individual routines differ, but most include the following: work in long tones, lip slurs, tonguing, finger and slide exercises, and intervals, played in various registers and at various dynamic levels.

Also of importance is the "warm-down." When players have been playing in the upper range for an extended period, or exerting physical demand on their embouchure, playing a few warm-down exercises in the low range relaxes the lips to prevent "stiffness," comparable to an adult's exercise to avoid that "morning-after" stiffness. The most common warm-down is to play short exercises softly, in the lowest register of the instrument (including pedal tones for more advanced players) with frequent periods of rest (the mouthpiece off the lips).

Long Tones

Long tones are essential. They provide a daily test of steady breath support, endurance, and a way to listen for and improve tone quality and intonation. Sustained tones are an excellent way to coordinate breathing, range, and dynamics simultaneously throughout the entire register. The player should concentrate on producing and projecting a centered tone regardless of how soft the dynamic level, as well as a well-focused attack and accurate intonation.

Lip Slurs

Lip slurs are the technique of changing pitches within a harmonic series by adjusting the embouchure only, without changing slide position or valve combinations. Students should practice lip slurs in all registers, beginning each day with the middle register and gradually extending to the upper and lower registers. Lip slurs help strengthen the important muscles of the embouchure and help coordinate breathing with embouchure change. If lip slurs are difficult for the player to perform successfully, it is usually because the upper note fails to respond. This problem may be caused by (1) failure to maintain a steady stream of air; (2) unconsciously making a break between the two notes of the slur; (3) not enough flesh of the lower lip in the mouthpiece to start the slur; (4) failure to increase the air speed necessary for a higher pitch on the overtone series—often resulting from students' confusion between the speed of the air and the amount of the air; and (5) failure to firm the muscles at the corners of the mouth for the upper tone (resulting in the increased speed of the airstream blowing the aperture too open). The airstream must increase in speed to slur upward cleanly and slow to slur downward; for most beginners, this is accompanied by a change of dynamic level from piano to forte and the reverse. Lip slurs are helped by arching the tongue (which can be demonstrated by having a student whistle and "slur" from a low pitch to a high pitch—this can be done only with the tongue) and by moving the lower lip in and out.

CONTROL

In the good old days a trumpet player was judged by his ability to whip through such favorites as the "Carnival of Venice," "Emmett's Lullaby," and the "Grand Russian Fantasia." Today, amateur performers are required to play what once was left to more advanced groups. The requirements for the "Carnival of Venice" and the trombone part of a Beethoven symphony are vastly different; but both make serious demands on the performer. The former, with all of its flourishes and runs, looks more difficult, but the symphonic part is just as difficult to play. To play a few isolated notes in various registers with perfect control may be more difficult than to play music that requires a dazzling technique. The first measure of Wagner's "Rienzi Overture" may frighten more trumpet players than does any solo in the literature. The following suggestions can help in achieving control.

1. Practice single attacks. Learn to play any scale or arpeggio one note at a time, removing the instrument from the lips after each tone. Then preface each single attack with one, two, or three articulated grace notes. Try to acquire the ability to play any pitch in the playing range at any level of volume in any style in tune. This procedure helps develop a "memory" of how the embouchure should feel for various pitches.

2. Practice intervals from any given tone. For instance, begin on second-line G in treble clef or a fourth-line F in bass, and play a major second, a major third, a fourth, and so on. Practice ascending intervals, descending intervals, and sequences of thirds, fourths, fifths, and sixths.

3. Write out a series of unrelated tones and practice them daily. Refer to Farkas' *The Art of French Horn Playing* for examples of this kind. Similar studies are available in various books. (See the bibliography at the end of the chapter.)

4. Work on tones that seem difficult to play accurately on the various brass instruments (e.g., the sixth partial F# concert on B♭ instruments).

5. Keep a record of your progress. Try to make fewer mistakes the second time through an exercise. Learn to practice critically. Players who habitually miss dozens of notes in their daily practice sessions are always at a loss to understand why they miss dozens of notes in a performance. Herbert L. Clarke relates that he hadn't actually been aware of his inaccurate playing until the day a friend commented on the large number of errors he heard.[3] He revised his practice habits and became the most famous cornetist of all time.

FLEXIBILITY

Many players lack the flexibility to slur upward—they cannot attain the upper note. Others get it by using an unmusical burst of air. Excessive pressure reduces flexibility and contributes to the difficulty of slurring. Players tend to pull the mouthpiece back into the lips to get that higher note. This use of pressure is not entirely wrong, but it should not be used as a crutch to overcome slurring difficulties.

Occasionally the trumpet or horn player must execute a lip trill. The lip trill is nothing more than a fast lip slur usually between notes a whole tone apart. Because a trill must be rapid to be effective, it must be practiced slowly, gradually increasing the speed to gain flexibility.

[3]Herbert L. Clarke (1934), *How I Became a Cornetist*, St. Louis: Joseph Huber, p. 50.

RANGE

It isn't easy to develop a good high range. The young player always hopes to find a secret that will suddenly empower him to soar flawlessly into the upper registers. Whereas a major scale can be practiced sufficiently in one evening to be played very fast, learning to play high notes takes a great deal of time and progress is usually slow. A good high register results from the combination of good embouchure and a supported airstream from the diaphragm developed through practicing sustained tones and lip slurs in a comfortable register at medium volume. As strength develops, the range and dynamic level may be extended.

High tones are produced by coordinating the breath, lips, and tongue, not by violent physical exertion. The corners of the mouth must be held firmly together to increase tension; the more developed the muscles become the greater is their ability to contract. The player must tense the corners of his mouth with the feeling that the corners of his lips are pressing against his teeth. He must exhale with greater abdominal pressure to increase the speed of the airstream and vibrate his lips faster. His tongue should be raised or arched as if forming an "ee" sound—the arch is in the middle of the tongue, not at the back (Figure 13–4). Tightening muscles or tension in the back of the tongue will close the throat. The lower lip must not be allowed to collapse into the mouth over the lower teeth or behind the upper lip. For the high range, the lower jaw will often rise somewhat so that the lip and teeth opening becomes smaller. Some horn players hold the head back to alter the angle of the flow of air entering the mouthpiece; a more acceptable alternative is to draw the lower lip back so it is slightly under the upper lip, keeping the lips together, and sending the stream of air downward. The brass player using the pivot system does the same thing. For the upper limits of the range, suddenly forcing the air out with greater speed will help produce the higher pitches. Students attempting to increase their upper range should play softly in that register—this approach aids the student in distinguishing between the speed and the volume of the air. Even a very soft, slight squeak (played with little mouthpiece pressure) is fine at first; a baby crawls before it walks and walks before it runs.

Learning to play in the high register demands practicing in the high register, but with care, frequent rest, and alternate low register practice (still with plenty of air support). Buzzing on the mouthpiece or with the lips can help strengthen the facial muscles.

When attempting to increase one's range, the habit of warming-down cannot be stressed enough. The player must take these few minutes to relax the facial muscles and increase the flow of blood to the muscle tissue.

Figure 13–4
Approximate Location of the Tongue for Low, Middle, and High Notes

ARTICULATIONS

As the term is defined in most dictionaries, *articulation* is how sounds are connected—that is, not only how a sound is started but how it ends. This definition is important because many wind players are adept at starting a pitch using the tongue, but far too many use the tongue to end the note. Use of the tongue not only results in an unpleasant sound but also handicaps the player in fast passages or long, soft, tapered phrase endings.

For attacks the tongue is used merely to clip off the "wind sound" at the beginning of each tongued note (i.e., the milliseconds between the point that the air is released and the point that a standing wave in the instrument produces a tone). The cleanest beginning of each note is achieved by letting the tongue touch the roof of the mouth just behind the upper teeth. Use the syllable "duh" because it is slightly less explosive than "tuh," although every brass player will eventually face an articulation that requires an explosive attack.

Students should experience the difference in tongue placement when vocalizing "tuh," "duh," "thuh" (which is *not* used in performance), and "kuh" (used in double-tonguing, but used here to demonstrate various ways one can start a tone). While tongue placement for the vowel sound is the same for each of these syllables, the tongue is used differently for each of the consonant sounds (the vowel "ah" is often used, but because it involves movement by the jaw it can lead to associating jaw movement with tonguing). The tip of the tongue is farthest forward and touches the teeth on "thuh," with the middle of the tongue touching the roof of the mouth for "kuh."

The tongue stays out of the way when inhaling and during the actual time the tone is being produced. It rises very quickly, touches the roof of the mouth when the consonant "d" is vocalized then quickly returns to the bottom or middle of the mouth (as if vocalizing "oe" in the low register and "ee" in the upper). Teachers must be careful in working with students who choke off the airstream; too much emphasis in keeping the tongue at the bottom of the mouth can result in tension and poor articulations. In general, students should be directed to keep the tongue relaxed and to tongue using the least amount of tongue movement. If teachers emphasize the appropriate vowel sound in vocalizing exercises and melodies, the tongue will respond properly. The rule of thumb (or tongue) is that the shorter the distance that the tongue must move, the greater the control, the quicker it can move, and the less fatiguing will be rapid and prolonged passages.

Most pitches are stopped when the air is stopped; they should not be stopped abruptly with the tongue except for jazz articulations. One of the most difficult concepts for a beginning brass player to understand is that notes are connected unless the music indicates something different. The words in this sentence are printed with spaces used to separate them; when vocalized or read aloud, however, the words run together and the vowel sounds are articulated by consonant sounds. Students must understand that notes in a musical phrase are analogous to the vowel sounds when speaking and are separated when tongued only by the consonant "d" used at the beginning of each note which quickly "disrupts" the airstream. In very fast passages, the tongue starts and stops tones with the same motion.

A common articulation problem is for students to hold the air until time to play the note. Holding the air prior to an attack will guarantee tension in the throat, neck, and chest, and makes it difficult to "restart" the airstream with control. To counter this habit the mouthpiece should be placed on the lips (which should be relaxed and completely at rest), the breath taken through the corners of the mouth "around" the mouthpiece, and released with no hesitation. At the instant that the air is released, the lips form the proper embouchure for the desired pitch (from memory), and the tongue moves to touch the area just behind the top teeth. The placement of the tip of the tongue must be the same for the same style articulation whether the note is played loudly or softly, and regardless of register. The player should blow through the note, not just blow "at" the note; golfers and musicians refer to this concept as "follow through."

Important to all wind players is speed of tonguing and evenness of rapid tonguing. Students should see, through demonstration, that taking a proper breath and vocalizing "duh, duh, duh, duh" will result in no movement in the face or jaw. If the students blow or vocalize as if playing a long tone and repeat "duh," the tongue will slightly and properly disrupt the air without stopping the air.

When controlled and accurate tonguing becomes a habit, and as demands in the music require, the student can gradually be introduced to the variety of articulations used by brass players. Syllables such as "luh, luh, luh" are appropriate and commonly used for legato passages; "tuh—tuh—tuh" for marcato passages.

Brass players (and flute players) have the advantage of being able to double-tongue and triple-tongue easily. Double-tonguing is done by "see-sawing" the tongue so that the tip touches the teeth alternating with the middle of the tongue in touching the roof of the mouth: "tuh–kuh, tuh–kuh" or "duh–guh, duh–guh." In learning multiple tonguings it is much easier to vocalize these syllables than to use them in playing an instrument. The student should then practice by starting a long tone, and very slowly articulating that pitch over and over by placing the tongue in the positions for the consonants "duh–guh" (Figure 13–5). This exercise should be repeated slowly until the articulations are even. This may require separate practice on the "guh" syllable, until it flows easily. The tempo should be increased gradually.

Figure 13–5 Initial Exercise to Coordinate the Tongue for Double-Tonguing

Only when the student begins to feel comfortable with the task of double-tonguing, and a moderate to fast tempo is achieved, should use of the valves be added minimally to the task (Figure 13-6).

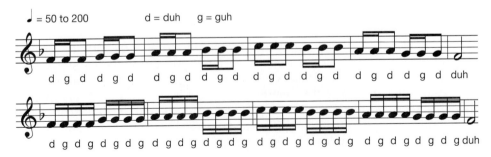

Figure 13–6 Initial Exercise for Coordinating Fingers with Tongue in Double-Tonguing

Finally, difficult passages may be introduced that require much greater coordination of lips, tongue, embouchure, and also the fingers (e.g., illustrated in Figure 13–7). Each of these types of exercises should be single-tongued, then practiced using only the "guh" articulation, and slowly double-tongued, striving for evenness and a good tone quality.

Figure 13–7 Coordinating Fingers with Double-Tonguing

In triple-tonguing, the tongue makes a somewhat circular motion repeating "tuh–duh–kuh, tuh–duh–kuh." Again, the same technique of starting slowly and gradually increasing speed and accuracy is used. This technique is followed by stages of adding valves, then the actual coordination of the embouchure, tongue, air, and fingers.

Other series of syllables work well for triple-tonguing and seem to be more natural for some players. The syllables which are not useful are "Tuh—kuh—tuh, tuh—kuh—tuh". "Tuh—kuh—tuh" seems natural for many students who learn to double-tongue first, and try to add another "tuh" after the double-tongued notes, but this pattern of syllables makes it virtually impossible to play the notes evenly.

Essential to every successful brass player is the ability to play with a wide variety of articulations, including: slurs (lip and valve), accents (emphasized notes), staccato (separated notes), legato, sforzando, double-and triple-tonguing (legato, staccato, etc.), and flutter-tongue (placing the tip of the tongue near the center of the roof of the mouth and vibrating the tongue like a greatly exaggerated "rolled r").

INTONATION

Two of the primary factors in intonation for a brass instrument are (1) the harmonics of the overtone series and (2) valve combinations. The overtone series, being a "natural" phenomenon, does not conform to the rules of the tempered scale; certain pitches are higher or lower than their equivalent in the tempered scale. In relation to the tempered scale, partials five and ten are somewhat flat; partials seven, eleven, thirteen, and fourteen are severely flat; partials three and six are sharp. When these partials are used, the player must make pitch corrections to play in tune with other instruments using the tempered scale. The fingerings commonly used by valved instrument players are suggested specifically to avoid these partials or to compensate for out-of-tune partials.

Nearly all instruments are made so that the slides must be pulled slightly to be in tune. The tuning slide should be pulled, and for the valved instruments, all the valve slides may be pulled, especially for the horn. The general rule is to pull the first slide twice as much as the second, and the third slide three times as far as the second. Any tuning is useless unless the player listens and uses the embouchure to make fine adjustments when playing. Many trumpets and cornets are designed with a ring on the third valve slide that is moved by the ring or middle finger of the left hand. Other brass instruments use a fourth valve and the trombone has a trigger. Most professional-line and many middle-line trumpets and cornets have similar devices on the first valve slide.

The brass player can alter pitch by changing the position of his lips or tongue, the direction of the airstream, or the amount of air pressure. The general rules are these: To raise the pitch, tighten the muscles at the corners of the lips; arch the middle of the tongue slightly by thinking "ee," as though moving to a higher register; increase the amount of air pressure (using the abdominal muscles) to increase the speed of the airstream; focus the airstream at an angle rather than straight into the mouthpiece (see Figure 13–2 on page 205). To lower the pitch, loosen the muscles at the corners of the lips; lower the tongue and jaw by thinking the syllable "aw," as though moving to a lower register; in the lower registers, direct the stream of air down into the mouthpiece. In the higher registers any angling of the airstream will sharpen the pitch, but in the low register a downward direction of the air can help flatten the pitch.

MUTES

Mutes in general tend to raise the pitch of the instrument in the lower register. They also make the instrument slightly harder to play and less responsive. Students should not practice excessively with mutes. Because they add resistance, they are considered by many teachers to be a viable means to build the embouchure, but it is impossible to work on tone quality when the instrument is muted, and tone quality is, after all, the most important element in musical skill building.

Straight mutes, except for the plastic variety, tend to raise the pitch. The straight mute produces a brighter tone but a thinner sound; the tone seems to be affected most in the lower register, somewhat less in the high register, and least in the middle register. The most popular straight mutes are of metal. The "stone-lined" mute is still a popular product and is less expensive. The metal mute sounds a bit raspier and was initially preferred by jazz musicians; now the metal mute has been refined and most trumpet players prefer it.

Cup mutes, frequently used in solo literature as well as in jazz ensembles, lower the pitch in the medium register. Tonal color cups, however, lower the pitch in the upper register. Use of the cup mute gives a velvety tone quality with the tone attenuated most in the lower register and less as the pitch rises.

Wah-wah and Harmon mutes tend to raise the pitch in the middle register and lower it in the high register. These mutes produce a buzzing sound or tone. They thin out the tone more in the extremities than in the middle range but are adjustable using the stem projecting from the center. Because these mutes fit snugly inside the bell of the instrument, and the cork completely surrounds the mute, the trumpet player must blow warm, moist air into the bell to create a layer of water vapor to keep these mutes in place.

DYNAMICS

After good tone quality, the factor that can most enhance the music is dynamic control. The player who has developed the complete dynamic range from pianissimo to fortissimo approaches professional standards. Whereas the amateur often has little besides an ear-shattering fortissimo and an ever-present mezzo forte, the professional seems to have every graduation from a whisper to a sforzando, all produced with a consistently fine tone.

Dynamic control depends upon breath support and control, a responsive and flexible embouchure. Powerful tone requires more air, soft tone requires less air. To develop volume, the student practices inhaling a large amount of air and getting rid of it rapidly. To play softly, he inhales the same amount of air but exhales it more slowly, making it last for a much longer time, and increasing his control to avoid wavers, quavers, and bends. More muscular control is necessary for soft playing; more embouchure control is necessary for loud playing, as an increase in the air pressure tends to force the lips open.

To maintain a pianissimo tone, the lips should be relaxed and close together, the throat open and relaxed, and the air blown with intensity as a small, thin, steady stream. If the lips are too far apart the tone may break. The ability to attack and sustain a note played pianissimo can be developed by practicing whole notes as softly as possible alternated with whole rests. The player should remove the mouthpiece from his lips on each rest and make a fresh start for each tone. A common problem in playing softly is the tendency to "hold onto" the air, even on soft passages. The tone must be projected and constant air support maintained. A valuable mental concept is to project the soft note to the back of the auditorium.

THE MOUTHPIECE

The mouthpiece on a brass instrument is as important as a reed on an oboe—it influences intonation, tone quality, and response, and it is a factor in accuracy, flexibility, and endurance. Fortunately, brass mouthpieces are not as fragile and temporary as reeds. If the player finds one that pleases him, he has it forever. Finding the right one is a problem; the mouthpiece can cause a dozen playing faults.

The dimensions of most mouthpieces are identified by number and letter. The same numbering system is not used by the three most popular manufacturers, so it is necessary to give both size and brand name when speaking of mouthpieces. With the Bach and Giardinelli, the low numbers indicate a larger cup diameter as measured across the inner edge of the rim (a Bach 3 is larger than a 7), whereas the opposite is true for Schilke numbers. A letter indicates the depth of the cup. The Bach A cup is the deepest; models without letters have medium-deep cups. Bach B cups are medium deep but slightly livelier than the unlettered cup, and the C cup is medium shallow.

There are four critical areas to consider in selecting a mouthpiece. They are the rim, cup, bore or throat, and backbore Figure 13–8 and Figure 13–9.

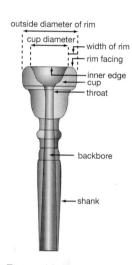

Figure 13–8 Mouthpiece for Brass Instrument

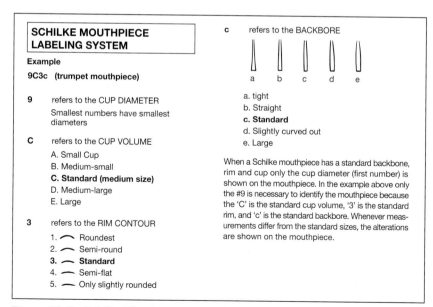

Figure 13–9   Schilke Mouthpiece Labeling System

The Rim

A medium-wide rim offers good flexibility without cutting off blood circulation to the lips. A wide, flat rim (as on the left) provides greater endurance by spreading the pressure from the embouchure toward the mouthpiece over a greater area, but possibly at the expense of flexibility and accuracy (Figure13–10a). The narrower rim (Figure 13–10b) enhances flexibility, but tends to decrease in endurance as it "cuts" into the embouchure more. Rounded outer and inner rims reduce the amount of flat surface coming in contact with the lips, tending to reduce endurance but enhancing flexibility. Wide-rimmed mouthpieces coupled with a round rim and a large cup diameter may result in a poor high register and less lip flexibility.

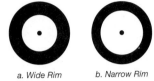

a. Wide Rim   b. Narrow Rim

Figure 13–10
Relative Difference Between Wide and Narrow Rim Pieces[4]

The rim of the mouthpiece may have a fairly sharp inner edge often called a "bite"; a rounded inner rim will give more comfort, but at the expense of control of articulation and accuracy. Of the two most popular brands of brass mouthpieces, Bach and Schilke, probably the most significant difference is that Bach mouthpieces have this "bite" and Schilke ones do not. On the horn, a sharp bite facilitates clean attacks but hinders the production of clean slurs; a rounded rim produces the opposite effects.

The Cup

Both Renold Schilke and Vincent Bach recommended the use of the largest possible cup diameter because the player is then forced to use his lip muscles correctly rather than pinching out the high tones (See Figure 13–11).

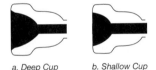

a. Deep Cup   b. Shallow Cup

Figure 13–11
The Black Area Illustrates the Area inside the Brass Mouthpiece Cup[5]

Warburton now manufactures the largest cup volume for each of the brass instruments. A narrow and shallow cup favors the upper harmonics, producing a sound that is thin, shrill, and almost nasal (See Figure 13–12).

If the dimensions are both shallow and small, the tone is choked, hard and stuffy, and a good tone is hard to produce (although it may be easy to get "a sound"), although the upper register is easier to attain. A deep, big cup gives increased volume and tone in the low and middle registers, but carried to extremes, results in a dull, unfocused tone. The smaller sizes are recommended for players who have weaker embouchures. In short, the deeper the cup, the darker the sound, and usually the more difficult the upper range.

With the horn, true euphonium, and tuba mouthpieces, the shape of the cup from the rim to the bore can be only slightly bowl shaped or nearly straight. The bowl-shaped cup will produce a somewhat darker and more resonant tone; the straight will result in a less resonant but smoother, lighter tone. This difference is caused by the angle of the "edge" at which the cup joins the throat.

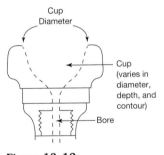

Cup Diameter

Cup (varies in diameter, depth, and contour)

Bore

Figure 13–12
Parts of the Upper Portion of a Brass Mouthpiece that Affect All Aspects of Performance

The Throat or Bore

Tone quality is also determined by the size of the throat opening in the mouthpiece, called simply "the throat" or "the bore." Larger throats enable the player to produce a darker or mellower sound and to play louder without overblowing or

[4] http://www.selmer.com.
[5] http://www.selmer.com.

distorting the tone; at the same time the larger throat often reduces control at softer dynamic levels. A large throat demands more muscular strength in the embouchure and greater endurance. Small size throats make the sound more brilliant and make playing in the upper register easier, but the sound usually becomes more and more shrill as the range is extended upward. Further, a tight throat can hurt intonation. For the average player a mouthpiece with an enlarged bore (many repair shops enlarge the bore) is not recommended because his lips are not in shape for long hours of playing. Many brass players will have a favorite mouthpiece bored out as their range and endurance develop.

With the horn, the shape of the cup from the rim to the bore can be bowl shaped or nearly straight. The bowl-shaped cup will produce a somewhat darker and more resonant tone; the straight will result in a less resonant but smoother and lighter tone.

The Backbore

The backbore of the mouthpiece must be related to the instrument as well as to the size of the rim, cup, and bore (Figure 13–13). If the backbore is small, notes in the high register can usually be played more easily, but tend to be stuffy; if too large, there is insufficient resistance in the instrument, resulting in poor endurance and airy, spread tones. Most mouthpieces are made with medium-size backbores for average players. The standard Schilke mouthpiece is made with a larger backbore than the Bach; the Bach is often bored out by more advanced players.

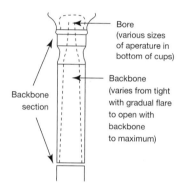

**Figure 13–13
Parts of the Lower Portion of a Brass Mouthpiece That Affect All Aspects of Performance**

General Considerations

The best mouthpiece for beginning students is probably a compromise of all the available sizes in the four parts of a mouthpiece; that is, a medium-size cup with a standard rim on a medium-size throat and backbore. As the student develops his embouchure and the teacher observes the player's strengths and weaknesses, a mouthpiece can be selected to help accommodate any weaknesses that cannot be remedied by good playing habits (Figure 13–14).

Students who have a tendency to play with excessive tension and a squeezed tone and cannot seem to relax the sound may benefit from a mouthpiece with less resistance. Conversely, those with a tendency to overblow may be helped by a more open mouthpiece. Split tones or a strident, thin sound are often a sign of too small and too shallow a mouthpiece.

If a student transfers from the trumpet to the horn, he may have embouchure difficulties. A transition mouthpiece, such as the Pottag 6A made by Reynolds, may be helpful to use until the player adjusts to the different demands of the horn and can move successfully to a standard horn mouthpiece.

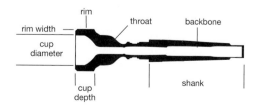

Figure 13–14 Parts of the Brass Mouthpiece

CARE, CLEANING, MAINTENANCE

All brass instruments accumulate a certain amount of dirt and grease. Brass instruments can be washed by pouring warm, soapy water through them, followed by a rinse in clear water to remove all the soap. Running clear, warm water through the instrument every few days is recommended. The outside should be dried with a soft cloth. Piston valves, rotary valves, and slides should be removed to clean them. When using a swab, the student should be certain the metal end is covered with a soft, lint-free cloth to prevent scratching the soft valve casings. The valves must be handled carefully, because even a tiny bump can cause them to jam. The valves and valve casings should be carefully wiped without the fingers touching them because dirt, perspiration, or acid from the hands slows valve action. After cleaning, the valves are returned to the instruments with the numbers of the valves matching the numbers on the casings. Valve slides (not trombone slides) should be slightly lubricated with slide grease.

Most of the dirt accumulates in the mouthpiece and leadpipe. A small flexible brush or cloth plus lots of warm water should be used to clean these areas regularly. Placing the mouthpiece in boiling water may be necessary if it is extremely dirty. When mouthpieces become stuck in the horn, they may be extremely dirty, the student may have driven the mouthpiece in with his hand, the horn may have been dropped, or the shank may be bent. If the mouthpiece does become stuck, it should not be removed by wiggling it back and forth. The use of a mouthpiece puller or the services of a repairperson are required. Almost any repairperson can recall fantastic tales of damage to instruments at the hands of well-meaning but uninformed parents. Proper preventive actions will eliminate this problem altogether. The player should remove the mouthpiece when he is through playing and keep the mouthpiece and receiver clean.

The tuning slides can also stick, due to a copper precipitate that builds up or to dirt and sludge resulting from saliva passing through the horn. Removing the slides often and keeping them greased eliminates this problem. If a slide becomes stuck, one can sometimes loosen it by inserting a handkerchief or belt through the tubing and exerting pressure. This move failing, it is best to call a repairperson who has special equipment to loosen these slides.

Daily care is important. The valves and slides must be kept lubricated, but too much lubricant can cause dirt and sludge to accumulate quickly. Saliva should not be substituted for oil because it is injurious to the valves and contains acids that in time will corrode the valve or casing. One way to oil a valve is to pull the first valve slide and allow the oil to run through, working the valves up and down and removing the excess oil from the third valve slide. This method prevents dirt from the air contacting the valve, keeps the valve from being handled so much, and reduces the chance of dropping it. Applying oil directly onto the valve or slide can help insure that the valve tops do not become corroded and stuck. The valve casing can be cleaned with a chamois cloth. The valve itself can be cleaned by a lintless paper such as a coffee filter without causing damage.

The dirt that tends to accumulate in the small ports in the valves can be removed by drawing a small cloth through the ports. The cleaning rod should not be used for this purpose as there is danger of denting the valve casings where the star aligns the valves. This dirt can be removed with a toothpick. Threads on caps should be kept clean to insure their easy removal when needed. The felt at the top of the valves becomes worn and must be replaced occasionally, as is also true of the corks on the valves.

New instruments should be flushed with warm water before they are used; otherwise dust that has worked its way into the instrument during packing and shipping may cause damage to valves or valve casings. Running a small amount of oil through the leadpipe will keep the acid in the saliva from producing a slimy copper precipitate inside the tubing. New valved brass instruments require frequent cleaning and re-oiling of the valves for a three-day period or until no trace of dirt or grime appears on the valves.

The student should not be carrying schoolbooks or the day's lunch in the instrument case. If the case has a special compartment, that should be used for instrumental accessories. All these items should be secure and out of contact with the instrument, because even the smallest dents on the mouthpiece or the mouthpiece shank will affect intonation and tone quality. Dents that occur must be removed immediately by a competent repairperson. All braces should be kept soldered to prevent weakening the instrument.

Sodas, candy, or other sugary foods should never be put in the mouth when playing. Sugar in the instrument can cause moving parts to stick. Rinsing out the mouth or better yet, brushing one's teeth, before playing will promote cleanliness of the instrument.

TROUBLESHOOTING

Equipment

Sluggish piston valves

1. Oil valves separately by loosening retaining cap and carefully lifting from valve casing; a small amount of olive oil may be added to the valve oil to make it stick longer. (Most brass instruments are constructed so that the leadpipe goes directly into the first valve; consequently, much oil is washed off by condensation.)
2. Make sure student is pressing valves straight down and not at an angle.
3. Remove valves and clean them and the casing with lint-free cloth; oil well, and replace.
4. Interrogate student to determine if he has instructions backwards. Vaseline on tuning slides; oil on valves.
5. If horn is well used, try stretching springs or rotating springs between valves.

Sluggish rotary valves

1. Place several drops of valve oil into first valve slide, holding instrument so that it runs down the tubing; work the other valves up and down; expel excess oil out third-valve water key or slide.
2. Oil the front bushing, and remove the valve cap to oil the bushing back—using rotary valves that are not oiled can quickly ruin the valves.

Trombone slide moves slowly, not freely

1. Place several drops of slide oil onto slide; expel excess oil out water key.
2. Make sure student is keeping right arm, hand, and fingers relaxed.
3. Inspect slide for slide cream-oil mixture. (Thoroughly clean and use either oil or slide cream–water.)
4. If student uses slide cream, spray with water until the water beads up on the slide.
5. Remove slide and lay on table; the slide should lie flat, as one raised "corner" indicates alignment problems.
6. Inspect slide for edges rubbing the tubing inside the slide; worn plating will cause brass against brass friction and excessive wear.
7. Interrogate student to determine if she was only half listening when you explained petroleum jelly (Vaseline) on *tuning* slide.

Air will not pass freely

1. Inspect F attachment on trombone for correct alignment.
2. Inspect for clogged leadpipe or bell. (Mouthpieces fit very snugly in the bell.)
3. Inspect for a dirty mouthpiece.
4. Make sure piston valves are in correct casings.
5. Make sure rotary valves are aligned.
6. Inspect for worn corks.

Mouthpiece wiggles

1. Shank too long. (Have competent repairperson remove short sections at a time). A mouthpiece shank that is too short causes moderate to severe intonation problems.
2. Shank out-of-round. (Again, have repaired by competent repairperson.)
3. Euphoniums and tubas may require a special size shank designed for the particular manufacturer.

Instrument leaks air

1. Inspect and if necessary replace cork on water key.
2. If around trombone's F valve casing, have resoldered by competent repairperson.

3. If around baritone's valve casing, have resoldered by competent repairperson.

4. If new instrument, have retailer replace it.

5. If leak is around the trombone slide, it is a very serious problem; try slide cream–water solution; replating is a costly alternative.

Buzzing sound

1. Inspect for broken brace(s); have resoldered.

2. Determine if a recent soaking may have loosened residue inside. (Rewash or use flexible brush.)

3. Inspect for loose receiver spring on trombone.

4. Be sure the trombone's receiver screw connects bell to slide tightly.

5. Determine if baritone mouthpiece is too small; purchase correct size.

Gurgling sound

1. If water gurgles without valves pressed, inspect for clogged water key (remove running slide and dump); expel any water, rotate baritone to pour out of an open slide tube, leadpipe, or bell section.

2. If water sounds with valves pressed (especially a problem with the second piston valve), remove valve slides to expel; tilt baritone to pour. (Many students forget that the third-valve must be pressed for the third-valve water key to work effectively.)

3. Horn: empty valve slides, unwind horn slowly to drain out excess water from the leadpipe; if left for too long, some will pass all three valves and must be drained through bell.

Tone

Thin, strident

1. Lack of air and/or air pressure.

2. Teeth together; drop jaw.

3. Aperture too small; have student pucker lips as if whistling then buzz without mouthpiece sound (pitches, scales, or tunes), then add mouthpiece, then add instrument.

4. Tongue tense or possibly too high. (Relax tongue or try pushing against the back lower teeth; use "taw" syllable.)

5. Tension in throat. (Drop shoulders; drop tongue as in yawning; rag-doll approach.)

6. Embouchure too stretched. (Relax mouth, tighten corners, buzz without mouthpiece.)

7. Mouthpiece too shallow and/or backbore too tight.

8. Aperture too flat. (Attempt to get student to pucker more—like a whistle; try a "doo" articulation rather than "dah" or "duh.")

9. Too much lip (especially upper lip) in the mouthpiece. (Keep the corners tight or try to think "em" with corners tight.)

10. For horn: right hand too straight or not inserted enough; cup more; try to cover more bell.

11. Tongue too high. (Try articulating "daw" rather than "dee".)

12. Practice breathing large amounts of air with the mouth in shape for vocalizing "o-o-o-o".

Dull, spread, or "unfocused" sound

1. Lips not buzzing evenly. (Buzz without mouthpiece, then with mouthpiece alone.)

2. Not enough air support. (Blow "fast" air.)

3. Cheeks puffing. (Practice buzzing without mouthpiece.)

4. Embouchure too slack. (Tighten corners and encourage student to focus pitch—blow a fast "pencil thin" airstream.)

5. Aperture too large. (Same as 4.)

6. Mouthpiece too large in diameter.

7. Chin may not be stretched flat. (Keep corners firm and teeth apart to flatten chin.)

8. Horn: right fingers may be apart. (Keep fingers together.)

9. Horn: head too high, tilted back. (Reposition horn so that student can bring mouthpiece to embouchure at approximately same angle as a clarinet.)

10. Horn: too much pucker in embouchure. (Buzz without mouthpiece.)

Forced sound with excessive edge

1. Mouthpiece too shallow or throat/backbore too small.

2. Throat too tight. (Relaxation exercises.)

3. Embouchure too stretched. (Attempt more pucker.)

4. Too much bottom lip. (Try two-thirds upper.)

5. Embouchure too stretched which flattens aperture. (Attempt to pucker more; buzz without mouthpiece, then with mouthpiece alone before adding trombone.)

6. Tongue is too high. (Articulate with "daw" instead of "dee" or "dah.")

7. Practice inhaling and exhaling large amounts of air with mouth in shape for vocalizing "o-o-o-o" and without "holding" the air.

8. Attempt to play while pulling mouthpiece away from embouchure.

9. Work toward mental image of "warmer" airstream.

10. Dirty mouthpiece or leadpipe.

11. May try a more funnel or V-shape mouthpiece.

Stuffy, fuzzy sound (airy)

1. Too much lip in the mouthpiece; try a larger sound mouthpiece or keeping corners tighter.

2. Lips pinched together.

3. Teeth together. (Drop jaw as in "aw.")

4. Air pocket behind upper or lower lip. (Keep corners of mouth firm and practice buzzing without and with only the mouthpiece.)

5. Cheeks puffing. (Buzz without mouthpiece.)

6. Closed throat. (Pull shoulders down; drop tongue as if there's a hot potato in your mouth.)

7. Head tilted. (Correct playing position.)

8. Fatigue. (Relax embouchure by "flapping" lips like a horse; buzzing without and on the mouthpiece alone; work on pedal tones with a focused sound [lips may not buzz evenly when they are tired and/or swollen; this can be caused by lack of proper warm-up, warm-down, trying for too many high notes too soon, or simply after a demanding practicing session].)

9. Too much saliva in mouthpiece/embouchure.

10. Improper mouthpiece placement. (Correct embouchure and posture.)

11. Embouchure may be too spread for the low notes, without keeping corners firm.

12. Horn: too much hand in bell.

Difficult with upper range

1. Excessive playing of low notes. (Rely more on air and less on pressure; corners of the mouth should be kept firm, attempt to pull horn and mouthpiece away from embouchure when playing.)

2. Blow air faster; a "pencil-thin" jet airstream.

3. Fatigue; lack of proper warm-up or warm down on previous day.

4. Mouthpiece too deep or diameter too large.

5. Try to direct air downward by rolling in lower lip.

6. Too much bottom lip in mouthpiece.

7. Embouchure may be too immature. (Be patient and work on lip slurs for strength.)

8. Improper mouthpiece angle. (Correct position for holding.)

9. Embouchure too tight. (Correct embouchure.)

10. Low brass: extensive work on pedal tones to open throat, keep air moving without excessive demand on embouchure endurance.

Articulation

Explosive attacks

1. Building air pressure behind tongue or "holding" onto the air before releasing it. (Try for better coordination between air and tongue); inhale to exhale without stopping. (Try practicing attacks completely without the use of the tongue.)

2. Tonguing between the teeth. (Work toward a "duh" articulation to replace "thuh.")

3. Stopping the previous note with the tongue. (Practice playing long tones while merely dis-

rupting the airstream with the tongue, notes are connected.)

4. Articulating with a "pah" or "mah" syllable.

5. Aperture too small. (Practice for a big, rich, full, but focused sound in all registers; flexibility exercises to keep from "closing-down" when going into upper register.)

6. Attempting to articulate with lips touching "puh" or "muh." (Work on long tones with "big, opened, focused tone" and use slow repeated "duh" articulations.)

7. Horn: head tilted back too far. (Reposition horn to keep head at approximately same angle as clarinet.)

Scooping notes, facial movement

1. Air taking too long to reach appropriate velocity. (Full breaths and complete diaphragm support.)

2. "Chewing notes;" excessive chin movement. (Tongue moving too far; replace "taw-taw" with "doo-doo".)

3. Inspect for chin bunching up. (Buzz without mouthpiece; stress keeping corners firm.)

4. Sometimes caused by students playing timidly; explain that mistakes are expected; encourage brass players to take a chance.

5. Slide not working smoothly. (Keep it well lubricated.)

6. Drop back of tongue.

7. Too much lip in the mouthpiece. (Practice forming an embouchure and buzzing without the mouthpiece, then trying to establish the same sensations when playing.)

8. Horn: head tilted back too far.

9. Jaw too closed. (Try opening jaw/teeth more at all times: inhaling, tonguing, exhaling.)

Difficulty with slurs on trombone

1. Smears on trombone. (Use legato tongue for all slurs: "duh" or "dah" articulation.)

2. Teach alternate slide positions.

3. Move slide very quickly.

4. Do not change embouchures if pitches are on the same harmonic series (i.e., slurring from a middle-line D to a fourth, line F uses the identical embouchure.)

5. Same as the previous 5.

Difficulty with valve slurs

1. Minimize embouchure change if valve slurs are within the same open partial (i.e., there should be absolutely no movement/change when slurring from a second space A to fourth line F.)

2. Too many long tones in daily practice schedule without a sufficient balance of flexibility studies.

3. Slam valves (i.e., press them very quickly.)
4. Steady airstream to avoid breaks.

Difficulty with lip slurs

1. Try directing air downward for slurs going up.
2. "Lean" into lower pitch for slurs going up; followed by the upper pitch played slightly softer.
3. Increase air speed (but not volume) when going to upper note.
4. Avoid excessive pressure on upper note; tighten corners of mouth instead and let air do the work.
5. Roll-in lower lip for upper pitch.
6. Do not let tone spread on lower pitches. (An easy habit to fall into because it is almost impossible to "undershoot" a low pitch.)
7. Too many long tones on a daily basis without sufficient balance of flexibility studies.
8. Mouthpiece rim too wide.
9. Keep airstream steady to avoid breaks.
10. For ascending slurs arch tongue "tah—ee".

11. Not enough lower lip in mouthpiece can make upward slurs difficult.

Endurance lacking

1. Too much pressure from mouthpiece onto embouchure. (Loosen grip in left hand; try using only a few fingers on left hand to hold instrument; or practice while holding the instrument as far from the embouchure as possible and still get a tone.)
2. Fatigue from too demanding practice sessions without enough rest periods.
3. Lack of proper warm-up and/or warm-down.
4. Not using corners of mouth properly (the strongest muscles in the face) and not relying on the air to do most of the work.
5. Mouthpiece placement may need correcting.
6. Lacking full intake of air.
7. Often due to mouthpiece being too low on embouchure.
8. Anxiety. (Relaxation and the realization that mistakes are going to happen—but it is not the end of the world.)

BIBLIOGRAPHY

Texts

Indicates out of print in 2001.

*ANDERSON, PAUL G. (1989). *Brass Solo and Study Guide*. Evanston, IL: Instrumentalist.

BAINES, ANTHONY (1993). *Brass Instruments: Their History and Development*. New York: Dover Publications; reprint of (1976) New York: Scribner's.

*BELLAMAH, JOSEPH L. (1976). *A Survey of Modern Brass Teaching Philosophies of Today's Leading Brass Specialists Including Trumpet, Cornet, Horn, Trombone, Euphonium and Tuba: Also Including Jazz Approaches to Brass Playing by the Leading Performers*. San Antonio, TX: Southern Music.

Brass Anthology: A Collection of Brass Articles Published in The Instrumentalist Magazine *from 1946 to 1999*, 10th ed. (2000) Northfield, IL: Instrumentalist.

*FARKAS, PHILIP (1989). *The Art of Brass Playing: A Treatise on the Formation and Use of the Brass Player's Embouchure*. Rochester Wind Music, reprint of 1962, Bloomington, IN: Brass Publications.

FARKAS, PHILIP, *The Art of French Horn Playing*, Evanston Il, Summy Birchard Publishing Co. (1956).

FASMAN, MARK J. (1990). *Brass Bibliography: Sources on the History, Literature, Pedagogy, Performance, and Acoustics of Brass Instruments*. Bloomington, IL: Indiana University Press.

FOX, FRED (1982). *Essentials of Brass Playing: An Explicit, Logical Approach to Important Basic Factors That Contribute to Superior Brass Instrument Performance*, enlarged ed. Miami, FL: Warner

Brothers; reprint of (1974) Pittsburgh, PA: Volkwein Brothers.

*HAZEN, MARGARET, and ROBERT HAZEN (1987). *The Music Men: An Illustrated History of Brass Bands in America: 1800–1920*. Washington, DC: Smithsonian Institution Press.

HERBERT, TREVOR and WALLACE, JOHN (eds.) (1997). *The Cambridge Companion to Brass Instruments*. New York: Cambridge University Press.

HUNT, NORMAN and DANIEL BACHELDER (1994). *Guide to Teaching Brass*, 3rd ed. Boston: McGraw-Hill.

JOHNSON, KEITH (1994). *The Art of Trumpet Playing*, 2nd ed. Denton, TX: Gore Publications.

*LEIDIG, VERNON F. (1960). *Contemporary Brass Technique*. Hollywood, CA: Highland Music.

MUELLER, HERBERT C. (1995). *Learning to Teach Through Playing: A Brass Method*. Milwaukee: Hal Leonard Publishing; reprint of (1968) Locke, NY: Author.

* REINHARDT, DONALD (1992). *The Encyclopedia of the Pivot System*. New York: Charles Colin Music Publishers; (reprint of 1964 edition).

ROBERTSON, JAMES (1994). *The Low Brass*. New York: McGraw-Hill.

*SCHILKE, RENOLD O. (n.d.). *The Acoustics of Inner Brass and the Acoustical Effects of Various Materials and Their Treatment*. Chicago: Schilke Music Products.

SEVERSON, PAUL, and MARK McDUNN (1983). *Brass Wind Artistry: Master Your Mind, Master Your Instrument*. Athens, OH: Accura Music.

*WEAST, RONALD (1965). *Brass Performance: An Analytical Text of the Processes, Problems, and Tech-

nique of Brass, 3rd ed. New York: McGinnis and Marx.

WHITENER, SCOTT and CATHY WHITENER (1997). *A Complete Guide to Brass: Instruments and Technique.* New York: Schirmer Books.

Journals

Brass Bulletin. Quarterly from Brass Bulletin, CH-1674 Vlar Marens, Switzerland.

Instructional Videos

Canadian Brass: *Master Class* (Canadian Brass, 1989). Reston, VA: MENC.

Canadian Brass: *Spectacular* (with principal brass players from the N.Y. Philharmonic and Boston Symphony Orchestra. 1989 Palatine, Il: Sharper Video Productions, Inc.

Canadian Brass: *Breathing and Posture.* 1991, Palatine, Il: Sharper Video Productions, Inc.

Canadian Brass: *Tonguing and Embouchure.* 1991, Palatine, Il: Sharper Video Productions, Inc.

Canadian Brass: *Performing and Playing in an Ensemble. 1989,*

Developing Brass Ensembles (Richard Wolf, 1990). Madison, WI: University of Wisconsin–Madison Videotapes.

Gordon's Brass Clinic: *The Seven Natural Elements of Brass Playing* (Claude Gordon, 1984). Elkhart, IN: Selmar Company.

14

The Trumpet and Cornet

HISTORY

The history of the cornet or trumpet is very old if the instrument is viewed as related to the first lip-voiced instruments such as a shell or elephant horn of the pre-historic era. More directly related is a trumpet made of wood, mentioned in Sumerian texts about 3000 B.C.E. The Swiss "alphorn" and Jewish "shofar" of the present are descendants of this early instrument. Various horns of different lengths and shapes can be found throughout history. They were generally connected with war or ceremonial events. Some historians trace the present-day rivalry between the cornet and trumpet back to earliest times. For centuries there had been a fluctuation of preference for either the conical or cylindrical instrument, depending upon the situation and sound desired. Actually the trumpet was preferred until about 1400. It was the more effective in the primary use of such instruments, that of causing fright or awe.

The first instrument that could be fingered was the "cornett" or "zink," traced to the Persians as early as C.E. 77, but not used widely until the Middle Ages. It was a conical instrument with a cup mouthpiece and holes in the body comparable to the clarinet of today. This instrument culminated in the serpent, ophicleide, and keyed bugle of the nineteenth century. The trumpet has undergone fewer major changes in design than any other instrument, and only the addition of the valve has had any lasting effect upon its basic design.

It was throughout history the instrument of royalty. By the sixteenth century, the trumpet had become such a specialized and "heroic" instrument that trumpet guilds that had been forming since the fourteenth century, were among the strongest "unions" in Europe—stretching from England to the Russian border, including central Europe and Scandinavia. Members were exclusively allowed to play at royal events, church services, and other civic events. Just as the finest violins at the time were being produced in Brecseia and Cremona (e.g., Amati, Guarneri, and Stradivari), Europe's trumpet center was Nuremberg. The first guilds were established there and grew northward to Scandinavia. Members of the guilds were status symbols themselves with the kings of Poland having as many as twelve, Saxony had eight, and Leipzig had four (including Gottfried Reiche for whom J. S. Bach wrote most of his post-1730 trumpet music).

The official duties, membership rules, and rights were written in 1623 by the Holy Roman Emperor Ferdinand II. Guild members (following two years of an expensive apprenticeship) were even given direct access to royalty in cases of dispute of complaints about nonguild members playing in public.[1] By the end of the sixteenth century, the Prince of Saxony had expanded the rights of guild trumpeters to include virtually all trumpet playing in Germany. Non-members had their instruments confiscated and were banished from the region; many were publicly punished for repeated offenses.

The trumpet was favored by Bach and Handel as well as other late Baroque composers. The Classical composers, however, did not like its shrill sounds, and not until Beethoven used it is his *Third Symphony* did it come to be a standard part of the orchestra.

The keyed bugle was invented by Kolbel of St. Petersburg in 1760. It was soon replaced, around 1815, by an instrument with a piston valve, the invention of Blumel, an oboe player from Silesia. Stolzel, who purchased the patent, adding a second-valve. By 1830 Muller added the third-valve so that the scale was complete above the second partial as we use it today. Although the valve trumpet was used by Halevy in *La Juive*, Wagner is generally considered the first composer to write well for the instrument. Wagner's use of the trumpet occurred almost simultaneously with the rise of the band and the great cornet virtuosos such as Arban, Levy, Smith, Bellstedt, Clarke, and Goldman at the turn of the twentieth century. Throughout the early part of the twentieth century, the cornet was associated with bands, the trumpet with orchestras and dance bands. Today, in the hands of most school musicians, the cornet and trumpet have very small differences in sound, but definite opinions are held by professionals as to the superiority of starting on one or the other. During the middle of the last century in the height of the large symphonic bands (conducted by masters such as William Revelli and Mark Hindsley), the cornet was preferred because it blended better with the woodwinds, while trumpets were reserved for true trumpet parts to project through the ensemble. With the rise of wind ensembles, and the more typical small band that is erroneously called a wind ensemble, the trumpet has become the preferred instrument of beginners, retailers, and school musicians. In the hands of an accomplished player, the difference is noticeable and important.

SELECTING THE INSTRUMENT

The length of both the B$\flat$ cornet and the trumpet is the same: approximately $4\frac{1}{2}$ feet. The trumpet is approximately two-thirds cylindrical with only one basic winding whereas the cornet is about 70 percent conical and the tubing has two windings. Technically the difference lies in the degree of taper. The tubing of the cornet tapers from the mouthpiece opening throughout its entire length except for the valve and tuning slides. The trumpet tubing is larger at the mouthpiece and remains cylindrical for most of its length. Although the bells are about the same size, the mouthpieces are not interchangeable between the two instruments. The sound differs between the two instruments because the cylindrical-bore trumpet enhances the higher partials whereas the conical bore cornet enhances the fundamental and the lower partials.

It matters little on which instrument a student begins instrumental music, so the child should be allowed to select the instrument with which he will be happiest.

---

[1] Don Smithers (1988), *The Music and History of the Baroque Trumpet before 1721*, 2nd ed. Carbondale, IL : Southern Illinois University Press.

In addition to different-size bores, instruments are obtainable with different-size bells. A large-bore instrument with a small bell produces "brilliance" rather than a "darker" tone. A darker tone can be obtained from a medium-bore instrument with a large bell if a mouthpiece with a medium to large cup is used. The bore size is measured at the second-valve port and the bell size is measured immediately before the flare.

Since 1980, companies offer detachable bells to convert B♭ trumpets to C trumpets (several offer an E♭, F, and G trumpet with three bells and three sets of tuning slides—of course, each configuration a compromise). The most esteemed trumpet maker today is Monette, which has made some actual acoustical changes to improve the instrument's pitch and control/use of the airstream.

There are also other important details of construction. Top-valve spring action is superior for all small piston brass rather than the spring placed below the valve. The instrument should be tight (i.e., no loose parts banging around when shaken) with the valves freely moving. It should give the desired response in a playing test.

When inspecting a used instrument for possible purchase, one should inspect the valves for undue wear at the bottom of each valve. One poor playing habit is to press the valves at a slight angle rather than straight down, a motion that creates wear and tear on the alloy coating on the valves. If this coating is worn off one can expect serious trouble from the instrument. Valves should also be tested to see if they "wiggle" in the valve casing, an additional sign of excessive wear, or if they bounce when pressed and then released—valves with good springs should not bounce up and down at the top of the stroke. And finally, but less serious, the outside of the instrument should be inspected for pits. Some brass players have excessive acid in their perspiration, and frequent handling of the instrument without wiping it off after playing can damage and pit the brass, especially around the valve casings.

All valve combinations should be checked with an electronic tuner to determine if they are inordinately out of tune. One should start with the open tones and then the various valve combinations, knowing that low D and low C♯ will be considerably sharp. First-line E may be a tad sharp and fourth-line D may be a tad flat; any other out-of-tune notes should encourage one's shopping. Compression in the valve slides are checked by pulling a valve slide, then depressing the valve and listening for the "pop."

The instrument being purchased should play responsively in all registers and not have too much or too little resistance. Most beginners find instruments with a small bore easier to play as they are not required to breathe correctly. (An example for the music educator is to blow through a trumpet mouthpiece with a very tight backbore and realize how much easier it is to buzz in the upper register than with the same diameter and cup size with an open backbore.) Because beginners can "get by" without plenty of air support, assistance from an advanced trumpet player or teacher should be sought when selecting an instrument. Most beginner-level instruments have a smaller bore to facilitate range and endurance; these crutches are not necessary for the young trumpet player; it is better to develop good playing habits from the beginning.

Whether to purchase an instrument with an easily adjustable first- and/or third-valve slide is generally a matter of personal preference and cost, but all trumpet players should at least have an adjustable third-valve slide by the time they reach high school. Trumpets designed with this adjustment are manufactured with the third-valve slide slightly shorter, bringing the low E♭ and all A's in tune. Some trumpets/cornets employ a trigger-operated device on the first-valve slide; the more common "hook" or "saddle" is preferred because it has no mechanism to break and makes removing the slide to drain water easier. If the first-valve slide is short enough to bring fourth-line D and third-space C♯ in tune, certain first-and second-valve combinations are sharp (such as the bottom-line E) requiring the player to extend the first-valve slide for that note. The professional-quality trumpet offers the player a choice of using either the first-or third-valve slide to adjust the most out-of-tune notes, low C♯ and D. Which slide to use depends on the fingering patterns and technical difficulty.

ASSEMBLING THE INSTRUMENT

Assembling the trumpet should not present any problems. It consists of merely inserting the mouthpiece. Mouthpieces for brasses can be damaged if they are forced or jammed into the instrument. Some players give the mouthpiece a slight turn after it is inserted to insure the proper seating and a reverse turn to remove the mouthpiece. Wiggling the mouthpiece back and forth to work it in can damage both the end of the mouthpiece and the leadpipe, allow air to leak, and affect intonation and tone quality.

HOLDING THE TRUMPET OR CORNET

The remaining principles discussed will refer to trumpet, but hold true for cornet. The correct hand position for playing the trumpet is shown in Figure 14–1. The trumpet is held with the left hand. One grasps the trumpet with the fingers around the third-valve casing and the thumb around the casing of the first-valve. It is important that the thumb not be too high or the student may support the instrument with his wrist. The wrist should be as straight as possible and in line with the forearm. If the wrist is bent, the wrist muscles will soon tire from supporting the weight that should be sustained by the entire arm. If the instrument is held so that the valves are slightly tilted to the player's right and the left wrist kept straight, the weight will be carried by the arm. It is then necessary for the player to experiment to find the point of balance of the instrument for maximum comfort. Most modern trumpets are balanced at or near the third-valve, so when properly held the point of balance in the left hand will be near the point where the bell tubing rests on the upper joint of the first finger.

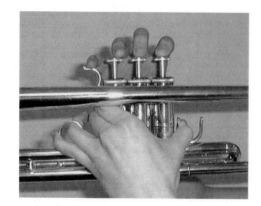

Figure 14–1
Left-Hand Position for Playing the Trumpet

If the instrument is held in balance and tilted slightly to the right with both wrists held straight, both elbows will be about even, comfortably away from the body so as not to hamper breathing, but not out so far as to require real effort to support the elbows. The head rests easily on the shoulders without bending. The wrists are straight and the arms form an angle of approximately 60 degrees when viewed from the front. Proper posture is complete when the student rests both feet on the floor and sits or stands "tall" (see Figure 14–2 on page 228). Improper posture prohibits correct breathing and contributes to muscular tension.

Whether the player should hold the trumpet parallel to the floor is a question upon which there is disagreement. Vincent Bach wrote: "Hold the instrument in horizontal position or slightly above—without leaning your head backwards ... Push the lower jaw forward so the lower teeth are in line with the upper ones."[2] Donald Reinhardt says, "Please do not take too seriously the greatly overrated mid-

---

[2]Vincent Bach (n.d.), *Embouchure and Mouthpiece Manual*, Elkhart, IN: Selmer; reprint of Genuine Bach Mouthpieces (1956) Mt. Vernon, NY: Vincent Bach Corporation, p. 11.

Figure 14-2
Sitting Position for Playing the Trumpet

Victorian phrase, 'hold the instrument in a horizontal position at all times.' Forget this nonsense and hold your trumpet to conform to your type of jaw."[3] The jazz trumpeter Snooky Young and the symphonic player Vincent Cichowicz both play with their instruments "pointed" downward. The best approach to the problem is to keep in mind that a slightly downward tilt is acceptable and to experiment in achieving the best tone by moving the instrument in an arc from the horizontal while keeping the head erect and relaxed. The position that gives the best sound should be adopted. Poor hand position can tip the bell downward, putting pressure on the lower lip, changing the angle of the air and jaw, and resulting in a dead tone. Conversely, although less likely, poor hand position in tilting the bell upward results in poor endurance in the upper register. Students with an overbite will probably find they obtain a better sound by holding the instrument somewhat below the horizontal.

Many aspects of trumpet playing are similar to those of the other brass instruments and were discussed in Chapter 13. These items are not repeated here.

The right hand should be in a position resembling a "C" (as if holding a tennis ball) placed so that the fingertips curve in a relaxed manner above the valve buttons; the right hand should not help hold the trumpet. If the fingers are too flat, if the wrist is bent, or if the right hand is too low or too close to the instrument, the valves will be pulled down rather than pushed. For example, if the trumpet is held with the valves exactly perpendicular to the floor, the right wrist can be kept straight only by holding the right elbow high and far away from the body; the left wrist can be kept straight only by keeping the left elbow jammed into the left rib cage. Playing should be done with the fleshy balls of the fingers, not on the knuckles or on the extreme tip of the fingers.

The right thumb should rest under the leadpipe between the first-and second-valve casing. This placement is important because it positions the fingers properly above the valves, allowing better use of the weak ring finger. The position of the thumb (1) provides support for fingers when they depress the valves, (2) aids in keeping the fingers up, (3) prevents the hand from drooping inward toward the side of the instrument, and (4) helps balance the instrument.

The finger ring or hook should not be used. The little finger should remain free to respond in sympathy with the third finger. The third finger is the weakest and should not be inhibited by a restricted little finger. The finger hook is used only when the player needs to hold the instrument with the right hand as in turning pages or placing a mute in the bell. Using the hook may also lead to excessive and damaging pressure on the lips. Some players use the hook as an aid to the upper register, but the added pressure on the embouchure results in less endurance and limited range, as there is a limit to the pressure the lips can stand. One can demonstrate to students the technique problem caused by using the finger ring: Ask a student to hold out his right hand and wiggle his fingers, then grasp and hold his little finger, completely restricting it from moving, and then ask him to wiggle his fingers—the resulting action is not only less comfortable, but the fingers simply cannot move as freely.

[3]Donald S. Reinhardt, (1992) *The Encyclopedia of the Pivot System.* New York: Charles Colin Music, p. 9.

EMBOUCHURE

The discussion of physical characteristics and their importance in trumpet playing is heard over and over, yet there are many exceptions to the rule. The older idea of thin lips for a trumpet player and thicker lips for the larger brass instruments has been largely abandoned. The following differences may be considered for a student wishing to start on trumpet:

1. Uneven teeth make if difficult for the player to seat the mouthpiece properly on the lips, although teeth that are only slightly irregular are not necessarily detrimental. Many good players have overcome a minor irregularity by placing the mouthpiece rim slightly to one side. The muscles of the face and tongue are sufficiently flexible so that with practice small variances can be overcome. When the player places the mouthpiece very much off-center, however, he has unequal muscular control. This imposes a strain on the embouchure muscles, limits range and endurance, and allows an uneven vibrating surface and improper position of the tongue that impedes tonguing. Two simple tests to determine whether the prospective player can place the mouthpiece in the center of his lips are: (a) whistle, to see if the whistle aperture is in the center of the lips, and (b) produce a buzzing sound with only the lips.

2. A severe malocclusion (overbite or underbite) or failure of the jaws to come together evenly results in strain and prevents the mouthpiece from receiving correct support. A small degree of malocclusion is normal. Projecting the jaw forward corrects some overbite.

3. A player whose lips are considerably longer or shorter than his front teeth may have trouble. Lips that are long in relation to the teeth tend to roll inward too much. If the upper lip alone rolls in too far, it is injurious to both endurance and range. Lips short in relation to the teeth may not come together sufficiently at the center to form a proper embouchure.

4. Front teeth that slant inward prevent the lips from providing a firm support for the mouthpiece.

5. Unusual lips such as injured facial muscles, harelips, and large scars should be carefully considered before allowing a student to begin on trumpet (or any other brass instrument).

To assist the formation of a correct embouchure, the student may be asked to place his lips in the position for vocalizing the syllable "em." Then he can raise the instrument to his relaxed lips and vocalize "pooh." This procedure will usually have immediate results. At this point, the student should be asked again to form his lips as if vocalizing "em," then tighten the corners of the mouth and buzz the lips until a tone is produced. Practice and careful instruction in shaping a proper embouchure along with proper breathing will result in rapid improvement.

Students who have initial difficulties producing a tone on the trumpet should buzz with the mouthpiece only, or buzz their lips without the instrument or mouthpiece. While buzzing the lips alone, the teacher can touch the student's chin to determine if the air is being directed too far downward. If so, the student should be reminded to project the jaw a bit more forward. Buzzing without the mouthpiece is also useful for those students who have a tendency to puff out their cheeks, as buzzing strengthens the appropriate muscles. It is virtually impossible for one to puff out the cheeks when buzzing without the mouthpiece, just as it is impossible to bunch up the chin.

**Figure 14–4
Side view,
playing low C**

**Figure 14–5
Side view,
playing middle C**

**Figure 14–6
Side view,
playing high C**

**Figure 14–3
Trumpet Embouchure**

A correct embouchure is shown in Figures 14–3, 14–4, 14–5 and 14–6. The mouthpiece should be centered on the lips horizontally and placed vertically so as to use one-third upper lip and two-thirds lower lip, which when observed using a mouthpiece visualizer is actually closer to half-and-half inside the mouthpiece. A visual half-and-half distribution on the lips (which means even more upper lip) may be acceptable. The corners of the mouth are tightened and pressed against the teeth. The center of the lips sympathetically tighten just enough to provide a fleshy cushion that vibrates when the airstream passes through it. Tightening the corners of the mouth also helps to keep the chin drawn flat.

Mouthpieces

The trumpet has attracted more mouthpiece manufacturers than any other brass instrument. Many "gimmick-type" types of mouthpieces are available, sometimes advertised as extending the upper range and capable of doing half the work for the trumpet player.

The student should select a mouthpiece from a reputable company and secure his upper and lower range by developing the embouchure and breathing apparatus. Among the best all-around, general-purpose mouthpieces for beginning players are the Bach 7C, Schilke 9 or 11, Stork Vacchiano 7C, and Yamaha 11C4. For advanced players, the more popular mouthpieces are Monette, Josef Klier Reeves, Warburton (making the largest, and one of the few manufacturers to set inside rim diameters at 17.5 mm, 17.25 mm, 17 mm, 16.75 mm, etc.), and two of the best-selling custom mouthpieces at the turn of the century—Stork Custom Mouthpieces and Marcinkiewicz.

As the student grows physically and the embouchure muscles grow stronger, he should try a larger mouthpiece under the guidance of a knowledgeable trumpet teacher. A larger mouthpiece (at least with regard to cup diameter and depth) allows for a richer, darker tone quality. A larger cup diameter allows the aperture of the embouchure to open more, with more of the lip vibrating, resulting in a clearer tone and a fuller tone without sounding overblown. These mouthpieces also require more air support for successful playing. For students who have not developed a strong embouchure, a larger mouthpiece will hurt the upper range. Students should not be exposed to bad habits in order to play in the upper register; therefore, the teacher must be careful of the demands placed on nascent trumpet players.

Jazz players, on the other hand, often prefer a shallower cup and tighter backbore to assist their endurance in the high register and to enable a variety of articulations and tone qualities. That is, they do not want to produce a deep, full trumpet tone. The primary considerations for these varied sounds are cup diameter, cup depth, throat or bore size, and backbore.

INTONATION

Intonation requires practice and good listening habits. Trumpet players in most ensembles are given a brief opportunity to tune their C or B with the unwarranted assumption that the rest of the pitches are in tune. Intonation on any instrument can be improved by knowing the natural tendencies of the instrument—this is especially true with the trumpet, as most trumpets share common intonation flaws. Figure 14–7 shows the intonation flaws of the majority of B♭ trumpets whether manufactured as student-line or professional-line instruments. The medium- or professional-line instruments with devices to extend the first-and/or third-valve slides help correct intonation.

The notes comprising the seventh harmonic are so flat that they are completely ignored; these notes are played by using valve combinations that lower the eighth harmonic.

↑= sharp; ↓= flat; hashes = increased degree

Figure 14–7   Trumpet: Pitch Tendencies of Certain Notes

Trumpet students should also be made aware of performance intonation tendencies. Students often play slightly flat in the upper register when tired but become quite sharp as they become even more fatigued and pinch for the high notes. Ideally, the fatigued trumpet player should immediately warm down and put the instrument away, but during the spring concert this response may not please the audience, conductor, or the rest of the section (especially during a Haydn symphony). Temperature and performance anxiety also affect intonation.

TONE QUALITY AND EFFECTS

Tone quality varies among professional players and even more so among students, but the trumpet student is going to sound only as good as his mental image of the ideal tone. Often the young student is so caught up in technique and range that tone quality is neglected. It matters little how fast a trumpet player can double-tongue or how many major and minor scales can be played; if the tone is unpleasant, the effort has been lost. Good tone quality depends on the student's ability to mentally conceive a good trumpet sound, to listen critically, and to evaluate the tone produced.

A fine teacher can encourage students to produce a better sound by demonstrating good and poor examples. For example, the student should strive for (1) a focused, centered sound so that the tone does not spread on crescendos or become pinched on decrescendos; (2) a full tone quality that results from steady air support and an appropriate size mouthpiece for each individual; and (3) a relaxed sound, not forced, relying on plenty of wind while maintaining a good embouchure. Excessive mouthpiece pressure is used to make up for lack of air or a developed embouchure. A trumpet has a great range of dynamics. The student should practice in all dynamic ranges and make dynamic changes while practicing to produce focused and clear tones. Long tones are a useful tool and can be made exciting to the student by an understanding and inspiring teacher.

In *The Art of Trumpet Playing*, Keith Johnson discusses the importance of "imagination and experimentation" in playing the trumpet. His stress is on imagination, allowing the student to produce new ideas from existing information. He emphasizes that for a player to improve his sound he must have existing information; that is, a firm grasp on how successful trumpet players sound, even though he may not want to emulate that exact sound.

This need for a model can be satisfied in several ways. (1) The music teacher can provide an example. (2) Private lessons may be the most optimum means for providing young students with models. (3) An exemplary high school player may be used. (4) For high school players, master classes taught by professional musicians or college students can provide a role model for good tone quality and other aspects of good musicianship. A young trumpet student can learn much and begin conceptualizing a good tone quality by listening to a professional flute player. As Johnson observes:

> Musical imagination, if properly used, is beneficial in several ways. First, it ensures receptiveness to new ideas that can be gained from listening to music of all types and sources. Trumpet players can gain unlimited ideas from fine singers, pianists, string players, and others. New ideas should be incorporated into one's playing. Occasional alterations in vibrato, increasing or decreasing the volume level for certain passages, or modifying an articulation in some subtle way will enhance the musical interest of any performance....
>
> In the process of acquiring new ideas, players should not be afraid to experiment. Many students are so conditioned to "right" and "wrong" judgments that they become overly cautious and afraid of making mistakes.... Fear of mistakes is a threat to imaginative, creative playing.... For substantial improvement to occur the student must be able to imagine a better sound than he has played previously, and in order to implement this new sound he must be willing to experiment.... The teacher should direct and encourage the student, guide his experimentation, and comment on the results with understanding and accuracy.... Any skill, artistic or otherwise, is learned through trial and error.[4]

Vibrato

The most common method of vibrato for trumpet and the easiest to develop, is hand vibrato. Hand vibrato is created by using the thumb of the right hand (which is resting gently under the leadpipe between the first- and second-valve casings) to

---

[4]Keith Johnson (1994), *The Art of Trumpet Playing*, 2nd ed., Denton, TX: Gore, pp. 20–21.

move forward and backward making subtle pulsations in the pitch (about seven per second). The pulsations should be even and the pitch not noticeably affected. Many jazz trumpet players use a wider, broader vibrato, especially on phrase endings of ballads. Again, students should listen to recordings or live performances of successful trumpet players, then let the ear determine what is most appropriate. Vibrato changes depend upon tessitura and style of the music. Some styles of music are best played with no vibrato, for example, classical orchestral literature.

Many trumpet players also use a lip or jaw vibrato, achieved by playing a straight tone and moving the lips or the jaw slightly (the latter as if vocalizing "wah—wah—wah" rapidly). Lip vibrato can be executed more subtly than hand vibrato, but can affect endurance and lip slurs if the teacher does not remind students to maintain a proper embouchure. When Adolph Herseth of the Chicago Symphony was asked how he produced a vibrato, he replied he didn't know. After a pause he said, "I guess I just wiggle my lips and blow."

FINGERINGS AND TECHNIQUE

The basic fingerings on brass instruments are easier to learn than those for the woodwinds. Having to rely on the embouchure to change the overtone series means that brasses are not necessarily easier to play than woodwinds. To play the entire range, tubing is added by the valves to lower individual notes of each overtone series. If the principle is understood, it is easy to memorize the seven valve combinations.

Good hand position is important in developing fingering skill. The player should learn to push the valves down firmly and feel a slight impact when the valve cap hits the valve top.

Technique comes with practice. Scale studies are indispensable for developing technique, but they should not be the entire substance of the student's musical diet. Fundamental tasks such as learning to play scales rapidly can be learned in a relatively short period of time. Other tasks such as good tone quality, extended upper range, and endurance require more practice and should not be neglected during any stage of the trumpet player's development.

Common and alternate fingerings are shown at the end of this chapter. Alternate fingerings should not be ignored, for they are needed for tuning and technique. Some passages are almost impossible to play without use of alternate fingerings. Alternate fingerings can also improve intonation.

A few illustrations of the use of alternate fingerings may serve to point up the discussion.

1. Valves 1 and 2 equal valve 3. Passages involving an awkward movement to 1—2 should be tried with 3 as a substitute. For example, a passage where low D (1—3) to bottom-line E (1—2) is repeated rapidly it is much easier to "trill" between these two notes using only the index finger as in Figure 14—8.

2. Valve 3 is sometimes preferable to 1–2 for intonation. For instance, first-line E is often too sharp when played with 1-2. It can be played with 3 (a little flat) and lipped up to pitch. The same substitution may make high A more in tune.

1-3 1-2 1-3 1-2 1-3 1-2 1-3 1-2   1-3 3 1-3 3 1-3 3 1-3 3

Figure 14–8   Third Valve Substitution for 1 and 3 for Rapid Passages

3. On some good trumpets (especially C trumpets), a preference is given to finger fourth-space E with 1–2 and fourth-space E♭ with 2–3.

4. Many quickly moving articulated passages are played more cleanly using alternate fingerings; a very simple example, but one with which young students can identify, are bugle calls which are played without valves or in a sense with alternate fingerings using any single-valve or combination of valves.

WHAT TO PRACTICE

One of the things that discourages youngsters from studying an instrument is boredom. Confinement to a single method book is guaranteed to contribute to boredom. There are many excellent books to which students may be exposed. Those listed at the end of the chapter are not intended as a comprehensive list, but are indicative of the variety of material available.

The psychological principle of working on a single problem at a time is sound, and certain materials are better than others for solving problems, developing confidence, and accuracy. Any of the complete methods offers a vast source of control exercises to challenge the virtually limitless combination of dynamics, range, articulations, and phrasing. For instance, the single-tonguing and interval studies in Arban's should be practiced very slowly part of the time, emphasizing the perfect placement of each tone and the absolute evenness of each tongued note. When the student is certain she can usually play any interval without errors, she is ready to audition.

Daily practice should include long tones while crescendoing and decrescendoing and also while maintaining the same dynamic level; flexibility studies (lip slurs) to insure continued embouchure development; studies on various articulations; technical studies to develop finger facility; and lyrical studies or melodic passages to promote expressive playing. Although this routine may appear somewhat long for first-year players, the teacher should remember that beginners' lip slurs may be between only two notes for each valve combination; the articulations only of long tones, tongued quarter notes, and slurs; and their technical studies may consist of only parts of the C and F major scales. Young students should frequently play pieces they already know. Familiar pieces build confidence and musicianship and enable the student to concentrate on musical aspects of playing.

One should never dismiss the value of "doodling around" or imaginative practice. Such playing by ear helps develop listening skills, versatility and technical facility, and often keeps students interested. Good instrumental music teachers encourage their students to play by ear.

CARE AND MAINTENANCE OF THE TRUMPET/CORNET

In general, brass instruments present fewer maintenance problems than do woodwinds, strings, or percussion instruments. The primary task of the young trumpet/cornet student is to keep the instrument clean. Care of the instrument on a daily basis should include wiping off the trumpet with a rag to remove acidic perspiration left by the hands. Some perspiration can destroy the finish and pit the brass over a period of time.

As with all brass instruments, students must always be reminded to treat their trumpets with care, not to leave them unattended on chairs or the floor, not to bang the music stand when bringing them to playing position, and not to play rhythms or "tunes" by popping the mouthpiece with the palm of their hand. Dents in the leadpipe, valve or tuning slides, and valve casings cause serious problems in tone, intonation, and/or technique. These should be removed by a qualified repairperson.

Students should know that the valves must be pressed in order to pull the slides; for example, the first-valve should be pressed before adjusting the first-valve slide. One of the most common problems among beginning trumpet players is the inability to remove saliva through the third-valve slide water key, a frustration due to not pressing the third-valve while blowing air through the instrument.

Valves should be oiled on a daily basis, and all slides pushed in when the instrument is not being played. This habit prevents stuck slides. The valve slides should be greased with petroleum jelly or slide grease at least once a month.

BIBLIOGRAPHY

Texts

•*Indicates out of print in 2001.*

ASPER, LYNN K. (1999). *A Physical Approach to Playing the Trumpet.* Hudsonville, MI: Wave Song Press.

BATE, PHILIP (1978). *The Trumpet and Trombone: An Outline of Their History, Development, and Construction,* 2nd ed. New York: W. W. Norton and Company.

BROILES, MEL (1989). *The Art of Trumpet Playing.* New York: Charles Colin Music.

*BUSH, IRVING R. (1962). *Artistic Trumpet Technique and Study.* Hollywood, CA: Highland Music Company.

COLIN, CHARLES (1994). *My Rendezvous with the 40s: Reflections II.* New York: Charles Colin Music Publishing.

*DALE, DELBERT A. (1985). *Trumpet Technique,* 2nd ed). New York: Oxford University Press

DAVIDSON, LOUIS (1975). *Trumpet Profiles.* Bloomington, IN: Author.

GOLLEHON, MAC (1991). *Embouchure Update.* New York: Charles Colin Music.

HAYDEN, SHEPARD, and VINCENT BACH (1978). *How to Build Up Endurance in Trumpet Playing.* New York: Charles Colin Music.

JOHNSON, KEITH (1994). *The Art of Trumpet Playing,* 2nd ed. Denton, TX: Gore.

MCNEIL, JOHN (1999). *The Art of Jazz Trumpet,* (complete edition with one CD). Brooklyn, NY: Gerard & Sarzin.

REINHARDT, DONALD (1992). *The Encyclopedia of the Pivot System.* New York: Charles Colin Music.

SHERMAN, ROGER (1979). *The Trumpeter's Handbook.* Athens OH: Accura Music.

SMITHERS, DON (1988). *The Music and History of the Baroque Trumpet before 1721,* 2nd ed. Carbondale, IL: Southern Illinois University Press.

TARR, EDWARD (1988). *The Trumpet.* Portland OR: Amadeus Press.

Journal

Journal of the International Trumpet Guild. Quarterly from the International Trumpet Guild, School of Music, Florida State University, Tallahassee, FL 32306-2098. Available from David Jones, ITG Treasurer, 241 East Main Street #247, Westfield, MA 01086.

Trumpet Studies

Easy—Medium (elementary or middle school)

Balasanian-Musser. *25 Easy Studies* (Belwin-Mills).

Balent. *Breeze-Easy* (2 vols.) (Warner Brothers)

Beeler. *Method for the Cornet* (2 vols.) (Warner Brothers).

Clarke. *Elementary Studies* (Carl Fischer).

Concone. (ed. Sawyer). *Lyrical Studies* (Brass Press).

Getchell. *Practical Studies for Trumpet* (Book I) (Belwin-Mills).

Hering. *The Beginning Trumpeter* (Carl Fischer).

Little. *Embouchure Builder* (ProArt)

Longinotti. *L'Etude de la Trumpette* (Henn & Henn)

Musser and Del Borgo. *Modes in Contemporary Music* (Alfred).

———. *Rhythm in Contemporary Music* (Alfred).

———. *Tonality in Contemporary Music* (Alfred).

Robinson, *Rubank Elementary Book* (Rubank).

Williams. *Modern Method* (Colin).

Medium (middle school and high school)

Arban (ed. Goldman and Smith) *Complete Conservatory Method* (Carl Fischer).

Bennett. *14 Melodic Studies* (King).

Bousquet. *36 Celebrated Studies* (Carl Fisher).

Broiles. *Private Practice* (Weissman Music).

———. *Trumpet Studies and Duets* (McGinnis).

Clarke. *Technical Studies* (Carl Fischer).

Clodomir. *70 Petits Exercices* (International).

Colin. *100 Original Warm-Ups for Trumpet* (Colin).

Concone. (ed. Sawyer). *Lyrical Studies* (Brass Press).

Davidson. *Trumpet Techniques* (Louis Davidson).

Getchell. *Practical Studies for Trumpet* (Book II) (Belwin-Mills).

Goldman, *Practical Studies* (C. Fischer).

Hering. *The Advancing Trumpeter* (C. Fischer).

———. *28 Melodious and Technical Studies* (C. Fischer).

Irons. *27 Groups of Exercises for Trumpet* (Southern).

Pottagim. *Preparatory Melodies to Solo Work* (Belwin-Mills).

Schlossberg. *Daily Drills and Technical Studies* (Baron).

Smith. *Lip Flexibility on the Cornet or Trumpet* (C. Fischer).

Advanced (high school and college)

Arban. (ed. Maire) *Celebre Methode* Complete (3 vols.) (Leduc).

Balasanian. *20 Studies* (International).

Balay. *15 Etudes.* (Leduc).

Bitsch. *20 Etudes.* (Leduc).

Bordogni. *24 Vocalises* (C. F. Peters).

Brandt. (ed. Vacchiano). *34 Studies and 24 Last Studies* (Belwin-Mills).

Broiles. *Have Trumpet—Will Transpose* (Colin).

Charlier. *36 Etudes Transcendantes* (A. Leduc).

Chavanne. *25 Characteristic Studies* (Leduc)

Clarke. *Characteristic Studies* (C. Fischer).

Colin. *Advanced Lip Flexibilities* (Colin).

Deutsch. *The Extended Trumpet Range* (Colin).

Dufrense and Voisin. *Develop Sight-Reading* (Colin).

Gally. *22 Exercises* (A. Leduc).

Harris. *Advanced Studies, Trumpet* (Colin).

Longinott. *Studies in Classical and Modern Style* (International).

Maxime and Alphonse. *20 Etudes Tres Difficiles* (A. Leduc).

Maxwell, Jim. *The First Trumpeter* (Colin).

Petit. 15 Etudes *Technique et Melodiques* (A. Leduc).

Sachse, E. *100 Etudes for Trumpet* (International).

Smith. *Top Tones* (C. Fischer).

Smith, Walter. *Studies for Embouchure Development* (C. Fischer).

Instructional Videos

Beginning Trumpet. (Mary Lazarus, 1989). Atlantic City, NJ: Music Foundation Video.

Belwin 21st Centrury Band Method: Trumpet Level 1 (Rolf Smedvig, 1996). Miami: Warner Brothers Publications.

Getting Started with the Trumpet (Leslie Grove, 1996). Spokane, WA: Getting Started Productions.

Keys to Trumpet Mastery (Allen Vizzutti, 1992). Palatine, IL: Sharper Video Productions.

Marsalis on Music, 4 videotapes (Wynton Marsalis, Yo-Yo Ma, Seiji Ozawa, Daniel Anker, and others, 1995). New York: Sony Classical Film & Video.

Steps to Excellence: A Video Clinic, Vol. 5. (Allen Vizzutti, 1984). Grand Rapids, MN: Yamaha Musical Productions.

Trumpet Course: Beginners & Intermediate (Clark Terry, 1981). West Long Beach: Kultur.

Trumpet, Vol. 1 & 2. (Mark Inouye and Thom Proctor, 1998). Miami: Warner Brothers Publications.

The Trumpet. (J. Drew Cremisio, 1991). Canoga Park, CA: MPV.

A New and Different Way of Getting More Music out of the Trumpet. (William Adam, 1997). Fairbanks, AK: Stewart Aull/Moving Images.

The Trumpet (Drew Cremisio and Mark Arnett, 1998). Canoga Park, CA: Backstage Productions.

Recommended Classical Trumpet Artists

Maurice André playing Hummel, Vivaldi

Wynton Marsalis playing Haydn, Purcell

Mike Tunnell playing Frankenpohl, Rouse

Ketil Christiansen playing Jorgenson, Haydn

Recommended Jazz Trumpet Artists

New Orleans Dixieland: Nick LaRocca

Dixieland: Louis Armstrong

Chicago Dixieland: Bix Beiderbecke

Swing: Cat Anderson and Harry James

Bop: Dizzy Gillespie

Cool (modal, Funk, Fusion, Avant-Garde, Harp Bop, Post-Bop): Miles Davis

Hard Bop: Clifford Brown

Avant-Garde: Don Cherry

"Young Lions:" Wynton Marsalis and Roy Hargrove

TRUMPET
Fingering Chart

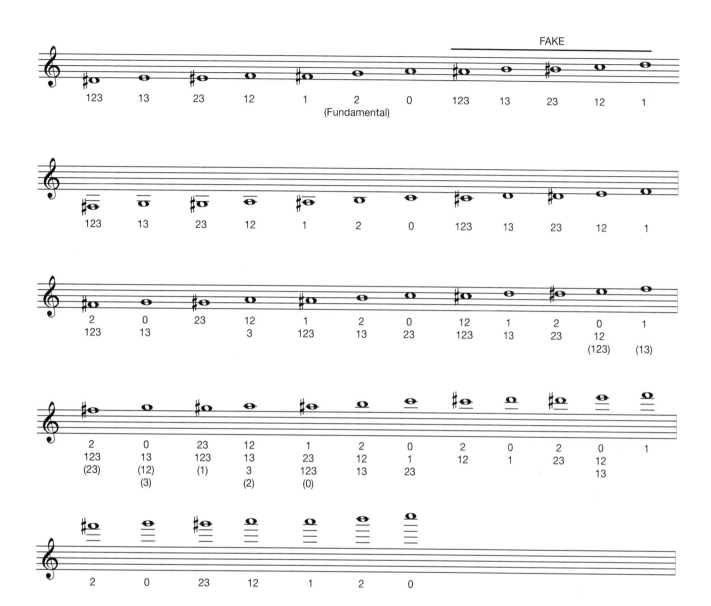

Common and Alternate Fingerings for the Trumpet (Note: Parentheses indicate the seventh partial—always a bad note [very flat] and best played with another fingering)

15

The Horn

HISTORY

The horn has been in use throughout Europe and Asia for more time than one would care to imagine—probably about thirty centuries, give or take a few. For all except the last three of these its existence had little to do with music. The ancient shofar of biblical times was used for war and worship; the nearer relative found in the Middle Ages was used for battle and hunting. These latter instruments were high pitched and brilliant, even raucous, and were carried over the shoulder. The *jagertrommet* was one of the earlier hunting horns; the *trompe de chasse* was a later development of French origin, which came somewhat closer to the modern horn with its more tapered conical bore, a wider bell, and longer tubing. The *waldhorn*, a German version of the *trompe de chasse*, was admitted to the orchestra at the end of the seventeenth century. Lully had used the horn as early as 1664 in the opera *Princess d'Elide*, but for color effects rather than as a real musical instrument.

The characteristic that hindered the use of the horn in the orchestra was not so much its tone quality as its incomplete scale. Having no valves or keys, it was limited to those pitches that could be produced by lip alterations above the fundamental tone. To increase its pitch possibilities, crooks were added around 1718.

Hampel's revolutionary contribution was the use of the hand in the bell. With the hand in a variety of positions in the bell, Hampel could not only mute the tone somewhat but also could change the pitch being produced, thus increasing the pitch flexibility of the instrument. During the later eighteenth and the early nineteenth century, the hand horn was popular and at its height for beauty of tone and appearance. The valved horn was introduced in the early nineteenth century and soon replaced the hand horn, though the latter was still played till the end of the century. The variety of crooks were discarded and gradually the F horn predominated over those in other keys. As orchestral music demanded increasingly greater power and higher range, the B♭ horn was thought to be the solution, especially for first and third horn parts with their higher tessitura. About 1900 the German firm of Kruspe produced the first double horn, designed to have the advantages of both the F and the B♭ horns.

Musically, the life of the horn began in the late Baroque period in Germany; Keiser used it in an opera in 1705. Bach made much of it, and Handel's writing for the horn is so characteristic as to be almost a trademark. In France, Rameau used it in his 1749 opera *Zoroastre*.

These composers usually used two hand horns. Beethoven added a third horn in his *Third Symphony*. In the *Ninth Symphony* he added the fourth, and composers after him wrote for either two or four, depending on their musical objectives. Schumann was one of the first composers to recognize the advantages of the valved horn.

SELECTING THE INSTRUMENT: B♭ OR F HORN

At the outset, the prospective horn player is faced with a choice of which horn to play. There are three horns to choose from, all equally legitimate. A choice among the B♭ horn, the F horn, and the double horn depends primarily on the desired sound.

The B♭ horn is nine feet long with a range lying a perfect fourth above the F horn. It is used to play lower because the fundamental of the F horn is so difficult to reach. It blends well with the other B♭ instruments of the band and orchestra in both intonation and tone color. Because it plays in a register in which the partials are similar to those of the trumpet, the beginner can learn to play with greater accuracy and confidence. Single B♭ horns have a different tone quality, a slightly harsher, more open sound than the F horn, but directors who use them are enthusiastic about them. Currently only Amati and Yamaha make student-line single B♭ horns. Figure 15–1 illustrates the partials produced on the F horn and the B♭ horn.

Figure 15–1 Horn: Partials on the Open (no valves pressed) F Horn and the Open B♭ Horn (in concert pitch)

The principal difficulties that the B♭ horn causes beginners are tone quality in the low register and often poor intonation on the beginning pitches used in the most popular group method books. The single B♭ horn also has a built-in disadvantage. When the hand is used to stop the tone and produce hand-stopped sound, the pitch is lowered three-quarters of a whole step rather than the half step of the stopped F horn. Because this pitch is impossible to correct by transposing, the hand alone cannot be used for muting. Some manufacturers have placed a fourth valve on professional-line horns that makes the necessary alteration in pitch when the hand is used for stopped horn. Some B♭ horns have a fifth valve that lowers the horn to F.

Tradition as much as anything else makes the F horn the preferred choice for beginners. The F horn has the most traditional horn quality. It is about 12 ½ feet in length, rarely has more than three valves, and has a practical range of approximately F♯ at the bottom of the bass clef to second-leger line C above the treble clef (these pitches *sound* a perfect fifth lower). Because the F horn plays in the upper partials of the overtone series rather than the lower partials nearer the fundamentals, the pitches playable with any valve combination are close together, more so in the upper register. Beginners can lose confidence and become discouraged over the difficulty of playing the correct note when the notes are so close together for any given valve combination.

Due to the difficulty of obtaining correct pitches on the F horn compared to other brass instruments, the double horn is standard in spite of its greater weight and price. The double horn is not a horn put into another key by adding a slide but is two horns with a common mouthpiece, leadpipe, and bell. The B♭ side of the horn is accessed by a fourth valve (activated by the thumb) that reduces the overall length of the brass tubing to roughly nine feet. The B♭ side of the instrument has the advantage that its fundamental is a fourth higher than the F horn, so it plays in a lower register of the harmonic series in order to sound the same pitches. Usually the player of a double horn uses the F horn in the lower register for its tone quality and the B♭ horn in the upper register for its accuracy and tone quality.

There is no unalterable spot at which one should change from one side to the other on a double horn; the right place is that which is the easiest, where the notes speak the best, and where the player can get the desired and most consistent tone quality. Often this is somewhere between written G♯ and C♯ in treble clef. Figure 15–2 shows where particular sides of the double horn are used.

F   B♭   F   B♭

Figure 15–2   Horn: Approximate Uses for F and B♭ Sides

When selecting a double horn, whether new or used, it should be played by an expert hornist and the student herself if she has been playing for several years, to verify that both sides are in tune with each other. If there is any question that the player lacks a discriminating ear or is in the habit of lipping certain notes in tune, it is best to use an electronic tuner for such a task, because stability of intonation is of great importance in selecting an instrument.

Horn players often purchase used instruments due to the relatively high cost of double horns. As when buying a used automobile, one should question why the owner wishes to part with it. The same concerns apply to all used instruments; the primary additional concern for a used horn is the dents it may have. Because the bell of the horn is so thin, it is very easy to dent; and though dents—not those in the bell—in the leadpipe especially, can cause intonation problems, repairs made by an unqualified horn repairperson can increase the intonation problems *and* add tone quality problems by destroying the consistent thickness of the metal. A bell on which the lacquer has worn off is of little concern. Any repairs to the braces can usually be identified; these can give an indication of the maintenance and previous damage to the instrument.

A used horn should be inspected for pitted brass where the hands touch the instrument. A certain amount of wear should be expected on the valve stems, but pitted brass can wear through and result in costly damage. Another concern is the cleanliness of the bore.

Horns have more resistance than any of the brass instruments—this resistance affects tone quality, flexibility, range, intonation, virtually every aspect of the instrument. This resistance should be constant and a characteristic of the horn itself, not due to years of accumulated dirt.

THE HORN AS A MARCHING BAND INSTRUMENT

In the early 1970s when corps-style marching bands began to emerge, there developed a desperate need for a midrange sound in the brass. Consequently, the mellophone that had been previously used primarily in jazz ensembles was improved by several manufacturers and marketed as a marching alternative to the concert horn. Presently, horn substitutes are labeled mellophones and marching horns; the marching horns are slightly more conical, use a horn mouthpiece, and have a tone more closely resembling a real horn. Mellophones are designed to use a trumpet mouthpiece but are commonly available with an adapter for a horn mouthpiece, a use that seriously affects the already poor intonation of the instrument.

The advantage of mellophones and marching horns is that they are bell-front instruments. Both are normally pitched in F, but an octave higher than regular horns, so trumpet fingerings are used. The upper register of the mellophone can be played with more confidence than on the concert horn, because the notes are spaced farther apart. The most universal criticism of the marching horn is that due to the proportion of conical to cylindrical tubing it is easily overblown, especially by trumpet players.

ASSEMBLING THE HORN

The horn is taken from its case by grasping the outside tubing in the vicinity of the valves. The tubing is reinforced for this purpose; the rest of the horn is more fragile than one would imagine a metal instrument to be. The metal is extremely thin—so thin that the bell can be dented by pressure from the fingers. Even the weight of the instrument will dent the metal when it is handled incorrectly.

The single step in assembling the horn is to insert the mouthpiece into the leadpipe with a gentle twisting motion.

HOLDING THE HORN

The player should sit on the right corner of a chair at about a 45-degree angle with the right leg positioned beside the chair and slightly to the rear, the leg supporting the horn. As players mature, they should be encouraged to play with the horn off the knee. The left leg should be directly in the line of vision with the conductor. This position facilitates seeing both music and conductor and keeps the player's back well away from the back of the chair. Some younger players may need a book on which to rest their right foot to keep the horn in the proper position for playing. See Figures 15–3 and 15–4 on page 242 for examples of playing position while seated.

Horn players also stand to play, especially in solo work, but they should not march. The body from the waist up should be in the same position whether sitting or standing, a naturally relaxed and efficient position. The right hand's function is to move in and out of the bell, correcting intonation and altering tone quality; when standing, the player must listen carefully as he uses her right hand partially for support; this use can affect intonation and tone quality.

The left hand holds the instrument and operates the valves. The little finger is placed within the hook to support the horn; the three middle fingers rest in a curved position on the valves. The horn uses rotary valves that are depressed considerably less than the piston valves used by most other brasses. Because of the left-hand grip, horn players must be reminded not to use it to apply excessive pressure

Figure 15–3
Horn: Sitting Position with Bell on Leg

Figure 15–4
Horn: Sitting Position with Bell off Leg

on the embouchure. The little finger should not clench and push the mouthpiece into the embouchure. On the single horn the thumb is placed around the tubing, resting lightly rather than grabbing the tubing. Some single horns have a hook for the thumb that may aid in the development of good habits. This hook is replaced by the thumb valve on a double horn. The left arm hangs loosely from the shoulder, as relaxed and natural as possible, with just enough angle or slant to help the fingers to move freely and rapidly.

The placement of the right hand affects both tone quality and pitch and enables the student to produce the effects desired by composers and the conductor. Because of the wide variety of hand sizes and shapes, it is not possible to be specific about the right-hand placement, shape, or use. The young student with a small hand will have a different placement than will a full-grown player in order to produce the same effects. The use of the right hand can make the difference between a beautiful horn sound and one that is unpleasant. Because habits are so hard to break once set, some hornists recommend positioning the beginner's hand as it will be used when the player reaches maturity even though the sound temporarily suffers.

Although there are several schools of thought on right-hand position, only one method is generally used in the United States today. The fingers are close together with no space between them and are extended with the finger knuckles almost straight. The hand is cupped, bending at the knuckles to form an angle somewhat larger than 90 degrees. The thumb lies next to the index finger, fitting flush so no open space exists between the thumb and the hand. The thumb is bent a little so the tip of the thumb lies almost on top of the index finger rather than at its side. The hand goes into the bell of the horn with the fingers held vertically rather than horizontally, the back of the fingers touching the inside of the bell on the side away from the player. If the player's hand is small, her thumb will not be brought over the index finger but will extend out from the hand, still joined. This formation makes it possible to close off the bell with the heel of the hand by moving the wrist to cup the palm more—the fingers remain as flat as they can and against the bell. The more the hand is inserted, the darker and flatter the pitch.

Figure 15–5 Horn: Normal Position of the Hand in the Bell

The hand is used to alternate between tone quality that can be described as "dark" or "brassy." The first involves inserting the hand farther than normal and the latter involves removing the hand almost completely. Good horn players adjust their hand position for the appropriate tone quality for the music played as well as for specific instrumentations; for example, hand placement is different when a hornist plays in a woodwind quintet than when he plays in a brass quintet.

The player determines how far the hand should be inserted into the bell by listening and adjusting. The hand is placed at the point where the tone quality is best and the pitch of the horn matches the pitch of the ensemble (examples of right-hand positions are shown in Figures 15–5 and 15–6). Horns are manufactured about one-quarter step sharper than other brass instruments to compensate for the placement of the hand in the bell. This affects upper-register response and pitch more than lower register. One idea is to place the hand in as far as it can go without muffling the tone, but the distance will not be the same for any two hands. The size of the hand alters tone as well as intonation, and the player must learn to produce the tone quality he wants with the hand he has. Cupping and straightening the hand is done gradually to avoid sudden changes of tone quality.

**Figure 15–6
Horn: Closed Position of the Hand in the Bell**

The horn should be held at an angle similar to that used for playing the clarinet. The mouthpiece, not the head, is tilted downward. The horn is held at an angle so that the leadpipe is about 15 to 20 degrees from the horizontal. Horn players should, on occasion, stand to determine a proper relationship of the horn to the body remembering that standing can adversely affect use of the right hand for tone quality.

The bell should not face directly into the player's body or directly to the side. An angle about half way between the two would cover nearly all correct positions for holding the instrument. The double horn may rest on the right thigh.

THE BEGINNING STUDENT

When the beginner knows that the horn is his instrument of choice, no valid reason exists for starting him on the trumpet. There are, in fact, many reasons for opposing it. Problems of embouchure increase the difficulties of the horn player who has previously played the trumpet, and there is little evidence that trumpet study contributes to a keener ear or better harmonic sense.

A source of frustration on the part of beginners is the fact that many beginning method books start all winds on F concert, a note that is comfortable and easily accessible for most winds but poor for the horn. Further, most beginning method books progress from that pitch downward. To have the F horn player play up an octave, third-space C, is not encouraged as this is the eighth harmonic for the horn, and the pitches both one step above and one step below are played with the same fingering, a discouraging factor. If the teacher does not wish to use a method book that starts the horn on a different pitch from the rest of the instruments, one alternative is to start horn players separately from other beginning wind players.

The B♭ horn and the double horn can be made accessible to an interested grade school student. Starting a pupil on a single F horn is easier at the middle school level as older students should have greater embouchure control (and strength) and a more accurate sense of pitch and intervals.

For students of small stature who have difficulty reaching both the bell with their right hand and the mouthpiece with their embouchure, a *competent, experienced* instrument repairperson can bend the leadpipe to a more comfortable position with little or no effect on the horn or overall tone quality. The leadpipe can later be bent back to its original position when appropriate.

EMBOUCHURE

In the United States, fairly standard practices govern embouchure although one frequently hears about the "einsetzen" and "ansetzen" embouchures. The terms refer to setting the mouthpiece *in* or *on* the embouchure. The einsetzen is rarely recommended, though a surprising number of players without formal instruction apparently feel that it is natural and right, especially for the lower register. It produces a fine tone but is limited in flexibility and upper range. With this embouchure, the mouthpiece is placed in the lips, about midway in the pink area of both upper and lower lips. For many it is placed midway "inside" the lower lip with the upper lip shaped for a more traditional embouchure. The outer lip area then curls around the mouthpiece. Because the delicate pink area of the lip furnishes support for the mouthpiece, developing endurance is more difficult. Players who successfully use the einsetzen usually have fuller, thicker lips.

With the ansetzen or normal embouchure, the mouthpiece is set on the lips after they have been properly shaped, Farkas's excellent description likens the mouth to a drawstring on a bag, drawing the bag tightly shut over a coffee can—the tautness of the bag results from pulling forward and backward at the same time.[1] The lower lip is turned in a little over the teeth; the chin must not bunch. (It may help to have the beginner exaggerate this slightly.) The teeth are somewhat apart and the mouthpiece is placed high on the lips. Having the mouthpiece entirely outside the pink of the lip reduces the range and produces poor tone; some middle-ground combination of *in* and *on* the lips is the more practical approach. If the jaw is flat, the corners of the mouth will not turn up into a smiling position. A correct embouchure is illustrated in Figures 15–7a and 15–7b.

Embouchure faults can develop when beginning students practice in the low horn register. The embouchure for this range is difficult to develop; for the extremely low pitches the player actually removes some of the lip from the mouthpiece, which seems unnatural and incorrect.

---

[1]Philip Farkas (1962), *The Art of Brass Playing*, Bloomington, IN: Brass Publications, p. 17.

Figure 15–7a
Horn Embouchure (front view)

Figure 15–7b
Horn Embouchure (side view)

INTONATION

Initial tuning is done in the following manner. All the slides are pushed in. Then, if the double horn is used, the F side is tuned first using the F tuning slide. Usually the slide will need to be pulled one-quarter to one-half inch to bring the F horn down to standard pitch. The next step is to tune the B♭ side to the F side using the B♭ tuning slide. Having the open tones on both sides in tune, the player may then bring the other notes into correct relationship by pulling the other valve slides, those on the F side first and then those on the B♭ side. The main tuning slide in the leadpipe that affects both sides of the horn is reserved for tuning with the ensemble. This entire procedure is to no avail if the right hand is not in the correct position during the tuning. The player must not tip or move his hand, or favor notes during tuning; if he does, he will not tune the instrument correctly. All instrument companies provide excellent booklets on how to tune a horn. Each player should be sure to read one and follow the procedures with patience. This entire procedure will be a waste of everyone's time if the student does not listen carefully and develop an understanding of good intonation.

For day-to-day tuning, players are often seen adjusting one valve slide and stopping. When one valve slide is altered, it is almost always necessary to adjust the others to it and to adjust both sides of the double horn. If only one valve slide is tuned, it will be incorrect when used in combination with others. The player should tune several notes, compare the B♭ and F sides, and adjust as necessary. Beginners will require the assistance of a teacher and possibly an electronic tuner—both are tools for developing the ear and not a substitute for listening.

The double horn has fewer intonation problems than the other valved instruments, providing that it is a quality instrument (See Figure 15–8 on page 246). Unlike the temperamental woodwinds or even the trumpet, the double horn can be played well in tune on almost all pitches throughout its range. This is not because it is more perfectly designed than the other brasses, but because it is actually two horns. Bad notes on one side can be avoided by playing them on the other side. The double horn player has numerous devices to help her play in tune: She can adjust the two tuning slides as well as the six valve slides which affect the over-

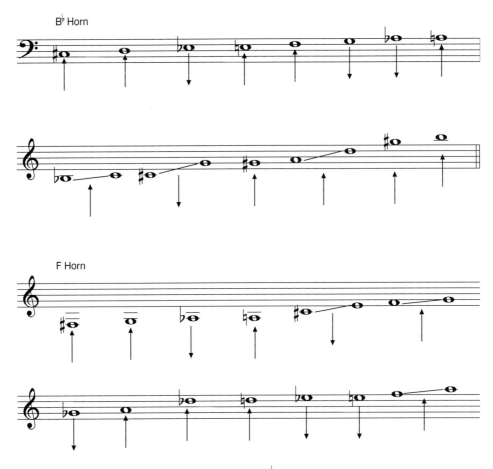

Figure 15–8   Horn: Intonation Problems of the Bᵇ and F Horns

all tuning; she can adjust her embouchure while playing to change the individual pitches. The player of a single horn (F or Bᵇ) adjusts pitches in the same way, with one tuning slide and three valve slides.

One of the unimportant but fascinating idiosyncrasies of the horn and other brass is that a chord may be produced on it. A few players have been able to do this, and there are compositions that call for it. One note is played while another that is a member of the chord built on the first note is hummed; this combination produces two other strong partials that are audible, resulting in a four-note chord. We know of no method for learning this trick other than experimentation. Except for the rare occasion when it is called for, this feat may fall into the category of "things not worth doing are not worth doing well."

Like all valved instruments, the tubing for each valve is a comprise required for equal temperament. For the double horn, some of the out of tune notes can be avoided by switching from one side to the other. In certain registers, however, when it is best to play on the F side or the Bᵇ side, there are pitch tendencies for particular notes. These are indicated in Figure 15–8.

TONE QUALITY

Horn tone is produced in the same fashion as on other brass instruments except that the horn player has an additional way of changing tone quality. On all brass instruments, the tone is chiefly controlled by the embouchure and breath support;

the horn player also uses his right hand in the bell to change the sound. Beyond these techniques, the most important factor is the ear. As on all wind instruments, tone quality is primarily determined by the player's mental image. On horn this is especially important because what the listener hears is different from what the player hears due to the position in which that horn is held and played. Further, the design and acoustics of the room affect horn tone quality more than that of any other wind instrument.

The player should listen to as many horn players and good recordings as he can and choose the kind of tone that he desires. He must then listen as he plays and keep adjusting his embouchure until the sound approaches his mental ideal. Tone quality of the horn is different from performer to performer and from band to orchestra, and recordings differ in timbre between performers who play with woodwind quintets and those who play with brass quintets. Advanced horn players learn to approach the instrument differently depending on the instrument's use, performing equally well with brass and woodwind groups, chamber groups, large ensembles, and as soloists. Twentieth-century music requires a distinctly different tone than that used for Romantic compositions.

The horn is so adaptable that it can blend with woodwinds, brass, or strings. It is also a beautiful complement to the human voice. It can be the accompaniment or solo instrument and by changing the tone quality can be used in nearly every combination of instruments. With all these challenging possibilities, players should never limit themselves to an embouchure that produces only one kind of tone. To play every passage with a dark sound or a light, bright sound is to ignore the musical style and the meaning of the passage. The player who enjoys the instrument the most is the one who widens his range of sounds from dark to light just as conscientiously as those from high to low.

Perhaps the single most important variable in good horn tone is the airstream. Because the horn has the most resistance of all brass instruments, it is quite easy to produce a sound with a minimum amount of air. The F horn is more than twice as long as a trumpet, requiring that the air must be constantly and consistently supported whether one is playing long lyrical lines or fast technical passages. Too much air, often a sign of an embouchure that is too tight, will promote overblowing and produce an overly brassy sound (this special effect is demanded on occasion).

A common problem among horn players is that they seem to crack more notes than the other brasses; this cracking is in part due to the closeness of the pitches with any given valve combination. Compared to the shorter brass and woodwinds, the length of the horn requires more time for the pressure wave from the embouchure to create the standing wave that makes the note speak. With experience and continued development of the breathing apparatus, hornists learn to time their attacks. Teachers should understand the horn player's dilemma.

The tone quality is also controlled by the embouchure: the size of the lip opening, the shape of the lips, the amount of mouthpiece pressure on the lips, and the angle at which the air enters the mouthpiece. A high palate and fairly large oral cavity also enhance the tone, but these are not within the power of the player to change. A more puckered embouchure, within reason, will give a smoother, mellower, darker sound. Too much pucker can make the tone so dark that it begins to resemble the baritone horn in quality. A more smiling, stretched embouchure will give a bright, brilliant tone, which can become brassy and harsh. The term *cuivre* or *schmetternd* designates this brassy, harsh sound, which is used for special effects in orchestral and band literature. In ordinary playing sufficient pucker is maintained to obtain a tone that is mellow but not overly subdued—the horn tone should have an element of brilliancy to it.

The horn produces a wide variety of tone colors and effects for which there are many foreign labels. For example, *mit dampfer* (with mute) is often used synonymously with *stopped, stark anblasen, gedampft* with "+" above the note marked forte, *gestopft* with *muted, con sordino,* or the British *closed.* The player has to remember specifically what each means, and then alter the practice with the conductor's wishes.

Some further explanation should be made of the term *cuivre.* Players are often puzzled as to whether this term indicates use of a mute. *Cuivre* means to play with a brassy tone; *schmetternd* and *blechern* indicate the same sound. The tone may be produced by forcing too much air into the horn or by using the mute (cheating) and forcing against it, creating sufficient air pressure to get the brassy quality required. If a forte passage is being played and some form of muting is called for, the *cuivre* effect is desired.

There are three primary effects on the horn in addition to the straight horn tone. These are (1) the stopped tone (hand tightly in the bell) used for special effects, (2) the muted tone produced by means of a regular mute, and (3) the brassy tone designated by *cuivre* or *schmetternd.*

The hand in the bell makes the tone more open or more closed. If the tone is too dull and thick, the hand should be withdrawn a little. The closed hand darkens and subdues the tone, whereas an open hand allows the tone to emit freely. The stopped bell, like the muted bell, is used only for special effects specified by a composer and is not part of normal playing. The position of the bell also affects the sound for listener and player, but that sound is never the same for listener as for player. The player may like the dark tone he gets with the bell turned into his body, but the listener may find it lifeless, dull, and uninteresting.

If the tone is not good, one should check for the following: Does the embouchure have enough of a pucker to get a good cushion on the upper lip? Is the upper lip free enough from pressure to enable it to vibrate? Are the teeth open enough to make a round tone? Think of forming an open vowel; "oo" is usually preferred, "oh" for a brighter tone, or "aa" or "ee" may help. Is the embouchure too tight or too smiling? Does the breath come from the diaphragm area through an open throat? Is the tongue bunched up in the back of the mouth?

Vibrato

Though at present vibrato is more widely accepted, horn players traditionally have not used a vibrato except occasionally in solo works. The French are an exception; they favor a thin tone with a vibrato, the same speed vibrato for all registers and dynamics. The vibrato seems to destroy the genuine horn quality, giving it a more sentimental, superficial character not in keeping with most of the music written for it. Although some hornists advocate diaphragm vibrato, the most popular method has been jaw vibrato.

Mutes and Stopped Horn

Ideally, a commercial mute is used for muted passages, and the hand is reserved for passages that call for hand stopping. When the hand is used, it goes into the bell of the F horn with the effect of shortening the overall length of the instrument (raising the pitch one-half step, or temporarily creating a horn in F♯). Normally, in order to play "hand stopped," the hand is inserted about 6 1/2 inches into the bell, but the distance will vary with the size of the hand. When a commercial mute is used, the pitch obtained may depend on the status of the mute's cork that wears and is affected by moisture. Players of double horns normally play muted passages on the F side of the instrument or use nontransposing mutes if the register being performed requires use of the B♭ side of the instrument.

Hand stopping is often referred to as stopped horn; other terms are *sons bouches*, *bouchez*, *chinuso*, and *gestopft*. The hand is useful for this purpose only to about the bottom of the treble clef because below that it is not powerful enough to resist the air pressure. A small hand may make the pitch too sharp even after transposing down a half step; a large hand may produce the opposite pitch problem. In these cases, the player may be forced to compensate by altering his embouchure, lipping up or down, or, if the stopped passage is a long one, retuning the slides. Today there are several manufacturers of special mutes that can be used for the appropriate sound and do not require transposition. These enable the hornist to use both the F and B♭ sides of a double horn. Criteria in selecting a nontransposing mute sound include good intonation as well as the desired muting effect.

The use of any mute creates intonation problems because the player cannot use his hand to bring the pitch into tune. He therefore must listen to the pitch created, make the necessary adjustments with the mute when possible, and adjust the pitch with his embouchure. Mutes are manufactured with a screw arrangement by which the player can adjust the mute to assist in intonation. These have not been widely accepted because they take too long to adjust. Recently mutes have been manufactured that allow a pitch adjustment on the outside that remains true throughout the register of the horn.

FINGERINGS

The horn is a transposing instrument. Pitched in F, the notes played sound a perfect fifth below. When a player switches to the B♭ side of the double horn, he continues to read the notes for horn in F but uses a different set of fingerings. Consequently these notes also sound a perfect fifth below those read and played, although they are played on a B♭ horn. The fingering chart at the end of the chapter shows the fingerings for both the F and the B♭ horns (as well as the double horn). An asterisk marks the most common fingerings (although depending on the particular passage, alternate fingerings and even the other side of the horn is frequently used). The chart covers a very broad range of written pitches for the horn; most public school horn players will never see music written to these depths or heights.

WHAT TO PRACTICE

Like every brass player, successful performance depends on the quality and quantity of practice; a positive relationship exists between performance and preparation. For the beginning horn student, use of supplementary material is perhaps more critical than for any other brass student. Discouragement can beset young horn players who see their colleagues advancing rapidly through the book and find themselves lagging behind often through no fault of their own.

The warm-up for horn players should include long tones at various dynamic levels and crescendos/decrescendos in all registers of the instrument (the player diligently attempts to keep the pitch and volume from wavering; blasting at the upper dynamic ranges should carefully be avoided). Lip slurs for flexibility and scales for finger dexterity should also be included.

As players develop, scales and arpeggios can be extended to cover a full three-octave range. This greater range improves accuracy, strength of the embouchure, endurance, control, flexibility over a wide range, and intonation.

Attacks are usually a frustrating problem for beginning horn students. Daily practice on attacks should include all dynamic levels and all registers. A valuable study is to write out a series of unrelated pitches (not unlike a tone row), each followed by a rest, and have students attack each note. Emphasis should be placed on the "duh" articulation, as the "tuh" articulation creates an exaggerated explosive sound on the horn and leads to even more cracked pitches. Because of the small size of the mouthpiece and the normally puckered embouchure, tonguing with accuracy is more difficult on the horn than on the other brass.

CARE AND MAINTENANCE

Moisture collects in the horn as in any other instrument. It presents more of a problem, however, because the horn cannot be swabbed, and the moisture doesn't run out the bottom. The addition of water keys is becoming more common, and some professionals have several water keys added to their instruments.

Horn players must unwind their instruments at every opportunity—they have enough trouble playing accurately without contending with bubbly notes. The valve slides should be emptied after each playing, more frequently if needed. Running water through the horn or forcing in a small swab is not a good idea—these practices may push the dirt and sludge into some inaccessible spot where it will lodge permanently. Some of the slides are shaped so they can be cleaned with water or a brush, and a little common sense can indicate which ones these are. Moisture left in the horn will retain dust and grease which in time will change the tone of the instrument. Because cleaning the horn after it becomes dirty is so much more difficult than draining it each time it is used, the latter should be enforced or at least urged upon the student.

Removing the slides should be easy. If the horn is cared for properly, the slides are removed often for emptying, adjusted continually for tuning, and shouldn't stick. Because students, however, have been known to fail to accomplish that which they have been asked to do, slides sometimes go for semesters unmoved. In such cases the slides should not be yanked out by grabbing with the hand and pulling, for the soft metal will yield to the pressure of the hand and take a different shape than that intended. A repairperson is recommended if any real force is needed. Students often discover that when they pull out a slide they can get a "pop," and slide pulling can become a favorite pastime. The popping action can result in leaks in the slide or the valve casing; students should be urged to find other amusement. The affected valve should be depressed when removing or returning the valve slide—one slide at a time—which will eliminate the pop and keep the instrument in better condition. The slides should be lubricated with slight amounts of petroleum jelly or slide grease.

The valves must be oiled regularly, with either special horn oil or regular valve oil. To oil these, pull the slides and insert three or four drops onto the slide. Replace the slide, return the horn to playing position, press and release the valve numerous times, then remove the slide and expel the excess oil. Some books suggest letting the oil run down the casing onto the valve, but this is not recommended because the oil picks up dirt and lint on its way and deposits it on the valve. At least weekly the valve bearings should be oiled (top and bottom).

The genuine corks on rotary valves are subject to wear and to hardening and should be replaced with a synthetic rubber "cork." Most manufactures use this synthetic material. The corks are crucial to valve alignment, which determines pitch and greatly affects tone quality.

The string on the valves needs to be replaced occasionally if breakage is to be avoided, perhaps once a year for players practicing an average amount. Strings do not break often but when they do it always seems to be at a critical time—the horn player must realize that unless the strings are replaced periodically, they are going to break—and if "Murphy" is correct, it will be two measures prior to a solo at the District Band Festival. Only one string at a time is removed and replaced. Of importance is to line the valve up at the exact level of the other two. Instruction in how to replace strings on rotary valves is too often ignored by instrumental music teachers.

The finish on the horn is a question of preference. Many horn performers play an instrument that has been stripped of all lacquer (sometimes just from the bell) or manufactured without lacquer. All student-line horns, however, are finished with lacquer to protect the brass from pitting. The finish can and should be preserved from damage caused by the acids of the student's hands by frequent wiping with a soft cloth. The horn lacquer is as durable as that on other instruments, but the hands come into contact with more of the horn, so the possibility of deterioration is greater. Left-hand guards made of plastic or leather help. Leather is preferred because of its greater softness and flexibility. Players like to polish the instrument to a beautiful sheen, but polishing should be done in moderation, as the lacquer is so thin that polishing can eventually remove it, particularly on the bell. Some manufacturers do not lacquer their instruments, and a new horn looks as dull as one used for 40 years.

BIBLIOGRAPHY

Texts

Indicates out of print in 2001.

*BERV HARRY (1977). *A Creative Approach to French Horn.* Bryn Mawr, PA: Chappell Music.

*BUSHOUSE, DAVID, and JAMES D. PLOYHAR (1983). *Practical Hints on Playing the French Horn.* Melville, NY: Belwin-Mills.

COUSINS, FARQUHARSON (1992). *On Playing the Horn,* 2nd ed. Chapel-en-le-Frith, England: Caron.

FARKAS, PHILIP (1956). *The Art of French Horn Playing:* Evanston, IL: Summy-Birchard.

*FITZPATRICK, HORACE (1970). *The Horn and Horn-Playing and the Austro-Bohemian Tradition from 1680–1830.* New York: Oxford University Press.

*GREGORY, ROBIN (1969). *The Horn: A Comprehensive Guide to the Modern Instrument and Its Music,* rev. and enlarged ed. New York: F. A. Praeger.

JANETZKY, KURT, and BERNARD BRÜCHLE (1988). *The Horn.* Portland, OR: Amadeus Press

LABAR, ARTHUR (1986). *Horn Players' Audition Handbook.* Miami, Belwin-Mills.

MONTAGU, JEREMY (1990). *The French Horn.* Princes Risborough, England: Shire Publications.

MORLEY-PEGGE, R (1973). *The French Horn: Some Notes on the Evolution of the Instrument and of Its Technique,* 2nd ed. New York: W. W. Norton.

REYNOLDS, VERNE (1997). *The Horn Handbook.* Portland, OR: Amadeus Press.

*SANSONE, LORENZO (1962). *French Horn Music Literature with Composers' Biographical Sketches.* New York: Sansone Musical Instruments.

SCHULLER, GUNTHER (1992). *Horn Technique.* New York: Oxford University Press.

TUCKWELL, BARRY (1983). *Horn.* New York: Schirmer Books.

*YANCICH, MILAN (1971). *A Practical Guide to French Horn Playing.* Rochester, NY: Wind Music.

Journals/Associations

The Horn Call. Semiannual journal of the International Horn Society. Available from 2220 N. 1400 East; Provo, UT 84604-2150 (URL:http://www.hornsociety.org).

Horn Studies

Easy—Beginning (elementary or middle school)—all start from low C to second-line G

Berv. *A Creative Approach to the French Horn* (Chappell).

Clevenger, McDunn, and Rusch. *The Dale Clevenger French Horn Methods* (2 vols.) (Kjos).

Clodomir. *Methode Elementaire* (A. Leduc).

Fearn. *French Horn for Beginners* (Theodore Presser).

Getchell. *First Book of Practical Studies* (Belwin-Mills).

Goldstein. *Book of Exercises* (Cor).

Hill and Froseth. *Introducing the French Horn* (w/recording) (G.I.A.).

Howe. *Method for French Horn* (Marvin Howe).

Musser, and Del Borgo. *Modes in Contemporary Music* (Alfred).

———. *Rhythm in Contemporary Music* (Alfred).

———. *Tonality in Contemporary Music* (Alfred).

Singer. *Embouchure Building for French Horn* (Belwin-Mills).

Tuckwell. *50 First Exercises* (Oxford University Press).

———. *Horn Tutor* (Oxford University Press).

Yancich. *Method for the French Horn* (Wind Music).

Medium (middle or high school)

Belloli. *8 Studies* (International).

———. *24 Etudes* (Sansone).

Borris. *Studies & Pieces* (2 vols.) (C. F. Peters).

Brophy. *Technical Studies.*

Concone. *Legato Studies* (Belwin-Mills).

———. *Lyrical Studies* (Brass Press).

Gallay. *Unmeasured Preludes* (Sansone).

———. *12 Grandes Etudes Brilliantes* (Elkan-Vogel).

———. *30 Etudes* (Sansone).

Getchell. *Second Book of Practical Studies* (Belwin-Mills).

Horner. *Primary Studies for the French Horn* (Theodore Presser).

Maxime-Alphonse. *40 Etudes Facile* (A. Leduc).

———. *70 Etudes Tres Facile* (A. Leduc).

Miersch. *Melodious Studies for the French Horn* (C. Fischer).

Musser and Del Borgo. *Modes in Contemporary Music* (Alfred).

———. *Rhythm in Contemporary Music* (Alfred).

———. *Tonality in Contemporary Music* (Alfred).

Pares and Claus. *Daily Exercises and Scales for the French Horn* (C. Fischer).

Pottag. *Daily Exercises* (Belwin-Mills).

———. *Preparatory Melodies to Solo Work* (Belwin-Mills).

———. and Andraud. *335 Selected Melodious, Progressive and Technical Studies* (2 vols.) (Southern Music).

Shoemaker. *Legato Etudes for Horn.* (Belwin-Mills).

Singer. *Embouchure Building for French Horn* (Belwin-Mills).

Advanced (high school or college)

Bitsch. *12 Etudes* (A. Leduc).

Bozza. *18 Etudes en Forme d'Improvisation* (A. Leduc).

———. *Graphismes* (A. Leduc).

Dufrense and Voisin. *Develop Sight-Reading* (Colin).

Gallay. *Unmeasured Preludes* (Sansone).

———. *12 Grandes Etudes Brilliantes* (Sansone).

———. *30 Etudes* (Sansone).

Falux. *20 Virtuoso Studies after Bach* (Elkan-Vogel).

———. *25 Progressive Studies* (Elkan-Vogel).

Fearn. *Exercises for Flexibility* (Elkan-Vogel).

Kling. *24 Horn Studies* (Woodwind).

———. *40 Characteristic Etudes for French Horn* (Southern Music).

Kopprasch. *50 Etudes for French Horn* (Southern Music).

———. *60 Selected Studies* (C. Fischer).

Maxime-Alfonse. *20 Etudes Difficiles* (A. Leduc).

———. *40 Etudes Moyenne Force* (A. Leduc).

Mueller. *22 Studies* (International).

———. *34 Studies* (2 vols.) (International).

Reynolds. *48 Etudes for French Horn* (G. Schirmer).

Sansone. *A Modern Method for French Horn* (2 vols.) (Sansone).

Singer. *Embouchure Building for French Horn* (Belwin-Mills).

Woude. *French Horn Studies.* (Summy-Birchard).

Instructional Videos

Belwin 21st Century Bands Methods. *Horn in F. Level 1 & 2.* (Lisa Bontrager, 1996). Miami, FL: Warner Bros.

The French Horn. (Phillip Farkas, 1984). Juneau, AK: Mobile Video Company.

Horn Drills & Excerpts, Vol 1 & 2 (James Decker, 1994). Los Angeles: IVSI, School of Music, University of Southern California.

Horn Playing: Past and Present (David Kirkpatrick, Tom Bartolomeo, Cathy Miller, Alan White, Pat Lippart, Joe Lovinsky, 1992). Ft. Mead, MD: U.S. Army Field Band.

Steps to Excellence: a French Horn Clinic Vol. 2. (L. William Kuyper, 1987). Grand Rapids, MI: Yamaha Music Products

Recommended Classical Horn Artists

Dennis Brain playing Mozart and Strauss
Eric Ruske playing Mozart
Barry Tuckwell playing Brahms and Strauss
Alex Shuban playing Gershwin and Bernstein

Recommended Jazz Horn Artists

Swing: Claude Thornhill
Bop: Julius Watkins
Cool: Sandy Siegelstein
Third Stream: Gunther Schuller
Hard Bop: John Clark
Post-Bop, Avant-Garde: Pete Levin

FRENCH HORN
Fingering Chart

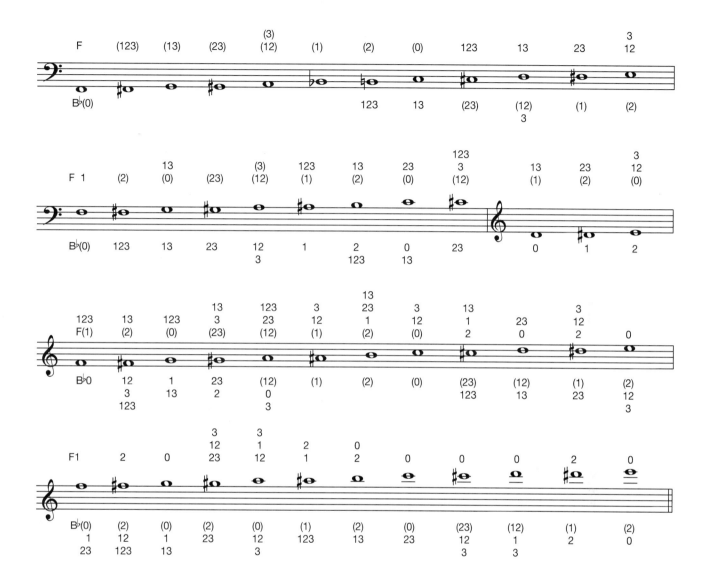

16

The Trombone and Baritone/Euphonium

HISTORY

The Roman armies marched to the calls of brass instruments, among which were those named *buccina*. This instrument, about 12 feet in length, vaguely resembled the trombone although it was shaped more like the letter C. The Romans seemed to have mastered the art of bending metal tubing, but this art was lost with the fall of Rome and not rediscovered until the Middle Ages; with the disappearance of this skill the buccina also disappeared.

In the fourteenth century a definite ancestor of the trombone was used, bearing the unpoetic name of *sackbut*. It appears in paintings before 1500, and by the end of the sixteenth century it was found in several sizes and ranges—a family of sackbuts similar to the family of stringed instruments, according to the common practice. These were useful instruments, because they could play the first four semitones below the open tone, so that with the use of overtones most of the notes of the chromatic scale could be obtained, a rare feat for a wind instrument. In the early 1500s, the fifth semitone was added, which made the complete scale available except for one or two low tones at the bottom of the range.

The sackbut was especially prominent in the tower music in Germany and in the church music of the Gabrielis, Monteverdi, and others of the Venetian school. The early concept of the trombone as a sacred instrument for use in the church remained prominent for many years. In spite of this it found its way into one of the first operas, *Orfeo,* by Monteverdi. It was used thereafter in opera and ensemble music continuously, more for color effects than as a legitimate member of the orchestra. Mozart's extraordinary sense of the potentialities of the trombone is shown in its use in the *Requiem,* in *Don Giovanni,* and in *The Magic Flute,* but only with the Beethoven *Fifth Symphony* did it find a place in symphonic music. The possibilities of the trombone seem to have been better understood following Berlioz' *Treatise on Orchestration,* and since that time (1844) it has been a standard member of the wind family.

Most of the history of the baritone and euphonium is identical to that of the tuba (the next chapter). During the early 1800s, the need for tenor brass instruments that could match the tone quality and dynamic range of higher brasses in wind bands and ensembles prompted the search that led to the baritone/euphonium. Between 1835 and 1850 instrument manufacturers used the Berliner-Pumpen and Vienna valves for a variety of instruments. In 1839, Pertinet of Paris introduced a modified Berliner-Pumpen valve that is still used in modern-day brasses.

Efforts by instrument makers and players continued through the nineteenth century to improve design and performance quality. One result was the compensating systems that appeared first in the 1850s. Compensating systems are designed to correct intonation (specifically the 1–3 and 1–2–3 valve combinations) on euphoniums and tubas by automatically adding extra tubing. In 1838, Moritz patented a five-valve bass tuba in E$^\flat$ and a four-valve tenor tuba. "Apparently there were many hybrid models of so called tenor horns, euphoniums, and bombardons that were called by various names from country to country with no standard nomenclature."[1] By midcentury this instrument was a fully developed euphonium with a larger bore invented by Sommer of Weimer. These instruments were called *Barytone* or *cor-basse* tenor in France, *barytone* in Germany, and *baritono* in Spain.

Today's instruments are made so that the euphonium is associated with the "baritone voice," whereas the baritone, like the trombone, is associated with the "tenor voice." In brass band literature there are separate parts for the baritone and euphonium.

For many years, students playing the baritone/euphonium have been those whose embouchure or facial characteristics impaired success on trumpet (or they didn't practice). Due to the relationship of its relatively large bore to its length, combined with a greater degree of conical taper than the baritone, the euphonium can produce among the most beautiful tone qualities of all brass instruments. In the hands of an accomplished performer, one with good listening skills, it can play virtuosic lines as well as any of the brasses.

SELECTING THE TROMBONE

The trombone is a cylindrical brass instrument (approximately two-thirds cylindrical, one-third conical) pitched one octave below the B$^\flat$ trumpet. Although both are B$^\flat$ instruments, only the trumpet transposes (sounding one step below the written pitch). The trombone, like all bass clef instruments, is a nontransposing instrument; it sounds the pitch that is read. Like the trumpet, the trombone and baritone play in the register encompassing their second to ninth or tenth partials.

In selecting a used trombone one should look for the following: (1) Possible leaks. These may be located by removing the slide from the bell section, stopping the threaded tube, and blowing through the leadpipe. Leaks can also be identified by immersing the slide in water and stopping one end with the hand while blowing in the other; bubbles will pinpoint the leak. A leak at the point where the slide section screws onto the bell section will be evident if condensation forms on the player's left hand. (2) Obvious wear. This is indicated by badly worn lacquer and, more serious, worn chromium plating on the inner slide. Worn plating will cause sticking due to brass rubbing against brass. (3) Slide alignment and valve alignment. The slide may stick and appear to be well worn in spots, indicating an alignment problem. The valve alignment may be checked by removing the valve cap and examining the position of the notches. The F attachment valve can be either a string valve, a mechanical rotary, or ball and socket. (4) Loose braces and worn corks. Bass trombones occasionally leak at the valve; this may be checked by removing the F tuning slide, pushing the trigger, and blowing into the mouthpiece while holding the hand over the open tubes.

---

[1]H. W. Schwartz (1938), *The Story of Musical Instruments*, Elkhart, IN: C.G. Conn Ltd., p. 232.

The F attachment is a device consisting of extra tubing that is switched into the basic length of the instrument by means of a thumb-operated valve or trigger. It makes accessible six pitches at the bottom of the range. The F attachment also adds a multitude of possible slide positions, offering alternative positions, trills, and other technically difficult passages. Why aren't all trombones made with F attachments? Purists insist that the attachment distorts the basic proportion of two-thirds cylindrical and one-third conical, thus changing the tone quality. Further, it creates a noticeable difference in tone quality where passages use the F trigger on only a few interspersed notes (not unlike the hornist who strives to make the B♭ side sound like the F side). The characteristic trombone sound is to be desired; anything that mitigates it is undesirable. The improved axial-flow valve provides improved response and clearer pitch changes, especially on large-bore bass trombones.

The B♭ tenor trombone is designed to play seven different fundamental positions. With the F attachment engaged, only six positions are available because the positions are farther apart on the stick. The B♭ trombone with F attachment is identical to the bass trombone in range and playing techniques but the difference in the size of the bore produces the difference in sound.

The bore of the B♭ trombone is approximately .485 to .547 inch; the bass trombone has a larger bore, at least .560 inch. A larger bore makes the lower tones more accessible and of better quality and, conversely, the tenor trombone is better suited to playing in the upper register. Because of the larger bore, the bass trombone needs a larger bell and larger mouthpiece to produce its best effects. Many players who transfer from the smaller to the larger instrument keep their old mouthpiece, which will fit the bass trombone with the use of an adapter shank; to do this destroys much of the true bass quality and makes intonation unpredictable at various dynamic levels. A better solution is to order two identical mouthpieces, one with a tenor shank and one with a shank for bass trombone. Both the deeper cup size and larger throat are needed in order to obtain the volume and richness desired from the bass trombone.

Choice of equipment has an important bearing on tone. The jazz trombonist is not likely to favor the large-bore instrument with a 10.5-inch bell used by the bass trombonist in a symphony, and the symphony player would probably hesitate to face the wrath of the conductor should she appear for rehearsal with a narrow-bore, small-bell trombone. The four physical factors influencing the degree of brilliance possible for any low brass are (1) size of bore, (2) size of bell, (3) type of metal used, and (4) mouthpiece. Larger bore, bell, and mouthpiece produce larger, deeper sounds. The sound closest to a real symphonic sound is achieved by most school musicians only on a bass trombone and not on a tenor trombone with an F attachment, even though many professional symphonic trombone players do play successfully on large-bore tenor trombones.

The bass trombone has no low B-natural on the conventional model. Low B can be obtained by pulling out the F tuning slide, but this is an awkward maneuver and produces a low B that is unusually sharp. The C above it is also sharp. A solution to the problem of low B is an F–E mechanism—two separate attachments. The second attachment adds more tubing and has an additional thumb valve to open additional tubing along with the F tubing. The result is a complete chromatic scale without the nuisance of manipulating the tuning slide.

Most jazz soloists play a small-bore tenor trombone with section players in big bands playing larger horns. The small-bore tenors allow more conservative use of the soloist's air and are more responsive to the great variety of jazz articulations.

A recent invention for the trombone is the Quadro® Slide Trombone. The slide tubing is wrapped twice, so instead of two tubes in the slide section that move, there are four. The advantage is that the length of each position is shortened by approximately half and gives beginners the opportunity to reach sixth and seventh positions. The tone quality at this writing is unknown. There will be the obvious limitations when the young student wishes to change to a "real" trombone. This instrument, however, may prove popular in the jazz idiom.

SELECTING THE BARITONE AND EUPHONIUM

The baritone and euphonium are alike in several respects: Both are brass tubes approximately nine feet long, pitched in B♭, approximately two-thirds conical and one-third cylindrical, with the degree of taper greater for the euphonium. Their appearance is similar and with beginning students their tone quality is somewhat similar. The baritone/euphonium's fundamental is the same as that of the trombone, with three valves lowering the pitches in the overtone series in a fashion identical to those used on a trumpet. The instruments are true bass instruments, and players should learn to read bass clef as most serious music is written in bass clef.

The euphonium has a larger bore (.555 to .651 inch) and requires a larger mouthpiece than the baritone horn. The euphonium bell is approximately three inches larger than that of the baritone. Most euphoniums come with the fourth-valve that lowers the fundamental to F below the bass staff. Whereas the F attachment on trombone extends the lower range and provides alternate positions to facilitate technique, on the euphonium the fourth-valve adds this range but its most essential feature is improved intonation. A few euphoniums have a low E extension (like a slide within a slide) on the fourth valve slide. The fourth-valve affords an extension of range to low B♭, with the exception of the low B-natural, which is not available unless the fourth-valve slide is pulled to E. A famous euphonium soloist, Brian Bowman, suggests that an instrument can be tested to determine if it is a true euphonium by reversing the tuning slide; the main tuning slide of a baritone will fit the instrument reversed due to its greater proportion of cylindrical tubing, the tuning slide of a true euphonium will not fit reversed because one end is larger than the other.[2]

The baritone is the preferred instrument for beginners because its smaller mouthpiece and smaller bore (.562 to .579 inch) require less air, making it more responsive and easier to control. Also it is generally less expensive. Most baritones are bell-front whereas the euphonium usually is made with an upright bell; thus the baritone has the more projecting and "focused" tone quality of the two.

Guidelines to follow in selecting a new or used baritone or euphonium follow:

1. Check if the partials are reasonably in tune.
2. The instrument should be checked for any air leaks.
3. On a used instrument the valves should be inspected for tightness of fit (i.e., do the valves "wiggle"?) and for excessive wear at the bottom edge of the valves. If the plating is worn, replating could be costly in time and money.
4. Compression can be checked by pulling the valve slides, then pressing the valve and listening for a "pop."
5. The instrument should have similar response and tone quality in all registers.
6. Because lacquer is the most common finish for baritones, it should be inspected for wear; pitted brass can be a problem. Lacquer that has worn off can usually be resprayed by a reputable repairman.

Baritones do come in four-valve models, but the three valves are far most common in the United States with four valves purchased on euphoniums.

---

[2]Brian L. Bowman (1983), *Practical Hints on Playing the Baritone (Euphonium)*, Melville, NY: Belwin-Mills, p. 23.

ASSEMBLING THE INSTRUMENTS

There are three parts to the trombone: the slide, the bell, and the mouthpiece. The slide and the bell are assembled by resting the bottom of the slide on the floor, being careful not to grasp the slide in the middle of both tubes (squeezing the tubing will ruin the alignment), taking the bell section in the left hand and carefully fitting it into the slide, then screwing the two together. The angle at which the two sections fit together is 90 degrees or less, varying with the individual player's hand size. The angle is usually less with the F attachment. The slide is made of thin, relatively soft metal. It can be dented by the slightest knock or bump, impairing intonation and slide movement. Care should be taken when removing the slide and bell from the case and in assembly so that the slide does not strike anything. Bumping a music stand often occurs when young students raise their trombones to play. At this point the slide can be unlocked. With older trombone players, it normally occurs when aiming a low C at the saxophone player sitting in front.

Assembling the baritone should present no problem except for its weight and size. The euphonium is even heavier. The instrument should be removed from its case by grasping it through the thumb ring with the right thumb and carefully lifting with the right hand; the left hand assists in steadying the horn by holding the bell section. The mouthpiece should be inserted with a slight twisting motion.

The mouthpiece for trombone and baritone is inserted with a slight clockwise twisting motion and removed by a simple counterclockwise twist; forcing will damage it. The mouthpieces should be kept in pouches so that they do not bounce about in the case and damage the instrument.

POSITIONS FOR HOLDING

The trombone, baritone, or euphonium player sits in an upright but relaxed erect position, bringing the instrument to her lips in such a way that mouthpiece pressure is distributed evenly between the upper and lower lip. During the early stages, the trombone should be held to the left side of the music stand so that the student can see "around" the bell and not hit the music stand with the slide. For all three instruments, the instrument is brought to the head, not the head to the instrument.

Trombone

The left hand holds the trombone by grasping the braces of the slide and bell section, the thumb around the brace of the bell section nearest the mouthpiece, the lower three fingers around the top brace of the slide and the slide receiver. The left index finger rests on the shank just behind the mouthpiece or leadpipe (the size of the student's hand, consequently, will determine the angle at which the bell section and slide are secured together). The entire weight of the instrument is borne by the left hand and arm. The wrist must be straight or tension will cause it to tire quickly. See Figure 16–1. On most trombones, a weight is usually placed in the back brace of the tuning slide that balances the slide in first position. The farther the slide is extended, the more the left hand must grip to keep the balance. Balance is often difficult for the beginner; if forced to hold the instrument in playing position too long, she may develop bad habits like propping her elbow on her waist.

The right hand manipulates the slide, grasping the slide brace lightly between the thumb and the first two fingers. Control is better when the thumb and middle fingers are closer to the lower than to the upper part of the slide. The right hand

Figure 16-1
Trombone: Sitting Position

and arm must be relaxed and loose. If the hand, wrist, or elbow is tense, flexibility will be limited. The right palm should face the player rather than the bell. Correct hand position for playing the trombone without an F attachment is shown in Figure 16-2.

Due to the weight of the trombone and the pressure of the counterbalance so close to one's head, students may develop the habit of tilting the head, which occasionally results in the bell section's resting on the player's shoulder. Tilting the head will affect the airstream and consequently tone quality, range, flexibility, and articulations.

The hand position for a trombone with the F valve is slightly different (see Figure 16-3). The weight of the trombone is supported primarily by the lower three fingers of the left hand and the index finger that is placed over the leadpipe. The thumb remains free to operate the valve mechanism.

Figure 16-2
Trombone: Hand Position
Without Using the F Attachment

Figure 16-3
Trombone: Hand Position
Using the F Attachment

Figure 16–4   Baritone: Sitting Position

Figure 16–5   Euphonium: Sitting Position

Baritone/Euphonium

The baritone and euphonium are held diagonally across the chest in an upright position, resting against the crook of the left arm. The left hand should be extended across the body of the instrument so that the left thumb reaches the ring of the tuning trigger (a very useful option) as in Figures 16–4 and 16–5, or grasps the bottom tubing wherever it is most comfortable. This position puts the weight of the instrument on bone rather than on muscle and helps to reduce fatigue.

Correct hand positions for baritone and euphonium are illustrated in Figures 16–6 and 16–7. Some euphoniums have the fourth valve mounted on the side

Figure 16–6   Baritone: Hand Position

Figure 16–7 Euphonium: Hand Position

where the left hand holds the large tubing; thus the index or middle finger on the left hand manipulates the fourth valve. Players who have instruments with the fourth valve next to the third valve may hold their horn to manipulate the fourth valve with the index finger on the left hand. Although this appears awkward at first, the left index finger is far more dexterous than the right-hand little finger.

The right hand and arm should bear no weight as the fingers must be free to operate the valves with maximum speed and accuracy. The fingers of the right hand are slightly curved. The instrument should not rest in the player's lap when she is playing. The teacher must be careful not to demand that the beginner hold the relatively heavy baritone in playing position too long.

THE BEGINNING STUDENT

The most important physical characteristic in a beginning trombone or baritone student is adequate size. If the desire is present, however, physical size is less relevant. Lung capacity is something that can be developed. Students who play the lower brasses need to have good listening skills. Smaller students have difficulty reaching sixth and seventh positions on a trombone. Although many method books avoid introducing sixth-position notes, teachers tend to begin with the B♭ major scale, thus forcing the beginning trombone player to go from the first note to sixth position on the first two notes of the scale.

Among the most difficult tasks for the beginning trombone player is simply holding the instrument, even one that has a counterweight. The muscles used to hold the instrument must be developed.

The procedures used for producing the initial sound on trumpet (Chapter 14) can be applied to starting baritone and trombone players. The low brass player may not be required to blow the air as fast as a trumpet player, but ample air support is crucial. The teeth should be farther apart than for trumpet—articulations such as "doe" or "toe" substitute for "duh" and "tuh." Buzzing with the mouthpiece alone reinforces the development of the embouchure, preventing cheeks from puffing, keeping the corners of the mouth firm, keeping the chin flat. Buzzing on the mouthpiece reinforces good intonation and pitch placement, but adding the instrument to the end of the mouthpiece makes it an entirely new task. A focused, well-centered tone will aid intonation.

Beginning low brass students should be taught the basics of low brass playing, especially the mental concept of a good tone quality for each instrument. Although they frequently sit next to each other in beginning classes and play the same parts, the trombone should not sound like the baritone and the baritone, should not sound like the trombone.

When students are transferred from trumpet, many teachers fail to provide careful instruction on tone production for the trombone or baritone. Trumpet players initially play the low brass instruments with a more "stretched" embouchure than is appropriate. Left unchecked, this embouchure results in a thin, cold tone quality and often a strident sound. Although the baritone is easier to play due to less resistance, trumpet players can get into the bad habit of being satisfied with a thin tone, instead of breathing deeply and projecting a thick, broad, lush sound.

EMBOUCHURE

A correct trombone embouchure is illustrated in Figure 16–8 on page 262. The mouthpiece is usually placed with two-thirds of the upper lip and one-third of the lower lip forming the embouchure. This is not a hard and fast rule; some trom-

Figure 16–8
Trombone: Embouchure

bonists play with about half upper and half lower lip. For young players with small faces, the mouthpiece may fit tightly against the nose and also cover part of the chin.

Ideally the trombone and baritone players should have a fairly square facial structure so that the large mouthpiece has a firm support. Players with a more V-shape jaw or a somewhat pointed chin will find the mouthpiece less well adapted to their facial conformation.

The mouthpiece should be centered horizontally. When the player watches the slide to avoid striking music racks or other players, she tends to pull it to one side, usually to the right. Moving the slide may move the mouthpiece on her embouchure unless she turns her head with the slide. When young players with short arms attempt sixth or seventh positions, they often slide the mouthpiece to the right side of their face; rarely does the mouthpiece recenter when the arm returns to a closer position.

The low brass player alters the airstream more than does any other brass player. Normally, for the lowest pitches on trombone—the pedal tones—the airstream is directed somewhat straight through the mouthpiece; the higher the pitch, the more the airstream is directed downward. The basic embouchure formation is similar to that for other brass instruments—lips relaxed across the front of the teeth, corners of the mouth tightened firmly and anchored firmly against the teeth. There must be sufficient lip in the mouthpiece. After the mouthpiece is set against the lips, the player can pull them back and out of the cup by clamping the corners of the mouth together if necessary, but she can't push more lip into the mouthpiece. A rigid embouchure should be avoided, as occasional adjustments are necessary. The lower jaw is dropped more than for a trumpet or horn embouchure. Playing the first, second, and third overtones can help expose embouchure faults as good sound cannot be produced in this range with a bad embouchure.

The two greatest embouchure faults are (1) stretching the lips too much, forming an aperture that is too flat and possibly too wide, one that does not provide enough lip to serve as a cushion for the mouthpiece, thus creating a harsh, edgy, and/or thin tone; (2) too much lip jammed in the mouthpiece and/or teeth too closed, causing an uneven aperture that creates a stuffy/thick tone. Both problems are difficult to identify because the trombone mouthpiece covers such a significant portion of the student's mouth.

A correct baritone embouchure is shown in Figure 16–9. It closely resembles the trombone embouchure.

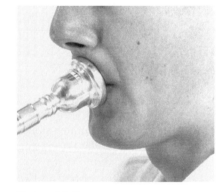

Figure 16–9
Baritone: Embouchure

MOUTHPIECE

The mouthpiece is critical for a quality trombone tone. It is possible for a trombone to play "sweet and lyrical" or with great edge and projection. The mouthpiece can enhance either of these two extremes; proper mouthpiece selection for most students must consider the player's strengths, weaknesses, and desired tone, or one which best enables her to perform in a variety of styles.

A small cup diameter coupled with a shallow cup facilitates the upper register—especially when attached to a narrow backbore—but it may become edgy at a lower volume level. A larger cup in rim diameter and depth enhances the lower register, increases volume, and provides a deep, dark tone. Its restrictions include making the upper register more difficult and reducing flexibility and endurance for those players with poorly developed embouchures. Some trombonists prefer a more funnel-shaped mouthpiece that produces a richer, mellower sound and eliminates all edge from the tone.

INTONATION

The trombone has the potential for being the only wind instrument with perfect intonation, and by the same token, it has the potential for having the worst. Playing in tune depends primarily upon two things: (1) tuning the instrument properly with whatever mechanical means are available and (2) listening. The general practice is to tune the trombone in first position by pulling the tuning slide to the exact intonation. For beginners, first position should be tuned slightly sharp. A few beginning instruments have a spring in the slide receiver that allows first position to be tuned normally and allows pitches such as D above-the-staff to be brought into tune by depressing the spring slightly. However, the advanced player usually tightens her lips for first position, enabling her to mechanically tune and still have the slide vibrato available. If the instrument has an F attachment, there is a second tuning slide on the attachment. The procedure for tuning with the F attachment is as follows. Adjust the B♭ tuning slide, and then tune the F tuning slide by playing fourth-line F on both the B♭ and F sides. After both slides are in tune, flicking the trigger that opens the extra tubing should produce a pitch matching sixth-position F on the B♭ trombone.

Few high school trombonists achieve their intonation potential. The cause is failure to listen. Proof may be had by simply watching young players as they measure pitch with their thumbs outstretched in a vain search for third or fourth position, or bump the slide against their teeth as they return to first position. Different partials have different pitch characteristics; two or three pitches played in the same position may each need a slightly different adjustment of the slide. One famous trombonist argues there are at least fifty-one positions on the trombone, not seven.[3] The player learns to play each tone as well centered, focused and in-tune as possible. Other brass players humor pitch by adjustments in the embouchure, but this is neither necessary nor correct for the trombonist.

High school players will play second and third position flat, and fifth, sixth, and seventh positions sharp. Teachers can remedy these pitch problems by pointing out that the difference between slide positions increases as the positions increase. The difference between first and second position is slightly less than the difference between fifth and sixth positions. Experienced music teachers will testify that beginning trombone players routinely play A-natural too flat and A♭ too sharp. To develop the ear and help distinguish different slide positions, it is advisable to have students play on a daily basis passages similar to that in Figure 16–10 on page 264 while starting on different first-position partials.

On most bass trombones, F below the staff is very flat and C below the staff is sharp; the F is tuned flat in an attempt to get C low enough. The best remedy is to play F in sixth position on the B♭ side. The double valve, the F attachment plus an E attach-

[3]Mark R. McDunn and Clifford Barnes (1965), *Trombone Artistry*, Kenosha, WI: G.Leblanc, p. 2A.

Figure 16–10
Beginners tend to play the E-natural and E♭
in the third position. They should practice
this exercise and listen for the difference—
E-natural is in the second position.

ment, prevents the low B from being so sharp. The double valve puts low B in tune and the player adjusts the rest of the pitches. Instruments with these attachments are very costly; few schools use them, and even fewer high school players own one.

The baritone and euphonium also have built-in intonation problems, many of which the euphonium solves with the fourth valve. The fourth-valve slide is slightly longer in length than the 1–3 valve combination so it can be tuned to play those pitches accurately, whereas the 1–3 combination is always sharp. Similarly, the 2–4 combination can be substituted for the 1–2–3 valve combinations. The fourth valve also serves to extend the lower register. Many baritones and euphoniums are equipped with devices for quickly altering the valve slides (such as the "rings" or "saddles" found on many trumpets). When the school purchases a euphonium, it is wise to invest in a top-of-the-line model with a fourth valve. When alternate finger-ings are used, the tone quality should remain unchanged. Practice with an elec-tronic tuner is useful for students to develop the habit of automatically lipping certain notes in tune as well as developing a good overall sense of pitch. Practicing intervals with the mouthpiece alone and checking intonation with a piano are also beneficial for developing the ear and controlling intonation.

The ideal broad, rounded sound of the baritone must not be misinterpreted as a spread, unfocused sound, a quality that produces very poor intonation. Good intonation depends on good tone quality. Intonation and tone quality go hand in hand. Players learn early which notes must be coddled for good pitch in order to keep the tone quality consistent. Pitches that are sharp often sound strident or thin; pitches that are flat usually sound muddy or stuffy. Figure 16–11 indicates the pitch tendencies for the three- and four-valve instruments.

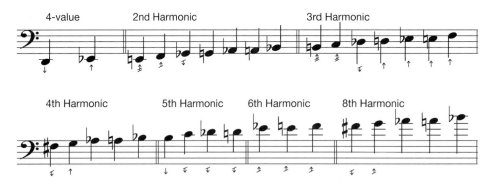

Figure 16–11   Baritone/Euphonium: Pitch Tendencies of Certain Notes

TONE AND EFFECTS

The trombone has a brilliant sound. The euphonium is more mellow, the smaller-bore baritone sounding somewhat lighter but also very warm and full. Thus the pri-mary difference in the two instruments of the same length and playing in the same registers is all in the sound desired. The preferred trombone tone quality has progressively darkened during the past century, and many players mistakenly copy the mellow sound of the euphonium rather than developing the instrument's own brilliant sound. A good trombone sound is produced by playing with enough breath support that the tone is in danger of cracking. If the player will practice cracking the tone (which most will do with great delight) then learn to stop just short of this, she will get the large, projecting sound characteristic of the symphonic trombone. By no means, however, should the tone be crude and obnoxious.

Absolutely essential to producing a good tone quality on any musical instrument is a well-developed mental image of what the tone should sound like. This is perhaps most critical for the young trombone player, who hears a wide variety of trombone tone quality in rock/funk tunes, Muzak, jazz, and "new wave" recordings. Without a mental goal for which to strive, the student trombonist is severely handicapped.

The average school player does not practice enough to develop a good upper register on a large-bore instrument. Arthur Pryor used a small-bore trombone that he played with the utmost virtuosity. The students of the late Emory Remington, famed trombone teacher at the Eastman School of Music, are almost unanimous in their choice of a large-bore, large-bell trombone.

Legato playing has a direct bearing on beauty and tone. Tommy Dorsey taught the world that a trombone can sing. This quality may have made the predecessor to the modern trombone predominant in the very early Renaissance church music with voices. Today the development of a true legato style is a must for the trombonist.

A fine legato depends upon the player's mastery of lip slurs, legato tonguing, evenness of sound, and rapid pitch change. Lip slurs are used for two kinds of musical situations: (1) a slow contrary-motion slur in which the interval ascends and the slide extends, or the interval descends and the slide moves in; and (2) a slur for two pitches played in the same position, for instance, B♭ down to fourth-line F.

Vibrato

The baritone uses vibrato more than does any other brass instrument, partly because it has many lyrical lines in wind literature. As with other instruments, baritone vibrato should be subtle, not distracting; enhancing, not dominating. The preferred method of vibrato is the lip/jaw vibrato.

The student must first establish and be able to maintain a well-centered, focused sound, then use the embouchure to create vibrato by forming "wah—wah—wah" without using the jaw as much as when these syllables are actually vocalized. The student should begin with slow metered pulses and gradually speed them up. Different styles of music, however, require vibrato of different speeds and width.

The trombone may be the easiest instrument on which to produce vibrato and among the most difficult on which to control it. Vibrato has traditionally been achieved by gently rotating the right wrist similar to a string player playing with vibrato with her left hand/wrist. The trombone player's right hand moves the slide slightly raising and lowering the pitch. Unfortunately, many young players attempt to play with vibrato before developing the fine muscular control required to play tastefully. More recently, jaw vibrato has become increasingly popular and preferred by most conductors and professional players.

SLIDE TECHNIQUE FOR TROMBONE

The *New Harvard Dictionary of Music* defines *portamento* as "a continuous movement from one pitch to another through all of the intervening pitches, without, however, sounding them discretely ... *glissando* remains the prevalent term for this effect in musical scores. Some writers have preferred to restrict the meaning of *glissando* to the motion in which discrete pitches are heard, reserving *portamento* for continuous variation in pitch, but musical practice is not consistent in this respect."[4] When a trombone player starts on an open tone and extends the slide to seventh position, she is actually playing a *portamento*, not a glissando. Legato tonguing is needed for all slurs for which the slide moves in order to avoid a smear or portamento effect. A soft "doo" or "dee" syllable is used for legato tonguing by "denting" or "disrupting" the air without stopping the airstream. This syllable is coordinated exactly with the action of the slide so that the sound is clean and the slide movement is not heard. If the slide is moved too slowly, the tonguing will not be able to cover the portamento effect. Usually the legato tongue is better than the lip slur for slurs in rapid tempo—the effect will be cleaner and clearer.

The feeling of legato is one of a constant flow of air, as in playing a long tone. The embouchure changes are necessarily minimal and smooth. Pitch changes should come from adjustments in the lips and in the airstream, never from tensing the throat. The prevailing school of brass playing favors the use of vowel singing ("oo—ee") to produce an ascending lip slur. All slurred passages on trombone should be treated as a legato tongue.

The slide always moves at the same rapid speed whether the notes are close or far apart, the music fast or slow. A common bad habit for trombone players is moving the slide slowly during slow passages. Rapid movement of the slide must be taught early, from the first lesson, for the habits of slow motion are hard to break.

There are at least three viewpoints as to proper slide technique. One states that the slide should move the shortest distance in fast passages. In the higher register, for example, nearly all notes can be played in adjusted positions one, two, and three, thus necessitating very little slide movement and requiring only a flexible wrist (Figure 16–12 Sequence 1). A second viewpoint advocates a circular motion wherein the slide continues to move in the same direction as long as possible (Sequence 2). This continuous movement in one direction is smoother, avoiding the jerkiness that may come from changing slide direction. Greater evenness of tone quality is possible because the use of all seven positions offers a wider variety of alternate positions. If the player plays in only a few positions, he will use both high and low partials, and these vary greatly in richness. The third viewpoint is a compromise, playing as many notes as possible in a phrase within the same overtone series (Sequence 3). Slide movement is of less concern; matching tone quality is the deciding factor. For example the opening music for *Der Rosenkavalier* would be:

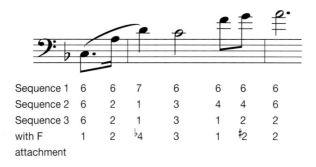

Sequence 1	6	6	7	6	6	6	6
Sequence 2	6	2	1	3	4	4	6
Sequence 3	6	2	1	3	1	2	2
with F	1	2	♭4	3	1	♯2	2
attachment							

Figure 16–12
Four Sequences of Slide Positions for a Single Passage
Covering a Thirteenth

[4]Donald Randel and Willi Apel (1986), *The New Harvard Dictionary of Music*, Cambridge, MA: Belknap Press of Harvard University Press, pp. 342, 648.

To be able to select the best method, the player must know all possible positions of every note, something not generally taught. The chart at the end of the chapter contains the most frequently used slide positions for the B♭ trombone as well as the most useful alternate positions; slide positions for the B♭ trombone with the F attachment are given below the regular positions. The trombone has harmonics that are often performed out of tune and slide positions that are sharp. The trombone player is expected and encouraged to develop her ear to hear these problems and correct them immediately. The altered slide positions for certain notes should become a habit.

WHAT TO PRACTICE

Trombones, baritones and euphoniums follow the practice routines suggested for all brass players. For the trombone, practice of technical passages which challenge slide technique is especially important because the slide presents problems not found on any other wind instrument. Daily drill on the following will develop slide technique for trombone:

1. Place the slide in position and play the written tone.
2. Move the slide to the next position quickly before starting the new tone.
3. Play one to two octave scales slowly in tenuto style and listen critically, striving to play each pitch in tune with the preceding note. Gradually increase the speed over a period of time.
4. Practice in front of a mirror to be certain that the slide does not move before a tone ends or after a new one begins.
5. In fast tempos, practice playing without stopping the slide at each tone. Learn to tongue in coordination with the slide so as to "pick off" each tone as it goes by. This is especially helpful for developing the ear and ridding one of the habits of feeling for third and fourth positions.
6. Practice slurring and tonguing all possible tones at one slide position from the fundamental up to the highest partial possible before moving on to the next position.

Practicing portamento is also desirable. To play it properly the student must use breath support and fill the horn with air. The widest portamento possible on a trombone is an augmented fourth—six half steps—because there are but seven slide positions. Shorter portamentos are possible when the notes permit a single slide motion or when they are in the same harmonic series. Arrangers and composers may write out all the notes in a portamento, or they may put down only the terminal notes with the marking *gliss.* between. Arrangers seem to be somewhat uncertain of the actual portamento possibilities of the trombone, so occasionally music contains notes impossible to play; the F attachment can be used to allow the use of different overtone series.

CARE AND MAINTENANCE

The care of the trombone is a problem of some dimension, whereas care of the baritone and euphonium is similar to that of the trumpet (Chapter 14). Beginners, both young and old, are inclined to drop the slide. The slide is remarkably delicate, with a wall thickness as small as .006 inch or about the equivalent of three human hairs. The clearance between slides is even less, being only the width of a single hair or of a single sheet of bond writing paper.

With this in mind, the following rules for care of the trombone will assume proper importance.

1. Keep the slide locked except when playing the trombone.
2. Assemble the instrument with care, so that hitting the slide is avoided. The case should remain on the floor and not on the lap.
3. Handle the case with care and always open it from the middle. Opening the case from one end puts a strain on the slide. The slide is in the lid and twisting the lid can damage the slide.
4. Never assume the slide is locked. Pick up the trombone by the two side braces.
5. Do not put objects in the case that might damage the trombone.
6. Keep a rubber tip on the bumper knob to prevent the instrument from slipping during rest periods.
7. Never leave the instrument balanced on a chair.
8. Be sure there is plenty of playing room so that the slide does not hit objects when extended to the lowest positions.

The slide is usually lubricated with cold cream or slide cream and water, or with oil, but never with both. The slide cream–water combination is good when the instrument is used every day; if the instrument is not used it becomes gummy and the slide sticks. There are now a number of commercially prepared cold creams for trombone slides (e.g., Superslick) that have fewer tendencies to gum up than do face creams.

Oil is probably better for beginners, but in applying it the player should be careful not to touch the glass dropper to the slide, for tiny particles of glass may come off which will then be rubbed into the metal by the slide motion. To add water to the slide cream, use a clean spray bottle such as that used to contain household cleaning products, and use clean water. A little water goes a long way, and in the case with most trombonists, it will go all the way to the clarinets, flutes, and trumpets.

In cleaning the trombone this procedure should be followed:

1. Fill the assembled slide with warm (not hot) water.
2. Clean the slide with a flexible wire cleaning brush and flush again with water. Do not use a cleaning rod, because it can easily damage the fragile inner slide.
3. Take the slide apart and place the inner slide-mouthpiece section in a safe place while working on the outer slide.
4. The outer slide may be cleaned with the cleaning rod wrapped in unbleached muslin, but when the rod is used the flexible brush must always follow it to move out any dirt or lint that has become lodged in the curve of the slide. Because this is true, it is easier and nearly as thorough to simply use the flexible brush. Always hold the side of the slide that is being cleaned—never hold one side while cleaning the other.
5. After cleaning, lubricate with oil or slide cream. Between cleanings, wipe the inner slides periodically and spray with water as needed. Avoid working the slides when they are dry.
6. The cork barrel next to the slide brace accumulates dirt that can get into the area between the slides and foul the action. Clean the barrel with a pipe cleaner.

7. Clean the tuning slide the same way that the slides are cleaned, using a flexible brush and warm water, not the rod. If the tuning slide becomes dirty and begins to stick, even the use of a cloth to help pull it out may dent it. When adjusting the tuning slide, use equal pressure in both directions from the middle of the two tuning braces.

When the trombone is taken outside for football games or parades, dirt is invariably blown on the slide. It should have a thorough cleaning before it is played again because dust and cinder particles on the slide will scratch it as it is moved. Often there are microscopic metal filings from the manufacturer that can scratch and damage the slide.

Trombones with one or two rotary valves require some additional care—a drop of oil applied beneath the valve cap each week. The valve should be dismantled annually and thoroughly cleaned. A repairperson should handle this or an older player may do it herself.

BIBLIOGRAPHY

Texts

* Indicates out of print in 2001.

ARLING, HARRY J. (1983). *Trombone Chamber Music: An Annotated Bibliography,* 2nd ed. Nashville, TN: Brass Press.

*BAKER, DAVID N. (1974). *Contemporary Techniques for the Trombone: A Revolutionary Approach to Dealing with the Problems of Music in the Twentieth Century.* New York: Charles Colin Music.

BATE, PHILIP. (1978). *The Trumpet and Trombone: An Outline of their History, Development, and Construction,* 2nd ed. New York: W. W. Norton.

BOWMAN, BRIAN (1985). *Practical Hints on Playing the Baritone (Euphonium).* Melville, NY: Belwin-Mills.

FINK, REGINALD H. (1977). *The Trombonist's Handbook: A Complete Guide to Playing and Teaching the Trombone.* Athens, OH: Accura Music.

*GRIFFITHS, JOHN R. (1980). *The Low Brass Guide.* Hackensack, NJ: Jerona Music.

GUION, DAVID M. (1988). *Trombone: Its History and Music, 1697–1811.* Newark: Gordon and Breach.

KLEINHAMMER, EDWARD (1963). *The Art of Trombone Playing.* Evanston, IL: Summy-Birchard.

———, and DOUGLAS YEO (2000). *Mastering the Trombone,* 2nd ed. Hayward, WI: EMKO Publications.

KNAUB, DONALD (1978). *Trombone Teaching Techniques,* Athens, OH: Accura Music.

LANE, G. B. (1999). *The Trombone: An Annotated Bibliography.* Lanham, MD: Scarecrow Press.

*LOUDER, EARLE L., and David R. Corbin. (1988). *Euphonium Music Guide.* Evanston, IL: Instrumentalist.

*McDUNN, MARK, and CLIFFORD BARNES (1965). *Trombone Artistry.* Kenosha, WI: G. Leblanc.

PHILLIPS, HARVEY, and WILLIAM WINKLE (1992). *The Art of Tuba and Euphonium.* Secaucus, NJ; Summy-Birchard.

RALPH, ALAN (1992). *The Double Valve Bass Trombone: A Method for Trombone with Single Valve in F, Double Valve in E, Double Valve in D and "Independent" 2nd Valve in G.* New York: Carl Fischer.

RANDEL, DONALD, and WILLI APEL (1986). *The New Harvard Dictionary of Music.* Cambridge, MA: Belknap Press of Harvard University Press.

*ROSE, WILLIAM (1980). *Studio Class Manual for Tuba and Euphonium.* Houston, TX: Lola Publications.

*WERDEN, DAVID, and DENIS WINTER (1990). *Euphonium Music Guide.* New London, CT: Whaling Music.

WICK, DENIS (1996). *Trombone Technique,* 2nd ed. reprinted with corrections from 1984 ed. London: Oxford University Press.

Journals/Associations

International Trombone Association. Box 5336, Denton, TX 76203.

Trombone Studies

Easy—Beginning (elementary or middle school)

Beeler. *Method for Trombone* (2 vols.) (Remick).

Cimera. *55 Phrasing Studies* (Belwin-Mills).

Cimera and Hovey. *Method for Trombone* (Belwin-Mills).

Endresen. *Supplementary Studies* (Rubank).

Fink. *Studies in Legato* (C. Fischer).

Gower and Voxman. *The Rubank Method Series* (Rubank).

Harvey. *Method for Trombone and Baritone* (Belwin-Mills).

Long. *Elementary Method for Trombone and Baritone* (Rubank).

Pares. *Scale Etudes* (Rubank).

Shuman. *Preparatory Studies for Trombone* (Leeds).

Williams. *Method of Scales for Trombone and Bass Clef Baritone* (Colin).

Young. *Elementary Method for Trombone or Baritone* (C. Fischer).

Medium (middle or high school)

Arban and Mantia. *Method for Trombone* (Rubank).

Blazhevich. *Clef Studies for Trombone* (Leeds).

———. *Sequences 26 Melodic Studies* (C. Fischer).

Blume. *36 Studies for Trombone* (3 vols.) (C. Fischer).

Campbell. *30 Contemporary Etudes* (Sam Fox).

———. *170 Studies* (Belwin-Mills).

Colin. *Artistry in Trombone Solos: From the Charles Colin Complete Modern Method for Trombone or Bass Clef Baritone* (Colin).

____. *Breath Control and Technique: From the Charles Colin Complete Modern Method for Trombone or Bass Clef Baritone* (Colin).

———. *Melodious Fundamentals, Trombone* (Colin).

Fink. *Introducing the Alto Clef* (Accura).

———. *Introducing the Tenor Clef* (Accura).

———. *Studies in Legato* (C. Fischer).

Gregoriev. *78 Studies* (International).

Kopprasch. *60 Studies* (vol. 1) (C. Fischer).

Ostrander. *Bass Trombone and F Attachment for Tenor Trombone* (Ostrander).

Pearson. *Standard of Excellence: Book 2 Trombone* (Kjos).

Remington. *Warm-Up Exercises* (Rochester Music).

Rochut. *Melodious Etudes* (Book I) (C. Fischer).

Schlossberg. *Daily Drills and Technical Studies* (Baron).

Slama. *66 Etudes in All Keys* (International).

Voxman. *Selected Studies* (Rubank).

Advanced (high school or college)

Bach. *Six Suites for Unaccompanied Violincello* (G. Schirmer).

Blazhevich. *Clef Studies for Trombone* (Leeds).

———. *Sequences 26 Melodic Studies* (C. Fischer).

Colin. *Advanced Lip Flexibilities, Trombone* Vols. 1—3 (Colin).

———. *Progressive Technique* (Colin).

Kopprasch. *60 Studies* (2 vols.) (C. Fischer).

La Fosse. *Complete de Trombone a Coulisse* (A. Leduc).

Mantia. *Trombone Virtuoso* (C. Fischer).

Miller. *Clef Studies* (C. Fischer).

Mueller. *Technical Studies* (C. Fischer).

Ostrander. *Bass Trombone and F Attachment for Tenor Trombone* (Ostrander).

Remington. *Warm-Up Exercises* (Rochester Music).

Rochut. *Melodious Etudes* (Books II–III) (C. Fischer).

Shapiro. *Modern Universal Method for Baritone and Trombone* (Cundy-Bettoney).

Tyrre. *40 Progressive Studies in the Tenor Clef* (Boosey & Hawkes).

Baritone/Euphonium Studies

Easy—Beginning (elementary or middle school)

Arban. *First and Second Year* (C. Fischer).

Archmede. *Foundation to Baritone Playing* (C. Fischer).

Beeler. *Walter Beeler Method,* Book I (Warner Brothers).

Cimera. *Method for Baritone.* (Belwin)

Getchell. (ed. Hovey). *First Book of Practical Studies* (Belwin-Mills).

Long. *Elementary Method for Trombone or Baritone* (Rubank).

Uber. *70 Beginning and Early Studies* (PP Music).

Williams. *Little Classics* (Colin).

Young. *Elementary Method for Trombone or Baritone* (C. Fischer).

Medium (middle school or high school)

Arban. (ed. Randall Mantia). *Complete Method* (C. Fischer).

Clark. *Technical Studies* (C. Fischer).

Colin. *Charles Colin Complete Modern Method for Trombone or Bass Clef Baritone* (Colin).

Endreson. *Supplementary Studies* (Rubank).

Fink. *From Treble Clef to Bass Clef Baritone* (Accura Music).

———. *Studies in Legato* (C. Fischer).

Getchell. *Second Book of Practical Studies.* (Belwin-Mills).

Gower. *Rubank Advanced Method* (Book 1) (Rubank).

Langely. *Practical Tutor for B♭ Euphonium* (4 valve, B.C.) (Boosey & Hawkes).

Pares. *Pares Scales* (Rubank).

Vandercook. *Vandercook Exercises* (Rubank).

Vobaron. *34 Etudes Melodiques* (Costallat).

Voxman. *Selected Studies* (Rubank).

Weber. *Tunes for Technique* (Belwin-Mills).

Advanced (high school or college)

Blume. *36 Studies* (C. Fischer).

Bordogni. (ed. Rochut). *Melodious Etudes* 3 vols. (C. Fischer).

Charlie. *32 Etudes de Perfectionnement* (Lemaine).

Concone (ed. by Shoemaker). *Legato Studies* (C. Fischer).

Goethe (ed. Ostrander). *60 Studies* (International).

Harris. *Advanced Daily Studies* (Colin).

Mueller. *Technical Studies* (vol. 3) (Fischer).

Schlossberg. *Daily Studies and Technical Drills* (Baron).

Slama. *66 Etudes* (C. Fischer).

Uber. *Warm-Up Procedure for Trombone* (Baritone).

Instructional Videos

Beginning Brass: Trombone, Baritone and Tuba (various artists, 1996). Long Beach, CA: Music Education Co-op.

Beginning Trombone (Michael Lasater, 1989). Atlantic City, NJ: Music Education Video.

Belwin 21st Century Band Method. Baritone, Level 1 (Kenneth Amis, 1996). Miami: Warner Brothers Publications

Belwin 21st Century Band Method. Trombone, Level 1 (Scot A. Hartman, 1996). Miami: Warner Brothers Publications.

Getting Started with the Trombone (Dave Matern, 1996). Palatine, IL: Sharper Video Productions.

A Master Class: Bass Trombone (John Rojak, 1999). Boston: The Boston Conservatory.

Steps to Excellence: A Video Clinic, Vol. 4 (Donald Knaub, 1984). Grand Rapids, MI: Yamaha Music Products.

Steps to Excellence: Fundamentals of Euphonium Playing, Vol. 6 (Paul Doste, 1989). Grand Rapids, MI: Yamaha Music Products.

The Trombone (Hal Harris, 1998). Canoga Park, CA: Backstage Productions.

The Trombone Care and Cleaning (Hugo Magliocco, 1996). Macomb, IL: School of Extended and Continiung Learning, Western Illinois University

A Trombone Clinic (Donald Knaub, 1986). Grand Rapids, MI. Yamaha Music Corporation.

Tuba & Euphonium: The Individual and the Instrument (Carlyle Weber and Donald Burleson, euphoniums, 1998). Ft. Mead, MD: U. S. Army Field Band.

Ultimate Beginner Series for Trombone, Vols. 1 & 2 (Tim Conner, 1998). Miami: Warner Brothers Publications.

Recommended Classical Trombone Artists

Christian Lindberg playing Sandstrom and Zwilich
Ron Baron playing Hindemith
John Swallow playing Berio and Milhaud
Josep Alessi playing Bernstein and Rouse

Recommended Jazz Trombone Artists

New Orleans Dixieland: Kid Ory
Chicago Dixieland: Miff Mole
Swing: Tommy Dorsey, Tricky Sam Nanton, and Jack Teagarden (also Dixieland revival)
Bop: J. J. Johnson
Hard Bop: Slide Hampton and Phil Wilson
Avant-Garde, Free Jazz: Roswell Rudd
Most influential trombonists 1980–2000: Bill Watrous, Delfeayo Marsalis, and Steve Turre

Recommended Classical Euphonium Artists

Jean-Pierre Chevaliller playing Handel and Danzi
Robert Childs playing Wilby and Clarke
Adam Frey playing Bitsch and Cosma

TROMBONE
Fingering Chart

Pedal tones   False notes without F attachment

Slide:	7	6	5	4	3	2	1	7	6	5	4	3
with F									♭7	♭6	5	♯4

Slide:	7	6	5	4	3	2	1	7	6	5	4
with F	♭2	1		♭7	♭6	5	♯4	2	1(♭7)	♭6	5

Slide:	3	2(7)	1(6)	5	4	3(7)	2(6)	1(5)
with F	♯4	♭2	1		♭7	♭6	5	♯4(♭7)

(used to
tune F attachment)

4(7)	3(6)	2(5)	1(4,7)	3(6)	2(5,7)	1(4,6)	3(5,♭7)
♭2(♭7)	5(1,♭7)	♯4(♭6)	♭2(5,♭7)	1(♯4,♭6)	♭2(5,♭7)	1(♯4,♭6)	♭2(5,♭6)

2(4,6)	1(3,5,7)	2(4,6)	1(3,5,7)	2(4,6)	1(3,5)	2(4,7)	1(4,♯3,7)
1(♯4,5,♭7)	♭2(♯4,♭6)	1(♭2,5,♭7)	1(♯4,♭6)	♭2(♯4,5)	1(♯4,5,♭6)	♭2(5,♭7)	1(♭2,5,♭7)

The flat and sharp signs associated with trombone positions indicate student tendencies to play these notes sharp or flat as reported to us by teachers.

BARITONE & EUPHONIUM
Fingering Chart

The most frequently used fingerings and alternate fingerings for Baritone and Euphonium; where they differ, fingerings for three-valved instruments are below the staff—fingerings for four-valved instruments are above the staff.

17

The Tuba

HISTORY

The tuba is the lowest of the brass instruments; its name, although applied specifically to one instrument, is a basic name for those bass-pitched brass instruments that are held in the vertical position rather than the horizontal. Typically, tuba refers to alto horns, baritones, and euphoniums as well as to the contrabass tuba. The tuba as we know it was invented in the early nineteenth century and has no direct ancestors with the same general characteristics and appearance. One might consider the serpent, invented by Guillaume about 1590, to be an early forebear of the tuba, though the similarities between the two are not great. The keyed serpent, or "ophicleide," appeared in the early 1800's. Originally pitched in B, two octaves and one half step below middle C, it was soon built in a variety of pitches. The "helicon" may also be considered an ancestor of the tuba. Known as the "rain catcher" because its bell opened upward, it was carried in an upright position, wrapped around the body. In Germany the helicon was called "bombardon" and was built in B♭, F, or E♭ with a wide, semiconical bore. According to Berlioz, the bombardon differed from the bass tuba in having only three valves and an inferior tone quality. There is no connection between the present-day tuba and the old Roman tuba, which was more like a cornet or bugle with a conical bore and a cup mouthpiece.

The question of who actually invented the tuba is unsettled. Stolzel and Moritz have both been credited with inventing the instrument, and both actually received patents for the tuba. The date for its invention is often given as 1835, but it was first used before 1835 by Wilhelm Wieprecht in the Trompeteer Corps of the Prussian Dragoon Guards in Berlin. It was an instrument in F with five valves, held in an upright position. For a short period a version of this instrument was produced which was held over the shoulder so that infantry marching behind the band could hear it adequately. The piston valve was added, and the first BB♭ bass was brought out by Cerveny of Koniggratz in 1845. Around 1848 Sax produced the E♭ and B♭ upright bass tubas similar in most respects to those of the modern orchestra, with a conical bore like the French horn and the oblong shape and cupped mouthpiece of the trumpet.

The Wagner tubas were developed for use in the *Ring* cycle, in which the horn sound was needed at low ranges. They were made in at least two keys, B♭ and F. They had a narrow conical bore and were played with a funnel mouthpiece like the horn. They were mellower and more agile than the regular tuba, but their sound failed to blend with the rest of the brasses.

A bass tuba similar in construction to the euphonium existed for a while but was gradually replaced by the inventions of Adolph Sax, the double instruments in E♭ and B♭. These two have remained in use to the present, although the EE♭ is rarely found outside the brass band today. The BB♭ tuba is used in the band, whereas the CC and F are preferred for orchestral work. The F instrument is found largely in German and French orchestras.

The sousaphone is a form of helicon bass tuba that was developed by Conn in 1898. The earliest sousaphones had a bell that opened upward; the bell-front version appeared about 1908 when it was officially adopted by U. S. military bands. The sousaphone rapidly replaced the helicon and has remained popular to the present, particularly in high school bands.

The best criterion for selecting a student to play tuba is desire, followed closely by the second criterion, a good ear. A teacher can point out the importance of the bass line; the essential part that the bass plays in all wind, string, and symphonic literature; and the necessity of having bright students with accurate listening skills to establish the foundation in a wind or orchestra ensemble.

The number of tubas for a well-balanced band or orchestra is a matter open to debate. With bands there is a tendency to have large numbers, perhaps because they often do not play as well as other members of the band, or perhaps because an entire row of sousaphones looks good in the marching band and the school letters can be spelled out on the bell coverings. One viewpoint says that using too many tubas makes a thick, muddy sound; three is plenty for the average band and one is the norm for orchestras. Probably never more than five should be used in a band, even with a 120 piece organization. The other viewpoint is that of E. F. Goldman, who at one time said that he believed 10 percent of the band should be tuba. Stauffer states it is better to have too many than too few. The kind of sound that the director wants and the competency of her players will be the deciding factor.

SELECTING THE INSTRUMENT

Picking the player by his size, to fit the size of the instrument, is unwise. Those big fellows who are picked in grade school to play the tuba frequently turn out to be the football heroes in high school, and the band loses its tuba section for the football season.

This lowest-pitched brass instrument has two basic forms, the recording tuba and the sousaphone, quite different from each other in appearance and tone quality. The tuba is available in both bell-front and the more popular upright models. Because of its weight and size, it is impractical for marching bands. A harness is made so that the tuba can be used in marching, but it is seldom used. The tone quality of the tuba is superior to that of the sousaphone and is consequently favored for concert playing.

The sousaphone had been the more common public school instrument because of its versatility, although many schools are now replacing it with convertible tubas that are held upright for concert playing; then leadpipes are changed; and for marching it is carried on either shoulder. Although the sousaphone has a tone quality superior to the convertible tuba, the "over-the-shoulder" instruments are usually easier to carry and less expensive.

Most better-quality tubas have valves that are rotary action similar to the horn, a highly efficient action that uses a shorter stroke and is quieter than piston valves. Unlike those on the horn, the rotary valves on most tubas do not use string, but rather a mechanical linkage made of brass or similar alloy. Ordinarily the mechanical rotary valve is slightly slower than piston action due to added resistance; however, the Mirafone tuba is an example of mechanical rotary valves that are satisfactory. European tubas commonly use a mechanical rotary action that has a shorter "stroke" than American rotary valves. Because of the added resistance, legato playing is more difficult with this valve type.

The rotary action permits the tuba to be tilted slightly to the left, making the right-hand position more comfortable, but it has the disadvantage of taking up space. Piston valves such as those used on trumpets and most baritones require the instrument to be held upright, making the right-hand position clumsier but keeping the instrument directly in front of the player. The worst feature of piston valves on the tuba is their long "stroke," which hampers technique. The majority of tubas constructed with rotary valves have a fourth valve which serves in the same way as the fourth valve on the euphoniums. Any new purchase, whether with rotary or piston valves, should include the fourth valve.

The sousaphone is comparatively easy to carry in marching. It rests on the left shoulder and the entire body carries its weight. When budget limitations do not allow purchase of both tubas and sousaphones, the sousaphone must be the choice for band and tuba for orchestra. Both instruments, although very different in appearance, consist of conical tubing of the same length (18 feet for BB♭) and bore (.610 to .926 inch, a large variance). The taper is shorter on tubas than sousaphones. Three piston valves are the norm for the sousaphone.

The advantage of rotary-valve tubas over piston-valve tubas, even piston valves advertised as short-stroke valves, makes it worthwhile for schools to invest in rotary-valve instruments.

An effort should be made to purchase concert tubas, saving the sousaphones for marching. During marching season the concert tuba can be kept at home for practice; then at the conclusion of marching season the sousaphone is kept at home for practice. Few parents are willing to purchase a tuba for a high school student, and even fewer students will be cooperative in lugging it home for nightly practice.

The concert tuba is made in two versions, the upright bell and the less common bell front. The upright bell produces a brighter sound and cleaner articulation; the front model spreads the sound and is less brilliant. Characteristics of the concert stage may make the upright bell disappointing; for example, if the stage ceiling is too high, the sound from the upright tuba will go straight up and never reach the audience. Experimentation with moving the tuba section to various positions on stage may produce good results. The upright bell has the definite advantage of cleaner articulations due to diffusing the sound more than the more directional bell front.

Tubas are available in a number of finishes: brass lacquer, brass epoxy lacquer, nickel plated (lacquered), and silver plate. Sousaphones are now available in the same finishes plus fiberglass, which is considerably lighter. Brass epoxy lacquer is the newest type of finish and is most durable. Like many other brass, silver plate gives the darkest sound, which is perhaps most suitable for tubas. Due to the size of the instrument, however, the cost of silver plate is much more than that of a lacquer finish.

The tuba is made in several keys: F, E♭ (both upright only); CC, BB♭ (both upright or bell front). The BB♭ tuba, pitched one octave below the baritone, is the most common school instrument. Presently Mirafone, Premier, and Yamaha make a relatively inexpensive small-bore BB♭ tuba for younger students that has replaced the single E♭ instrument.

The F tuba has become the choice for solo and chamber music in the United States. For orchestral playing, with its greater demands on the low register and frequent transposition, the CC tuba is the preferred instrument. Compared to the BB♭, the CC instrument has a better tone quality, has greater flexibility and better intonation, and is generally more full and powerful. The ease and certainty of the CC's high range give it an additional advantage in orchestral works. Wagner, for example, wrote for E above the staff and higher, in which case it is handy to have the CC or an F tuba.

Guidelines to follow in selecting a new or used tuba are:

1. Consider if the partials or overtone series is reasonably in tune (open, second valve, first valve, and all combinations).
2. The instrument should be checked for any air leaks.
3. On a used instrument the valves should be inspected for tightness of fit and excessive wear at the bottom edge of the valves.
4. Valve compression can be checked by pulling the valve slides, then pressing the valve and listening for a "pop."
5. The instrument should have similar response and tone quality in all registers.

Some tubas have more resistance as more valves are added; this is a serious handicap for a good sound and consistent technique—such an instrument should be bypassed in selecting a tuba. Valuable options include extra braces and a strong protective butt plate on the bottom curve.

ASSEMBLING THE INSTRUMENT

Assembling the tuba should present no problem except for its weight and size. The instrument should be removed carefully from its case by grabbing it through the thumb ring with the right thumb and lifting, the left hand assisting in steadying the horn by the bell. The mouthpiece is inserted with a slight twisting motion. The tuba may also include attaching the bell or putting the instrument in its stand. On school instruments, even putting on the mouthpiece may not be necessary, for it may not have been removed for years.

HOLDING THE TUBA

The tuba may be placed on a chair stand, in which case the stand is adjusted to fit the player's height. If a stand is not used, the instrument is held with the left hand in a position comfortable for the embouchure to meet the mouthpiece. The instrument may rest on the chair between the player's legs or in the player's lap (see Figures 17–1 and 17–2 on page 278). Adjusting the angle of the mouthpiece is important; the two mouthpiece bits that come with sousaphones are for this purpose. The player should not need to strain or put his head and/or neck in an unnatural position to get to the mouthpiece; he should adjust the angle of the instrument so that it is comfortable for him as he sits in a relaxed, upright position or slightly forward. He may have to sit on books straddling the tuba (resting on the chair) or possibly straddle the tuba that is resting on books or a cushion—in either event, it is important that the student experiment to determine the correct height of the mouthpiece to his embouchure.

With a large instrument, the player often has a tendency to move his face and lips to the instrument. The player who adjusts himself to the horn asks for trouble; his posture will be poor, he will develop unnecessary tension, have trouble getting

Figure 17–1
Playing Position for Tuba (from front)

Figure 17–2
Playing Position for Tuba (from side)

Figure 17–3
Playing Position for Sousaphone

adequate breath support, produce a poor tone, and become easily fatigued. If the player holds the tuba, he must shift the instrument to the place where the mouthpiece meets his embouchure comfortably.

The proper position for holding the sousaphone is even simpler (Figure 17–3). The player gets into the instrument, rests the upper part of the circular tubing on his left shoulder, and adjusts the mouthpiece for his comfort. Sponge pads for the left shoulder are desirable for carrying the sousaphone any distance and may also be used when the player is seated.

EMBOUCHURE

The proper tuba embouchure (Figure 17–4 and 17–5) may be said to more closely resemble that of the horn than the trombone. The embouchure is slightly more puckered than for the trombone, and the teeth are farther apart than for any brass instrument. The placement of the mouthpiece is less critical for the tuba because less pressure is needed (but due to the larger mouthpiece and bore, more air is needed). Like other brasses, the corners of the mouth should be kept firm, not tight.

The best way to find the starting point for the bass embouchure is to have the student buzz without the mouthpiece to identify the aperture in the lips. Then guide the student to center the mouthpiece on that aperture.

There may be a definite advantage in starting the tuba player on the mouthpiece only—success on the mouthpiece alone may build confidence and perhaps courage before the student tackles a large brass pipe sometimes as big as himself. Buzzing on the mouthpiece also helps the student use the air more efficiently and helps to develop the ear.

The embouchure for the tuba is similar to that for all brass: The reader should review Chapter 13 carefully. The placement of the mouthpiece is less critical for the tuba because less pressure is needed. Still, the player needs to experiment until he finds the placement that gives the best results. Because the mouthpiece and the bore are larger, the upper and lower teeth are farther apart and less mouthpiece pressure is used. The additional space between the teeth is necessary to create a larger mouth cavity for the escape of air. A wider portion of the lips vibrates, so more air must be projected to set the lips in motion. One problem is an embouchure that has more tension toward the center of the lips than toward the corners of the mouth. A smile-type embouchure or air leaking at the sides of the mouth may be an indication of this problem.

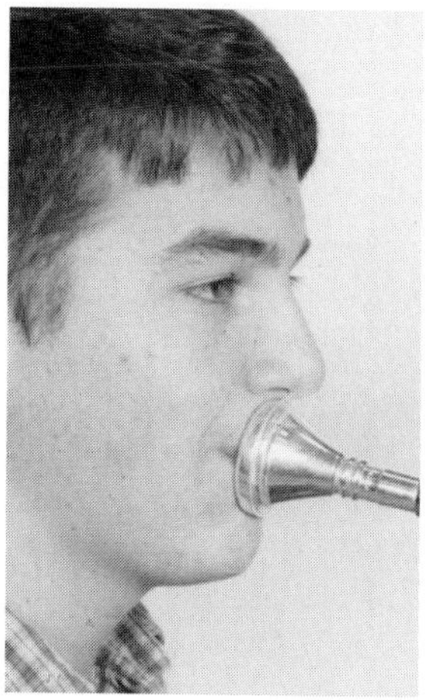

The beginning tuba player often has difficulty finding enough air to support the tone. Less pressure is required than for the higher brasses, but more air must be moved through the instrument because its bore is considerably larger than the upper brasses. A smile-type embouchure makes the lips too thin and destroys the cushion necessary for good tone. The cushion does not imply loose, flabby lips. A dull or airy tone will result from loose lips that push too much into the mouthpiece cup. For tuba, on the lower pitches from about B♭ below the staff down, the bottom lip does thicken and actually extends into the mouthpiece. For pitches above this, the tension must be adequate at the corners of the mouth to keep the lips from bunching up inside the mouthpiece. Because the mouthpiece covers such a wide area of the lips/face, many students should drop the entire lower lip from the mouthpiece to inhale large amounts of air required for good tone on the tuba. Beginners should initially be encouraged to breathe whenever necessary.

The embouchure can be strengthened and developed more quickly if one buzzes on the mouthpiece with regularity. The most common problems among young tubists are: (1) lips too tight, which especially affects flexibility; (2) too much puckering often accompanied by a bunched-up chin; (3) chewing each note; (4) teeth too close together (occasionally a piece of 1.5 centimeter cork can be held between molars to keep them apart); and (5) the tongue too high in the mouth.

Often the initial buzzing on the mouthpiece is "high" in pitch; if so, the student needs to drop her jaw to open the teeth more. This additional space between the teeth is necessary to create a larger mouth cavity for the escape of air.

Although no exact rule-of-thumb exists for tuba mouthpiece placement, most successful players place it so that more upper lip appears to be in the mouthpiece. Harvey Phillips advocates that the upper lip remains anchored to the mouthpiece, retaining its shape regardless of range and changing only slightly when ascending into the upper range. He writes that the lower lip changes shape, tension, thickness—becoming "larger, thicker, and looser when approaching the low register and thinner and tauter when approaching the upper register," keeping the flexibility of the lower lip's movement, altering the size of the oral cavity that serves as a resonating chamber.[1]

With transfers from other instruments, the problem is usually not one of too much relaxation but of too much lip tension. Former trumpet players have difficulty realizing that the teeth should be fairly far apart and that little embouchure pressure is required for producing the tone. To open the teeth sufficiently and produce a rounder tone, Jarvis suggests using the syllable "doe," first spoken, then

**Figure 17–4
Tuba Embouchure
(side view)**

**Figure 17–5
Tuba Embouchure
(front view)**

[1]Harvey Phillips and William Winkle (1992), *The Art of Tuba and Euphonium*, Secaucus, NJ: Summy-Birchard pp. 26–27.

blown, then blown through the mouthpiece, and finally blown into the horn. Use of "doe" drops the lower jaw to keep the teeth open and creates a large oral cavity, but at the same time it keeps plenty of cushion in the center of the lips. The embouchure may change for the lower pitches, the jaw dropping and moving slightly back as the pitches descend. A rule sometimes given is that for B♭ below the staff the teeth are sufficiently open to allow the first knuckle of the index finger to be placed between the teeth. For lower notes the opening is even wider. The corners of the mouth remain firm and do not change, even though the center of the lips is relaxed. In the middle and upper range, the syllable formed by the lips and oral cavity is similar to "doo," with "dee" for the extreme top of the register (teeth closer together and middle of tongue closing the oral cavity).

If the student closes the aperture in the embouchure by stretching the lips (smiling), the resulting sound is a distorted tone. The air must move faster through the instrument, not just through the mouthpiece. Because this increased amount of air is accompanied by greater air pressure, the lips have a tendency to "blow open." Students must be patient while their embouchure strengthens. Practice on pedal tones will help loosen the embouchure after demanding practice in the upper range and will keep the throat relaxed and open. Practice on pedal tones also helps to keep the corners of the mouth firm.

When the embouchure is too loose and relaxed or there is insufficient breath support, the tone will be airy and fuzzy. If the embouchure is too tense and not open enough, the sound will be raspy, cracked, or explosive.

Young tuba players may get in the habit of letting their jaw move when changing registers. This habit may start by the emphasis on dropping the jaw for the low register. Excessive jaw movement results in poor articulations, unstable pitch, and notes resembling a "wah-wah" guitar.

Mouthpieces

Although the tuba mouthpiece is the most expensive mouthpiece of any wind instrument, parents must realize that these mouthpieces are less expensive than the instruments purchased by the parents of other wind instrumentalists. Students should be required to purchase their own mouthpieces because they do not have to purchase their own tubas, if for no other reason than to promote pride of ownership. Presently beginners use a Bach 30E or 32E, Yamaha 65, Denis Wick 4L or 5L, advancing to larger diameters with deeper cups such as the Bach 18 or 12, Yamaha 67C4, Schilke or Conn Helleberg.

INTONATION

Good pitch is an essential aspect of good tuba playing. It is also a very difficult task. Problems include hearing intonation discrepancies in the low register; control of pitch with such a large embouchure opening; lack of control when so much air is needed; and frequently the problems associated with neglected school-owned instruments. Yet good intonation is required of the tuba player and tuba section for a well-tuned band or orchestra, as the perception involved in listening to the pitch of any chord is based on the lowest or fundamental pitch.

Notes below the staff, those most difficult to hear, are also the most troublesome in intonation. Figure 17–6 contains pitches that are commonly flat or sharp for the BB♭ tuba.

Good intonation begins with an instrument that is in good condition. Due to the size of the tuba, it is usually not cleaned as often as it should be. The bass play-

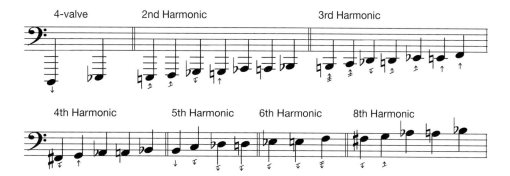

Figure 17–6   Tuba: Intonation Problems for BB♭ Tuba

er must work toward achieving control so that a steady, clear pitch—which is *reliable*—can be played. Good intonation requires that the student play in tune with the ensemble as well as herself. Many high school tubists play slightly above the "center" of the pitch, the resonant pitch for each valve combination, and need to relax and open up the oral cavity.

Several things can be done to improve intonation. First, the tuning slides may be used. Besides the general tuning slide, each valve has its own slide, similar to the other valved brasses. Most tuba players seem to be unaware of their existence; they never touch them, don't know how to use them, and depend entirely on the general tuning slide. Because of the length of the tubing and the lower range of the instrument, the slides must be pulled much farther than on the higher instruments to change the pitch. An inch or more is not uncommon, and the player should go ahead and pull the slide boldly—if he makes too great a change he can adjust it, but he may never get to the correct pitch if he timidly pulls little by little. The tubist must learn to alter the first-valve slide while playing to flatten those pitches that require adjustment and then push that slide back in for other notes which use the first valve.

Second, the tuba, like all brass instruments, becomes sharper with increased temperatures, but does so at a pace nearly twice that of the higher instruments. Therefore, if the temperatures are likely to be markedly warm (during a concert, for instance), tuning the rest of the group slightly sharper than normal will allow for the tuba's rise in pitch. The tuba cannot pull the slide sufficiently to match pitch if the tuning standard remains at A=440 throughout the concert.

Third, vowel formation or the position of the tongue and lower jaw can affect the pitch. As on other instruments, a more closed vowel causes the pitch to rise slightly; a more open vowel lowers the pitch. Consequently, the tuba player is always struggling to maintain a consistent tone quality and centered pitch across the different registers of the instrument. This consistency requires the practice of long tones in different registers, patience, and a copious number of hours working with an electronic tuner. If the sound is somewhat choked, it will also be sharp. This sharpness can be remedied by pulling a slide or two, but this procedure does not help the tone quality. The student should attempt to open up the vocal cavity and throat, and drop the tongue; each alteration will require the student to breathe properly. The immediate change will be a flatter, more open sound. The flatness can easily be fixed by adjusting the tuning slide.

A fourth help for intonation is a trigger on the first-valve slide. A player can also push the slide down for any notes he needs to make sharper. When the slide is released, it will immediately return to its normal position. The spring mechanism is easily controlled with a flick of a left finger. This trigger is an expensive item and unfortunately rare on school-owned tubas.

FINGERINGS

The fundamental that sounds when no valves are depressed is easily produced owing to the wide bore of the tuba. The entire low range is very sonorous because of the limited number of harmonics. When the fourth valve is added, it is a substitute for one and three and it improves the normally sharp intonation of this valve combination and the 1–2–3 combination which can be played fourth and second. The fourth valve also extends the range an additional fourth because it can be used in combination with the other valves to reach even lower pitches. The fingering chart at the end of this chapter contains the common fingerings as well as alternate fingerings for three-and four-valved tubas.

A fifth valve is sometimes recommended to help solve intonation problems on tuba. It produces a pitch between a major second and a minor third so that much adjustment of intonation is possible. When alternate fingerings are used, the tone quality should remain unchanged.

Music for the tuba is often badly written and may need to be altered to achieve musical results. Among the common changes a director may expect to make are these: (1) The part may need to be moved up or down an octave. (2) Rapid slurred passages are often impossible for the entire section to play clearly and precisely (especially with piston valves); the usual solution is to have only the first chair play the passage as written, with the others tonguing every other note or a combination of tonguing and slurring. (3) Orchestral transcriptions frequently contain passages originally written for the string bass that make unreasonable demands upon the tuba player. These should be simplified, not only for the player's morale but also for the sake of musical clarity and accuracy. It may improve the player's technique to wrestle with impossible passages, but when these are genuinely unsuited to the instrument's capabilities it is better to rewrite them than to expect the student to master the impossible.

TONE AND EFFECTS

The element having most influence on the tuba tone is plenty of air, plus consistent support for that air, and a relaxed throat and jaw. The more open the throat, the better the tone, provided there is adequate breath support from the diaphragm. Most players try to tighten the lips too much. They defeat their own purpose by putting forth too much effort. The cheeks should not puff out, which is more of a tendency for tuba than for other brasses. If the lips and jaw are relaxed (corners of the mouth tight), there will be less danger of air in the cheeks.

One problem unique to the tuba, due to the long way the air has to travel, is the time lag between initiating the tone and its sounding. The tuba, as foundation of the band or orchestra, must be precisely on the beat, so the tuba player must anticipate the beat slightly. The lag, which can sometimes occur unnoticed by the tubist, prohibits the director from obtaining a precise, crisp, synchronized sound from the group. This problem is further aggravated if the student has difficulty with instrument response—the bane of many tuba players. A proper warm-up is essential for control and for a responsive embouchure.

A fuzzy tone on tuba results from too much relaxation of the embouchure or diaphragm. The center of the lips should be loose and free, the jaw relaxed, but the corners of the mouth must remain firm and the diaphragm offering firm support. A raspy or cracked tone may be due to a tongue that is arched too high in the middle or to insufficient breath support. It may also be due to jaws that are clamped shut restricting the airflow. A more open throat and jaw help eliminate rasping and cracking. On the other hand, a cracked or blasting sound may be due to the player's taking a breath for each note. Although beginning players should breathe when they need to, they should immediately begin striving to play longer phrases, until breathing with the phrase is habitual. If the problem is difficulty with sounding the very low notes, the solution is more air support and a more open jaw and throat.

Most tuba players at all stages of development need to practice in the lowest register of the instrument. Long tones with crescendos and decrescendos while attempting to produce a "deep, dark" sound will help. Playing in the low register including pedal tones helps the student's breathing and helps to establish good playing habits such as opening the throat and dropping the jaw.

Vibrato

Vibrato is seldom used by tuba players in ensembles as the tuba establishes the pitch for the entire group whether it is orchestra, band, or brass quintet. Most fine tuba soloists use jaw vibrato for solo literature.

Mutes

Mutes are little used in tuba literature, though they are not completely unknown. In certain selections such as Persichetti's *Symphony for Band* and much orchestra literature mutes are required for tuba. These mutes are made in shapes to fit either an upright-bell model or bell-front tuba. As with other brasses, tuba mutes tend to sharpen the overall pitch.

CARE AND MAINTENACE OF THE TUBA AND SOUSAPHONE

All too often, tubas are purchased by the school without cases. This is merely asking for trouble. A hard, quality tuba case will increase the usability of any brass instrument by years. The tuba especially is prone to nicks, dents, scratches, and so forth due to its size. Schools that have purchased cases often find the time required to assemble the rather bulky instrument detracts from rehearsal time, so the cases are not used on a daily basis. The tuba and sousaphone are normally relatively maintenance-free instruments. The most important and often neglected aspect is cleaning the inside of the instruments. They should be taken apart like the other brasses and soaked in a bathtub of warm water, then flushed with great amounts of water to remove loosened particles of debris. This cleaning involves removing the slides, the bell section if possible, and piston valves if they are used on these instruments. A flexible brush (or "snake brush") should be used to clean at least the leadpipe and tuning slide and including the bits. While the horn and slides are soaking, the valves should carefully be wiped clean with a lint-free cloth and the valve ports inspected for dirt or grime; these can be cleaned with a cotton swab or pipe cleaner. The teacher should either do this task or make it very clear to the student that 18 feet of brass tubing filled with water is manageable only with care.

The instrument should be dried with a soft cloth, the slides replaced after lubrication with petroleum jelly or slide grease, and the valves oiled well and replaced. Most piston valve tubas have springs at the bottom of the valve casing. These should be inspected periodically and stretched or rotated between valves. Rotating works well with four-valve tubas whereby the first-and second-valve springs are exchanged with the third-and fourth-valve springs, thereby postponing the replacement of all four springs.

Brass rotors on the tuba can be left in the instrument while soaking. Once a year, however, they should be removed and cleaned. All moving parts will require lubrication; valves need oiling on a daily basis.

Additional items of importance for the tuba and sousaphone are the following. The mouthpiece bits for the sousaphone as well the mouthpiece should be cleaned weekly. The bits should not be boiled if they are lacquered because boiling will remove the lacquer finish. Warm water and a brush are sufficient. The mouthpiece should be removed when the tuba is not being played and stored in a mouthpiece pouch (vinyl or leather) to protect the rim and shank from nicks and scratches. Silver polish should be used on silver-plated instruments, and soap and water on fiberglass sousaphones.

Many rehearsal rooms have hooks for storing the sousaphone, but these are often the kind where the instrument can be knocked off by a careless passerby. The use of newer materials such as fiberglass in the sousaphone has greatly reduced the problem of dents in the bell and large tubing; however, the valves, valve tubing, mouthpiece, and bits are still metal. Most structural problems invariably occur where the plastic materials are joined to the metal pieces.

The tuba or sousaphone should never be placed on the floor with the bell down. The weight, resting on both the bell and the tuba, can cause a dent or bend in the bell. For storing, the instrument should be in its case, away from traffic.

BIBLIOGRAPHY

Texts

* Indicates out of print in 2001.

BELL, WILLIAM, and WINSTON MORRIS (1967). *Encyclopedia of Literature for the Tuba.* New York: Charles Colin Music.

BEVAN, CLIFFORD (2000). *The Tuba Family,* 2nd ed., reprinted and revised from 1978. Winchester, England: Piccolo.

BIRD, GARY (1994). *Program Notes for the Solo Tuba.* Bloomington, IN: Indiana University Press.

*GRIFFITHS, JOHN R. (1980). *The Low Brass Guide.* Hackensack, NJ: Jerona Music.

LITTLE, DONALD (1985). *Practical Hints on Playing the Tuba.* Miami: Warner Brothers.

*MASON, J. KENT (1977). *The Tuba Handbook.* Toronto: Sonante Publications.

MORRIS, R. WINSTON (1996). *The Tuba Source Book.* Bloomington, IN: Indiana University Press.

PHILLIPS, HARVEY, and WILLIAM WINKLE (1992). *The Art of Tuba and Euphonium.* Secaucus, NJ; Summy-Birchard.

*REGER, WAYNE M. (1967). *For All Bass Tuba and Sousaphones: Wayne M. Reger Presents the Talking Tuba.* New York: Charles Colin Music.

*ROSE, WILLIAM (1980). *Studio Manual for Tuba and Euphonium.* Houston, TX: Lola Publications.

STEWART, M.D. (1987). *Arnold Jacobs: The Legacy of a Master: The Personal and Pedagogical Recollections of Thirty-One of His Colleagues, Students, and Friends.* Northfield, IL: Instrumentalist.

Journal

T.U.B.A. Quarterly journal of the Tubist Universal Brotherhood Association. Available from Paul Ebbers, School of Music, Florida State University, Tallahassee, FL 32306.

Tuba Studies

Easy—Beginning (elementary or middle school)

Arban. (ed. Prescott). *First and Second Year* (C. Fischer).

Beeler. *Method for Tuba* (2 vols.) (Warner Brothers).

Bell. *Foundation to Tuba Playing* (C. Fischer).

Endresen. *BB♭ Tuba Method* (Cole).

Getchell. (ed. Hovey). *First Book of Practical Studies* (Belwin-Mills).

Hovey. *Elementary Method* (3 vols.) (Rubank).

Kuhn. *Method for Tuba* (Belwin-Mills).

Rys. *50 Easy Studies* (A. Leduc).

Uber. *25 Early Studies* (Southern Music).

———. *Warm-Up Procedures* (Colin).

Medium (middle or high school)

Arban. *Arban-Bell Method* (Colin).
Bell. *Tuba Warm-Ups* (Colin).
Blazhevich. *70 Studies for BB♭ Tuba* (vol. 1) (King).
Bobo. *Mastering the Tuba* (3 vols.) (Bim).
Bordogni. *43 Bel Canto Studies* (King).
Concone. *Legato Studies.* (C. Fischer).
Endresen. *Supplementary Etudes* (Rubank).
Fink. *Studies in Legato* (C. Fischer).
Geib. *Geib Method for Tuba* (C. Fischer).
Hedfa. *Etudes* (Boosey & Hawkes).
Hilgers. *Daily Exercise* (Reift).
Jacobs. *Warm-up Studies* (Encore).
Rochut. *Melodious Etudes* (C. Fischer).
Slema. *66 Etudes* (International).
Pease. *Bass Method* (Book I) (Pro Act).

Advanced (high school or college)

Bach. *Bach for Tuba* (Book II) (Western International).
Bernard. *40 Etudes pour Tuba* (A. Leduc).
Cimera. *73 Advanced Tuba Studies* (Belwin-Mills).
Delguidice. *Dix Petits Textes* (Eschig).
Gallay. *30 Studies* (King).
Grigoriev. *78 Studies for Tuba* (King).
Knaub. *Progressive Studies for Tuba* (Belwin).
Kopprasch. *60 Selected Studies* (King).
Kuehn. *28 Advanced Studies* (King).
———. *60 Musical Studies* (Books 1–2) (Southern Music).
Lachman. *25 Etudes* (Hofmeister).
———. *26 Etudes* (Hofmeister).
Ostrander. *Shifting Meter Studies* (King).
Rys. *50 Finishing Studies for Tuba* (A. Leduc).
Sear. *Etudes for Tuba* (Cor).
Tyrrell. *Advanced Studies for BB♭ Bass* (Boosey & Hawkes).
Uber. *Concert Etudes* (Southern Music).
Vaslev. *24 Melodious Etudes* (King).
Vandercook. *Studies for E♭ or BB♭ Bass* (Rubank).

Instructional Videos

Beginning Brass: Trombone, Baritone, and Tuba (various artists) Long Beach, CA: Music Education Co-Op.
Belwin 21st Century Band Method. Tuba, Level 1. (Kenneth Amis, 1996). Miami, FL: Warner Bros.
The Tuba. (Mathew B. Borger, 1991). Canoga Park, CA: Backstage Pass Productions
Phillips on Tuba. (Harvey Phillips, 1986). Madison, WI: University of Wisconsin-Madison.
Tuba & Euphonium: The Individual and the Instrument. (Jay Norris and Scott Cameron, tubas, 1998). Ft. Meade, MD: U. S. Army Field Band.

Recommended Classical Recording Artists

Arnold Jacobs performing Strauss, Monti, and Clarke
Roger Bobo performing Galliard, Barat, John Stevens, and Thomas Stevens
Gene Pokorny performing "Orchestral Excerpts for Tuba"
Sam Pilafian performing Anderson and Dinicu
Jeffrey Jarvis performing Ford, Taggart, and Penn

Recommended Jazz Tuba Artists

Dixieland and Classic Jazz: Joe Tarto
Cool: Don Butterfield
Fusion: Billy Barber
Bop, Post-Bop: Bob Stewart
Hard Bop: Ray Draper

TUBA
Fingering Chart

18

Percussion Instruments

Percussionists classify their instruments into four families: idiophones, membranophones, aerophones, and chordophones. Idiophones are instruments that produce sound by the entire body vibrating, such as cymbals, claves, and triangles. There are also tuned idiophones that include the mallet percussion (e.g., the whole bar on the marimba vibrates). Membranophones are those instruments that produce a sound when a membrane is struck, primarily drums. Timpani and some Latin and marching instruments are tuned membranophones. Aerophones are the percussionists' toys: These instruments require wind (e.g., train whistles, slide whistles, sirens, and bull roarers) to produce sound. Chordophones produce their sound by striking a string with a hammer or similar device (e.g., piano and dulcimer; because a harpsichord is plucked, it is considered a string instrument like a guitar). Cook's category of electrophones includes electronic percussion such as the drum machine. Gary Cook is often cited in this chapter due to the completeness and currency of his excellent text.[1]

Together, percussion consists of the most ancient and primitive instruments known, as well as the most modern. Humans learned to rub and strike objects together before they learned to blow into a hollow reed or pluck a taut string. Idiophones (castanets, sticks, clappers, and similar instruments) are as a class more venerable than the drum. Stick clappers date back at least to 3000 B.C.E., rattles to 2500 B.C.E., and cymbals to 1100 B.C.E.

The possible origin of the more sophisticated percussion instruments is a stimulating topic. Often the original instrument little resembles its present-day descendant. For example, the chimes grew out of a stone slab that was suspended and struck; the xylophone was once nothing more than a wooden slab or two placed across the legs and struck. Some instruments reached a high degree of beauty and refinement early in their history; the Peking bell in China is over 4,000 years old. Drums as a class are somewhat more sophisticated than the idiophones, because making a head for a drum out of a stretched hide demands some previous thought and planning rather than simple accidental discovery. Opinion is that drums probably were invented rather than found by chance; they were used very early as signals and may have been created for that purpose.

Most of the percussion entered the orchestra as late as the Classical or Romantic period. Kettledrums, or timpani, were the earliest to be admitted. They

---

[1] Gary D. Cook (1997), *Teaching Percussion 2nd ed,* New York: Schirmer Books.

date from C.E. 600 in Persia and came into Europe with the Crusaders about 1300. They entered the orchestra about 1675 in connection with operatic effects. For many years, the timpani were tuned to the trumpets, but Beethoven broke this tradition with the *Eighth Symphony*, in which he tuned them in unison with the bassoon. Although the tambourine is spoken of as early as Genesis and Exodus in the Bible, called the *tabret* or *timbrel*, it was not until Weber used it that this instrument was put into the symphony. Gluck had used the triangle as early as 1779; Haydn in *The Seasons* introduced a number of programmatic sounds including thunder, the whistle of a quail, gunshot, and the chirp of a cricket. Wagner and Tchaikovsky used the glockenspiel, Tchaikovsky made the celeste famous, and Mozart had a broom beating the edge of a drum. In almost every case, these were introduced for a programmatic effect, but once used this way they began to be utilized for strictly musical effects and gradually became legitimate members of the percussion section. Contemporary music has made great use of them and has invented some new ones, such as brake drums and kitchen chairs, instruments that would have astonished even Papa Haydn.

In spite of their ancient age, the percussion instruments have not been quite respectable until recently. They have had no literature of their own, no good texts or method books, and no systematic approach for learning the necessary techniques. Merv Britton, Michael Colgrass, and Mike Udow demonstrated the musical worth of the percussion instruments by writing solos and ensembles that go beyond mere noisemaking and have artistic merit. Teachers should provide real learning situations and also motivation for the percussionist. Percussion ensemble music offers challenging parts and demands real musical knowledge from the players. Percussionists benefit as much from small ensemble experience as the wind and string players do from their specialized ensembles.

Due to faulty teaching methods, many percussionists do not develop real musical skills; they are not asked to read melodic lines or to sing. They should be able to count accurately, but many cannot. An added deterrent to their musical growth is the tendency toward specialization. Often, snare drummers play only snare drums, timpanists play only timpani, and so forth. This makes the student desultory and unoccupied. If he were expected to play all the percussion instruments, he would have occasional melodic parts (in addition to the rhythmic), he could double on instruments in the same composition, and he might even practice to improve his competence in using sticks, mallets, and especially listening.

An increasing number of ensemble programs schedule the percussion in a separate class. This does provide the opportunity to teach musicianship to the percussionists, but the obvious disadvantage is missing the percussion parts during the daily rehearsals—a loss of *esprit de corps,* and a possible second-class mentality.

In the typical situation, the teacher must make every attempt to include every student in the musical learning process, including note reading, discussions about rhythm, tone quality, and musical interpretation. The small ensemble is as important to percussionists as it is to the strings and winds and should participate in public performances, contests, and festivals. A percussion ensemble (including ethnic-based ensembles such as steel drums and an African drumming ensemble) can be the pride of the school.

SELECTING THE INSTRUMENT

In spite of their ancient age, it has been only since 1950 that percussion instruments have gained the serious attention of musicians. Beginning with Paul Price and his students and extending through the twentieth century, composers recognized the potential of percussion and began to write better parts for school orchestras and bands as well as ensemble and solo literature.

Contemporary composers use varied percussion instruments for color and musical effects. The days of assigning a student with a bad ear to "beat the drums" are over. Modern-day percussionists (not drummers) must be as competent musically as any member of the ensemble, to read both treble and bass clef as well as listening for balance, blend, and musical understanding. Piano instruction is of value to all instrumentalists, but it may benefit percussionists the most.

Beginning percussionists should purchase or rent the full "beginner percussion kit" that includes bells, a snare drum, two stands (essential for a good foundation for percussionists), a practice pad to keep neighbors happy, mallets, and sticks—all in one case. Recruiting percussionists into a sixth-grade beginning band and allowing them to invest in only a drum pad and sticks while encouraging other students to invest in expensive instruments is recycling the decades-old problem of percussionist neglect—commitment, musicianship, and responsibility.

THE PERCUSSION SECTION

Percussion instruments can be expensive and few school budgets are unlimited. With care and regular maintenance percussion instruments can last many years, allowing the teacher to purchase additional equipment over time. To extend instrument life, all students must be convinced that marimba and timpani covers are just as important as an oboe case and are to be used, that timpani are not to be used as coffee tables, and that only percussionists (not the trombone players) are to "club" the percussion instruments.

Students should be expected to provide and care for their own sticks and mallets, with mallets shared by the section (e.g., tam-tam and large bass drum beaters) purchased by the school. A heavy-duty, quality stand for all mounted percussion is a necessity. These should be adjustable to each player's height and should have deep protective guide arms to hold the instruments in place. Cases should be purchased for all small drums and assorted equipment. Large storage areas are needed in which to secure the equipment so that instruments do not remain in the room for "problem solving" by every hopeful amateur.

The school system should, as with all instruments, invest only in professional-quality instruments. Over a period of time, or as a part of equipping a new building, the high school band and orchestra percussion section should accumulate the following:

1. Four snare drums (one $3\frac{1}{2}$ x 13 or 14 inch piccolo, one 5 x 14 inch, one $6\frac{1}{2}$ x 14 inch, and one marching band snare with the pitch lowered) and gut snares to use as a field drum.

2. Bass drum (18 x 36 inch) with a suspended stand that can be tilted; skin heads on both sides require care and should never be used in the marching band "pit" due to frequent changes in humidity and temperature. Fiberskin heads are less trouble, less expensive, and sound the same to the common ear.

3. Two pair of medium crash cymbals (18 inch medium heavy and 20 or 22 inch medium heavy) with leather straps (lighter weight crash and suspended cymbals with a higher sound are more appropriate for marching band).

4. Two suspended cymbals (16 inch and 18 inch).

5. One $2\frac{1}{2}$ octave steel bells.

6. One $3\frac{1}{2}$ octave xylophone (rosewood or kelon).

7. One $4\frac{1}{2}$ octave marimba (rosewood or kelon).

8. One 3 octave vibraphone with variable speed motor.

9. One set of chimes (with $1\frac{1}{2}$ inch tubes).

10. Six tom-toms (6, 8, 10, 12, 14, and 16 inch).

11. Four timpani: 23, 26, 29, and 32 inch (the basic requirement is a pair of 26 and 29-inch timpani. When additional drums are used, they are the 32 inch and then the 23 inch).

12. Tam-tam (30 inch) with stand.

13. Accessory percussion: the collection should include two triangles (6 inch and 8 or 9 inch with a variety of beaters) and clips, a variety of tambourines, bongos, two sizes of conga drums, timbales, ratchet, at least two sizes of cowbells, woodblocks of various sizes, claves, maracas, guiro, sleigh bells, agogo bells, castanets, cabasa, crotales, bell trees, wind chimes, finger cymbals, sirens, slide whistles, bird calls, and whip cracks.

14. A drum set including 4-5 x 14 snare; an 18 x 22 bass drum; 10, 12, and/or 14 inch mounted toms; a 16 x 16 floor tom, 13–14 inch hi-hat; 20–22 inch (medium) ride cymbal; 18 inch (medium-thin) crash/ride cymbal; throne; pedal; and other necessary hardware.

The middle school percussion section requires about one-half the instruments of the complete high school section including two timpani (at least a 26-inch and a 29-inch pair), a 3 octave xylophone, a 3 or $3\frac{1}{2}$ octave marimba with synthetic bars, and $2\frac{1}{2}$ octave concert bells.

SNARE DRUM

Purchase

A good-quality drum will have these characteristics: 10 tension lugs, a snare release, and gut, wire, or nylon snares. The shells may be made of a synthetic material, wood, or metal, with metal producing the most brilliant sound and wood the warmest. The snare release is essential to prevent the drum from "buzzing" due to sympathetic vibrations when other winds or strings are played and to enable the snare to be used as a tom-tom. Gut snares are generally more articulate than wire snares, making them important for marching snare drums, but wire snares are fine for concert work. Student-line snare drums have wire snares.

The size of the snare is determined by the use for which it is intended, the texture of the music, style, and the number of accompanying drums in the passage (although only one concert snare plays at a time). Figure 18–1, for example, contains four of the many popular snare drums. The 12 x 14 wooden snare would have the warmest sound with good control over a variety of dynamics whereas the 12 x 15 chrome drum would have a higher loud end of the dynamic range, but a brighter sound overall. The brass $6\frac{1}{2}$ x 14 enhances articulations, but sounds very bright, whereas the 5 x 14 drum enhances articulations even more and sounds a bit darker. The two latter drums allow an extended soft end of the dynamic range continuum and are more likely to blend into a band or orchestra much better than the 12 inch deep drums.

The field drum for marching percussion used by competitive bands and drum corps have become standardized

Figure 18–1
Four Concert Snare Drums (left to right: wooden 12 x 14, chrome 12 x 15, brass 6½ x 14, and aluminum acrolite 5 x 14)

using new technology at 12 x 14 (with Kevlar heads). Most companies, however, still make marching band drums with traditional technology in 12 x 14 or 12 x 15 sizes; the larger drums sound better.

Heads and Sticks

Snare drumheads are available in either plastic or calfskin (with Kevlar used by competitive marching bands). Although professionals often prefer a calfskin head, plastic heads are fine. They require less maintenance, are unaffected by weather, are cheaper, and sound and feel like skin heads. The snare head (bottom) should be as thin as possible, the batter head (top) of medium thickness. The batter head must be thicker in order to wear well. Plastic heads are available with a coating to enable effective brush usage. Thinness is important for the snare head because its role is to *respond* to the standing air set in motion by a stroke on the batter head.

The batter head has an outer ring or flesh hoop made of metal. The snare head is held onto the shell by a metal counterhoop through which the tension rods are placed and evenly tightened. On bass drums the counterhoop is wooden. Percussionists must learn how to tighten the drumhead without having the head (especially calfskin heads) pull out of the flesh hoop.

The internal snare drum muffler is used to adjust the ringing in concert playing. It should be adjusted to barely touch the batter head. The adjustment is made with the snares off in order to hear the ring.

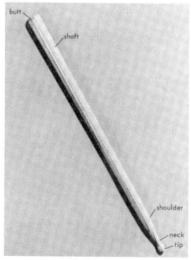

Figure 18–2
Drumstick

The stick appears to be the simplest piece of equipment used for making music, but it comes in a variety of sizes, shapes, weights, and materials, and the knowledgeable player needs to understand what these differences will do for his playing. The parts of the stick are tip, neck, shoulder, shaft, and butt, and varying the size, especially of the tip and neck, affects the sound (see Figure 18–2). Each snare drum player should use the same type and size of stick when playing unison parts; a unison should not occur in orchestra or band but does occur with marching bands. Multiple snare players in concert literature are required only when special effects are desired.

Generally, the more useful stick is one with a short taper. A short taper places the balance point farther forward with more of the stick weight in the tip end. A long taper facilitates the playing of the concert buzz roll up to about mezzo forte, but does not have the weight at the tip to achieve a good fortissimo.

According to Cook, the size of the tip is among the most important elements of the stick's effect on the drum. A smaller tip results in clearer articulations and a softer sound; a larger tip helps in playing loud passages, but is more difficult to play cleanly. The percussionist either compromises the musical effect or has numerous sticks at his disposal. Sticks were once classified with a letter and a number, the larger number usually indicating a larger stick. These numbers are no longer universal, each company having its own designation for length, taper, head size, material, and weight.

Too light a snare drumstick should be avoided even though students seem to prefer them. As students purchase all snare drum sticks, a teacher recommendation is necessary. A medium-heavy stick is easier to control and generally has a wider range of usefulness. The sticks must be balanced, made of straight-grained hickory with each stick pitched identically and not warped (the director should roll them on a table to ensure they are straight). Sticks with the higher pitch are preferred (tap them on a table and listen to the pitch). Plastic sticks should be avoided.

Brushes

The two types of brushes are those with wooden handles and the more traditional tube type that allows one to extend the brush to a desired length. Two faults often occur with the tube type: (1) The brush is used fully extended, making too large a fan and producing a spread, uncontrolled sound. The brush should extend far enough to leave one to one-half inch of the handle showing at the back end of the tube and hold in that position. (2) The player's responsibility—making too large of a curricular pattern on the head.

SNARE PERFORMANCE

Position for Holding Sticks

There are generally two types of grips: the traditional and the matched grip, with matched grip generally preferred. The traditional grip (Figure 18–3) resulted from the angle of the drum when played by military drummers. Timpanist and keyboard mallet players have always used matched grip. Snare drum stands allow one to position the snare drum at an angle that also facilitates the matched grip (Figure 18–4). One advantage of the matched grip is that the same wrist muscles are used for the vertical motion (lift and play) for each major percussion instrument. With traditional grip, different muscles are used requiring additional practice to perform accurate rhythms and obtain the desired musical effects with a different grip in each hand.

The first concept in playing the snare or any percussion instrument is to avoid bodily tension. Tension begins with an incorrect grip. The essential element in holding the snare sticks is to locate the balance point. The balance point is the fulcrum of the stick that enables it to rebound freely 6 to 10 times.

The essential element in holding the sticks is to locate their balance point, that spot which when used as a fulcrum will enable the sticks to rebound freely several times. If the stick stays on the head or rebounds just once or twice, it is held too far back and too much weight is in front of the fulcrum. If the stick strikes the head only once and then remains in the air, it is held too far forward with too much weight behind the fulcrum. Most percussionists hold the stick slightly back of the balance point. Although it appears that the stick is held between the thumb and first finger, these fingers merely control placement; the stick actually rests in the curve of the second finger. There should be as little tension in the thumb and first finger as possible. To avoid gripping the stick with the thumb and first finger, the student should spend some time practicing balancing the stick without them. When he has the hang of it, he can add the two controlling fingers and learn to strike the head in a specific spot. As he progresses, the student will gradually be able to use more and more finger grip without tension. When he starts using the fingers for control too soon, he may develop tension which hinders facile and smooth technique.

The left-hand stick is held differently from the right when the drum head is played at an angle. This position is a result of using a military type sling. A movement is growing, however, to use slings that position the drum head horizontally for both marching and concert work. Should the slanted head position be used, the conventional grip for an angled drum is as follows: the left hand stick is placed between the thumb and first finger with the balance or fulcrum point resting on the crotch formed by these two fingers. The palm is approximately at right angles to the floor, or turned up slightly. For tension-free playing, the left hand should initially control the stick as it rests in the crotch of the thumb and first finger without other fingers to hold, guide, or manipulate. The stick will rest on the second phalanx of the ring finger with the first and second fingers curved above, but not gripping it. The player may later wish to exert some control from the fingers, and in this case the index finger will curl around the stick somewhat, but will remain as relaxed as possible.

When the drum is held horizontally, the right hand must be adjusted to a lighter use of the stick. The hand moves less and consequently needs less speed than with the angled drum.

After sufficient mastery of the recommended position, the reflective percussionist will experiment to find the exact position that facilitates the most musical performance.

The Matched Grip The drumstick should balance on the middle finger as the balance point acts as a fulcrum. Slight adjustments can be made later. Avoiding any tension, grasp the stick at the fulcrum between the thumb and first joint of the index finger. Stay relaxed; dropped sticks is a better situation than tensely grabbed sticks. The remaining fingers loosely fold around the stick for possible support and to reduce tension in the grip. This is done with the palm up, the thumbnail pointing down the shaft. The stick is held naturally about half the distance between the base of the little finger and the start of the wrist—across the midpoint of the palm. In playing position, the hand actually resembles an angled "knock-on-the-door" hand position. The proper position places the *wrist* in its best position for vertical motions. Even though the thumb and index finger are at the balance point, there should be little tightness—definitely no squeezing. The stroke is with the hand and the wrist. There should be no twisting or horizontal rotation of the wrist or horizontal movement of the hands.

Figure 18–3
Snare Drum: Traditional Grip

The Traditional Grip The traditional grip is taught by using the right thumb and index finger to "dangle" a stick in order to determine its balance point. The shaft is slid butt end first over the web between the thumb and first finger of the left hand with the right first finger supporting the balance point an inch or two in front of the palm. As for all grips and embouchures, slight adjustments are made later. The ring finger is brought under the stick to replace the supporting right finger with the little finger beneath the ring finger. Then the thumb closes over the top, touching the first finger between the two joints, and the index finger wraps comfortably over the stick beside the index finger. Then the palm is rotated upward.

One must be careful not to play with the palm "up," but actually with the palm facing the player. Control is by the thumb and the index finger with the stick resting on the knuckle of the ring finger. The stick pivots at between the thumb and base of the index finger requiring a grip from the side.

Figure 18–4
Snare Drum: Matched Grip

A critical element in playing most percussion instruments is the height of the instrument in relationship to the body. For matched grip, the snare drum is placed 8 to 10 inches from the body, about waist high, and level or tilted slightly toward the player. A stand adjusted too low or too high creates tension throughout the performer's entire body. The proper height places the players' forearms nearly parallel with the floor. With the stick head resting on the instrument, the elbows should be at the players' side or slightly forward. The position should feel natural.

The Stroke   "Principal" strokes begin with the stick about three inches above the batter head, then raised to about a foot above the batter head with the wrist, and are useful for developing wrist muscles and exaggerated motion to internalize the pulse.

The fulcrum of each stick can be marked with a pen. The skillful drummer is careful to equalize the bounces of the sticks to give his playing a smooth, even sound (rudiments are helpful in developing this technique). The striking area should be small, within a diameter of 3 to 3 1/2 inches. Striking area is important because the sound differs depending on where the head is struck. The center of the head has the most resonance and ring (unless heavily muffled), whereas striking near the rim gives a clear, dry sound. Generally strike the head about halfway between rim and center although rudimental drummers often play in the center for volume, moving toward the edge for softer passages. Experimenting for the best musical effect is the task of all percussionists.

Rudimental Drumming

Rudimental drumming is a means through which percussionists learn to control the stroke, the bounce, grace notes, and the roll. Later this control is applied to "music." Rudiments are criticized when they are played unmusically, but they need not be; their primary value, however, is in the development of technique. Rudiments emphasize control of sound through sticking, speed and dynamics—not unlike string and wind players practicing scales and arpeggios that can also be played musically or unmusically.

Rudiments must be practiced slowly, softly, and loudly, then fast (softly and loudly), then faster, and so on—one returns to them by playing slowly with control, accelerating (maintaining stick control), and then decelerating with control, while remaining relaxed throughout the entire body. Tension and speed are almost synonymous unless these rudimental strokes are practiced in a relaxed manner at all tempos and dynamics such that one expects beginners initially to lose control and even drop a stick from time to time. Control is the tone color of the percussionist and comes only with practice. Rudimental drumming practice is balanced with practice on materials that focus on phrasing and reading notation accurately and expressively. When rudiments are played starting slowly then increasing to one's maximum speed and then slowed again, the loudest notes are at the slower speeds. The drummer plays softest at his maximum speed because he cannot lift and control the stick when it is far above the drumhead at the fastest tempo.

The single-stroke roll is played by alternating hands at a speed that creates a sustained sound. Speed comes from the wrist on the single stroke that is also used on the timpani, suspended cymbal, mallets, timbales, and other percussion instruments. Professionals can play sixteenth notes at mm=200 using a single stroke. Buddy Rich has been clocked at 208 and Dave Snavely, a Hollywood studio player, at 221. High school snare drummers might strive for mm=140 for about a minute, but this must be done with no (or very little) increase in arm or body tension. Only allow a speed contest among your percussionists when you can observe possible bad habits.

The *drag* (formerly called the *ruff*) is a principal stoke preceded by two grace notes. The first stick plays an unaccented tap followed by a controlled bounce (controlled by the third, fourth and fifth fingers) followed immediately by the principal stroke. A precise drag is basic to much musical playing and requires considerable practice.

The *flam* appears early in most method books and is also a difficult rudiment to control and play evenly. A flam is written as a principal note preceded by one grace note. One difficulty with flams is the natural tendency to raise the stick for the grace note too high; half inch above the head is ample, whereas the stroke begins as much as 9 inches above the head, yet both sticks are to strike the head almost simultaneously. In jazz, flams are frequently played very open for style and to "kick in" a wind section (often called "fa—lam").

The 26 Standard Rudiments (Figure 18–5 on pages 296–297) are variations of the basic strokes. The relationship between the stroke, the bounce, and a smooth roll is controlled by the fingers, wrist, and arm.

Concert Playing

All percussionists should start instruction on the snare drum and bell kit illustrated in Figure 18–6. With heterogeneous instruction the percussionist is usually the most ignored person except to be told to play quieter. The teacher must be imaginative and teach the students that listening to others is part of becoming a musician. When the percussionists play bells in these classes, everyone learns notation together.

Figure 18–6
Percussion Starter Kit. *Photo courtesy of The Selmer Company, Inc.*

Playing the snare drum expressively and musically in a beginning heterogeneous class is a challenge, and one player at a time on the snare is sound advice. Without melody or harmony, snare drummers must rely on stick control for expressive qualities.

Faults of snare drumming are usually due to the lack of control of the stroke and/or bounce. The faults may be due to any or all of the following:

1. Incorrect stick grip—excessive use of fingers and grip too tight
2. Incorrect hand position—hand turned out, in, or up too much
3. Uneven balance in sound between sticks due to uncontrolled height above the drumhead
4. Wrist bent because the arm is held too close or too far from the body resulting in wrist, arm, and body tension and lack of relaxation
5. Using too much arm rather than wrist, thus producing large movements when small, agile, ones are required, although this is more a problem with advanced performers
6. Not using a firm blow in the stroke
7. Not hitting the correct spot on the head for the sound desired
8. Not matching sounds—one stick hitting in a different spot than the other stick
9. Incorrect stickings
10. Lack of controlled bounce (too many or not enough)

The Thirteen Essential Rudiments

Figure 18–5   The Standard 26 Drum Rudiments (National Association Rudimental Drummers)

The Thirteen Rudiments To Complete The Standard
26 American Drum Rudiments

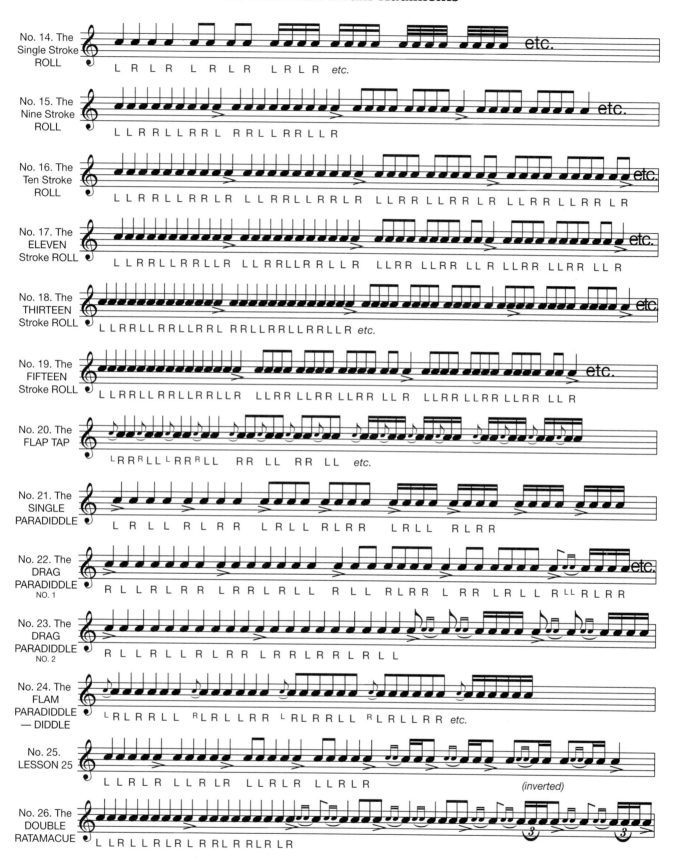

Figure 18–5 *Continued*

Care and Maintenance of the Snare Drum

The snare should be placed in its case when not in use. It is a good habit and reduces the risk of the drum being kicked off its stand. About twice a year, the snare drum should be taken apart, oiled, and cleaned. All the movable parts should be oiled with a light all-purpose oil such as "3-in-1." One drop for each rod thread is enough. Any dirt between the flesh hoop and the counterhoops should be removed. Marks on the head may be erased with an art gum eraser. All loose screws and nuts should be tightened. If the springs inside the lugs are loose and buzz from sympathetic vibrations, a small piece of cotton can remedy the problem.

After use, the snare drumhead should be left at the same degree of tension. The snares should be left on when the drum is stored to prevent the head from shrinking or warping. Heads should be replaced before they break. Replacing both batter and snare heads should be a yearly activity. For serious drum-corps-style marching bands, heads are tightened so much to project the sound that they require frequent replacement.

Plastic heads are durable and require little maintenance. Their disadvantage traditionally has been a weak fundamental and excessive ring. Improvements during the last quarter century have virtually eliminated these problems. More care is required if one is fortunate to obtain quality calfskin or goatskin heads. The best preventative measure to maintain the collar and springiness of the head is to tune the drums before putting them away at the end of rehearsal or practice, thus leaving them with proper tension.

BASS DRUM

After the snare drum, the bass drum may be the most frequently used percussion instrument (Figure 18–7). A regulation bass drum stand to suspend the drum prevents extraneous vibrations and enables the drummer to adjust the angle of the instrument to direct the sound.

Purchase

The width of the shell, rather than the diameter of the head, is the determining factor in volume. Shell depth for concert bass drums vary from 16 to 18 inches, with a diameter of 34 to 40 inches. A 16 inch drum is useful for middle schools; an 18 inch width is necessary to produce adequate volume for high school organizations—18 x 38 is best. Overall, the lower the sound, the better. Further, with the help of several quality mallets, a larger bass drum can be played with a good soft tone quality more easily than a small bass drum can be played forte and with good tone. A drum that is too small will have a tenor quality and be unable to produce the boom desirable in a bass drum. The best sound is produced by real calfskin heads, with fiberskin second. A common compromise is calfskin on the batter side and a plastic head on the resonant side. Good bass drum heads are worth the extra money.

Figure 18–7
Bass Drum: Size 18 x 40
(pictured with plastic heads)

Tuning

The bass drum is the lowest non pitched member of the percussion section. The heads are tuned by tuning the lugs, alternating across the batter head first and then thumping the head near each lug to hear the same pitch. The batter head should be tuned as low as possible without getting a flapping sound or loss of good tone. The resonant head should be tuned slightly higher. Unlike many drum corps snare and tenor players who attempt to tune to specific pitches, the concert bass has no exact pitch, but rather has more of a resonant "effect."

Playing

The right-handed player stands somewhat to the right of the drum, not directly behind it, with the drum tilted or, in some occasions laid almost flat. The sound is projected from the resonant head to the floor where it is reflected in all directions. With loose heads and the normal delayed sound, if the bass drummer actually plays precisely on the conductor's beat (as most conductors repeatedly demand), the sound will always be a fraction late—sending many conductors rapidly toward a nervous breakdown.

The beater should be held with the right hand using the same basic grip as used for the snare drum. The arm should be flexible and the wrist relaxed like a string bass player playing pizzicato. The blow used most of the time is a direct stroke on the head with the idea of drawing the tone out of the instrument. The slightly glancing blow is used most frequently in marches. A sharp perpendicular blow to the middle of the head produces a "cannon-shot" sound and the maximum volume. Most playing is done in the area about one-third to one-half of the distance to the center. Rhythmically active figures should be played closer to the rim because there is less ring there to muddy the articulations. The area next to the edge should be avoided. The bass drum is played for dynamic as well as rhythmic effects; it is struck harder and lighter and in different spots on the head. Marches require playing on a different spot on the head than the spot for overtures or symphonic transcriptions. Contemporary music for band, orchestra, and percussion ensemble calls for considerable experimentation and dexterity and cannot be played thoughtlessly or in routine fashion. The bass drummer must be a musician just like any other member of the organization.

Special effects can be made on the bass drum, not only by different strokes but also by various kinds of beaters, muffling effects, and by striking it in different places on the head. These effects, retained perceptually, should be part of the drummer's repertoire. They will be useless, however, if the drummer cannot slightly anticipate the beat so that the sound occurs on the beat.

At least four different beaters should be available: lamb's wool, hard felt, a large timpani stick, and a wooden beater. The drummer will also need a car-wash mitt.

Contrary to the snare drums, muffling is often external. Muffling can be accomplished by use of a hand or the car-wash mitt. The fuzzy mitt facilitates a variety of muffling effects depending on how much and how hard it touches the resonating head. When the bare hand is used for muffling, usually just after the stroke, just the fleshy tips of the fingers are placed on the drum. A complete muffle is with the entire left hand placed on the playing head, as illustrated in Figure 18–8. Muffling is also accomplished by placing the right foot on a chair or small step as in Figure 18–9 and using the knees.

The more common bass drum effects are achieved as follows:

1. Accents are played closer to the center.
2. Pianissimo passages are played with harder, heavier sticks to achieve clarity and to avoid muddiness.

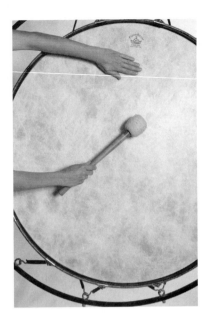

Figure 18–8
Bass Drum: Left-Hand
"Complete" Muffle Position

Figure 18–9
Bass Drum: Right-Knee
Muffling Position

3. A sharp staccato, a crack, or a shot are produced by using a hard beater or a timpani stick and striking in dead center of the head.

4. A thud is made by striking the center with a soft mallet.

5. A roar is produced by striking very hard with a pair of woolen beaters about one-third the distance between rim and center.

6. The thump sound is made by striking softly with a hard stick in the middle of the drum, then muffling immediately.

7. The roll is best accomplished on a bass drum by using two bass drumsticks (not borrowing a pair from the timpanist).

8. There should never be more than one bass drum in a band or orchestra unless there is a special requirement written in the score.

Care and Maintenance of the Bass Drum

When the drum has a calfskin head and is to be left without playing for two or three days, tightening this head is essential. The only exception is when the equipment is very old and the room is subject to changes of humidity and temperature. In this case the hoops may warp unless the head is loosened. Warped hoops should be replaced as soon as possible. The calfskin head will lose its resiliency under continued beating, but the liveliness can be easily restored by applying a damp cloth to the head. This "wetting down" will need to be done once a year. It involves removing the head from the drum, moistening it with a damp cloth on both sides of the skin, replacing it on the drum, and allowing it to dry. At other times it may need to be moistened slightly and allowed to dry while on the drum.

Cleaning should be done twice a year, the rods oiled once every year. The nuts and screws on the tension rods work loose and fall into the inside of the drum; they should be tightened frequently to prevent this. Ensemble members including violists seem to be tempted to stuff things into the airholes of the drum, a capital offense in many ensembles.

MALLET PERCUSSION

The major keyboard percussion instruments are similar in their playing techniques and are discussed together. They are the marimba (in a variety of ranges), vibraphone, concert bells (or glockenspiel), and xylophone.

Marimbas have thinner wooden blocks than the xylophone with resonators to enhance the sound, providing a greater dynamic range. Marimbas are designed with a $2\frac{1}{2}$ octave range for beginners (a very limited range), a 3 octave, $3\frac{1}{2}$ octave, and the $4\frac{1}{2}$ instrument. The "concert grand" marimba has 5 octaves (adding notes descending to the C below the 4 octave marimba) and may be required for solos and some ensemble literature.

Vibraphones have a $2\frac{1}{2}$ to 4 octave metal keyboard that produces vibrato by revolving fans, electronically powered, that open and close the resonators. A variable speed mechanism allows the player to select the speed of the vibrato. Note in Figure 18–10, the "black" bars are on the same level as the "white" keys, unlike the other mallet instruments; this facilitates playing on the ends of the bars, or in the center, the placement affecting subtle changes in tone quality.

Concert bells or glockenspiels have $2\frac{1}{2}$ octaves starting on G above the treble staff and soaring into the range of the piccolo. Their sound is the most penetrating of any keyboard percussion instrument.

The xylophone sound is produced by the vibration of hard wooden blocks arranged from $2\frac{1}{2}$ to $3\frac{1}{2}$ octaves (the latter extending into the range of the piccolo). Xylophones may have resonators on a few of the lower notes to enhance the sound. The xylophone is played with hard rubber or plastic mallets (student owned) to produce its brilliant, projecting tone quality.

Mallets

The mallets for each of these four instruments are held with the matched grip used for snare drum and timpani. As illustrated in Figure 18–10, the wrists is an extension of the arms and the hand in a "knock-on-the-door" position—the body rotates rather than the wrist to play the appropriate notes as well as the player sidestepping up and down the keyboard as necessary.

Keyboard mallets are held near the end with no more than an inch extending from the back of the hand. The student puts his arms at his side, and then raises both hands to form the matched grip; the result is usually a reasonable angle for holding the mallets.

Marimba mallets are made with a broad variety of hard to soft cores and hard to soft yarn or cord wrapping of these cores. Most mallet makers color code the mallets. Each percussionist should have a variety including at least two pair of each of the following: soft core–soft yarn, soft core–medium yarn, soft core–medium yarn, hard core–medium yarn, and hard core–cord-wrapped mallets.

**Figure 18–10
Mallets: Two-Mallet Playing
Position for Vibraphone
(marimba and xylophone)**

Vibraphones also require a wide variety of mallets. Because the bars are metal, cord wrapped rather than yarn-wrapped mallets produce the clearest sound. Two pair each of soft, medium, and hard cord-wrapped mallets are the minimum for each percussionist. A few contemporary composers have scored for hard plastic and even brass mallets for the vibraphone; these should be played with great care to prevent denting the aluminum bars.

Concert bells or glockenspiel have the hardest bars and require the hardest mallets. Because four-mallet work on these instruments is virtually unknown, the minimum set of mallets should include a pair of hard plastic (e.g., acrylic), a pair of hard rubber, and a pair of brass mallets.

Xylophones generally use harder mallets than marimbas because of the difference in the thickness and density of the bars; a hard mallet will detract from the tone quality and permanently damage the fragile wood of a marimba. For xylophones, three pair of mallets are the minimum. These should be one pair of wood, one pair of vulcanized rubber or plastic, and one pair of hard-core yarn-wrapped. Xylophone mallets are 12 inches in length for regular playing and 16 inches for four-mallet work. Fiberglass handles are excellent, being durable and nonwarping, and rattan is acceptable.

Playing

Instrument height should allow the player's forearms to be parallel to the floor, creating a logistical problem when the section has players of differing heights. For keyboard percussion, the instrument must be elevated to accommodate the tallest player by using small wooden blocks under the wheels. Shorter players will need to have their personal riser's to play. These risers must be sturdy. The body is positioned a few inches from the edge of the bars, centered according to the music, the body shifting to keep the shoulders parallel to the keyboard and at the proper angle for the mallets. It is incorrect to rotate the body to play the higher and lower notes, as this movement ruins the positioning of the mallets, hampering technique. The shoulders are never moved and the elbows rarely. The hands are held approximately 4 inches over the keyboard (or where the little finger can touch the bars); wrist action is used to make the stroke, which is light, fluid, and melodic in motion. There is a slight flexing of the sticks in the hand to maintain a floating feeling.

The arms make only two motions: (1) right and left on the keyboard and (2) to reach for the black notes. Two octave scales are practiced as the sticking is reversed in the second octave. The motion is in the wrists with no tension in the arms or shoulders.

Striking the bar where the string passes through it will result in a dead sound and is used only for special effects. The lower manual of keys is struck in the center of the bar over the resonators, or when techniques requiring close to the upper manual, whereas the upper manual (the black notes) must be played near the edge to facilitate performance.

Four Mallets   When three or four mallets are required, the Musser grip is the easiest as the sticks do not cross inside the hand (Figure 18–11). Also, it is based on the matched-grip position. The Musser grip can be taught using the techniques listed (teach with palm up).

1. The outside mallet is held between the middle and ring fingers with shaft secured against the fleshy part of the palm. It is secured by wrapping the ring and little finger around the shaft.
2. The inside mallet is held between the thumb and index finger (a pivot point) with the second finger wrapped around near the bottom of the shaft for support (similar to the matched grip).

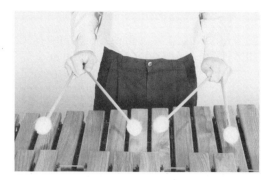

Figure 18–11
Mallets: Four-Mallet Musser Grip for Marimba
(xylophone and vibraphone)

Figure 18–12
Mallets: Four-Mallet Traditional Grip for
Marimba (xylophone and vibraphone)

3. With the hand closed around the two mallets, they should appear parallel.

4. Intervals between the two mallets are adjusted by rolling the inside mallet at the pivot point and using the index finger to determine the interval.

The traditional grip is not uncommon in four-mallet work (Figure 18–12). The following steps are used to teach the traditional grip (again, easier to teach with palm up).

1. Hold a mallet in the matched-grip position, securing the mallet between the index finger and thumb (the pivot point).

2. Slide the second mallet into the grip between the index and middle fingers.

3. The shaft of the second mallet crosses the first mallet's shaft at approximately the middle of the palm and on top (palm up).

4. The end of the second mallet (the crossed shafts) is secured by the ring and little fingers against the palm.

5. The interval is opened by sliding the thumb under the shaft to a position next to the index finger (palm down) and moving the thumb away from the index finger (an octave is about 90 degree).

6. The interval is closed by squeezing the shafts back to position using the middle, ring, and little finger while the thumb slides back to position outside the primary mallet (or inside if palms are down).

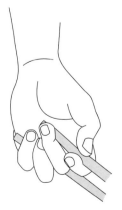

Figure 18–13
Drawing of the Stick and Finger
Placement of the Musser Grip

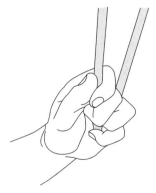

Figure 18–14
Bottom View of the Musser
Two-Mallet Grip

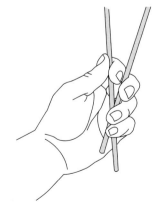

Figure 18–15
Bottom View of the Traditional
Two-Mallet Grip

Concert Bells or Glockenspiel

Concert bells are expensive and some directors substitute a marching bell-lyra (2 octave range). The marching bell-lyra's difference in sound is appreciable and the substitution should be avoided. The substitution is made because orchestra bells are expensive as they are hand hammered. In securing second hand bells, one should check for chips in the plating of the bars. Orchestra bells usually have a range of 2 ½ octaves, sounding G above the treble staff to C. Composers, however, write concert bell music two octaves below where it sounds.

Care of Mallet Instruments

The only in-house maintenance required for mallet instruments is occasional adjustment of the cord and screws that hold the bars in place, and checking for proper padding under the bars. Any retuning of the bars is done by a professional repairperson.

    The mounting cords on the keyboard instruments wear thin and break after much use and should be checked periodically. Bars should be wiped off after each use with a soft cloth. They should be inspected annually for cracks and checked for intonation.

TIMPANI

The timpani are considered by many to be the chief or most exalted member of the percussion family. Even in symphony orchestra programs, the timpanist is listed separately from the percussionists. It is the only primary percussion instrument that requires students to tune as they play. Each drum has a normal compass of a perfect fifth, but is frequently stretched to a minor sixth with plastic heads.

Tuning

The timpanist must often change the pitch of his instruments during a number; hence, he must be a sensitive musician with an acute ear. Scales, arpeggios, and simple tunes assist in familiarizing the timpanist with the sound of common intervals. Tuning is achieved by a foot pedal (after the heads have been tightened to the appropriate range for each drum). The composer usually indicates at the beginning of the work what notes will be required of the timpani. Tuning is indicated in the music by "change" or "muta." Until the ear is trained, timpani are tuned by reference to a pitch pipe, the player mentally fixating the pitch, then tuning the drum by releasing the pedal to the lowest note and glissandoing up to the desired pitch. The pitch is verified by tapping lightly with the finger or drumstick in the playing spot and double-checked around the head near each lug at the approximate playing distance from the rim (4 to 6 inches).

    When tuning to the extreme pitches of the drum, attention should be given to the big pedal spring at the bottom of the bowl. If the low notes will not hold, the spring should be turned to the left to loosen it; if the high notes will not hold, the spring should be turned to the right to tighten.

    Timpani sound best when played in the middle register of their range, or a little higher. The ranges are shown in Figure 18–16.

Figure 18–16 Timpani: Ranges

Heads and Mallets

Striking in different areas of the head will produce different sounds. The best sound is generally about 4 to 6 inches between the rim and the center of the head. Soft passages are played closer to the rim, but even extremely loud passages are seldom struck closer to the center than the normal playing area. Most timpani come with plastic heads, and they are, as for the other drums, entirely satisfactory, being durable, economical, and reliable.

Mallets are available in assorted lengths and materials, each with a specific purpose, as the instrument relies largely for its expressive character upon the type of mallet used. Mallet heads are typically $1\frac{1}{2}$ inches in diameter and vary in consistency from soft felt to wood. Mallet handles should be at least 9 inches long. Longer ones are satisfactory if the player can handle them. In order to elicit a good tone from the head, the center of the stick head should consist of some noncompressible material. Often, inexperienced timpanists use felt heads that are too large, too fluffy, and too fat, when a firmer, smaller felt head would produce better results. When a student timpanist plays an entire number or even an entire concert with the same pair of mallets, it clearly indicates that the player has not learned the essentials of his art.

Students need to experiment with various timpani mallets to find the heads that fit their style of playing "based more on allowing for a natural rebound, drawing tone from a drum, or playing into the drum"[2] as well as the instruments themselves, the performance hall, the ensemble (for balance), and for the proper length and weight. Study with a professional timpanist who can provide direction in selecting appropriate mallets is recommended.

Playing Techniques

There are two accepted ways of holding the timpani sticks, each with advantages and disadvantages. The French grip is vertical to the drumhead, the thumb on top of the stick and the four fingers cupped directly underneath (Figure 18–17). This grip requires rotary action from the wrists. The second, or German grip (Figure 18–18), requires the thumb to be on the side of the stick; the palm down; the hand, wrist, and forearm making a straight line. This matched (German) grip may feel more natural and is often modified to resemble the matched grip used on the snare drum and other mallet instruments.

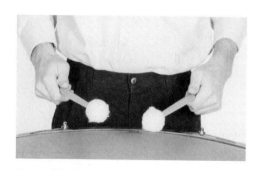

Figure 18–17
Timpani Hand Position: "French"

When the player sits on a stool, his forearms are nearly parallel with the floor. With the mallets resting on the instrument, the elbows should be at the player's side or slightly forward, so that striking 4 to 6 inches from the rim on the two center drums feels natural. The stool should be of the proper height to allow the arms and hands to play in a natural and comfortable position. If more than one student plays the timpani, different stools may be necessary or a stool of adjustable height. The timpani are frequently played while standing with the sticks held with an unchanged grip and the stroke begun with the sticks nearly parallel to the floor. The player's height requires some adjust-

Figure 18–18
Timpani Hand Position: "German"

² Ibid., p. 168.

ment in posture, as the height of the sick above the head must be adjusted for tone color and dynamics.

The timpani must be placed close together but not touching. Too many timpanists attempt to arrange multiple drums into a tight arc around themselves. This arrangement affects their performance, body movement, and resonance of the outside drums (making tuning difficult). The largest drum is on the player's left, smallest to the right (the opposite is a German setup).

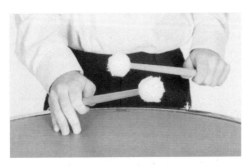

Figure 18–19
Stopping the Timpani Ring While Continuing to Play ("on the fly")

The timpani sticks are held parallel to the instrument, and the body rotates from drum to drum or if sitting, the entire upper torso. The position of the timpani must be so that when the body rotates the sticks remain parallel to the instrument. The stroke is a short, sudden, perpendicular stroke. The stick should bounce the instant it touches the surface of the head, as if the player has touched a hot iron and is drawing the sound out of the timpani. Only the wrist is used in making the stroke. Once struck, the sound will ring for a long time unless cut off, so each note may have to be stopped as well as started. The tone is stopped "on the fly" by placing the fleshy area of the fingertips on the head (Figure 18–19). If all the fingers are placed on the head at once, an unattractive and unmusical slap is created at the end of the tone. To avoid this sound, drop the fingers on the head, starting with the little finger and with a rapid rolling motion, placing all the fingers on the head ending in a position illustrated in Figure 18–20.

Single sticking is used to practice equal notes of slow or moderate duration; alternate sticking is the more common practice depending upon the effect desired. Rolls are usually played faster on the higher-pitched drums and slower on the lower drums. Dynamics are changed by alternating the stick height.

Figure 18–20
Stopping the Ring Completely, Followed by a Rest

By exerting different pressures on the stick with the thumb and first finger, different intensities and tone qualities can be created. For instance, a crisp staccato needs a tighter grasp by the thumb and forefinger than does a legato passage. A more intense tone needs more finger pressure. A different type of blow from the perpendicular will occasionally be needed; for example, an extreme legato is produced by a glancing blow.

Timpani sticking, like snare drum sticking, is learned by listening and watching professionals. Hard and fast rules are not as useful as discerning what sounds right. A few commonsense practices illustrate this point. Although alternate sticks are usually used, there are passages where more musical sense would be achieved by using the same stick. Crossing of sticks is done to reduce movement and thus gain greater control; the crossing stick passing over the stationary stick (Figure 18–21).

Composers are not always careful about timpani writing; the player must use her ear to determine a note's proper length in relationship to the music. In *forte-piano* rolls, the player should wait briefly after the *forte* note is struck before beginning the *piano* roll so that the *forte* will have time to fade. Because the area closer to the rim is better for soft playing, crescendo

Figure 18–21
Cross Sticking

passages should begin in that area and move out to the usual playing spot. For diminuendo passages, the reverse takes place.

Placing a handkerchief, wallet, or chamois on the head at the spot directly opposite the striking area mutes the instrument. *Coperto* means to put a cloth on the head to produce a distant sound; *scoperto* means to remove it.

Care and Maintenance of Timpani

Plastic heads are as satisfactory as calfskin heads and require less care and maintenance (and are less than a one-fourth the cost). Their disadvantage has been a weak fundamental and excessive ring. Maintaining the collar is essential if the low tones are to be accessible; the extra slack the collar offers is required when the tension is relaxed for the lowest notes. The heads should occasionally be wiped with a damp cloth to get rid of accumulated grease from fingers and air pollution. Plastic heads should be replaced every two years or so, with excessive scratches affecting tone quality.

Covers for the timpani heads should be used. Nothing should be placed on the timpani head, certainly no books, instrument cases, and sharp objects. Percussionists should lay their sticks on an extra music stand or put them away in their stick bag; sticks should not be left on the timpani head.

Other elements of care include getting rid of a creaking pedal. This sound indicates that the bowl of the kettle needs cleaning: The head should be removed, the rounded underside cleaned with a fine steel wool, and the edge that touches the rim of the kettle rubbed with paraffin wax. The head is then replaced exactly as it was by lining up marks on the head. This alignment is essential, otherwise the head will never seat itself for a good tone.

Dents in the bowl may be straightened with a rawhide or rubber hammer. The procedure is to tap gently, holding a piece of wood as a bevel against the outer side of the bowl. Dents most frequently come from careless pushing of the drums. Students should be taught to drag the drum behind them rather than pushing. This helps insure its remaining upright. Timpani should also never be moved by grasping the rim or tension handles, only by the bars running down the sides of the drum.

CHIMES

Chimes are a set of long, tubular bells, covering a chromatic range of about $1\frac{1}{2}$ octaves from middle C to F. They are suspended by a gut string and struck at the top of the tube by a rawhide mallet. The regulation mallet weighs about 6 ounces. It is usually too hard and may be softened by making cross cuts on the striking end or by covering the end with chamois or other soft leather. Playing technique involves striking, with a rapid rebound, the top striking cap of each chime with the mallet and simultaneously dampening the previously struck chime with the free hand. Some chimes have a damper pedal, which is used with chord changes and allows the player to use two mallets, a frequently required technique in contemporary music. If the chimes seem to be out of tune, they may be sent to the factory for alterations.

TENOR DRUM AND TOM-TOMS

The term *tenor drum* is a carryover from early marching band days. The instrument is actually quite old and is referred to as tamburo, cassa-rullante, caisse roulante, tambourin roulant, or ruhrtrommel, all indicating a field drum of approximately 12 x 15 to 18 inches with snares off, and tuned considerably lower than modern day marching snare drums. It is played like the snare drum, but usually with heavier sticks.

In modern marching bands, the tenor drum has been replaced with toms, that is, "triples," "quads," "quints,"—seemingly all the drums that one's spine can carry. These multiple drums were adapted from tom-toms used in concert work; they provide marching percussionists with a wide range of pitches. Tom toms differ from tenor drums in that they have only one head. Most band and orchestral pieces that call for toms require four different sizes; many percussion ensemble works call for six to eight. A concert snare with snares off can be used as a quick substitute for a tenor drum or a single tom.

CYMBALS

Cymbals are rarely given the treatment that their importance to an organization warrants. When directors look upon them as noisemakers that anyone can bang together, they become just that, with no care given to their purchase or their playing. The cymbal has an important contribution to make to the sound of the band and orchestra, and the quality of the sound is important. Though it is obviously not a complex instrument, there are techniques of playing and levels of quality in the physical characteristics of the instrument that make it either an asset or a detriment.

Selection of good cymbals is important. Nothing can destroy a fine sounding organization faster than to have in a climactic moment the clanging together of two plates seemingly borrowed from the kindergarten rhythm band. Because a poor cymbal is hardly better than a pie plate, the director should know what makes a good one.

The difference in quality of cymbals is judged by the quality of tone produced, the rapidity with which the cymbal reaches full vibration, and by the lack of a single predominant pitch. The best cymbals do not produce one dominant pitch. They produce overtones of such size that they create the desired ringing crash rather than a specific pitch. Nevertheless, a certain amount of pitch in each cymbal is necessary for the sound to be musically pleasing. Pairs are made so that the pitch produced by one is a second or a third from the other.

Cymbals come in various sizes, weights, thicknesses, and pitches. They also come in a choice of materials, hand-hammered, medium-hammered, and spun brass. Hammered brass has the better tone and is more widely used in good organizations.

Size does not determine the pitch. Small cymbals *can* be lower in pitch than large ones. Size does determine the proportion of noise produced from striking the two instruments together. There will be some noise in striking, but with larger cymbals, less noise and more tone is produced. Cymbals too large, however, become unmanageable in the hands of student players. A variety of sizes will offer flexibility of sound and avoid limiting the organization to the gong-like quality of the oversized cymbal.

At least seven weights of cymbals are available from most reputable manufacturers, ranging from paper-thin to extra-heavy. The thinner and smaller the cymbal, the faster it will speak, this property being determined by the total amount of metal in the instrument. Medium and medium-heavy cymbals are the most popular. Too light a cymbal may sound better at close range, but it lacks the overtones, and carrying power of the thicker instrument. Listen to it from a distance before deciding on its acquisition. A danger with lighter and thinner cymbals is that a fortissimo crash will turn them inside out because they lack the weight to resist the blow. It is poor economy to buy a thin cymbal in the larger size unless its only use is to produce a gong-like tone. A heavier cymbal of reasonably good quality is usually the best choice.

Good cymbals should be played using leather straps; never use the wooden handles that bolt on the cymbal. Wooden handles detract both from the quality of the sound and from the life of the cymbal. They deaden the tone, eliminating almost all of the overtones, leaving only an uninteresting, plain sound rather than the rich welter of conflicting partials that the good cymbal offers.

Cymbals also sound better if the lamb's wool is removed as it interferes with the full range of overtones. Because comfort is a major concern for the cymbal section of a competitive marching band, have players wear thick gloves and incorporate spots throughout the show where the cymbal players ground their equipment (and possibly join the pit for a musical selection).

Playing

The cymbals are held by gripping the strap with the thumb on top and the other fingers underneath, most of the pressure being exerted by the thumb and forefinger (as in Figure 18–22). This position gives the most opportunity for control by fingertips, knuckles, and wrists. It is tiring when the cymbals must be held for a long period without relaxing the grip, for marching the hand can be inserted into the strap. The fingertips and knuckles should be utilized for control, requiring a small felt or leather pad. The lamb's wool pad makes it impossible to bring the hand in contact with the reverberating metal, consequently limiting control of the cymbals.

The left cymbal is held almost stationary parallel to the floor (for a dark sound) to no more than a 60 degree tilt from the floor (for a bright sound) for right-handed players. The right cymbal is moved against it with the top edge leading into the stationary cymbal. This is the standard approach for right-handed players; left-handed players may reverse it. A straight blow is unsatisfactory; rather than producing a ringing crash, it traps the air inside the two cymbals as they come together and results in a muffled "pop." A glancing blow is more effective, but this also can be carried to extremes because the sound will be too delicate and fragile if the blow is too glancing. The best sound is produced when the cymbals are held fairly close together with the right cymbal a little below the left (Figure 18–22), and struck by moving the right cymbal up in a modified glancing blow which begins striking the left cymbal at a point about 3 inches from the top as the left cymbal starts down (Figure 18–23).

Figure 18–22
Cymbals: Ready for Crash

Figure 18–23
Cymbal Point of Impact

Figure 18–24
Cymbals: Follow Through

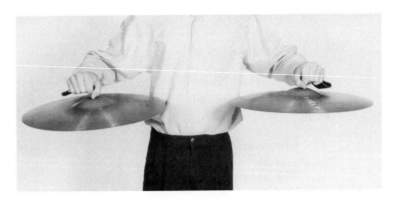

Figure 18–25
Cymbals: Position for Ringing

The right cymbal begins to move first and makes the more vigorous movement; the left cymbal moves down to meet it. After a crash, the cymbals are opened toward the audience, then usually held parallel to the floor. A good crash cannot be made if the cymbals start too far apart. A long-running start is unnecessary to produce a huge sound; a vigorous push and a short stroke will suffice. When several crashes in a row are demanded, the left hand remains perfectly still. When successive blows (not crashes) are called for at a moderate or slow speed, the right hand will start the first one and then the hands alternate for each blow after that—the hand that has moved down in the preceding blow being in position to start upward for the next one.

Moving both cymbals in opposite directions before, during, and after the crash is described by Cook as a technique developed by Sam Denov, formerly of the Chicago Symphony Orchestra.[3] With this technique right-handed players move the left cymbal downward and the right cymbal upward for the crash and a follow-through where the right wrist rotates palm up and the left wrist rotates palm down (Figure 18–24). The advantage to this technique is that a different sound is made by the cymbals' angle to the floor when crashed; perpendicular to the floor is a brighter sound, with a position nearly parallel to the floor, much darker.

Whenever possible, the cymbal tone should be allowed to ring until it dies of its own accord (Figure 18–25). When the music calls for short sounds from the cymbal, it must be stopped before the ring is over. Stopping the sound is accomplished by placing the cymbal edge against the chest or upper torso at the precise moment the tone is to cease. The player initially will not be able to tell how long to let the cymbals ring and when to stop them. After the number has been played a couple of times, she will know what follows the cymbal crash and how long a ring is appropriate.

For soft crashes, Cook suggests aligning the cymbals together (the edges of each cymbal), then separating for the preparation only an inch or so and closing them gently with a quick rebound.[4] Striking the inside facing of the left cymbal with the right as in loud crashes results in a soft sound, but poor tone quality.

The two-plate roll, also called the double-cymbal roll, is made by placing the cymbals together about an inch or two off-center so that air will not be trapped between them. A fast clapping motion is then made with both hands and arms, resulting in a loud, harsh sound. The swish, also called "angels' wings," is achieved by rubbing the edge of one cymbal lightly across the inside face of the other. A similar effect is produced by rubbing only the edges of the cymbals together.

[3] Ibid.
[4] Ibid.

The suspended cymbal, preferably a 16 to 18 inch thin instrument, can be struck in many different places and with nearly every object imaginable to obtain a variety of effects (Figure 18–26). It may be struck directly or with a glancing blow on the edge, middle, two edges at once, and so on, with wood, nails, knife blades, saw blades, coins, and soft mallets. Regardless of the effect desired, the cymbal, like the gong, is slightly set in motion with the fingers before striking. A glancing blow is better for the instrument than a direct one because the direct blow tends to warp the edge. When wooden sticks are used, it is recommended that the blow be struck down and out with the thick part of the stick, the same motion with a felt-tipped mallet. The roll is produced by striking with small, rapid, alternate blows on either side of the cymbal, equidistant from the center so that a balance with the suspended disc can be maintained. Hard-yarn mallets or fairly hard timpani sticks are most successful.

Figure 18–26
Suspended Cymbal: Position for Playing

Loud crashes are made by striking the edge a glancing blow with a stick. If the note has a slur-type marking over a following rest (usually with the abbreviations *L.V.*), then the cymbal should be left ringing. Nonmetallic sizzling sounds are produced by placing the snare drum stick under the cymbal and striking on top with another stick; metallic sizzling is made by placing metal filings or keys on top of the cymbal and striking with a padded stick. Debussy, for example, wanted a metal coin scraped on the surface for a specific effect in *Fetes*. The only limiting factor to the cymbal's use seems to be the imagination of the composer, player, and teacher.

A suspended or mounted cymbal of any type should not be screwed too tightly to its holder. It must be left free enough to vibrate well, which reduces the danger of cracking around the center hole.

Care of the Cymbals

Cymbals must not be left in excessive heat or in the direct rays of the summer sun. They are tempered with heat, and dead spots can result when they become extremely hot for any length of time. The edges are relatively fragile and can be chipped—being dropped on the floor or knocked together affects their temper and the director's.

Dirt and sediment dampen some of the overtones, so cleaning will help retain the brilliance of tone. Cymbals should never be buffed with a buffing wheel. The heat of the friction has exactly the same effect as the heat of the sun or overly warm radiator—the temper of the instrument will be destroyed and dead spots will result. Cymbal polish can be purchased if a high sheen is desired, though most professional percussionists believe the polishing ruins the tone quality.

TAM-TAM

For generations the term gong has been used synonymously with *tam-tam*. In truth, a gong is a pitched instrument that has a very pronounced tone. A tam-tam is a large disc that produces a nonspecific pitch. Composers also mistakenly score for gong when they desire tam-tam. Unless a specific pitch is written, one can assume a tam-tam is the correct instrument.

The spot for striking the tam-tam will probably be a little off-center, but the best approach is to test the entire surface to find the area that gives the best sound. Because tam-tams are hand hammered, they will be thicker in some spots than in others. Before being struck, the tam-tam should be set in motion by touching it inaudibly several times with the hand; otherwise, the tone is cold with little staying power. This procedure is also important in cold weather (such as marching band performances) as the tam-tam may crack if not properly warmed up. For best resonance, the tam-tam should be hung with gut bass-viol string; if possible it should be positioned at the height at which either the knee or the free hand can be used to dampen the sound after the tam-tam is struck—this will usually be about three feet off the floor. Like the cymbal, the tam-tam can produce different effects by being struck in different spots with a variety of beaters. It is often scraped with a coin to produce a mysterious effect.

Because the tam-tam has a delayed response, there is general disagreement as to its use. Cook indicates that the larger tam-tam should be "played" before the sound is desired in order to have the instrument sound at the proper time; McBeth indicates that modern composers are aware of the delay and a delayed sound is wanted.[5]

TAMBOURINE

The tambourine is an interesting instrument, capable of producing many different sounds. The 10 inch is the most common size, with both larger and smaller sizes available. Tambourines are presently made of metal, plastic, and wood, and can be found with and without heads. A true tambourine has a skin head and is made of wood (metal is heavy and difficult to control; plastic is not very durable).

Little upkeep is necessary, but the pins that hold the jingles should be examined occasionally as they work loose with playing. If the head becomes slack, it can be moistened with a wet cloth and allowed to dry out slowly.

Playing

The tambourine is held in one hand and struck with the other (Figure 18–27). The instrument is held immobile, and the striking hand moves, so that extraneous jingles resulting from moving the instrument can be kept to a minimum. For a right handed person, the instrument is held in the right-hand with the thumb on the outside of the rim and the four fingers gripping the inside and muffling the head. The center may be struck with the fleshy part of the left hand fingertips, the heel of the hand, the knuckles, or on the knee. The rim may be struck with the fingers, with timpani sticks, or snare drumsticks. It may be shaken, played with a wet thumb to achieve a thumb roll, or muted with a handkerchief. Most of these are indicated in the music, but some are left to the discretion of the player.

Loud playing is usually accomplished by striking with the fleshy part of the first three fingertips or with the knuckles, in the approximate center of the head. This technique is adequate for moderate or slow passages at forte volume. For rapid rhythmic passages, a differ-

Figure 18–27
Normal Tambourine
Playing Position

[5] Cook, ibid., p. 239; and McBeth, 1972, p.291.

ent technique is necessary. Here the knee and the knuckles are used: The foot is placed on a chair so that the knee is bent, the tambourine is held head down just above the knee (Figure 18–28). The instrument is then moved up and down in the rhythm required, alternately striking the knee and the knuckles at the speed and volume required. In this fashion complex rhythms can be played forte with considerable precision.

Soft, fast passages are played by setting the tambourine head down on a soft pad and using the hands or timpani sticks on the wood of the rim (Figure 18–29). Soft passages are also played by holding the tambourine parallel to the floor, head down, as though the instrument were resting on a pad or cushion, and striking the rim with fingers of the other hand. For any speed or any dynamic level, articulations are generally cleaner when the head is parallel to the floor. Muffling may be appropriate for any situation and is accomplished by placing a handkerchief on the inside of the head.

Figure 18–28
Tambourine: Knee Position

Long rolls are produced by rotating the instrument with the wrist. A short, quiet roll of one or two counts may call for the thumb roll, which is a way of vibrating the jingles by means of friction between the thumb and head (Figure 18–30). The thumb is wetted, then rubbed around the edge of the head close to the rim with the tambourine tilted toward the empty hand. The friction sets the jingles in motion. This is a somewhat hazardous practice, as the player is never sure when the thumb is going to suddenly become dry.

Figure 18–29
Tambourine: Position for Controlled Playing

Figure 18–30
Tambourine: Thumb Roll

Some players use powdered rosin rather than wetting the thumb. An even more secure solution is to use wax around the edge of the head or to glue a thin strip of emery paper around the edge. Regular sandpaper is less satisfactory; it begins to wear away the skin of the thumb if many rolls are required.

TRIANGLE

The pitch of the triangle is determined by its size. Two triangles varying from 6 to l0 inches are considered adequate for most playing needs. As with all other instruments, they should be of good quality. A poor-quality triangle is hardly preferable to having none at all; the tiny sound of a cheap piece of metal will make its use ridiculous rather than musical.

The twine or string that comes with the instrument should be replaced with a fine gut string or fishing line and this attached to a holder. When the triangle needs to be suspended from the music stand, the clip serves as the fastener. The triangle remains suspended when not in use and when both hands are required to play it. The triangle should not extend more than $1\frac{1}{2}$ inches below the clip as it will rotate if the cord is too long.

In sound, a tinkle is preferred to a definite pitch. Because some strikers produce more specific pitches than others, the sound varies with the striker used. The regular triangle beater should be at least 10 inches in length and from $\frac{1}{16}$ to $\frac{3}{8}$ inch in diameter. They can be purchased as a set that includes a storage bag and a vari-

Figure 18–31
Triangle: Normal Position,
Single Stick Rolls and Fast
Rhythmic Patterns

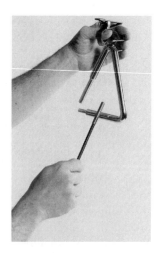

Figure 18–32
Triangle: Single Stick
Position for Special Effects

Figure18–33
Triangle: Full Kit (assorted
beaters) and Triangles

ety of triangle beaters. Other strikers such as spike-size nails, medium-size metal nail files, pieces of wire coat hangers, and the wire handles from telescoping snare drum brushes, should also be collected. Most of these are for special effects, of course; the triangle beater is the most frequently used.

For single stick rolls and fast rhythmic patterns, the beater should extend approximately 2 inches through the triangle (Figure 18–31). Soft rolls are played close to the closed angle, with little motion. Louder rolls will be wider, player farther away from the angle to allow for more vigorous striking and producing more volume. Rolls are started on the base (Figure 18–32).

Place the beater inside the triangle and strike the base about one third of the way in from the closed lower corner. A single beat is often played outside, either on the closed face of the triangle or on the base, but rhythmic patterns are easier to control when the beater is placed inside and played on the base. Fast rhythms require striking both base and side. An extremely fast passage may necessitate the use of two beaters, one in each hand, with the instrument suspended by one or two clips (to insure the triangle will not rotate). Triplets also are more successfully executed with two beaters. They tend to sound like a roll when a single beater is used.

LATIN AMERICAN INSTRUMENTS

Castanets

Castanets are of three types: single, double, and the castanet machine. The Epstein machine places the castanets into a holder, allowing the player to obtain greater precision, control, dynamic ranges, and even rolls.

The single castanet has one pair of blades, or clappers, attached to a wooden handle that serves as the sounding board (Figure 18–34). The double castanet has two sets of clappers (Figure 18–35). It is held by gripping the handle with the bottom three fingers, the thumb resting lightly wherever comfortable, and the index finger furnishing control.

Figure 18–34
Castanets: Single Clappers

Figure 18–35
Castanets: Double Clappers

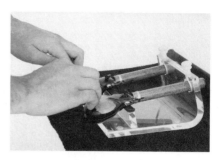

Figure 18–36
Castanet Machine

Slower passages require use of the double castanet or the machine (Figure 18–36) for dynamics from mezzo piano to fortissimo. Softer passages in moderate or slow speeds will use the single, which may be struck in the normal manner—on the open palm, on the knuckles of the closed fist, or on the leg.

Rolls are produced by striking a double castanet rapidly against the knee. Use of the castanet machine allows more control over dynamic levels. Tremolos are produced by using a set in each hand.

Terms for castanet playing are derived historically from Spanish dancers: G*lopé* indicates a single stroke with a single clapper or the machine. *Double glopé* are two castanets playing a single stroke with single clappers or the machine. And the *carretilla* is played on the machine as three or four grace notes to the primary beat; the grace notes are played beginning with the little finger leading to the index finger or thumb (as if drumming one's fingers impatiently).

OTHER ETHNIC PERCUSSION

There are other percussion instruments whose chief use was originally Latin American dance rhythms, but are used in a wide variety of music by today's orchestra and band composers. For Latin American rhythms: There should be conga drums, timbales, cowbell, and of course, a drum set. The samba uses the snare drum with the regular drumstick in the right hand and the wire brush in the left. The right hand plays the first note on the edge of the drum, and the left hand brushes the second note near the center of the head. The snares should be off. The tambourine may be used to double the snare, and maracas are used on quarter notes. The characteristic bolero rhythm is a triplet on the second half of the first beat. In Latin American music, the bolero is simply a slow rumba, but all of its other specific characteristics have dwindled in importance until the only one left is the triplet rhythm. Don't improvise the tango. When substitute players are used to augment the percussion section, the percussionists should be kept on the timbales and maracas because these demand more skill; the nonpercussionists can play the claves, guiros, and cowbells.

Maracas

Maracas are used in pairs. The left hand is in front of the body holding the lower pitched instrument, the right hand alternates over the top of the left hand (Figure 18–37 on page 316). They are usually played with a single beat in the left hand and a double beat in the right with a flick of the wrist. For soft passages, the maraca is held with thumb and bottom three fingers, and the base is tapped with the index

Figure 18–37
Playing Maracas

Figure 18–38
Common Rumba Rhythm Played on Maracas

finger. Maracas are used for mambos, guarachas, Cuban boleros, rumbas, beguines, tangos, congas, and paso dobles. The rumba rhythm is played with straight eighth notes, as in Figure 18-38.

Temple Blocks

Authentic temple blocks are actually Korean blocks, each made of one piece of balsa wood and painted. They are very fragile, chip easily, and should be played near the edge with medium-hard rubber or yarn marimba mallets. True temple blocks are becoming more and more difficult to find and are increasing in cost.

Most percussion sections today substitute "block" temple blocks as in Figure 18–39. They usually come in sets of five, although many more are available. These temple blocks allow a greater variety of tone colors by using different mallets (soft-to-medium rubber as well as all-yarn mallets). Very hard mallets can be used at soft volume levels for a resonant, projecting sound—snare sticks may damage the blocks. Even more durable models are available in plastic at a much lower cost, and they sound reasonably authentic.

Woodblocks

The woodblock is related to the temple block, but oblong in shape. They are made from various hardwoods and come in different sizes.

The block is held in the left hand and struck with a hard rubber-mallet or butt of a snare stick (Figure 18–40). For the best sound, the long tone slot should face the audience and be at the top of the block rather than at the bottom, the performer practicing until he determines the spot with the greatest resonance. When multiple wood blocks are needed, or the music requires two mallets, a holder is used to mount them. At least two should be available, a high and a low. Playing on the solid and on the hollow parts of the block produces different sounds.

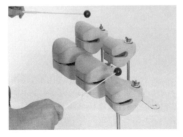

Figure 18–39
Playing Five-Pitched Temple Blocks

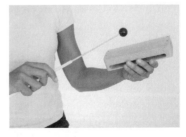

Figure 18–40
Playing a Woodblock.

Claves

Claves are two small, round sticks of rosewood or grenadilla, played by striking together (Figure 18–41). They are the most important instruments in the rhythm section for Cuban rhythms. One is placed on the partially closed knuckles of the left hand with the palm turned upward, being held in place with the thumb. It is struck with the other clave, held loosely in the right hand. They furnish a steady beat in the mambo, Cuban bolero, rumba, and beguine. They are not used in the conga, samba, or paso doble.

Figure 18–41
Playing Claves (note cupped left hand)

Some of the most common rhythms are shown in Figure 18–42.

Forward Clave Rhythm

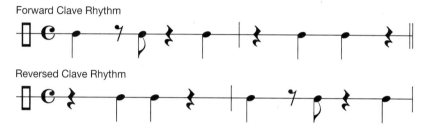

Reversed Clave Rhythm

Figure 18–42   Common Clave Rhythm (note reversed rhythm)

Cowbells

A regular cowbell could be used with the metal striker removed, played with a snare drumstick, and it will sound like one purchased at the local music store. Cowbells are useful on fast rumbas, congas, and the montuno. Two bells of different pitches are used on the conga and the montuno. The bell, available today in different sizes, is held in a cupped left hand (as in playing claves) and struck with the part of the snare stick that produces the sound desired. Muffling with adhesive tape deadens the tone. A finger touching the cowbell at various locations also produces different sounds. This muffled bell is a "concerto" and is used for the conga and the montuno.

Common cowbell rhythms are shown in Figure 18–43.

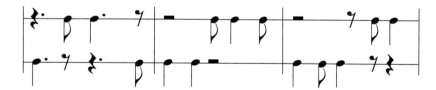

Figure 18–43   Common Cowbell Rhythm

Conga Drum

The conga drum is a deep, barrel-shaped drum made of wood or fiberglass, with a head of mule hide. It may rest on the floor or be held in a conga stand with the smaller drum traditionally to the player's left. At least two tunable sizes should be used with the smaller drum traditionally to the player's left. They may rest on the floor or in a conga stand. Congas range from 10 to 13 inch heads and are approximately 30 inches long. Cook divides all conga playing into three basic sounds:

Figure 18–44
Playing Conga

1. Open sound—striking the head between the center and edge with a "relaxed open hand and fingers and allowing the fingers to strike the head and spring back to a straight position with the back of the hand."
2. Closed sound—played with either the heel of hand or a cupped hand, or fingertips.
3. Slap—played like an open sound, but "grabbing" at the head.[6]

The left hand plays rim shots with flat fingers, holding the fingers against the head after striking (Figure 18–44).

Bongo

Bongo drums are played in pairs, the most common pair being $7\frac{1}{4}$ and $8\frac{1}{2}$ inch heads. They are made with a calf, mule, or goatskin head and are used principally for boleros, rumbas, mambos, and similar dance types. The instruments should be tunable with the two drums about a fourth apart.

As the smaller instrument plays predominantly, it should be placed on the left. The tips of the fingers and the thumb are used near the edge for a ringing sound, with softer sounds produced toward the center of the heads. Players should experiment with the various ways to strike the bongo, and with combinations of hand, fingers, and thumbs, to discover the remarkable number of sounds possible.

Timbales

In France the term *timbales* indicates the timpani; in the United States it refers to two small tom-toms on a single stand (Figure 18–45). The player must be sure of the composer's intention and select the right instrument.

Figure 18–45
Playing Timbales

Timbales are larger than the bongo drums, but tuned similarly with 13-and 14 inch heads. They are usually made of brass, although other metals are used for less expensive models. The sticks are either quarter inch dowel rods or rattan. The timbales are commonly used in beguines, in which they serve to accent the first afterbeat typical of beguines.

Different areas of the timbales are used for various effects: shell, rim, center, and so forth. In Latin or Afro-Cuban jazz, the timbale player is the master percussionist. A cowbell is occasionally attached and played with one stick while the other plays the drums.

Cabasa

The cabasa is very much like a maraca, except that the "rattlers"—small hard beads—are on the outside rather than the inside, strung on a ribbon that wraps around the ball. A cabasa is available from Latin percussion specialty companies in three sizes. It is held by the handle and struck with the palm of the other hand (Figure 18–46). It is effectively used in sambas.

[6] Cook, *Teaching Percussion*, p. 256.

Figure 18–46
Playing a Cabasa

Figure 18–47
Playing a Guiro

It can also be held in the right hand, the beads selectively covered with the left, and the instrument spun back-and-forth. The beads may be tapped with the left hand to produce a third effect. The samba pattern is usually two taps followed by a spin with the right hand.

Guiro

The guiro is a gourd-shaped instrument with a corrugated surface that is scraped with a small piece of wood, wire, or bamboo (Figure 18–47). A wooden guiro produces the best sound. These are used principally in the rumba. The most common guiro rhythm is an ostinato (Figure 18–48).

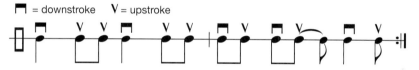

Figure 18–48   Common Guiro Calypso Rhythm

OTHER TRAPS AND AUXILIARY PERCUSSION

The list of items usable in percussion effects is nearly endless, depending upon the originality of the composer and the inventiveness of the player. The following list suggests the scope of possibilities; it is not inclusive: wind machine, anvil, steel drums, whistles, brake drums, rattles, slapstick, bird whistles, Quijada, agogo bells, talking drums, log drums, calypso maracas, 14-inch ka-me-so, sleigh bells mounted, *tablas, bata, djembe,* and dumberg drums (a combination Conga and bongo drums). Of these ethnic instruments, the most popular is the *djembe* due to is various sizes and its ability to project (Figure 18–49). In 1998–2000, several drum and bugle corps used them so many marching bands have followed suit. The djembe appears frequently in percussion ensemble music.

Figure 18–49
Playing a Medium-Size
Djembe in a Stand

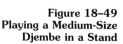

THE DRUM SET

The drum set is one of the most visibly exciting instruments and often the instrument that makes the study of percussion attractive. The irony is that most students are offered little or no opportunity to learn about the drum set in school curricula. Those who are fortunate enough to purchase a drum set are often left to "figure it out" on their own due to lack of instruction or lack of information from their director. Drum set playing is not just for the after-school garage band. It is used in serious competition, and many of the sought-after orchestral percussion positions include drum set playing in the audition process. Drum set (or its effects) is found in marching band shows, percussion ensembles, concert band music, orchestral scores, chamber works, and the traditional combo or jazz-band settings. We have not found it used with the school orchestra. Drum set playing requires the utmost concentration and focus, but with relaxation, limbs work interdependently and without tension with each other. The most important skill a student gains from drum performance on a set is not the physical coordination, but the ability to "multitask," to use a 1990s buzzword.

In order for the limbs to be *physically* coordinated, they must first be *mentally* coordinated. The increased mental agility is a major benefit of learning to play the drum set and is manifested in other areas of percussion performance.

Two types of drum sets are in use today: (1) those with double bass drums and several hundred pounds of toms and cymbals that were made popular by rock bands in the 1980s, and (2) those that have evolved from jazz playing in which the drummer established the meter and decorated or enhanced the rest of the ensemble with background figures and short fills between phrases. In today's music programs, the latter type is preferred, although it may not be as flamboyant as the large rock-band drum set.

Drum, Cymbal, and Head Selection

The basic modern-day drum set usually consists of a bass drum, a snare drum, two mounted toms, a floor tom, three cymbals (ride, crash and, a hi-hat cymbal) and the hardware (bass drum pedal, cymbal stand, tom-tom mounts) that link the pieces together. The composite array of these sounds makes up the "drum set" or "drum kit." (The expanded rock sets generally include two bass drums of different sizes, five mounted toms, two floor toms, three crash cymbals of different sizes, a splash cymbal, two ride cymbals, two snares, plus enough hardware to build the skeleton of a baseball stadium.)

The most popular "jazz kit" includes a 16 to 18 x 22 inch bass drum, a 5 x 14 inch snare drum, two mounted toms (8 x 10 inch and 9 x 12 inch) and a 16 x 16 inch floor tom. A cymbal setup should include at least a 20-inch ride, an 18-inch crash/ride, 14-inch hi-hats, and possibly a 20-inch swish or China cymbal. The throne, pedals, stand, and hardware are also required (Figure 18–50).

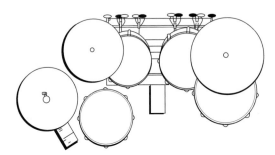

Figure 18–50
Jazz Kit (viewed from overhead)
Showing approximate locations
of Drums and Cymbals

Cymbal selection also differs from cymbal selection in the orchestra or band (crash and suspended) and might feature a 22 inch ride (with a large bell), multiple crash cymbals, 14 inch hi-hats, and a variety of special effects. Appropriate drum and cymbal selection is generally influenced by the overall volume of the music, the stylistic context in which they are to be played, and, of course, personal taste. In a jazz setting, the responsibility for "the groove" lies with the ride cymbal and the hi-hat—finding a great ride cymbal–hi-hat pair is essential. In a rock or funk setting, the increased volume warrants explosive crash cymbals—a crisp ride with a powerful bell.

The dramatic difference in volume between these two examples also affects the drumhead best suited for the music. Because brushes are frequently used in jazz drumming, drumheads that have a coated surface are most desirable; however, some jazz drummers select heads manufactured to emulate the sound of natural calfskin, attempting to recreate the sound of traditional jazz drums prior to the advent of plastic heads. Alternately, the increased volume of rock or funk settings may encourage the use of a noncoated head that allows a sharp attack, strong projection, and increased durability (thicker). The best compromise is a plastic-coated batter head that is loosely tightened, but not to the extent that the snare stick dents the head when playing. Toms should use fiberskin heads with medium tension—the top and bottom heads should be tuned the same. Experimenting with different heads and muffling devices (both internal and external) while listening to the drummer from a distance with the ensemble is necessary to select the best tuning of the most appropriate heads.

The Setup

Creating the arrangement of drums and cymbals must allow for the necessary independence of four limbs (plus feet separately). This freedom of movement and unrestrained comfort is the most important aspect for the set player in determining the arrangement of the drum set (Figure 18–51). Unlike the other percussion instruments that are played while standing, one of the early challenges of learning the drum set is to overcome the limitation of mobility created by sitting.

Because of this relative "grounding," the importance of placing cymbals and drums in relationship to one's body shape is important not only for the enhancement of performance but also for injury prevention. Sitting at the correct height is perhaps the most important factor. When adjusting the seat (throne) height, a stu-

Figure 18–51
Drum Set

dent should strive to sit so that the upper legs are just slightly above parallel to the floor and his back straight. With the knees bent, the bass drum and hi-hat should be placed at a distance away from the body that prevents the ankles from "flexing" when the legs are at rest. The bass drum is placed in front of the throne while the hi-hat is placed to either side, depending on the player's preference.

The angle between the knees can be determined by having the student "sit comfortably" on a drum throne; doing so will insure that the angle is body-specific and natural for the student. Once this is determined, the student should place his hi-hat and bass drum pedals in the same relationship. Careful monitoring of toms and cymbal heights will allow a student's shoulders to droop, encouraging the arms to stay relaxed, and allowing the entire drum set to be played with an economy of motion. "Boom-type" cymbal stands are recommended because they allow a greater range of adjustment when placing cymbals in the most appropriate spots.

Sticks

Selecting the right or "appropriate" stick is just as important as selecting the appropriate drums, heads, and cymbals for a particular kind of music. The overriding factor should be personal comfort but a stick's size and tip shape (along with a player's stroke) can dramatically affect the resultant tone produced on drums and cymbals. Great care should be taken to select a stick that not only "feels" good but also is shaped and weighted in a way that helps the drummer produce the appropriate sounds for a specific type of music. For example, a stick generally used for a "combo jazz" setting is generally thinner and lighter than a stick used for a "rock" setting. More important than volume, recognizing which instruments within the drum set can portray the core of the rhythm/style is vital when selecting an appropriate stick. The core of a swing/jazz sound comes from the ride cymbal; the perpetual ride cymbal pattern becomes the impetus that inspires star players. A stick that produces an articulate ride cymbal sound is more important than producing a high-volume drum tone. Conversely, in music where the center of the groove is found in the snare drum backbeat, stick selection centers on the quality and fullness of the drum sound, and less on that of the ride cymbal sound.

Styles

One of the most difficult decisions a student faces is when the director calls up a selection, and as he is "counting off" the tune the student speculates, "What's a Bossa Nova?" Having a wide knowledge base of music and styles is a necessity for the drum set player. To gain that knowledge base requires listening and watching great players of various styles. Although the language of world music includes many different styles, swing, rock, bossa nova/samba, Latin/mambo, fusion, and funk are those that most frequently occur. These styles serve as starting points for the drum set student.

Once a number of great recordings have been purchased, the student should listen for specifics: What is the overall rhythmic subdivision? (swing eighths/triplets versus. straight eighths) Where are the strong and weak beats of the music? From where does the "feel" originate? (hard beat as in rock, syncopated bass lines as in funk, phrasing around the clave as in Latin music). Where are the harmonic cadence points of the music (always on one, never on one)? What are some of the patterns/grooves that other instrumentalists play (bass, piano, guitar, etc.)? What is the actual groove that the drummer is playing? How do the drummer and percussionist interact? At what point do they alter what they are playing and what do they play instead? What is the characteristic sound of the instruments? Small drums? Large drums? Tuned high or low?

MARCHING PERCUSSION

The emphasis on percussion as an integral (and expensive) component of corps-style marching bands has grown steadily since the mid-1970s. Using drum and bugle corps as models, high school marching band directors have borrowed many percussion instruments, concepts, and techniques. To cover fully the complex and ever-changing area of marching band percussion is beyond the scope of this text. References, which provide more detailed guidance, are listed at the end of this chapter.

Marching band percussion presents a number of concerns for every director, one of which is size and instrumentation. It is not easy, however, to determine that a band of X size should have a percussion section of Y size with Z instrumentation.

The primary activity of the marching band should determine the size and instrumentation of the percussion section size. Corps-style competitive marching bands can have anywhere from four to twelve snares, three to six individuals who carry tenor drums, three to six pair of cymbals, three to nine bass drums, and a virtually unlimited array of percussion in the pit: timpani, tam-tam, suspended cymbals, concert vibes, marimbas, xylophone, bells, tom-tom, chimes, and more. The tremendous variance between percussion sections may require an arranger to alter the percussion scoring of many band scores. Although almost any band has the wind instrumentation to play the published stock arrangements, percussion parts often must be augmented or simplified to conform to the instrumentation and expertise of the performers.

Due to the complexity and intricacy of the competitive drum section, directors often hire specialists to train and teach the percussion section as a separate ensemble. Further, since 1975 the rules of Drum Corps International have allowed the pit to remain stationary. Marching bands naturally followed suit.

The percussion section is largely responsible for creating the energy and rhythmic drive of the marching band. An ideal piece of music for marching band might have predominately long notes in the winds to allow greater control of dynamic levels, intonation, and articulation, giving the percussion most of the rhythmic aspects. A better marching sound can be achieved by letting the tubas play half and whole notes and write movement in the bass drum parts.

Marching Snare Drums

Snare drums are the foundation of the marching band percussion sections. Most teachers place their best percussionists on snare as it plays the most intricate rudiments (in contrast to the essential 26 listed early in the chapter, drum lines use more than 100 rudiments) and because the use of multiple snare players for volume increases the need for precision (again in contrast to what we advocate that only one snare should play in concert percussion).

Marching snares are now virtually all 14 inch with a 12 inch shell (only two manufacturers make a 13 inch marching snare). Snare drums have become more "standardized" due to desired weight. The popular floating head design allows a multiple-ply shell to float inside a cage that contains all the instrument's hardware. This design eliminates tightened heads from collapsing the shells, and allows for more precise tuning as the number of lugs is increased. Additional vent holes are also drilled in the shell.

Most major percussion companies make marching snare drums of varying quality and price. Directors should make every attempt to purchase the best-quality marching snare drums for their bands' activities—and to keep them in good playing condition. Marching snare drums, for example, will usually mean the student will have to adjust individual snares. Too many directors believe their "drummer" could never tune a gut snare or tune the drums to a common pitch. If students can learn to adjust reeds and can learn to play with good intonation, then certainly snare drummers can learn to adjust snares.

The number of snare drummers needed in a marching band is difficult to determine. Many directors overestimate the number required to balance the winds. On the other hand, additional snare drummers allow each player to play softer and with more control. A rule of thumb is to have one snare drummer for every eight to ten brass players.

The most difficult task for the marching band snare drummer is precision. In any given arrangement, drummers average many more notes than those played by the first trumpet. With 10 to 12 students playing these notes in unison, rhythmic precision of the ensemble is a formidable task. Because the visual elements of stick heights, stick angles, drum angles, and any gimmick-type stick visuals are expected, the task of teaching (and learning) can become extremely time-consuming. When the marching formations and maneuvers are added to the playing, the role of marching band percussionists challenges the student who thought being a drummer required little practice.

Fortunately for percussionists, the days of slings or straps are over. Schools should purchase lightweight adjustable carriers. These carriers disperse the weight of the drum evenly across the upper torso, enabling the drums to remain steady. They keep the drum level to facilitate matched grip and make the snare line look even, and usually fit under the uniform jacket.

Most successful marching drum lines spend time each day "warming up." Marching snare drum exercises are available in a number of sources (see the end of the chapter bibliography). These exercises are based on repeating sixteenth note patterns while alternating one of sixteenth notes with a double (thirty-second notes with the same stick), then a double substituted for several of the sixteenth-notes, and so on. Most good snare lines will play an exercise repeatedly trying to achieve the precision to sound like a single individual.

Tenors—Multiple Drums

The band director who is enlarging the marching band drum line must decide whether to purchase "triples," "quads," or "quints." Then he must determine the sizes. The dilemma of the number of drums confronts the arrangers and publishers of commercial marching band arrangement.

Figure 18–52
Marching Tenor ("Quint") Line

The first notable use of multiple percussion in a marching group occurred in the 1960s when the now famous drum and bugle corps director Bobby Hoffman carried a pair of timbales with the Hawthorne Caballeros. Since that time, drum and bugle corps (and bands) have tried elongated triples that look like elephant tusks, congas mounted, bongos split to each side of a snare drum, and other arrangements in an attempt to "carry" as many drums as possible onto the field (Figure 18–52).

The development of lightweight drum shells and carriers has allowed 6-, 8-, 10-, 12-, 13-, and 14-inch tenor drums to be mounted in threes, fours, or fives in any combination. The most popular is a 6—8—10—12—14 quintuplet mounted on a lightweight vest. Cutaway tenors are also available.

The decision as to what size drum to purchase is guided by pitch. Conceptually, the multiple drums are used to "fill the gap" between the snare and bass drums. If the snare drums are using older 15-inch drums that cannot be tuned as high as 14-inch drums with Kevlar heads, then one would select "quads" in 10-12-13-14 inch sizes. The pitch, however, of four larger drums may "bleed over" into the pitch range of the bass drums if the bass drum section is large and uses small drums.

Realistically, what to purchase is determined by cost. Multiple drums are expensive, and the lightweight carrier is essential. Consider fielding one multiple drum player for every two or three snares. A smaller drum line may have only one multiple and one snare player; this arrangement provides greater musical contrast, interest, and ensemble support than two snare drums.

Marching Bass Drums

Traditionally the band bass drummer has been the most singled-out, fussed-at, unappreciated musician in the ensemble. Three reasons can be given: (1) Band directors have often assigned one of their weaker players to this seemingly simple instrument; (2) it is one of the most important instruments in the ensemble; and (3) the director insists that the bass drummer watch and try as-the-student-might, the delayed sound may cause the director to seek therapy.

The smallest number of tonal bass drums that can be used effectively is three, arranged in a 22, 24, and 28 combination. The fourth drum would be a 26-inch drum and the fifth a 20-inch bass drum.

The more common lines consist of five drums. Most large bands field as many bass drums as possible in the "battery." Matched bass drums are made in 9 sizes:

Figure 18–53
Five Member Bass Drum
Line Practicing

16—18—20—22—24—26—28—30—32. Colleges use as many as 9 bass drums when precision is not crucial and the large numbers help balance a large band (drum corps have a 130-person maximum size).

There are, however, marching percussion specialists who advocate larger drums, such as a 36-inch drum, which is useful for special effects. The largest drum used successfully in recent years has been the 42-inch Pearl custom-made bass drum for the Garfield Cadets. It was not carried, but mounted in the pit. Unless needed for a visual effect, the 36 drum also belongs on the sideline.

It is important to purchase good-quality bass drum carriers. A number of good quality padded, nonpadded, high-rise, and other carriers are available.

Cymbals

Generally the cymbals selected for use in marching band are of lighter weight than those used in concert. They come in 14, 16, 18, and 20 inch sizes and in brilliant, medium, or medium heavy weights. Weight becomes especially important when the cymbal players are required to hold the instruments extended for the snare players to play side cymbals. Whereas the lamb's wool pad is usually removed for concert use, a small pad helps protect the marching cymbalist's knuckles. Most players are also more comfortable when wearing lightweight leather gloves. The newest innovations have been cymbals manufactured in a choice of colors. Their tone is not improved; they merely provide an additional visual effect for the marching band.

The Pit

In 1975 Drum Corps International (DCI) altered its rules to allow tonal mallet percussion instruments on the field. For years, drum and bugle corps students marched around the field carrying bells, marching xylophones and marimbas (both smaller than concert instruments), and even chimes. A few years later, DCI altered its rules to enable those percussionists to "ground" their equipment; to place percussion equipment just off the sideline, allowing it to remain stationary throughout the show. Band directors followed the DCI model, although bands marched bell-lyra's (and continue to do so) for decades before drum corps did.

Presently, drum and bugle corps and most corps-style bands utilize a variety of stationary instruments on the sideline near the drum major's podium. Each provides a new sound to enhance the band's overall musical performance, but most are expensive.

The most beneficial sounds are produced by the mallet instruments. The pit enables a concert marimba, with Kelon bars, to be placed on the sideline. Bells, xylophone, and vibraphone are also useful—in that order. Great care must be taken to keep these instruments in good repair; moving these instruments from the rehearsal room to the practice field on a daily basis shortens their useful lives regardless of how carefully they are treated and maintained.

Also commonly found in the pit are Latin instruments, color instruments, special effect instruments and a variety of ethnic percussion (and stringed) instruments. Although these instruments are less costly than keyboard instruments, their usefulness is more limited. Spanish and Latin tunes provide a welcome variety to the audience.

Tenor tom-toms (mounted on a concert stand), timpani, tam-tam, and suspended cymbals all can provide beautiful colors to any musical ensemble and especially to the marching band. But, again, these instruments are expensive and difficult to move. Few instrumental music programs can afford a set of timpani for concert work and a second set for marching band. Still fewer programs can provide the personnel required to move two to four timpani, four keyboard mallets, a dozen Latin instruments, tom-tom, tam-tam, and the like on and off the field for every rehearsal and performance.

Marching bands that have attempted to place the entire percussion section in the pit, have often suffered from phrasing, balance, and inadequate percussion problems to such an extent as to make these attempts of questionable educational importance.

BIBLIOGRAPHY

Texts: Concert Percussion

*Indicates out of print in 2001.

BAJZEK, DIETER (1988). *Percussion: An Annotated Bibliography.* Metuchen, NJ: Scarecrow Press.

BECK, JOHN H. (ed.) (1997). *Encyclopedia of Percussion* (Garland Reference Library of the Humanities, Vol. 947). New York: Garland Publications Trade.

*BENVENGA, NANCY (1979). *Timpani and the Timpanist's Art: Musical and Technical Development in the 19th and 20th Centuries.* Goteborg, Sweden: Goteborg University.

BLADES, JAMES, and J. MONTAGU (1970). *Early Percussion Instruments from the Middle Ages to the Baroque.* London: Oxford University Press.

————, and JOHNNY DEAN (1992). *How to Play Drums.* New York: St. Martin's.

CARUBA, GLEN (1996). *Afro-Cuban Drumming: A Comprehensive Guide to Traditional and Contemporary Styles* (w/CD). Milwaukee, WI: Hal Leonard.

COMBS, MICHAEL (2000). *Percussion Manuel.* Prospect Heights, IL: Waveland Press.

CIRONE, ANTHONY (1975). *The Orchestral Snare Drummer.* Menlo Park, CA: Cirone Publications.

————.(1977). *The Orchestral Mallet Player.* Menlo Park, CA: Cirone Publications.

————. (1978). *The Orchestral Timpanist.* Menlo Park, CA: Cirone Publications.

————, and JOE SINAI (1977). *The Logic of It All.* Menlo Park, CA: Cirone Publications.

————. (1998). *Art of Bass Drum and Cymbal Playing.* Ft. Lauderdale: Meredith Music Publishers.

COOK, GARY D. (1997). *Teaching Percussion,* 2nd ed. New York: Schirmer Books.

DENOV, SAM (1985). *The Art of Playing Cymbals: A Complete Guide and Text for the Artistic Percussionist,* rev. ed. Miami: Warner Brothers.

DWORSKY, ALAN, and BETSEY SANBY (1994). *Conga Drumming: A Beginners Guide to Playing with Time* (w/CD). Minnetonka, MN: Dancing Hands Music.

*GOODMAN, SAUL (1985). *Modern Method for Timpani.* Miami: Columbia Pictures.

KLOWER, TOM (1997). *The Joy of Drumming: Drums and Percussion Instruments from Around the World.* York Beach, ME: Samuel Weiser.

LANG, MORRIS, and LARRY SPIVACK (1997). *Dictionary of Percussion Terms.* Brooklyn: Lang Percussion.

*LUDWIG, WILLIAM F. (n.d.). *The Development of Drum Rudiments.* Chicago: Ludwig Drum.

*MACCALLUM, FRANK (1969). *The Book of the Marimba.* New York: Carlton Press.

MAFFIT, ROCKY (1999). *Rhythm and Beauty: The Art of Percussion.* New York: Watson-Guptill.

MCBETH, FRANCIS W. (1972). *Effective Performance of Band Music, Solutions to Specific Problems in the Performance of 20th Century Band Music.* San Antonio, Tx: Southern Music Company.

MOIO, DOMINICK (1996). *Latin Percussion in Perspective* (w/CD). Pacific, MO: Mel Bay Publications.

*PAPASTEFAN, JOHN J. (1978). *Timpani Scoring Techniques in the Twentieth Century.* Mobile, AL: University of South Alabama.

Percussion Anthology: A Compendium of Articles from the Instrumentalist, 4th ed. (1995). Evanston, IL: Instrumentalists.

PINKSTERBOER, HUGO (1993). *The Cymbal Book* (w/CD). Milwaukee, WI: Hal Leonard.

RICH, BUDDY, HENRY ADLER, and HENRI KLICKMANN (1997). *Buddy Rich's Modern Interpretation of Snare Drum Rudiments.* New York: Music Sales; reprint of (1942) New York: Amsco.

SALLOUM, TREVOR (1997). *Bongo Book* (w/CD). Pacific, MO: Mel Bay.

SOUL, DOUG (1996). *The Soul of Hand Drumming* (w/CD). Pacific, MO: Mel Bay.

STONE, GEORGE L. (1998). *Stick Control for the Snare Drummer.* Randolf, MA: George B. Stone.

WHALEY, GARWOOD (1993), *Percussion Education: A Source Book of Concepts and Information,* reprint of (1989). Reston, VA: Music Educators National Conference.

Texts: Jazz Set

BRIGGS, FRANK J. (1994). *The Complete Modern Drumset* (w/CD and/or videoape). Pacific, MO: Mel Bay.

LATTA, JIM (1997). *Rock, Jazz, and Funk Drumming.* New York: Koala Publications.

MALABE, FRANK, and BOB WEINER (1994). *Afro-Cuban Rhythms for Drumset.* Miami: Warner Brothers.

PAYNE, JIM (1993). *Funk Drumming (w/CD)*. Pacific, MO: Mel Bay.

ROTHMAN, JOEL (1999). *Play Rock Drums (Step One)*. New York: Amsco.

ZUBRASKI, DAVE (1997). *Rock Solid Drum Patterns: Grooves, Patters and Fills You Can Learn Today!* (w/CD). New York: Music Sales.

Percussion Studies

Easy—Beginning (elementary or middle)

Brown. *Combination Method for Snare Drum and Mallets* (Belwin-Mills).

Coffin. *The Performing Percussionist*, Book 1 (C. L. Barnhouse).

Feldstein. *Mallet Student* (Belwin-Mills).

———. *Mallet Technique for Bass and Treble Clef: Two Mallets* (Belwin-Mills).

Firth. *Vic Firth Snare Drum Method*, Book I (C. Fischer).

Green. *George Hamilton Green's Instruction Course for Xylophone* (Meredith Music).

La Rosa. *Contemporary Drum Method*, Book 1 (Somers Music).

Payson. *Beginning Snare Drum Method* (Payson Percussion).

———. *Elementary Marimba and Xylophone Method* (Payson Percussion).

Peters. *Developing Dexterity for Snare Drum* (Mitchell Peters).

Whaley. *Basics in Rhythm* (Meredith Music).

———. *Primary Handbook for Mallets* (Meredith Music).

Medium (middle or high school)

Beck *Flams, Ruffs and Rolls for Snare Drum* (Meredith Music).

Bellson and Breines. *Modern Reading Test in 4/4* (Belwin-Mills).

———. *Odd Time Reading Text* (Belwin-Mills).

Berle (ed. Feldstein). *Mallet Independence* (Belwin-Mills).

Cirone. *Portraits in Rhythm* (Belwin-Mills).

Coffin. *The Performing Percussionist*, Book 2 (C. L. Barnhouse).

Delecluse. *20 Etudes* (Alphonse-Leduc).

———. *30 Etudes*, Books I–III (Al. Leduc).

Firth. *Mallet Technique—38 Studies for the Marimba, Xylophone and Vibraphone* (C. Fischer).

———. *Vic Firth Snare Drum Method*, Book II (C. Fischer).

Goldenberg. *Modern School for Xylophone, Marimba and Vibraphone* (Hal Leonard).

Green. *George Hamilton Green's Instruction Course for Xylophone* (Meredith Music).

Houllif. *20 Bach Chorales* (Music for Percussion).

Kraus. *Phil Kraus—Modern Mallet Method*, Book 1 (Belwin-Mills).

Lang. *14 Contemporary Etudes for Mallet Instruments* (Belwin-Mills).

———. *15 Bach Inventions for Mallet Instruments* (Belwin-Mills).

Macmillan. *Basic Timpani Technique* (Belwin-Mills).

———. *Masterpieces for Marimba* (Belwin-Mills).

Podemski. *Musical Studies for the Intermediate Mallet Player* (Meredith Music).

———. *Podemski's Standard Snare Drum Method* (Belwin-Mills).

———. *Primary Handbook for Timpani* (Meredith Music).

———. *Solos and Duets for Timpani* (Meredith Music).

Advanced (high school or college)

Albright. *Contemporary Studies for the Snare Drum* (Belwin-Mills).

———. *Rhythmic Analysis for the Snare Drum, with Introduction to Polyrhythms.* (Award Music).

Burton. *Four Mallet Studies* (Ludwig).

Cirone. *Portraits in Rhythm* (Belwin-Mills).

Delecluse. *30 Etudes*, Books I–III (Alphonse-Leduc).

Fink. *Sight Reading and Audition Etudes* (Fink).

———. *Timpani Tuning Etudes* (Fink).

Gates. *Odd Meter Duets* (Sam Fox).

Goldenberg. *Modern School for Snare Drum (with a Guide Book for the Artist Percussionist)* (Hal Leonard).

———. *Modern School for Xylophone, Marimba and Vibraphone* (Hal Leonard).

Green. *George Hamilton Green's Instruction Course for Xylophone* (Meredith Music).

Kraus. *Phil Kraus—Modern Mallet Method*, Books 2 and 3 (Belwin-Mills).

Payson. *Concert Etudes for Snare Drum* (Payson Percussion).

Peters. *Advanced Snare Drum Studies* (Mitchell Peters).

Stevens. *Method of Movement for Marimba* (Marimba Productions).

Stout. *Etudes for Marimba,* 2 vols. (Paul Price and Alfred).

Instructional Videos

Drum Basics Step One (Sandy Gennaro, 1994). Miami: Warner Bros.

Snare Drum for Beginners with Mat Britain. Van Nuys, CA: Backstage Pass Productions.

The Bongo Drums One Step with Brad Dutz. Miami: Warner Bros.

African Drumming (1993) Babatunde Olatunji Brattleboro VT: Interworld Music Associates.

David Eagles *Drum Basics* (1994). Chatsworth, CA: Music Video Products. (Learn simple note-reading, tuning, tome colors, coordination exercises).

Drumming Made Easy: A Complete Guide for the Beginner 1991. Woodstock, NY: Homespun Video. Holding the sticks, reading music and timing, exercises.

Yamaha Fred Sanford *"Marching Percussion,"* vols. 1–2, includes book. Schaumburg, IL: Sharper Video.

Beginning Snare Drum (1989). Atlantic City, NJ: Music Education Video.

Clinic Presentation: Frank Epstein (1995). Miami: Warner Brothers.

Clinic Presentation: Emil Richards (1995). Miami: Warner Brothers.

Getting Started on Congas; Technique for Two and Three Drums, Fundamento I & II (Bobby Sanabria, 1996). Miami: DCI Music Video.

The Conga Drum Style (Brad Dutz, 1995). Miami: CPP Media Group.

Richardo Gallardo Traditional and Contemporary Mexican Percussion Instruments (1995). Miami: CPP Media Group.

Clinic Presentation: Patricia Sandler (1995). Miami: CPP Media Group.

Clinic Presentation: Bob Moses (1995). Miami: CPP Media Group

Practical Drum Set Application, Afro-Caribbean Rhythms (Chuck Silverman, 1992). Miami: CPP Media Group

Belwin 21st Century Band Method. Percussion, Level 1 (Jack Bullock and Anthony Maiello, 1996). Miami: Warner Brothers.

Belwin 21st Centruy Band Method. Keyboard Percussion, Level l, (Jack Bullock and Anthony Maiello, 1996). Miami: Warner Brothers.

Alex Acuna, Live From PAS '95 (1996). Miami: CPP Media Group.

Luis Conte, Live From PAS '95 (1996). Miami: CPP Media Group.

Bill Molenhocf (1995). Miami: CPP Media Group.

The Percussion Family (1979). Bloomington, IN: Agency for Instructional Television.

Concert Percussion: A Performer's Guide (Anthony Cirone, Sam Denov, Cloyd Duff, and Fred Sanford, 1989). Alameda, CA: Masterplan.

Music Educator's Guide to Percussion (Michael Combs, 1987). Knoxville, TN: University of Tennessee.

Percussion and Vibration Techniques (1976). Boston, MA: Sargent College of Allied Health Profession.

Jazz Percussion Videos

Drum Course for Beginners with Louis Bellson (1981). W. Long Branch, NJ: Kulter International Films. Basic grip, plus four rudiments.

Drum Method I: Joe Morello—A–Z (1993). Pound Ridge, NY: Hot Licks Production.

Drum Method II: Joe Morello (1993). Pound Ridge, NY: Hot Licks Production.

Mel Lewis. Mel Lewis and the Jazz Orchestra—Jazz at the Smithsoniam (Kulture 1273). ClickSmart.com, 400 Morris Avenue, Long Beach, NJ 07740

Henry Adler. Hand Development Technique (1992). Miami: CDP Media.

Getting Started on Congas; Conga Basics (Bobby Sanbria, 1996) Miami: Warner Bros.

Hands on Drumming. Universal Keys to Hand Drumming Session 1. (Paulo Mattioli, 1996). Topanga, CA: African Publishing.

19

Principles for Strings

HISTORY

By the sixteenth century, instruments resembling the modern violin, viola, cello, and bass were widespread in Europe. The Italian instrument makers of Brescia and Cremona, German artist-craftsmen in Mittenwald, and makers in France (who became better known for bows) remain legendary. During the attempt to perfect string instruments, the Brescia group flourished for about two centuries but was overshadowed by the astonishing perfection of the Cremona instruments. Among the string instrument makers of Cremona were Amati, Guadagnini, Ruggieri, Guarneri, and Stradivari. Although it is usually assumed that each of these famous violin makers also crafted violas, cellos, and basses, it is primarily the violins that have survived.

Early bows were shaped like hunting bows from which they were probably derived. The current design, with its inward curvature of the stick, was developed in France during the late Baroque period.

One of the traditional pitfalls in many string classes is a lack of teacher imagination. String classes can profit from abandoning the books and playing by ear to immediately begin ear training and allow the student to focus on his relationship with the instrument. The ability to play a tune (pizzicato) early in the training is a powerful incentive to perform traditional melodies. Tuning, harmonics, and use of all four left fingers should also be taught early.

PHYSICAL CHARACTERISTICS

The four string instruments that comprise the modern string orchestra have much in common. All are made of wood and are similarly constructed. All use a bow drawn across the strings, the hair of which when properly rosined actually grabs the string and serves as a tone generator. All alter pitches by placing the left fingers at various locations on a fretless fingerboard or by playing on a different string.

Inside each string instrument is a bass bar, sound post, and corner blocks. The bass bar is the critical element in each instrument's tone quality. Serving to reinforce the top of the instrument, the bass bar is a strip of narrow wood glued along the length of the body below the lowest string that influences tone quality and dampens excessive vibration of the lower string. Figures 19–1 and 19–2 illustrate the parts of the string instruments.

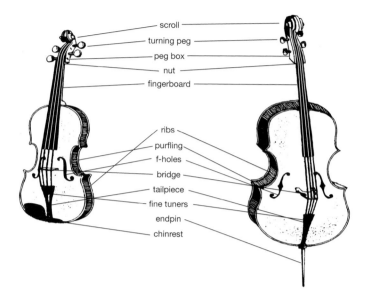

Figure 19–1   **Parts of a Violin and Cello: Front View**

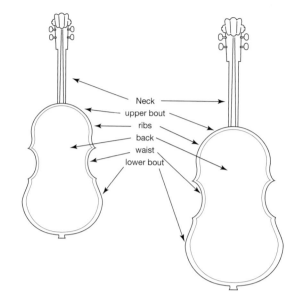

Figure 19–2
Parts of a Violin and Cello: Back View

The sound post is a dowel, which fits vertically between the front and back of the instrument. The sound post is generally positioned slightly to the bottom and right of the edge of the bridge, the exact placement being a position that produces the best tone quality. Figure 19–3 illustrates the position of the bass bar, corner blocks (*inside* the "points" above and below the waist), and sound post.

Sound Post

A string instrument should never be played without a sound post. The resulting strain can easily ruin the instrument. Sound posts do come loose occasionally and need to be reset. In resetting, the grain of the post should be kept at right angles with the grain of the top of the instrument. The quantity of vibration that the body of the instrument absorbs can occasionally shake loose not only the sound post, but eventually the bridge and even the tailpiece. The teacher can temporarily reset these but precision setting requires a skilled repairperson.

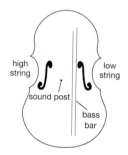

Figure 19–3
Top of Violin Showing Location of Bass Bar and Sound Post Inside the Body

The nut is a critical component usually made of ebony and fitted across the top of the fingerboard. It determines the height and spacing of the strings, and when it is an inappropriate size for the instrument must be adjusted or replaced by a competent repairperson.

The Bow

Most student-line bows consist of a stick made of fiberglass, graphite, or a composite material, and synthetic hair. Higher-quality bows are made of pernambuco, rosewood, or brazilwood with the hair from a horse mane or tail. Synthetic materials to replace expensive horsehair are rapidly improving in quality. Fine-quality composite bows are increasingly available. Figure 19–4 illustrates the parts of the bow.

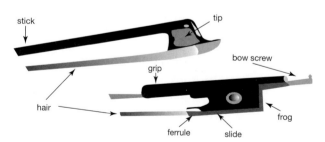

Figure 19–4   **Parts of the Violin Bow**

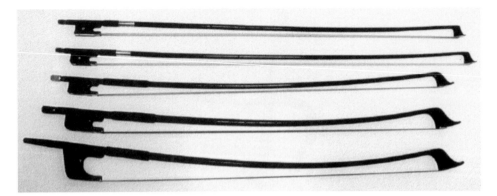

Figure 19–5 Violin, Viola, Cello, and French and German Bass Bows

Viola bows are heavier and longer than violin bows. The cello bow is thicker and shorter, with the bass bow the shortest and heaviest (Figure 19–5).

The bow hair is tightened or loosened by holding the frog with the left hand and turning the bow screw with the right. The hair is loosened when returning the bow to the case to prevent the stick from warping. Rosin is applied to the bow hair to increase friction when the bow is drawn across the strings. The correct tension of the hair is a matter of trial and error and depends upon the sound desired and the performing maturity of the student. It should not be stretched so tightly that the bow straightens. A good rule of thumb is to leave a space between the stick and hair the width of a pencil for violin and viola, and the width of a thumb for cello and bass. Getting the proper amount of rosin on the bow hair is also learned by trial and error. To apply rosin, the bow is held at the frog and drawn back and forth on the rosin that is held in the left hand. To prevent unnecessary dirt or damage to the bow hair, avoid touching the hair.

The Bridge

The bridge is critical to tone quality as well as technique. Its purpose is to space the strings evenly near the tail of the instrument and serve as a conduit for vibrations from the strings to the body of the instrument that is the resonator. A high bridge assists beginning students to position the bow on only one string. Each time the pegs are adjusted to tune a string instrument, there is a tendency for the bridge to be pulled toward the fingerboard, causing it to tilt or become warped.

The bridge should fit tightly between the top of the instrument and the strings, with the feet uniformly in contact with the instrument. The bridge is never glued in place (except by an occasional frustrated parent), but fits snugly, and tilts slightly away from the fingerboard. Most new bridges are too thick and are designed to be thinned and professionally adjusted and fitted.

Bridges are placed on the instrument between the notches of the f holes by string instrument repair specialists, but every string teacher should be prepared to adjust bridges to a position that is appropriate and usable *until* the bridge can be checked by an expert. The top of the bridge is shaped to approximate the contour of the fingerboard; it is better to have the top of the bridge too curved than too flat to avoid playing on more than one string. The bridge is too curved if the bow scrapes the instrument when playing on the highest or lowest string.

If a string instrument lacks responsiveness and has a sober tone, a thinner bridge can improve its sound. If the sound is somewhat too bright, a thicker bridge will help darken the sound.

Tuning Pegs and Fine Tuners

Four tuning pegs are used on the violin, viola, and cello to macrotune the four strings. The bass uses a mechanical device to achieve the same purpose. The pegs are inserted into the peg box (Figure19–1). These pegs adjust the pitch and should remain in position once set. To adjust when tuning rather than turning the peg to the desired pitch and then pressing it into the peg box, pressure should be gradually applied toward the peg box as the peg is turned. When pegs slip (do not hold the pitch), a specialized peg compound should be used that is not as abrasive as chalk and does not affect the oil in the wood. Pegs slip when they do not fit properly. The fit of the peg can be determined by inspecting the shiny mark which should have the same shiny width all around the peg. If the shine is only in spots, or there are spots on the peg where there is no shine, the peg does not fit correctly. The problem may be an irregular peg hole, a peg that is worn, or one that is the wrong size. This problem should be fixed by a qualified string instrument repairperson. A well-fitting peg is one that does not have to be "eased off" in tuning or require a final "jam" to keep it in place.

Fine tuners on the tailpiece are used with metal strings to adjust the microtuning on most violins, violas, and cellos reducing the need to adjust the pegs.

Mutes

Mutes are required at times on all four string instruments to produce a contrast in tone quality. The most convenient are rubber "slide on" mutes. These are attached to the instrument in an "off" position and are moved into position when required (see Figure 19–6 and 19–7).

Strings

There are three types of strings: gut core strings, steel core strings, and synthetic core or multistrand strings. Each type of string enhances specific aspects of the sound. The single most important criterion for a good string is that it produce a pure fundamental tone without distortion from overtones or pitch fluctuations.

Beginners seldom use gut strings, a string that produces a warm sound with complex overtones. Gut strings do not last as long as other types, and they are the most sensitive to temperature and humidity.

Figure 19–6
Violin Mute: In the "Off" Position

Figure 19–7
Violin Mute: In the "On" Position

Steel strings were developed as a reliable alternative to gut strings and are often found on violins, violas, and cellos, and should be considered for bass. Steel strings have a simple, clear, pure sound, with few overtones; the primary criticism is a somewhat brilliant and thin sound.

Synthetic core strings sound more like gut strings, don't stretch as much as gut, respond faster, and provide a more consistent sound than gut strings.

Each type of string is available in three thickness or gauges: thin, medium, or thick. The thin and medium are sometimes labeled "forte" and "piano" or "orchestra" and "solo". Thicker strings provide greater volume and are generally more powerful but are less responsive and require more tension. Excessive string tension can damage the bridge or the instrument.

The best match of strings to an instrument is accomplished through trial and error, although steel strings are usually applied as a set. A good choice is to start with medium-gauge steel core strings. Over time any quality string loses its edge, and becomes unresponsive and needs to be replaced. Because this change is so gradual many students fail to notice it. Wrapped strings should also be replaced if windings begin to unravel.

As all strings break, teachers and students need to know how to replace them (string players always carry a spare set of strings that match those on the instrument). The knot on the loop end is first inserted in the correct hole of the tailpiece or the loop is placed over the fine tuner; the other end of the string is fed through a hole in the proper peg winding it over the end to prevent slippage and tightened by turning the peg outward. The appropriate maneuver is one that results in keeping the string as straight as possible between the nut and the peg. The string should not overlap itself on the peg.

Students should be aware that new strings need time "to mellow" and may vary in pitch for a few days. Thus, strings are not to be changed the day of a performance, but several days prior in order to give than time to "settle."

New strings can be false and unpredictable in the way they vibrate. A false string produces unreliable harmonics that would require altered fingerings when playing in higher positions. It should be promptly discarded.

SELECTING A STRING INSTRUMENT

String instruments are either copies, models, or originals. The advances made by string manufacturers during the last century mean that most new string instruments are adequate.

The primary criteria for selecting string instruments are condition (for a used instrument) and the sound the instrument produces. Because the sound potential is impossible for the beginner to determine, an expert is invaluable in helping students, parents, and the novice string teacher select the appropriate instrument.

When purchasing a used instrument determine if the neck is centered between the f holes, check for cracks and that any repaired cracks are level on both sides. Other considerations include: is the soundpost cracked, the fingerboard smooth, the peg box solid, the tailpiece properly positioned, the bow warped or cracked, and whether the nut is the appropriate size. Check that the pegs work and that there are no buzzes when the instrument is plucked or bowed.

LEFT-HAND FUNDAMENTALS

Harmonics

Harmonics are produced by lightly touching the string at its nodes; for example, gently placing a finger approximately at the middle of a string will cause it to sound an octave higher. Placing the finger at one-fourth the length of the string from the bridge (or from the nut) will sound the note two octaves above the open string. Touching the one-third point very lightly on the string (either node) will sound the pitch a twelfth above the fundamental or open string. Obviously, long fingernails will affect the ability to play these harmonics and possibly other notes.

Early practice of rote exercises is recommended for all string instruments. The notation for natural harmonics is a small circle for an open string (to sound an octave higher). A diamond over a note (appearing as a double-stop) indicates a "false" or artificial harmonic that is played with a lower finger (usually first finger) stopping the string and an upper finger lightly touching the node. First have students play an open D pizzicato, then slide the fourth finger toward the bridge touching the string to find the octave harmonic (half way up the string). The student listens to match the pitch and the best sound for the octave (first harmonic), which is a position where the student does not feel vibrations with the finger. This exercise should be repeated on all four strings using fourth, third, second then first fingers for violin and viola, and third, second, first, and thumb for cellos and basses (this introduces the thumb to the low strings in preparation for thumb positions). Second position provides an excellent introduction to harmonics.

Advantages of this "harmonic" approach are that it includes ear training, teaches a relaxed left hand (avoiding a death grip that can develop if the student stays in first position for weeks or months), uses much of the fingerboard to prepare for shifting, and instills the feeling of relaxation throughout the body. The left-hand's position for the first harmonic is also an easier place to hold the violin and viola than the first position.

Continuing to play by rote and "from memory" is important. Playing the instrument in guitar position, without the bow, and by rote promotes the habit of listening carefully to one's own performance. Students should be expected to play a large number of familiar and unfamiliar songs "by ear," always listening carefully and deciding what could be improved. Playing by ear enables students to focus on intonation, rhythm, and when playing with others, balance and blend.

When the bow is introduced, students should continue to practice playing by ear Notation is also introduced early conveying the idea that all musicians play by ear *and* with notation. The notation should never interfere with developing the ear. Likewise, playing by ear should not promote inexact performance from notation. Both skills are critical; a well-developed ear allows one to hear notes mentally before they are played and make immediate adjustment with a piano or ensemble. Examples of harmonic exercises are in Figure 19–8.

Figure 19–8 String Harmonic Exercises (notated for violin)

Shifting

Shifting refers to transporting the left arm and hand in order to place fingers in a new position. Shifting is used for key changes, modes, tone color, and playing passages that are awkward in one position. Early shifting is recommended as it facilitates a flexible left hand, eliminates a tense grip on the neck, and promotes a free left arm.

Students are reluctant to shift when the method book contains too much material in first position or they fear faulty intonation. When learning to shift is delayed, shifts are often jerky and students usually stop the bow between shifts. With the initial "ear approach" to string playing, shifting "games" are suggested. Paul Rolland called his shifting game "ghosting," as the sound obtained by students moving their left hand up and down the fingerboard sounded eerie.

Shifting may be introduced on each string instrument through harmonics which develops a fluid and relaxed left hand and thumb. This relaxed, flexible left arm/hand approach should help convey the importance of a relaxed right bow arm and hand.

In shifting, the thumb needs to be flexible. When shifting down, the thumb leads, preceding the hand and leaning into the direction of the shift. Regardless of whether the shift is up or down, the thumb and wrist both lean in the direction of the new position. The player anticipates the shift by leading with the arm, moving the thumb along the neck, and sliding the fingers into the new position. Cello and bass players also shift when playing in thumb position. Whenever a shift is performed, the player must steal from the duration of a note as a shift takes time. The decision whether to cheat the last note of the old position or the first note of the new position, depends on the musical context.

The string pedagogue Jerrie Lucktenburg has simplified the teaching of shifting by placing shifts in three categories:

1. Shifting on one finger
2. Changing fingering from a lower-numbered finger to a higher-numbered finger
3. Changing fingering from a higher-numbered finger to a lower-numbered finger

One choice a student must make is which finger to use to slide to the new note on a shift. Using Lucktenburg's categories, category 1 offers no choice. Category 3 always follows the rule that upward and downward shifts are on the lower-numbered finger. Category 2 is more complicated: The shift is made on the "old finger" for Baroque and Classical music, whereas Romantic music calls for upward shifts to use the "new finger" and downward shifts to use the "old finger."

When bow changes accompany shifts, students may stop the bow completely. For shifting with a bow change, the rule is that "new finger" shifts are made after the bow changes direction and "old finger" shifts occur during old bow direction. When the left-hand shifts take place with a new bow, they are usually accomplished closer to the tip of the bow.

Finger Action

The fingers of the left hand determine the pitch of notes other than the pitch produced by the open strings. Markers on the fingerboard indicate where to place the fingers is a teaching device to indicate approximate pitches. Rather than hindering listening, markers enhance the ear by encouraging confidence in the playing of octaves and other intervals. Interval practice begins with the interval of a fourth on the string bass and chord tones on the other string instruments. The student obtains a mental image of the intervals and then matches the image with his performance. The mental image must initially be checked frequently by the teacher or with an in-tune piano or other device. There is an eventual element of artistry in the use of the left-hand fingers as there is in all aspects of string performance. The string must be depressed sufficiently to produce a clear tone yet the finger and left forearm remain relaxed. Excessive finger pressure contributes to tension in the left hand, tension that often seeps into the wrist, arm, and elbow, and throughout the body. Not only must the strings be touched in a fluid, artistic manner, the release is equally important. Fewer motions are more unmusical than a string bass player releasing all fingers at the same time.

Physical

Although problems of tension have been mentioned, there cannot be an overemphasis on the physical aspects of string playing. String instruments are simple to play so that any challenge to performance excellence results from either an untrained ear or failure to understand human physiology and how the muscles of the body need to be used to perform technically demanding music. Correct breathing is often ignored. Adequate string performance is a head to toe operation; failure to understand the interrelationships of the body parts (more than simply the muscles) will result in not only awkward performance but also possibly actual pain. More musicians have physical injuries than do athletes, although admittedly on a different scale. Learning to play a string instrument well requires constant observation by the player, his teacher, and interested others for signs of tension and/or lack of freedom of motion. Although it may seem strange to hear string teachers suggest that one plays from the center of the body or from the head, these concepts make sense. A physical emphasis in string pedagogue has been present in the literature since at least the time of Carl Flesch, but its importance and complexity have increased with the increased knowledge in physiology.

Because slouching and bad posture are related to playing while seated, violin, viola, and bass players should practice some or all of the time standing, as standing is the most natural, free playing position. With all string instruments the elbows move freely and are away from the body. One should be able to flex toes, knees, elbows, and more without affecting one's performance.

Double Stops

A double stop is produced by simultaneously bowing across two adjacent strings. Double stops appear regularly in solo and ensemble literature for violin, viola and cello. Basses seldom see double stops and when required they are usually played divisi.

The bottom note of any double stop is the dominant pitch in forming the interval. Major and minor thirds and sixths, in which one of the two notes is an open string, are the most frequently written double stops and easily played on violin, viola and cello. Fingered thirds and perfect fifths, without an open string, are deceptively difficult to play in tune.

Two difficulties in playing double stops are (1) fitting the fingers in the physical space required by the interval and (2) bowing as more bowing precision is required to play two notes evenly and together.

Playing string instruments may require more physical energy than the winds and percussion, as there must be musical intensity with minimum or no tension in any muscle in the body. Locked knees when standing or an awkward posture while sitting affects not only the technique but also the sounds produced.

RIGHT-ARM AND HAND MOVEMENT

The Bow

The right hand guides and pulls the bow. Position and freedom of motion are both important. Since most tunes in beginning string methods could be executed by holding the bow like a baseball bat, bad habits are easily formed.

The bow is held with a light touch and a relaxed right arm and hand. The bow is initially close to the bridge with a light feeling. The first and second fingers may contact the bow stick at various points depending upon the tonal intensity desired and what seems natural for the player's fingers. A technique to get in the habit of correct right hand positon is to use a cardboard tube or special device to control the horizontal movement. Practicing in front of a mirror is always recommended.

Paul Rolland advocated a changeable bow hold, with beginners using a higher bow hold to compensate for the bow's weight, especially when it is lifted from the strings. As the muscles strengthen, the hand gradually moves to the position pictured in Figure 19–9. When playing, the weight of the bow should not produce tension as it is supported by the strings, not the arm or wrist. When playing near the frog, the bow is controlled by the second and third fingers, the fourth finger for violin and viola being on top of the stick. When playing in the middle of the bow, the forearm and wrist are straight. When playing at the tip of the bow, the wrist is relaxed but rotated slightly downward. In all three positions the hand and two fingers move naturally to provide balance for the bow. Movement is through the large muscles—shoulder to elbow to wrist.

Figure 19–9
Correct Bow Hold for Violin

The bow hold changes as it crosses strings so the hand position will vary slightly depending upon the string being played. Crossing strings is a smooth operation, rolling the arm and bow together. Bass players think of reaching out as they "roll" to a higher string.

The bow draws the tone from the string. The basic motion is either down or up bow (with notation as ⊓ and V , respectively) alternating for each note unless otherwise indicated, such as a slur or other specifically notated bowings.

The three factors essential to perform dynamics with good tone are (1) the placement of the bow (contact point) on the string, (2) the weight of the bow on the string (as controlled by the right shoulder and arm,) and (3) the speed of the bow. They are not mutually exclusive as increased weight applied to the bow may require moving the bow closer to the bridge and vice versa, exact bow placement differing slightly by instrument.

The tilt of the bow is a fourth factor. In order to maintain the same volume level and the same tone quality throughout the duration of a long note, the bow is held flatter to enable more hair to contact the string. Lower string instruments use a flatter bow.

BOWING

Emphasis should be placed on use of the full bow to "pull" the tone from the string. With beginners, however, the full bow is often overemphasized, resulting in tension. Initially short rhythm patterns should be played on open strings. Students with short arms should use one-half or two-thirds of the bow to ensure correct posture. Common problems are touching a second string and maintaining a parallel bow. The use of initial bow strokes on two adjacent strings (a double stop) is a useful way to help keep the bow stroke prependicular to the strings. The right elbow should straighten on a long down-bow with the wrist remaining flexible as the hand travels slightly away from the body.

Speed, Weight, and Point of Contact

Speed and weight of the bow, (in addition to having a quality instrument), are the chief ingredients of tone, though by no means the only ones. Too much weight of the bow on the string can produce a scratchy, dull sound because the upper overtones are suppressed, and excess pressure, coupled with too slow a speed on the upper strings, will make a raspy, harsh tone, extremely unpleasant in quality. Weight has more affect on tone as one plays closer to the frog unless the weight of the bow is reduced as it nears the frog. To improve tone quality ease bow weight, appropriately increase the speed (usually), or shift the point of contact on the string. A scratchy tone may also be due to the bow not being at right angles to the string. Opposite tonal problems arise from the reverse bowing faults. If too little bow weight is applied to the string, coupled with a fast bow or playing too far from the finger board, the tone will be hoarse and thin because of the lack of the fundamental. (*Sul tasto* bowing over the fingerboard, of course, calls for just this type of fast, light bowing.) To correct a thin tone, increase bow weight, slow the speed, or play nearer the fingerboard. Volume of tone depends upon a good-quality instrument and bow speed—the faster the bow, the greater the sound produced. For this reason, a short forte note may use more bow than a short *piano* note. Louder tones are played nearer the bridge, softer tones nearer the fingerboard. Because using the bow near the bridge requires more weight, this weight is inextricably involved in volume though it is less a factor than speed.

A full bow produces the best sound on the violin, so teachers encourage students to use a full bow as early and often as feasible. For beginners, however, this procedure may result in too fast a bow. The full bow technique for expression is not applicable to cello or bass even though the bows are shorter. For comparable effects the bass player uses about one-half the bow length and the cellist about two-thirds the length.

Dynamics

The downbow results in a natural decrescendo, the upbow a natural crescendo. Because the bow is heavier at the frog and lighter at the tip, more weight must be exerted in the tip area if the sound is to stay constant. The listener wants to hear constant intensity throughout the length of any note, requiring the rate of change to be greater near the frog. This rate of change explains why intelligent use of the bow is so difficult to master and why so many students are prone to avoid it. The weight on the bow is from the whole arm, not the fingers alone, but the arm weight is transferred to the bow through the fingers, especially the index finger. At times, however, the second, third, and fourth fingers are also used to increase bow weight depending on the section fo the bow being used.

Loudness is affected by increased speed and weight, the amount of hair on the string, and placing the bow closer to the bridge. Too much weight will cause the tone to crack. Too fast a bow will produce a surface tone, as will moving the bow too close to the bridge. Good tone quality on a quality instrument is produced by the friction of the stroke—the right proportion of bow speed and bow weight on the string. Friction is increased by slowing the speed of the stroke and applying greater weight. The position of the bow is also a factor; it must be at the right contact point between the bridge and fingerboard and tilted at the correct angle so that the appropriate amount of hair contacts the string. The tension of the bow hair itself has an effect on the tone quality.

When the left hand shifts to a new position, the bow also moves slightly in the same direction in order to keep the same proportion of the string vibrating.

Arm weight is increased by rolling the forearm in toward the body. Speeding up or slowing down the bow on a single note affects both tone and volume unless the player changes his speed at the tip where more bow is needed, or at the frog where less is required. To keep an even tone quality and volume, different speed and weight are needed not only for upbow and downbow, but also for the different strings. On the higher strings and in the higher positions, bow speed should generally be greater. The heavier strings require more weight and less speed.

Attacks and releases are an important part of bow technique. There are at least two general methods of initiating sound: the attack and the touch. The attack is produced by placing the bow on the string in advance with weight at the instant the bow initiates motion; this method is called *martelé* (also for chords). The touch attack is produced by setting the bow in motion before the final weight is applied; the bow is pressed down rather gently to begin the tone. To assist with the release a somewhat circular motion of the arm and bow is necessary if an attack and release are not to be abrupt and awkward. It is a figure-eight motion with its principal characteristic not the figure it makes but the smooth turning movement at the beginning and closing of the phrase. If the release comes at the tip of the bow, the player may perform it smoothly by slowing down, changing the balance from the index to the middle two fingers, and letting the bow drift noiselessly toward the fingerboard.

Position of Bow on String

The bow must be drawn straight across the string to help keep the intensity constant and maximize the bow's function. To counteract the tendency to pull the bow clockwise, the player should push the right wrist outward to keep the bow straight. The general rule is that the hair is at right angles to the string and the bow is about halfway between the bridge and the fingerboard, with variations for the lower strings—and lower string instruments (Figure 19–10). When bowing at the tip, the first finger is firmly on the bow; at the frog, the third and fourth fingers do the work, almost lifting up on the bow. The middle area between bridge and fingerboard is used for most playing; here the bow can be moved fairly rapidly with medium to high weight, or slowly with low or medium weight, without changing the tone quality.

Figure 19–10
**Violin: Bow at Right Angle
to Strings**

The slant of the hairs on the string must not be confused with the angle of the entire bow. As the bow moves perpendicularly, it may be flat enabling all the bow hair to touch the string, or it may be tilted. Cello and bass players use a flat bow most of the time. The full hair of the bow is used most of the time, particularly in the upper half of the bow close to the frog it is desirable to use less hair since the bow is stiffer. More hair is used on the lower strings than on the higher; more is used for *forte* and *fortissimo* than for *piano* and *pianissimo;* more is used at the tip than at the frog. Lower string instruments with shorter bows use bow weight as a major factor for dynamics as their bowing is generally flat. The full hair is used for a bouncing bow with the bouncing motion reduced by tilting the bow. A more brilliant tone is produced with the edge of the bow hair, which favors the higher partials, and conversely a more mellow sound results from more hair on the bow.

Abrupt stopping and starting of the bow within a phrase is unmusical; a new stroke is begun by the arm before the hand and wrist have brought the bow to the conclusion of its present motion—the arm begins to move into the up-bow just as the down-bow is being completed so that the motion is continuous and smooth. The elbow is held out enough to help create the flowing movement, but not so far as to create tension. The motion of the forearm does not cease until the end of the phrase and a follow-through motion. The continual curving motion means that the down-and up-bows move on different planes; to stay on the same plane would require a complete halt and a shift to the opposite direction, creating a dead spot in the string. The point of contact on the string generally does not change, but the angle of the bow does, except in shifting, gradual dynamic changes, and other technical and expressive requirements. The pedagogue Lynn Harrell claims he never thinks about the contact point, but listens and allows the bow to move where the music sounds most effective.

Some writers advocate using as little shoulder movement as possible; others suggest that a rotary motion in the shoulder will make for a smoother bowing action. The wrist is more flexible in fast bowings, but the action still originates in the body—through the shoulder, upper arm, forearm, and wrist. The tendency to tense the upper arm while playing fast notes, in an effort to exert more energy to the wrist, must be avoided.

Because a beautiful tone is the ultimate goal of fine string playing a brief summary of the factors and determinants of beautiful tone is appropriate.

Tone comes from a combination of articulation of fingers and bow, quality of attack and release, finger application, vibrato, proper point of contact, control of bow speed, quality of the instrument, condition of the bow hair, quantity of rosin on the string, and the acoustics of the room. A harsh tone is produced by too much bow weight, too slow or tired bowing, or the bow placed too near the bridge, or a thin tone is caused by insufficient bow weight, the bow placed too close to the fingerboard, or the bow moved too rapidly in relation to the weight applied.

The overriding factor is relaxation; the whole body must maintain good posture and remain tension free. If one part of the arm or hand is stiff, it is nearly impossible for the rest of the playing mechanisms to be relaxed.

Bowings/Articulations

Bowings are a lifetime study, individual and orchestral. Each can and should be practiced on each of the string instruments.

Abbreviations are used to define six divisions of the bow:

W.B.—Whole bow   Pt.—Point (upper third)
U.H.—Upper half (lightest part)   M.—Middle (middle third)
L.H.—Lower half (heaviest part)   Fr.—Frog (lower third)

Dynamic levels are generally altered by one or more of several techniques:

To play louder:
- Increase the focus (allow more bow hair to pull the string).
- Add more bow weight.
- Use a faster bow speed.
- Move bow closer to the bridge and with more focus on the core sound.

To play softer, opposite actions are required including using less bow weight and a faster bow (floutando).

Détaché Alternating down-bow and up-bow for each note is *détaché,* the most commonly used bowing. Bow direction is alternated smoothly for each note (Figure 19-11).

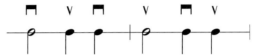

Figure 19–11   Bow Markings for *Détaché*

In order to play this passage smoothly and with the same dynamic level, start at the frog and play the first note $\frac{1}{2}$ down-bow, up $\frac{1}{4}$ bow, and the last note of the first measure $\frac{1}{4}$ down-bow arriving at the starting point. The second measure would be up bow using $\frac{1}{2}$ bow, then down $\frac{1}{4}$ bow, and back up $\frac{1}{4}$ bow ending the measure at the middle of the bow. A fuller sound at the same tempo is achieved by doubling the amount of bow used for each note. Changes of direction are done smoothly, without stopping or hesitation.

Staccato Staccato is played with a detached, swift bow movement while leaving the bow on the string. Unlike the *détaché* bowing, there is a brief silence after each note. Alternating bowing direction, the note begins and ends precisely. The area of the bow and speed of the bow are dictated by the dynamic level desired and the note duration (quarter–or eighth note). One uses the upper half of the bow for a softer staccato and closer to the frog for *forte.*

Slurs Slurs between open strings are the most successful way to introduce playing two notes without a change in bow direction. Any part of the bow can be used depending on the music that precedes and what follows the slur (Figure 19–12).

Figure 19–12   Introduction of Slurs

Slurred Staccato and Hooked Bow These techniques are similar to slurs in that the bow moves in the same direction while playing several notes. For slurred staccato, the bow stops between each note to give definition and a slight silence. The first line of Figure 19–13 illustrates an introduction to slurred staccato.

Preparation for hooked bowing is introduced in Figure 19–14 at a slow tempo using meters that the student has previously mastered. Hooked bowing is similar to staccato slurs, but is used most frequently on dotted eighths and sixteenths, or quarter and eighths in 6/8, and is added to avoid distribution problems in *détaché* passages or to unify section bowings.

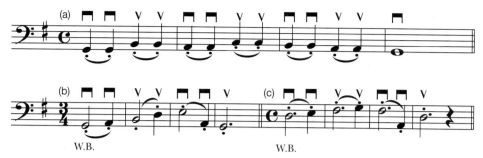

Figure 19–13 **Introduction of Slurred Staccato**

Figure 19–14 **Hooked Bowing**

At an extremely fast tempo, beyond the player's ability to play hooked bow, *détaché* is used.

Spiccato An articulation unique to strings is *spiccato*. This technique uses the right arm, wrist, and fingers to bounce the bow on the string in either a brushing or crisp motion. It is normally played at the middle of the bow and alternates direction for each note. Figure 19–15 illustrates spiccato notation.

Rolland suggests that an unhurried bouncing of the bow on a string is the best preparation for spiccato. Letting the bow bounce on the string helps to develop balance and control of the bow. He also encourages students to hold the bow lightly; there is no need to grasp the bow tightly.[1]

Figure 19–15 **Introduction of Spiccato**

Tremolo Tremolo is executed by playing alternating down-and up-bows very rapidly using only a small amount of bow. Tremolo is notated ♪ ♪ . It is played near the tip of the bow.

Marcato and Martélé Marcato is used to refer to the style of the music itself whereas *martélé* refers to the bowing used to achieve a marcato style. It is notated with the term, the abbreviation for marcato, or the house top accent mark: ▲ ▲

Martélé is like a heavy staccato bowing and seldom is used in soft passages. Bow weight is increased just before the bow moves, then immediately reduced.

Portato Also called *louré*, portato is used to play several notes with the bow moving in the same direction. Portato differs from slurred notes and slurred staccato in

---

[1] Paul Rolland (1990), *Basic Principles of Violin Playing*, American String Teachers Association, Reston, VA: Music Educators National Conference.

that there is a definite "beginning" to each note, but each note is held as long as possible. This is achieved by giving slightly more weight to the longer note. Portato is notated in Figure 19–16.

Figure 19–16 Introduction to Portato

Advanced Bowings A complete list of terms for bowings and string articulations would easily comprise an entire chapter in itself. Several sources are included in the end-of-the-chapter bibliography. Some of the more commonly encountered bowings are:

1. *Détaché lancé*—a very slight separation between notes, but without an accent.

2. *Détaché porté*—a light swelling produced at the beginning of the note, followed by a diminuendo at the end. Similar to *louré*, but separate bows rather than the same bow are used for each of the notes in the passage.

3. *Collé*—detached notes produced with very short strokes near the frog. The bow digs in, not heavily, but suddenly.

4. *Sautillé*—a springing stroke resembling a very rapid spiccato but used at faster tempos than when spiccato is used. The bow stroke is rapid and short, and played near the balance point of the bow, allowing the natural bounce of the bow to provide the articulation. Speed is controlled by the movement of the hand and wrist.

5. *Staccato volante* (or flying staccato)—marked like a slurred staccato is used in fast tempos. The bow is placed on the string and allowed to bounce as a series of notes are articulated in a single bow stroke. It is easier to perform in the up-bow direction than the down-bow direction but both are required. Weight in the arm or hand is alternately applied and released through the bow in a "trembling" motion.

6. *Ricochet*—unlike staccato volante, which starts with the bow on the string, the bow is dropped from above the string and allowed to bounce. This can be done only with the down-bow stroke and rarely involves more than two or three notes at a time. Speed is regulated by the bow's position.

7. *Fouetta* (or whipped bow)—produced near the tip or point, usually with an up-bow. After a down-bow, the bow is lifted slightly off the string and comes down with a fast, energetic attack.

8. *Col legno*—striking the string with the wooden part of the stick rather than the hair. It is a special effect usually used for rhythmic ostinatos.

9. *Ponticello*—the bow is placed very near the bridge. Light, swift strokes produce a tone with many of the upper partials and a weak fundamental.

10. *Sul tasto*—bowed over the fingerboard, the result is a soft, "dark," "wooden flute" tone quality. It is sometimes referred to as "flautando."

Jazz

Jazz performance can and should be in everyone's repertoire. Jazz musicians do not consciously violate any of the physical performance concepts of any of the instruments, and jazz string players are well aware of the consequence of failure to play relaxed. The importance of teaching jazz is that it requires the players to listen carefully to themselves and others. They start early (at the first lesson perhaps) and make improvisation part of their daily practice. Improvisation may start with the open strings unless instruction begins in third position and continues as notes and rhythms are learned. Students can take turns, leading an echo, or playing an improvised phrase over an ostinato.

Suzuki

No discussion of strings would be complete without reference to the methodology of Shinichi Suzuki. Suzuki may be no more important than Dorothy Delay or Paul Rolland, but his ideas on string (and wind) performance have become a baseline for discussion.

Suzuki's basic principles are twofold: Ear training which is accompanied by intensive and continuous listening beginning at birth and a building block approach to skill development. In a building block pedagogy, one skill at a time is mastered. When a second skill is added, the two skills are practiced together. First skills are continuously reinforced in the context of the newer and more advanced competencies. Suzuki would suggest a sequence of exposure, imitation, encouragement, repetition, addition, and finally improvement and refinement.

The Suzuki method is particularly attractive to contemporary music educators in that it makes use of continuous evolving and improvisation. Basic to the method is the concept that all children can learn to play a musical instrument.

Perkins describes five characteristics associated with Suzuki.

The Mother-Tongue Approach All children are born with the same capacity to learn music as to learn their native language. Language is learned primarily from parents through exposure, imitation, and repetition. The mother-tongue approach does not begin at age three with the first string instruction; it beings at birth with focused listening.

Environmental Condition Parents play a critical role in the Suzuki method. He advocates an explicit partnership between the student, parents, and teachers for learning. The parent or, in extreme situations, a sibling is to learn the instrument first. The imitation between mother and child is important for learning on an instrument, as for learning one's own language. Most learning is from the family, not the teacher. Learning is a pleasurable game with instruction beginning only when the child asks to try. He is given an imitation instrument (box) and bow to play with while the mother is playing her instrument. When he receives his instrument, careful review of what he has learned on the pre-instrument is conducted.

Tone and Life Tone development is emphasized in the belief that tone is a clear projection of the "inner voice" and a manifestation of the "living soul"; the struggle to improve tone quality parallels the growth of individual character. The Suzuki principles transfer to many of life's activities. Praise is an important concept and blame for errors not assigned. Praise is important to assist a child in recognizing that music and life have goals, the musical goals being intermediate or short-term goals. Goals are matched to a child's attention span, Suzuki claiming to have given a lesson as short as 30 seconds. An idealist, Suzuki expects his students to become finer human beings as a result of their musical experiences.[2]

In Japan, note reading is introduced gradually when students begin Book Four at age seven or eight. Music reading does not receive the attention in the Japanese version that it has in the United States, as Japanese students learn to read music in their school music classes.

Music reading is introduced to beginners through a combination of activities derived from Dalcroze, eurhythmics, and Kodaly, initially away from the instrument. In the *Suzuki Violin Method*, Book One, students sing pitches using syllables while clapping, walking, running, swinging their arms, miming bowing movements, shaking hands, and jumping in rhythm and introduced to notation earlier than in Japan. Further, students are expected to listen to a specific set of recordings to enhance ear training, and absorb expressive playing from performing artists or ensembles.

Suzuki created the present 10 volumes of the *Suzuki Violin Method* by assembling a collection of music, chosen for its musical validity and its appeal to children. Each selection has been "child tested." A new teaching point is introduced in nearly each piece, moving from the simple to the complex. Music is not used in Japanese lessons; students are required to memorize each piece, review frequently, and refine each piece until it becomes a part of their personal repertoire. In the United States notation is gradually introduced with emphasis retained on the ear. Few scales, exercises, or etudes are found in any of the 10 volumes. American Suzuki has added scales, shifting exercises, string crossings, and similar exercises as an addendum to the bowing exercises retaining the emphasis on tone quality. The curriculum is sequential and fixed.

Suzuki's ideas are based on research results from his institute on how children learn, not on how they learn music. The student is to become his own teacher.

Breathing and Body Movements   Tone as a result of proper bowing is continually stressed. Students can explain how the bow hair sets the string in motion and how bowing can change the tone. Short but carefully crafted bows are used with the student advancing to full bow. Breathing and body movements are necessary for musical expression—all stem from an inseparable spiritual base. He instructs students to "breathe life" into their performance to produce a "tone with a living soul."[3] Suzuki does not, however, provide information for breathing (e.g., inhaling with up-bow's and exhaling with down-bows). While the primary stance is centered over the left foot, he encourages small movement of the right foot. Altering the weight results in many Suzuki students moving naturally and subtly with the music.

Developing Musical Sensitivity   Developing musical sensitivity is achieved in a number of ways in the Suzuki Method. In addition to listening to recordings of the great violinists, constant repetition, and refinement of the standardized repertoire, students play variations on well-known tunes stimulating their musical imagination. Physical problems are minimized—high bow hold, tunes on the E string, and relaxation exercises are important. Contrary to other methods, the student is secure in bowing on the open strings before the left hand is introduced. Quality of bowed sound is of the essence. When the left hand is introduced, three fingers are employed simultaneously to reinforce proper left hand position.

Suzuki, interestingly, is aware of the Japanese emphasis on social conformity; consequently, he recognizes how a method can stifle creativity. He continued to

---

[2] M. M. Perkins (1995), *A Comparison of Violin Playing Techniques*, Bloomington, IN: A.S.T.A., pp. 131–132.
[3] Ibid., p. 166.

learn and grow throughout his long life—reducing the possibility of the method becoming a stagnant cult. He has written much about how the development of the whole child will assist in fostering intuition, the root of creativity.

CARE AND MAINTENANCE OF INSTRUMENTS AND BOWS

Rosin dust will fall from the bow during practice or rehearsal. Because rosin is an abrasive, the dust should be gently wiped off the body of the string instrument and bow stick with a soft cloth. If rosin becomes caked on the instrument or bow, have a string repairperson remove it.

The body of the instrument can be polished a few times a year with a commercial polish *made for string instruments* that is available from most string instrument retailers or manufacturers. Continued handling of a string instrument's body will eventually eat through the varnish. Do not let students use commercial furniture polish, even if it does smell better.

The instrument is better protected if there are adequate storage facilities with temperature and humidity controls. Portable racks for cellos and basses are one solution if instruments must remain in the rehearsal space. Bows and instruments have their place, a place off limits to music, books, lunches, and extra tennis shoes.

Hair

The bow hair wears down each time the bow is used. With metal strings, the hair will wear out fairly rapidly. Worn hair does not hold rosin well and a clear, full tone becomes difficult to produce. This change can be so gradual that the student does not notice the change. Further, as the student develops, her bow strokes may improve at a pace matching the decline of the condition of the bow hair, so that there is a seeming lack of improvement in tone quality. The bow hair needs to be inspected and replaced at least once a year.

Frequently, a single hair or two will come loose from one end of the bow. The hair(s) is removed by cutting with scissors or a nail clipper. Although students delight in using their teeth to yank out these hairs, the bow can be damaged unless the yank is sophisticated.

STRING TROUBLESHOOTING

Physical Problems

Body

Buzzes and rattles

1. Items inside or touching instrument.
2. A loose tuner (screwing it back on tightly.)
3. A loose chinrest (special chinrest tool or paperclip in a pinch).
4. Tailpiece contacting the chinrest.
5. Loose purfling.
6. End of string in peg box rattling against something.
7. Cracks or open seams.
8. Loose screw on endpin, or endpin itself.

Endpin does not hold or set

1. Endpin must be sharp or holder provided.
2. The restrainer is broken or twisted so the thumbscrew cannot reach the endpin. (Broken restrainers and thumbscrews must be repaired by competent repairperson.)

Strings

Strings break or are difficult to tune

1. String breaks at bridge. Bridge notch may be too narrow, or bridge has been planed so thin it cuts the string. Have bridge re-cut or replaced.
2. String breaks at nut. Notch is cut too narrow and string is pinched.

3. Gut and wound strings are difficult to tune.(Loosen string, remove from notch, and run lead [graphite] pencil in the notch several times. If unsuccessful see competent string repairperson.)

Gut strings

1. Frayed, particularly where fingers frequently touch the strings. (Snip off the frayed pieces if there is ample string.)

Wound strings

1. Winding separates or breaks and unwinds, due to flawed string, sharp edge on nut, fingernails too long, or simply wear. (Correct cause, replace string.)

False string

1. Gives off irregular vibrations sounding overtones more than the fundamental. (Replace string.)

Bow

Difficult to loosen or tighten

1. Bow hair too short or too long or threads on bow screw stripped. (Have repaired.)

Individual or "hunks" of hair pull from tip

1. Individual hairs indicate a problem with knot or bonding of hair at tip. Larger portions indicate a loose bonding of hair at tip of bow. (Rehair. If the problem remains, exchange bow or replace.)

Bow becomes warped

1. Failure to loosen bow after playing. (Repairperson can reshape fiberglass.)
2. Uneven distribution of hair. (Rehair bow.)

Tip breaks

1. Faulty grain in wood or a damaged tip. (Replace.)

Bowing

Difficulty in smoothly manipulating the bow

1. Thumb is inserted too far through the bow.
2. Thumb bends in instead of out.
3. Thumb is positioned too far from frog.
4. The fingers are spread too far apart. Move closer together, maintain relaxation.
5. Little finger is flat instead of curved. Instrument and/or bow too large. Place finger in correct position.
6. Change the angle of the bow to the string through the rise and fall of the wrist and the inward pull of the ring finger.

Difficulty in changing bow styles

1. Instrument is held too high or too low.

Finger facility is hampered and shifting is too slow

1. Arm is held too far to the left putting the fingers in an awkward position and creating problems in shifting. (Encourage the student to make the elbow mobile.)
2. Instrument resting too low in crotch of hand between thumb and index finger. (Base of index finger should be the contact point with the neck of the instrument.)
3. The left wrist is bent in so that it touches the neck of the instrument, which slows the shifting fingers.
4. The left wrist is bent too far outward, straining the wrist and forearm.

Bow direction or change

1. Place bow on the string with sufficient pressure.
2. Slow bow speed and weight prior to change, lift weight more at change, and follow through: The arm and elbow change direction first, then the wrist, then fingers and bow. Avoid rigid bow hold or wrist.
3. Nonlegato connection of bow use a slightly circular path with the frog circling toward the player at the change of direction.
4. Curve the fingers in when reaching the frog and stretch them back out toward the tip.

String crossings

1. Prepare bow by moving near the new string.

Poor détaché bowing

1. Emphasize release in initial movement coasting to a gradual stop. (Lift bow on approaching the frog on the up-bow.)
2. Increase bow weight and weight of the thumb.
3. Tension in the bow arm. Relax.

Spiccato

1. Reluctance to relinquish control over the bow. (Lighten bow hold and the rotary motion of forearm.)

Intonation

Out-of-tune notes

1. Vocalize scales, arpeggios, and melodic passages; overreliance on finger placement aids; poor initial tuning; relying on kinesthetic feel rather than ear.
2. Playing too fast. (Encourage listening.)
3. Awkward left-hand position, preventing the natural dropping of the finger. (Adjust hand position based on physical characteristics.)
4. Poor orientation of the fingers to conform to the contour of the neck and fingerboard. Mold

hand to proper finger position. Use finger aids such as pencil marks or small stickers on the fingerboard.

6. Poor concept of tonality in general and finger patterns in particular. Increase instruction in scales, interval spacing, and multiple strings.

7. Poor concept of distances when shifting. Loosen the finger contact points.

8. Inability to match pitches. Practice vocalizing scales, and sight singing.)

9. Inability to improve resonance and clarity. Adjust pitch to achieve maximum resonance.

Tone Quality

Thin and small

1. Failure to draw bow parallel to strings.
2. Lack of rosin on bow.
3. Failure to "pull" sound from string.
4. Lack of knowledge of the relationship of bow speed, point of contact, and bow weight. Have students play whole notes while changing one of these variables and compensating by altering the other two.
5. Keep elbow high in the upper half of the bow, weight to string.
6. Unbalanced or unmatched quality of strings. Use less pressure or replace.

Limited dynamic range

1. Check relationship of bow to string.

Shallow tone, sluggish response

1. Use more left-hand finger pressure.
2. Use more bow weight and rotate forearm.

Shifting

Jerky or not smooth

1. Allow fingers to lead hand to new position. Focus attention on closing motion of elbow and a leading or anticipatory motion by the arm.
2. Lighten the contact points. Anticipate finger movements by a slight arm movement.
3. Unnecessary accents. (Decrease the bow speed and bow weight during the shift by a slight right arm motion.
4. Pulling string out of line. (Practice following the string direction; watch for tendency to push string to the left.)
5. Loss of balance of hand en route to new position. (Give attention to contour of hand position.)
6. Speed of shift is inappropriate to speed of passage. (Make appropriate adjustment.)
7. Failure to move out and over the ribs of the instrument when shifting above third position.
8. Out-of-tune shifting. (Play in same position.)

Vibrato

Irregular

1. Locking hand to instrument's neck. (Release support of hand, usually base of first finger and/or thumb.)
2. Irregular or convulsive pulsations: tension in the left arm.
3. Attempting to vibrate at right angle to string. (Slide finger up and down the string to reinforce orientation. Compel the first joint of the finger to move with the hand.)
4. Excessive arm vibrato. (Useful for double stops, particularly octaves, arm vibrato can be controlled by third-position practice.)

Low String Instruments

1. Distance shifting. Requires lightness of movement.
2. Use open strings and harmonics for quicker shifts.

Left-Hand General Principles

1. Use natural spaces. Don't squeeze the fingers together.
2. Moving the thumb back in thumb position gives the left hand more power.
3. Play with a flat, unbent wrist.
4. Fingers less perpendicular to the fingerboard.
5. Play with the fleshier part, but not with flat fingers.
6. Change fingers by rotating the whole hand.
7. Never stop the movement of the left arm when shifting. During a shift upward, lift the elbow first and as the arm does a natural circle downward in a clockwise motion, release the hand and shift to the note. Use the weight of the arm to move on the fingerboard.
8. When shifting back, let the elbow do a circular motion counterclockwise. As the elbow naturally rebounds upwards, shift back.

Right-Arm General Principles

1. Use weight of the arm to create friction with the bow. Dynamics are produced by changing the amount of weight on bow. Fingertips should be on the top edge of the bridge when transferring weight of arm onto the bridge.
2. Begin bow movement by moving the upper arm first. The elbow anticipates the bow change and leads the bow arm motion.
3. Feel the third and fourth fingers on the bow at the frog, the first finger on the bow at the tip.
4. With fast short bow strokes, move the lower arm.
5. Right elbow higher than the lower arm unless on a lower string.

Upper String Instruments

Technique

Inability to keep elbow centered

1. Instrument is too far left or right.
2. Instrument is held too much at an angle, causing the right elbow to move too low for the top string distorting bow arm. (Correct position.)
3. Instrument held too flat, causing the right elbow to move too high for the low string, distorting the arm, and putting excessive strain on the hand and neck.

Lack of finger dexterity

1. Left arm too close to body.
2. Wrist is collapsed against neck of instrument.
3. Neck has dropped into slot between thumb and forefinger.
4. Fingers should approach strings approximately perpendicular.
5. Thumb gripping neck.
6. Holding left elbow still. (Elbow must rotate to right for lower notes and left for higher notes.)
7. Failure to raise hand higher when moving to lower note. (Reposition curvature of fingers.)

BIBLIOGRAPHY

Texts

* Indicates out of print in 2001.

ALTON, ROBERT (1990). *Violin and Cello Building and Repairing.* Brighton, MI: Native American Book Publishers.

APPLEBAUM, SAMUEL (1986). *The Art and Science of String Performance.* Alfred.

———. & LOUIS B. GORDON (1972–1977). *Applebaum String Method: A Conceptual Approach.* Miami, Belwin-Mills.

*BELWIN-MILLS (1975). *Building Better Strings and Orchestras: A Manual for the String Teacher and Orchestra Director: Including a Complete Guide to the Belwin Course for Strings by Samuel Applebaum,* 4th ed. Melville, NY: Author.

BERMAN, JOEL, BARABRA JACKSON, and KENNETH SARCH (1999). *Dictionary of Bowing and Pizzicato Terms,* 4th ed. American String Teachers Association with National School Orchestra Association. Reston, VA: Music Educators National Conference.

*BOLANDER, JOHN A. (1981). *Violin Bow Making.* San Mateo, CA: B. Poulsen.

*COOK, CLIFFORD A. (1957). *String Teaching and Some Related Topics.* Urbana, IL: American String Teachers Association.

DILLON-KRASS, JACQUELINE, and DOROTHY A. STRAUB (1991). *TIPS: Establishing a String and Orchestra Program.* Reston, VA: Music Educators National Conference.

DONINGTON, ROBERT. (1981). *String Playing in Baroque Music.* New York: Simon and Schuster.

EDWARDS, ARTHUR C. (1985). *Beginning String Class Method: For Violin, Viola, Cello, and Bass,* 4th ed. Dubuque, IA: Wm. C. Brown.

EISELE, MARK J. (1980). *The Writings of Paul Rolland: An Annotated Bibliography and Biographical Sketch.* Reston, VA: American String Teachers Association.

GERLE, ROBERT (1983). *The Art of Practicing the Violin.* London: Stainer and Bell.

———. (1991). *The Art of Bowing Practice.* New York: Schirmer Books.

*GIGANTE, CHARLES (1986). *Manual of Orchestral Bowing.* Bloomington, IN: American String Teachers Association; Frangipani Press.

GOODRICH, KATHLENE and MARY WAGNER (1994). *Getting It Right from the Start: A Guide to Beginning and Maintaining a Successful String Orchestra Program.* American String Teacher Association with National School Orchestra Association. Reston, VA: Music Educators National Conference.

GREEN, ELIZABETH A. H. (1990). *Orchestral Bowings and Routines.* Reston, VA: American String Teachers Association.

———. (1987a). *The Dynamic Orchestra: Principles of Orchestral Performance for Instrumentalists, Conductors, and Audiences.* Upper Saddle River, NJ: Prentice Hall.

———. (1987b). *Teaching Stringed Instrument Classes.* Bloomington, IN: American String Teachers Association.

*HENKLE, TED (1982). *The String Teacher's Handbook.* Cleveland, OH: Ludwig Music.

HUTCHINS, CARLEEN (1976). *Musical Acoustics: Violin Family Functions,* 2 parts. New York: Academic Press.

*HUTTON, TRUMAN (1970). *Basic Bowings for the String Section.* Hollywood, CA: Highland Music.

KLOTMAN, ROBERT H. (1996). *Teaching Strings: Learning to Teach Through Playing,* 2nd ed. New York: Schirmer Books.

KREITMAN, EDWARD (1998). *Teaching from the Balance Point.* Western Springs, IL: Western Springs School of Talent Education.

LAMB, NORMAN, and SUSAN L. COOK (1994). *Guide to Teaching Strings* 6th ed. Dubuque, IA: Brown & Benchmark.

MUSIC EDUCATORS NATIONAL CONFERENCE (1991). *Teaching String Instruments: A Course of Study.* Reston, VA: Music Educators National Conference.

PATERSON, JENNIFER, and JEAN HORSFALL (1995). *Early Days II: A Guide to the First Stages of String Playing.* London: Rhinegold.

RABIN, MARVIN, and PRICILLA SMITH (1990). *Guide to Orchestra Bowings Through Musical Styles; A Manual to Be Used with Video,* rev. ed. Madison, WI: University of Wisconsin, Division of University Outreach.

ROLLAND, PAUL (1990*). Basic Principles of Violin Playing.* American String Teachers Association
_____ MARLA MUTSCHLER, and A. HELLEBRANDT (1974). *The Teaching of Action in String Playing; Violin and Viola,* rev. ed.; revised in 1986 and 2000 by American String Teachers Association; Available through A.S.T.A. of Reston, VA.

*SMITH, G. J. (1973). *Teaching Strings with Paul Rolland.* Reston, VA: National School Orchestra Association.

STRAUB, DOROTHY A., LOUIS BERGONZI, and ANNE C. WITTE (1996). *Strategies for Teaching Strings and Orchestra.* Reston, VA: Music Educators National Conference.

Journals/Associations

Australian String Teachers' Association, 5 Oakridge Road, Aberfoyle Park, S. Australia 5159 Australia.

Association of Canadian Orchestras, 56 The Esplanade, Suite 311, Toronto ON M5E 1A7 Canada.

American String Teachers Association, 1806 Robert Fulton Drive, Suite 300, Reston, VA 22091.

American Symphony Orchestra League, 1156 Fifteenth Street NW, Suite 800, Washington, DC 20005-1704.

Instructional Videos

Shin'ichi Suzuki in Lecture-Demonstrations on the Mother-Tongue Method (1976). Stevens Point, WI: American Suzuki Institute.

The Teaching of Action in String Playing (9 vol.) (Paul Rolland, 1989). Urbana, IL: Rolland String Research Associates (University of Illinois).

20

The Violin

HISTORY

The history of the violin is filled with hundreds of ancestors from dozens of countries. Their common characteristic is a sound produced by means of a stretched string. The most direct precursor of the violin was the vielle. Known by a wide variety of names, the vielles came to Europe from Asia, probably in the ninth century. The vielles dropped their drone string(s), retaining three to five melody strings tuned similarly to those of modern Western stringed instruments.

Scholars continue to debate if the violin was a direct descendent of vielles as both were used widely in fifteenth and sixteenth century Europe. The first non-fretted fingerboard, F-shaped sound holes, and waist are often attributed to Gaspar Tieffenbrucker (actual name Duiffoprugcar), but many authorities hesitate to assign an exact origin. It may be Vuillaume who patterned (1827) the violin on the viola da gamba, but the great instruments were made between the mid seventeenth to mid eighteenth centuries—by Amati, Guarnerius, Stradivarius.

The violin is the soprano member of the string family and is available in $\frac{1}{32}$, $\frac{1}{16}$, $\frac{1}{10}$, $\frac{1}{8}$, $\frac{1}{4}$, $\frac{1}{2}$, $\frac{3}{4}$, and full sizes. All violins have four strings that are tuned as shown in Figure 20–1.

The majority of string students start on violin. Because literature for the violin is plentiful and the instrument itself can be obtained at a price many families can afford, the violin is an ideal beginning instrument.

a   **b**

Figure 20–1
Open strings (a) and Range of the Violin (b)

SELECTING THE VIOLIN

The size of the violin is important for young players, because bad habits result from too large an instrument. Bad bowing positions, poor wrist and finger action, and an incorrect arm position can result when the violin does not fit the player. The correct size is determined by extending the left arm while holding the violin. The fingers should comfortably extend around the scroll with the elbow slightly bent (see Figure 20–2a). When instruction is begun in the primary grades, schools should invest in the smaller sizes so parents do not constantly have to trade to a larger size.

Figure 20–2a
Checking Violin Size (correct size)

Figure 20–2b
Checking Violin Size (too large)

Students should not advance to larger physical instruments until physically ready. If the violin is too large, the arm must stretch uncomfortably to reach first position and the fingers will not be in the correct position on the strings (see Figure 20–2b.). If the violin is too short, the arm will cramp, the left elbow bend excessively and create tension—the major cause of poor violin performance.

Chinrests

The chinrest provides an elevated, contoured surface that enables the performer to lever the violin with the left edge of the jaw. Chinrests are made in many sizes, shapes, and prices to accommodate the many sizes and shapes of jaws, chins, arm lengths, and parents' purses. There are two types of chinrests: one that straddles the tailpiece, and one that clamps to the left of the tailpiece. In either case, the chinrest is for the chin, not the side of the face. It should have a fairly definite ridge at the top and on the side, and otherwise be flat enough to fit the chin. It is made so that it does not rest on the violin body, leaving the body free to vibrate. The chinrest helps the player adjust the instrument to the length of his neck and also protects the wooden body from the sweat and oils of the face.

Rolland suggests the following considerations in selecting a chinrest:

1. A chinrest that has a well-molded back ridge and a contact surface that slopes slightly downward toward the top of the violin. Avoid chinrests that have a surface that rises toward the direction of the scroll.
2. The jawbone should rest far back on the chinrest, its inner arch pulling back against the ridge of the chinrest. The jawbone should cross over the lowest point of the chinrest, at the left side of the ridge.
3. If the player has a large fleshy jaw, she should use a broad, flat chinrest. The player with a long neck requires a higher chinrest. Players with short arms usually like a rest that moves the violin to a position rather high on the shoulder.[1]

Chinrests are mounted over the tailpiece and are either centered directly over the tailpiece or lie to the left of the tailpiece. Those that assist the student in holding the violin to the left of the front of the body are by far the most useful.

If the chinrest touches the tailpiece, an irritating buzz is possible. The chinrest should be padded with cork and securely tightened down with a chinrest tool.

[1]Paul Rolland and Marla Mutschler (1974), *The Teaching of Action in String Playing, Teacher's Manual*, Urbana, IL: Illinois String Research Associates, p. 62.

Shoulder Pads

Shoulder pads are designed to reduce the distance between the back of the violin and the player's left shoulder so that the player doesn't have to move her head down or raise her shoulder—both sources of tension. Shoulder pads for violins are made in dozens of shapes and sizes. Shoulder pads can be constructed from foam rubber that is inexpensive, can be cut to any shape, and can be stacked in multiple layers. Whether to use a shoulder pad is determined by the student's physical characteristics, especially the length of her neck. A pad is needed if the student must move the head or shoulder to "balance" the instrument.

Guitar Position

The banjo or guitar position is one approach to starting beginners, especially very young children. With the guitar position, the student obtains the proper feel of the instrument, can play tunes by fingering with the left hand and plucking (strumming) with the right and if care is given to left-hand finger positions (determined by the angle of the violin) can establish a solid foundation that is unchanged when the instrument is raised to the neck (See Figure 20–3). A great advantage is that this position allows the teacher and student to focus on intonation. The transfer from guitar position to under-the-chin pizzicato playing or use of the bow is natural.

In guitar position, the side of the left thumb and base of the first finger knuckle lightly touch the neck. Well-trimmed fingernails point toward the bridge, not the ceiling. The palm faces the instrument.

Figure 20–3
Violin Held in Guitar Position

HOLDING THE VIOLIN

The violin is held on the left shoulder slightly less than 45 degrees to the front of the body. The end button pin touches the neck. The instrument rests on the inner part of the shoulder close to the neck and over the collarbone. The fingerboard should be nearly parallel with the floor, but will change slightly as the player's technique advances.

To teach the proper holding position, ask the student to stand erect while facing you. The stance should be erect, but relaxed with the feet shoulder width and the left foot slightly forward for balance and the arms in a natural position by the sides. Have her swing her arms, flex her knees to ensure total body relaxation. Place the violin on the shoulder and have the student rotate her head toward the chinrest. The side of the jaw is used as leverage for holding the violin. The palm of her left hand can be placed on her right shoulder, making a "shelf" for the violin and helping to keep the instrument nearly parallel to the floor. The instrument should be balanced between the relaxed shoulder and the relaxed jaw/chin; it is not gripped.

Have the student continue to hold the instrument with the jaw and chin with her line of vision on the scroll. Stand close enough to catch a dropped violin. She should then turn the head slightly, facilitating her view of both the music stand and the teacher.

While holding the violin lightly but securely with the jaw, chin, and shoulder (avoiding tension), have the student bring her left hand to the neck of the violin without changing the hold on the instrument. Check that her teeth are not

Figure 20–4
Correct Position of the Thumb and Hand on the Neck of the Violin

Figure 20–5
Correct Holding Position for Playing Violin While Standing

clenched—avoidance of tension at all steps of instruction is critical to good violin playing. The violin neck is partially supported or at least steadied between the left thumb and the base of the first finger as illustrated in Figure 20–4. The wrist is straight.

The inside thumb is held lightly against the side of the violin neck providing minimal support. The thumb must be free to move and may extend slightly above the neck depending on the length of the student's fingers. The thumb, must not be locked in a rigid position, but must be able to move to maintain the proper posture of the four fingers of the left hand that are over the fingerboard. The violin is taken from the shoulder and held in the lap for rest position.

Common faults in holding a violin include the following:

1. The instrument is angled too far in either direction, causing unnatural movements for the bow arm and for the left arm.
2. The angle of the instrument is too flat; not only does this strain the head and neck, but forces the student to raise her arm inordinately to play on the lowest string.
3. The instrument is held too low or too high; both interfere with left-hand shifting and right-hand bowing.
4. The left elbow is too far to the left; this is awkward for the left fingers and is detrimental to shifting. Finger placement takes precedence over elbow position.
5. The instrument when supported in the "crotch" of the left hand makes good fingering and shifting impossible, as the violin will bounce from excessive movement under the neck.[2]

LEFT-ARM AND HAND MOVEMENTS

The traditional approach to the position of left-hand is often a case of folklore. Apparently the authors of most method books were all taught by a short, pudgy little man who had to have his left elbow as far to the right and under the instrument as possible, in order to place his fingers correctly on the strings. Because this was his greatest problem, he drilled his students on the importance of keeping the left elbow well to the right regardless of how uncomfortable this might be for the six-foot-six guy with long arms (who probably became so uncomfortable in orchestra that he was an easy recruit for basketball). This six-foot-sixer could always play more easily in third position on his violin's G string than in first position on the E string—for good reason. The moral, we hope, is obvious: the position of the left elbow is only important to the extent that it helps the finger position.

[2]Norman Lamb, and Susan Cook (1994), *Guide to Teaching Strings,* 6th ed. Dubuque, IA: Brown & Benchmark; p. 86.

The elbow should be placed where it enables the fingers to fall perpendicularly on the strings in a fairly straight line. The fingers are placed on the string so that the fingernails do not touch the string, but not as far back as the fleshy part used for playing wind instruments. The proper spot is somewhere in between—right at the end of the fingers, fingers that have not been unduly stretched or flattened. The elbow position changes depending on (1) the position being played, (2) the left thumb position, (3) the use of vibrato, (4) shifting, and (5) special effects made by the left hand.

A good check for proper elbow placement is to see where it puts the middle knuckles. These should be approximately level with the fingerboard. If these knuckles get above the level of the fingerboard, the fingers will curve too far and touch the string too close to the fingernail. If they are too low, the weight will fall away from the fingertips creating tension in the hand and fingers. Muscular action will then be impeded and some of the driving force needed to press the string down will be lost. If the hand is high enough, the finger should automatically have as much power as needed to depress the string. It is not a matter of great muscular strength (this is reserved for marching with the string bass), but of posture.

These principles must be modified for players with short arms or hands and individuals with fingers of unusual length. If the little finger is inordinately short, as occasionally happens, more wrist and thumb movement will be necessary when this finger is used, but this change by no means counteracts the need for proper knuckle level. With the average hand, the little finger should fall in line on the strings just like the others.

The hand, wrist, and forearm are usually straight, except when playing in half position; fifth position and above; performing unusual extensions; and double, triple, or quadruple stops. The hand should barely bend at the wrist, either to the side or back and forth. There will be some turning but this should come as a result of changing positions. If the wrist is bent out too much, the first and second fingers may not be affected, but the third and fourth will not be able to obtain the necessary leverage, and the tone quality, especially on the E string, will be ugly. If the hand is turned out too much—that is, if the wrist is turned in, to facilitate the higher strings—the palm of the hand will be flattened, the third and fourth fingers will have some advantage, but the first two fingers will be cramped.

Emphasis should be placed on the idea of an "open" hand. The instrument is never cradled in the palm or crotch of the thumb. The angle of the left-hand fingers changes for different strings. For rapid playing in which large movements of hand and arm are undesirable, the fingers are placed over one of the two middle strings and moved to the other strings by changing the angle of the fingers rather than by moving wrist or elbow.

Third position may be more natural for young students—students who are playing by ear to whom the names of the notes are relatively unimportant. What feels *natural* without tension is key. For players with large hands, the common position is to hold the thumb high, the violin neck near the base of the thumb and below the knuckle of the first finger, but not so low as to rest on the flesh connecting the thumb and forefinger. Too low a thumb for these individuals can make the fingers stiff because it forces the fingers to curve excessively. The opposite thumb position is necessary with short-fingered students; in this case, the thumbnail is placed close to the neck so that the little finger can easily reach the lowest string. With small hands and fingers, the thumb's position may be almost under the neck of the instrument and the wrist held as straight as possible to give the fingers ample flexibility. A low thumb will help to reduce excessive movement for a small hand. The general rule, then, is that a large hand can use a higher thumb than a small hand. If the neck slips into the soft flesh of the palm, the hand position will be too high. Teachers of string instruments adjust positions to fit individual students.

Sufficient finger pressure on the string is imperative for a clear pitch. There must be springy resistance from the string for the bow to function properly. Left-hand support creates this resistance. The fingers of the left hand should not strike the string percussively from directly above because this nearly always results in tension, but drop lightly like springs to maintain relaxed flexibility. Two opinions exist as to the source of the correct pressure: the hand knuckles or the whole arm. These opinions actually complement each other for the action of the knuckles is moved by the fingers, and a strong "push" from this area of the hand produces a good solid feeling on the strings. But this action must be backed up with a relaxed arm that adds to the strength of the hand. There will be little tonal support from the arm unless it is relaxed and free, with the movement originating in the left shoulder and upper arm; a stiff arm will force the player to depend upon her fingers alone for striking the strings. The energy in the finger movement of both hands can actually be traced to the player's back, where the strongest muscles are. This was a primary conclusion in Paul Rolland's research—he found that the energy emanates from the back, through the shoulder, down the upper and lower arms, through the wrist to the fingers. It is essential that all the "connecting" points be free of tension to allow the energy to flow.

In establishing the shape of the hand for any one position, the player should think of a *flexible* "frame." The frame of the hand is that distance between the outside two fingers—first and fourth—that will produce a perfect fourth on one string and an octave interval on two adjacent strings. For example, if the hand has the proper frame in first position on violin, the first finger on the G string will produce A and the fourth finger on the D string (adjacent) will produce A an octave higher. The same frame when used on the violin's D and A strings in first position will produce an octave interval on E. The feeling for this distance will change in the higher positions, but a flexible frame gives the young player a stable interval by which she can judge where to place her fingers. The young player can increase her security of pitch by leaving the first finger down whenever possible—as long as the finger does not become rigid and contribute to tension—and placement of the other fingers can be measured from it. This practice contributes to security, but if used when no longer needed, it inhibits a good vibrato and leads to a stiff hand.

All master string teachers have advocated tension-free playing. When standing, the violinist must maintain flexibility in her knees, legs, hips, and the rest of her body. She must make any adjustments necessary that aid in maintaining freedom to move those parts of the body even while playing. The player should be able to transfer weight from one leg to another, whether she is a beginner playing pizzicato in guitar position or an advanced performer. Violin playing uses nearly all of the muscles in the body, and the movement of one reflects a movement, however slight, in other muscles. Observation of accomplished players reveals a freedom in the legs, body, shoulder, and neck as well as both arms, their hands, and fingers.

RIGHT-ARM AND HAND MOVEMENTS

The Bow Hold

Using both hands the student holds the bow stick near the tip in the left hand and with the right hand on the frog. The teacher then guides the right hand into a proper bow hold (as illustrated in Figures 20–6, 20–7 and 20–8). Difficult to describe in prose: The tip of the thumb is placed on the bottom of the stick with the left side of the thumb touching the grip (or wire) and the right side of the thumb touching the inside, lower edge of the frog. The first joint of the thumb is bent slightly outward. Suzuki teachers allow very small children to place the thumb

Figure 20–6
Correct Hand Position from Front of Bow Hold

Figure 20–7
Correct Hand Position from "Back" of Bow Hold

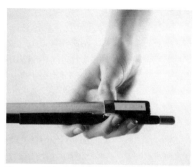

Figure 20–8
Correct Position of "Bottom" of Bow Hold

under the frog. Rolland suggested that young students will initially profit from the high bow hold, 4 inches or more up from the frog. This hold allows the hand to be closer to the balance point.

In a "mature" violin bow hold, the first three fingers curve over the top of the bow with all of the knuckles slanted toward the tip. The first or between the first and second joint of the first (index) finger rests gently on the grip (or wire). The second finger curves over the stick and across the thumb. The third finger curves over the stick. The tip of the little finger is in contact with the top of the bow stick near the third finger. The second and third fingers touch each other while there are spaces between the index and the middle fingers. The space between the fingers is best determined by the individual's hand when it is relaxed and hanging at one's side. As hands differ, so does the spacing of the fingers. All of the fingers should be relaxed and bent.

A common fault among young players is failure to use the lower and upper thirds of the bow although Suzuki advocates short bow strokes. With older players, avoiding the lower third is avoiding the uncomfortable feeling of having to adjust the wrist and lower the right elbow to make use of that portion of the bow. Also, it is more difficult to make a smooth change of direction at the frog, because the wrist is in its most bent position, several inches above the frog, the point that is most natural for young players.

Exercises taught by rote such as the one in Figure 20–9 can be fun when played by the entire class practicing on bowing while keeping the notes simple. This exercise can be played *détaché,* staccato, spiccato, all near the frog (using a circular motion for motion freedom).

then staccato, then spiccato, then...

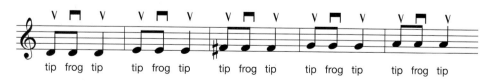

tip frog tip   tip frog tip   tip frog tip   tip frog tip   tip frog tip

then all at frog.

Figure 20–9 Sample Rote Exercises for Proper Intonation and Bowing.

Violin students must be cautious when playing near the frog, as there is a strong tendency for the thumb to cave in, causing tension in the wrist and restricting the wrist from the bending required to keep the bow straight. The natural result is that the violin moves slightly out of position on the shoulder and toward the center of the body, again restricting the natural follow-through of the right arm.

As the Suzuki approach so well illustrates, rote playing for beginners has a number of advantages over starting students with notation. If the student echoes rhythmic and tonal patterns, and learns to make simple music on the instrument by rote, she can concentrate on her bow position movement. For Suzuki, a secure right hand is necessary before the student is taught use of the left hand. Rote learning can teach students to *listen* to the sounds produced.

TUNING

Students should have fine tuners on all four strings. Initially, the student may rest the instrument in her lap and while plucking the string with one hand; turn the fine tuners with the other to obtain the correct pitch. If the pegs are set close to the pitch (perhaps with the help of the teacher), the fine tuners are adequate for these tuning exercises. When the instrument is under the chin, it should not be removed by the teacher to tune. The teacher may occasionally adjust the fine tuners (or the pegs) with the student as a "partner" in deciding when the string is in tune—but some students are quite competent if given the opportunity.

When the student is ready to learn to use the pegs, she rests the base of the violin in her lap with the bridge facing her and, while tuning the peg for the A string with her right thumb and index finger, plucks the string with the left thumb. She continues plucking while turning the peg. The left hand turns the G and D pegs while the right hand plucks the string. The pegs should be turned toward the violinist (to lower the pitch), then raised to the correct pitch while pushing in.

When the student is able to balance the bow on two strings without tension she should tune while bowing the notes with the upper half of the bow and turning the peg or fine tuner with the left hand. It requires practice (and patience on the teacher's part) for the student to learn to tune the A string, then even more practice and *opportunity* to tune the E string to the A.

Figures 20–10a and 2–10b illustrate tuning a violin with the left hand turning the left pegs (G and D strings) then the right pegs (A and E strings).

Figure 20–10a
Tuning G and D Pegs

Figure 20–10b
Tuning A and E Pegs

Figure 20–11
Tuning with Fine Adjusters and Bow

HARMONICS

During the very first lessons, the violinist should play harmonics. These are essential to facilitate getting around on the fingerboard; for ear training; for developing a flexible left hand and thumb; and for developing a relaxed, loose elbow, shoulder blade, and left hand/arm.

In first position, the student should pluck an upper string (D or A for the heterogeneous class) and then touch the string with the fourth finger to produce the second harmonic using finger weight no greater than that of a Ping-Pong ball. Next, the student should be shown how to slide the fourth finger noiselessly on the string lightly toward the bridge to find the same pitch. Then, she should play the open string and slide the fourth (the third, then second, then first) finger up the string to match the octave (first harmonic). Repetition, alternating pizzicato and bow, alternating fingers and, strings, and adding rhythms are all ways to enhance practice shifting to this and higher positions.

When fingerings in first position are started, continue to work on harmonics by rote with exercises such as in Figure 20–12.

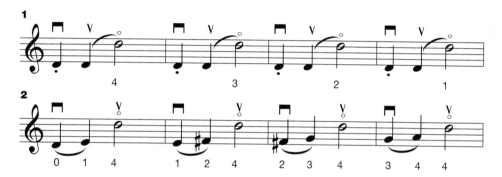

Figure 20–12   Rote Exercises for Harmonics—Using a Light Touch

THE SHIFT

Shifting on the violin refers to smoothly sliding the entire left hand toward or partially toward the bridge and back toward the nut. Shifting is used to extend the playing range of the instrument and to avoid awkward fingerings. Learning to shift smoothly and musically is of critical importance. Proper shifting is tension-free.

Figure 20-13 shows four examples of shifting. Examples A and C use harmonics. The harmonic shift in example C could also be played using the second and third fingers. Example B is a small, nonharmonic shift. When the shift is audible, it is a portamento shown in example D.

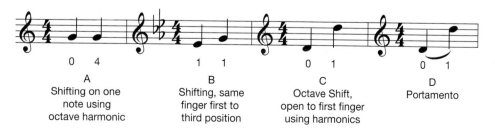

Figure 20–13   Examples of Shifting

Without shifting, string players would be limited to a range from the lowest open string to the distance the little finger could reach on the highest string. Shifting extends the range of each string and in the case of the violin extends the upper range of the instrument by two octaves.

Shifting on violin is accomplished by loosening the minimal left-hand points of support: thumb, base of first finger, and finger on the string, while maintaining a firm hold with the chin and shoulder. The elbow bends when moving to a higher position, and the actual shift requires the hand and arm to begin moving, with the finger on the string the last to leave its position.

A second pattern requires a change of fingers in shifting. One either shifts with the old finger (movement toward the fingerboard) or with the finger to be used for the new position. With shifting, the size of the shift should never be overestimated, as being slightly flat at the completion of the shift allows the player to "lead into" the exact pitch, which is usually more appropriate, especially in Romantic era music. Thus, some violinists have a "shifting rule," ascend with the old finger in pre-Romantic music, ascend with the new finger in Romantic and later music.

With the third pattern, the player shifts ascending and descending by leading with the finger designated to play the next note.

All shifting requires both mental and physical preparation. For example, the balance in the left hand is shifted prior to the shift so the balance is appropriate at the end of the shift. The old note is often thought of as helping, thus making it acceptable to hear the pitches produced by the old note (or helping note) finger during the shifts. The tempo of the music may cover some of the sound that naturally occurs during the shift but also this "extra" sound is one of the important tonal characteristics of string instruments.

The music and the player's ability level affect the type of shift used. Normally, the hand position maintains the same contour, retaining the feeling of balancing or supporting the instrument while the hand is moving. The speed of the shift usually matches the tempo of the music. Students must decide whether to cheat the duration of the old or the new note to allow for the time involved in shifting. Again, the music dictates. To achieve a smooth shift, the left hand must be relaxed.

Figure 20–14 illustrates the third position for each violin string. This position extends each string by a fourth. When the student shifts to third position on the E string, the first finger can be placed on an A that can be checked with the next open lower string. These checkpoints can be important when students first begin to shift.

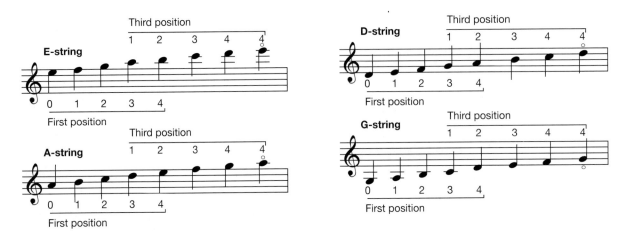

Figure 20–14 Notes Played in First-and-Third Position Violin
Note the top note of each scale indicates use of the harmonic for that string using the fourth finger.

TEACHING VIBRATO

As soon as students display a secure left-hand position and some evidence of a pitch center, they are ready to start using or learning vibrato. Preparation for vibrato is taught by having the students tap on the fingerboard. Students should initially be taught true vibrato on the violin by a back-and-forth rolling motion of the entire hand. From the wrist, the violinist rolls from the center of the pitch causing small fluctuations in pitch. Some arm movement can be used in producing vibrato.

Vibrato should be taught in third position to enable the hand to rest against the violin, providing support while the fingers attempt something new. One reason for teaching vibrato in third position is to enable the left arm, wrist, and fingers to move in a more relaxed fashion, close to the central focus of the player. Another reason is to allow gravity to assist in the initial and formative phases of the alternating movement, so important in the beginning stage of developing vibrato. Vibrato will usually start fairly easily with the second finger in third position, after which the student should try third finger. Early vibrato training often reduces the tendency toward tension in the left hand.

WHAT TO PRACTICE

Emphasis should be placed on intonation in the beginning string class and reiterated daily. Too much emphasis, however, leads to tension. Students must be encouraged to practice using double stops with open strings, to tune octaves, and especially perfect fifths. Frequent audio recording with students critiquing themselves and others emphasizes the importance of good intonation.

To improve technically—on intonation and shifting—violinists should practice scales. The D, G, and A major scales, one octave, are generally the first taught by class string method books. Students should be encouraged to strive for accuracy with speed and given a rhythm chart to play rhythmic patterns on each pitch. The next scales learned are generally a two-octave G scale and the F scale (with arpeggios), after which d minor can easily be approached. As violinists progress on the scales with good intonation and speed, they should be encouraged to attempt three octave scales using a variety of shifting to play a variety of rhythms and bowings.

Small ensembles are essential to every string student's personal growth. The amount of literature at various levels for string groups is remarkable—dating from original Renaissance music. These small ensembles help individual students develop their concepts of intonation, balance, and expressive musicianship.

Practicing should be done in front of a mirror and with frequent videotaping.

BIBLIOGRAPHY

Texts

* Indicates out of print in 2001.

ALTON, ROBERT (1990). *Violin and Cello Building and Repairing.* Brighton, MI. Native American Book Publishers.

*ATEN, JANE, and MARJORIE KELLER (1973). *Success Through Strings: Dallas Plan: Suzuki Oriented String Instruction.* Dallas: Dallas Independent School District.

AUER, LEOPOLD (1980). *Violin Playing as I Teach It.* New York: Dover Press; reprint of (1930), New York: F. A. Stokes.

BAILLOT, PIERRE MARIE FRANCOIS DE SALES (1991). *The Art of the Violin.* Evanston, IL: Northwestern University Press.

BORNOFF, GEORGE (1948). *Finger Patterns, a Basic Method Book for Violin.* Toronto: G. V. Thompson; reprint available from Newton Highlands, MA: FASE.

BOYDEN, DAVID D. (1989). *Violin Family.* New York: W. W. Norton.

BRONSTEIN, RAPHAEL (1981). *The Science of Violin Playing,* 2nd ed. Neptune, NJ: Paganiniana Publications.

COMMON, ALFRED F. (1999). *How to Repair Violins and Other Musical Instruments.* London: W.

Reeves, Ltd.; reprint and revision of 1909 edition.

COWDEN, ROBERT (1996). *Highlights from the American String Teacher (1984–1994) Viola Forum.* Bloomington, IN: American String Teachers Association.

CREMER, LOTHAR (1984). *Physics of the Violin* (trans. by John S. Allen). Boston: MIT Press.

EISELE, MARK (1980). *The Writings of Paul Rolland: An Annotated Bibliography.* Reston, VA: American String Teachers Association

FLESCH, CARL (1979). *Violin Fingering, Its Theory and Practice.* New York: Da Capo Press.

———. (1990). *And Do You Also Play the Violin?* London: Toccata Press.

GALAMIAN, IVAN (1999). *Principles of Violin Playing and Teaching,* 3rd ed. Ann Arbor: Shar Music.

GLASER, MATT, and STEPHANE GRAPPELLI (1981). *Jazz Violin.* New York: Oak Publications.

HART, GEORGE (1977). *The Violin and its Music.* Boston: Longwood Press.

HAVAS, KATO, and JEROME LANDSMAN (1981). *Freedom to Play: A String Class Teaching Method.* New York: Alexander Broude.

HILL, WILLIAM H., ARTHUR F. HILL, and HILL ALFRED EBSWORTH (1989 reprint). *The Violin Makers of the Guarneri Family, 1626-1762.* New York: Dover Publications.

HODGSON, PERCIVAL (1958). *Motion Study and Violin Bowing.* Urbana, IL: American String Teachers Associations.

ILLINOIS STRING RESEARCH ASSOCIATES (1971). *Holding the Violin Bow; Violin Playing at the Middle of the Bow.* Bryn Mawr, PA: author.

JACOBY, ROBERT (1985). *Violin Technique: A Practical Analysis for Performers.* Borough Green, Sevenoaks, Kent: Novello.

KENDALL, JOHN D. (1985). *The Suzuki Violin Method in American Music Education* rev ed. Princeton, NJ: Suzuki Method International.

KRAYK, STEFAN (1995). *The Violin Guide for Performers, Teachers and Students,* 2nd ed. Reston, VA.: American String Teachers Association.

LIEBERMAN, JULIE (1995). *Improvising Violin.* New York: Huisksi Music.

MENUHIN, YEHUDI (1981). *Violin: Six Lessons with Yehudi Menuhin.* New York; London: W. W. Norton.

MENUHIN, YEHUDI, and CHRISTOPHER HOPE (1986). *The Compleat Violinist: Thoughts, Exercises, Reflections of an Itinerant Violinist.* New York: Summit Books.

MENUHIN, YEHUDI, and WILLIAM PRIMROSE (1991). *Violin and Viola.* London: Kahn and Averill; reprint of 1976 edition.

PERKINS, MARIANNE M. (1995). *A Comparison of Violin Playing Techniques: Kato Havas, Paul Rolland, and Shinichi Suzuki.* Reston, VA: American String Teachers Association.

POLNAUER, FREDERICK F. (1974). *Total Body Technique of Violin Playing.* Bryn Mawr: Theodore Presser.

PRIMROSE, WILLIAM (1970). *Technique Is Memory: A Method for Violin and Viola Players Based on Fingers Patterns.* New York: Oxford University Press.

ROLLAND, PAUL (1972). *Prelude to String Playing.* New York: Boosey & Hawkes.

——— (1978). *Movement in String Playing: As It Relates to Violin Hold, Bowing, Shifting and Vibrato.* Urbana, IL: Illinois String Research Associates.

*ROLLAND, PAUL and SHELIA JOHNSON (1984). *Young Strings in Action: Basic Materials and Motion Techniques for Individual or Class Instruction: Updated and Rewritten Text of Prelude to String Playing by Paul Rolland (Teacher's Text).* New York: Boosey & Hawkes.

ROLLAND, PAUL, and MARLA MUTSCHLER (Revised by Clara Rolland) (2000). *The Teaching of Action in String Playing.* Urbana, IL: Illinois String Research Associates.

ROLLAND, PAUL (1990). *Basic Principles of Violin Playing.* New York: Boosey & Hawkes; reprint by ASTA with National School Orchestra Association through Reston, VA: Music Educators National Conference.

ROLLAND, PAUL, MARLA MUTSCHELER, RICHARD COLWELL, DONALD MILLER, and ARTHUR JOHNSON (1971). *Final Report: Development and Trial of a Two Year Program of String Instruction.* U.S. Department of Health, Education, and Welfare.

ROSS, BARRY (1989). *A Violinist's Guide for Exquisite Intonation.* Bloomington, IN: American String Teachers Association.

STARR, WILLIAM (1976). *The Suzuki Violinist: A Guide for Teachers and Parents.* Secaucus, NJ: Summy-Birchard.

STOLWELL, ROBIN (ed.) (1993). *The Cambridge Companion to the Violin.* New York: Cambridge University Press.

SUZUKI, SHINICHI (1959). *Position Etudes.* Princeton, NJ: Summy-Birchard.

——— (1969). *Nurtured by Love.* Smithtown, NY: Exposition Press.

——— (1978). *Suzuki Violin School* (10 vols.). Miami: Warner Brothers.

——— (1986). *Talent Education for Young Children.* New Albany, IN: World-Wide Press.

——— (1990). *Man and Talent.* Ann Arbor, MI: Shar Music.

SZENDE, OTTO, and MIHALY NEMESSURI (1971). *The Physiology of Violin Playing.* London: Collet's.

YAMPOLSKY, I. M. (1977). *The Principles of Violin Fingering.* London: Oxford University Press.

Violin Studies

Easy—Beginning (elementary and middle school)

Applebaum. *Building Technic with Beautiful Music* (Belwin).

Herfurth. *A Tune A Day Scale Book* (Boston Music).

Hrimaly. *Scale Studies* (G. Schirmer).

Kelobar. *Elementary Scale and Chord Studies* (Rubank).

O'Reilly. *Fiddle Magic* (Kjos).

———. *Fiddle Rhythms* (Kjos).

Rolland. *Action Studies.* (Boosey & Hawkes).

Rose. *Progressive Studies for the Young Violinist.* (Kjos).

Schloat. *Introduction to the Violin* (Schloat Prod.).

Seveik. *Exercises in the First Position,* Part 1 (C. Fischer).

Sitt. *20 Etudes in the 1st Position* (vol. 1) (G. Schirmer).

Whistler. *First Etude Album.* (Rubank).

———. *Scales in 1st Position.* (Rubank).

Wohlfahrt. *40 Elementary Studies.* (G. Schirmer).

———. *50 Easy Melodious Studies,* Book 1 (G. Schirmer).

Medium (middle school and high school)

Brown. *Two Octave Scales and Bowings* (Ludwig).

Kayser. *Elementary and Progressive Studies* (C. Fischer).

McConnell. *The New Dancla-Beriot Position Method* (C. Fischer).

Mazas. *Forty Selected Studies* (G. Schirmer).

Neumann. *Violin Left Hand Technique* (Theodore Presser).

Schradieck. *Scale Studies.* (C. Fischer).

———. *School of Violin Technics.* (2 vols.) (C. Fischer).

Seveik. *School of Violin Technics,* Parts II and III (C. Fischer).

———. *20 Etudes in the 2nd, 3rd, 4th and 5th Positions* (G. Schirmer).

Sitt. *20 Etudes in the 2nd, 3rd, 4th and 5th Positions* (vol. 2) (G. Schirmer).

———. *20 Etudes with Change of Position* (vol. 3) (G. Schirmer).

Trott. *Melodious Double-Steps* (2 vols.) (G. Schirmer).

Whistler. *Developing Double Stops* (Rubank).

———. *Introducing the Positions* (2 vols.) (Rubank).

———. *Preparing for Kreutzer* (Rubank).

Wohlfahrt. *50 Easy Melodious Studies,* Book II (C. Fischer).

———. *60 Studies* (vols.2) (C. Fischer).

Advanced (high school and college)

Blumenstengel. *Scale and Arpeggio Studies* (C. Fischer).

Dont. *24 Etudes and Caprices* (G. Schirmer).

———. *Progressive Studies with a 2nd Violin.* (G. Schirmer).

Fiorillo. *36 Studies or Caprices* (G. Schirmer).

Flesch. *Scale System.* (C. Fischer).

Galamian-Newmann. *Contemporary Violin Techniques* (Galaxy).

Gavinez. *24 Studies* (G. Schirmer).

Hrimaly. *Scale Studies* (G. Schirmer).

Kreutzer. *42 Studies or Caprices* (G. Schirmer).

Mazas. *18 Artists Studies,* Book III (G. Schirmer).

———. *25 Melodious and Progressive Studies* (G. Schrimer).

———. *27 Brilliant Studies,* Book II (G. Schirmer).

———. *30 Special Studies,* Book I. (G. Schirmer).

Rode. *24 Caprices* (G. Schirmer).

Rovelli. *12 Caprices* (G. Schirmer).

Schradieck. *Chord Studies* (G. Schirmer).

Spinosa, Frank, Rusch, and Harold. *The Artists' Studio for Violin* (Kjos).

Wieniawski. *8 Etudes-Caprices* (G. Schirmer).

Instructional Videos

Basic Violin Video (Ed Marsh, 1998). Levelland, TX: Texas Music and Video.

Beginning Fiddle Video, 2 vol. (Jim Wood and Murphy Henry, 1994). Winchester, VA: The Murphy Method.

The Heifetz Master Class at University of Southern California, 8 vol.(Jascha Heifetz and various students, originally recorded in 1962, converted to videocassette in 1984 & 1985). Ann Arbor, MI: Shar Products Company.

Josef Gingold Master Class, 4 vol. (Josef Gingold and students, 1982). Ann Arbor, MI: Shar Products Company.

The Joy of Shifting and Double Stops: A Violinist's Guide to Ease and Artistry (Jerrie Lucktenberg, 1991). Madison, WI: University of Wisconsin-Madison Department of Continuing Education in the Arts.

Kató Havas: A New Approach (Kató Havas, 1991). Cumbria, England: Lakeland Home Music.

Suzuki Method, Video Guidance. No. 1 (Shin'ichi Suzuki, 1999; in Japanese with English voice-over). Matsumoto, Japan: International Suzuki Association.

Master Teacher Series Lessons with Ivan Galamian, 5 vol. (Ivan Galamian and students, 1981). Ann Arbor, MI: Mark Video.

Rabin on Strings (Marvin Rabin, David Becker, Priscilla Smith, and Rosemary Poetzel, 1986). Madison, WI: University of Wisconsin-Madison Department of Continuing Education in the Arts.

Mel Bay's Anyone Can Play the Violin (Coral White, 1990). Pacific, MO: Mel Bay Productions.

The Teaching of Action in String Playing (Paul Rolland, along with *Sustained and Detaché Bowing; Bouncing the Bow; Developing Finger Movements and the Basic Shifting Movements; Holding the Violin Bow; Establishing the Violin Hold* (2 parts); *Developing Flexibility: Changing the Bow; Extending the Bow Stroke; Establishing Left Hand and Finger Placement in the First Position; Principles of Left Hand and Finger Action; First Steps in Vibrato Teaching; Rhythm Training,* 1970). Mesa, AZ: Rolland String Research Associates (1616 W. Mountain View 85201).

Ultimate Beginner Series: The Fiddle (Robert Aviles, 1999). Miami: Warner Brothers Publications.

Ultimate Beginner Series: The Violin (Dana Freeman, 1999). Miami: Warner Brothers Publications.

The Violin (Bill Scutt, 1998). Canoga Park, CA: MVP

Violin in Motion: An Ergonomic Approach to Playing for all Levels & Styles (Julie Lyonn Lieberman, 1995). New York: Huiksi Music.

Recommended Classical Violin Recording Artists
(there are many to choose from)

Zino Fanscesatti playing Beethoven and Saint-Saëns

Jascha Heifez playing Mozart and Franck

Fritz Kreisler playing Mendelssohn and Paganini

Anne-Sophie Mutter playing Crumb, Lalo, and Stravinsky

Recommended Jazz Violin Recording Artists

Dixieland, Swing: Joe Venuti and Stephane Grappelli

Fusion, Post-Bop: Jean Luc Ponty and Didier Lockwood

Avant-Garde: Leroy Jenkins

Dixieland Revival: Michael White

Crossover, Post-Bop: John Blake

21

The Viola

HISTORY

The viola is the patriarch of the string family and was the more common instrument until the violin was perfected. The viola is still considered by some to be less perfect than its relatives, requiring strings that are too thick and too heavy for its length. As a consequence, it produces a tone not as rich in overtones as the violin and cello. Its characteristic and plainer color, however, makes it indispensable for orchestra and chamber ensembles, in which it blends well with violin and lower strings, and endears it to contemporary composers and audiences, who love the less "typical" sound. It has been featured in the works of Berlioz, Holst, Fauré, Brahms, Hindemith, and many others.

Interestingly, the role of the viola is still evolving in this century. Few can deny that the viola was "second fiddle" to the violin in the nineteenth and most of the twentieth centuries. There is something about the viola sound, however, that is attractive to the contemporary listener. The viola does not impress with flaunting, virtuosic technique (unlike the violin), but with its haunting tone quality. William Primrose is one individual who helped establish the viola's integrity as a beautiful, expressive solo instrument. Premier composers wrote for him and he promoted works written for the instrument. Primrose was the first major player/teacher who considered the viola to be more closely related to the cello than to the violin.

Pitched a fifth below the violin, the viola is the alto member of the string family and plays alto and treble clef. It is larger than the violin with longer finger spacings and consequently different patterns. This difference creates a problem for many students switching from the violin as speed and flexibility are affected not only by the finger patterns but also by the wider instrument and the weight difference of the instrument. The weight difference alone is justification for starting transferring violists in third position.

Violas are made in several sizes. All violas are tuned as shown in Figure 21–1.

The viola benefited from design changes during the twentieth century, used to develop an instrument with a bigger sound without approaching shrillness or distortion.

The viola continues to serve primarily in an accompaniment role—both rhythmic and

Figure 21–1
Open-strings (a) and First Position Range of the Viola (b)

harmonic—in most string literature. The viola's rich, mellow tone quality balances well with the upper and lower strings, and blends with horn and woodwinds. String orchestra viola sections usually are comprised of just under half the number of violins.

While a large bone structure, including large hands and fingers, may be detrimental to the violinist, broad fingers are an asset to violists, aiding in the production of the full, round sound that resonates from the instrument's thicker strings and larger body. Once all obstacles are dealt with, the viola becomes, for the composer, "an ideal medium for all the expression of life's innermost feelings"; in the audience's response, "unmatched richness and beauty of tone" and in the violist's reaction, "a perfect instrument for tapping the reservoir of man's culminating artistic achievement."[1]

SELECTING THE INSTRUMENT

Violas are measured by their body length and are available in three basic sizes: junior, intermediate, and standard. Junior sizes have a body length of $13\frac{1}{4}$ or $13\frac{1}{2}$ inches. Intermediate size instruments are 14 to $14\frac{1}{2}$ inches in length. Advanced, or full size, violas are 15 to $16\frac{1}{2}$ inches in length (with some professionals playing instruments as long as 18 inches).

A viola is matched to the student's size; a beginning violist should play the largest instrument that fits him. The tone quality obtained is directly related to the viola's size. The fingers should be able to reach around the scroll, with the fingertips actually curled around it. It is important that the student can maintain the rounded hand ("C shape") when playing in the higher positions. Smaller violas simply cannot provide the true viola sound—they are useful for beginners and allow early success in technique for many students, but the student should be transferred to a larger instrument as soon as feasible. This importance for playing an instrument of adequate size is one reason for school-owned "undersized" instruments. Figures 21–2a and 21–2b illustrate a viola too large and one that fits well for the student respectively.

HOLDING THE VIOLA

To assume a playing position, the student keeps his head straighter than he would for violin and uses a jawrest rather than a chinrest (Figure 21–3). With a well-fitting jawrest that has a slight lip or edge and adequate shoulder padding, the viola

Figure 21–2a Checking Viola Size (too large)

Figure 21–2b Checking Viola Size (correct)

[1]William Primrose (1970), *Technique Is Memory: A Method for Violin and Viola Players Based on Fingers Patterns*, New York: Oxford University Press, pp. 107–108.

Figure 21–3
Playing Position for Viola

Figure 21-4
Rest Position for Viola

should be balanced in playing position without any hand support and without any muscle constriction that could cause tension. Any tension in the holding position will spread throughout the body. The jaw works as a counterlever on the chinrest along a vector that goes down and in, creating leverage; there is no squeezing of the "jawrest." Shoulder pads may not be needed by violists to make the instrument "flatter"; their use is often simply to provide the necessary friction against clothing and the slippery varnish of the instrument. Although, in theory, the instrument is held without support of the left hand, some support usually reduces tension in the jaw that results from fear of dropping the instrument.

The pad of the thumb is held lightly against the side of the viola neck for support and will usually extend slightly above the neck depending on the length of the student's fingers. The thumb, at all times, must not be locked in a rigid position; its role is gently to support the proper posture of the four fingers of the left hand.

Sufficient finger pressure on the string is imperative. Slightly more weight is required than for the violin due to the string's heaviness, but most of this comes naturally. As a good firm attack on the string by the bow provides the tone quality, the bow, as with the other string instruments, must meet a springy resistance to produce a good sound. Left arm, hand, wrist, and finger support create this resistance in the string. It is, again, important to avoid striking the string percussively directly from above with the fingers because this nearly always results in undue tension. The artistry is more in lifting the fingers—in a graceful, curved motion.

When a beginner first experiences placing the viola under the chin, his inclination is to retract his neck or to move the head out-and-down, resulting in misalignment. The teacher may have to demonstrate for the timid student that the instrument rests primarily on the collarbone and shoulder and does not require the left hand to hold it. The jaw is so relaxed that one should be able to talk while holding the instrument. In contrast with the violin, the viola is held flatter with the scroll lower, which should allow for greater flexibility. If the viola drops some in playing, this can be natural and not tension producing.

LEFT-ARM AND HAND MOVEMENTS

Like the violin, the viola player's left upper arm is the source of energy that moves down through the entire arm to the fingers. The differences between violin and viola include the increased strength required for supporting a heavier instrument, and a left elbow that rotates more to the left and some to the right to facilitate the natural power to depress the strings (while maintaining a reasonably straight line from the elbow through the forearm and wrist to the hand). The arm is extended more to reach the neck of the viola than is necessary for the violin. This can be fatiguing and give an unnatural feeling for a student switching from violin, but the viola position will soon become equally natural. The greatest danger from fatigue and any unnatural feeling is that arm tension can occur. When the muscles tire, practicing should cease.

The Thumb

Usually positioned opposite the second finger, the left thumb plays a more important role in viola playing than in violin playing. When playing the violin, the thumb maintains a relative position to the fingers as they move up and down the fingerboard. On the viola, however, the thumb equalizes the greater downward weight of the fingers on the thicker strings. It gently supports the neck without gripping. The thumb rotates to the left so the nail almost touches the neck in low positions (as in Figure 21–5) and naturally moves slightly lower under the neck for higher positions.

When playing in third position and higher, the thumb is positioned more directly under the neck to allow the fingers to reach the notes. Again, the thumb position depends upon the size and dimensions of the player; the thumb can be a source of tension in the left hand if it does not remain relaxed in all positions.

**Figure 21–5
Correct Position of
Thumb and Fingers
on Fingerboard**

The Fingers

On a full-size viola the distance for playing whole steps in first position is about $\frac{1}{8}$ inch greater than on a full-size violin. This distance adds an additional $\frac{1}{2}$ inch for the left- hand fingers to cover. On a $16\frac{1}{2}$ inch viola, the difference in distance is more than twice that of a 15-inch viola. The fingers do not stretch more; the change occurs in the palm of the hand.

Players with small hands must compensate with "minishifts" and adjusting the balance of the left hand to avoid stretching and straining the fingers. Again, what feels natural before bad habits take over is often correct. Mobility of the left hand is the key; to reiterate, students must not "learn" that any part of the left hand is used to hold the viola (as illustrated in Figure 21–6).

**Figure 21–6
Correct Position of the
Fingers and Hand on
the Neck of the Viola**

Viola technique requires the performer to apply sufficient pressure on the strings, but this is often overemphasized. The difference from violin is not great. To attain this firmness more of the pads of the left fingers are used than on the violin—the violinist uses his fingertips. The correct position has the pad of the fourth finger centered on the string. One result of pad use is a wider vibrato and a less brilliant tone quality—a darker, richer sound.

With the proper hand position, the fingers are angled toward the bridge at about a 40 degree angle if viewed from the top. The fingers drop vertically (90 degrees) on the string from the base knuckle of each finger. The weight originates in the upper arm and travels through the forearm, through the wrist and hand, to the fingers. Harmonics utilizing the full length of the fingerboard are excellent exercises not only for training the ear but also for learning to play without tension.

Intonation

Good intonation on viola requires a proper posture, proper instrument holding position, and no muscular tension in the left arm or hand. Although all string players require ear training and the keen ability to match pitches, the violist often makes more minor intonation adjustments due to; the need for unison playing with violins and cellos, the viola's harmonic role in voice leading, and having to provide for the crucial thirds and sevenths in standard harmonization.

SHIFTING

The principles of shifting on viola are the same as for the violin and are often similarly delayed in being introduced to students. The viola pedagogue, Henry Barrett, observes that these principles are so simple that teachers should be amazed when students have difficulty with this technique.[2] He attributes the violist's lack of success to the failure to prepare mentally or physically for the task. In most cases the player is trying to shift with the fingers and not with the arm.

Preparation includes loosening the contact points: base of the first finger, thumb, and the finger playing the note while the jaw and collarbone assume greater support of the instrument. The finger movement in shifting is anticipated by a slight motion in the hand and arm.

Barrett outlines the steps of shifting on the viola:

1. Shift executed by the bending of the elbow and controlled by the ear.
2. Left-hand contact points lightened.
3. Anticipatory motion in the arm and hand before the finger leaves the position.
4. Glide the fingers along the string lines.
5. Use a flatter angle of the finger while shifting.
6. Maintain the contour of the hand position and retain the feeling of balance in the center of the hand.
7. Match speed of shift to speed of passage.
8. Hold out the note preceding the shift for full value (we believe, however, that the note to be held depends upon the music).
9. Slow the bow at the moment of the shift to deemphasize the left-hand movements.
10. Slide on the finger that is making contact (for either up or down shifts), until the new position is reached; then drop the new finger in place.
11. Give special attention to the quality of sound of the note preceding the shift and the note following the shift.
12. Do not hurry. Shift slowly and deliberately. Feel the pull of the entire arm.
13. Practice without the viola or bow to improve coordination of the two arms working together.
14. Shift without the thumb touching the neck to reduce friction, lighten the hand, and improve mobility. "In performance, the thumb will find its way."
15. The bow approaches the bridge on high shifts to provide a better sounding point for the shorter vibrating string.
16. In extremely high positions, the base of the thumb moves over the ribs of the viola.[3]

Figure 21–7 on page 372 illustrates positions I–V for viola.

[2]Henry Barrett (1978). *The Viola: Complete Guide for Teachers and Students*, 2nd rev. ed., Tuscaloosa, AL: University of Alabama Press, p. 64.
[3] Ibid, p. 64–65.

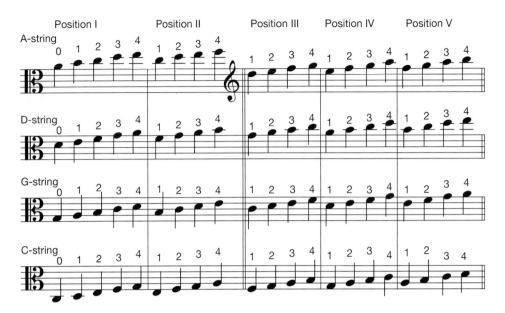

Figure 21-7   First Five Positions for Viola

VIBRATO

Viola vibrato is generally slower and slightly wider than violin vibrato. The flatter part of the finger pad is used; the wrist must remain relaxed. If a student were to play with identical vibrato on the violin and viola, the listener would hear the viola vibrato as slower because the length of the string and its thicker gauge make it slower to respond to pitch fluctuations. Instruction in vibrato should begin early.

LEFT-ARM AND HAND MOVEMENTS

The entire body works together as a dynamic, changing system, making analysis of viola (and all string) playing difficult. The center of balance is near the second and third fingers. The position of the violist's left hand moves more than the violinist's, yet shifts less than it does on the lower string instruments. These larger (than violin) movements vary with fingerings, string crossing, vibrato, trills, double stops, arm and finger length, and the amount of pad of the fingertips; they are a challenge to the performer in expressive and articulated performances. Components of the left-hand movements must be isolated for teaching, learning, and practicing.

RIGHT-ARM AND HAND MOVEMENTS

The Bow Hold

The viola bow for a 15 to 16 inch instrument is slightly longer than the violin bow. It is also heavier, thicker, and has a wider spread of hair. It has a curved end at the frog instead of the sharp angle of the violin bow.

Because the viola bow is heavier and plays on larger strings, it requires a firmer hold than the violin hold in order to draw out the rich tone quality. A more aggressive approach to bowing is suggested: First, the bow is held higher than a violin bow, the thumb is moved slightly more under the stick and set opposite the

a) View from Front   b) View from Back   c) View from Bottom   d) View from "Inside"

Figures 21–8 a–d   Viola Bow Hold from Various Angles

third rather than the second finger. Second, the first finger drops on the stick resting on the first joint and providing additional control. The little finger rests on top over the pearl counterbalancing the weight of the bow.

The flat part of the bow hair is used the most, with the side of the bow hair used only for *soto voce*. In general the violist uses slower bow speeds and shorter strokes due to the difference in strings, and strives for a "core" sound (like cello and bass).

Figures 21–8a-d illustrate a correct viola bow hold from various angles.

Bowing

In general, the larger muscles such as those of upper arm and forearm are used for power and for crossing strings. The fingers that hold the bow and contribute to articulations are controlled by the next larger muscle. That is, the fingertips are controlled by the fingers, then the base joint of the fingers, then the hand, up to the shoulder. Violists should practice double stops to improve bowing technique; this practice will also help single notes, sharpen the ear, and strengthen the left hand. The smaller muscles in the hand and fingers are used for more subtle bowing actions and various types of articulations/bowings.

Like the other strings in both up- and down-bows, the bow is kept perpendicular to the strings in a curved, smooth, natural curved motion. The bow arm is low and closely follows the height of each string. Practicing octaves is a helpful exercise. The bow weight, speed of bow, and point of contact each contribute to dynamic levels and tone color. The bow is placed closer to the bridge than for violin in order to attain a characteristic sound. Bowing procedures and techniques, as with all strings, are determined by the music and the effect desired. Bowing technique is a prime difference between viola and violin.

TRANSFERRING FROM VIOLIN

Transferring from violin to viola offers the player greater opportunities to participate, much interesting contemporary viola solo and chamber music, and the chance to be "special." When a violinist approaches the viola with his violin playing technique, the results are a shallow sound with little or no depth, and a light tone that is unpleasant and unsatisfying. He should be encouraged to use more bow weight, particularly any natural weight achieved through the use of the rotary motion of the right forearm. He should also use more left-hand finger weight. Finally, the student should be taught to anticipate every entrance, as the strings do not respond as quickly as they do on the violin.

The new violist is also confronted with the greater distances not only in fingering but with extensions and shifting. The change of clef is an additional challenge for the transfer student. One trick, for example, is to play viola music like violin music but read each note down a third lower than printed. However, these tricks do not work well for long, as the finger patterns are different.

The best solution is for the violinist turned violist to learn to read the alto clef. This is achieved by first singing the note names while following the alto clef, then fingering through the music before attempting to play it. By no means should the new violist learn the music by rote without reading alto clef.

BIBLIOGRAPHY

Texts

Indicates out of print in 2001.

*ATEN, JANE, and MARJORIE KELLER (1973). *Success Through Strings: Dallas Plan: Suzuki Oriented String Instruction.* Dallas: Dallas Independent School District.

*BARRETT, HENRY (1978). *The Viola: Complete Guide for Teachers and Students,* 2nd rev. ed. Tuscaloosa, AL: University of Alabama Press.

BORNOFF, GEORGE (1952). *Bornoff's Patterns in Position: Viola.* Toronto: G. V. Thompson; reprints available from Newton Highlands, MA: FASE.

COMMON, ALFRED F. (1999). *How to Repair Violins and Other Musical Instruments.* London: W. Reeves, Ltd.; reprint and revision of 1909 edition.

COWDEN, ROBERT (1996). *Highlights from the American String Teacher (1984–1994) Viola Forum.* Bloomington, IN: American String Teachers Association.

DOLEJŠÍ, ROBERT (1973). *Modern Viola Technique.* New York: Da Capo Press; reprint of 1939 Chicago: University of Chicago Press.

*HODGSON, PERCIVAL (1958). *Motion Study and Violin Bowing.* Bloomington, IN: American String Teachers Associations.

MENUHIN, YEHUDI, and WILLIAM PRIMROSE (1976). *Violin and Viola.* New York Schirmer Books London: Kahn and Averill, reprint of (1976).

*PRIMROSE, WILLIAM (1970). *Technique Is Memory: A Method for Violin and Viola Players Based on Finger Patterns.* New York: Oxford University Press.

RILEY, MAURICE W. (1993) *The History of the Viola,* 2nd ed. Ann Arbor, MI: Braun-Brumfield.

———. (1991) *The History of the Viola,* Vol. II. Ann Arbor, MI.: Braun-Brumfield.

TERTIS, LIONEL (1991). *My Viola and I: A Complete Autobiography: With Beauty of Tone in String Playing and Other Essays.* London: Kahn and Averill; reprint of (1974).

Viola Studies

Easy—Beginning (elementary or middle school)

Applebaum. *Third and Fifth Position String Builder* (Belwin-Mills).
Benoits, Henri & Renne. *Elementary Method* (2 vols.) (A. Leduc).
Berger. *Basic Viola Technique.* (MCA).
Bornoff. *Finger Patterns* (Thompson).
———. *Fun for Fiddle Finger* (Thompson).
———. *Patterns in Position* (Thompson).
Carsé. *Viola School,* Book I (Augener).
Cavallini. *Elementary and Progressive School* (2 vols.) (Ricord).
Kayser. *36 Elementary and Progressive Studies* (G. Schirmer).
Lifschey. *Daily Technical Studies* (C. Fischer).
———. *Scale and Arpeggio Studies* (2 vols.) (G. Schirmer).
O'Reilly. *String Power* (N. Kjos).
Whistler. *From Violin to Viola* (Rubank).
———. *Introducing the Positions* (2 vol.) (Rubank).
Wohlfahrt. *Foundation Studies* (G. Schirmer).

Medium (middle or high school)

Bruni. *25 Studies* (C. Fischer).
Carsé. *Viola School,* Books II–III (Augener).
Fischer. *Selected Studies and Etudes* (Belwin-Mills).
Flesch-Karman. *Scale System* (C. Fischer).
Herman. *6 Concert Studies.* (International).
———. *Technical Studies* (International).
Hoffmeister. *12 Studies* (Peters).
Kayser. *36 Elementary and Progressive Studies* (G. Schirmer).
Matz. *Intonation Studies* (Breitkopf & Hartel).
Mazas. *Special Etudes,* Books I and II (G. Schirmer).
Preston. *Direct Approach to Higher Positions* (Belwin).
Primrose. *The Art of Practice of Scale Playing on the Viola* (Belwin-Mills).
———. *Technique Is Memory* (Oxford).

Schradieck. *School of Viola Technique* (International).

Seveik-Lifschey. *Selected Studies* (G. Schirmer).

Wohlfarht. *60 Studies* (2 vols.) (Peters).

Advanced (high school or college).

Anzoletti. *Dodici Studi* (Ricordi).

Campagnoli. *41 Caprices* (G. Schirmer).

Carse. *Viola School*, Books IV–V (Augener).

Dont. *24 Studies*. (International).

Dont–Bailly. *24 Viola Studies* (G. Schirmer).

Dont–Svecenski. *20 Progressive Studies for Viola* (G. Schirmer).

Fiorillo. *31 Selected Studies* (International).

Fuchs. *Fifteen Characteristic Studies* (Oxford).

Gavines-Spitzner. *24 Etudes* (International).

Green. *12 Modern Etudes for the Advanced Violist* (Elkan-Vogel).

Kievman. *Practicing the Viola, Mentally Physically* (Kelton).

Krevz. *Select Studies*, Books III–IV (Augener).

Magers, Spinoza, and Rusch. *The Artists' Studio for Strings* (Viola) (Kjos).

Massias. *12 Etudes* (Jobert).

Mazas. *Etudes Brilliant* (International).

_____. *Etudes Special* (International).

Mogil. *Scale Studies* (G. Schirmer).

Paganini. *24 Caprices* (International).

Rode-Blumenau. *24 Caprices* (G. Schirmer).

Wieniawski. *Studies and Caprices* (Marks).

Instructional Videos

The Art of Primrose: A Presentation (David Dalton, 1997). Boston: The Boston Conservatory.

Master Teacher Series with Donald McInnes (Donald McInnes and Charles Avsharian, 1985). Ann Arbor, MI: Shar Products.

William Primrose; A Violists's Legacy (Wiliam Primrose and David Dalton, 1979). Ann Arbor, MI: Shar Products.

The Viola (Rudiger Barth and Dana Freeman, 1999). Miami: Warner Brothers Publications.

The Viola (Katherine Rodriquez, 1993). Canoga Park, CA: Backstage Pass Productions.

Viola with Kathryn Rodriquez for Beginners (Kathryn Rodriquez, 1991). Van Nuys CA: Backstage Pass Productions.

Recommended Classical Viola Recording Artists

Yùr Bashmet playing Britten and Shostakovich
Nobuko Imai playing Hindemith and Mozart
Kim Kashkashien playing Pendericki and Brahms
William Primrose playing Brahms and Beethoven

Recommended Jazzl Viola Recording Artists

Hard Bop, Post-Bop: Martin Stenger
Swing, Crossover: Mimi Rabson
Avant-Garde, Free Jazz: Philipp Wachsmann

22

The Cello

HISTORY

The name "violoncello" (or cello for short) first became current in the mid-seventeenth century, but bass violins of one kind or another are mentioned in several literary works of even earlier centuries. The cello actually originated in the early sixteenth century as a member of the violin family.

Martin Agricola, writing in 1529, describes instruments of the early violin family with different ranges, including a bass instrument with three strings tuned F–C–G (with F being the lowest string, then ascending in fifths). Hans Gerle, writing in 1532, describes an instrument with the same tuning as our modern cello, C–G–D–A, in ascending order. Both performers were lutinists. An instrument tuned a whole note lower (B♭–F–C–G) continued to be popular in England and France into the eighteenth century. The earliest known makers of instruments that would be recognized today as cellos were Andrea Amati of Cremona (who died before 1580), Gasparo da Salo (1540–1609) of Brescia, and his pupil Giovanni Paolo Maggini (1581–1632). Their cellos were larger than modern cellos (up to 80 centimeters in length).[1]

One famous cello made by Amati is called "The King." The cello has paintings of the arms, devices, and motto of King Charles IX of France. The physical characteristics of this violoncello are not much different from the modern-day cello; violoncellos have not changed much.[2] Some sixteenth-century cellos still exist. The move toward a smaller cello took place in Bologna in the 1600s when silver-wound lower strings were invented. Many luthiers were making cellos before the famous Stradivari; however, it was Stradivari who decided around the year 1707 to construct the instrument with a length of about 75 centimeters, which has become the standard. In the early eighteenth century, cello makers experimented with five-string cellos. Some think that Bach may have had the five-string cello in mind for his Sixth Cello Suite.

It was not until the late Baroque that the instrument was used, by classical composers such as C. P. E. Bach and Haydn, for more than the basso continuo accompaniment. Many Romantic composers seized upon it as the ideal expression

[1]Elizabeth Cowling (1983), *The Cello*, 2nd ed., New York: Scribner's pp. 26–27.
[2]Ibid, p. 28.

for some of their most beautiful works. This tradition has continued through to the twenty first century with composers such as John Tavener, among many others.

The cello sounds as the tenor voice of the string family. Its design and construction are virtually identical to an oversized violin and viola with the addition of an endpin. The endpin extends to the desired length to enable the player to hold the instrument properly. The endpin is to the cello what the chin and jaw rest are to the upper strings. The endpin must securely support the cello through any gyrations of the performer. A sharp endpin helps, but no matter how sharp, there are impenetrable floors. The cellist should never be without a strap or board on such occasions, a strap that attaches to the chair leg and is permeable to the sharpened endpin. The endpin needs to be sufficiently sharp to provide solid support in carpets with the deepest pile. A third solution is the rockstop, which, when properly used, provides adequate support.

Cellos are made in various sizes including $\frac{1}{16}$, $\frac{1}{8}$, $\frac{1}{4}$, $\frac{1}{2}$, $\frac{3}{4}$, and full size. The cello is tuned one octave below the viola as shown in Figure 22-1.

The cello has a range of more than four octaves. Due to its size and the gauge of its strings, it has an enormous range of dynamic levels—from delicate and thin to powerful and full. Orchestras tend to use a few more cellos than violas.

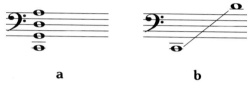

a   **b**

Figure 22–1
Open Strings (a) and First Position Range (b) of the Cello

SELECTING THE INSTRUMENT AND BOW

As we have reiterated for more than a dozen chapters, band and orchestra directors should not decide what instrument a student should play based on his or her physical characteristics. Interest is the primary criterion. A large hand and/or long fingers are an advantage but not an absolute necessity for playing the cello. Technically, playing requires stretching the hand for finger positions, and the strength, speed, and facility required for technical passages present difficulties with a hand that is too small, but there are many examples of successful small performers who compensate successfully. The stretch required between the first and fourth finger is necessary for basic playing but facility can be developed through practice. Players with small hands adapt by developing flexible and mobile hand movements.

Most sixth-graders are physically mature enough to play a three-quarter size instrument. Height of the instrument is adjusted with the endpin to ensure correct playing posture for students of varying size. The middle of the chin comes even with the scroll when standing. When seated, the top part of the lower bouts should be at knee length. The top of the instrument comes to the center of the breastbone. The student could hug the instrument. The instrument is too large if the endpin cannot be adjusted and the student has to drop her right shoulder and body to play at the tip of the bow. Full-size cellos differ in size. Before purchase, a professional should determine if the size is appropriate and that the bridge and fingerboard are matched to the instrument and the student.

The bow for the cello is heavier and shorter than the violin or viola bow, and like the other string instruments, a good bow plays a major role in tone quality and technique. Heavier bows on thicker strings require slightly more effort as the bow changes direction and crosses strings.

The cello bow must have greater tension on the hair than those used by the upper strings in order to apply adequate weight to the strings (too much tension, however, will allow the bow to slip across the strings unless rosined well). In the middle of a tightened bow, there should be a distance of half to three-quarter inch between hair and stick—considerably more distance than for the violin bow. The cello bow should be matched to the instrument.

A quality case for storage is important. As these are available with wheels, the weight of the case may no longer be a critical factor in deciding between a quality cloth case and the more protective plastic.

HOLDING THE CELLO

Though the principles of string instrument playing are applicable to all four major members of the family, cello and bass differ the most due to their size and playing position. The left-hand positions on cello, for example, are different because the pitches are spaced farther apart than on the violin or viola. Further, the orientation of the left-hand and arm must adapt to an up-and-down motion for the cello and bass (up-and-down bow for cello and bass is a metaphor).

The cello player is invariably seated with the instrument's weight resting primarily on the endpin. Interestingly, the endpin was not invented until the late nineteenth century by Adrien Seivais. This invention made cello playing easier. The endpin is placed slightly to the right of the player's center. The cello is tilted toward the player and positioned by placing the lower bouts between the legs (with the lower ribs just above the knees) and the lower right tuning peg (the low C) slightly behind the left ear. The small projection extending from the back of the instrument that braces the neck should be at the player's breastbone.

The cello is turned very slightly to the right to position the strings more directly under the bow.[3] The player distributes her weight evenly and securely between both feet. The student should be able to stand up comfortably (from the seated position) without adjusting the position of her feet. This principle can be taught by describing a triangle from the left leg to the sternum to the endpin. The position of the strings should run down the center of the body with the right leg free from the instrument. The result is that the cello is held slightly to the left of center.

Although the endpin allows adjustment to the height and tilt of the cello for tension-free posture, the chair is an important consideration. It is essential that the cellist sit on the edge of the chair when playing with chair height just right. As the player sits erect, she sometimes gives the impression of leaning forward slightly, but there is no need to bend over to see how things are going. Music industry manufacturers make chairs $18\frac{1}{2}$ inches tall for high school and adult players, with a forward slanted seat designed to free the cellist to lean slightly into the instrument. Smaller players usually find themselves in a position in which their hipbones are higher than their knees. Tall performers may need to raise the chair or even bend the endpin to avoid high knees.

Most players want the center of gravity to be on their feet or an imaginary tripod between the feet and the cello. This feeling is achieved by moving forward on the chair from the hips, and leaning *into* the instrument, rather than letting the instrument lean on them. The shoulder should not be turned because of instrument placement. An endpin that is extended too far can force the player back into a position that is physically and psychologically contradictory to good posture. Figures 22–2 and 22–3 illustrate the playing position for the cellist. This aspect of being able to "embrace" the cello is what makes the choice of chairs so crucial. The knees are used to support and steady the instrument only while tuning with the pegs.

[3] William Pleeth (1982), *Cello*, New York: Schirmer Books, p. 146.

Figure 22–2
Cello Playing Position (front)

Figure 22–3
Cello Playing Position (side)

THE BEGINNING STUDENT

It is important to devote extra time to the beginning cellist. Although the beginner benefits from the first lessons which explain names of the parts of the instrument, the cellist should also be allowed to explore her "larger" instrument by plucking, trying the bow immediately, and discovering the various sounds, including harmonics, which the instrument can produce. For example, let her explore the full length of the fingerboard and realize how the pitch changes. Playing by ear is as important for cellists as for violinists.

William Pleeth believes that teaching isolated techniques on the cello for beginners will create mechanical performers. Instead, the teacher should teach *basics* of technique and allow the student to alter slightly these basics to a "system" that works for him. All aspects of performing are based on relaxation, flexibility, and naturalness.

Because class method books are designed primarily for the violin, the cellist is introduced earlier to challenging fingerings. Good left-hand habits begin with attention to the slope of the left-hand, a slope that determines the angle with which the fingers meet the strings and enhances finger flexibility.

The "square hand" or "block" is advocated by many method books and teachers—that is, the fingers are to be at right angles to the string—but this hand position is actually based on only the middle two fingers being at right angles. This position enables players with large hands to easily play in tune.

A "sloped" left-hand position gives the beginner a better chance at more naturally controlling the space between the fingers and encourages flexibility when the pads of the four fingers are placed on the strings. This "sloped" hand position resembles the hand position on the upper strings, but upside down. (The little finger should also be sloped and not collapse.) The sloped left-hand position seems more natural for players with smaller hands. Students should not start with the first finger—starting with the fourth finger depressed keeps all fingers more relaxed.

Students need to get the feeling of motion in the left-hand—they should feel the position of the second partial and play the harmonics, then the third partial. Simple songs should be played with natural harmonics—by ear. The thumb is eventually used on the strings necessitating relaxed fingers and hand.

Because the upper arm is where the strength and energy to perform are initiated, the sloped hand is advantageous as a straight line can be formed through the hand to the elbow. Students should experiment with the shape of the hand to determine the angle that allows the greatest flexibility for the fingers and that feels comfortable and natural.

The thumb should lightly touch the neck of the cello about $3\frac{1}{2}$ inches from the top of the neck. The cellist's fingers are in first position when the thumb is opposite the second finger. Again, a mobile and flexible thumb is critical to making rapid progress on all string instruments—the thumb "floats" when playing the cello and bass. The angle of the upper arm (elbow) varies according to the string being played, the left elbow rising for the low strings and lowering for the higher strings.

Bowing for beginners should be taught in a natural, comfortable way. Due to the weight of the bow and the angle of the instrument, students need to be reminded that the strength to "dig into" the string and prevent slipping starts in the right shoulder and moves through the upper arm, elbow, forearm, and down to the wrist. If any one of these body parts becomes tense, the entire process is hampered. There should always be a straight line from the elbow, down to the forearm and to the wrist and hand. When the bow is at the frog, the wrist may be slightly convex, but never concave around the palm, or the straight line to the elbow is disturbed. As the bow is drawn, the elbow will not only bend outward but also move away from the body until about midbow. At that point the forearm also begins to move away from the body to continue the movement that began in the shoulder. Through the full bow, the wrist remains aligned to the elbow.

Tuning and Intonation

Too many teachers take too much class time to tune the student's cellos, which takes precious *learning time* from the students, as students must eventually tune their own instruments. Playing left-hand pizzicato is a good exercise to begin intense listening. All string instruments should have fine tuners on all four metal strings (except bass) to facilitate this learning step. Tuning begins as a cooperative project between teacher and student but soon is the student's responsibility. If she can't hear when the string is tuned, she can't play in tune.

If the instrument does not have tuners on all four strings, the instrument is turned to face the seated player to be tuned. The C and G strings are plucked with the right thumb while the left-hand turns the pegs; the D and A strings are plucked with the left hard while the right hand turns the pegs. Obviously, the importance of fully operational tuning pegs cannot be stressed enough. The pegs are turned and set as on the violin.

When the cellists have become adept at plucking, bowing, and tuning individual strings to tune each string, they should develop the skill to tune the four strings from a single string—usually the A. Because the tuning pegs slip more easily in the tuning process on the cello than on the upper strings (due to the increased weight and tension of the string), fine tuners are important. Students should also use the bow rather than plucking to tune as soon as they are comfortable using the bow. The upper half of the bow is used, starting at the tip to tune the A, then the D and A strings together, a double stop. It is important that the lower string predominate in these double stops. Students need opportunities and a patient teacher to develop the skill of hearing the "beats" of an out-of-tune perfect fifth, and the ability to adjust the fine tuner on the D string to eliminate them. An advantage of the cello is that these "beats" are easier to hear than with violin and viola due to the larger size of the instrument and the greater dynamic level possible. Students should also begin early in their instruction to play the octave A harmonic and the one-third string harmonic for a unison A.

Harmonics

As suggested for the upper strings, cellists should begin soon to play harmonics. The thumb prepares for thumb positions in the highest positions.

One easy and fun exercise used to explore the upper register on harmonics is contained in Figure 22–4, "Taps." Students know the tune, so good intonation can be achieved quickly.

The use of harmonics requires a flexible thumb and left hand/fingers. It develops good habits with the elbow and explores the entire register of the cello when combined with the method books that usually begin in first position.

Figure 22–4 "Taps" on Cello Played With Two Different Harmonic Systems

LEFT-ARM AND HAND MOVEMENTS

The best left-hand position is one in which the forearm forms a straight line from the elbow to the wrist. This position enables the full energy of the arm to flow to the fingers. The wrist, held as an extension of the forearm, forms a straight line. The arm cannot hang down in a totally relaxed position, as this will send the energy or weight to the elbow and no farther. The arm should be held out so that the forearm and hand are approximately parallel to the floor. The most active movements are in the upper arm. The lower arm remains relatively passive and the wrist steady. The forearm rolls back and forth in response to the movement of the upper arm and the hand. If the wrist is too flexible and active (i.e., not remaining in line with the forearm), the power coming from the shoulder will be lost, resulting in little energy being sent to the fingers.

The thumb, except for vibrato, remains opposite the second finger when playing in the lower positions (Figure 22–5). The thumb touches the middle of the

Figure 22–5
Thumb Position: Opposite Second Finger

back of the neck to insure that the fingers are farther away from the fingerboard (above the strings—as if holding a tennis ball). For playing on the C and G strings, the left elbow moves forward and the thumb slides to the left, under the fingerboard, enabling the fingertips to more easily reach the lower strings. The left-hand fingers normally encompass a minor third without extending, but the player must learn to stretch the hand without losing power—the little finger should be as firm on the strings as the first finger.

The fingers are slightly curved with the tips pointing down at an angle on the strings demonstrating the "sloped" hand position (Figure 22–6). The fleshy parts of the left-hand fingers stop the strings. It is important that the thumb not squeeze against the neck as this results in the other four fingers squeezing, limiting flexibility.

Figure 22–6
Left Finger Position: Sloped

On a full-size cello, the first finger is placed more than 3 inches from the nut to produce a whole step. This distance is reduced in graduated steps with each smaller-size cello. On a half size cello, an E is played on the D string by placing the first finger about $2\frac{1}{4}$ inches from the nut. When the first finger is placed about 3 inches from the nut on the D string to play an E, each finger can play a half step. Without forward or backward extensions, the notes are shown in Figure 22–7 played in first position:

The left-hand must continually prepare for the next note. Because keys of D major, G major, A major, and F major predominate in today's method books, the cello is one of the first string instruments to be introduced to extensions.

Figure 22–7   First-Position Cello Notes on Each String

Extensions

Extensions are used to avoid slides, glissandos, and unnecessary shifts. Extensions can be improved by exercises that develop hand muscles if these are introduced early. Backward extensions are introduced when the student plays an E♭ or a B♭ using low first finger. Forward extensions occur between the first and second fingers. Any additional stretch is unnatural, and should be treated as a shift of a half position with the hand pivoting on the first finger.

Extensions are difficult for beginners but can be improved by exercises that develop the hand muscles, accustom the hand to stretching, and build strength in the left-hand and the left fingers. In extending the hand, the tip of the first finger remains in place, pivoting slightly; the middle fingers and thumb move a half step forward from the first finger. The hand must turn so that the first finger is stretched upward and the thumb, with the weight of the arm, remains behind the middle finger. In effect, the arm and hand shift down (toward the bridge) a half step while the first finger is in place for hand orientation and to serve as a pivot.

The backward extension is required in first through the higher positions. The backward extension involves moving the first finger back one-half step while leaving the hand and arm in place. The side of the finger is used instead of the pad, and the finger is not curved. The *remaining* three fingers are in first position configuration, as shown in Figure 22–8.

Figure 22–8   Backward Extension on Each Cello String

The middle two fingers and the thumb do shift the center of the arm's weight if necessary (usually in higher positions). Most teachers believe that the backward extension should be taught first since it is more natural and requires less adjustment from the whole hand. Also, among the first notes learned are E♭ and B♭, pitches requiring a lowered first finger.

Half position, more common on string bass, occurs when the first finger is used to play one-half step above the open string and the remaining three fingers are adjusted back one-half step as shown in Figure 22–9.

Figure 22–9   Half Position Notes on Cello

Forward extension requires the left-hand to move down the neck/fingerboard using the first finger as a hinge. The space between the first finger and the second finger is increased, leaving the first finger once more in a "straightened" position and pointing toward the player's left ear. The thumb remains opposite the second finger, enabling the fingering shown in Figure 22–10.

Figure 22–10   Forward Extension Notes on Cello

This fingering and the notation for extensions are used frequently by the cellist, especially in minor tonality. Scale drill will assist students to anticipate which fingers to use on which notes. In the example above, a student playing the passage on the G string may be confused as to whether the B should be played with second or third finger. By anticipating the need for the fourth finger for C#, the student would know that the B should be played with the second finger.

Shifting

There are three registers on the cello, each of which uses a different hand position. The first register includes the first four positions. Here the thumb is in its normal place behind the second finger. The second register consists of positions five, six, and seven. The thumb is still placed behind the neck of the cello, but the fingers reach down to the fingerboard that lies over the body of the instrument. The elbow should not drop nor the wrist rise. Rather the hand should remain in a position resembling first position, except the fingers are closer together; the thumb can move slightly up the left side of the back of the neck if it feels natural and tension is avoided. The positions of the fingers are similar to the finger position for the violin: A whole step can be reached from the first to the second finger and from the second to the third finger. In other words, rather than requiring four fingers to span a third, it can be done in this register with three fingers. The third register includes all positions above seventh. In these positions, the thumb is placed across the A and D strings and kept down at most times.

These highest positions are called "thumb positions." In them the edge of the thumb presses down the A and D strings while always remaining one whole step behind the first finger. These highest positions are the most demanding for the hand—the thumb's position is awkward to maintain and the fingers must be lifted higher in order to depress the string with sufficient weight. On the lower, heavier strings, the difficulty is slightly increased because of the resistance and thickness of the strings—thumb weight must be sufficient if a good tone is to be produced. In practicing or performing scale passages in thumb position, both the thumb and the lower fingers remain down when the higher fingers move. This makes shifting easier and avoids the need for excessive movements of the fingers. When the lower fingers depress the string, less movement (because of less pressure) is required of the higher fingers.

The thumb position is important for octaves, thirds, in the higher positions. Thumb exercises strengthen the thumb and provide security. With the first finger in fourth position, substitute the thumb. Then check the natural harmonics by checking with the open strings above. If they match, the position should be remembered and used to practice the major scale and arpeggios.

Adjusting the left-hand to the different positions of the three registers, performing the shifts between positions efficiently, and making use of the extended position of the hand require turning of the hand and arm. Further, cellists frequently employ a slight rotation of the body, the left side of the body rotating slightly forward on an upward shift (left-hand moving toward the bridge) and vice versa. This movement helps relax the body and assists in a smooth shift. In addition to this slight body rotation, the left elbow is slightly elevated when shifting to a higher position and lowered when moving back toward the scroll. This rotation seems to come naturally when shifting is introduced to young players. In fifth position, the whole arm has to be raised somewhat; in the upper positions, turning the upper part of the body may be necessary to get the fingers in the best position, particularly when 1–2–3 fingerings are used. Because the hand needs to move rapidly into place for the next note or the next shift into a new position, the hand will often parallel the strings slightly more than normal. Sometimes the interval of a half step is played with the same finger sliding to the new note in order to avoid a bad shift.

Fourth position is considered the easiest position on cello after first position. The thumb stops where the neck joins the body, so the position is easily located for accurate intonation. The fingers don't have to stretch as far as in first, second, and third positions, nor do they have to apply as much pressure to the strings as in the higher positions. Often, fourth position is introduced before second and third or even first because it provides quicker success for the student in shifting, as this shift is easily checked if students have been taught to tune using harmonics.

Shifting to a higher position can be taught using the analogy of throwing a baseball. The upper arm moves toward the bridge slightly before the lower arm and hand. Students should be taught to keep the finger on whatever note precedes the shift, on the same string (with barely any contact) to assist in moving the hand in a straight line. Keeping the finger on the same string (even if it is not the finger used for the note after the shift) allows the cellist greater freedom in relaxing the left thumb and supporting fingers without fear of losing the hand's orientation during the shift. The overall movement should resemble a graceful curve.

Vibrato

Cello vibrato differs from that for the violin and viola. The forearm is used. This larger to smaller muscle route requires the forearm to move back and forth in a linear motion with the fulcrum above the elbow (making it necessary for the thumb to leave its customary place when the fourth finger is on the string and in the higher positions). Because the finger is at a right angle to the strings, the fleshy pad of the finger rolls back and forth on the string to produce the fluctuation in pitch. This is in contrast to upper strings where the fingertip and knuckle joint move.

Forte passages are played with a wider vibrato than softer passages. Speed is a matter of individual taste, although for the lower strings, a slower vibrato is preferable to one that is too fast. Cello vibrato must be wide enough to establish a true feeling of the natural voice. If it is too narrow and fast, it sounds like stage fright; if it is too wide and slow, it sounds contrived. Students should learn to play vibrato with a wide range of pitch fluctuations, speed, and intensity. The vibrato serves to assist the bow in communicating the art inherent in the music.

THE RIGHT-ARM AND HAND MOVEMENTS

Bow Hold

While the left-hand is an expression of the cellist's thoughts, the right hand is the cellist's voice. To teach the proper bow hold, have the student take the cello bow in the right hand by the bow screw, with the bow hair facing to the left while holding the bow securely with the left-hand at the tip. (This allows a clear view of the following steps.) First, the thumb is inserted under the grip with the joint bent outward and the tip of the thumb securely placed on the stick and the right side of the thumb touching where the stick meets the grip. Second, the first finger rests over the bow against the wire between the first and second joint. The second finger goes over the bow and down the side of the frog touching the ferrule (where the hair enters). The third finger, like the second, goes over the bow and rests on the side of the frog (with the third finger on the silver mount and the second touching the bow hair at the spot where it joins the frog). Finally, the little finger wraps over the bow to about the middle of the frog—the tip reaches just to the right of the pearl eye. Figures 22–11a and 22–11b on page 386 illustrate this bow hold.

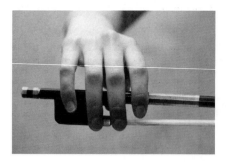
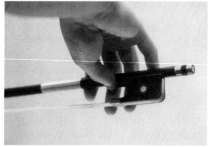

a) View from Front   b) View from Back   c) View of Frog

Figure 22–11 Cello Bow Hold from Various Angles

Since the cello bow is shorter, thicker, and heavier than the violin bow, it requires more support. The fingers guide the bow on the string, and only "grip" it when controlling "off the string" bowings and then the little finger serves both as support and as a counterbalance. The fingers guide the bow on the string, initiating the up bows and down bows, shifting the weight from one part of the hand to another. On the up bow, the first two fingers may control the beginning of the motion, shifting control to the last two fingers as the bow nears the frog.

In the playing position, the stick is tilted slightly toward the scroll. The right wrist is slightly arched when the bow is on the string near the frog (Figure 22–11c), and works like a hinge when changing bow direction. When the down bow stroke brings the tip of the bow to the string, the wrist is straight or slightly bent—but it should not be dropped.

The weight of the arm must be kept on the bow to prevent it from slipping downward. Because the bow tends to drop toward the floor, weight must be applied to keep it from slipping sideways and sagging completely out of playing position. On the other hand, too much weight stifles the resonance of the tone, making it dull. A happy balance must be achieved where the right hand is sufficient to control the bow, but relaxed enough to "pull" the best possible tone from the instrument in relation to speed and bow weight. The ear determines the best appropriate tone.

Common problems of the bow hold include (1) thumb inserted too far under the stick; (2) thumb is locked; (3) fingers dropping too far below the frog, resulting in holding the bow in the palm of the right hand; (4) the hand slants too far forward toward the tip or toward the bow screw; and (5) the back of the hand tilts forward, placing the bow at the wrong angle to the string.

Right-Arm and Hand Movements

Movement starts with the body weight and moves through the upper arm, coming from a relaxed shoulder. Lack of movement in the shoulder indicates unnecessary tenseness. The upper arm is the strongest part of the arm and is used for the extra pull required for the cello bow. Strength originates in the right arm, through the forearm, and allows the "wrist" to follow through the motions. The forearm must be relaxed to rotate as needed and serves somewhat as a device to refine the upper arm's strength into the wrist. During the change of bow direction, for example, the forearm changes direction slightly sooner than the fingers on the bow itself (the follow-through as discussed in the principles of strings chapter).

The right elbow's position is correct when the arm is held comfortably out from the body. When the bow is held correctly, with the tip placed on the strings, a straight right arm or one that is bent only very slightly should result. When playing at the frog, the inside of the forearm almost touches the edge of the cello, the fingers are almost straight, and the wrist is higher than when playing at the tip. Many texts exaggerate the different positions of the wrist in cello bowing. It is not necessary that the wrist form an arch when playing at the frog nor be lowered when playing at the tip. A common problem is that after an up-bow, some students fail to drop the elbow as they approach the frog on the down-bow. A slower bow is used on the C string.

The correct direction of the wrist is "up" at the frog, "down" at the tip, but not to the extreme—only enough to keep the bow controlled and keep the wrist in a straight line through the forearm to the elbow. Playing at the tip depends almost entirely on the muscles of the arm. An arm stretched to its full length and using the smaller muscles of the hand and wrist is not appropriate.

Pizzicato

In playing pizzicato on the cello, the thumb is placed at the side of the fingerboard. Plucking is done on different areas of the string for different effects: nearer the bridge for loud pizzicato and over the fingerboard for softer dynamics. The right thumb is placed against the right side of the fingerboard about four or five inches above the end of the fingerboard. The bow is held in a "fist" of the second, third and fourth fingers, while the first finger plucks the string about 2 to 3 inches above the end of the fingerboard to get the clearest tone and pitch. A sharper, more strident tone is created by plucking closer to the end of the fingerboard. The strings are pulled to the side rather than up because an upward pull would create a downward slap against the fingerboard.

In spots where the pizzicato must be played very quickly after the bowed note, it is easier to keep the bow in its regular position and to turn the hand enough to pluck with the second finger. In a simultaneous three-note pizzicato chord, the thumb takes the bottom note, the first finger the middle note, and the second finger the top note (arpeggiated). A four-note chord is almost always strummed with the thumb.

WHAT TO PRACTICE

Scales and études are a must for any musician. As students progress, they should be encouraged to play their scales two octaves with a variety of bowings and rhythms. Several octave arpeggios may be used for practicing shifting.

Études are designed to work on specific skills like smooth bow changes or shifts. A number of étude books are listed at the end of this chapter at three ability levels. Students should supplement class activities with these materials.

Thumb position is a technique required of all cellists. Mentioned earlier, thumb position is when the thumb comes to the front of the fingerboard and plays on the low string, while the other fingers curve more "over" the fingerboard. There is a common tendency to play sharp in thumb position. Possible solutions are:

1. Open the left-hand and observe the natural gap between the thumb and first finger, unlike the gap between the other fingers. This space is too easily transferred to the fingerboard.
2. Remain vigilant with the first finger, keeping it back; if the first finger is sharp, the other fingers will also be sharp. Practicing in front of a mirror is a means of checking one's position—check for naturalness and relaxation.

BIBLIOGRAPHY

Texts

Indicates out of print in 2001.

BORNOFF, GEORGE (1962). *Finger Patterns: With Addenda: A Basic Method Book for Violoncello.* Toronto: G. V. Thompson; reprints available from Newton Highlands, MA: FASE.

COWDEN, ROBERT L. (1995). *Highlights From the American String Teacher (1984–1994) Cello Forum.* Reston, VA: American String Teachers Association.

*COWLING, ELIZABETH (1983). *The Cello,* 2nd ed. New York: Scribner's.

DE RUNGS, MARIA (1970). *Cello Syllabus.* Boston: Branden Press.

*EISENBERG, MAURICE (1980). *Cello Playing of Today.* Borough Green, Sevenoaks, Kent: Novello.

EPPERSON, GORDON (1980). *The Art of Cello Teaching.* Bloomington, IN: American String Teachers Association.

HOARSFALL, JEAN (1974). *Teaching the Cello to Groups.* New York: Oxford University Press.

MANTEL, GERHARD (1995). *Cello Technique; Principles and Forms of Movement* (1st paper). Bloomington: Indiana University Press.

*PLEETH, WILLIAM (1982). *Cello.* New York: Schirmer Books.

POTTER, LOUIS A. (1980). *The Art of Cello Playing: A Complete Textbook—Method for Private or Class Instruction,* 2nd ed. Princeton, NJ: Summy-Birchard.

SAZER, VICTOR (1995). *New Directions in Cello Playing.* Los Angeles: Of Note.

SMITH, G. J. (1993). *Cellist's Guide to the Core Technique,* 2nd ed. St. Louis: American String Teachers Association.

STOWELL, ROBIN (ed.) (1999). *The Cambridge Companion to the Cello.* New York: Cambridge University Press.

Cello Studies

Easy—Beginning (elementary to middle school)

Applebaum. *String Builder* (Belwin).
Dotzauer. *Violoncello Method,* Book I (C. Fischer).
Grant. *First Position Studies* (Ludwig).
Herfurth. *A Tune a Day* (2 vols.) (Boston Music).
Lee. *40 Easy Exercise* (Leeds).
Matz. *The Complete Cellist* (Tetra).
O'Reilly. *String Power* (2 vols.) (Kjos).
Popper. *15 Easy Studies* (International).
Sato-Suzuki. Sato *Cello Method* (Summy-Birchard).
Such. *New School of Studies* (Augener).
Werner. *Practical Method for Violoncello,* Book I (Suvini Zerboni).
Whistler. *Introducing the Positions for Cello,* Book I (Rubank).

Medium (middle to high school)

Benoy-Sutton. *Introduction to Thumb Position* (Oxford).
Deak. Modern *Method for the Violoncello (2 vols.)* (Elkan-Vogel).
Dotzauer. *Violoncello Method, Book II* (C. Fischer).
Duport. *21 Études (2 vols.)* (G. Schrimer).
Epperson. *A Manual of Essential Cello Techniques* (Fox).
Frank. *Scales and Arpeggios* (Schott).
Grant. *Basic Thumb Position Studies for the Young Cellist* (Concert Music).
Kabelensky. *Major—Minor Études* (Leeds).
Klengel. *Daily Exercises (3 vols.)* (Breitkof & Hartel).
Kummer. *19 Études Melodiques* (Peters).
Marcelli. *Cello Method* (C. Fischer).
Matz. *25 Studies* (Dominis).
Merk-Klengel. *20 Studies* (International).
Piatti. *Cello Method,* Book II (Augener).
Popper. *Intermediate Studies* (International).
Schroeder. *170 Foundation Studies. (3 vols.)* (C. Fischer).
Whistler. *Introducing the Positions for Cello,* Book II (Rubank).

Advanced (high school and college)

Cossman. *Concert Studies* (International).
Duport. *21 Études* (G. Schirmer).
Epperson, Spinoza, and Rusch. *The Artists' Studio for Cello* (Kjos).
Francesconi. *Practical School for Violoncello,* Book III (Suvini Aerboni).
Franchomme. *Caprices* (International).
———. *12 Études* (International).
Gruetzmacher. *Daily Exercises* (G. Schirmer).
———. *Technology of Cello Playing (2 vols.)* (International).
Guerini-Silva. *13 Studies* (Ricordi).
Klengel. *Technical Exercises* (International).
Kreutzer-Silva. *42 Studies* (Peters).
Lee-Rose. *40 Melodic Studies* (G. Schirmer).
Magg. *Cello Exercises* (Borlke).
Schultz. *26 Technical Studies* (Schirmer).
———. *Technical Studies for the Advanced Cellist* (Schott).
Such. *New School of Cello Playing* (Stainer & Bell).
Yampolsky. *Violoncello Techique* (MCA).

Instructional Videos

Casals Master Class, 3 vol. (Pablo Casals with Cathrine Graff, 1961). Ann Arbor, MI: Shar Products Company.

The Cello (Manon Robertshaw, Rudiger Barth, and John Scott, 1999). Miami: Warner Brothers Publications.

The Cello. (Doug Bruestle, 1993). Canoga Park, CA: MVP.

Cello with Doug Bruestle for Beginners (Doug Bruestle, 1991). Van Nuys, CA: Backstage Pass Productions.

Cello Master Class with Bernard Greenhouse, 2 vol. (Bernard Greenhouse, 1993) Ridgefield, CT: Crescent Software.

Cello Sounds of Today (9 Vol.): 1. *Introduction*; 2. *Positioning the player and His Cello and The Fusion of the Right Hand and the Bow;* 3. *General Orientation of the Fingerboard and Placing the Left Hand, Flexibility of the Webs and Intonation;* 4. *Scales and Scale Bowings;* 5. *Diatonic Sequences and Scales in Broken Thirds, Solid Thirds, and Sixths;* 6. *The Independence of the Fingers in Multiple Stops, Chords, Embellishments, and Arpeggios;* 7. *Exercises in Thumb Positions;* 8. *Symphonic Cello Soli, Selected Tutti Passages from the Symphonic Literature;* 9. *The Mechanics and Aesthetics of Modern Cello Playing* (Fritz Magg, 1985). Bloomington, IN: Indiana University Audio-Visual Center.

Maestro Music Instrument Instructional Video for the Cello. (Douglas Bruestle, 1998). Van Nuys, CA: Backstage Pass Productions.

Suzuki Cello School. (6 tapes, 1984). Princeton, NJ: Summy-Birchard Music.

Recommended Classical Cello Recording Artists

Julius Berger playing Bloch and Kilmeyer
Colin Carr playing Brahms
Pablo Casals playing Beethoven and Bruch
Yo Yo Ma playing Schumann and Stravinsky

Recommended Jazz Cello Recording Artists

Bop, Cool: Harry Babasin
Cool, "Third Stream"; Fred Katz
Hard Bop: Doug Watkins
Hard Bop, Post-Bop: Richard Davis (also classical)
Avant-Garde, New Age: David Darling
Avant-Garde, Free Jazz: Abdul Wadud

23

The Double Bass

The double bass survived the evolution process with less change than did the other strings. With its sloped shoulders, it is similar to the Renaissance bass viol. The present bass is an octave lower than the older instrument and in this respect more nearly resembles the rare double bass viol popular through the seventeenth century.

The string bass is sometimes treated as the stepchild of the string family. Typically, much less attention is given to its mastery in heterogeneous string classes. There is also far less material written "about" the bass than the other string instruments.

The bass is the lowest voice of the string family. The bass is found in full, half, and three-quarter sizes. The full size bass is seldom seen in public school; the three-quarter is most popular. Whereas the other strings are tuned in fifths, the bass is tuned in fourths and sounds an octave below the notation shown in Figure 23–1.

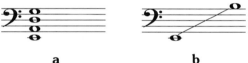

a   b

Figure 23–1
Open Strings (a) and First Position Range (b) of the Bass

The bass differs slightly in design having sloping and more rounded shoulders than the other string instruments. Basses have large and small bouts, 40 inch or 43 inch strings, a flat or swell back, and adjustable bridges. They also use a mechanical tuning mechanism, due to the string's mass, length and tension, rather than wooden pegs as illustrated in Figure 20–10 (Chapter 20). The bass mechanism (Figure 23–2) holds the string more firmly and precisely than do pegs and with a string winder reduces problems of replacing a broken string.

In many respects the bass is the most difficult instrument for the young player—not only due to its size, but because its longer and thicker strings require more strength yet the same control as the other string instruments. When bowing, the bass is slower in response. Further, the intervals for the fingers are farther apart and the low pitches are more difficult to hear.

The role of the bass in the orchestra is of paramount importance. The bass establishes the basis for balance of the

Figure 23–2
Mechanical Tuner for Double Bass

ensemble and provides the harmonic foundation for orchestral music, it also serves as a rhythm instrument.

Wind ensembles and symphonic bands use the bass to good advantage. Currently there is an increase in the number of high school bands and wind ensembles that are including a bass in the group. The school's jazz band will find the instrument indispensable; in the jazz band pizzicato becomes the primary playing technique.

The single greatest obstacle for the development of a bass player is its expense and its transportation. Young players cannot be expected to carry the bass home each day to practice; ideally the school could provide one for school use and one for home practice.

SELECTING THE INSTRUMENT

Although basses are available in smaller sizes, teachers, students, and parents should consider half and three-quarter size instruments. Because most bass purchases are made by the school, teachers should limit their purchases to half and three-quarter size instruments (with about 75 percent at the three-quarter size). Most basses are constructed of a solid spruce top with a solid neck and scroll. The tuning screws (rather than pegs) are preferably solid brass with nickelplating. The fingerboard should be examined by an expert to ensure it is not too high for the beginning student.

Chromium steel strings are best for beginners, but students should experiment with gut-core strings as they progress. What is essential is the spacing of strings along the fingerboard. Sometimes bridges are not cut exactly, preventing evenly spaced strings. Teachers should inspect beginners' instruments and refer those instruments in question to a string repairperson.

The bow should be made of Brazil wood with an ebony frog and nickel silver ring. Most students start the bass with a French bow, but by the second year they should be instructed on German bow technique and provided the option of using a German bow. The French bow is easier to monitor in a class setting, but many private teachers or the students themselves may prefer the German bow.

The case for the bass is an essential investment. A fleece-lined canvas or cordubon case that fits well is the very minimum. A bow holder as illustrated in Figure 23–3 is useful for extended pizzicato sections and jazz bassists who use the bow infrequently. Placing any bow on the music stand is asking for damage, especially for the widest bow in the string family.

Figure 23–3
Bow Holder for Double Bass

HOLDING THE BASS

Whether the bass is played while seated on a stool or standing, the main task is to establish a position that is comfortable and allows the left arm and hand and right arm and hand to move appropriately. Standing is more appropriate when instructing beginners. As with the cello, the endpin must be adjusted to facilitate playing position and correct posture. It must be sharp to provide instrument stability and is positioned eight or nine inches in front and slightly to the right of the left foot. The peg adjustment usually places the player's left-hand at chest level when playing in half position.

Figure 23–4
Holding a Half Size Double
Bass in a Standing Position

Figure 23–5
Holding a Three-quarter
Size Double Bass Using
Stool

One's legs should be spread about shoulder width, at right angles, and the body's weight evenly distributed. The knees are not locked and probably should be slightly bent to allow the player to flex them at any time. Likely a bit more of the player's weight will be on the right foot—the important word is *slightly*. The endpin, preferably with a rubber tip, should be extended so that the right forearm is perpendicular to the floor and even with the top of the bridge. Place the side of the bass against the left side of the abdomen, near the groin, and allow it to balance (have student raise his hands in the air). The student should strike for a "weightless" bass, when the left-hand is free to move flexibly up and down the fingerboard and the right hand can attend to bowing (Figure 23–4).

If the player sits on a stool, a strap may be used, designed to stretch from the leg of the stool with spaced holes in the strap for the endpin. Experimenting with the endpin will determine the length needed to position the bass comfortably and at the proper angle, as illustrated in Figure 23–5. When sitting, the nut of the instrument should align with the forehead and the left-hand positioned to "shake hands" with the bridge. Of importance is the ability to bow near the bridge without leaning over the instrument.

When seated, the player sits with the left leg forward. The bass is tilted back and to the right so that the upper right bout rests against the left side of the body just below the rib cage. For a sixth grade student of average height, a half size bass should allow the lower right bout to rest against the left knee.

The left knee may be used to partially support the instrument, but not the left shoulder. The left thumb serves to balance the bass and prevent it from rotating, but is not used to support the instrument, as the thumb must remain mobile. The body needs to be able to move and cannot be locked into place by the instrument. The angle of the instrument varies with the student's size, but is generally tilted 60 to 75 degrees from an upright position.

The thumb touches the back of the neck opposite the first finger, with the hand rounded as if holding an orange. The thumb however needs to feel natural, fall where it is comfortable, and move to assist the left fingers without ever becoming "locked" in any given position. The upper arm is well away from the body—only slightly below horizontal. The forearm angles upward to allow the wrist to be in a position that enables the fingers to touch the strings at a perpendicular angle.

LEFT-ARM AND HAND MOVEMENTS

The upper left arm is held away from the player's body, with the wrist and the arch of the hand away from the neck so that the fingers can contact the string from as great a distance as possible. The elbow is up and shoulder down. The muscular strength for the left fingers starts in the body, moving from the *back*, through the upper arm, and runs through the arms to the fingers. As with the cello, the bass strings are depressed using the muscles at the base of the fingers. The distance between the wrist and the fingers is important to generate the extra weight needed.

The wrist is almost a straight extension of the elbow with the elbow held high enough to allow the fingers to be approximately perpendicular to the strings (see Figure 23–6). The second and third fingers are placed at right angles to the strings. The idea of a rigid frame for the left-hand has been overemphasized; the position of the fingers is of importance and a slight downward slant of these fingers is not incorrect. The thumb reaches to about the center of the neck, but does not hold the instrument; it simply rests against the neck to aid the motion of the opposite fingers. The little finger may be pointed slightly downward. Fingers must be placed firmly on the strings, with enough of the fleshy part of the tip used to cover the thick string, but not so much that the tone is deadened. On the bass the resistance offered by the heavy, long strings is such that the fingers must actually stop the string—push it down to the fingerboard—rather than touching it only enough to change pitch. A lighter touch may produce a slight change of pitch or a harmonic but also can produce a rumble or a buzzing sound.

**Figure 23–6
Left-Arm and Finger
Positions for Playing a
"Balanced" Bass**

Fingers become sore, especially beginners', but they soon toughen with daily practice. Students often initially play first in the upper positions where the need for left-hand finger pressure is less. Most teachers begin with third position rather than first. Open string playing is usually delayed. Shifting is usually accomplished with the finger that is down rather than with the finger that is to play the next pitch. Players often shift more frequently than necessary to avoid using the weaker little finger. This is not a good habit. With sufficient use, the fourth finger gains greatly in strength and can reduce the need for excessive shifting. One technique is to play major scales on one string using all four fingers with shifts, which assists with ear training as well as left-hand technique. Then practice chromatic scales of one or two octaves on each string, using shifts, and gradually increasing the speed. Octaves on the bass are performed by skipping a string, using the first finger on the lower string and the fourth finger on the higher string. Bass players make many adjustments of the left-hand, pivoting rather than shifting, using the third finger and in some cases a collapsed hand. The third finger is commonly used for F♯ on the G string. Bass players who do not follow good principles of motion and achieve tension free playing spend considerable time in the doctor's office.

The most common left-hand problems stem from holding the elbow too low and from using the left-hand to help support the instrument. Unless the elbow is high enough to allow a straight wrist and fingers perpendicular to the string, tension will build, the wrist will fatigue and/or cramp, and the forearm will stiffen. If the instrument is leaning on the hand for support, shifting is difficult. The hand must be relaxed and free to move quickly and easily; it cannot be burdened by the weight of the instrument. Students must avoid the following:

1. Vice grips with the left-hand.
2. Pincers between the thumb and fingers.
3. Letting the hand collapse and the thumb slide under and around the neck (often called the "Babe Ruth grip").
4. The 1–2–4 finger spacing should resemble a cello extension; that is, the second finger should not be too close to the first.

Tuning

There are two common methods for tuning the instrument, both using the bow. The most common method (or what is taught first) is to lightly touch the string with the left third finger half way between the bridge and the nut. The sound will be an octave higher (first harmonic) and enable the student to hear the pitch more clearly and accurately. A second method is to use harmonics that will produce octave pitches from adjacent strings. For example, the first finger, as described in the first method, touches the D string at the midpoint to sound an upper D. With the hand in a "normal" playing position, the fourth finger lightly touches the G string about one-third the distance down the neck, producing the second harmonic on the G string that is also a D.

Left-Hand

Bass players must learn to listen to their own playing as do all fine instrumentalists. The bass string is so long that bass players can be "close" to the pitch and it may seem acceptable. But playing the fundamental of the chord in the low register and with a string of great length makes it even more important to strive for good intonation. Visual aids can help, but the ear is the best judge. Playing harmonics that are easier to hear also provides kinesthetic landmarks.

Many students in school music programs learn to play bass in first position. On a three-quarter-size bass, the distance from the nut to the first finger is approximately five inches. The left fingers require equal distances between first, second, and fourth. Students can practice this position by holding Ping Pong balls between these fingers. Gary Karr also uses Ping Pong balls on the bow to demonstrate the importance of a horizontal bow stroke.

The left hand is curved with the wrist and arch of the hand away from the neck. It is essential for bass technique (finger action, vibrato, shifting) to keep the hand somewhat open and elongated. If the hand is too close to the neck, technique is limited. The palm should not rest against the neck.

Vibrato

Vibrato on the bass is produced by the left forearm and wrist, nearly identical to that for the cello. The motion is from the elbow. Bass vibrato is usually slower and wider than for any of the other strings. The motion makes the fleshy finger pads roll on the string. Strength for playing with vibrato, especially on long notes for which it is used most frequently, is achieved by keeping the fingers close together rather than spread. This "block" hand must be able to move readily back to a "melodic" position to cover moving notes. The best vibrato seems to be produced when the student attempts to oscillate the pitch at the same frequency she feels the string is vibrating.

RIGHT-ARM AND HAND MOVEMENTS

There are two types of bass bows, both widely used: the French and the German. These require different bow holds. The French hold is more widely used by symphony players in the United States because it offers more flexibility and freedom of movement than the German hold. The position for holding the bass French bow is similar to that for the cello (Figures 23–7a and 23-7b). The chief difference is that the index finger grips the bow at the middle joint rather than at the first joint. The inside corner of the thumb is placed in the corner of the frog, with the thumb bent and flexible. The third and fourth fingers contact the concave side of the frog; the little finger is over the stick about the length of a fingernail. The wrist is generally straight but flexible. When playing at the bow tip, the index finger and thumb use a twisting motion to apply weight to the tip; at the frog, the bow is lifted and bal-

a) View from Front

b) View from Back

Figure 23–7 The French Bow and Bow Hold

anced by the thumb, first, and little finger. American-made French bows are generally identical to German bows except for the frog; in reality the French bass bow should be shorter than a German bow due to weight.

With the German bow, used by Gary Karr and Jeremy Miller, two outstanding contemporary bassists, the frog is placed between the thumb and little finger and against the web of the thumb and fingers (palm up). The first, second, and third fingers rest along the under right side of the stick for support, with the first finger providing most of the support. The little finger must remain curved to prevent a tense wrist. Gary Karr calls the holding position the bow cradle, not a bow grip, to emphasize comfort and flexibility (Figures 23–8a, 23–8b, and 23–8c).

Control of the bow is necessary to produce all the effects on the string bass. The elbow should not protrude to the right when bowing, but should generally fall along the line formed by a straight (though relaxed) arm. A free wrist action is necessary for a smooth bow change and for varying the types of bow stroke used. Because the bow position is controlled by the bow hold, the bow is tilted, resting on the inner edge of the bow hair. Because the weight applied to the bow is greater than for the other strings, most—and sometimes all—of the hair actually comes in contact with the string in spite of this tilt. The bow is usually placed as close to the bridge as possible to "pull" the darkest, richest sound possible. Gary Karr suggests the distance from the bow's contact point to the bridge is dictated by the length of the string (or left finger position) the player always trying to vibrate as much (length of) the string as possible. Another example: If given the option of playing A on the D string or open A, the open A is more desirable as it allows more string to vibrate. The bass player has proportionally much less bow hair available to her to produce a satisfactory tone and must continually experiment, changing bow speed when changing the contact point and also changing speed and bow length when

Figure 23–8 The German Bow and Bow Hold

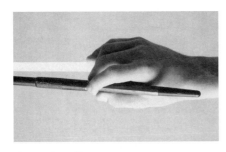

a) View from Front

b) View from Back

c) On Strings

playing at the frog and the tip. String crossings also require adjustments in bowing to retain evenness in tone quality.

Because the bass bow requires some strength, the German bow and hold is increasing in popularity in the United States. A final, but important, point is that the bass often needs to use a slower bow speed (relying on weight) than the higher-pitched string instruments to get to the core sound. Many teachers call for full bow from the entire ensemble, which forces the bass players to use too much bow speed.

WHAT TO PRACTICE

The student should start with pizzicato playing using a wide circular motion, rotating the entire right arm at the shoulder to pluck the strings and "pull" the string sound from the bass. The first efforts at bowing should use short strokes to emulate the sound of the pizzicato playing.

Next, as for the other string instruments, the bass player should pluck harmonics by rote. The first harmonic is half the distance of the string, next the second and third harmonics are played. The tune "Taps" using the thumb as "another" finger, is shown in Figure 23–9. As with cello, "Taps" is a fun piece to help develop a gentle, relaxed left-hand touch and motion, good left elbow and arm position, and it should be played pizzicato and arco.

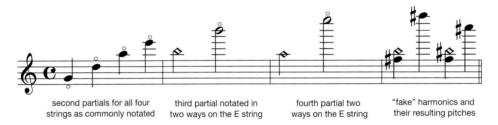

| second partials for all four strings as commonly notated | third partial notated in two ways on the E string | fourth partial two ways on the E string | "fake" harmonics and their resulting pitches |

Figure 23–9 Bass Harmonics.
With natural harmonics in first position student can get notes a third apart depending on high and low position. Artifical harmonics are not feasible in the lower positions.

The bass strings are not only longer, they are thicker and heavier, requiring more weight on the string for it to respond. Students should apply the greatest bow pressure at the beginning of the bow stroke—that is, "dig into the string"—then immediately adjust the pressure to produce the appropriate dynamic level. The weight of the bow does not change drastically, especially in forte or fortissimo passages, but there is a slight reduction for softer tones, only to have the weight reapplied and/or tilted so that more bow hair makes contact with the string when the stroke approaches the tip.

This technique of using a "bite" or somewhat harsher articulation is easier to do at the frog than at the tip. Bass players practice both. Bass players also strive to reduce the harshness of the initial articulation so that it becomes more controlled.

As with all string instruments, the bow is kept parallel to the bridge (see Figure 23–8c) and at a contact point between the bridge and fingerboard where the best tone is produced. Because the bow is farther from the eyes than with violin, this positioning is more problematic. This "level" bowing plane is a kinesthetic motion that needs to become automatic and requires the new player to practice with a mirror to learn the parallel "feel" of the right arm and wrist when playing on the four different strings.

On a half size bass, to play an E on the D string the first finger stops the string about 3¾ inches from the nut; consequently, in order to play the ascending F♯, one must use fingers two, three and four with four stopping the string in the appropriate spot for the pitch. On a three-quarter bass, the E requires the first finger to be about 5 inches from the nut with greater spacing between the fingers in order for the fourth finger to reach F♯.

In general the third finger is used to support and strengthen the fourth finger when playing bass (until position VI is reached). The third finger, in positions I–V, is rarely used as a substitute for a fourth or second finger pitch. For example, on the open D string the first finger plays E, the fourth finger plays F♯, explaining

Figure 23–10 First Seven Positions for Double Bass

why the bass is tuned in fourths rather than fifths like the other string instruments. The next string would be G.

Due to the size (length and thickness) of the bass strings, and it's sounding an octave below the notes written, there is some leeway with regard to finger placement for accurate intonation.

The E string on the bass is the lowest sound in the orchestra (except for bass extensions and the organ). It is traditionally played with a slower bow motion than any other string in the string family and a bow weight that requires digging into the E string almost to the extent that it is pushed to the A string.

The size of the bass means that students find their way around the instrument kinesthetically rather than looking at their fingers and bow motion.

CARE AND MAINTENANCE

Care of the instrument includes purchase of a quality soft case. The case is expensive, but a wise investment. If one spends $3,000 or more on a fine musical instrument, why not spend another $400 to make it last and depreciate less? Hard cases, with wheels, are also a possibility. Carrying the bass by the bouts or the neck is preferred over carrying it by the fingerboard; the wheel attachment is available for replacement for the endpin, so heavy lifting can be minimized. Picking the instrument up from the floor should be done by gently rolling it on its ribs rather that sliding it along the floor, so that the edges are not rubbed and damaged.

Protectors are now available for the bouts when the bass is placed on its side. Also useful are the bow holds that attach to the tailpiece. Bass rosin must be used on the bow hair—it is stickier than the rosin for the other string instruments.

BIBLIOGRAPHY

Texts

* *Indicates out of print in 2001.*

BENFIELD, WARREN, and JAMES DEAN (1973). *The Art of Double Bass Playing.* Evanston, IL: Summy-Birchard.

BORNOFF, GEORGE (1953). *Bornoff's Patterns in Position: Bass.* Toronto: G. V. Thompson; reprints available from Newton Highlands, MA: FASE.

COWDEN, ROBERT L. (1995). *Highlights From the American String Teacher (1984–1994) Double Bass Forum.* Reston, VA: American String Teachers Association.

*GRODNER, MURRAY (1974). *Comprehensive Catalog of Available Literature for the Double Bass,* 3rd ed. Bloomington, IN: Lemure Musical Research.

*KROLICK, EDWARD J. (1957). *Basic Principles of Double Bass Playing.* Washington DC: Music Educators National Conference.

STANTON, DAVID H. (1982). *The String (Double) Bass.* Evanston, IL: Instrumentalist.

TURETZKY, BERTRAM (1989). *The Contemporary Contrabass,* rev. ed. Berkeley: University of California Press.

Double Bass Studies

Easy—Beginning (elementary or middle school)

Applebaum. *Bass Methods* (Belwin).

Baklanova. *10 Easy Pieces* (Leeds).

Berryman. *Intonation Plus* (Hal Leonard).

Findeisen. *Complete Method* (4 vols.) (International).

Gale. *Gale's Practical Studies for Double Bass* (Double Bass Music).

Marcelli. *Carl Fischer Basic Method for the String Bass* (2 vols.) (C. Fischer).

Nanny. *Complete Method for the Double Bass* (A. Leduc).

Simandl. *New Method for the Double Bass* Book I. (C. Fischer).

Ward. *Elementary Method for Double Bass* (Rubank).

Zimmerman. *Elementary Double Bass Method* (G. Schirmer).

Medium (middle or high school)

Applebaum. *Building Technic* (4 vols.) (Belwin).

Bille. *New School for Double Bass* (Ricordi).

———. *Orchestral Bowing Etudes* (Belwin.)

Bottesini. *Metodo Per Contrabasso* (Ricordi).
Butler. *Progressive Method* (2 vols.) (C. Fischer).
Dragonetti. *Five Studies* (Carish).
Flesch. *Scale System* (C. Fischer)
Grodner. *An Organized Method of String Playing* (P. International)
Hause. *96 Etudes* (Theodore Presser).
Kayser-Winsel. *36 Studies* (International).
Kreutzer-Simandl. *18 Studies* (International).
Lee. *Studies.* (International).
Storch-Hrabe. *57 Studies* (2 vols.) (Universal).

Advanced (high school or college)

Drew, Spinosa, and Rusch. *The Artists' Studio for Strings* (Bass) (Kjos).
Hrabe. *86 Etudes* (International).
Janowsky. *Rhythmic Studies in Velocity* (Encore).
Schwabe. *Scale Studies* (International).
Simandl. *Gradus ad Parnassuma 24 Studies* (2 vols.). (International).
———. *30 Etudes for the String Bass* (C. Fischer).
Slama. *66 Studies in All Keys* (International).
Sturm. *110 Studies* (2 vols.) (International).

Instructional Videos

All Star Bass Series—Left-hand Bass Techniques with 10 artists' in-depth look at techniques, rhythm ideas, developing speed, and variety of fingerings for scales arpeggios, and chords.
All Star Bass Series—Right Hand Bass Techniques with 10 artists' in-depth look at techniques, speed, bowing technique, open string use, and more.
Basic Bass, Part I—Stringing, rhythm and harmonic theory, basic scales and bass patterns.
Basic Bass, Part II—Tuning with harmonics, technical exercises, neck familiarization.
Basically Karr (Gary Karr, 1992). Palatine, IL: Sharper Video Productions.

Jazz Bass Videos

Double Bass: Vocabulary 1. (Jeff Salem, 1997.) Toronto: Salem Drum Co.
The Acoustic Bass; Musicianship and Improvisational Techniques (Mike DeMicco, 1999). Woodstock, NY: Homespun Video.
Karr Tunes (Gary Karr, 1991). Madison, WI: University of Wisconsin, Madison.

Recommended Classical Bass Recording Artists

Willi Beyer playing Debussy and Schenberg
Lucas Drew playing Gibson and Surinach
Gary Karr playing Dvorak and Ramiser
Wolfgang Gutler playing Bottesini and Hindemith

Recommended Jazz Bass Recording Artists

Chicago Dixieland: Ed Garland.
Swing: Walter Page & Milt Hinton ("The Judge," has appeared on more recordings than any other individual; continued through the 1990s).
Bop: Oscar Pettiford.
Bop, Hard Bop, Post-Bop, Avant-Garde: Charles Mingus.
Hard Bop, Post-Bop: Ron Carter.
Hard Bop, Avant-Garde, Free Jazz: Charlie Haden.

24

Rehearsal Routines

The word *rehearsal* is familiar to musicians. It comes from the Old French word *rehercer*, meaning "to harrow again" (also the word from which the word *hearse* was eventually derived). Interestingly, one of the definitions of *harrow* is "to torment." A more positive note is that harrowing is, of course, used to prepare the field for seed, part of the process of producing a good crop. However, to extend the discussion, there are rehearsals that do not harrow in either sense, rehearsals that are satisfying enough to the student but are not effective for learning. For example, there are those that drill endlessly on a few contest selections, those that simply entertain the students, and those that rehearse music chosen only to entertain the public.

In examining the rehearsal as preparation, considerations in these two chapters are given to the following:

Chapter 24

1. Score Preparation
2. Rehearsal Planning
3. Daily Routines
4. Tuning and Intonation
5. How to Practice

Chapter 25

6. Focusing the Rehearsal
7. Selection of Music
8. Phrasing
9. Tone, Balance, Blend, and Instrumentation
10. Musical Independence
11. Tempo, Meter, and Rhythm
12. Musical Interpretation
13. Bowing
14. The Jazz Program
15. Concerts

The rehearsal depends on the conductor. Ideally, she has the following qualifications. First, she has a passion for music, for teaching, and for people. Second, she is a good musician who can read a full score with an understanding of the music and its compositional and performance history. She knows how to isolate, teach, and rehearse the subtleties of the music and how to identify the major technical problems. Third, as a good teacher she is acquainted with bowings, fingerings, and the unique problems of *each instrument* in the ensemble. Fourth, as a good conductor she can use the baton to help her group understand what she wants from them and is able to teach the individual members to respond to specific gestures. Fifth, as a receptive human being, her mannerisms, appearance, and attitudes do not alienate her from students nor does she attempt to be their peer but demonstrates a model of professionalism. She is receptive to the mood of the group and able to use that mood to advance individual learning. She knows how to establish a rapport with most of her students. She understands the importance or need of the group's sense of accomplishment as well as that of each individual. She has a sense of humor and enough security to admit her own mistakes.

Some conductors view themselves as actors. It is imperative to exude energy and enthusiasm for the task at hand even when one feels crabby. Expressing enthusiasm should not all be an act. While rehearsing the daily routines that gradually improve the ensemble's sound, precision, and musicianship over long periods of time, anyone who is not genuinely enthused by observing students grow musically should pursue another profession. Each one of us was, in varying degrees, attracted to music education by dreams of conducting great masterworks performed by professionals—your students must become professionals. In reality, the goals of music education require a better teacher than a conductor... and, ideally, someone outstanding as a teacher and performer.

Another characteristic of successful ensemble directors/teachers is their ability to engage students to work together as a team. Not unlike a sports coach, the orchestra/band director must help the group develop pride, *esprit de corps*, group dynamics, cooperative learning, responsibility, a work ethic, and respect for the contribution each person makes to the performance. (Phil Jackson's autobiography *Sacred Hoops* is a wonderful discussion of taking the last-place Chicago Bulls and getting the players to work together to win multiple national championships.) When the last-stand second violins or back-row clarinetists feel they are making a contribution to something important, they will remain motivated. The teacher must believe it herself and convince the students that the whole is greater than the sum of its parts while encouraging everyone to be aware and respectful of the individual parts.

As mentioned in Chapter 2, "Objectives," guided activities and cooperation among members of an ensemble require effort and that thought is based on explicit individual and group objectives established cooperatively by the teacher and students. For many students, instrumental music will be the most important influence during their school years. Experiences should be selected and guided toward the development of positive attitudes (enhanced by experiential objectives), personal growth (knowledge, skill, and understanding), and the ability to think critically when evaluating music or musical performances. These objectives lead to musical independence—a primary goal of music education.

The overall purpose of each rehearsal (each a new venture) is to develop musical understanding; secondary purposes are to prepare a concert while enjoying the experience, focusing on and developing character and the qualities of good citizenship. Focusing on the first facilitates the secondary objectives. Because effective rehearsing is dependent on objectives, the daily objectives must be attainable. The director should clearly formulate a rehearsal plan, including types and levels of objectives and rehearsal procedures—and then follow the plan. After the rehearsal, a review, reflection, and evaluation complete the venture. Video or audiotaping one's teaching for self-assessment cannot be overdone.

Because the primary focus of this text is instrumental music performance, the objectives of interest are those that meet performance and conducting goals. Again, refer to Chapter 2.

SCORE PREPARATION

There is no single "best" procedure to prepare a score. All conductors *must* know a work in order to rehearse it efficiently, and the extent to which the director knows the score determines how much she can accomplish. Knowing the music and the score thoroughly is the conductor's first responsibility, but all too often administrative details interfere and she resorts to sight-reading along with the ensemble. When the conductor "discovers" elements of the work when she is already on the podium, an effective rehearsal is impossible. Score preparation makes the rehearsal possible.

Orchestra and band directors who learn the music along with their students are infamous. During the initial sight-reading and first few weeks of rehearsal, these conductors do not know the score well enough to give needed cues. By performance time, however, the poor ensemble is cued to death—at the time the members least need them.

The music is in the sound, not in the printed notation. Alice Parker defines music as what is *not* on the page. Scores are marked for learning, not as a guide to conducting. Teachers who conduct only their markings are generally insecure and mechanical, do not listen beyond what is "highlighted," and are not prone to enjoying creative and "special" moments during performance. Battisti and Garofalo write: "The conductor should approach score study as an imaginative musician, a creator, and not simply as a decoder of notation."[1]

Studying a score is similar to touring a house, only with more effort. Like the architect who draws detailed plans, the composer constructs a musical outline that is as accurate as Western notation allows. What the contractor, builders, decorators, and residents do with the architect's drawing is to make it come alive and express the human experience; they determine the character of the house. What the conductor is able to do with a score is like what the contractor does with the blueprint: turns it into something real, something tangible. Hearing the score is like taking a tour of "the home"; one enters the front door, looks about the foyer, takes a tour of the living room or kitchen, then into another room, sometimes connected by long hallways, sometimes no hallway at all—each room different in shape and size, different in color schemes, different in lighting and trim and decorations. The conductor must learn to trust the composer as well as her own intuition and imagination to *create* as well as to *build* the structure solidly with technical and musical skills.

The score is learned and prepared in various stages. First the score (full or condensed) is perused to determine if it is appropriate for the ensemble's instrumentation and the quality of the literature as it pertains to teaching specific objectives such as form, craftsmanship, and performance skills. It is then examined again, this time for overall form and specific style. As the work is studied for subsequent rehearsals, more details are uncovered. The process of learning the score, depending on the artistic magnitude of the work, will continue until the score is virtually memorized; and the better the quality of music, the more detail and musical meaning will be discovered through score study. Also, the ability to "hear" a score (audiation) will improve with experience.

[1]Frank Battisti and Robert Garofalo (1990), *Guide to Score Study for the Wind Band Conductor*, Ft. Lauderdale, Meredith Music p. 1.)

During the initial score study, all key, tempo, or meter changes are noted. In some scores tempos are marked with metronome markings, while in others, words such as "moderato" are used. In the latter case, one must examine the melodic line to get a "feel" for what *moderato* indicates. Also, the density of the notes should be observed: any exposed parts (and who), which sections are responsible for the foreground line, middle ground, and background, and passages of rapid rhythms.

The next stage is to study the score with a metronome. Early stages of studying a score are both a cognitive and an affective process whereby the conductor draws on her knowledge of music theory and history as well as her imagination, emotions, intuition, and passion. Score study reveals the overall continuity of the piece that will continue to develop in the mind's ear, producing an "intuitive musical feeling for the expressive content and form of the [mental] image."[2]

Although the metronome may be set at a tempo slower than that desired for performance, the steady beat will help the director audiate to determine the overall flow, rhythm, and direction of the work. This procedure will also help the director determine which rhythms, technical passages, or articulations may cause the ensemble to stumble—and hence become candidates for warm-up and technical drill. During this phase of the study the director should not stop, but continue through the entire work or until the metronome must be changed.

Initially, a detailed analysis of isolated rhythms or articulations is not necessary. With the metronome maintaining a constant tempo (performance tempo, or close), the director should follow through the score with her eyes moving from line to line attempting to audiate the ensemble sound. (Practice with an occasional check with the piano develops the conductor's ability to hear chords and lines over time.) Although few new teachers will be able to hear in their "mind's ear" exactly what the score sounds like, it is important in rehearsal preparation to read through the score and glean as much as possible. As the director becomes more experienced, these initial perceptions will become more accurate. With the metronome forcing one through the score, the director may select to attend to any underlying rhythmic accompaniment in the middle or background or to the melodic figure in the foreground. Subsequent study will disclose many more musical features. The eye and "inner ear" will soon discover more elements in the notation and the form of the work will gradually be outlined in the mind.

The next stage is to go through the score aurally, humming or singing various lines of the score. For many new directors, this stage of humming the melodic lines is needed (especially in polyphonic sections) before the formal sections of the music can be understood and outlined (i.e., before larger sections and smaller sections, periods, and phrases within the periods can be determined). The director should first sight-sing the lines to get an idea of the flow and the most appropriate tempos to maximize the phrasing. The piano is used later to check accuracy.

As the score becomes more familiar, she then studies and analyzes bit by bit to include specific rhythmic elements, melodic elements, harmonic elements, texture, and orchestration. The director should examine and highlight in pencil any desired changes in tempo or meter. The relationship between tempos of large sections and whether these tempos are used to help establish a specific mood (such as an underlying driving rhythmic figure used to accompany a slower melodic line) should be observed. Temporary changes in the tempo such as ritardandos and accelerandos should be noted with respect to "where they are going," the quickness of the change, and their effect on any established mood or style.

Melodic aspects of score study include locating the primary melodies, or whatever part(s) belong in the foreground, and countermelodies (always a back-

[2] Ibid. p. 22.

ground and often a middle ground) and identifying the instruments playing them. Markings should be used to indicate when a middle ground part moves to the foreground or a foreground part moves to the background. In addition to the overall form, each melodic section will have form, climax, and point of rest within the specific style. The contour of the melodic lines is important to each phrase and for contrasting styles, and their contribution to the contour of the entire work is basic to interpretation of the sections and phrases that make up the whole. The variety of ways the composer develops the melodic material should also be identified.

After your imagination and your musicality have constructed a musical work from the score and several pages of "notes," it is time to delve deeper into the piece:

1. One should not listen to a recording right away, but rather allow the musical mind to develop the structure, mood, phrasing, tempo, and the desired artistry.

2. Continue to analyze the score to make an *informed* interpretation of the piece.

3. The score is analyzed to learn and know these components of the composition:
   - Foreground parts (or melody)
   - Middle ground parts
   - Background (or harmony)
   - Tempo and meter
   - Orchestrations (doublings, exposed parts)
   - Form
   - Texture (density)
   - Dynamics
   - Articulations that generally determine style
   - Most important, expressive elements and terms

These elements assist in the conductor's adding musical nuances.

Garofalo recommends to begin a harmonic analysis determine the tonal centers at the beginning and end of the work's large sections.[3] The second step is to identify the harmonic basis of the various sections—the harmonic language—and how sections move harmonically to the next section. Each section is then analyzed in terms of the harmonic motion that gives the music its momentum and direction, including the common cadences, but a large number of works for band and orchestra written in the late twentieth century and early twenty-first century make use of cadential devices that expand beyond the limits of common-practice theory/composition.

The melodic and harmonic components of the work together determine the dynamic levels. The dynamic levels notated should be observed, and any special effects (such as *sfz*) should be marked for special treatment and possible technical drill. The director and performers will add nuances beyond those indicated in the score as suggested to them by the melodic contour and underlying harmony. Except for special effects, seldom do any two measures remain at the same dynamic level in an artistic performance.

---

[1]Robert Garofalo (1976), *Blueprint for Band*, Portland, ME: J. Weston Walch, pp. 30–36.

Instrumentation is a primary concern for many conductors when they prepare a score. How to compensate for a less-than-perfect instrumentation? Often score study will reveal that major lines intended for missing instruments are doubled or cued in other parts; many times a solo is cued for another, more common instrument. However, study of the score may indicate that sections need to be altered or rewritten. For example, analysis of a band work may indicate that the basses, bassoons, baritone saxophone, and contrabass clarinet all play an important rhythmic ostinato in unison, but the band does not have a bassoon, baritone saxophone, or contrabass clarinet, and only one tuba. Further study of the score and a bit of common sense may indicate that the work is not appropriate for this band beyond a sight-reading experience, if that. If the work is appropriate for performance, the section in question may need rewriting: Instead of the tuba simply playing louder, borrow some string players from the orchestra, or the part may be performed by the trombones (with due diligence), baritones, or even horns. Orchestras frequently must double viola parts with violins or cellos.

Often the teacher's growth in preparing a score is achieved without listening to a recording—letting her audiation, imagination, analysis, and creativity roam. Promotion recordings are sometimes sterile and unmusical, designed primarily to provide an overall impression of the work. A musical teacher is imaginative and a risk taker. There is much to learn in all music—one never knows until she tries.

REHEARSAL PLANNING

Rehearsal time is a precious commodity. To use the time most effectively, the director must not only plan each rehearsal but also establish a routine.

Many successful directors maintain a master schedule. Starting with critical dates—concerts, holidays, and state tests—it is possible to outline the rehearsal objectives for every day of the school year. The piece(s) to be rehearsed each day can be indicated and matched with warm-ups and technical drills and include sight-reading selections and time for listening activities.

Most teachers can sight-read the score (or fake it) faster than the students and can snooker the students by selecting a piece of music at the last minute to fill rehearsal time. The effective rehearsal is usually planned to include a variety of activities selected with a goal in mind. With good planning, the teacher can include in one rehearsal period some sight-reading, technical drill, form and style recognition, and intensive musical understanding of one or two concert numbers, with a few minutes for "fun music," old favorites, or a listening period. There is nothing wrong, however, with intensive work when the students and you are in the mood and motivated. Experienced teachers use the chalkboard for most announcements and to indicate the order of the music. The chairs and music stands should be in their proper place before the students enter the room, and every action aimed toward accomplishing planned objectives during allotted rehearsal time.

At least the first 20 percent of the available rehearsal time each day should be spent in a routine that includes initial procedures and activities that address basic musicianship. These include procedures to improve tone quality, breath support, intonation, technique, phrasing, bowings/articulations, and a bit of musical knowledge and listening. Students who aurally know where a phrase peaks or ends, who feel dynamic level within the context of the composer's markings needed to achieve a proper balance, who have a repertoire of bowings or articulations to apply when needed, are en route to being musically educated.

What occurs during the first portion of every rehearsal is crucial to the development of any outstanding instrumental music program. The term *warm-up* has unfortunately been associated with only the physical preparation of lips, fingers, and bow arms, to the neglect of the mental preparation. Activities that improve tone, intonation, ensemble precision, and individual musicianship are part of every warm-up. The term *routine* implies that the student *knows what to expect.*

Students often do learn in spite of the hit-or-miss approach to teaching, camouflaging much inadequate instruction. Writing lesson plans is part of college training, including writing procedures for attaining specific objectives. Preservice teachers, however, seldom note that instrumental conductors continually reflect on objectives, procedures, and systematic assessment. Teaching well looks easier than it is.

Long-range objectives were discussed in Chapter 2. Short-term objectives must be further organized into monthly, weekly, or daily objectives. Most important, for instrumental music education to improve, the focus must balance the attainment of group and individual objectives (unless every student receives private lessons). Finally, instrumental music educators must evaluate students at both the group and the individual level. Group assessment, in the form of public concerts, festivals, and contests, has been the norm for many generations.

In *every* rehearsal someone should play a solo or solo part. Through the course of the year, each student should play for his or her peers—not just when the director is searching for "wrong notes," but something that student can play well. Research studies indicate that playing for only peers is more anxiety producing than a contest performance. Thus, this routine is important in building self-confidence.

Lesson Plans

The purpose of lesson plans is to enable teachers to *think* about what they wish to teach, why, and how they will accomplish that task. Useful lesson plans are those written or outlined that include the daily class lessons for weeks and possibly months. Each can later be altered according to what was accomplished and the needs identified on the previous day. Notes of success and failure should be kept as a type of evaluation, as teachers learn while procedures or activities work and which leave the students frustrated or in a daze.

Lesson plans are especially useful for new teachers to stay "on course" and limit the temptation to drift toward addressing unexpected performance problems. No matter how tempting it may be to pursue the remedy of a major performance problem that is "suddenly" noticed, staying with the lesson plan will accomplish the day's objective(s) and allow time for the teacher to give thought to the best ways of addressing the new problem(s) with the greatest efficiency (unless it is a minor problem that can be quickly corrected). Staying on task is not meant to discourage providing immediate feedback on all problems.

There are many forms and ways to write lesson plans. Each lesson plan, however, should begin with brief, prefatory material such as the class, date, and so forth, then at least the group objectives should be explicitly stated. Use these objectives to plan the musical experiences designed to achieve them. Most objectives directed toward skill acquisition are stated in behavioral terms—that is, what the students should know and be able to demonstrate. A lesson plan contains detailed procedures that include what is to be accomplished in each portion of the daily routine.

The lesson plan includes possible means of assessment and clever ways to provide feedback to the students. Providing feedback and honestly and clearly informing students individually, as sections, and as a large ensemble about their progress during the day's rehearsal is the most neglected component of instrumental music education. The importance of explicitly informing students of the extent that they achieved the objectives for the day should seem obvious; unfortunately, it is seldom done. Assessment of the group objectives (by teacher and students) and as much truthful feedback to individuals as possible should be part of every rehearsal.

Planning for Pacing

The director's responsibility is to keep the rehearsal moving. Pacing is of paramount importance; rapid pacing tends to be preferred by students. It is better for the ensemble members to be surprised that the period is over than have them looking at their watches throughout the rehearsal.

1. Plan every aspect of the rehearsal to within minutes.
2. Seldom work with a single section in the ensemble for more than a few minutes or other students become bored, frustrated, and could be disruptive as the percussionists practice juggling with the drumsticks and other loose equipment.
3. Many corrections can be made by replaying the selection if a nonverbal hint has been given on the error, rather than stopping to speak. Facial expressions and body gestures (in addition to conducting) can communicate anything from a precise entrance by the third cornets to correcting inappropriate behavior by a violist.
4. Refuse to be interrupted by students who need a "late or absence slip" signed. The telephone should have an answering machine, and you should avoid responding to irrelevant questions and most "cute" behaviors.

Planning for Sight-Reading

Students learn to do what they do, and sight-reading is an essential skill for musical independence. Music for sight-reading should be selected before the school year starts. The director should go through the music library or the card catalog and select interesting music by objectives, teaching for form, key, technique, style, and technical and musical difficulty. These selections should then be ranked from simple to complex in each category to facilitate for sequenced instruction.

One of the most frequently discussed objectives of music education is perceiving and performing music from notation. Daily attention to sight-reading leads to attaining this objective and numerous others; for example, sight-reading is one way to acquaint students with a wide variety of musical forms and styles, keys, and so on, because the ensemble is limited in the number of works that can be prepared for performance. To sight-read is to use all the learned skills, perceptual, aural, technical, and cognitive. It may not be feasible (or even desirable) to sight-read at every rehearsal, but several rehearsals per week should include sight-reading.

If the sight-reading piece draws on skills taught during the first concert selection (key, accidentals, dynamics, articulations, rhythms, etc.), it can reinforce and transfer the skills that were taught and the teacher can assess whether these were accomplished.

Students should scan the selection for a few minutes before performing it; the time for scanning gradually reduced (keeping length of the work in mind). Rhythm and tempo are the first elements to be stressed. Students may miss notes, or fumble in rapid passages but maintaining the musical movement is most important.

It is essential to draw attention to the successes in the sight-reading (another reason the director must listen and not become preoccupied with sight-reading the score). Compliments must be specific; terms such as *ok* or *not bad* are insufficient and provide little feedback that leads to education. If the music is simple enough, the ensemble should sight-read well; compliments on what should be expected can be counterproductive.

Previously Learned Music

It is important to end a rehearsal on a positive note (the oldest pun in the business), and this should be planned for. The easiest way to do so is to schedule music that the ensemble enjoys and can play well. A cohesive ensemble can also enjoy a challenge even at the end of a long rehearsal.

DAILY ROUTINES*

Instrumental teachers have a routine for rehearsals, usually in the following order (1) individual warmup and preparation time as the students enter the classroom (putting away their books and getting out their instruments); (2) short announcements that remind students to look at the calendar or changes in a schedule; (3) a warm-up of scales and a technical study and/or chorale (with tuning); (4) rehearsal of concert music; and (5) sight-reading experience; (6) a very short verbal conclusion and dismissal. Novice and insecure teachers spend, and allow students to spend, more time in preparation and make longer announcements than more successful teachers, leaving less time for ensemble warm-ups.

Routines enable the ensemble to accomplish tasks efficiently. There is one for high school band students arriving at the school for a Friday night football game, just as there is a different routine for the orchestra when it travels to the District Festival.

With 30 to more than 100 students in an ensemble, routines are needed to keep everyone (including the teacher) on task. Student comfort level rises when he knows what to expect and do. Students desire structure. Students must know what their responsibilities are and what to expect, enabling the teacher and ensemble to progress through the class period with maximum time devoted to instruction.

A warm-up routine is critical, including focus on time signatures, key signatures, and the aspects "about" music. But this material is very low on the taxonomy of cognitive knowledge (though essential); it can easily be learned by beginners and intermediate players outside the rehearsal. A few selected music theory workbooks from several dozen listed in the bibliography of this chapter are best used as homework with specific pages assigned for each school term and graded, with students provided the opportunity to correct their work, as mastery of the knowledge is the objective.

Procedures

Procedures are the teaching strategies used in a rehearsal. They are directed toward clear objectives that are *shared with the students*. A frequent occurrence in the classroom, alas, is that of an orchestra director stopping to tell the violas to "play at measure 48." What must go through the minds of these individual students? They reflect on their performance of measure 48. The command is accepted but the purpose is a mystery. Worse, after they play the passage and receive no feedback, the conductor asks the second violins to "play at 48." This searching is a daily occurrence when the conductor should have added another phrase such as "so we all use the up-bow

---

*Written for the elementary or beginning ensemble.

on the eighth note." If expectations, objectives, and strategies are made explicit, students will meet them. If only the conductor knows the objectives or expectations of the procedures, students are left out of a very important process: educating.

A myth is that lengthy warm-ups or routines are boring to most students. They are boring only when students are unaware of their purpose or objectives and are not challenged by the experience. To prevent these essential procedures from becoming boring, the teacher finds different ways of explaining skills and most importantly makes every aspect, even performing scales, *musical.*

Warm-Ups

Starting the rehearsal was discussed under Daily Routines. The purpose of the ensemble warm-up is to address the basics of ensemble playing; it is an extension of the individual warm-ups and helps ready the ensemble to tune, blend, and balance. Remembering your musical goals throughout these procedures and keeping a positive rehearsal atmosphere while working on small details will keep routines interesting and challenging and the ensemble members motivated in each rehearsal. The warm-up should help students learn what they need to practice at home, how to listen, what to listen for, and how to develop ensemble precision.

If the teacher is required to take roll, there are ways to accomplish this quickly. The quickest method is to have the chairs and stands in place, a quick glance around the ensemble revealing any vacant seats. (This requires effort before the rehearsal.) The prepared director has arranged chairs and stands, written the order of the rehearsal material on the board, posted any necessary announcements to avoid using rehearsal time, and has a band parent present if ancillary tasks need completing such as collecting fund-raiser money. This preparation allows the director to make herself available to students at the beginning of class.

Individual warm-ups are useful for getting the students to focus on music making as well as physically preparing the body, bow arm, embouchure, fingers, and tongue. It should be a beneficial segment of every rehearsal, never a chaotic waste of time and energy. The director should stand by the podium (not *on* the podium) ready to assist students in their warm-ups and answer questions. (A student quartermaster can field requests for music, reeds, valve oil, and a replacement string that has just broken.) The point is that students need several minutes to warmup individually and to check their equipment, (especially the mandatory pencil), but they must be taught the procedures on *how* to warm up, tune up, and when to shut up.

After a few minutes of individual warm-up, which includes individual and section tuning, the director signals for quiet by stepping onto the podium. This is one of the procedures as the disorganized teacher who waits on or off the podium until everyone is quiet is doomed to wait longer and longer each day.

Announcements should be brief—no more than a minute with longer announcements made when a short break is needed. Only the most essential and pressing issues need to be addressed, as most needed information is on the rehearsal room chalkboard or in their folders to be taken home. The ensemble warm-up should begin immediately after the general announcements. Established procedures enable a director to step on the podium, raise the baton, and give a downbeat for the daily physical relaxation warm-up exercises or the first note of a technical drill.

Breathing Exercises

For bands, at least three rehearsals each week should start with at least four to eight minutes of breathing exercises to relax the body and focus the mind, to continue to develop the breathing apparatus over time, and to maintain good habits of posture and proper breathing. Teachers should emphasize the benefit of breathing exercises and stress that learning the habit of proper breathing takes place over months and years, not in just a few rehearsals. Daily group practice on breathing not only improves virtually every aspect of wind performance but also emphasizes the importance of proper breathing to each member. See the discussion in Chapter 7, Principles for Winds.

The types and styles of breathing exercises are limited only by the teacher's imagination. What each should have in common, however, is good posture and a relaxed, slow inhale that fills the lungs at the bottom, then the middle, then the upper part without raising the shoulders. The inhale should be silent as any noise indicates tension in the throat or mouth. Relaxation during inhaling is important to allow the appropriate parts of the body to expand.

Exhaling must also be taught and practiced. The exhale should be like a sigh which should expel all the air in a second or less. One exhaling exercise is to have the students hold a sheet of music about six inches in front of their faces. After inhaling a slow full, relaxed breath, exhale by attempting to blow the paper straight away from the face. If the paper flaps and flutters, there is inconsistent airflow.

Yawning and silent sighing promote the best relaxation and are used to demonstrate proper breathing. These breathing exercises segue into playing scales slowly or tuning exercises, while maintaining the sensation of relaxed but full breathing.

String orchestras naturally spend less time on breathing exercises—only for relaxing, although string players coordinate breathing and bowing. The percussionists should participate, as it is difficult to talk while inhaling.

Technical Drill

At least five to ten minutes of technical drill should follow specific individual and section feedback on the success of the tuning process. During the technical drill, the director continues his sequential instruction designed for instrument mastery. One objective is to develop uniform ensemble style (e.g., articulations, marcato style, and uniform bowings). To be meaningful, the material covered during the technical drill should build on previous work and be recognizable as sequential improvement.

Technical drills for orchestra often consist of rote performance of scales and arpeggios that require use of all positions and harmonics. Scale technique transfers to concert literature competence, both musically and kinesthetically, more than any other technical exercise. Different bowings are also addressed or reviewed with these scale/rhythmic exercises.

Technical study is a progressive, sequential approach from basic to advanced articulations/bowings, and mastery of rhythm patterns from simple to complex. Rhythm patterns are memorized for home practice and along with tonal patterns make excellent assessment material for spot-checking.

Rehearsing technical problems with the full ensemble should not replace individual drill, but focus on the ensemble's precision. Although it may be appropriate for middle school ensembles to drill on scales and arpeggios in order to learn fingerings and bowings, high school players should know these fundamentals and focus on ensemble techniques drawn from the music.

A loud, fast march or stylized dance is fun to play but useless for tuning. Usually the best music for progressing from tuning to intonation is a chorale or harmonized scale or chord study.[4] The cleverness of the director has much to do with maintaining students' interest when using such studies. Merely playing through

---

[4]After several years of being out of print, the Raymond Fussell and Leonard Smith band drill books are now back in print. These and others are listed in the end of bibliography.

them without attempting to make some improvement is a waste of precious time. Explaining what the students should improve and *how* is essential.

The most useful technical drills are those from drill books and those created by the teacher that clearly are moderately challenging and are played musically. The advantage of books is that they contain interesting rhythms and harmonics and are designed to facilitate transfer. The disadvantage is when students are confronted with notation they tend to focus on the page instead of the sound.

Drill on isolated rhythms and articulations can benefit listening skills and playing by ear. In this type of drill the director gives each section its beginning note and asks these students to echo the pattern she gives them, using that pitch or perhaps a simple scale-wise movement.[5] Such drills are all done by ear, but at some point the students should see how the rhythm is notated.

Musicianship cannot be learned unless it is taught. Practice is necessary to develop most musicianship skills, so ways must be found to make practice attractive. Contests between groups can be fun, especially if the groups are selected in whimsical ways: blondes against brunettes, talls against shorts, low instruments against high, and so forth. No new piece of music should be attempted without consideration of the student's readiness to understand its key, meter, form, rhythm, melody, style, accidentals, dynamic markings, and interpretive terms. This is the stuff of music—time must be made to teach these musical things during the routines that begin each rehearsal.

Chorales

Chorales for band provide excellent warm-up material because chorales are fairly simple and students can concentrate on following the conductor while listening and adjusting intonation, balance, blend, and tone quality—the components of good performance. Again, students must be taught what to listen for and taught the meaning of the conductor's gestures.

Chorales are also used to teach attacks and releases, for ear training, and for shaping phrases. The director can ask students to memorize a phrase quickly and then focus on conducting cues for tempo, dynamics, intonation, balance, and blend—the director should then shape that phrase in a variety of musical ways. Chorales are also good material for vocalizing (regardless of octave displacement), which is prerequisite for superior intonation.

Chorales are interesting and fun when approached with imagination. During the five or six minutes of rehearsal time devoted to chorales, the group may work on only a single phrase or single modality, because it is more important that the ensemble perform that phrase well than play through several chorales.

Musicality (or passion, emotion, or art) is what chorales are all about. The objective of musicality fails where the band or orchestra plays through a chorale once and is satisfied if the notes are correct. The point we attempt to make here is that simple notes played expressively can result in extraordinary musical expression, musical direction, or flow—the components of the art of music.

TUNING AND INTONATION

Students are quite capable of discriminating high from low on standardized music tests, but the transfer of this competence to their instrument in not readily apparent. The saxophone pedagogue Donald Sinta exclaims that poor intona-

---

[5] Daniel L. Kohut (1996), *Instrumental Music Pedagogy: Teaching Techniques for School Band and Orchestra Directors*. Champaign, IL: Stipes, reprint of (1973) Upper Saddle River, NJ: Prentice Hall, pp. 219–20.

tion is *learned.* Apparently putting a music machine to use in the hands of students is quite different from discriminating high from low; but, if Sinta is correct, good intonation can be expected if taught from the beginning of instrumental instruction.

Among orchestra and band conductors, there are those who champion *listening* for more accurate intonation and those who make use of pitch measuring devices such as electronic tuners. Although the objective is the same—to develop pitch consciousness and improve intonation—the results differ. Tuning is the process of listening and adjusting one's instrument to the perceived pitch. This requires "thinking" the pitch before producing it. Whether by ear or by an electronic device, a trumpeter should "lip-up" or "lip-down" only long enough to find the correct pitch and then adjust the tuning slide appropriately. Intonation is the process of thinking and then playing pitches that match others. Use of an electronic tuner holds the risk that students will come to consider tuning as a "visual" thing (always a concern).

When a group is in tune, it produces a clear sound; when it does not it has a muddy sound, ranging from annoying to blood chilling. Tuning each instrument to a single pitch is generally wasted time as tuning any instrument requires listening to more than one note. A little knowledge is a dangerous thing, and pitch is an area about which many have only a little knowledge. It is amusing to hear some directors report that they tune their group to "A=441," only to observe that the room temperature is 85 degrees, and then hear the group. What is needed is less pseudo-science and a great deal more listening.

Thinking the correct pitch before playing is the final and essential step before playing.

Interestingly, most children who start band or orchestra already have an ear for good intonation or the ability to match pitch. If the instrumental music teacher were to administer one of the available standardized music tests, it is likely that most children in the ensembles would do well on the pitch discrimination part. The problem lies in putting a new piece of equipment in their hands and helping them apply what they already know to its use.

Remaining in tune while playing a melodic or harmonic line requires adjusting each pitch if necessary with the embouchure, alternate fingerings, or general adjustment of the fingers for string players. Faulty intonation is among the most distracting aspects of performance by string ensembles and wind bands. Simply asking students to adjust pitch is not enough. Once the instrument is tuned, students must listen to play in tune—teach them how to adjust their fingers and/or lips to alter the pitch. Establishing a good early foundation for the orchestra and band requires the use of compact discs or piano accompaniment during the initial critical years. Hearing recordings of their own rehearsals will make ensemble members more cognizant of intonation.

Tuning

Tuning should precede and follow breathing exercises and be incorporated into technical drill and chorales. The orchestra rehearsal room should have an A sounded by an electronic device as students enter the room. This allows each student to try to tune as one takes his or her instrument from the case. The only way to learn to tune is to practice tuning. Some orchestra directors are impatient and tune the instruments for the students. If the young student has trouble tuning his open strings to a constant electronic pitch, he will noticeably contribute poorly to the ensemble's intonation when it is time to apply the left-hand fingers. Thus, a string teacher should never take the instrument from the student, tune it, and give it back. Such action indicates that the director believes the student is able to play in several positions, with all types of bowing—but lacks the basics of string performance: tuning.

Band and orchestra teachers should make use of singing and humming. Orchestras play unison D and A major scales virtually on a daily basis, but seldom are students asked to sing the scale.

One commonly used rote exercise for tuning bands (in concert pitch) is shown in Figure 24–1.

Figure 24–1 Wind Warm-Up Example

Intonation may be refined further if the lowest voices sustain an F throughout. Orchestras can benefit from similar rote studies. Playing by rote allows more concentration on listening. Having students sing each two-measure slur before playing it, with emphasis on proper vocal production, is good practice: The playing "teaches" the singing while the singing refines the playing.

Throughout the tuning process, the director must monitor the breathing of wind players. Attention to proper breathing should continue through the entire rehearsal. The routine of tuning, the breathing exercises, chords, unison scales, and chorales are intended to transfer to the music under study.

Because many students have never dreamed that they must do anything special to play in tune, they must be taught the pitch tendencies of their instruments. In general, brass instruments and flutes tend to go sharp and clarinets flat on a crescendo; on diminuendos, the opposite. All instruments vary according to the player and the register. There are many exercises designed to improve intonation. Ask students to sing a triad and then play it. If they are typical, after the initial giggling, the singing will probably be more in tune than the playing.

Intonation Through Balance

Francis McBeth advocates improved intonation through appropriate balance—with his procedure, good intonation is dependent on good balance. This relationship between balance and intonation is similar to the relationship between good intonation and tone quality. These two are inseparable, both depend upon equipment, proper breathing, a good embouchure, and critical listening. Tone quality can be improved through emphasis on good intonation, and vice versa, however, the two are not interchangeable.[6]

According to McBeth, intonation problems cannot be solved until balance problems are resolved. At any given dynamic level the higher-pitched instruments should be playing softer than the lower-pitched instruments. To demonstrate this concept to a band or orchestra, McBeth suggests dividing the band or orchestra into four groups: soprano, alto, tenor, and bass. For band, the sopranos include the piccolo, flutes, oboes, first and second clarinet, first and second trumpet; the altos: alto saxophones, third clarinets and third trumpets, first and third horns; the tenors: first and second trombones, baritones, bass clarinets, tenor saxophone, second and fourth horns, and first bassoon; and the basses: tubas, euphonium, contrabass clarinet, and second bassoon. For strings the sopranos include violins; altos: violas, tenors: cellos; basses: double basses.

---

[6] Francis W. McBeth (1972), *Effective Performance of Band Music, Solutions to Specific Problems in the Performance of 20th Century Band Music,* San Antonio, TX: Southern Music p. 11.

Then the following steps are used to teach ensemble members to listen to achieve a better balance:

1. Record the full ensemble while playing a chord at pianissimo and crescendo-ing to fortissimo.
2. Repeat the process, this time with bass instruments providing the full crescendo while the tenors play three-fourths of the crescendo, the altos one-half, and the sopranos one-fourth.
3. Finally, the ensemble plays the chord again, but with the balance reversed; that is, sopranos playing a full crescendo and basses one-fourth of the crescendo.
4. When this tape is played for the ensemble, it is very likely that their first or "normal" crescendo will sound more like the one with the reversed balance than like the "pyramid-type" balance.
5. It is also likely that the second (balanced) crescendo will sound like a superior ensemble.
6. The director should point out that multipart sections such as the clarinets and trumpets should use this type of balancing within their individual sections (i.e., the first trumpets should be able to hear the third trumpets).

The usefulness of this procedure is that when proper balance is achieved, players are enabled to hear the lower voices. If each individual is playing softer than those students playing lower pitches and louder than those playing higher pitches, students are able to tune to the fundamental of the chord.

A few suggestions conclude this discussion of intonation. In today's economy, virtually every orchestra or band member can afford to purchase his own tuner and have visual proof of his inability to sustain a tone at a constant pitch. Daily practice while thinking of this constancy contributes to good intonation. The offenders in sour-sounding groups are often students who see their instruments only during rehearsal time.

Rehearsal of Concert Music

Rehearsing concert/performance music is the heart of the rehearsal, and the reasons the students are there. The bulk of the rehearsal is devoted to this music, whether it is actually scheduled for performance. This music has been selected purposefully, with a variety of objectives, both long and short term, in clear view.

Observation of student response is critical to this part of the rehearsal. The teacher must "read" the students to determine the extent that they understand, whether they feel a sense of accomplishment, and to make sure they do not become fatigued or bored. Teacher intuition and experience determine when additional explanation or help is needed; these observations are sound pedagogical strategies and allow progress from the known to the unknown.

When giving directions for starting at the beginning, the director should state them once (using musical terms when possible)—twice at most—and begin. When directions are repeated several times, students fall into the habit of ignoring the first two or three statements and listen only the last time, if then. The directions must, however, include what is to be improved beyond "violas, take it at 16."

The director must be thinking of what to say before stopping the group. Repetition is good, especially for teaching and learning the basics and technically challenging passages. But drilling a passage without feedback can be counterproductive and dangerous; if notes or rhythms are to be corrected, for example, the teacher must have a strategy for enabling the problem to be understood and mastered. When drilling a musical passage, only one musical element should be changed at a time to prevent information overload.

As the group approaches performance level, playing a variety of recordings (including their own rehearsal) is valuable. After the ensemble has an idea of the music and can perform it acceptably, the use of recordings is invaluable. Listening to several interpretations of the work in preparation can demonstrate (1) phrasing and musical line, (2) intonation, (3) style, (4) articulation, (5) precision of attacks and releases, (6) rhythmic accuracy, (7) balance, (8) blend, and (9) melodic and harmonic direction and movement. In addition, students can reflect and discuss the group's own recording and ways it can be improved. The best self-appraisal occurs with group objectives.

However, listening to recordings should be postponed until mid-rehearsal or later. Otherwise conductors (and students) are prone to try to interpret the score "in the manner of" the Chicago Symphony Orchestra or the University of Illinois band—such a mental concept won't bolster the confidence of the ensemble members as they struggle to sound like these groups and may lead to the early retirement of the conductor. All directors should be aware of the core literature of their performance medium. The recordings listed at the end of this chapter not only serve as model ensembles but also are representative of the "core repertoire."

HOW TO PRACTICE

The conductor/teacher is a coach who must place the responsibility for musical progress where it belongs: with the individual students. *Rehearsals are* not *practice sessions. Practicing is done at home to allow the ensemble to rehearse.*

Individual home practice is an essential element of improvement in instrumental music performance. Training in how to practice is often overlooked in the teaching process. Bad habits begin in string and band classes when a page or two is performed during class and the class is merely told to practice the next page for the next lesson.

Younger students cannot practice "what they don't know." All too frequently, in the next class the teacher will spend considerable time correcting errors learned in home practice, leaving less time to teach. The solution? Ask students to practice what was taught "today" in class, trying to make it "better," "smoother," "more even," "more in time," "keeping bows perpendicular to strings," and so on. If "today's" teaching helped the beginners in developing a mental concept of tone quality, smooth articulations, change of bow direction and phrasing, then "tomorrow's" class time can be spent more effectively.

Most heterogeneous method books are fairly well sequenced, so that learning "page 12" in class, then practicing "page 12" at home to learn it better, will enable more efficient teaching of "page 13."

An insightful look into how to practice is to study performers who have mastered the highest levels of performance and their coaches and apply this knowledge at an understandable level for students.[7] Talent does play a role in attaining mastery of performance skills, but research indicates that the differences between so-called "talented" students and those students with "desire," who put forth effort, decrease when students practice effectively.

[7] Harold Jorgensen and A. C. Lehmann (1997), *Does Practice Make Perfect?: Current Theory and Research on Instrumental Music Practice.* Oslo: Norges Musikkhogskole.

Effective practice requires cognitive study of the music to determine bowings, phrases, where to breathe, style, appropriate articulations, and other musical attributes that contribute to artistic interpretation.

The research reported by Jorgensen and Lehmann indicates that students' natural practice habits parallel their learning styles. For example, a measure of learning styles is determined by the *Learning Process Questionnaire.*[8] This device measures whether students adopt a "deep" or a "broad surface" approach to their learning. Students who score higher on a "deep approach" to learning tend to practice with primary concern for musical ideas, striving for technical skills needed to achieve those ideas. Students who scored high on the "surface approach" usually learned by rote, focused on technique, and practiced repetitiously without concern for musical expression.

The most common, perhaps glaring, difference among students is the frequency of practice and why they practice. Many students do not practice on a daily basis if they can "get by" and practice only for an audition, a performance test, or when a parent insists. Therefore, teachers must instill in beginners the idea that individual home practice is a natural, expected part of being in instrumental music. Initially, 30-minute home practice sessions should be the norm in order to make minimal progress.

After playing for a few years, students should want to practice as much as an hour each day. The teacher should suggest interesting and musical supplementary materials for students (such as the materials listed at the end of each instrument chapter) and regularly monitor students' progress. Teachers must expect to spend time listening to students play from the Arban, Primrose, or Klose book to monitor technical and musical skills. Instrumental music teachers must set aside time in the morning, during lunch periods, and after school for 10 to 15 minute private lessons to ensure students are practicing regularly, practicing appropriate material, and striving to play everything musically and expressively. As we have stressed before, every rehearsal or music class should allow several students to play for their peers to demonstrate their progress.

Practice Content

Warm-Up Students must be taught to warm up. This process differs for each instrument or each family of instruments. All should begin practicing scales and arpeggios, with a metronome, then long tones for winds, rudiments for percussion, while strings practice scales or rote exercises. Brass players should rest between each two-octave scale. If the long tones are 30 seconds or more, brass players should rest 30 seconds before attempting the next. Warming up should be done at various dynamic levels.

As students develop musically and technically and their practice time increases, more materials are added to the warm-up. Examples are: a memorized étude, a melodious study for expressive playing (while maintaining a steady rhythm by subdividing beats), a favorite orchestral excerpt, music from the school ensemble folder, or other materials that demand changes in style, bowing/articulations, and dynamic levels. Each piece or selection should be played accurately (with the metronome) and expressively.

The full warm-up at all stages of development should generally require a third of the total practice time.

---

[8]J. Biggs (1987). *Study Process Questionnaire: User's Manual,* Hawthorne, Victoria: Australian Council for Educational Research.

Technical and Musical Study After a proper warm-up, a technical study or several pieces that are being learned should be practiced. These should always be technical material in a stage of learning that the student continues to strive to master, so that it eventually can become part of the warm-up section just discussed. New scales and arpeggios may fit into this category as well as études, technical studies for range, and string studies for double stops, shifting, or thumb positions. This category may also include works from the school ensemble under preparation that need home practice.

The term *technical study* does not imply that only fast and flashy works are to be practiced. These should balance between expressive, melodious music and those that have dense notation. All challenge the fingers, tongue/bow, hands, embouchure, arms, wind, bow speed, and brain.

This portion of the practice period should be the longest. And this portion is when students learn to use a variety of strategies to master the demands of the music.

Strategies Students should isolate a technical challenge, visually study or analyze it, and practice it repeatedly. Slowing the tempo is usually required (to a tempo at which it can be played correctly), with a gradual increase of the speed to the proper tempo. Examples might include a triple-tongued passage for brass, a rapid sixteenth-note run for woodwinds that crosses a register, or a rapid sixteenth-note passage for strings that requires shifting. Slowing the tempo and gradually increasing it should always be done with the metronome "ticking away" in order to maintain evenness of the passages.

During this type of drill, students must maintain the musicality and expressiveness in "directing" the line and ensuring a proper phrasing in the context of the entire work. Other strategies that students should be taught include how to isolate a difficult passage and vary the rhythm, slurs, inventing related exercises to address the problem.

Another strategy is marking parts. This is especially useful for bowings and for wind players who may need to use alternate fingerings.

Beginners frequently start at the beginning of a piece and play to the end repeatedly; they should learn how to listen to their playing, how to isolate a problem, and deal with it. Playing through a piece in its entirety often includes practicing an error until it is engrained in the passage. Students must learn to listen to themselves critically and evaluate their performance with today's inexpensive cassette recorders. There is tremendous benefit in requiring students to record themselves and listen to their own playing. As their knowledge of musical performance increases, they become more astute in their evaluation.

Related to this, the school's instrumental library should include a variety of compact discs and cassette tapes of master performers (many of whom are listed at the end of each instrument chapter) for students to check out. This enables students to develop a mental image of proper tone quality as well as an outstanding performer to serve as a model.

Summary

The ability to practice effectively is not a natural component of being a musician. Instrumental students must "learn to learn."[9] Most important is a broad musical knowledge base that enables students to accurately determine the task, identify

---

[9]Susan Hallam (1997), "Approaches to Instrumental Music Practice of Expert and Novice: Implications for Education" (p. 103) in Jorgenson and Lehmann *Does Practice Make Perfect?*

problems and recognize errors, evaluate their own progress and develop/use strategies to address these problems. This knowledge base comes with experience but can be enhanced by instrumental teachers spending class time in short periods of listening to bands, string orchestras, soloists, wind ensembles, and full orchestras. Further, allowing students to borrow "model" recordings as well as encouraging them to purchase CDs, cassette tapes and videotapes speeds the process of developing this broad knowledge base and also a mental image of good musical models.

The strategies for practicing must also be taught and monitored. The strategies used by musicians increase as their performance level increases, but still require instruction and formative evaluation by the instrumental teacher.

BIBLIOGRAPHY

Texts

* Indicates out of print in 2001.

BATTISITI, FRANK L. (1995). *The Twentieth Century American Wind Band/Ensemble: History, Development and Literature.* Fort Lauderdale, Meredith Music.

BATTISITI, FRANK L., and ROBERT GAROFALO (1990). *Guide to Score Study for the Wind Band Conductor.* Ft. Lauderdale Meredith Music.

DALBY, MAX F. (1993). *Band Rehearsal Techniques: A Handbook for New Directors.* Northfield, IL: Instrumentalist.

DEL BORGO, ELLIOT (1994). *Rehearsal—The First Ten Minutes: Developing Musicianship in the Concert Band.* Douglassville, PA: Educational Programs.

GAROFALO, ROBERT (1976). *Blueprint for Band.* Portland, ME: J. Weston Walch.

———. (1995). *Instructional Designs for Middle/Junior High School Band: Teacher's Manual.* Ft. Lauderdale Meredith Music.

———. (1996). *Improving Intonation in Band and Orchestra Performance.* Ft. Lauderdale Meredith Music.

GILLIGAN, RUSSELL (1991). *Perfect Practice Promotes Progress.* Stevens Point, WI: R. Gilligan.

GREEN, ELIZABETH, and NICOLAI MALKO (1992). *The Modern Conductor: A College Text on Conducting Based on the Technical Principles of Nicolai Malko as Set Forth in His The Conductor and His Baton.* 6th ed. Upper Saddle River, NJ: Prentice Hall.

HALLAM, SUSAN (1998). *Instrumental Teaching.* Oxford: Heinemann Educational.

INSTRUMENTALIST COMPANY (1996). *New Director's Handbook: Practical Answers for Beginning Teachers.* Northfield, IL: Instrumentalist.

JACKSON, PHIL (1995). *Sacred Hoops: Spiritual Lessons of a Hardwood Warrior.* New York: Hyperion.

JØRGENSEN, HARALD, and A. C. LEHMANN, (1997). *Does Practice Make Perfect?: Current Theory and Research on Instrumental Music Practice.* Oslo: Norges Musikkhogskole.

*JURRENS, JAMES (1991). *Tuning the Band and Raising Pitch Consciousness.* San Antonio, TX: RBC Publications.

*KINNEY, GUY S. (1987). *High School Music Teacher's Handbook: A Complete Guide to Managing and Teaching the Total Music Program.* West Nyack, NJ: Parker Publishing.

KOHUT, DANIEL L. (1996) *Instrumental Music Pedagogy: Teaching Techniques for School Band and Orchestra Directors.* Champaign, IL: Stipes reprint of (1973) Upper Saddle River, NJ: Prentice Hall.

*KUHN, WOLFGANG E. (1970). *Instrumental Music: Principles and Methods of Instruction,* 2nd ed. Boston: Allyn and Bacon.

KVET EDWARD (1996). *Teaching Beginning and Intermediate Band.* Reston, VA: Music Educators National Conference.

———. and JANET TWEED (1998). *Strategies for Teaching High School Band.* Reston, VA: Music Educators National Conference.

LABUTA, JOSEPH A. (1997). *Teaching Musicianship in the High School Band,* rev. ed. Ft. Lauderdale: Meredith Music.

*McBETH, W. FRANCIS (1972). *Effective Performance of Band Music, Solutions to Specific Problems in the Performance of 20th Century Band Music.* San Antonio, TX: Southern Music.

SCHLEUTER, STANLEY L. (1997). *A Sound Approach to Teaching Instrumentalists: An Application of Content and Learning Sequences,* 2nd ed. New York: Schirmer Books.

*STAUFFER, DONALD W. (1954). *Intonation Deficiencies of Wind Instruments in Ensemble.* Washington, DC: Catholic University of America Press.

*THORNTON, JAMES (1976). *Ear Training for Band.* Delaware Water Gap, PA: Shawnee Press.

Music Theory Workbooks

BENWARD, BRUCE. (1985) *Music in Theory and Practice: Workbook.* Dubuque: W.C. Brown, 1985.

BENWARD, BRUCE, AND GARY WHITE (1997). *Music in Theory and Practice.* Boston: McGraw-Hill.

BOWMAN, CHRIS. (1996) *Music Theory Owner's Manual: Books I and II: A Teaching Workbook with Illustrations and Examples for You to Write and Check Your Answers On* Navarre, FL: Bow and Arrow Music.

BRANDMAN, MARGARET (1987). *Margaret Brandman's New Theory Workbook. Books 2–4: A Contemporary Practical Approach.* Woolloommooloo, N.S.W.: Chappell & Intersong Music.

DOUGLAS, CHARLES H. (1967) *Basic Music Theory.* Athens, GA: McKenzie.

———— (1970). (ed. Wesley McKenzie) *Basic Music Theory.* Park Ridge, IL: General Words & Music.

ETLING, FOREST R. (1979).*Workbook for Band.* Elgin, IL: Author

HILL, FRANK W., ROLAND SEARIGHT and DOROTHY SEARIGHT HENDRICKSON. (1992). *Study Outline and Workbook in the Fundamentals of Music.* Dubuque, IA: W. C. Brown.

LINDSAY, MARY. (1997) *Grade Two Theory Workbook: For Use with Music Theory Question and Answer Book.* Kingston, Ontario.: Ellis, Ivison & Lindsay Music.

PETERS, CHARLES S., AND PAUL YODER. (1963–1968). *Master Theory.* (vols. 2–6). Park Ridge, IL: Neil A. Kjos Music.

SURMANI, ANDREW, AND KAREN F. SURMANI. (1998). *Alfred Essentials of Music Theory: Lessons, Ear Training, Workbook.* Van Nuys, CA: Alfred.

TALL, JOHANNES. (1983). *Introduction to Music Theory: Workbook.* Dayton, OH: Heritage Music.

TUREK, RALPH. (1996). *Workbook for the Elements of Music: Concepts and Applications.* New York McGraw-Hill.

Warm-Up Materials

Band

CHIDESTER. *Chorale-Time for School Bands and Orchestras: 55 Chorales and Warm-up Exercise* (C. Fischer).

CLARK.. *Five Minutes a Day* (Barnhouse).

CURNOW. *Chorale Masters* (Hal Leonard).

ERICKSON. *66 Festive and Famous Chorales* (Alfred)
————. *Artistry of Fundamentals* (Alfred).
————. *Band Fundamentals* (2 vols.) (Warner Brothers).
————. *Rhythms and Rests.* (Alfred).

FORQUE, and THORTON. *Harmonized Rhythms for Concert Band: Progressive Melodic Rhythms for Rhythmic Studies* (Kjos).

FUSSELL. *Exercises for Ensemble Drill.* (Warner Brothers).

GORDON. *42 Chorales for Band* (Bourne).

HAINES and MCENTYRE.. *Division of the Beat* (3 Books) (Southern Music).

HALE. *Rhythm Slides.* (Author).

HARRIS. *Directional Warm-Ups.* (Warner Brothers).

HOVEY. *Advanced Technique for Bands.* (Cole).
————. *Tips for Band* (Warner Brothers).

HUDADOFF and WARD. *Sight-Reading for Young Bands* (2 vols.) (Shawnee Press).

LAKE. *16 Chorales by J. S. Bach* (Hal Leonard).

MCLEOD and STASLEA. *Scale Études: Int. Accuracy and Rhythmic Precision.* (Warner Brothers.)

PLOYHAR. *I Recommend.* (Warner Brothers).
————. *Technique Today* (3 vols.) (Warner Brothers).

PLOYHAR, and ZEPP. *3-D Band Book* (Belwin-Mills).
————. *Tone and Technique through Chorales and Etudes.* (Belwin-Mills).

RHODES and BIERSCHENK. *Symphonic Band Technique* (Southern Music).

RUSCH. *24 Arban, Kloes, Concone Studies* (Warner Brothers).
————. *55 Ensemble Studies* (Warner Brothers).

SMITH *Sight-Reading for Young Strings* (2 Vols.) (Shawnee).
————. *Symphonic Rhythms and Scales* (Smith).
————. *Symphonic Technique* (Hal Leonard).
————. *Symphonic Warm-Ups* (Hal Leonard).

SMITH. *The Treasury of Scales* (Belwin Mills).

STARER. *Rhythmic Training* (Hal Leonard).

SWEARINGEN. *First Chorales for Band* (Barnhouse).
————. *127 Original Exercises in Unison for Band or Orchestra* (Belwin).
————. *101 Rhythmic Rest Patterns* (Warner Brothers).

WEBER. *Rehearsal Fundamentals.* (Warner Brothers).

WILLIAMS and KING. *Foundations for a Superior Performance* (Kjos).

YAUS. *50 Chorales for Band.* (Warner Brothers).

Orchestra

ALLEN, GILLESPIE, and HAYES. *Essential Technical Development: International Technique Studies* (Hal Leonard).

ANDERSON. *Essentials for Strings: A Systematic Approach to Technical Development* (Kjos).

APPLEBAUM. *Etudes for Technic and Musicianship* (3 vols.) (Warner Brothers).
————. *Scales for Strings* (2 vols.) (Warner Brothers).

CHIDESTER. *Chorale Time for School Bands and Orchestras: 55 Chorales and Warm-Up Exercise.* (C. Fischer).

CURNOW. *Chorale Masters* (Hal Leonard).

FORQUE, THORTON, and GERALD ANDERSON. *Harmonized Rhythms for String Orchestra: Progressive Melodic Rhythm Studies* (Kjos).

FRISCHBACK and FROST. *Viva Vibrato* (Kjos).

ISSAC. *The First Ten Minutes: Warm-Up Exercises for Strings* (Wynn Music).

MULLER. *28 Études for Strings, Selected from the World Famous Etudes by De Beriot, Alard, Wohlfahrt, Has Sitt, Kayser, and others* (Warner Brothers).

O'REILLY. *String Rhythms* (Kjos).

REESE. *22 Studies for Strings for Individual or Class Instruction in Unison or Ensemble Adapted from Wohlfarh—Hohmann and Henning.* (Warner Brothers).

THURSTON. *Bach Chorales for Strings: 28 Chorales* (Southern Music).

WITT. *A Rhythm a Week.* (Warner Brothers).

YAUS. *127 Original Exercises in Unison for Band or Orchestra* (Belwin).

Recommended Band Recordings

Cincinnati Wind Symphony—Eugene Corporon, Conductor; *"Emblems."*

Dallas Wind Symphony—Frederick Fennell, Conductor; *"Trittico,"* Reference Recordings, 1993.

Eastman Wind Ensemble—Donald Hunsberger, Conductor; *"Live in Osaka,"* Sony Classics, 1992.

Eastman Wind Ensemble—Frederic Fennell, Conductor; *"Ballet for Band."*

Ithaca College Wind Ensemble—Rodney Winther, Conductor; *"The Centennial Recording."*

New England Conservatory Wind Ensemble—Frank Battisti, Conductor; *"Contemporary American Wind Music."*

The Northshore Concert Band—John P. Paynter, Conductor; *"European Tradition."*

North Texas Wind Symphony—Eugene Corporon, Conductor; *"Tributes."*

Northwestern University Symphonic Wind Ensemble—John P. Paynter, Conductor; *"Paynter Conducts Arnold."*

St. Olaf Band—Miles H. Johnson, Conductor; *"The St. Olaf Band."*

Netherlands Wind Ensemble—Heinz Hollinger, Conductor; *"Strauss—Music for Wind Ensemble."*

Tokyo Kosei Wind Orchestra—Frederick Fennell, Conductor; *"Fanfare and Allegro."*

Tokyo Kosei Wind Orchestra—Frederick Fennell, Conductor; *"Hands Across the Sea."*

University of Georgia Symphonic Band—H. Dwight Satterwhite and John N. Culvahouse, Conductors; *"The Symphonic Band."*

University of Houston Wind Ensemble—Eddie Green, Conductor; *"The Planets."*

University of Illinois Symphonic Band—Harry Begian, Conductor; *"The Begian Years Volume III."*

University of Illinois Symphonic Band—Harry Begian, Conductor; *"The Begian Years Volume VII."*

University of Illinois Symphonic Band—Harry Begian, Conductor; *"The Begian Years Volume XIV."*

University of North Carolina, Greensboro Wind Ensemble—John R. Locke, Conductor; *"Celebration!"*

Recommended Orchestra Recordings

The selection is sufficiently rich that recommending four or five is a matter of personal choice.

A comparison can be made between Bernstein's recordings of the Mahler symphonies with Loren Maazel's recording of Mahler's 8 with the Vienna Philharmonic.

Mozart 35–41 with Karl Bohm and the Berlin Philharmonic.

Beethoven 9 and Von Karajan to compare two different conductors with the Berlin Philharmonic.

Bach's *Brandenburg Concerti* with the Musica Antiqua of Koln.

Recommended Recordings For String Quartet

The Kronos Performs Philip Glass

Additional Recommended Recordings

Leonard Bernstein and the New York Philharmonic answering "What Is Jazz"

The Youth Symphonies in the United States are nearing professional performance standards, and one can select recordings from the youth symphonies of almost any major city—New York, Los Angeles, Boston, Dallas, Atlanta, and more are excellent models.

25

Rehearsing
Concert Literature

Teaching varies in important ways; the student is only one of the variables. Teaching students to play their instrument is one kind of teaching; melding the talents and abilities of a group of competent students to make beautiful music together is a different task. Music provides different opportunities for enjoyment: Practicing alone is satisfying; performing alone or in public with or without an accompanist is personally rewarding. Chamber music experiences are to be relished, but there remains the literature for the large ensemble that delights in ways that solos and small ensembles cannot. There is also the personal satisfaction of contributing meaningfully toward accomplishing a musical objective.

FOCUSING THE REHEARSAL

The experience of being part of a large group of equally competent musicians working together with near-perfect precision can be unforgettable. The conductor has the critical role in creating this experience. The statement that no ensemble is better than its weakest player is only partly true; closer to the truth is that no ensemble is better than its conductor. The conductor should possess musical insights far exceeding those of individual players, insights that enable her to call forth the best in every player. The public school music educator is primarily a teacher on most days, but in the rehearsing and conducting of good literature the teacher also becomes a performer, contributing musically to the process with the other members of the ensemble. Both conductor and the players must understand the music, as there is almost always an interpretive role for each player within the framework and vision established by the teacher/conductor.

Rehearsals require variety in order to serve more than one purpose; student interest is one of the purposes, but the more important purposes focus on accomplishing numerous objectives at varied levels of sophistication. There is, of course, no magic pattern for the daily rehearsal. The mood and interests of students and teachers are not that predictable, although one learns through daily habit that rehearsals mean focus, concentration, and a positive attitude toward "digging in" to improve oneself and the group. An interesting and varied rehearsal contributes to this positive, concentrated atmosphere. Just as one's tone needs to be centered, the rehearsal needs to be centered on one or possibly two primary objectives that

421

are clear and understood by all students (and the teacher). Variety implies music of different styles, music requiring different levels of concentration, and music in different stages of preparation, as well as a range of experiences that contribute to the development of musicianship, knowledge, skill, and perception in individuals and the group. And, of course, the rehearsal should have an atmosphere of productive enjoyment—it should be fun. There will be intense periods where everyone is "sweating" to get it just right and periods of relaxation that make orchestra and band different from other classes. A few elements are sacred—warming up, tuning, and the musical objective of the day—but even these can be varied, not so much for the sake of variety as to "scale" all sides of the mountain of musical excellence.

The primary focus is that all performance must be musical, including warmups, tuning, and technical exercises. Time devoted to rehearsing a few students or a section is justified because without this teacher assistance the objectives for the large ensemble are inhibited. In certain places in the concert literature, the entire ensemble requires the assistance of the conductor, whether on notes, rhythms, bowings, intonation, expression, or a common vision and interpretation of the composer's intention. Emphasis on the technical elements, the "technique" of group performance, must not overshadow the focus on musical structure and seeking the musical line. Wrong notes, within limits, seldom interfere with conveying to the students the composer's intention and the appropriate musical style. There are recordings of great pianists and harpsichordists who frequently miss notes but whose musical interpretation is so stunning as to place these recordings among the best of the genre. Notes are important, of course, but students should recognize that mastery of the notes, rhythm patterns, progressions, and expression marks is the means to reach the goal of musical performances. A level of musical sophistication has been achieved when students recognize just how the melodies, cadences, modulations, and rhythmic elements contribute to musical coherence, enabling the listeners (including the performers) to grasp the primary musical ideas and to know when those ideas are being developed and when the composer is offering a romp between musical ideas.

There are many effective ways to introduce a new work to the student ensemble, the basic way being that of synthesis—analysis—synthesis in its numerous variations. If the approach is to sight-read the music, the emphasis should be on establishing in the ears of the students the overall structure of the work—the form, the style, and the elements that create musical climaxes whether rhythms, harmonies, melodic lines, or a combination of these. Another type of introductory synthesis is to briefly discuss such aspects of the work as its place in the composer's oeuvre and in the history of music, its distinctive qualities, *or* its relationship to other arts, and so forth. Or the discussion might point out the importance of various sections and solo parts, indicating the relative importance of these to the musical sense of the work and also to the rest of the ensemble as they develop supporting materials.

Another synthesis would be to have the group "walk through" the music, with the eyes only and without instruments. Here, the emphasis of the discussion is on requiring each student to musically perceive in his or her mind the sounds to be produced and to be able to verbalize the perception. Discussions in music classes are never exclusively verbal; singing is often required to communicate one's understanding of the composer and the music. Another approach to synthesis is to use recordings to provide the initial musical impression of the work. Comparisons of several recordings of the same work can illustrate the meaning of ensemble/conductor interpretation and of individualistic style. Other works by the same composer or in the same style can be briefly examined to good effect. There are arguments against the use of recordings to provide a synthesis but these arguments are outweighed by the possible advantages with high school groups. Students can recognize that the purpose of this initial synthesis is to obtain a rough or initial idea of the work and that there will be miles to travel before the ensemble has established its own interpretation of the work.

Having section leaders demonstrate melodies, countermelodies, and rhythmic structures performed at the approximate correct tempi along with teacher comments is still another way to establish synthesis, enabling students to "picture" the form and how their parts contribute, in simple and complex ways, to the structure. Depending upon the teaching situation, there are undoubtedly other sound ways of introducing a new piece to an ensemble.

The analysis part of our lesson plan has as many variations as there are teaching situations. The conductor prepares by analyzing the music in terms of the strengths and weaknesses of her ensemble, she rehearses her conducting of probable "trouble" spots, and she uses a variety of means to mentally hear all of the parts and combinations: The students practice their parts at home and in sectionals, and it is not impossible that some "drilling" by the entire group will occur to get the attacks, releases, balance and blend, bowing, phrasing, and so on, both precise and musical. There have been legendary public school and professional conductors who teach primarily through the initial synthesis and lots of analysis with almost no attention to the final synthesis. It has been reported that William Revelli has performed with the final synthesis occurring only at the public performance—an extreme approach for most public school ensembles! Too often, however, there is an overemphasis on the final synthesis when the primary emphasis should be on the first two parts of the synthesis—analysis—synthesis sequence of instruction.

Rehearsal can be productive or almost a total waste of time, as anyone who has been a member of several different ensembles has experienced. Rehearsing concert literature requires planning by the conductor—primary plans and backup plans based on the most probable contingencies. One learns these probable contingencies through experience—especially by student teaching and by observing many ensembles. These observations help to make intelligent planning possible, even in the first rehearsals in the first job. Because the music chosen for performance will be diverse, and because objectives vary from one situation to another, there are exceptions to any suggestions about the "best" way to rehearse. Nevertheless, certain priorities guide planning for and conducting rehearsals of musical literature. These approximate priorities follow:

- Musical form
- Style and genre
- Conventional musical interpretation
- Metrical organization and rhythmic precision
- Melodic and harmonic lines
- Feeling for tonal centers and modulations
- Attacks and releases
- Phrasing
- Musical movement
- Tone quality and intonation
- Contrasting elements
- Expressive devices
- Balance and blend
- Bowings and articulations
- Notes

The role of the conductor interpreting literature for the school ensemble is, (1) to demonstrate the musical sense of the work and (2) to assist individuals and sections in the technical issues that have not yet been mastered and that may require rote instruction and learning. In conveying ideas while rehearsing, the conductor becomes a teacher, projecting her voice to the entire group and generalizing the technical problem in a meaningful way, although it is possible that the trombones won't understand. As with all instruction, eye contact with students is important. The only time the conductor talks while looking at the score is when she and the students are together counting measures to identify a musical problem or to establish where to begin. Even when singing a phrase or two to model a musical idea, the conductor should not look down at the score while modeling; she either knows the phrase or holds the score as a vocal soloist would. The purpose is to communicate with the ensemble, best done by a sparing use of words or modeling while looking at, and focused on, the students. If everyone is concentrating, the students are as anxious as the conductor to get on with the task of "making music."

This chapter is not about conducting; those reading this text should already understand how to lead a musical group. Although the conductor should always "look professional," our focus here is on the goal of enabling the ensemble to sound like a *musical* ensemble. First, a few axioms for the conductor.

1. Mark the score in ways that will enhance efficient learning by students, enabling each one to understand and deal with the complexities of the music

2. Conduct the music in the way that makes the most musical sense. The conducting should communicate musical ideas to the students. It is essential that the meaning of conducting gestures be explained to the students, and more than once.

3. Conducting is coaching, communicating the plans for the performers and the performance through nonverbal means. Conductors can prevent problems by cuing, reinforcing players with approving motions, giving signals alerting the musicians as to forthcoming changes, and assisting those who are struggling with a bit of special attention. These nonverbal messages range from brief eye contact to conducting every beat or even subdivisions of the beat.

4. Listen to and be concerned about the full group; the balance may benefit from changes in intensity of the accompaniment rather than from the melody being played louder. Avoid following the first violin or first trumpet part as this often overemphasizes the melodic line and allows the conductor to avoid reading the full score.

5. Clarity depends upon everyone being able to see the beat, both the downbeat and its rebound. Save any exaggeration and large beat patterns for special effects; a normal, clear, visible beat pattern goes a long way in communicating with the ensemble. As the performers are watching the conductor out of the "corner of their eye," it is important that any change in the beat pattern or its size not destabilize the performance of individuals and sections, as will occur if the beat pattern becomes excessively small or large for no musical reason.

6. Expect students to respond to not only the downbeat but also all musical gestures. It seems that students are able to learn quickly that they will be given a second or third chance to respond to conducting gestures. More than one research study has found that ensemble members can explain fewer than half of the common conducting gestures. This fact may partially explain the need for several trials, but more often it results from the failure of the conductor to expect a minimum level of concentration on rehearsal procedures.

7. When sections or the entire ensemble lag behind the beat, the conductor must act. Stopping and explaining is one possibility. Stopping and demonstrating tempo with a metronome is another. Continuing to conduct but changing the beat size, often to a smaller beat pattern, may signal to the players the presence of a problem. Some drill may be required when the players are struggling to keep up because of technical problems.

8. If students are not in the habit of closely following the conducting pattern, a good practice is to use a simple piece of music to "rehearse" both abrupt and gradual tempo changes, even if they make little musical sense. The objective is for the student to learn how to watch both the conductor and the music.

9. Videotapes of conducting can reveal a lack of clarity in the beat pattern and conducting gestures. Practicing conducting is necessary as every piece of music presents unique situations. The more helpful the teacher is to the students, the more learning will occur in the rehearsal.

10. The music flows not only from the baton but also from the conductor's stance, motions, and expressions. The conductor becomes the music, stylistically and generically. Even the audience can be enlightened by observing a sensitive conductor.

SELECTION OF MUSIC

A number of factors influence the selection of music to be used in rehearsals. Music should be selected for what it can teach of and about music, and also for its interest, its motivational value, and for variety. Everything placed in the folder will have educational value including the music for "pops" concerts and athletic events. Orchestra and band directors, with their extensive education and passion for music, have been known to select primarily "heavier" pieces of music they would like to be able to conduct, but which are too difficult to be of educational value to the ensemble. Music must also be selected keeping in mind the multiple audiences, the students, their parents, the school personnel, and the general public. There is ample "good" music for satisfying these multiple audiences, but it may not be in the files. Selecting good music is a task requiring considerable time and expertise; if this were not so, there would be less worthless music performed by school ensembles. The reviewing of scores must be a continuing process for the teacher, analyzing both new and old publications. The music that was inappropriate for last year's ensemble may be today's best learning experience. In addition to the reviewing of scores, music selection must be part of one's professional development and part of a continuing conversation with colleagues.

Considerations for selecting music should account for (1) the instrumentation as well as student achievement level; (2) the audiences; (3) the conductor's competence; and (4) *the quality of the music*—selections (including, but not limited to, masterworks) that are well written, authentic, and allow for artistic performance. There is not a direct relationship between the difficulty of the music and a successful concert; a Grade VI band or orchestra playing good Grade III compositions has the potential for a great musical experience.

The numbers selected for public performance, and the order in which they appear on the program, must consider the audience(s). The initial number must be one that is reasonably short and about which the ensemble members feel secure in performing. Ideal is one that builds confidence for the rest of the program and allows students to think about their intonation, the balance and blend, and their ability to see and respond to all conducting gestures. Longer numbers are usually placed early in the program, both to accommodate to the audience's attention span and to ensure that the performers will have the physical endurance to perform well. A long warm-up or last-minute rehearsal before the concert may reduce the flexibility and endurance of the players' lips, hazarding cracked tones and missed high notes in the concert. Very few concerts are too short ... but many are too long; there is no need to demonstrate everything that the students have learned in one concert.

In the process of music selection, there are a number of elements that can be the focus. Technical skills are those most frequently considered because music is generally "graded" according to playability, dissonance, changing and irregular meters, and unusual and syncopated rhythms. If the rehearsal time is sufficient only to master these technical skills, that music is too difficult and was inappropriately selected. The ensemble situation is not the place where one should learn to play his instrument; rather the ensemble setting provides the opportunity not only to make "real music" but also to develop musical understandings not possible in the practice room. Style, intonation, balance, blend, precise attacks and releases, and many expressive devices can best be taught in the full ensemble—competencies that are not quickly or easily understood. As graduates of the music program, the students should be discriminating listeners, and discrimination is based more on the subtle, musical elements of a performance than on the technique of the performers or the antics of the conductor.

Directors should select music that will challenge and improve performance skills (perceptual, technical, and musical as well as sight-reading) in a context of good literature that provides useful information *about* music—that is, historical and/or structural information, craftsmanship, and the intangibles that allow music to touch the soul. Orchestras have a broader choice of quality literature from various historical periods than do bands. When in the 1970s band directors attempted to perform only original wind music, they denied themselves the tremendous resource of fine transcriptions and denied students a valuable component of their music education. Wind ensembles are superb teaching vehicles, especially for contemporary music, but they also have their musical limitations. Rehearsing, listening to, and comparing music of different genres from various historical periods is an important learning activity for both wind and string players.

Music from various historical periods is especially appropriate for teaching form. The vast majority of music written for wind bands has been written since 1960 and is in an ABA format or slight variant. To develop an understanding and aural recognition of forms such as sonata, allegro, rondo, fugue, and larger forms such as the symphony and dance suites, requires the use of transcriptions, or alternatively, of listening to recordings.

Techniques for studying a score for possible purchase are similar to studying a score for rehearsal. The teacher should first determine the approximate grade level and whether the work requires an instrumentation that is feasible for her. Second, the teacher should observe the ranges and tessitura for each instrument, the rhythmic complexity and tempo, unusual demands on a particular section (e. g., must the trombones double-tongue or are there outrageously fast *détaché* passages for viola?), the dynamic range in the context of register, the group's instrumentation, and any awkward modulations or hard-to-hear approaches in dissonant sections. An important consideration often ignored is the length of phrases or overall length. For example, there are several band transcriptions of Ralph Vaughan William's *Linden Lea*; although the overall piece is fairly short and technically easy, it is demanding due to the lengthy phrases and the consistent requirement to perform each line with intensity and momentum.

PHRASING

The *phrase,* a natural division of the melodic line, is usually marked by a cadence; the *art of phrasing* is musical movement from cadence to cadence. Musical sequences (two or more phrases) become understandable in much music by following tension and release points. Bach chorales are among the best tools for teaching phrasing.

In Western music, upward movement often implies a strain or struggle against a descending pull. This upward pull takes various forms. In general, the highest note is usually the point of greatest tension within the phrase, and the music should move toward this point. From the point of greatest tension the phrase continues to a point of rest, indicated by one of several kinds of cadences. (The term *cadence* is from the Latin infinitive, *cadere,* "to fall.")

Rhythmic intensity rather than melodic height may create tension, with its end a point of musical climax. An unexpected change in the rhythmic flow—faster melodic movement or a sudden slowing—can also contribute to creating a focal point of a phrase. To talk about the high point of the phrase is complicated, but hearing it is usually easy.

Whether every musician can explain tension and repose is not as important as understanding that phrasing defines melodic movement. Language is organized in phrases and uses punctuation in writing and vocal inflection in speaking to indicate its cadences. When one ends a sentence, the voice drops to a lower pitch, a full cadence. A question is expressed with a rising inflection, analogous to a half cadence in music. All performers must understand the relative role of half, full, and deceptive cadences, and most should know about additional cadential devices. Cadences differ in their finality: a half cadence indicating only a pause, a I–IV–V^7–I cadence more final.

Students should mark the phrases, as the ends of phrases provide opportunities for changing bow direction or taking a breath. Long phrases may call for staggered breathing by the winds and staggered bowings by the strings—that is, students on each stand take a breath or change bow direction at different places in the phrase so that the section as a whole may sustain the musical idea. Often, the peak notes of a phrase are located and marked. Students should audiate the shape of each phrase and understand what is meant by musical line. The dynamic markings in some music should be regarded skeptically when they contradict the musical sense. Playing with awareness of the musical form brings coherence to the performance, every note having an important function and each note leading to the next.

Sustained or repeated tones are not performed at the same weight or level except for special effects, and they always increase or decrease the intensity of the line. These suggestions apply not only to melody but also to the accompaniment, and every member of the group must play being conscious of the form. Finally, phrase endings should be smoothly tapered with an appropriate release, because, in Western music, the tension is usually reduced at cadence points.

Many of the great instrumental soloists of the past claimed they learned how to "sing" on their instruments by studying the performances of great singers. One can learn much about phrasing from recordings of Dietrich Fischer-Dieskau, Bryn Torfel, or Dawn Upshaw.

Harmonic Phrasing

Harmony and melody are so interwoven in creating form that consideration of them as separate elements is possible only for purposes of discussion. Bach chorales provide excellent practice in harmonic phrasing. The interaction of melody and harmony is especially noticeable at cadence points in Baroque music.

Harmonic structure (less so in polyphony) is the basis for any feeling of tension and relaxation in the music and determines how a phrase should be played. The tonal center and the tonic chord represent release or relaxation—the absence of tension—so that the farther the harmony moves from the tonal center, the greater the tension produced. When playing a chorale, all students should be able to sing "do" at any moment or spot in the music. Also, the more unexpected the harmonic movement, the greater the tension. A brief summary of the way in which harmony helps create movement would include these elements:

1. Cadences are points of relaxation; cadences not on the tonic imply continuation, whereas cadences on the tonic produce finality.
2. Movement away from the key center creates tension; the more distant, the greater the tension.
3. Return to the tonal center releases tension.
4. Modulation to a new key that requires a decisive cadence in the new key, not just the appearance of an altered chord or a secondary dominant, is an expressive device, signaling greater tension.
5. Chromatically altered chords produce tension, and the altered tones require more stress, followed by relaxation as they resolve.
6. Dissonance is relative, and the style of the music determines the consonance or dissonance of any particular chord.
7. Today's ears are jaded from overfrequent exposure to dissonance and to uncommon key relationships, requiring a cognitive effort to recognize the emotional effect of a modulation.

Knowledge about the music is necessary for the conductor who wishes to approximate the composer's intentions. A chord highly dissonant in the music of Mozart would be tame in the music of Schoenberg. That which appears dissonant in classical music is often consonant in romantic music and innocuous in contemporary music. The inherent tension of a particular chord is relative; the level of tension of that chord is determined by the other chords in the composition, or the melodic direction in polyphony that takes precedence over harmonic direction.

Players are often vaguely aware of the harmonic movement of the music without understanding it or without listening specifically for it. If the director teaches chord structure and harmonic progressions, and how harmony functions in developing phrases and climaxes in the music being performed, the students come to understand more of the music.

Attacks and Releases

Satisfactory playing of any music demands not only that the group understands musical direction (melodic and harmonic) and responds to it, but also that students begin and end each phrase precisely, even when there are overlapping phrases. Good attacks depend upon these elements:

- The instrument must be in playing position.
- The player's finger position, bowing position, or breathing must be prepared.
- The player must be watching the conductor.
- The conductor must have a definite, clear preparatory beat and downbeat or lift/cut off which the player understands.
- The student must hear the note before playing it.

None of these elements is difficult to achieve, but constant attention must be given to them until the group has formed the habit of clean attacks through on- and off-the-string attacks, breathing exercises, technical drills, and *careful* listening.

The releases are equally important and require the same level of mental and musical alertness and sensitivity. Although most directors are adept at identifying sloppy attacks and drill repeatedly on precise attacks, relatively few bother with releases. A precise release at the end of a tapered phrase, followed by resumption of tempo at the next phrase, is as important as correct notes.

Releases are difficult to execute with precision unless the players have been taught to give full value to these ending notes and to observe the section leader— great ensembles develop a "feel" for a musical release and follow-through. When the conductor signals for release at the end of a phrase or sequence, she must use a clear gesture of baton or hand so that the precise instant of release can be seen and understood.

Students should always have pencils at the ready and develop the habit of marking in their music anything that will help them play better; for example, difficult spots to practice at home, an accidental that is hard to remember, bowing changes, breathing places, added nuances, expression marks, tricky intonation spots, and special attacks and releases. A uniform procedure for marking, such as illustrated here, should be used.

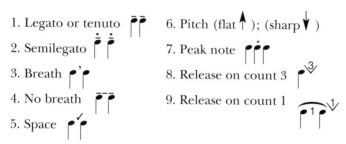

1. Legato or tenuto   6. Pitch (flat ↑); (sharp ↓)
2. Semilegato   7. Peak note
3. Breath   8. Release on count 3
4. No breath   9. Release on count 1
5. Space

Not one band or orchestra in a hundred plays with exact precision, yet precision is the easiest problem to detect. Aspects of ensemble performance such as intonation, tone quality, phrasing, balance, and blend are subtler and impinge on performance in varying ways. A group is precise or it is not. The group that has rhythmic precision and plays with clean attacks and releases is such a surprise and joy that many other errors can be forgiven. When groups are sloppy it is not because they lack ability. The conductor is to blame.

TONE, BALANCE, BLEND, AND INSTRUMENTATION

Music teachers are fond of claiming that a beautiful tone is the single most important factor in good playing. Most musicians agree with this, but the public does not seem overly concerned about beauty of tone, judging by the best-selling compact discs, the television programs with high ratings, and the famous name performers. Loud and distorted guitars, a bass with no tonal center, raucous saxophones, and edgy-toned trumpets abound. Department stores and record stores are more likely to stock the week's newest alternative garage-band than flute solos by Rampal or cello concertos by Yo Yo Ma.

Before players will play with a good tone they must hear examples of good tone. This is one excellent reason why listening time in the rehearsal period is an excellent practice, as is allowing students to check out CDs from the orchestra or band library. Tapes (both audio and video) and compact discs can be used to develop the mental concept of beautiful tone. The director may be an accomplished instrumentalist and hearing her illustrate types of tone will be valuable to the students, but she cannot adequately illustrate the entire range of instrumental sounds nor the desired ensemble sound of a fine band or orchestra.

When all the players have a good tone and all sections blend internally, the battle still remains unfinished; the overall tonal blend and balance of the organization must still be worked out.[1] This problem is the teacher's, as it is the teacher who must adjust the components of her ensemble to match her mental concept of the desired sound. Such adjustments are easier said than done, as many variables interfere: instrumentation, scoring, acoustics of the rehearsal room and the performing facility, and strengths and weaknesses in sections, not to mention subjective judgments by conductors. The conductor listens constantly to judge the balance and blend of the group, but when she is close to the group she may get a very different impression from that obtained several yards away. Occasionally, rehearsals on the stage of a larger hall may allow the balance and tone to be heard better, and the players as well as the conductor will hear the difference. The conductor should turn the baton over to a student director and move back into the hall to listen for tone quality, intonation, blend, and balance. What she hears may be very revealing, especially if rehearsals are ordinarily held in a "bright" room in which the sound runs together. The best rehearsal rooms are similar to the performing hall, which one would hope is not the school gymnasium.

Balance does not mean that every section plays at the same dynamic level. The music will partially determine which sections need to predominate at any given moment, the melodic parts usually being of more interest than those that are strictly accompaniment. Because each musical composition is different, it is useless to elaborate the point except as a reminder that in band the saxophones or trumpets should not always be dominant, and that not everyone in the ensemble plays at precisely 15 decibels.

Instrumentation to achieve a satisfactory balance requires planning. An ideal instrumentation is impossible to achieve in most situations, but some general rules can be followed. First, one seldom hears a band criticized for having too many clarinets or an orchestra for having too many violas. Second, for bands, good balance will not be possible if the brass section is equal in number to the woodwinds. For orchestras, two cellos simply cannot balance two dozen violins. Starting with recruiting and encouraging students to transfer early in their program are the only ways to ensure an instrumentation that can achieve an acceptable balance.

For wind ensembles that have one player on a part, the foregoing statements concerning balance do not apply. A wind ensemble should not attempt to sound like a band, nor vice versa. Many band directors are attempting wind ensemble concerts with what are basically small symphonic bands—the change of names for them is only a way of selecting the best players into one group. If such a group is to sound like a wind ensemble, the literature must be appropriate, and the instrumentation must be thinner than that of a symphonic band. If one does not have a first trombone who has the endurance to perform the entire concert, then perhaps a wind ensemble approach is inappropriate.

Capable players on all the parts will contribute to ensemble balance; placing the best players on the first parts with the weakest players on the third parts results in a dreadful balance. Few bands or orchestras have enough good players to form an ideally matched ensemble, but thoughtful distribution of the talent is one way to balance the group. There should be strong players on second violin and viola (even

---

[1]Balance generally refers to the degree that sections in an ensemble dominate over others—in a well-balanced chord played by an orchestra, all instruments are heard equally well and no note of the chord sounds louder than the others. Blend indicates the quality of individuals' and sections' fitting together inseparably. At times the brass should blend into a brass sound rather than a sound that is distinctly trumpet, horn, trombone, and tuba; an individual player with substandard tone quality or dynamic level will not blend and will hurt his section's blend.

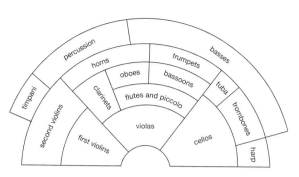

Figure 25–1 Symphony Orchestra 1

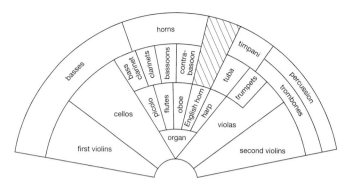

Figure 25–2 Symphony Orchestra 2

if it means encouraging successful violinists to switch to viola), just as strong players should be assigned to all the clarinet parts in a band. This aspect of "instrumentation" relies greatly on recruiting. Too many beginning band directors allow far too many students to start on saxophone or drums; far too many orchestra directors do not start enough violas or cellos.

Finally, balance and blend are affected by seating arrangements; these should be altered until the most acceptable balance is found for the group. The conductor who leaves her seating arrangement the same from year to year does not listen carefully to her group. Changing seating arrangements is an attempt to improve balance, blend, and the overall ensemble sound. Seating should be planned to assist the sound production of weak sections. Brass instruments are "directional"—they project their sound mostly in front of them. Other instruments such as woodwinds and strings are "nondirectional" and radiate sound all around them. The instruments on the outside edge of the group are easier to hear and should be those that produce the least volume. For orchestras, a very rough, general rule-of-thumb is about one-third the number of violas as violins, a similar number of cellos, and a few less basses than cellos. Few professional orchestras, however, follow such a rule rigidly as the literature calls for various instrumentation.

The seating arrangements for full orchestras in Figures 25–1 and 25–2 are both commonly used by professional and school orchestras. Both have the winds centered, with woodwinds in front of the brass, and both have the principal first violinist, violist, and cellist near the conductor. The sound produced by the seating in Figure 25–1 would create a greater contrast between upper and lower registers within the strings, as the upper strings are to the left and the lower strings to the right, with violas centered (who play both with the upper parts and with the lower parts). The arrangement illustrated in Figure 25–2 could result in a more blended sound with the high and low strings mixed, but with the flexibility of enhancing the highs (by having all violins in the front) and the lows (by having the basses closer to the audience than in Figure 25–1 and right behind the cellos).

Figure 25–3 is the traditional seating arrangement used by most school string orchestras. Teachers should experiment with string seating rather than routinely adopting the traditional seating. The arrangement in Figure 25–3 is less effective with a small viola section; a better ensemble sound may be produced if the violas are switched

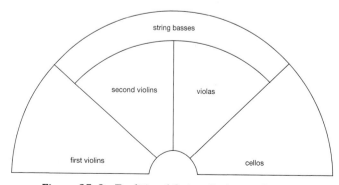

Figure 25–3 Traditional String Orchestra Seating

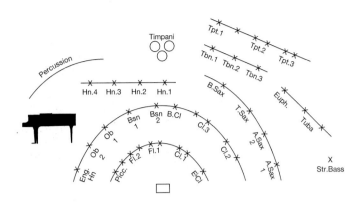

Figure 25–4
University of New Mexico Wind Symphony;
Eric Rombach-Kendall, Conductor

with the cellos. In instances of only a few second violins, switching them with the cellos and moving the basses behind the cellos may produce a better ensemble sound. Ensemble directors should experiment throughout the year, not only to determine the best ensemble sound but also to provide students with opportunities to hear different parts.

Individual seating within the section can also affect the total sound. As indicated above, to put all of the best players in the first sections and the weakest players in the last is good for neither musical nor pedagogical results. Musicianship, technical ability, and also personality, temperament, leadership, and experience should be considered. One might alternate players who have a strong and weak sense of rhythm, good and poor bowing, good and poor intonation, so that the better players may help the weaker ones. Timid but promising students may be placed in leadership spots.

Placing the first-desk players in wind ensembles and orchestras as close to the center of the ensemble as possible will facilitate listening for intonation, and uniformity of articulations, style, balance, and phrasing.

Figures 25–4 and 25–5 illustrate seating arrangements that are popular among wind ensemble conductors. Both have one on a part except for doubling the tuba to provide a more solid foundation to the pyramid-balanced ensemble sound (discussed in the previous chapter). The arrangement in Figure 25–4 aligns the principal brass players toward the center, clustering woodwind families: The principal double-reed players are together and the principal single-reed players are closer to the audience.

The wind ensemble illustrated in Figure 25–5 is creative in that it uses straight lines to achieve not only projection but also ensemble blend by positioning the clarinets in the center with midrange saxophones behind the flutes (highs) and low clarinets behind the oboes (highs): The midrange horns are close to the saxophones for blend and the trumpets are positioned to project and blend, by their location near the trombones and euphoniums.

The band arranged in Figure 25–6 is for 53 wind players; clarinets and flutes sit in rows near the audience. The low

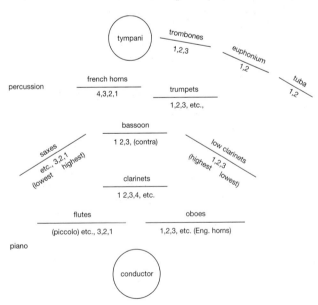

Figure 25–5
New England Conservatory of Music Wind Ensemble;
Frank Battisti, Conductor

brass are centered in the back to play through the high brass and woodwinds for a full, balanced ensemble sound. The arrangement is controversial in that the horns have their bells directly to the audience.

Figure 25–7 is a common seating arrangement for fully instrumented symphonic bands. The symphonic band conducted for decades by Harry Begian at the University of Illinois had an established instrumentation of about 100 players with all parts doubled (except the obvious: piccolo, E♭ soprano clarinet, saxophones, and trumpets). He aimed for a blended clarinet sound by his unique seating arrangement of those instruments (Figure 25–7), clustering the lowest instruments around the timpani and at the same time keeping the brass choir together.

When instrumentation and seating are maximized, the conductor and players can better focus on the ensemble's tone, intonation, balance, and blend. As with good tone and intonation, good blend is the result of listening. The student whose playing is loud, shrill, or nasal should be controlled. There is little room for individualism. Avenues to achieving blend include careful listening, good tuning, and proper dynamics.

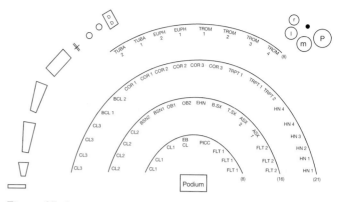

Figure 25–6
University of North Carolina—Greensboro Symphonic Band; John Locke, Conductor

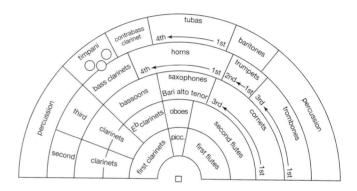

Figure 25–7
University of Illinois Symphonic Band under Harry Begian

Achieving a properly balanced ensemble may require that students transfer to different instruments. Any transfer needs to be approached carefully. Encouraging conscientious students who learn quickly and providing a school instrument and private lessons from the teacher are often viewed as a reward by both the students and their parents.

MUSICAL INDEPENDENCE

Most instrumental teachers will recognize this situation: The orchestra plays a familiar warm-up number with a good tone and intonation and fair balance; next they move on to scales. The notes are accurate and the students play with a fair degree of technical skill as they play different rhythms and modulate. With warm-ups completed, the ensemble begins to rehearse their concert music. Suddenly the group sounds like a parody of itself. The playing is out of tune, sections are screeching, and the conductor struggles to be heard above the din. It is obvious that she knows what the piece should sound like, but her group appears less certain. They stop, and she listens to various sections alone. The errors she finds seem incongruous, considering the time spent on technical drill. Students have missed key signatures, players seem unaware of tonality and balance, and many fail to understand basic musical principles (i.e., no one in the viola section remembered to carry an accidental through the entire measure). However, the director has infinite patience and corrects each mistake she finds, no matter how painstaking the process. The orchestra begins again, and the chaos is slightly less. Some of the errors the director pointed out have been reduced. With the next new composition, the cycle begins all over again.

Is this exaggerated? For many bands and orchestras, it is not. How many times does the typical ensemble director have to stop to remind a section that staccato means detached? The solution is to teach more music through music, and to teach for transfer during the warm-up routine so that it actually transfers to the music. If difficult numbers cannot be mastered without sacrificing musicianship, then simpler numbers are called for. Time spent on sight-reading, ear training, listening, and drilling on technical exercises to make them *musical*, may in time produce musicians capable of performing the more difficult numbers. If the conductor does envision a developmental program of musical learning for the band and orchestra, she must plan that program, because learning comes only through logical steps that proceed in orderly fashion from the simple to the complex.

The director of school groups must realize that the ability of grade-school students to concentrate and stay on task is usually less than that of high school students. Further, younger students do not always have the stamina to play for a full hour, much less 90-minutes in a block schedule. Time must be allocated for physical rest, and it is during these periods that other tasks can be introduced. For example, as the students begin to show signs of fatigue, observant conductor/teachers will continue to work on the music by clapping rhythms, singing parts and scales, listening, and other activities.

Musical independence can also be promoted through the way a director corrects mistakes. Performance errors will occur—it is essential that directors demonstrate this understanding to students. As the correcting process continues, the director should involve the students in making musical decisions as well as in identifying and correcting technical problems.

To the director, it may seem much faster to stop the group and quickly give directions to improve the performance. However, if time can be taken to listen and then lead a discussion on how to shape a phrase or where a crescendo might be added to make a section of the music more effective, or to ask the clarinet section leader to devise an "easier" fingering, or to ask the tuba section members if they feel the percussionists are rushing, more learning will occur, more critical observation/listening will take place, musical judgments will be made—in short, musical independence will be fostered. Students seldom make mistakes on purpose (well, maybe the trombones), but it can become habit forming for students to plod along satisfied with their own mediocrity if the director doesn't prod them to greater alertness. Encouraging students to analyze a problem and devise a solution leads to musical independence, if they have a mental model of what the ensemble should sound like.

Musical independence leads to individual musicianship. And working with a room full of musicians is a genuine pleasure. Students can help determine why a mistake was made and often they can determine how to fix it. They should not always need a director to point out the mistake and tell them how to fix it. They never need a director to embarrass them in the process.

It is essential that young people realize that mistakes are a part of learning. Directors can clearly model this by admitting their mistakes. Ensembles strive for perfection but it is a goal that is never reached. Students can learn to anticipate errors and avoid them (often simply by paying attention), and with time the director can establish herself as a source of information and guidance to help them reach their goals—not a tyrant who rules "her" group with an iron fist where every mistake results in humiliation.

The teacher's positive attitude helps tremendously. No one enjoys falling below a teacher's expectations. Success should be met with reward; limited success should be met with limited rewards. Success gives rise to success. The director must provide opportunities for every student to attain some degree of success or sense of accomplishment.

Finally, musical independence is demonstrated in part by students' individual practice. In today's busy adolescent life, students have difficulty making time for practicing their instruments. Being talented helps a student achieve, but efficient and consistent practice helps more.[2] Students have to *learn to practice*, however. The ability to practice is no more natural than the ability to finger an oboe—both require instruction.

TEMPO, METER, AND RHYTHM

A composition need not be played at its performance tempo during sight-reading. Most conductors initially practice music at slower tempos until problems of technique are under control. It is true that musical values are lost when numbers are rehearsed at slower tempos, but a slower tempo helps with error detection especially for young teachers as well as the students. However, line, metrical and rhythmic aspects, and interpretation can become mechanical and sterile if the slower tempo is maintained for too long. Also, attempts at shaping phrases and melodic/harmonic direction at the slower tempo may not be appropriate when the tempo is increased to the proper speed. Further, string players may have an impossible time using correct bowings at a slow tempo (unless each note is played shorter).

It is fallacious to imagine there is a single correct tempo for a composition. Compare, for example, recorded versions of the Beethoven symphonies as performed by Bernstein and by Boulez. Bernstein was often criticized for his fast tempos, but there is a range of acceptable tempos for music of all styles. Tempo is determined within reason by each conductor's interpretation and unfortunately sometimes constrained by the technical abilities of members of the ensemble.

Students must learn to follow the conductor. Maintaining a steady tempo is nearly always a problem in school groups because of the tendency of amateurs to rush through passages with lots of rapid notes and to drag passages with fewer notes. Loud parts of compositions usually bring out the impulse to speed, soft music the instinct to lag. The conductor is responsible for making her musicians obey her tempo. Players must see the baton as well as their music. They should adjust their music stands at a proper height to make both visible. The conductor can encourage closer attention during occasional rehearsals by intentionally beating time erratically. By adding a fermata here and there and by changing tempo, she can insure that players are paying attention. This technique is especially useful when playing the warm-up chorales during which every eye is focused on the conductor rather than the notation.

Players must maintain the established tempo on rapid passages and in places where they are prone to speed up or slow down (such as on notes of long duration or rapid technical passages, respectively). Most rushing or dragging of fast passages stems from lack of command of fingering and articulation or sheer fright at the

[2]Richard K. Weerts, (1976), *Handbook of Rehearsal Techniques for the High School Band*, West Nyack, NY: Parker Publishing pp. 9–17.

Figure 25–8 **Various rhythm approaches to learning rapid sixteenth note passages by strong players**

density of black notes. Often technique can be developed by playing through the passage with altered rhythms rather than mere repetition. For instance, a passage in rapid sixteenth notes may be practiced with the rhythms of Figure 25–8.

Subdivision

Watching the conductor is merely the beginning of attempting to establish precise tempo, meter, and rhythm with an ensemble.

The entire basis for rhythm is *subdivision* of beats. Experienced directors are aware of the difficulty students have in keeping a steady beat, often initially realized by players during their first confrontation with a metronome. One solution for both bands and orchestras is for each person to touch knees with the person sitting on either side, then all pat their feet through technical drills or the concert music. This assists weaker players and helps internalize the pulse.

Subdividing an unsteady beat moves one step away from precise rhythm. Lack of a uniform tempo from the director for a passage that is uniformly subdivided by the players results in a devastating "muddy" ensemble sound. The ability to maintain a tempo and accurately subdivide the beat is part of score preparation with the metronome ticking and is what the ensemble is drilled on in technical drills. The problem is compounded when articulations by the various sections differ. A difficult skill is to hear who in the ensemble is not subdividing correctly. This skill improves with experience and can be improved more quickly by recording rehearsals, then diligently analyzing the recordings.

Teachers must teach members of the ensemble to internalize the pulse by subdividing beats—to feel the pulse and subdivide into quarters, eighths, sixteenths, until that subdivision also is internalized from much repetition (Figure 25–9). This practice should start at the beginning level at which the ensemble players are playing quarter notes in band and orchestra. Mentally subdividing whole notes into sixteenth notes is probably the most challenging.

One method to help students learn to subdivide beats is to start a selection by counting off but then not conducting it. When the ensemble does not need a human metronome, the conductor is freed from the task of providing the beat and can shape phrases, dynamics, interpretation, and expression. She becomes the chief listener and consensus maker.

Although many students will learn to feel the pulse (a quarter note), the underlying subdivision at the very first level (eighth notes) may at first be difficult to feel. To feel the eighth-note level and subsequent levels of subdivision requires opportunity and practice. The more the students can delve into subdivision, the more precise the music as well as the generation of greater energy, direction, flow, and excitement.

Figure 25–9 **Basic Progression of Subdivision**

Meter and Rhythm

A performing group is united by its perception of the metrical pattern of a composition, using subdivision at the eighth-note or sixteenth-note level. This perception is based on what each player knows, hears, and sees. The relationship between meter and tempo and what the conductor does is worthy of attention at every rehearsal. No march or waltz accompaniment, for instance, can be perfected without training players to feel the underlying pulse of the music.

Singing, speaking, and clapping rhythms are probably the most effective ways to achieve precision and unity. Singing is closer to the real music in question, but speaking, counting, or chanting can create more vitality in rhythm practice, and clapping can get the feel of the rhythm into the muscles. Many teachers shy away from singing and so do their students, although it should be natural enough for musicians to sing. The way to get a group of students over self-consciousness in singing is to model, as you sing or clap the rhythm or give it words and telling them to respond similarly.

One difficulty in rhythmic correctness is the distribution of "weight" on the tones. Sometimes the pattern indicates equal weight but is played with one tone stressed, actually lengthening the stressed note and cheating others. Rhythms such as ♩ ♪ ♩ ♪ are more accurately spaced when the sixteenth note is played as a "grace note" to the next beat rather than on the "last-fourth-of-the-beat." Its association with the following beat rather than the previous beat will result in greater precision and may prevent rushing. Perhaps the most common rhythmic inaccuracy occurs in the playing of this dotted eighth–sixteenth pattern as if it were 6/8 time. Further, the dotted-eighth and sixteenth pattern with a 6/8 feel is correct for jazz style and is played even differently in a waltz or a march.

Uncommon Meters/Rhythms

One of the most difficult obstacles in performing twentieth-century literature is the frequent use of asymmetrical meters. Most beginning method books and junior high literature are limited to 4/4, 2/4, 3/4, and 6/8 meters, so the first time a group encounters 5/8 or 7/8, they flounder.

Asymmetrical meters should be introduced in the portion of the rehearsal routine devoted to technical drill, and *before* such a meter is encountered in the music. Many of the newer technical drill books listed in the bibliography of this chapter contain such drills. In drilling scales, different pitches of the scale can be stressed depending on the subdivision of the 7/8 measures (that is, 2–2–3, 2–3–2, or 3–2–2).

The director should explain that 5/8 is simply a lopsided 2/4 and 7/8 is a lopsided 3/4 (with one of the beats having an "extra" halfbeat). She will conduct the 5/8 and 7/8 like a two or three pattern with a delay after the "long" beat equal to the "extra" eighth note—here it is helpful to count aloud "one-and, two-and, three-and-and."

Style

Style might be thought of as the way the music flows. Everyone remembers the scene in *Hamlet* in which Hamlet directs the actors to "Speak the speech, I pray you, as I pronounce it to you, trippingly on the tongue. But if you mouth it, as many of our players do, I had as lief the town crier spoke my lines." Amateurs are bound to experience some difficulty in "speaking the speech" as it is intended. In musical terms, delivery is in part a matter of understanding legato and staccato as opposites. March style, for instance, is usually characterized by vigor and a light, detached kind of delivery, with each strain in a specific style.

From the purely physical standpoint, legato playing is connected and smooth with a continuous flow of tone. True legato is probably one of the most difficult problems for wind players. Staccato should be considered as "separated," not "short," because the space between tones varies with tempo and music. Students should be able to differentiate between the degrees of separation, ranging from the most detached to the most connected, and to recognize their markings.

Styles are usually dictated by rhythms and/or articulations. Adding space in rhythmic patterns is also important to maintaining tempo. The habit of rushing is common whenever off beats or repeated dotted figures appear and the group is not subdividing. When the tempo is fast, a very general rule is to require a space after any longer note that is followed by a shorter note. The point is that we often overlook the problems that are fundamental to music, while we worry about eight-to-five on the football field or whether to tune to a Pythagorean scale in the concert hall.

Simple pencil markings plus "codes" devised by the students themselves will help them remember how an accent mark is to be played in one selection and how it is played in another. Figure 25–10 contains quarter notes indicating markings that progressively decrease the space between the notes.

Figure 25–10 Range of Markings (from most detached to most connected)

Style is dependent on the articulations that are appropriate to the music (e.g., historically and/or rhythmically). For example, there is a difference between "weight" on a note and accents—two separate articulations, either of which may or may not be appropriate. The director must be aware of basic rules of interpretation—for example, eighth notes are generally detached at a fast tempo and have full value at a slow tempo (unless otherwise marked).[3] An example of this can be demonstrated by having the ensemble play a strain of a 6/8 march with all of the notes played full value then again with the eighth notes played shorter. Most students will agree that the second style sounds "better," or more appropriate. Such styles are determined by tempo, notated articulations and any style markings (e.g., *marcato, pesante, scherzando, grazioso,* Latin, bossa-nova, etc.), and the general character of the music.

Style characteristics of traditional *marches* include the following:

1. An effervescent first strain, followed by
2. A dramatic second strain (with brasses in the foreground on a tune and occasional brass tune and woodwinds playing with power in the background),
3. A lyrical, singing trio (often enhanced by having brass and percussion tacit the first time), and
4. A martial, marcato break strain (when the brass finally open up)

This description clearly indicates the importance of the woodwinds in march style—yet many directors equate the march with blowing brass. More importantly, the "march style" requires four contrasting styles based on balance, articulation, and dynamic levels.

---

[3]Technical drills should include fast legato eighth notes to develop that skill when it is required

No director can expect the band or orchestra to perform beyond what she conducts. If she expects a band to play *marcato*, she must conduct that way; if she expects the group to play grazioso, then she must conduct differently. She can stop and explain these differences to the group, which will have an impact for a few measures, or conduct appropriately and save time and obtain the desired effects.

MUSICAL INTERPRETATION

Every year at contests and festivals, adjudicators undergo one or more experiences such as this: The band uses as a warm-up number a traditional march played very straight ahead, with all of the notes and most of the rhythms played correctly; the tempo slows slightly at the trio and continues to slow to the end as the band tires—the result of "getting used to" a tempo variation in rehearsal. The orchestra selection is a Vivaldi sonata in fugue form, chosen for its difficulty and played very slowly because the strings have not mastered it well enough to play it at the proper tempo. Some winds have double parts, although the work is written for strings alone. The band performs an arrangement of a movement from a Brahms symphony, playing all the notes at the same volume regardless of whether they are melody, countermelody, harmonic support, or bass and snare drum parts added by the arranger. The adjudicators should, and do, mark the group down. When interpretation and expression of the music are lacking or erroneous, technical accuracy and precision cannot take its place. The *music* is missing.

Command of a variety of tonguing and bowing styles, from legato to staccato, is necessary for a variety of interpretations. Command of a wide dynamic range from pianissimo to fortissimo and a tonal range from "dry" to "lush" is also necessary.

Emphasis on interpretation must not wait until the notes and rhythms are mastered. Artistic manipulation of lines and harmony can furnish students an incentive for greater control of tonguing, tone, and dynamics (and all other musical factors), because interpretation is what makes the music alive and worthy of the effort.

Interpretation includes everything: tempo, rhythm, tone, balance, dynamics, phrasing, attacks and releases, and melodic/harmonic direction, in short, that which makes the notation musical. Interpretation must be appropriate to the style of the music and must conform to the accepted practices of the period from which the music comes. Interpretation means observing all of the movement within the music and playing in such a way as to enhance what is on the page. The movement of melodic lines, of motifs, of harmonic progressions, of countermelodies, and of counterrhythms is the essence of music. Bringing these out effectively so that they are heard in proper balance, from the smallest passing tone to the total formal design, is interpretation. This can be done only when the players recognize movement and can hear how their parts fit into the whole. The notation is a blueprint for the music; players learn this through explanation and example from the conductor and also through guided listening.

For the conductor/teacher to explain what the inner voices do, to subordinate a countermelody to the principal melody, to show how contrasting tone colors help produce motion, to help bring out the altered note in an altered chord, to trace the melody and all its variations through the composition so that they may be emphasized—these processes are time-consuming but teach the player about music as no single element can.

Most music teachers get a smattering of knowledge about style from their college courses, especially their applied music lessons and music history, but this should be augmented by listening to authoritative performances. The form of the piece also has bearing on interpretation: A baroque fugue is played in a stricter tempo than a baroque toccata; a romantic song is relatively contained and intimate, whereas a romantic tone poem can run the gamut of dynamic variety; contemporary music may be lyrical or austere; classical music may be serious or filled with humor. The conductor must know what is appropriate.

McBeth has observed that the conductor is the ensemble member who has the obligation to recreate what a composer/arranger intends—in other words, to communicate about the music. The conductor must prepare the score—know the score—and guide the ensemble to appropriate interpretation, thus narrowing the distance between composer and listener. If the conductor is conscientious, the gap can be narrowed. If the conductor is less than prepared, the audience may perceive an entirely new creation and inevitably of a lesser quality than that written by the composer.[4] The challenge is teaching expressive or artistic interpretation to groups of teenagers. Musical expression requires conceptual teaching.

Although several of these concepts have been mentioned, the following approaches are organized in steps. The simple concepts presented here will assist rehearsal procedures. These exercises can be incorporated in the warm-up routines discussed in the previous chapter.

1. Upward motion of a line generally generates a feeling of motion, almost a search for "resting point." The point of rest may be very slight or virtually insignificant rhythmically, but the artistic expression comes from the anticipation of arriving at that "target note."
   a. Exercises can include having the band or orchestra sing a major scale and gradually sing a ritardando when approaching the upper tonic.
   b. Encourage the ensemble to mentally think of the top note when they sing the lower triad to help them understand the motion.
   c. The notes just preceding the top note are the essential artistic interpretation. Students will eventually learn to feel the subtle pull toward that resolution. Leonard Meyer has written that the longer the delay, the greater the meaning evoked by the final resolution: the emotional or feelingful response by the musicians and audience.
   d. The point of rest or "resolution" may last only a moment as the phrase continues in another direction to create more tension and release.
2. Downward motion of a line can equally evolve these feelings of motion and meaning, similar to the concepts of upward motion; downward direction promotes a journey in the mind as it seeks a target note for a moment of release.

BOWING

The orchestra director and her concertmaster are responsible for deciding or creating the uniform bowings for the string section. If there is any truth to the general impression that the orchestra is a more elite ensemble than the high school band, it is because of the *musical* responsibility associated with bowing. The novice may think of music as consisting of a series of notes, bowed consecutively, down-up-down-up, and so on. This unimaginative bowing pattern would produce only the notes—the *music* would be absent and the listener robbed of the enormous potential of the string instrument. A string orchestra, well disciplined in bowing practices, can be a complete musical experience.

---

[4]McBeth, W. Francis (1972). *Effective Performance of Band Music, Solutions to Specific Problems in the Performance of 20th Century Band Music,* pp. 34–39. San Antonio:Southern Music Co.

Various bowings were described in Chapter 19, "Principles for Strings," and the soloist has considerable freedom in using the various bowing patterns where they make musical sense and/or follow traditional musical practice. Bowings are often marked when the composer/arranger has specific sounds in mind; when the bowings are indicated, the player merely needs to practice them to perfect the marked articulations.

An appropriate bowing is determined by the music and by reasonable considerations for its physical execution. Bowing patterns should not be tension producing; good string performance depends on remaining as relaxed and free as possible. Bowings are selected because they facilitate the desired sound (tone color), articulations, and musical style. The bow itself makes a major difference in the sound produced on a string instrument, and for this reason some bows are worth as much or more than the instrument. Because the sound produced by a down-bow is seldom identical to that produced by an up-bow (although one constantly practices to make them sound as similar as possible), it is important that the instruments playing the same part agree on the bowing; if it is not indicated in the music, it should be penciled in.

More than 20 variations of sound production are available to the string student, with a primary decision being whether a passage should be played *on* or *off* the string. Playing on the string means that the tone is initiated with the bow already on the string. Even with the ability to "dig in" to the string with on string bowings, the initial attack and follow-through will produce a different quality of tone. A careful study of the history of string performance practices is a better method of determining appropriate bowing than the memorization of set rules, although both may be helpful. Before Tourte (1747–1835) improved the bow, off-the-string bowings were impractical. The challenges of playing the new music of the time brought about improvement to the bow; John Dodd and Wilhelm Cramer both produced bows similar to that of Tourte at about the same time. (This history of the bow is informative, as is the fact that shifting was difficult and not a common practice prior to the invention of the chinrest around 1820.)

There is a great deal to learn about musical styles and the chief composers of music for strings. Though there is also much to learn about bowing, no one thought it necessary to compile a list of guidelines for orchestral bowing until Elizabeth Green's book, *Orchestral Bowings and Routines.*[5] This slim volume is the one "basic" book of orchestral bowings; it has served the profession well for half a century. Green illustrates the various bowings with musical examples, and although some of the music is quite advanced, her suggested bowings clearly make sense when applied to the musical excerpt selected from the best orchestral literature. It is simple to explain that a pickup note or notes are played up-bow in order that the first beat of the measure can receive the normal emphasis or accent with a down-bow. Other bowings, however, are more difficult to explain without musical examples.

Stylistic Considerations

Baroque music is marked by a single tone color throughout. There are well-defined levels of expression, and most of the contrast is produced by concertato procedures. Motives are sharply defined, and there is always a strong drive toward arrival points in the music. The frequent use of imitation requires the bowings to be imitative. Rhythmic patterns are commonly derived from dance music of the time, thus the rhythm is quite steady except for recitatives and fantasias. This simple

[5]Elizabeth A. H. Green (1990), *Orchestral Bowings and Routines,* 2nd ed. Reston, VA: American String Teachers Association.

rhythmic organization along the lines of symmetry and asymmetry of phrases informs the string student that the down-bow will be used on the first beat of every measure and on the third beat whenever possible. Although the bowing would have been on the string during the Baroque period, the strength of the music and its themes would indicate that off-the-string bowing is appropriate to initiate the motives, the strong characterization of expressive qualities, and the steady, energetic rhythm. Rhythms that are written as a pattern, such as a dotted eighth note followed by a sixteenth note or a dotted quarter followed by an eighth, are often played on one bow and on the string, either slurred or using a technique referred to as a "hooked" bowing. Long notes would be full bow, beginning near the frog for down-bows with the fast rhythmic patterns played more in the center of the bow. The index finger applies pressure to the bow, enabling each player to adjust his sound to match that of other players. (With the variety of instruments, bows, and strings found in most school orchestras, careful listening to match tone colors is required of all string players.)

In the classical period, the motives became melodies; the music became limpid and brilliant, requiring a variety of tone colors. As the tonal system became firmly established, emphasizing cadences became important in interpreting the music. The tessitura moved up, there was considerable use of crescendos and diminuendos, powerful rhythms, and syncopation to emphasize the importance of the metrical organization.

In general, one can play with more power at the bottom (frog end) of the bow than at the tip. Crescendos are usually played up-bow in order to provide the necessary control of the decrescendos that are played down-bow. Along with others, Mozart began to experiment with dissonance within his crystal-clear tonalities, and, prompted by his vivid imagination and relationship with the best performers, he used timbre for variety even in passages of exact symmetry. As the rhythmic figures were still derived from dance rhythms, the syncopated patterns are usually played on an up-bow in order to play the returning regular metric pattern down-bow on the first and third beats. Rests seldom affect the bowing motion as they do not interrupt the musical line. Chords, extensively used, are most often played down-bow, especially when there are rests between chords that allow for this off the string down-bow and stress on the top note of the chord (usually the more important note in a double or triple stop).

The relatively sharp accents in music of the classical period indicate a down-bow . Expression marks at either extreme, *pp* or *ff* (*sfz*), influence bowing, especially when contrast is employed. The loud passages require more down-bows as well as *détaché* bows; the soft passages (if not extremely fast) call for more continuous bowings. Some soft passages in classical music are also intense, requiring rapid single bowing in the middle of the string. Selection of the proper bowing is crucial to solidifying the rhythmic structure of the music. The bow stops before the various rhythm patterns, such as a group of four sixteenths or more complicated pattern, in order that the performer may begin most rhythm patterns down-bow. The exceptions are many and there is no substitute for knowing the music. Haydn's string quartets are tonal, but he apparently delighted in interweaving his melodies, minimizing the strong rhythms characteristic of the period and avoiding the strong half and full cadences that marked his symphonies. Mozart also has the listener chasing the melody, the listener aided by uniform tone color in two, quite distinct, ranges.

With romantic music, the cadences remain important but are weaker, and now the melody becomes a more prominent organizer for the bowing. Melodies in the minor mode require more emphasis than in the classical period. As a rule, the music of this period is more intense than that of the classical period, but the wide range of the music makes it even more critical to understand the individual composer and his or her style. Compare, if you will, the Brahms *Quintet in F minor* with Mendelssohn's *Hebrides Overture* or Strauss's *Till Eulenspiegel's Merry Pranks* for the musical effects desired. Longer melodies mean that bowing units may take two measures to "resolve" and return to a down-bow on the first beat of a measure. Dotted eighths followed by a sixteenth and similar two- and three-note patterns are generally played on one bow with the bow stopping between notes, when the tempo allows, to provide the precision expected. The Romantic period is the period of the virtuoso performer, and many examples can be found where there is inadequate time to stop the bow between the notes, and of course the ability of the student is also a consideration. (This bowing with a stop between notes is called "linked" or more commonly "hooked.") Long notes followed by a short note or two are also played linked. This increased tempo and greater expectations of the player with unslurred, cross-string requirements, means that ease of playing becomes a primary consideration. Upper notes in fast passages may be played up-bow with violins and violas and down-bow with cellos and basses to manage the intricate passages more easily. Up-bows can be accented by digging into the string, a technique described as accented *détaché*.

Chords are usually executed on the bow, although the player may have to "roll" the bow if there are three or four notes in the chord. Staccato notes, grouped, are often hooked in one direction. When spiccato bowing is called, for it is usually played off the string; the spiccato stroke that might be desired in a Strauss waltz is a "brush"-type spiccato stroke. Experimenting for the "right" (most appropriate) sound is to be encouraged.

Obviously, slurs of two or more notes are played either up-or down-bow in one direction. On-string *détaché* is more likely to be played in the middle of the bow, whereas off-string *spiccato* will begin closer to the frog. All bowings are also affected by whether the desired sound is better played close to the fingerboard or to the bridge; the lower strings generally play closer to the fingerboard, as was suggested in the separate chapters on strings. Short, heavy sounds are played closer to the bridge with some bow pressure on the strings; piano markings with either short or long notes will be played farther from the bridge, with long bows but with less pressure. There are many advantages to playing in the middle of the bow in classical and romantic music; *détaché, sautillé,* and trills are commonly played in the middle of the bow (tremolo is usually played at the tip). The bow must be kept straight lest it excite the longitudinal vibration and "squeak," a most unpleasant sound.

Not all bowings can be described by specific motions. The variety in tone and effect that strings are capable of is produced primarily by a combination of the speed of the bow, the placement of the bow on the string, and the control of the speed by the action of the right finger on the stick. *Martélé,* for example, is produced by pressure and quick release of the first finger on the stick at the beginning of each stroke and usually played in the upper half of the bow. Knowing the terms and approximately what sound is indicated is essential for efficient communication between conductor, concert mistress, and the section. However, some experimentation will be required for all but the most experienced players.

Modern music uses all of the devices of the preceding periods plus additional sounds. Much contemporary music is percussive and brilliant—tone colors are expected to appeal directly to the senses. Bartok's *Quartet No. 5* treats the strings percussively with returning themes that presage minimalism. Contemporary composers often desire contrasting tone colors between strings and other instruments in the orchestra, rejecting the blending of tone color that predominated from the Classical through the Romantic Period. The task of the musician is to shape the action of the music to assist the listener in perceiving. The "Hymn to Joy" from

Beethoven's *Symphony No. 9* requires a smooth, continuous treatment with the speed of the bow controlling the volume more than the type of bowing. Continuity is the concept to be conveyed in this Beethoven, a principle for all extended melodies just as that used by Franck in his *D Minor Symphony*. Wagner's continual building to subclimaxes requires that each melody begins as a separate section, building and then relaxing before beginning again at another attempt to reach the climax. Wagnerian melodies are played legato, and the player would want to avoid changing bow direction in the middle of a legato passage. Greatly increased intensity of bowings has inspired attempts to improve the instrument to withstand some of the violent ricochet bowings, but all efforts to date have been unsuccessful. The most recent improvement in string instrument design was to raise the bridge and provide a longer and stronger bass bar to withstand the increased pressure needed in maximizing the vibration of the top of the instrument. Playing closer to the bridge "forces more of the string's vibrations through the bridge into the top of the instrument and more tone is produced, also forcing more energy into a smaller space, since the string describes a smaller arc near the bridge, vitalizing the tone."[6]

Rhythmic Considerations

As attention to the rhythm is critical in classical music, so the rhythm is usually the influencing factor on bowing practices in contemporary music. Rhythmic clarity is important, melodies tend to be short, and a brash, clear sound is desired. Popular music requires glissandos and portamentos; country music achieves its inexact pitches either through delayed shifting or through bowing. To enhance rhythmic importance, the duration of tones just prior to complex rhythmic passages is often cut short in order to start the bow in the best position for completion of the "pattern." Usually the bow comes off the string after these rhythmic patterns.

Orchestral bowing is similar in all respects to bowing as a soloist except for the usual requirement to bow together. The upper arm leads the stroke, the elbow drops, and the hand follows. On bow changes, the elbow is dropped anticipating the down-bow and raised in anticipation of the up-bow. Advanced players may also curl their fingers as the bowing approaches the frog and extend them as the bow approaches the tip in order to maintain a continuous sound. The player continually listens for the "sounding point" with the particular speed and pressure of the bow, as the bow moves more slowly at the frog with decreased pressure to maintain the same sound. The weight, of course, needs to be increased when playing at the tip to maintain a constant sound. On all instruments it is important to have a mental (aural) concept before playing, but for string players this mental image must include not only the next note but the next measure or two (or even longer) requiring that string players look and think ahead. With musical understanding, proper bowing becomes a habit and bowing is not as complex as it may seem, although it is equal in importance to tone production on wind instruments.

Elizabeth Green's list of 14 principles emphasizes the importance of a good down-bow, suggesting that the player always count the number of pickup notes prior to an important, accented first beat; an even number of separated pickup notes start down-bow, an uneven number, up-bow (which "readies" the player for an appropriate down-bow emphasis to beginning notes which often establish the mode as well as the style of music). Preparation is required for long slurs as the unwritten rule is never to run out of bow before the musical idea is completed. The ear, a sense of style, and good command of the instrument are essential to any discussion of the number of appropriate bowings.

[6] Ibid., p. 77.

THE JAZZ PROGRAM

A major component of the complete secondary instrumental music program is the jazz ensemble(s). This section is devoted to providing the instrumental music educator a general background to assist in starting or maintaining jazz bands and/or combos.

If an active band program exists, it is easy to establish a jazz ensemble. One only needs to be wary not to let the "tail wag the dog," meaning that jazz becomes the focus of the performance program. The jazz band has numerous advantages: exciting literature, small size and mobility, and more performance opportunities than the larger ensembles have.

The typical middle and high school jazz band consists of two alto saxophones, two tenor saxophones, a baritone saxophone, five trumpets to cover the four parts (doubling the lead part), four trombones, and a real bass trombonist or tuba for the bottom part. Instruments needed to complete the ensemble, such as string bass (if not included in the symphonic band), piano, and guitar(s), can be recruited from the school population.

Publishers make arrangements for varied instrumentation: "Lab band" arrangements can be found that include horns, flutes, clarinets, tuba, and additional percussion, as well as string parts.

Starting a Jazz Band

Auditioning the rhythm section presents the most problems. A jazz player who is not a member of the band, though possessing a good ear and technique, may not be able to read music. Selecting nonband members who are not familiar with the way a well-disciplined organization operates requires evaluation not only of their technique but also of their attitude, genuine interest, willingness to learn, and reliability—all difficult to assess. One procedure is to observe their efforts in a full ensemble rehearsal, their cooperation, and their interest in the music (many rock-oriented guitarists may scoff at jazz standards such as "In the Mood"). Further, their participation and attitude toward other school activities *may* be helpful information.

Pianists are selected on the basis of rhythmic feeling. Many classically trained students may find jazz music quite foreign. The pianist should strive to maintain the correct rhythm, "holding time," and the ability to "grab" as many notes as possible. Practicing, listening to recordings, studying jazz method books, and videotapes can help pianists become contributing members of the rhythm section. Ability with fills and "turnarounds" should be of secondary importance and improvised solos third.

Acoustic bass players are preferred for jazz and combos. The bass player provides the pulse to the rhythm section, and so should demonstrate a strong beat when playing scales, arpeggios, études, or solos. A good ear is also essential. Electric bass players can make an important contribution but must be willing to learn to use published jazz materials and to play many styles.

Most high school set players can emulate rock drummers, but jazz band and small combo playing may be a new and different experience. The audition for a set player should include a solo as well as participation with the group. The set player should be able to maintain a steady and tight hi-hat cymbal on beats two and four, maintain a steady ride pattern on the ride cymbal, use a light bass drum, accent wind tutti "impacts" with the snare, and, *most important*, stay "out of the way." It may not be necessary for the individual to read the drum set part if she can hear and learn the arrangement by ear. It would be unfortunate, however, if a student did not learn to read music while participating in any music performance ensemble.

Guitarists, like drummers, are more apt to be rock than jazz oriented. The guitarist needs to be open to jazz styles, willing to listen to the subtle background playing of essential "timekeepers" such as Freddie Green with the Count Basie Band. The ability to read chord symbols is a must as is the ability to improvise in both rock and jazz styles. For all the instruments in the rhythm section, there are ample self-instruction books, recordings, play-alongs, and videotapes available.

Jazz Band Seating

There are several accepted ways to seat any jazz ensemble. Each has its advantages and limitations; the decision is based on the group's stronger and weaker sections. The rhythm section sits close together in order to hear the lead wind players (usually positioned in the center) as well as themselves (especially hearing the bass), to achieve balance within the rhythmic section, and to enable a player to glance at another's part for an improvised solo. Trumpets traditionally stand when playing to enhance projection and for the sound to project through the trombones for a fuller effect on full, thick jazz chords. The use of risers is visually appealing and improves the sound.

Because the majority of improvised passages are for first tenor, second trumpet, and second trombone, these instruments are usually placed closest to the rhythmic section. In the block setup (Figure 25–11) the bass should always be elevated (at least the amplifier). Figure 25–12 is used frequently with young players. The individuals can hear each other well, and the left side is available for a string section, horns or mellophones, vocal groups or "other" imported instruments.

The V-shaped seating arrangements illustrated in Figures 25–13 and 25–14 differ in that the former requires stronger, more confident players—but allows for greater eye contact among the performers. The latter is for a saxophone section that may not be as solid as the brass and benefits from the brass playing behind them for confidence.

Figure 25–15 is used frequently with younger, maturing players. The group can hear each other very well, and the left side is available for a string section, horns or mellophones, vocal groups, or other instruments imported from the lab band. Similar to the setup of Figure 25–14, a possible disadvantage is the bells of the brass are not directed to the audience, which might require additional microphones.

Figure 25–16 illustrates a common rehearsal setup used by lab bands and these groups learning to improvise.

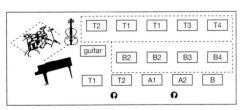

Figure 25–11
Block Set After Most Popular Setup During Big Band Era

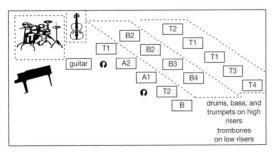

Figure 25–12
Angled Block as Suggested by Robert Ambrose

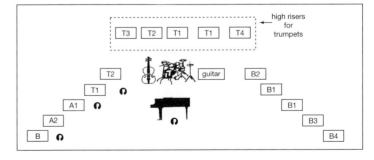

Figure 25–13
"Inverted V" After Stan Kenton

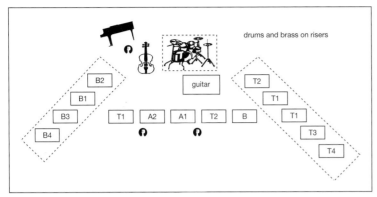

Figure 25–14
Triangle Set up for Projection

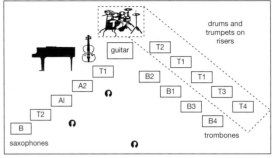

Figure 25–15
Block "Inverted V" Set-up

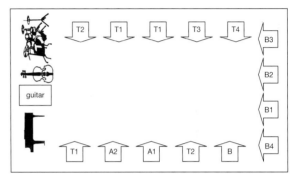

Figure 25–16
Rehearsal Setup (lab band,
improvisation lessons, sight-reading)

Articulations in Jazz

In Latin jazz, and other styles, such as rock, played with straight eighth notes, a "ta" attack is appropriate for all winds and the sound is stopped with the tongue (on short notes), whereas a softer "da" attack is used in traditional jazz for all winds (a "doo-dle-oodle" approach). The sound is still stopped with the tongue, but often more harshly by the brass, in an almost exaggerated manner ("doooit"). For example:

With only these articulation markings, the players are expected to interpret the style.

It is the section leader's responsibility to determine the articulation and the other player' responsibility is to follow. In most jazz bands the *primary* responsibility rests with the lead trumpet, with other section leaders quickly following those articulations (and changing them if the lead trumpet determines a better style) and the other winds following their section leaders.

The Rhythm Section

As indicated earlier, the greatest challenge facing most instrumental music educators in forming a jazz ensemble is the rhythm section—the most important aspect of any jazz combo or band. The rhythm section may perform as an ensemble of its own (e.g., the Oscar Peterson Trio).

The rhythm section usually consists of a set drummer, a bassist, a pianist, and a guitarist. Arrangements may call for extra percussion on Latin and other percussion instruments. The bass should be electric or amplified acoustic. The guitarist uses the electric instrument switching to an acoustic for Basie-style arrangements. *The rhythm section must practice together frequently.*

Piano

Piano parts are sometimes written out, making comping much easier for an inexperienced jazz pianist, or notated by chord symbols only, leaving the voicings and rhythms to the individual pianist. Currently the most common notation used by publishers of jazz arrangements is shown here in the third example in which the chord symbol and rhythm are provided leaving only the voicing to the pianist. See Figure 25–17.

The first example of Figure 25–17 can be used by most young pianists, but they should be encouraged to experiment continuingly with different rhythms and voicings. A general principle is that the more notes the pianist plays the easier it is for the wind soloists to improvise without seeming to play wrong notes. However, other groups such as the Chuck Mangione Quartet used no piano or guitar, giving the soloists even more "room" to improvise.

The notation in the second example of Figure 25–17 is often interpreted (incorrectly) to be played with straight quarter notes, the chords in root position. The pianist, while he concentrates on listening to the full ensemble to ensure his part is in the style of the music (rhythmically), also experiments with voicings to determine the best sounds. The director provides creative ideas and positive feedback when appropriate to help guide the pianist who may not have had to take risks and experiment on his own. The experienced pianist prefers this type of notation; rhythmic and harmonic freedom is the luxury of the jazz pianist.

Figure 25–17   Three Types of Piano Notation in Jazz Arrangements

The pianist is also expected to fill gaps in the music between the winds' solo sections. Sometimes the drummer plays a fill, but the pianist should always be prepared—especially on a Count Basie tune (or a Sammy Nestico arrangement). These fills are seldom written, so like the rest of the rhythm section, the pianist should learn the arrangement's structure by ear (remembering there are relatively few forms in traditional jazz styles), and fill the gaps, no matter how short the gap. These short fills are usually in the upper register of the keyboard and may consist of major seconds.

Though piano solos are often notated in easier jazz literature, the player must learn not to play the solo exactly as written, but rather in the style of the music. Articulations are seldom notated, as the player is expected to listen and learn the style of the entire arrangement and play the solo in the appropriate style.

With experience, the jazz pianist should expand his playing to include authentic improvisation. Listening to jazz recordings and focusing on the rhythm section is a terrific help. (The Jamey Aebersold recordings are especially helpful as the rhythm section comps throughout.)

The following list borrows from ideas from Ferguson and Feldstein regarding the piano's role in the rhythm section.[7]

1. The pianist need not play all the time, but punctuate chords, play fills, a "shine" on ballads. Overuse muddies the rhythm and punctuation. Use the hand for sustained chords as needed, avoiding the pedal.

2. Practice with a metronome.

3. Experiment with the printed part, leaving some chords out, substituting some, and altering others.

4. Play with correct style and rhythm when playing written solos attempting to make them sound improvised.

5. Leave thumb glissandi for Yanni and the like.

6. Listen for gaps in the music and try to fill them. Experiment with printed notes or chords in the upper register with correct rhythmic patterns.

7. Learn good voicing by studying published materials (especially transcribed solos) and transpose them to all keys.

8. Use silence as a rhythmic device (harmonic direction), and try not to be too busy with comping. On repeated chords, try to change the voicing.

9. Listen to recordings with the jazz director (e.g., Bill Evans, McCoy Tyner, Keith Jarrett, Chick Corea, and other big band favorites).

10. Don't play the bass line if there is a bass player in the band.

11. On rock and Latin charts an electric piano is adequate, but an acoustic piano is used for straight jazz.

Bass (String and/or Electric)

The role of the bass is to define the chords being played and to guide the movement of the music from one chord to another. The bass also provides a rhythmic drive to the music being played, a role often shared with the drums. When the bass takes control of the rhythm, the percussionist can concentrate on "decorating" the music, playing fills, and "kicking" in the winds at new sections of the music. Jazz bass players need to keep the steady beat driving and avoid overwhelming the band or combo. The bass line is a virtual metronome.

[7]Tom Ferguson and Sandy Feldstein (1976), *The Jazz Rock Ensemble*, Port Washington, NY: Alfred pp. 92–93.

Either an amplified acoustic or an electric bass is adequate for most big bands. Ideally, use both, as the electric bass sounds better on rock selections whereas the acoustic bass is preferred for swing. In most rock-oriented literature, the bass part is notated and comprises larger intervals and more repeated notes than jazz. Jazz arrangements also contain notated bass parts, but chord symbols are the norm.

Because the bass links the rhythm and harmony, the bass is often the instrument around which the music is organized. The most basic notes the bass player must learn are the I, II, IV, V[7] chord tones in the keys that are frequently played (which are usually not traditional orchestra keys). The bass player must also learn the major and melodic minor scales and the blues scales (1, 2, $\flat$3, 4, $\sharp$4, 5, $\flat$7, 8) in all keys.

The root and the fifth are probably the most important notes of any chord. These notes are always safe, too; but the walking bass line traditional to most types of jazz makes use of chord tones and simply approaches each chord change from a half step below or above the tonic note.

The most common special effect for bass is the slap bass. The slap bass originated during the swing era on acoustic bass. The bass player slaps the bass to make the bass lines stand out. Slapping the bass actually helps a young student to keep better time. The string is pulled with the first or second finger and allowed to slap back, then slapped against the fingerboard with the left hand. The technique is timed so that the hand slaps on counts two and four in 4/4 meter.

Again, Ferguson and Feldstein offer a list for the bass player:[8]

1. The bass line should be on the simple side rather than the busy side in jazz; busier with ostinato syncopated parts in rock.
2. The steady beat is the primary function.
3. All notes should be sustained as much as possible in all styles.
4. Staccato is avoided except for special effects, or improvising.
5. The bass line should be as linear and diatonic as possible in jazz tunes, with larger intervals and repeated notes in rock.
6. The conductor must listen to bass at all times for the beat and for helping the player with volume.
7. The lower register is used most frequently, with the upper register reserved for improvised solos.
8. Listen to professionals who lead groups (e.g., Stanley Clarke, Charles Mingus) as well as professional big band bass players.
9. The bass player must not compete with the drummer, but cooperate as one rhythmic unit.

Drum Set

The drum set (or trap set) player is the driving force that enhances entrances and soloists, solidifies tutti horn lines and punctuations, and establishes styles (i.e., swing, rock, Latin rhythms, ballads, shuffle, etc.). Also, and just as important, the trap set serves as a timekeeper with the bass.

The drummer should play simple time until she learns the arrangement by ear and can use her feet and hands independently to add accents and punctuation with the winds, fill between spots (allowing the pianist to fill when appropriate), and play ride cymbal behind soloists. One of the most common problems with drummers is "getting in the way" or trying to play too much—wait for the drum solo. In most 4/4 jazz tunes the right-handed player plays ride cymbal with her

[8]Ibid., pp. 99–100.

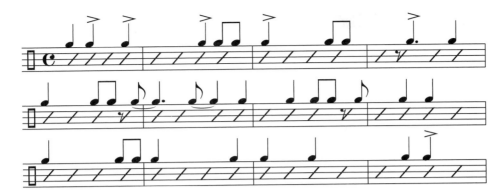

Figure 25-18 Typical Drum Set Part

right hand and the hi-hat on beats two and four. The left hand is free on the snare and toms for accents, and the bass drum is lightly played on all four beats to help deepen the bass sound and for accents or punctuation of the wind parts.

Drum parts are usually only a sketch that indicates where the ensemble has accents and where the drummer should perhaps play a fill. It is wise to leave the drummer's part in the folder and have her listen to the ensemble and learn the arrangement rather than attempting to watch this sketch and fail to concentrate on tempo, decorating ensemble parts, bringing in the groups, adding color, and change styles. An example of a typical drum part is shown in Figure 25-18.

Eight examples of drum set patterns for jazz are illustrated in Figure 25-19. The first is a basic jazz pattern. The top x's are the ride cymbal and the bottom x's are the hi-hat. The "top" notes are for snare (which would change much during a straight ahead jazz tune), and the bottom notes are the bass drum. Any notes in between would be toms. The second example is slightly accented on two or four, but with the straight eighths on the ride cymbal it would provide a Latin feel or even a jazz feeling.

The third pattern is used frequently as it fits most jazz tunes; the snare might alternate with rim shots (light or hard) depending on the horn parts. The fourth

Figure 25-19 Eight Jazz Patterns for Drum Set

example is for extremely fast tempos with the left hand playing snare and toms on various beats for accents and punctuation.

The fifth pattern is a shuffle, often played with brushes on the snare. Thad Jones arrangements use this pattern. It can be an exciting pattern in certain tunes. The sixth is a variation of the first and used for up-tempo tunes; the snare "pops" accents and punctuations on various drums and cymbals.

The seventh pattern is the only one that uses the snare and toms to create a driving rhythm, not the ride cymbal. This would not be appropriate throughout an entire jazz arrangement, but works well for rhythmic emphasis. The last example borrowed from Ferguson and Feldstein is a simple pattern used in any of the previous figures to break the set pattern. It is the type of pattern that is used after a drum solo to reestablish time.

Guitar

The guitarist has a part similar to the pianist's (or uses the same part) and holds time while occasionally adding rhythmic color. An amplified acoustic instrument is preferable to an electric guitar for jazz, but if an electric guitar is used, it should be adjusted to sound as much as possible like an acoustic. And the guitar, except for solos, *always* plays at a piano dynamic level.

The two primary jazz styles are to play straight quarter notes in the background (as Freddie Green did with the Basie band) or to play chords with a rhythmic feel similar to the tutti rhythms in the full ensemble. Like the drummer, the guitarist has to stay out of the way and not play "too busy."

In the rock styles, the electric guitar is preferred and the use of wah-wah pedals and other distortion devices are best decided by the director and used in good taste. The parts are played out and enhance the entire ensemble as a rock group.

JAZZ INTERPRETATION

As with other rehearsals, planning and organizing the jazz-band rehearsal is required to maximize rehearsal time. Sharing the rehearsal's objectives with the students makes instructional time more effective. Stating the objectives of the next rehearsal helps students to be prepared (especially those still learning to read chord symbols, improvise, or master difficult technical spots).

The primary stylistic interpretation for any jazz style is how the eighth notes are played: either straight (as written), or with a swing feel (6/8 feel). Rock, Latin (bossa nova, samba, etc.), Latin-Rock, and tunes with a classical flavor are played with straight eighth notes in the specific rhythmic patterns characteristic of these individual styles. Swing, modern jazz, Be-Bop, Post-Bop, and Dixieland are played with swing eighth notes.

As in all examples of musical performance, enough cannot be said for the importance of listening to recorded models. Many of the arrangements can be found on old or new recordings (even demos from publishers). Students should spend time in every rehearsal listening to recordings (a practice especially useful for the rhythm section).

All music requires interpretation, providing the director with considerable flexibility in interpreting wind and string literature. Jazz compositions and accompaniments also require interpretation, but the parameters are more strict. Ferguson and Feldstein make the comparison

> In "classical" music, if a performer plays the pitches and rhythms indicated by the composer, the music would sound correct. It will lack the interpretation qualities necessary for artistic performance, but it will be musically correct. In

jazz this is not true. If the performer plays the pitches and rhythms indicated by the composer, it will not be correct and will not sound like jazz. The same is true of rock, but to a lesser extent."[9]

The symbols common in jazz (and rock) notation follow:

—	(tenuto)	Indicates use of a legato tongue and hold full value.	*Sound:* "tah" or "daah"
•	(staccato)	Indicates short, detached notes.	*Sound:* "tat" or "daht"
>	(accent)	Indicates emphasis or stress to a note; the previous note should be played shorter. Consecutive accented notes are detached. The beginning of the note is not tongued harsher than any other note.	*Sound:* "tah" or "dah"
∧	(shorter accent)	Indicates more emphasis on the beginning of the note and is played shorter than regular accents.	*Sound:* "Taht"
∧•	(still shorter accent)	Indicates "punch" almost as short as the note can be played with a definite pitch.	*Sound:* "TaT"

Jazz rhythms are very seldom played the way they are written, with eighth notes played with a 6/8 feel, emphasis is placed on beats two and four in common time and on the offbeats when eighth-note passages are written ("do-dah", "do-dah" sound with slightly more air on "dah").

Most jazz is slurred or legato tongued with very few sharp, biting articulations. These do occur at times in jazz for special effects, especially on phrase endings and in accompanist figures that emphasize a note in the melody.

Improvisation

Improvisation is a primary characteristic of jazz. Most written arrangements of advanced-level music may put all the solos in one part per section; however, the teacher should allow all students to improvise. When members of the band are experienced improvisers, one of the most exciting features of a jazz concert is not knowing who the conductor will point to for a solo during a selection. Students should be free to play one or two choruses then make eye contact with the director that he is ready to end so that another soloist can be selected or the ensemble can regroup at a tutti passage.

Jazz tunes are based on a 12-bar blues, 16-bar blues, AABA form (each section 8 bars in length), or ABA song form (A=8 bars, B=16 bars). In a jazz arrangement in which the director inserts a solo section, she (or the students) can also collectively devise backup figures based on the chord progressions.

With the strict harmonic form, using the rhythm section to play the 12 to 32 measure progression, it is easy to open a "chorus" (i.e., the 12 to 32 bar progression) for individual solos, for students to "trade fours" (each improvising 4 measures, then alternating), or even a collective improvisation for the last improvised chorus before the ensemble regroups for the last time through the written arrangement.

[9]Tom Ferguson and Sandy Feldstein (1979), *The Jazz Ensemble,* Port Washington, NY: Alfred p. 39.

After the first complete statement of a rock-style selection, or after a transition and just prior to a complete statement of the tune, a two-bar repeated vamp can be inserted and repeated as long as necessary. If the tune is in a major key, the easiest vamp is a bar of the I (tonic) chord and a bar of the IV[7] chord in the key of F major, as shown in Figure 25–20.

This vamp would not be as appropriate in a swing or jazz selection as in a rock selection. Written chord progressions are provided to aid with improvisation in jazz and to keep the rhythm section playing the same riffs.

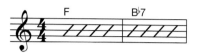

Figure 25–20
Chord Progression That Can Be Inserted and Repeated in Any Rock Tune After Any "Complete Section"

Teaching Improvisation

There are several approaches to teaching improvisation or at least helping students learn to improvise. First, it is essential to convince them that everyone (with a very few gifted exceptions) learns by trial-and-error. One must expect both rhythmic and tonal errors. What may initially sound like a wrong note may later be a key tone in a melodic passage in an attempt to go "outside," a practice that made Charlie Parker and Miles Davis famous.

Today, one means for students to practice and gain confidence in improvising is the Jamey Aebersold method. Students learn dorian, mixolydian, blues , and other scales that fit with specific shards in specific keys. In the key of C major, for example, a G[7] chord calls for a G mixolydian scale; a d_m chord calls for a D dorian scale. Another advantage of the Aebersold series is that it is published for C, B$^\flat$, and E$^\flat$ instruments, enabling clarinets, flutes, tubas, violins, and others to benefit from them.

A second approach to improvisation is advocated by the jazz pedagogue Jerry Coker. He believes there are five factors: intuition, intellect, emotion, sense of pitch, and habit.

> His intuition is responsible for the bulk of his originality; his emotion determines the mood; his intellect helps him plan the technical problems, and with intuition, to develop the melodic form; his sense of pitch transforms heard or imagined pitches into letter names and fingerings; his playing habits enable his fingers to quickly find certain established pitch patterns. Four of these elements of his thinking—intuition, emotion, sense of pitch, and habit—are largely subconscious. Consequently, any control over his improvisation originates in the intellect.[10]

Coker then trains the student in triads and seventh chords, which notes of these chords are best, and which can be used as primary tones. His approach is more intellectual than Aebersold's as his ideas stem from the notion that the student must learn fundamental theory before playing.

A third approach is to have the band play and at the improvisation section limit the soloist to one note. The improvisation is thus limited to rhythms and articulations, which are essential to the jazz concept. The director may need to help find "the" note, but the tonic or fill is normally safe. After getting a rhythmic feel, a second note is added. This process continues until the student is able to discriminate notes that belong with certain chords and notes that are best avoided. Essential to this approach is that, as notes are added, the student is encouraged to make up a "melody" so as to avoid too many "blurps" and "gurgles" that pass for high school improvised solos.

[10]Jerry Coker (1964), *Improvising Jazz*, New York: Fireside p. 31.

Two factors determine how well a student improvises: (1) how well she can play her instrument and (2) how much she listens and *hears* recordings of improvised solos.

The aspiring improviser should practice scales, including blues scales, in a circle of fourths plus arpeggios. The arpeggios should start with the notes of the triad, leading to the three notes of the fourth above and so on; minor and augmented triads come afterward. Next, four note arpeggios should be learned around the circle of fourths and based on the Major seventh, Dominant seventh, and minor seventh chords. Next, arpeggios should be expanded to nineth chords in Major, and dominant nineths, and the arpeggios need not always ascend. Trying not to intellectualize these types of exercises and experimenting with various meters and articulations aurally builds the type of motor skills that are needed in improvisation.

Students must realize these exercises are for learning to command the instrument (and endurance, range, etc.) and to train the ear to hear chords and chord functions. The exercises are not intended to later serve as "licks" to be inserted into solos.

CONCERTS

Every concert should be preceded by at least one rehearsal in the performance auditorium and preferably several. This rehearsal is important for adjusting balance, checking blend, and listening for any unexpected problems; it is also important for practicing and emphasizing concert poise, because every school band and orchestra has new students in it each year. Although the director has many aspects of the performance on her mind, each group need to at least discuss in detail how its members will enter the stage, how to exit if another group is performing, and appropriate behavior during the concert. Section leaders and other student leaders can attend to most of these details.

Concerts must start on time and not be too long. Small details such as clean and polished instruments (and shoes), proper dress, and good posture make a group look good. Another small detail that is a wise investment is a classy looking program that will present the proper image and reflect the hard work that went into preparing the concert.

Concerts can be outstanding, wonderful, and extremely enjoyable—but they will never be perfect. The concert is the natural outcome of rehearsals, and as Wolfgang Kuhn points out, it can have a maximum educational value only to the degree that it leads toward the development of the musicianship or music appreciation of the performers and the listeners. It must be of artistic quality.

BIBLIOGRAPHY

Texts

* Indicates out of print in 2001.

AMERICAN SCHOOL BAND DIRECTORS ASSOCIATION (1997). *The New ASBDA Curriculum Guide.* Miami: Warner Brothers.

*AMMER, CHRISTINE (1971). *Musician's Handbook of Foreign Terms: Containing the English Equivalents of Approximately 2700 Foreign Expression Marks and Directions Taken from French, German, Italian, Latin, Portuguese and Spanish Scores.* New York: Schirmer Books.

BRADY, SUSAN (1994). *Building an Ensemble: A Program to Motivate the Individual Performer.* Portland, ME: University of Southern Maine.

BURTON, RALPH (1995). *The Games of Music. Teacher's Guide.* San Antonio, TX: Southern Music.

*BUTTS, CARROL M. (1981). *Troubleshooting the High School Band: How to Detect and Correct Common and Uncommon Performance Problems.* West Nyack, NY: Parker Publishing.

CUTIETTA, ROBERT A. (1999). *Strategies for Teaching Specialized Ensembles.* Reston, VA: Music Educators National Conference.

*DART, THRUSTON (1984). *The Interpretation of Music.* New York: Hutchinson's University Library; reprint of (1954) London.

*DOORMAN, FREDRICK (1982). *The Interpretation of Music: The History of Music in Performance.* Westport, CT: Greenwood Press; reprint of (1942) New York: W. W. Norton.

FRAEDRICH, EILEEN (1997). *The Art of Elementary Band Directing.* Ft. Lauderdale: Meredith Music.

GALAMIAN, IVAN (1999). *Principles of Violin Playing & Teaching,* 3rd ed. Ann Arbor: MI: Shar Music.

GAROFALO, ROBERT (1992). *Guides to Band Masterworks.* Ft. Lauderdale: Meredith Music.

———— (1976). *Blueprint for Band.* Portland, ME: J. Weston Walch.

———— (1995). *Instructional Designs for Middle/Junior High School Band: Teacher's.* Ft. Lauderdale, FL: Meredith Music Publication.

———— (1996). *Improving Intonation in Band and Orchestra Performance.* Ft. Lauderdale, Meredith Music.

GILLESPIE, JON A. (1998). *The Wind Ensemble Catalog.* Westport, CT: Greenwood Press.

GREEN, ELIZABETH A. H. (1968). *Orchestral Bowings and Routines,* 2nd ed. Ann Arbor, MI: Campus Publishers.

INSTRUMENTALIST PUBLISHING COMPANY (1996). *New Director's Handbook: Practical Answers for Beginning Teachers.* Northfield IL: Instrumentalist.

*KELLER, HERMANN (1965). *Phrasing and Articulation, A Contribution to the Rhetoric of Music, with 152 Musical Examples.* New York: W. W. Norton.

KVET EDWARD (1996). *Teaching Beginning and Intermediate Band.* Reston, VA: Music Educators National Conference.

———— and JANET TWEED (1998). *Strategies for Teaching High School Band.* Reston, VA: Music Educators National Conference.

LABUTA, JOSEPH A. (1997). *Teaching Musicianship in the High School Band,* rev. ed. Ft. Lauderdale: Meredith Music.

LISK, EDWARD S. (1989). *The Creative Director: Alternative Rehearsal Techniques.* Ft. Lauderdale: Meredith Music.

MCBETH, W. FRANCIS (1972). *Effective Performance of Band Music, Solutions to Specific Problems in the Performance of 20th Century Band Music.* San Antonio:Southern Music Co.

MILES, RICHARD B. (1998). *Teaching Music Through Performance in Band,* 2 vols. Chicago, IL: GIA.

MILLER, WILLIAM CLAYTON (1997). *Band Director: Secrets of Success.* Lakeland, FL: Aiton.

*RASMUSSEN, RICHARD (1988). *Recorded Concert Band Music, 1950–1987: A Selected, Annotated Listing.* Jefferson, NC: McFarland.

REIMER, BENNETT (ed.) (2000). *Performing with Understanding: The Challenge of the National Standards for Music Education.* Reston, VA: National Association for Music Educators (MENC).

REUL, DAVID G. (1994). *Getting Started with Middle Level Band.* Reston, VA: Music Educators National Conference.

*RIGHTER, CHARLES B. (1945). *Success in Teaching School Orchestras and Bands.* Minneapolis: Paul A. Schmitt.

SHATTINGER MUSIC COMPANY (1997). *Resource Guide: Wind Band Discography.* St. Louis: Shattinger Music.

STIM, RICHARD (1998). *Music Law: How to Run Your Band's Business.* Berkeley, CA: Nolo Press.

STONEHAM, MARSHALL (1997). *Wind Ensemble Sourcebook and Biographical Guide.* Westport, CT: Greenwood Press.

STRAUB, DOROTHY A., LOUIS BERGONZI, and ANNE C. WITTE (1996). *Strategies for Teaching Strings and Orchestra.* Reston, VA: Music Educators National Conference.

*TIEDE, CLAYTON H. (1976). *The Practical Band Instrument Repair Manual,* 3rd ed. Dubuque, IA: W. C. Brown.

*WEERTS, RICHARD K. (1976). *Handbook of Rehearsal Techniques for the High School Band.* West Nyack, NY: Parker Publishing.

WHITWELL, DAVID (1984). *History and Literature of the Wind Band and Wind Ensemble,* multivolume set. Northridge, CA: Winds (Box 513, Northridge, CA, 91328).

WILLIAMSON, JOHN E., and KENNETH NEIDIG L. (1998). *Rehearsing the Band,* 2nd ed. Cloudcroft, IL: Neidig Services.

WISE, PHILLIP C. (2000). *So—You're the New Band Director, Now What?* Boston: Pearson Custom Publishers, reprint of (1996) Oskaloosa, IA: Barnhouse.

ZERULL, DAVID S. (1994a). *Getting Started with High School Band.* Reston, VA: Music Educators National Conference.

———— (1994b). *The Wind Ensemble and Its Repertoire: Essays on the 40th Anniversary of the Eastman Wind Ensemble.* Rochester, NY: University of Rochester Press.

Instructional Videos

The London Symphony Orchestra, Music Explorer (Colin Davis, 1996). Reston, VA: Music Educators National Conference.

Musicality in a Band Performance (Vaclav Nelhybel, 1992). Reston, VA: Music Educators National Conference.

Balance and Pitch in a Band Performance (Francis McBeth, 1992). Reston, VA: Music Educators National Conference.

Index